CIVIL WAR AND THE
SOCIAL

MW00834549

Can civil war ever be overcome? Can a better order come into being? This book explores how the Roman civil wars of the first century BCE laid the template for addressing perennially urgent questions. The Roman Republic's collapse and Augustus' new Empire have remained ideological battlegrounds to this day. Integrative and disintegrative readings begun in antiquity (Vergil and Lucan) have left their mark on answers given by Christians (Augustine), secular republicans (Victor Hugo), and disillusioned satirists (Michel Houellebecq) alike. France's self-understanding as a new Rome – republican during the Revolution, imperial under successive Napoleons – makes it a special case in the Roman tradition. The same story returns repeatedly. A golden age of restoration glimmers on the horizon but comes in the guise of a decadent, oriental empire that reintroduces and exposes everything already wrong under the defunct republic. Central to the price of social order is patriarchy's need to subjugate women.

MICHÈLE LOWRIE is Andrew W. Mellon Distinguished Service Professor of Classics and the College, University of Chicago. She is the author of *Horace's Narrative Odes* (1997) and *Writing, Performance, and Authority in Augustan Rome* (2009) and edited *Oxford Readings in Classical Studies: Horace's Odes and Epodes* (2009); she also coedited *Exemplarity and Singularity: Thinking through Particulars in Philosophy, Literature, and Law* (2015) and *The Aesthetics of Empire and the Reception of Vergil* (2006).

BARBARA VINKEN is chair of French and Comparative Literature at Ludwig Maximilian University, Munich. Her most recent books include *Krieg als Opfer? Franz Marc illustriert Gustave Flauberts "Legende des Heiligen Julian"* (2021), *Bel Ami: In diesem Babylon leben wir noch immer* (2020), and *Flaubert Postsecular: Modernity Crossed Out* (2015).

CLASSICS AFTER ANTIQUITY

Editors
ALASTAIR BLANSHARD
University of Queensland
SHANE BUTLER
Johns Hopkins University
EMILY GREENWOOD
Yale University

Classics after Antiquity presents innovative contributions in the field of Classical Reception Studies. Each volume explores the methods and motives of those who, coming after and going after antiquity, have entered into a contest with and for the legacies of the ancient world. The series aims to unsettle, to provoke debate, and to stimulate a re-evaluation of assumptions about the relationship between Greek and Roman classical pasts and modern histories.

Other titles in the series:
Classics and Celtic Literary Modernism: Yeats, Joyce, MacDiarmid and Jones
Gregory Baker
ISBN: 978–1–108–84486–4

Brecht and Greek Tragedy: Radicalism, Traditionalism, Eristics
Martin Revermann
ISBN: 978–1–108–48968–3

The Nero-Antichrist: Founding and Fashioning a Paradigm
Shushma Malik
ISBN: 978–1–108–49149–5

Dionysus after Nietzsche: The Birth of Tragedy in Twentieth-Century Literature and Thought
Adam Lecznar
ISBN: 978–1–108–48256–1

Feeling and Classical Philology: Knowing Antiquity in German Scholarship, 1770–1920
Constanze Güthenke
ISBN: 978–1–107–10423–5

The Vernacular Aristotle: Translation as Reception in Medieval and Renaissance Italy
Eugenio Refini
ISBN: 978–1–108–48181–6

Afterlives of the Roman Poets: Biofiction and the Reception of Latin Poetry
Nora Goldschmidt
ISBN: 978–1–107–18025–3

The Perpetual Immigrant and the Limits of Athenian Democracy
Demetra Kasimis
ISBN: 978–1–107–05243–7

Borges' Classics: Global Encounters with the Graeco-Roman Past
Laura Jensen
ISBN: 978–1–108–41840–9

Classical Victorians: Scholars, Scoundrels and Generals in Pursuit of Antiquity
Edmund Richardson
ISBN: 978–1–107–02677–3

Modernism and Homer: The Odysseys of H. D., James Joyce, Osip Mandelstam, and Ezra Pound
Leah Culligan Flack
ISBN: 978–1–107–10803–5

CIVIL WAR AND THE COLLAPSE OF THE SOCIAL BOND

The Roman Tradition at the Heart of the Modern

MICHÈLE LOWRIE

University of Chicago

BARBARA VINKEN

Ludwig Maximilian University, Munich

CAMBRIDGE
UNIVERSITY PRESS

Shaftesbury Road, Cambridge CB2 8EA, United Kingdom

One Liberty Plaza, 20th Floor, New York, NY 10006, USA

477 Williamstown Road, Port Melbourne, VIC 3207, Australia

314–321, 3rd Floor, Plot 3, Splendor Forum, Jasola District Centre, New Delhi – 110025, India

103 Penang Road, #05–06/07, Visioncrest Commercial, Singapore 238467

Cambridge University Press is part of Cambridge University Press & Assessment, a department of the University of Cambridge.

We share the University's mission to contribute to society through the pursuit of education, learning and research at the highest international levels of excellence.

www.cambridge.org
Information on this title: www.cambridge.org/9781009014281

DOI: 10.1017/9781009029995

First published 2023
First paperback edition 2023

A catalogue record for this publication is available from the British Library

ISBN   978-1-316-51644-7   Hardback
ISBN   978-1-009-01428-1   Paperback

For Lucas and Moritz, who grew with the book

Autre façon de dire: on ne trahit jamais que son frère. Le fratricide est la forme générale de la tentation, la possibilité du mal radical, le mal du mal.

In another turn of phrase: we never betray only our brother. Fratricide is the pervasive form of temptation, the possibility of radical evil, the evil of evils.

Jacques Derrida, *Politique de l'amitié*

Contents

List of Figures		*page* xi
Preface		xiii
Acknowledgments		xv
	Introduction	1
1	Figures of Discord	9
	Roma contro Roma	9
	Naming Civil War	15
	The Tropes of *Discordia*	20
	Conceptual Conflict	25
	Discordia and *Stasis*	29
	The Inner Orient	34
	Sacrifice, Conversion, Perversion	38
	Twisting the Trope	42
	Rome's Eternal Return	44
2	Oriental Empire: Vergil, *Georgics*	47
	Disruption	54
	Abject Rebirth	61
	Restoration as Collapse	65
	Triumph and Civil War	69
	Violence Generalized	73
	Art's Promise Withheld	76
3	Empire without End: Vergil, *Aeneid*, and Lucan, *De bello civili*	82
	Typology	86
	Twinned Cities	89
	Civil War Externalized	121
	Rome Ever Imperial	131
	Sacrifice/Suicide	133
	The Poetics of Empire	141

4   The Eternal City: Augustine, *De civitate Dei*   144
    Rewriting Rome   148
    Roma aeterna?   157
    Rome: Universal Civil War   160
    Exemplary History: Roman *Virtus*   169
    Two Earthly Romes in Milton   172
    Providential History: Jerusalem Divided   174
    Division within the Soul   181
    Suicide: Rome's Exemplary Sin   184
    God's *pulcherrimum carmen*   188

5   The Republic to Come: Hugo, *Quatrevingt-treize*   193
    Synecdochic Author   194
    Children of the Republic   203
    Lantenac: Heartless Sovereignty   205
    Tellmarch: Charity versus the Law   209
    The *Convention*: Revolution as Civil War   213
    Plus quam civilia bella: All in the Family   218
    La Tourgue: A Spectral History   222
    The Word Made Flesh: St. Bartholomew   224
    Lantenac and a Higher Sovereignty   232
    Noble Gauvain in Crisis   237
    Gauvain and Cimourdain: Earthly and Divine Republics   240
    Romanticism's Republican Testament: *Gauvain en gloire*   243
    Le sacre de la littérature   253

6   The Empire to Come: Houellebecq, *Soumission*   256
    Satura tota nostra est   267
    Roma temporalis   272
    Babel: Narrative Blackout   277
    Historia magistra vitae   281
    Some Sex and No Love   288
    Liberté, égalité, fraternité   295
    L'homme régénéré   300
    La sacrée littérature   308
    Con/Perversion   312
    Qu'est-ce que la littérature?   324

Bibliography   326
    Editions   326
    References   327
Index   356

Figures

2.1 Boscotrecase, Egyptian motifs, Metropolitan Museum   *page* 51
     of Art, New York
2.2 Boscotrecase, Sacro-idyllic landscape, Museo Archeologico   57
     Nazionale di Napoli
2.3 Jean-François Millet, *The Gleaners*, Musée d'Orsay, Paris   58
2.4 Jean-François Millet, *The Keeper of the Herd* (1871/4), Art   59
     Institute of Chicago
2.5 Ara Pacis Augustae, Tellus relief, Ara Pacis Museum, Rome   77
2.6 Ara Pacis Augustae, detail from the acanthus frieze, snakes   78
     eating chicks, Ara Pacis Museum, Rome; photo by Ralph
     Lieberman.
5.1 Jacques-Louis David, *The Lictors Bring to Brutus the Bodies*   208
     of His Sons, Musée du Louvre, Paris
5.2 Olivier Merson, *Christ en gloire*, mosaic (1923), Sacré-Coeur, 250
     Montmartre, Paris
6.1 Horace Vernet, *Barricade de la rue de Clichy* (1820), Musée du 282
     Louvre, Paris
6.2 Jean-Honoré Fragonard, *Jeune fille et son chien / La Gimblette*, 296
     Alte Pinakothek, Munich

Preface

We never imagined when we taught two seminars together in 2012 that the language of civil discord we were tracing in the Roman literary tradition would return with such a vengeance in our own political reality. The American election of 2016 and the nationalist populism spreading through Europe play out an age-old dynamic: the energy of internal division fuels hatred of others. The refugee crisis in Europe and the hysteria over immigrants in America project our own dysfunction before a rapidly changing world onto a foe depicted as reassuringly alien. The Islamophobia underlying what has been called a clash of civilizations we read as a fundamental misunderstanding motivated by anxiety over the putative decline of the West. This discourse and its structure have been familiar since the collapse of the Roman Republic, when the civil wars were figured as foreign wars against an Orientalized enemy.

Public discourse currently hammers home the metaphor of civil war throughout the media and the political classes. Technically, there is no formal warfare, but the discord within polarized nations and even within parties – the Republican and Democratic parties in the disunited States – comes in the mantle of an idea that derives from ancient Rome. When pundits from the *New York Times* have recourse to comparing an electoral candidate to increasingly obscure Roman emperors, and a name-check from Michel Houellebecq, bestselling novelist, means Augustus is being recognized more and more, we see the Roman analogy as a symptom of our collective fear that history is repeating itself all over again: republics are collapsing everywhere into tyrannies.

Our book analyzes a long-standing tradition that has become current in our times. This tradition reads contemporary history as a repetition of Roman history to ask the ever-urgent question: whether human beings can overcome the internal divisions that alienate us from each other and from ourselves. Our texts give answers conditioned by the historical circumstances and political and aesthetic commitments of their various authors. The structure of history remains a pressing question. Orientalism recurs as trope that obfuscates the real threat of internal enmity. As always, sex, love, and family are the intimate battleground for public affairs. Bloody civil wars provide material for thinking through the challenge of restoring the social bond ever threatened by civil discord.

Acknowledgments

Translations are our own, unless otherwise noted. Where we do use others' translations, we occasionally revise them for greater fidelity to the original. We have been unable to update bibliography systematically since September 2019 and regret that we were not able to cite M. S. Kochin and A. Spektorowski (eds.), *Michel Houellebecq, The Cassandra of Freedom: Submission and Decline* (Leiden).

Numerous institutions gave us support and shelter to carry this project through – at the University of Chicago: the Franke Institute for the Humanities, the Neubauer Collegium for Culture and Society, and the Georges Lurcy Visiting Professorship; in Munich: the Centre Flaubert and the Center for Advanced Studies at Ludwig Maximilian University; in Berlin: the Wissenschaftskolleg and the American Academy. In addition to conversation at these institutions, we are grateful for the possibility of discussing our project with students and colleagues at our home institutions, as well as at the University of Michigan and the Zentrum für Literatur- und Kulturforschung in Berlin. Their hospitality generously accompanied and soothingly softened the strenuous phases of writing.

We extend warm thanks to the series editors, Alistair Blanshard, Shane Butler, and Emily Greenwood. John Henderson deserves special appreciation for his fiercely friendly engagement. Answering their generous and thoughtful responses has made this a stronger book. We thank the Twombly Foundation for their generosity in authorizing our use of the cover image.

We are grateful to all who helped us through the editing process, most especially to Katharina Simon for her tenacity in checking references and compiling the index and to Kathleen Fearn from Cambridge University Press for her keen good sense and sharp eye for detail.

We fondly remember the waters we swam in during our months of sisterly effort: Lake Michigan, Wannsee, Lido, Krumme Lanke, Starnberger See, Riegsee, and the Lario – Lago di Como.

Introduction

It is not evident that a bestselling author addressing the so-called "clash of civilizations" between Islam and the West should choose to make an analogy to ancient Rome.[1] Yet in his 2015 novel *Soumission*, Michel Houellebecq twice compares the leader of the dystopian Muslim regime in France's near future to the emperor Augustus. In doing so, he mobilizes a tradition central to French literature: the retelling of French history in Roman terms. He also mobilizes a discourse central to European culture, whose roots go back to the civil wars that destroyed the Roman Republic in the first century BCE.[2] Houellebecq calls the implosion of the Fifth French Republic a civil war. When the new regime of the Muslim Brotherhood emerges from the ashes of a violent election, Houellebecq's figuration of it in the language of civil war does more than present the new French Empire in the guise of Augustus' new imperial order; it participates in a discourse that uses civil war as a locus to query the nature of the social bond and its collapse, to ask whether a ruptured social order can ever be healed, and to question the very nature of history. This discourse figures history in Roman terms and turns on whether Rome comes back in the guise of a republic or as an empire in an oriental mode.

The five authors we examine in this book represent different moments in the long history of this discourse. Vergil's *Georgics* and *Aeneid*, Lucan's *De bello civili*, Augustine's *De civitate Dei*, Victor Hugo's *Quatrevingt-treize*, and Houellebecq's *Soumission* share an organizing principle. All write under conditions of urgency, some during or shortly after actual civil war. But whether or not armies of citizens are fighting one another in their times, they think through the question of healing the social bond within history and on this earth through the figure of civil discord and its

---

[1] Huntington's (1996) phrase.

[2] Jal (1963) 2: Civil war is more than a "theme" of Latin literature; it is a discursive "tradition," whose terms remain relevant to the conflicts of our time. Ginsberg and Krasne (2018) 2: Civil war provides "a wider conceptual framework through which Romans understood themselves."

tropes. Our reading highlights the continuity of this tradition, in which a consistent substrate of metaphors for civil war figure history as repetition, particularly of the civil wars that tore apart republican Rome.

Our choice of texts is hardly exhaustive. To cover this tradition even within French literature would entail an encyclopedic project, ranging from Théodore Agrippa d'Aubigné, through Gustave Flaubert, Claude Simon, and Assia Djebar, among many others. The discourse begun at Rome bubbles up across European and American literature in high and popular culture – in Heinrich von Kleist's *Hermannschlacht*, Henry James's *Bostonians* and William Faulkner's *Absalom Absalom*, in Giacomo Puccini's *Tosca*, Salman Rushdie's *The Golden House*, George Lucas's *Star Wars*, and John Le Carré's *The Most Wanted Man*.[3] These texts see their own history through the lens of Roman civil war discourse and rewrite its metaphors to make sense of their own circumstances, according to the aesthetic modalities and political potentialities of their times.

The French texts we analyze are exemplary for appropriating the Roman civil wars as a figuration of history according to a Christian paradigm. They are representative because they reveal with astounding clarity the shocking tradition of interpreting *translatio Romae* not as a return of a Roman Republic or Empire in the guise of political stability and well-being, but rather as a *translatio belli civilis*. Paris, a universal imperial capital, became a figuration of a new Rome in the nineteenth century. Rome's model, whether Republic or Empire, was an inevitable figuration. Rome succeeding Rome came as fulfillment or curse, virtuous or decadent, new Jerusalem or new Babylon. It defined the terms with which literature in the nineteenth century and through the twenty-first has judged history, with France as universal history's particular instantiation.

Literature revisits the Roman civil wars of the first century BCE repeatedly as the scene of a dispute transcending historical particulars, which remains perennially unresolved. Can a new foundation emerge from civil war's violence, or does it fruitlessly destroy the social bond? The classical tradition is largely pessimistic about Rome's potential to overcome its internal divisions. Vergil, despite a pervasively bleak outlook, proffers a faint glimmer of hope in the *Aeneid*, that Augustus could end the cycle of internal violence inscribed into Roman history from its first foundation. Lucan's raging despair denies any possibility of historical change in Nero's imperial Rome. Vergil's open future becomes in his Christian reception

---

[3] Henderson (1998) xi: "The politics of the Roman revolution have never lost their relevance to the princes and peoples of the West."

a promise that can be revealed only with the changed conditions of history attending Christianity's advent. Hope for a new world order becomes a foundational concept for salvation history, which imagines a newly healed social bond. The tonal modalities set by Vergil and Lucan are tragedy and the grotesque. Vergil mourns the recurring violence that ushers in an empire predicted to last without end, while the Roman Republic's destruction appears irredeemable and permanent in Lucan. Everything is civil war, literally or metaphorically, everywhere, all the time. Any ideal Rome arises *ex negativo*. Lucan's deconstruction of the *res Romana* ultimately affirms what Rome should be but never was.

Augustine viscerally rejects Rome as exemplary of the highest virtue – for him not *virtus* but love. *De civitate Dei* retells the Roman civil wars as the negative figuration of God's universal city to come, the only source of concord, the only solution to discord. Secular history, in Augustine paradigmatically Roman, is inscribed into the fabric of salvation history: Rome, with all its civil wars, is the perverse antitype of the city to come. As such, Roman history is told in the mode of the grotesque. Rome – Republic and Empire alike – becomes shorthand for the eternal return of the curse of terrestrial history. Augustine assimilates all Roman paradigms, integrative and disintegrative alike, and sets them against a vision of a brighter future based on a new paradigm. Civil war governs earthly politics under the *civitas terrena*, so that the pagan Romans altogether become emblematic of worldliness as a dead end. To move beyond a politics of destruction requires the advent of the *civitas Dei*, which organizes humanity toward a republic of love. Augustine retains the Roman concept of citizenship as the category of belonging but transfigures it for the new Christian dispensation. This new order is for him a historical reality always in the process of becoming: It has been imagined but is imperfectly achieved within the world as we know it. Full realization remains to come.

The advent of Christianity and the French Revolution are two great breaks that inform conceptualizations of history's potential to start anew.[4] These share a promise to leave Rome behind with a new beginning. Like Rome, France becomes a universal paradigm in political thought. Hugo in his republican mode secularizes the Augustinian paradigm, and *Quatrevingt-treize* is exemplary for the republican political imaginary in nineteenth-century France. According to this model, the French Revolution will succeed in fulfilling the new covenant the Christian promise has failed to bring about. In the newly founded French

---

[4] Barrera (2021) follows the thread of universalism in civil war discourses.

Republic, one and indivisible, the Christian promise of a healed social bond will finally be realized and set a revived Republic on a firmer footing. The republicans recast the Catholic monarchy as the very Roman imperial tyranny the Christian promise was to overcome; instead of vanquishing the Roman paradigm of civil discord, throne and altar hypocritically reinscribe it. By figuring the monarchy's failure to overcome Rome, however, the republicans establish a model that will haunt their own attempts to leave Rome's ugly history behind. Rome always returns and reinscribes the inevitability of imperial decadence into all attempts at republican revival. This is the Roman paradigm's predicament.

In *Soumission*, Houellebecq vehemently unmasks this republican hope just as the republicans had unmasked the monarchy: The French Republic, in his story, has miserably failed. It creates no bond but fragments society into capitalist monads. As a consequence of civil war, Rome returns, not as a revitalized republic, but as an oriental empire, now in the mode of the next world religion after Christianity. The ostensibly Islamic reforms take all the dysfunction of the French Republic to a clarifying extreme. Yet again, Rome's figurative return brings no restoration and only makes things worse.

Perversion is a central rhetorical gesture in representations of civil war. By perversion, we mean the discursive turning of a trope in a direction that the speaker or text judges to be wrong. We consistently use perversion as a technical term, without judgment on our part, to capture the structural continuity between an integrative trope and its disintegrative turn. The revelation of prior, ostensibly wholesome (republican, Christian) values as distorted or decadent (imperial, monarchical, capitalist) is a common means of refiguration, either to condemn or to illuminate. If a better future can be imagined over history's horizon, the lost wholesome values need reintegration into a new value system to transcend their decadent perversion.

Decadence's preeminent coloring is oriental. Orientalism emerges as a trope for civil war in Augustan literature, specifically in depictions of the battle of Actium.[5] The projection of internal discord onto a foreign enemy figured as effeminate, sexually perverse, morally corrupt, and tyrannical – the Egyptian Cleopatra – reassuringly displaces onto an Eastern other the hatred that rends the social bond within Rome. This figuration becomes

---

[5] Jal (1963) 152 n. 2: Antony is a *Romain orientalisé* ("orientalized Roman"); Henderson (1998) 165: "othered foe"; Reed (2010) 67; Lowrie (2015c). "'Othering' the enemy in a civil conflict," however, starts earlier in Latin letters; Damon (2015) 118–19 on Caesar.

a central organizing principle for subsequent discourses of civil discord in the tradition of *Romanitas*. In Vergil's *Georgics*, the bee society, a microcosm of civil war and self-destruction analogous to both Rome and oriental cultures, preeminently Egypt, requires a solution also from Egypt. Whether the *bugonia* succeeds is one of the most fraught interpretive cruxes in Latin literature. In the *Aeneid*, the distinctions between Roman and Trojan, Roman and Carthaginian, Roman and Egyptian, assiduously maintained by the epic's characters, break down in a multiplicity of crisscrossing myths of origin.[6] The lack of distinction between Roman and other circulates as a textual secret to be discovered through philological labor. Lucan drags this secret onto the textual surface, thereby revealing the oriental figuration of the civil war enemy as false consciousness. *De bello civili* ends with Caesar embroiled in an adulterous affair with Cleopatra in Egypt. With the Roman Republic's demise, Caesar, who brings on the new imperial order, ends up in bed with the very Egyptian foe Augustan literature uses as cover for the ugly fact that, in civil war, Romans fight other Romans. Lucan reveals the Roman Empire as the oriental other the Augustan victory at Actium was meant to defeat: The victor of the civil war comes from Egypt and does not overcome Egypt. Instead of a restored republic, Rome becomes its own imagined enemy. The Augustan refoundation vanishes in the gap between Caesar and Nero. The poem refuses to narrate any intervening history.

Augustine, like Lucan, recasts the Romans as the orientals their own discourse vilifies. *De civitate Dei* rejects all Roman history – Republic together with Empire – as Babylon's equal. The Christian promise is to overcome the corruption, perversity, and tyranny the Romans view as oriental, but Augustine exposes as in fact Roman. Christians think to overcome the split of civil discord by becoming one in God. The Catholic church universalizes this promise of unity to the chosen citizens of God's new foundation. The orientalist projection would theoretically melt away in the realized city of God. The French Revolution's new beginning replays the structure but transfers the institutions. Republican discourse casts the Roman Catholic monarchy as the perverse, corrupt, effeminate, and tyrannical heirs of the now-conflated orientalized and Roman Empire. In Hugo's *Quatrevingt-treize*, the Terror fulfills French history as Roman history in its oriental mode. Hugo aspires to found a new republic on secularized Christian values. Like Augustine, he believes in a *civitas* based on love. He hopes to realize the promise of the French

---

[6] Toll (1997); Lowrie (2005) 971–6; Syed (2005); Reed (2007) 7–13 and (2010) 70, 74; Giusti (2018).

Revolution in the secularized city of God, that is, in the French Republic to come. As with the Catholic promise, the republican promise is extended universally to all citizens.

Houellebecq denounces French republicanism as a failed promise in *Soumission* and reveals the West's true identity as fully oriental: It is in reality the other it abhors. He literalizes the oriental nature of the civil war opponent under the name of a false Islam that instantiates everything the West pretends is alien to itself. France is on the road to becoming a new empire, run by the Muslim Brotherhood and modeled on the Roman Empire, a hellish perversion of republican values. In *Soumission*'s new empire, republican liberty and equality among men vanishes, leaving only domination or submission. Its new *fraternité* realizes the one remaining value of the French Revolution in a ruthlessly masculinist vein. Women are driven out of power from the highest to the lowest rank and degraded to sex objects or maternal caretakers. Augustus' new empire is refigured without republican virtues. It embraces the oriental decadence generally attributed to the later Empire. But the new empire turns out to be nothing but the internal decadence of the old republic fully exposed.

The consistent tarring of the civil opponent as oriental is a gesture of self-alienation that structures the double bind of civil discord's discursive representation. The promise of overcoming Roman civil war paradoxically replays the very structures understood to articulate it. The projection of the internal split onto an orientalized other, a gesture meant to keep internal discord under wraps, is uncovered in literature as ideological blindness. Orientalizing is a central figuration of civil discord, one that persists in the Roman political imaginary, which has – surprisingly – endured to this day. It is easily misread as if it expressed belief in a literal truth about the other, who has been subjected to this ideological rhetoric. Such misreading supports, in our view, a misunderstanding of Vergil as an apologist for, rather than critic of, empire, as if the *Aeneid* endorses a degrading view of Egyptians who deserve to be conquered, rather than exposing the projection of degradation onto Cleopatra as a way of refusing to face the fact that young Caesar was fighting Antony, a fellow Roman.[7] Those invested in taking the orientalist projection as a truth about others and not a rhetorical act of self-delusion – Fascists and National Socialists,[8] currently the right-wing and Islamophobic populist

---

[7] Veeser (1994) 2: It is a fundamental principle of New Historicism that acts of critique and resistance use the tools they condemn, at the risk of falling prey to the practices they expose. Wedeen (1999) 25.

[8] For the Nazi and Fascist appropriation of Vergil in particular, Thomas (2001) 222–59; on orientalism (238, 242–4). However, those opposed to both also found their *Aeneid* (260–77): "The victims of fascism readily identified with the victims of Aeneas and his Trojans" (276).

movements sweeping nations that self-identify as Western – have appropriated this figuration and taken it literally. They lack awareness that they are
thereby exposing their own conflict with their own societies.

Civil discord poses a challenge for narration. As a breakdown within all
spheres that make sense of the world – soul, family, sex, generation, the
cosmos, the gods[9] – civil war threatens the symbolic order. Such self-
on-self conflict within and across spheres is intolerable. Therefore cultural
discourses develop a host of representational strategies to avoid, displace, or
externalize a pain that nevertheless repeatedly and symptomatically rears its
ugly head. Vergil and Lucan establish two opposing representational
strategies: encoding a mythic foundation as an untold civil war and naming
and narrating civil war as such. Vergil's beautiful and linear narrative tells
a story of successful foundation in the epitome of the classicizing style. The
classical is not, however, monolithic. It includes its exclusions in style and
outlook. Discord underwrites concord as Alexandrian elegance underwrites Homeric grandeur. Vergil's representation of discord results in
ellipsis, textual fragmentation, palimpsestic allusion, and a density of
figuration. Traces of discord scatter across the apparently unified textual
surface. His narrative style is a coping mechanism that allows pain to be
kept under wraps, but it also makes available a story that cannot otherwise
be told to a reader willing to decipher the signifiers. The Vergilian tradition
builds on his foundational model of literary discourse in its encoded
modality.[10] By contrast, Lucan makes the civil war between Pompey and
Caesar his overt theme, but discord rips apart his narration: the disjunctive,
nonlinear story comes in tortured language, where strained grammar,
idiom, and expression mirror the wound to the body politic it represents.
His model becomes paradigmatic for an alternative tradition.

Augustine and Hugo narrate civil war overtly and without tortured
language because they believe Christianity's promise, which makes it
possible to imagine the cessation of civil war and a turn to redemption.
Augustine's satiric wit tells the horror of Roman civil war in rhetorically
heightened terms that take their tone from Lucan and bring the abject into
graphic vividness. Augustine reserves his sublime register to convey the
beauty and healing power of God's grace. Hugo similarly represents civil

---

[9] For cosmic expansion across spheres (nature, society, language), Breed, Damon, and Rossi (2010) 6–
7, 11. Loraux (1997b) 80–1: The city's governmental structures model the soul's governance of
sexuality through reason in Plato.

[10] Starting with Parry (1963), Vergilian encoding has been called "two voices." Thomas (2000):
Ambiguous interpretations of Vergil are already attested in Servius; for modern approaches (391
n. 29). In (2001), he tells European history through Vergil's reception.

discord in a Lucanian register. He, however, redeems the grotesque through the sublime in the aesthetics of secular Romanticism, which owes much to Augustine. Houellebecq's satiric irony arouses disgust in the reader, who sees through to the ugliness that appears normal to his benighted characters. Houellebecq, for whom no redemption lies on any horizon, reinscribes Vergilian techniques of encoding to undo the Christian promise but rages with Lucan to show that civil war is inescapable. The aesthetic choices of all – classical or sublime, satiric or grotesque – form an inherent part of their substantive response to the pressures of their times, responses that recall, replay, and reconfigure prior versions of the perennially anguished question, whether and under what conditions we may all learn to get along. Civil discord comes to light with greater or lesser degrees of clarity in this discourse.

From Vergil to Lucan, from Augustine to Hugo, and now with Houellebecq, civil war is only ever apparently overcome in the here and now. Its recurrent violence plagues history: from the French wars of religion (1562–98), through the Thirty Years War (1618–48), the English Civil War (1642–51), to the French Revolution (1789) and all the subsequent revolutions of nineteenth-century French history, the German *Befreiungskriege* (1813–15), to the Italian *Risorgimento* (1815–70) and the American Civil War (1861–5), the two World Wars, the current outbreak of global violence in the post-9/11 New World (dis)Order, the attack on the American Capitol on January 6, 2021 – terms whose classical Roman roots have been mediated through the Roman Christian tradition have shed light on these conflicts. Civil war's continual actual return in history is only half the story. The Roman tradition gives the lie to any declaration of closure; literature's representations of civil war as overcome reinscribe all its figurations in its very overcoming. The methods for bringing it to an end – empire and sacrifice, classical and Christian alike – are always shown to bring it back with a vengeance. The attempt to quell it not only tragically fails but, in a further perversion, twists the screw all the tighter.[11]

---

[11] Esposito (2011): Defensive measures redound on the defender in the logic of an autoimmune disorder.

CHAPTER I

Figures of Discord

"Literature" is a Latin word. Its belonging was never simple – literature travels, immigrates, labors, and is translated. Its Latin filiation is
exported and bastardized beyond confines and affinities, but always
along frontiers. Literature does not travel under just any conditions. It
does not use just any vehicle or shape of transport. Whatever the
idiomatic diversity of our maternal tongues, when we say "literature" – supposing we succeed in communicating – we speak and
understand each other from a Latin source, in the constraining
hospitality or violent welcome of Latinity.

Jacques Derrida, Demeure: Maurice Blanchot

Roma contro Roma

The title of Giuseppe Vari's film says it all: One Rome against another
Rome turns out to be the same Rome returning as a zombie. The collapse
of the Roman Republic in civil war and the political "solution" of this crisis
in Empire is the primal scene of the tradition we analyze. Literature at the
time tried obsessively to cope with this self-imposed wound to the political
imaginary, and subsequent literature keeps returning to this unresolved
scene.[1]

Imperial ideology claims that empire's establishment heals the wound of
civil war.[2] The unity of empire and morality aims to restore the body
politic through chaste procreation in a biopolitical gesture. The imperial
self, regenerated after civil war, allegedly does not destroy but fulfills the
ideal republican self: male, virtuous, and in control, particularly of women.
The flip side is the projection of effeminacy, decadence, tyranny onto an
oriental other. In antiquity, the civil war other was Cleopatra. In current

---

[1] The palimpsest characterizes Latin literature, Boyle (1993b) 1–2, Hinds (1998). Political and social
fragmentation is encoded through form: Quint (1993) 9: the attachment of "political meaning to
narrative form"; Lowrie (1997) 138–86; Bartsch (1997) 5–7 for Lucan.
[2] Body-politic imagery, especially wounding, is endemic to civil war discourse. Armitage (2017a) 9.

discourses, it is Islam. Those who construct the West as monolithic also construct a fictitious, equally monolithic East as its countertype in an act of self-blinding.[3] The circumstantial congruence between myth – generated from fear – and actuality in some instances is generalized, as if it could apply to a whole.[4] When orientalism talks about Cleopatra, about Islam, it talks about its own internal divisions, its own desire for self-mastery and control. The imagined other masks the uncanny truth that the civil war enemy is none other than the self.

The strand of literature we examine, however, reveals, through a persistent bass line of civil war tropes, the hollowness of the imperial claim. This tradition asserts that real-world empires perpetuate civil war's logic all the more perversely for avowing they have ended it decisively. Restored virtue, sexual morality reimposed and the reinforcement of traditional gender roles, a newly fertile birthrate, boundaries reestablished between self and other, friend and enemy, West and East, Occident and Orient – imperial ideology reassures by policing borders literature insists on crossing. As central to Western self-understanding as the imperial fantasy is literature's ability to deconstruct this fantasy, to turn the tables on "Western" identity constructed in opposition to the reviled other. Literature reveals – and sometimes denounces – the orientalist projection as false consciousness. After internal collapse, Rome comes back in this narrative, not restored but as horror. Where imperial ideology posits a clash of civilizations, literature reveals perpetual civil war.

Several of our texts have been charged with complicity. Without empire, Vergil could not have written the *Aeneid*, nor Lucan *De bello civili*. Without Islamophobia, Houellebecq could not have written *Soumission*. Such dependency is true, but banal. Without existing ideologies, there could be no framework to unravel. These authors have further been accused of celebrating what we, among others, argue they undo. We submit that careful reading will show that the fully celebratory interpretation cannot be maintained. Their works put ideologies on display to show the depth of internal contradiction. Augustine and Hugo, in a different strategy, denounce empire and establish alternative worlds, respectively the *civitas Dei* and the republic to come, in which civil war can be imagined as finally overcome. They did their utmost to bring these worlds into being,

---

[3] Said (1978).

[4] In her critique of Syrian ideology, Wedeen (2019) 164–5 describes how othering works to displace "unbearable fears . . . allaying anxieties by transferring unacceptable attributes onto a fantasy Other." Her specific example is attributing the causes of civil violence to "'terrorists'." Actual militant groups, such as the Islamic State, "made the process of Othering easier everywhere."

Augustine through the church, Hugo through politics, despite full awareness of these institutions' limitations.

These are not the only ways to undo empire. Postcolonial literature gives
voice to those othered by imperial ideology. Writing against empire from
within empire is the primary gesture, to cite Ashcroft, Griffiths, and Tiffin,
The Empire Writes Back (1989). From the beginnings of Latin literature, the
voices of conquered Greeks ring through. In Horace's words, "conquered
Greece conquered its fierce conqueror" (*Graecia capta ferum victorem cepit*,
Epist. 2.1.156). Latin literature in its entirety could therefore be taken as the
original postcolonial literature. But this is a different point. Only a whisper
of defeated voices from their own perspective emerges in our texts. In the
ecphrasis of the battle of Actium on Aeneas' shield, for instance, young
Caesar's triple triumph ends with a depiction of the conquered River Araxes,
chafing at being bridged (8.728). The Dahae are characterized, in the same
line, as "unconquered" (*indomiti*), giving the lie to the fiction of totalizing
empire. But the tradition analyzed here pours energy into displaying how
empire encodes the civil war it claims to end, how orientalism only papers
over social discord at home, and how Latin literature set the paradigm for
internal critique. We do not attempt to answer an important question,
whether othered voices can speak to empire from outside this tradition. In
keeping with our topic, our texts show their own societies unmaking
themselves from within in the very gesture of their remaking. These works
query categories and borders essential to Western identity. To speak cat-
egorically, we believe any work that deserves to belong to the so-called
Western canon must undo its own hegemony from within.

History told as a reenactment of the Roman civil wars appears in French
literature with varying degrees of explicitness, from direct naming to
quotation, subtle allusion, and the indirect retroping of Latin literature's
figures for civil war.[5] The story repeatedly revolves around central and
urgent questions. Can civil war ever be overcome, or is history doomed to
its continual reenactment? Can ending it bring restoration, or does renewal
inevitably entail imperial domination, which perpetuates under wraps all
the violence of republican contestation, thereby making life even worse?

Civil war disrupts categories. From the Latin *bellum civile*, the concept
denotes formal warfare among citizens.[6] But narratives often exceed the

---

[5] Putnam (1965) vii–xi calls for further reading of the *Aeneid* through its "individual metaphors and
patterns of verbal similarity," "repetitions of metaphor and image," "unifying imaginative patterns,"
"salient images," and "symbolic unity." For the palimpsest as literary strategy, Lachmann (1990). On
civil war as an "intertextual project" in Latin literature, Ginsberg and Krasne (2018) 2, 12–13.

[6] Armitage (2017a) 32–5, 48–58.

bounds of the bare concept with a broad set of metaphors attaching to *discordia*: violence within the family and between the sexes. We argue that Roman civil war also becomes the name of a trope that disrupts any neat limitation to formal war or citizenship and folds in the metaphors of discord.[7] The current use of civil war in ordinary language as a metaphor for any strong internal dispute or collapse of social norms is true to a long tradition.[8] At the center of a paradoxically unifying tropology from Roman times to the present, civil war is understood to shatter the social bond – the *vinculum societatis* or *sociale*, terms shared by Cicero and Augustine[9] – up to the cosmos and down into the soul. The concept of civil war obfuscates and hides the original and more fundamental crime of discord; the metaphors reveal the concept's concealments. By telling of civil war in Roman discord's terms, literature displays the concept's limitations and reveals a blind spot.

Rome stands as shorthand for world history, whose perennial condition is civil war. The Romans lived and breathed their own history as universal. Astonishingly enough, this paradigm continues to maintain its hold on the political imaginary to this day. Roman terms still inform contemporary frameworks: Republic, Empire, liberty, security, and civil war remain current in political language.[10] The frequency with which Roman emperors – the negative example par excellence of luxury, tyranny, and corruption – crop up in the media may measure the speaker's alarm.[11] We

---

[7] Maschek (2018) integrates archaeological and textual records; civil war was not just a political but "above all a social and cultural phenomenon" (12).

[8] For partisan infighting, Jess McKinley, "New York Democrats Ended a 7-Year Civil War. Now Comes the Hard Part," *New York Times*, April 5, 2018, www.nytimes.com/2018/04/05/nyregion/new-york-democrats-idc-future.html. As a metaphor for political conflict, Linda Greenhouse, *New York Times* op-ed, "The Supreme Court and the New Civil War," April 26, 2018, www.nytimes.com/2018/04/26/opinion/supreme-court-new-civil-war.html.

[9] For example, Cicero, *De republica* (1.49); Augustine, *De civitate Dei* (15.16). This metaphor underlies the binding of *religio* in its Late Antique etymology. See Maltby (1991) 522–3 for the controversy of whether *religere* or *relegere* was the root; the oldest attestation of binding religion is Lucretius (1.932), affirmed by Lactantius.

[10] Roman terms pervade the institutions of law and the Catholic church. Legendre (1964).

[11] Such comparisons dogged Donald Trump as president. Ross Douthat ran through Caesar, Nero, Caligula, and Elagabalus: for example, "Waiting for Caesar," *New York Times*, August 1, 2018, www.nytimes.com/2018/08/01/opinion/trump-caesar-republican-tax-cut.html. Connolly (2017), Kapust (2018), Freudenburg (2018a) and (2018b). Germany enacted a similar tyrannical trope by deporting sixty-nine refugees as a present to Horst Seehofer, Germany's interior minister, on his sixty-ninth birthday. The incident gained notoriety because a young man hanged himself on arriving in Afghanistan (https://thruttig.wordpress.com/2018/07/11/die-seehofer-69-wirklich-nicht-bestellt-erster-suizid-in-kabul/). Boris Johnson, who purged members of parliament from his own party trying to cleave Britain from Europe, compared his acts to Octavian's proscriptions. The *Guardian* suggests other things he could learn from his model: www.theguardian.com/politics/2019/sep/05/five-lessons-boris-johnson-could-learn-augustus-caesar.

stress civil war's Roman background, not because the Romans invented internal political violence, far from it. Witness the house of Atreus, patricidal Oedipus and his fratricidal sons born of incest[12] – the stuff of tragedy – and Thucydides' historiographical account of *stasis* during the Peloponnesian War. Nor because *bellum civile* has become the organizing concept for internal political violence in modern legal and political discourses.[13] We focus on Rome because conflict in modernity is frequently retold in Roman history's guise.[14] Marx declares in *The Eighteenth Brumaire of Louis Napoléon Bonaparte* that the French Revolution of 1789–1814 came draped first in the costume of the Roman Republic, then of the Roman Empire.[15] This ever-repeated travesty stands for history's incapacity to change.[16] Rome always returns, whether in tragic mode or as farcical zombie.

We set the stage by analyzing the origins of this tradition in formative texts of Latin literature. Vergil lends the civil and social wars of the first century BCE a central role in preparing for a new foundation under Augustus, and Lucan counters with a version of the conflict between Pompey and Caesar where civil war undoes any foundation. We progress to a canonical Christian text of Late Antiquity, Augustine's *City of God*, which globalizes and universalizes the original scene. Civil war appears as the basic structure of secular history across all time and space, starting with Abel in the Old Testament, and its only alternative is the *civitas Dei* that transfigures earthly history. As modern case studies, our two exemplary narratives are radically opposed in their answers and in their aesthetics: Victor Hugo's *Quatrevingt-treize* and Michel Houellebecq's *Soumission*. Nevertheless, their shared retelling of French history as Roman history and in the tropes of Roman literature mediated through Augustine allows us to outline the stakes and structure of this tradition.

As a self-declared new Vergil operating within an Augustinian paradigm, Hugo spells out all the stages of the *res Romana* as the model of a universal history instantiated in France. Victor Hugo offers the hope that the corruption of the *civitas terrena*, figured as Roman history, can be redeemed in a new order to come. In place of the *civitas Dei*, the locus of redemption for the Church Father, the father figure of French literature promotes a secularized Republic that retropes Christian concepts, ideals, and institutions. Hugo's last novel, *Quatrevingt-treize*, retells French

---

[12] In Latin literature, these myths figure civil war, Mac Góráin (2018).   [13] Armitage (2017a).

[14] Rome remains a site for elucidating contemporary history: of America, Murphy (2007), Smil (2010); in Hollywood, Wiseman (1995) 151–4, Wyke (1997).

[15] Marx (1960) 115.   [16] We thank Christoph Menke for this interpretation of Marx.

history in straightforwardly Roman terms. Allusions reside on the textual surface; quotations are only slightly distorted. Still, this tradition has become unreadable to our generation, fast losing hold of the classical tradition. Our reading brings this heritage to light. Hugo's message is that the universal republic to come is realizable not in a *civitas Dei* but in the *saeculum*, that it will overcome Rome and set society on a new foundation of secularized Roman Catholic values. While his message shares Augustine's optimism, he tells the story overtly, with Lucan's explicitness. Civil war in all its cruelty – battles of French on French, between men related by family – is the novel's topic and "guerre civile" occurs every several pages. His Vergil fundamentally believes in a new foundation. Hugo's tragicomic tone, modeled on Shakespeare, is ultimately redemptive.[17]

Michel Houellebecq reweaves the strands of this story. The Roman Empire has a roaring comeback in *Soumission*; his recent analysis of civil war's return retropes the canon. Fully within the French tradition, this realist novel brings an old strategy to contemporary ideological struggles: telling French history through Roman topoi.[18] His complex and manifold tropological inversions make pinning his texts down ideologically challenging. Houellebecq is usually read as Fascist, right-wing, misogynistic, and Islamophobic. This is too literal. His work is satire; it shows up the glaring ugliness of sexual domination and the hypocrisy of projecting internal division onto the oriental other. Satire denounces without necessarily offering any better alternative. Houellebecq leaves a disquieting void in the space left by the norms he shows in collapse.

The realist mode, which informs Houellebecq's novel, turns out to be surprisingly allegorical: it tells its story via another. French nineteenth-century literature retells the history of revolution from the *grande révolution* – which founded modern, republican nation states – through the Terror to the Commune as a history in Roman dress and shot through with civil war. Flaubert's method is paradigmatic for this tradition.[19] His novels employ the tropes of classical and Christian Rome without flagging them as such. His textual strategy, a refined reweaving of ancient intertexts, uncovers as false consciousness the republican ideologies that, in manifold forms, declare so energetically that they have ended discord: The discord eternally returns. His oeuvre is paradigmatic of cryptic inscription, where

---

[17] In the "Preface to Cromwell," Hugo repeatedly cites Shakespeare as a model for literature in his own times, Thierry and Mélèze (1963) 422 and *passim*.
[18] Vinken (2001), Zollinger (2015).   [19] Vinken (2009a).

translatio Babylonis comes under the cover of *translatio Romae*. Flaubert avails himself of oriental Babylon as Roman imperial decadence's twin, a figure in circulation since Augustine. Flaubert's poetics furthermore take their cue from language's fragmentation at the tower of Babel. His ornate and exotic code uses nothing straightforward: indirection, covert figuration, allusion – all require deciphering.

Flaubert and Hugo represent the disintegrative and integrative traditions of nineteenth-century French literature, respectively. For Flaubert, literature reveals an irredeemable condition, namely the eternal curse of Rome in history, while Hugo searches for a remedy. Flaubert's political message corresponds to Lucan's assessment of politics as grotesque, but his cryptic poetics match Vergil's method and tragic outlook. Both traditions rewrite the Roman obsession with the tragedy of civil discord in all its articulations. Like Lucan, Houellebecq names civil war and deconstructs supposedly virtuous republicanism as indistinct from the oriental empire that succeeds it. His method of representing discord's horror, however, takes its cue from the indirect expression of Vergil and Flaubert. His revived satire, the genre the Romans claimed as their own, encodes layered retroping – both rewriting and twisting – of the tradition with cryptic allusiveness.

Civil war becomes a paradigmatic sign of *Romanitas*: the Roman tradition constructed retrospectively in letters and by the letter, *après la lettre* and *d'après la lettre*.[20]

Naming Civil War

The difficulty of defining civil war has become a commonplace among historians.[21] Andreas Kalyvas offers an authoritative definition in political science: "armed combat within the boundaries of a recognized sovereign entity between parties subject to a common authority at the outset of the hostilities."[22] David Armitage's recent conceptual history recovers the

---

[20] Curtius (2013). Lowrie (2001) on Derrida (1998); see this chapter's epigraph. Vessey (2005) 174–5, in his analysis of Derrida's question "concerning the Latin-Europeanness of literature," notes that Curtius gives short shrift to Augustine's *Confessiones*. The same is true of the *De civitate Dei*. The trajectory of our book goes some way to filling the gap by recognizing Augustine's pivotal role between classical and modern *Romanitas*. Schwindt (2013) describes how memory, distancing, and forgetting the Republic and the civil wars in Augustan literature constitute a self-conscious culture, a tradition of remembrance across the break of a new foundation. His analysis is paradigmatic for how literary traditions operate.

[21] Price (2001) 32; Lange (2016a) 502 (long version, 1–4); Armitage (2017a) 48; Ginsberg and Krasne (2018) 7–10.

[22] Kalyvas (2006) 5.

Roman origins underlying modern understandings of civil war.[23] In Latin, *bellum civile* originated in a precise historical context: the power struggles that destroyed the Roman Republic and that the new imperial regime was established to contain. Armitage emphasizes how *bellum civile* highlights formal warfare as its mode and citizenship as its primary category of belonging and underlines the *longue durée* of the Roman concept's influence in political and legal thought.[24]

Attempts at refining increasingly precise distinctions have produced a hydra-like splitting and multiplication of terms. We view attempts to define civil war as an intellectual struggle to contain the uncontainable. Distinctions between *stasis, seditio, coniuratio* (conspiracy), *bella civilia, bella servilia* (slave revolts), *bella socialia* (war among allies), revolution, insurrection, insurgency, revolt, rebellion, uprising, guerrilla warfare, mutiny, *jacquerie, coup d'état*, putsch, riot, tumult, and terrorism are all attempts to put boundaries in language around intolerable transgressions. Latin juggles any number of allied terms.[25] Furthermore, naming actual civil wars caused discomfort.[26] *Bellum civile* was and is no master category.

The decision to call conflict civil war per se or by some other name is an ideological choice driven by struggles for legitimacy. Central questions are the justice of the cause (*bellum iustum*), the status, power, and degree of organization of the combatants, where boundaries are drawn, whether conflict can ever end and, if it does, whether anything better may come in its wake. Tumult and riot lack the legitimacy of organized opposition. Instead of insurrection or insurgency, calling the conflict civil war may elevate low-ranked or low-power combatants by emphasizing the justice of their grievances as citizens and give them near-equal status to a state viewed as tyrannical.[27] A recent example is Syria.[28] Boundaries are not just a legal

---

[23] Armitage (2017a); responses to his book, *Critical Analysis of Law* (2017) 4.1.

[24] Armitage (2017a); Rosenberger (1992) 157.

[25] *Oxford Latin Dictionary, civilis* 2: "civil and domestic evil" (*malum civile ac domesticum*, Cicero *Cat.* 4.15); "civil dissension" (*civilis dissensiones*, Caes. *Civ.* 3.1.3); "civil discord" (*civilis discordiae*, Cicero, *Fam.* 16.11.2); "internal wars, slaughter, rape and looting, civil discord were pleasing" (*bella intestina, caedes, rapinae, discordia civilis grata fuere*, Sallust *Cat.* 5.2); "civil rage" (*rabies civilis*, Lucan 6.63). Breed, Damon, and Rossi (2010) 4–8 on *discordia*. Lavan (2017) 21–4 surveys Latin terms for revolt: the imperial perspective "blurs all social and political specificity and sees only a shared antagonism to the Roman order, troped variously as disturbance, disobedience, treachery, or defiance" (24).

[26] Rosenberger (1992) 40–4, 150–63 shows complexity in Roman names for individual wars. Naming a war after the opponent necessarily reveals which side the speaker supported; various obfuscations elided terminological differences between internal and external warfare, allowing conflict to be mentioned without calling it *bellum civile*. Civil war proper happens only at Rome (158).

[27] Armitage (2017a) 13–14.

[28] Wedeen (2019) examines complex attachments, strategies of legitimation, and dynamics of power in her critique of ideology in Syria.

matter, but one of perspective. "World wars" and "cold wars" are conceptualized in national terms that preserve the sovereignty and unity of peoples and legitimate externally directed aggression. Once Europe is conceptualized as an entity, the world wars of the twentieth century become thinkable as civil wars. Kalyvas's emphasis on sovereignty and authority vanishes from a universalizing point of view: "We might say that all warfare, insofar as its combatants all belong to the human family, is a form of civil warfare."[29]

A war coded as just often goes by some other name. An innovation important for the French context is revolution, which finds legitimacy by allegedly bringing about a new and better order, construed as universal.[30] It is the demand for newness that makes Marx's comment about the French Revolution being acted in Roman garb so ironic: The new order comes in a costume out of style for close to two millennia. Napoleon's self-fashioning as a new Caesar, then a new Augustus, aimed to legitimate his actions but ended up undercutting the promise of the French Revolution; it came not only as civil war, but as sad history's inevitable return.[31] The Haitian Revolution, occurring in parallel in 1789 against the French colonizers, likewise undercut the French Revolution's promise of universalism. Toussaint Louverture converted a slave revolt, inspired by the ideals of the French Revolution, into a successful revolution. However, the French Empire denied equality and liberty to the Black population – thereby depriving them of fraternity as well. Slavery was finally abolished only during the Second Republic (1848).[32] Revolution's legitimating and inspiring discourses continually run afoul of age-old power politics.

Hannah Arendt analyzes the French and American Revolutions as attempts to open a window in history through new birth.[33] She stops short, however, of affirming the possibility of any fully new beginning. The French undercut their claims to novelty and therefore legitimacy by not finding an alternative to Roman models. The American

---

[29] Quint (2011) 283. On cosmopolitan thought, Armitage (2017a) 26.

[30] For a conceptual history of the distinction between civil war and revolution, Koselleck (2004) 46–57. Koselleck puts a revolutionary break in the concept of revolution at the Great Revolution of 1789. The permanent, legitimized revolution sets all classical oppositions on a new, somewhat-apocalyptical footing: "The concept that contrasted with the civil wars of the past was that of the state. And the traditional doctrine of *Staatsräson* considered wars to be a vent preventing civil wars ... all wars have been transformed into civil wars. In this situation it becomes increasingly uncertain which sphere the social, industrial, and emancipatory process of revolution might occupy" (57).

[31] Morrissey (2010), Huet (1999).   [32] For this story in French literature, Lammel (2015).

[33] Arendt (1963) 141–214; natality, 211–12.

revolutionaries' conceptualization of their Revolution as a unique historical instance – the establishment of a new freedom on their own home-
grown authority – tends in the direction of exceptionalism. They
nevertheless felt a need to undergird their new start on the basis of
Hebrew and Roman models. While the French Revolution fell into
a tragic cycle of repetition through the nineteenth century up to the
Second World War, the American experiment looked more robust when
Arendt was writing. The failure to resolve questions of belonging and
citizenship that resulted in the American Civil War – particularly the
integration of the formerly enslaved population and now that of immigrants – troubles American politics to this day. Arendt's analysis takes
a tragic turn when it broadens to other revolutions. They more generally
result in "revolutionary dictatorship, designed to drive on and intensify the
revolutionary movement," to ultimately set "the world on fire" in what
comes to resemble nothing more than permanent civil war.[34] The so-called
"permanent revolution" of dictatorial revolutions is a refusal to move
beyond beginning to foundation.[35] The Roman paradigm raises the question of whether conflict can ever actually establish a new foundation. Hugo
has high hopes of overcoming the Roman model through the secular
instantiation of a Christian one. Houellebecq answers no, there is no
revolution, but only ever internal collapse. Rome, always present, comes
back wearing a burka.

Civil war has become a dominant category again in current public
discourse, but its metaphorical register is perhaps even more salient than
precise classifications according to political science. A year into the Syrian
conflict, for instance, the BBC decided it should be called civil war when
they found a mother whose sons were fighting on opposing sides. The
tropes of discord authorized the name. There are, however, alternatives.
The choice of vocabulary can indicate political commitments and align-
ments, although terminology and its entailments may shift. In Arabic, the
disturbances were initially called "the events," and Arabists are uncomfort-
able with civil war as the right term.[36] The question whether it began as or
has become a sectarian war is fraught.[37] Some see the conflict in Syria as

[34] Arendt (1963) 158–9.
[35] Romans through the Augustan period understood their state as correcting constitutional deficiencies
through the repeated foundation of new institutions. Whether these refoundations entailed return
to the past or a new beginning was disputed, Lowrie (2010a) and (2013).
[36] We thank Robyn Creswell, Ghenwa Hayek, and Lisa Wedeen for in-person analysis.
[37] Wedeen (2019) 141–62 analyzes the uptick of sectarian identifications in Syria in light of the debate
in political science as to whether sectarian attachments cause conflict or come to expression in
"otherwise motivated" disputes (161).

a proxy war between Iran and Saudi Arabia, and, for a while, it looked like a proxy war between the United States and Russia, until the American president lost interest in opposing the cold-war foe and abandoned traditional allies. It is not simply that foreign powers get drawn in after the fact. Citizenship, one among other ways of belonging, entails only one set of loyalties. If citizens fight, they do so not *qua* citizen, but under some other category: partisan of Caesar or of Pompey; Guelf or Ghibelline; of Union or Confederacy; Protestant or Catholic; Republican or Monarchist; Communist, Democrat, or Fascist; Shiite or Sunni. If citizenship commanded the highest loyalty, civil war as such would arguably not take place.

Issues of civil war – whether violence is among citizens or others, whether violence is formal warfare – currently shape discourse on "terrorism." They inform Sylvie Kaufmann's editorial on the Paris attacks in 2015: "In Europe, the terrorists we are confronted with are our fellow citizens, born and bred in our societies."[38] Terror, in her definition, comes not from without, but from within; violence is inflicted not by others, but by citizens; terrorism as a category evades sovereignty and formal warfare. The resurgence of civil war's categories is the sign and symptom of a speaker's diagnosis that the political order, whose main *raison d'être* is to prevent civil war, has failed. Globalization has, among other things, globalized the discourse of civil war.

To call an outbreak of violence "civil war" is never an innocent act. The task of defining concepts is blind to the performative consequences of the act of naming. The definition of any war elicits conflict. To name violence warfare organizes phenomena according to graspable patterns. Such decisions reassure. A prime example is the dispute over the conflict now commonly called the "First World War." Besides the retrospective grant of priority in light of the Second World War, or national differences in appellation – *Weltkrieg, la Grande Guerre* – naming this historical event was a matter of contemporary debate. In his letters, the painter Franz Marc says this violence was not a war between nation states, but "a European civil war, a war against the inner invisible enemy of the European spirit" ("europäischer Bürgerkrieg, ein Krieg gegen den inneren, unsichtbaren Feind des europäischen Geistes") and "the terrible blood-sacrifice of Europe's fraternal strife" ("das entsetzliche Blutopfer des europäischen Bruderkrieges").[39] A historian might insist that blood sacrifice is a metaphor, while war is the proper term. We underscore

---

[38] *New York Times*, November 17, 2015, www.nytimes.com/2015/11/17/opinion/frances-war-within.html.
[39] Franz Marc, *Das geheime Europa* (*Secret Europe*), in Lankkheit (1978) 163. Vinken (2009b).

that the choice of language has profound consequences, because it elicits an active response. What to call the Catilinarian conspiracy, what to call the Commune, is a matter of life and death.

It is not only the choice of concept – "sedition" or "civil war" – that is ideological. The very choice to describe such acts in conceptual terms is an ideological choice that veils the rhetoricity and performative dimension of all acts of calling. Conceptual history respects definitions, that is, boundaries. We use the methods of metaphorology, which analyzes transfers across them.[40] Metaphorology reveals that civil war is a structure reenacted across levels of meaning (nation, family, religion). Civil war violates boundaries: What should be kept outside forces its way in; what should be contained bursts out. Existing structures that form the social body dissolve through internal violence; the internal enemy is externalized as other. These shifts make defining civil war challenging, because the object of analysis changes shape through the act of naming. The fact that the denomination confers recognition only in retrospect reveals it is an ideological choice: "Civil war" is a tool, to legitimate or delegitimate the conflict. After the fact, "revolution" legitimates the winners.[41]

The proliferation of terms and the slippage in Latin between *discordia* and *bellum civile* reveal that "civil war" is no master concept that successfully distinguishes one type of violence from another. The Roman metaphorics used to discuss such violence capture the paradoxical interrelation between the transgression of boundaries, blindness to such transgressions, and their exposure. The Roman poets shed light on the perversity of ideological attempts at normalization and explode restrictive conceptual categories. The subsequent tradition takes up this literary inheritance from Latin, even as the civil wars of their own times masquerade in the dress of Roman history.

The Tropes of *Discordia*

Latin literature often narrates *bellum civile* in the register of *discordia*, etymologically a ripping apart of the heart. The end of Catullus 64 is a concise and early articulation of the collapse of the social bond through the corruption of family and sexual relations.[42]

---

[40] On the friendly battle between Koselleck and Blumenberg, Haverkamp (2009).
[41] Price (2001) 32–5; with analysis of contested terms in the Jewish rebellion (70 CE) and American Civil War: Both sides legitimated mutual slaughter, Northerners calling it a "War of Rebellion" and Southerners "The Second American Revolution."
[42] Konstan (1977): The entire poem indicts Rome; this passage is possibly a contemporary *roman à clef* (82–4). Skinner (2003) 23–4: Catullus' corpus critiques contemporary mores.

sed postquam tellus scelere est imbuta nefando
Iustitiamque omnes cupida de mente fugarunt,
perfudere manus fraterno sanguine fratres,
destitit extinctos gnatus lugere parentes,
optavit genitor primaevi funera nati,
liber ut innuptae poteretur flore novercae,
ignaro mater substernens se impia nato
impia non verita est divos scelerare penates.
omnia fanda nefanda malo permixta furore
iustificam nobis mentem avertere deorum.
quare nec talis dignantur visere coetus,
nec se contingi patiuntur lumine claro.   64.397–408

After the earth was dyed with unspeakable crime and all drove Justice to
exile with their lustful intentions, brothers drenched their hands in brother's
blood, the son stopped grieving for his dead parents, the father chose death
for his firstborn son so he could freely gain possession of the flower of an
unwed stepmother, the impious mother, spreading herself under her
unknowing son, did not fear defiling the divine gods of household lineage.
All things speakable, unspeakable, mixed through and through with wicked
fury, averted the gods' just mind from us. Wherefore they do not deign to
visit such gatherings, nor do they suffer themselves to be met by the clear
light of day.

Likely written in the 50s BCE, when Rome devolved into street violence
before the civil war battles of the 40s, this passage condenses into short
compass figurations that become standard for the collapse of the social
bond: fratricide, incest, the father's desire to kill his firstborn son to enjoy
a woman not yet his wife.[43] Chthonic abjection in family relations stains
the earth; law and religion break down with Justice in exile and the gods
abandoning humanity. The mix of speakable with unspeakable conveys
religious pollution while challenging language's expressive capacity. In
a strange resonance, Peleus' and Thetis' wedding guests gather at
Pharsalus in the narrative frame (64.37). An unresolved question lingers:
could the poem have been written as late as the battle between Pompey and
Caesar in 48 BCE?[44] A covert civil war context would lend specificity to the
ending's social degradation.

---

[43] Perverted sexual relations, beyond generational and lateral family bonds, become a strong trope of
discord. By contrast, the comparable passage in Hesiod, *Works and Days* (182–9), omits breakdown
between men and women but includes guest and host. The fleeing goddesses are Shame and
Retribution. The Near Eastern parallels cited by West (1978) *ad loc.* correspond closely to Hesiod
and omit sexuality.

[44] Vergil, who, as Gale (2013) 289–90 shows, refers back to Catullus' description of the emptied
countryside (64.37–42) at *Georgics* 1.506–8, where Pharsalus and Philippi are conflated,

Lament for Roman values' corruption specifically in civil war starts in the heat of the 30s BCE, the climactic decade that ended with young Caesar's victory over Antony and Cleopatra at Actium (31 BCE). If Catullus 64 joins a series of tropes for social disorder and only hints at civil war per se, Horace clearly evokes *bellum civile* with tropes of discord in *Epodes* 7.[45]

> Quo, quo scelesti ruitis? aut cur dexteris
>   aptantur enses conditi?
> parumne campis atque Neptuno super
>   fusum est Latini sanguinis,
> non ut superbas invidae Karthaginis
>   Romanus arces ureret,
> intactus aut Britannus ut descenderet
>   sacra catenatus via,
> sed ut secundum vota Parthorum sua
>   urbs haec periret dextera?
> neque hic lupis mos nec fuit leonibus
>   umquam nisi in dispar feris.
> furorne caecos an rapit vis acrior
>   an culpa? responsum date.
> tacent et albus ora pallor inficit
>   mentesque perculsae stupent.
> sic est: acerba fata Romanos agunt
>   scelusque fraternae necis,
> ut inmerentis fluxit in terram Remi
>   sacer nepotibus cruor.   *Epodes* 7

Where, where are you rushing, accursed criminals? Or why do you join hidden swords to your right hands? Has too little Latin blood been poured over fields and Neptune's realm, not so the Roman may burn the proud citadels of hated Carthage or the unconquered Briton descend the Sacred Way in chains, but so this city may perish – according to the vows of the Parthians – by her own right hand? This was never the custom for wolves or lions, wild only against the unlike. Or does fury snatch you, blind, or a sharper force or guilt? Answer! They are silent, and white pallor dyes their faces, and their minds, shaken, grow dumb. So it is: Harsh fates drive the Romans and the crime of a brother's murder, when the accursed blood of Remus against any desert flowed into the earth.

---

retrospectively constructs this passage as about civil war. Ambuhl (2016) adds Lucan's rewriting of both and queries the tradition of dating Catullus 64 to before Pharsalus (305).

[45] Wiseman (1995) 16: The death of Remus in this poem "could only make sense as a symbol of strife and violence."

Hyperbolic comparison to wild animals suggests violation of natural law – even the lion and Roman wolf, paradigms of savagery, do not match the atrocity of civil war. The city's suicide and the perversion of self-directed warfare confound reason. That foreign enemies would be a worthier target becomes a commonplace in Augustan literature.[46] The soul's fury is the essential problem, handed down from generation to generation as a curse. The climactic trope is fratricide.[47] Romulus' foundation generates chthonic pollution. Exclamation and rhetorical questions, finding no answer in the silent people, ventriloquize the voice of an orator powerless to change the course of events.

In the early Augustan period, Horace elaborates what becomes a central trope of civil war: perverted sexual and familial relations under a debased religious order.[48] A prime example is *Odes* 3.6, written in the 20s and published by 23 BCE.[49] The poem opens with a call to rebuild the temples – until then, Rome will continue to pay for the sins of the ancestors. A close link between "sedition," which has nearly destroyed the city (*seditionibus*, 13), and marital prostitution (21–32) binds social with political collapse. In a dizzying disruption of cause and effect, the poem's fifth stanza makes it impossible to assign priority.

> Fecunda culpae saecula nuptias
> primum inquinavere et genus et domos:
>   hoc fonte derivata clades
>   in patriam populumque fluxit.   *Odes* 3.6.117–20

> Centuries fecund with blame first stained marriages and the race and houses; destruction derived from this source has flowed into the fatherland.

Indistinction between political and social discord is the point. They violate divine order together: all beginnings, all ends should be conducted in subordination to the gods (5–6). Causality and representation go both ways. The corruption of marriage passes from a mere symptom of social disorder to a strong trope for the internal breakdown of the political order in civil war, and civil war conversely figures the collapse of the social bond. The link is now firm in the Roman imaginary. This poem is paradigmatic for how Latin literature reveals the social nature of the collapse of the civil

---

[46] E.g., Horace, *Odes* 1.35.33–40.

[47] On fratricide as Rome's ancestral curse, Jal (1963) 407, Nisbet and Hubbard (1975) 399, Watson (2003) 283–6.

[48] For the link between uncontrolled female sexuality and the general breakdown of order, Edwards (1993) 42–7.

[49] Lowrie (2018), with comparanda in Tacitus and Machiavelli.

wars through the corruption of the institution of marriage. The tropes of temples in disrepair and adultery attested in this poem crystallize and become conventional.

Odes 3.6 calls not just for restoration, but the expiation of what Christianity would call an original sin. Augustus answers this call by reinforcing political peace with an authoritarian and biopolitical social intervention.[50] The center of the so-called Augustan program entailed patriarchal legislation regulating marriage, procreation, love affairs, and adultery, as well as the restoration of no fewer than eighty-two temples.[51] Augustus aimed to bring closure to civil war in the symbolic order through moral and religious renewal. Horace continually sidesteps any direct affirmation of the Augustan program through ambivalent rhetorical gestures that defer praise.[52] Even in the *Carmen saeculare*, Rome's declared social renewal, grounded in the marriage legislation and affirmed in the indicative (71–2), depends on divine favor (65).[53] The "good and sure hope" (*bonam spem certamque*, 74) it declares reassures but defers to the future. Horace's story – fighting at Philippi on the losing side, an uneasy accommodation with Augustus, civil war's continued discursive disruptions to his poetic voice – complements the tradition we survey in long-form genres.[54] Suffice it to say that *Odes* 3.6 and the Cleopatra Ode (1.37) help solidify the violation of norms of sex, gender, and their institutions as tropes of civil war.[55]

Much of our book takes seriously Gadamer's premise, that tradition works behind our back.[56] But sometimes it stands out with great clarity. Tacitus, *Histories* 1.2, neatly packages together a set of civil war tropes, many from Horace: civil wars mixed with foreign, ruined temples, polluted rites, the Capitoline burned at the hands of citizens, adultery, bloodstained waters.[57] Beyond broken marriages, social order breaks down when slaves and freedmen betray the family, friends crush those lacking an enemy. Machiavelli in turn condenses this passage from the *Histories* into a sometimes word-for-word translation:

> If he then considers minutely the times of the other emperors, he will see them atrocious because of wars, discordant because of seditions, cruel in

---

[50] In history, the poem likely responds to rather than determines Augustus' program.
[51] *Res gestae* (8, 20). On the marriage legislation, Treggiari (1991) 277–98; Edwards (1993) 37–42; Milnor (2005) 140–1.
[52] Lowrie (1997) 224–65, 317–52; (2007).   [53] Putnam (2000) 147; Lowrie (2009) 135–7.
[54] Lowrie (1997) 138–86, (2010b).   [55] Oliensis (1998) on Canidia; Lowrie (2015c).
[56] Gadamer (1975).
[57] Cleopatra, Antony's stand-in, threatens the Capitoline at Horace, Odes 1.37.6–8. For waters stained by Roman blood in civil conflict, *Odes* 2.1.33–4.

peace and in war; so many princes killed with steel, so many civil wars, so
many external ones; Italy afflicted and full of new misfortunes, its cities
ruined and sacked. He will see Rome burning, the Capitol taken by its own
citizens, the ancient temples desolate, ceremonies corrupt, the cities full of
adulterers. He will see the sea full of exiles, rocks on the shores full of blood.
Machiavelli, *Discorsi* 1.10.5

Civil war's tropes, where marriage's perversion correlates social with political collapse, become cemented in convention. Their transmission now
flows succinctly.

The French novels we analyze inherit a Roman tropology that expresses
the violence behind civil war. Threats to the social bond disrupt natural,
political, and religious order. The discord of civil war represents the
violence politics is meant to overcome. To use *bellum civile* together with
the revelatory tropes of *discordia*, which cast civil war in light of the social
bond's violation, is to declare that order has collapsed, the categories of
friend and foe have blurred, and along with them, the categories that make
sense of the world.

Conceptual Conflict

> for Rome a *bellum civile* in any case represented a perverse oxymoron.
> Schmitzer, "Roman Values in Velleius"

In an overly schematic opposition, the crucial difference between Greek
and Roman conceptualizations of internal violence would rest on the
operative categories of belonging. Hellenism typically stresses bonds of
ethnicity through family and kinship, "blood" relations, culture, and
language, while Romans emphasize citizenship defined in legal and political categories.[58] Such differences would posit a conceptual gulf between
their outlooks.

These neat distinctions crumble in the Roman literary tradition. We
submit that the tropes of *discordia civilis* reinscribe all that *bellum civile* as
a concept for warfare between citizens hides, namely the disturbance of
family, sexual and reproductive ties, notions of self and other that civil war

---

[58] For Greek ethnicity and the tendency toward family and kinship as classificatory principles, Loraux
(1997b) 202–21, Hall (1997) 17–66, especially 36–7; for Roman citizenship as a political and legal
category, its universal extension under Caracalla in 212 CE, and its reception in political thought,
Ando (2015) 7–28, (2016); for further developments in the distinction between ethnic (*ius sanguinis*,
"the law of blood") and cultural (*ius soli*, "the law of soil") belonging and its consequences for
Germany and France, Kristeva (1989), Lacchè (2016).

brings within the city. Even when speaking of civil war, literature reaches for the larger category, discord, whose primary figurations are fratricide, parricide, and suicide; rape, adultery, and the perversion of marriage, which together couch civil war as *bellum domesticum*.[59] Its worst instantiations are incest, war between sexes and generations, between mother and daughter, father and son. For republican Romans, the *ne plus ultra* is the father killing his son; for Augustine, it is the daughter killing her mother. In modernity, the perversion of erotic relations becomes the dominant note. The tropes of civil discord bind *bellum civile* in an intimate embrace. They reveal what the concept hides in its core – civil war's violence targets not just fellow citizens, but nearest and dearest; it unmasks the concept as an attempt to cover over abjection.

A paradox of *bellum civile*, as perverse as it might seem, is to hide its horror under the legitimacy granted by formal battle and legal definitions. Whereas the literary record presents civil war regularly as dishonorable and shameful,[60] political practice can normalize the conflict. Making it one more variation among others justifies what is otherwise judged reprehensible.

> What kind of war then could there be in which the fortune of the Republic has not exercised him [Pompey]? War civil [*civile*], African, Transalpine, Spanish – mixed with citizens and the most bellicose nations – with slaves, with ships, varied and diverse types of wars and enemies, not only waged by this one man, but even brought to an end – these wars declare that no matter has been placed in military practice which could escape the knowledge of this man. Cicero, *De imperio Cn. Pompei* 28[61]

Cicero's argument that Pompey should receive an extraordinary command against Mithridates turns him into a model of Republican masculine virtue. He is the best because he masters war of all kinds, including civil, and wins all possible glory. Augustus' laconic style similarly lists foreign and civil warfare as two possible types.

> Wars civil and foreign on land and at sea I often waged on the whole globe of the lands; and as victor I granted pardon to all citizens who asked. Augustus, *Res gestae* 3

---

[59] Jal (1963) 469–70; Thomas (1981) 653, 690–95: the "dangerous contiguity" of *pater patriae* (father of the fatherland) and *parricida* (parricide); Loraux (1997b) 218. For *bellum domesticum* (internal war), Rosenberger (1992) 159.

[60] Jal (1963) 450–64.

[61] Lange and Vervaet (2019b) hypothesize that Sulla invented the term *bellum civile*, so it was already circulating when Cicero used it here.

Augustus betters Pompey in a Caesarian vein; hardly ashamed of waging civil war in itself, he can vaunt clemency in victory.[62] Such shamelessness is already manifest among his predecessors. Despite discomfort, Romans in fact celebrated triumphs for their victories in civil war, provided the triumph was not over a civil enemy alone. Carsten Lange lays out the evidence, contrary to the denial of many historians, ancient and modern.

> a commander could in practice expect to triumph after a civil war victory if it could also be represented as being over a foreign enemy, even if the principal opponent was clearly Roman. Significantly, the civil aspect of the war did not have to be denied . . . the idea of civil war as "normal" reflects the way civil war permeated the politics and society of the Late Roman Republic.[63]

Declaring that civil war enemies were *hostes* eased the practice: Being an "enemy of state" converted internal into external enemies. Also legitimating were defending the Republic against an opponent who had initiated civil war and liberating the state from faction. Bandaging over the wound of civil war with foreign war or liberation was enough for generals to reap the fruit of glory at the expense of their own defeated fellow citizens.

The register of civil war elides neat distinctions, not only between internal and external enemies, but even between the presence or not of battle, any antithesis between familial and legal categories of belonging. Latin literature frequently refers to civil war with the broader category *discordia* and often figures it in family terms.[64]

> The civil wars of the dying Republic were frequently represented through the myth, no doubt all too often a reality, of strife within the family: the supreme example is the conflict between Caesar and Pompey, father-in-law and son-in-law, while a more generally available image is that of fratricide, with the particularly nasty variation of twin fratricide. In civil war the orderly succession of generations through father and son is cut off by mutual destruction within one generation. Hardie (1993) 93[65]

Roman narratives tell civil war in mythic familial and sexual terms that inscribe more intimate relations into warfare between citizens. Ethnic and

---

[62] Lange (2019): Augustus' *Res gestae* justifies his role in the civil wars.

[63] Lange (2016b) cover blurb. Lange (2013): Although Sulla and Pompey inched closer, "Caesar's Spanish triumph in 45 . . . unequivocally broke the taboo on civil war triumphs" (77). On dissimulating the fact of civil war, Rosenberger (1992) 42–3, 155.

[64] The political context – the people's *fasces*, kings' purple, the warfare implied by reference to the Dacians – framing *agitans discordia fratres* ("discord driving brothers," *Georg.* 2.496) makes it clear that Vergil's phrase pertains to civil war beyond familial strife.

[65] Austin (1977) at 6.830 remarks of Caesar's and Pompey's appearance as in-laws: "Virgil has given Epic cachet to what was originally a gibe of the lampoonists." Lefèvre (1998) 107.

familial paradigms of political belonging, arising more organically in Greek, prove irresistible to Roman authors, who heighten the horror of violence of like on like through family and sexuality.

As a concept, civil war bears internally the normalization granted by the Republic, even as its historical actuality destroyed the very Republic that normalized it. What the concept covers over is the horror of a more primal violence that continually resurfaces. By restricting its scope to legal citizenship and war as conflict between armies, *bellum civile* conceptually limits the political sphere. It represses the familial ground of politics recognized since Aristotle (*Nic. Ethics* 1162a16–18, *Politics* 1252a25; Cicero, *De officiis* 1.54) and excludes the feminine in a masculinist vein.[66] It sublates blood ties into the political metaphor of an exclusively male fraternity that haunts all forms of republicanism from Rome to its modern articulation in Rousseau's *contrat social*.[67] *Bellum civile* represses the internal violence familiar from Greek myth: war within family and tribe, between women and men, parents and children.[68] As a concept, *bellum civile* whitewashes a stain and makes it possible to speak of internal violence via the clean and proper terms of a masculinist republicanism. It declares this war's *champ de bataille* one like any other: between men, between armies. It legitimates what literature shows cannot be legitimated.

The first phrase of Lucan's poem, *bella . . . plus quam civilia* ("wars more than civil," 1.1), figures the semantic difference between *bellum civile* and *discordia* at the same time as collapsing the distinction between them. The classic interpretation of this passage is that war in the family, namely between Pompey and Caesar as father- and son-in-law, is worse than civil war.[69] Lucan, however, does not in fact identify family breakdown by name but lets it be assumed; the reader is expected to infer it. Familial discord bubbles up as a worse horror within the cleaned-up and contained

---

[66] Owens (2017) addresses civil war's extensive exclusions.   [67] Vinken (1993).

[68] For the overlap of Greek myth and Greek history, Loraux's (1997b) chapter on brothers, especially 205. Greek classificatory categories come largely from parentage: The brother becomes first a companion, then a citizen (206, 215). In *stasis*, the persons killed are "other selves" ("ces autres soi-mêmes," 216). In *bellum civile*, the predominant figuration is son killing father (217), but see Bannon (1997) 150–1 on brothers. Thomas (1981) distinguishes the legal category *parricidium*, specifically, murder of a father, from literary figurations, which generalize violence to all family members (714–15).

[69] Della Corte (1984–91), under *guerre civili*, reviews the ancient distinction between *bellum civile* and *bellum plus quam civile* (more than civil war); in the latter, the principals' relationship extends beyond citizenship to family. Jal (1963) 35–37, Ahl (1976) 313, Conte (1988) 17–20: compare Seneca, *Phoenissae* 354–5: *non satis est adhuc / civile bellum: frater in fratrem ruat* ("civil war is not enough so far: let brother rush against brother"). Henderson (1987) 135 = (1998) 187 retails the Lucanian excesses unleashed by the phrase.

concept of civil war. In four short words, the phrase enacts with concision a complex structure: It names civil war, hides the broken familial bonds, and renames civil war to include the excluded terms, which are borne along with civil war under erasure. The narrative then spells out the familial horror. Whitewashing the abjection underlying civil war is a perversion of language that the tropology reveals to be inadequate to the reality of the thing. Through such tropological refiguration, civil war is made to bear within itself the familial discord the concept taken literally (war among citizens) would cover up. That the tropes of *discordia* become figurations of *bellum civile* indicates that civil war has a general tendency to become more than itself.

The Roman tropology of civil war in civil discord's conventional metaphors explodes conceptual restriction. Civil discord is revealed to be intrinsic to the political, because the tropes of Rome's foundation are the same as its tropes, namely fratricide and rape. Romulus' murder of his brother Remus and the rape of the Sabines establish the political and social orders respectively.[70] Latin literature avails itself of civil war's metaphorical potential as discord and extends its logic of internal violence across spheres: fratricide and parricide within the family, cosmic turbulence in the weather, internal division within the soul, sexual violence, adultery, suicide – all become tropes for civil war.[71]

The Roman term *bellum civile* remains powerful because it captures a paradox: Civil war is always more than itself.

Discordia **and** Stasis

Greek *stasis* is often identified as *bellum civile*'s correlate, but these terms do not align exactly.[72] Starting from Greek, it makes more sense to translate *stasis* into Latin as *discordia*. These are the broader categories encompassing political strife of many kinds short of and including warfare. What Benjamin Straumann says of *stasis* also pertains to *discordia*: "Every civil war is necessarily a *stasis*, but not every *stasis* amounts to a civil war."[73] *Stasis*

---

[70] Interpretation of the Remus myth is fraught. Wiseman (1995) speculates it was created in the fourth century BCE as an allegory of the conflict of the orders, with each element arising dynamically through the classes' competition to control its meaning. The murdered brother corresponds to the repeatedly thwarted plebeian demand for participation in governance. The myth contains a veiled foundation sacrifice that responds to early third-century political events, later sanitized as the solution to a security crisis (summary 126). By the triumviral period, the myth becomes a trope not just for political contestation, but for civil war (143–4).

[71] For the psychological dimension of *stasis* in Thucydides, Price (2001) 25, 36.

[72] Armitage (2017a) 21, 37–45.   [73] Straumann (2017) 142.

slides from discord to outright war.[74] Greek qualifies *stasis* with *emphulos* or *emphulios* (tribal) when specifying conflict internal to a given polity, but the implication of blood relations inherent in the *phule* lends a valence different from the Latin emphasis on citizenship in *civilis*. When warfare needs specification, Greek uses *polemos*, which, like *stasis*, may be qualified with *emphulos* or even *oikeios* (belonging to the household).[75] Like *bellum*, *discordia* may be qualified with *civilis*.[76]

Nicole Loraux shows that the Greeks always end up defining political violence in terms of family.[77] Discord within the polis can come as *polemos oikeios* (a war of one's own / in the home). This is a scandal demanding immediate remedy, where the household provides the model for reconciliation. Discord can also come as a fact of destiny or nature, in which case they called it *haima homaimon* (bloodshed of like blood). This sees violence within the family as inevitable and tragic. Mediating between inevitability and possible remedy, between formal war and indiscriminate bloodshed, *stasis emphul(i)os* (tribal discord) also names blood ties and locates internal conflict in ethnicity. Because the polis is defined in familial and tribal terms, internal political violence is similarly structured. Whether as source of violence or source of reconciliation, family and blood always provide the framework.

Loraux describes a continual dynamic of crossing terms. If the city is defined as a *phule* (race or tribe), it follows that *stasis* reveals the category of belonging as grounded in nature. If you define the city as an *oikos* (a household), a locus of reconciliation appears on the horizon to quell the *polemos* (war).[78] There is no synthesis between natural and institutional categories, but a continual circling of ambivalence in which *stasis* provides a kind of "cement of the community."[79] Giorgio Agamben links Loraux's analysis to Christian Meier's thesis about the attempts in fifth-century Athens to define the city in strictly political categories and describes *stasis* as

---

[74] Lange (2017): *Stasis* covers a sliding scale up to outright warfare and therefore only partially overlaps with *bellum civile*. Historiography's focus on pitched battles rather than guerrilla warfare is misleading. He emphasizes untidy conceptual boundaries in both Greek and Latin between foreign and domestic warfare, the ideological blurring of narratives, and the importance of family ties.

[75] E.g., Cassius Dio, στάσεις καὶ πόλεμοι ἐμφύλιοι ("disturbances and tribal wars," 52.27.3); Plato, ὁ οἰκεῖος πόλεμος ("war in the household," *Menexenus* 243e2).

[76] E.g., Cicero, *Ad fam.* 16.11.2.3; Sallust, *Cat.* 5.2.3, *Jug.* 78.1.2. Vergil's juxtaposition of *discordia* with *civis* (*Ecl.* 1.71) does the same work.

[77] Loraux (1997a) 38.   [78] Loraux (1997a) 62.

[79] Loraux (1997b) 63; in her chapter "Le lien de la division," her analysis of *dialuo* (92–3), which can mean both to divide and to reconcile, among other ambivalent words, shows *stasis* to be essential to maintaining the social bond in Greek political thought (90–120). She brings the psychoanalytic categories of repression and denial to her analysis of *stasis* in addition to ambivalence (59–89).

a zone of indifference between the apolitical space of family and the political space of the city.[80] He rearticulates Loraux's and Meier's theses about Greek terminology and Athenian politics in more general terms to make the claim that the structure of *stasis emphul(i)os* captures the ambivalent logic of the political sphere.

Agamben describes the political as a dynamic field defined by tension between the extremes of *oikos*, namely family, and of *polis*, which putatively sets up surrogate bonds of fraternity among citizens.[81] *Stasis* functions as a threshold where an excessive pull toward familial bonds repoliticizes the family and an excessive pull toward the *polis* reinscribes family bonds within it. *Stasis* for him becomes an essential and perhaps the fundamental logic of politics. It obeys what for Agamben's thought is a basic structure: the internalization of the external and vice versa. At the threshold between two ways of belonging, *stasis* constitutes a zone of indistinction between them that continually renegotiates their inability to separate. If the sovereign's legitimacy, as Hobbes paradigmatically claims, resides in the ability to prevent civil war, Agamben is skeptical about its eventual success, given his thesis that *stasis* is politics' very articulation.[82] Like Machiavelli, he puts contestation at the heart of the political, but for Machiavelli, contestation does not necessarily lead to out-and-out bloodshed.

The early Roman Republic provides a positive model for Machiavelli in that it succeeded in structuring contestation for centuries with only occasional turmoil, such as the plebeian secessions, and little bloodshed; it devolved into civil war only later, with the turbulent Gracchi. The challenge for Machiavelli is to keep a republic from falling into corruption and to renew it once it does.[83] For Agamben, violence is part and parcel of contestation. It cannot be overcome and its denial – preeminently through Christianity and its secularizations – fundamentally deforms the political sphere. The stability etymologically encoded in *stasis* – standing – takes the disturbance as a unity, an "autarchic process," something like a "principle."[84] Agamben describes the current political world as this structure universalized.[85] Thucydides also universalizes *stasis* as fundamental to all

---

[80] Agamben (2015) 23.   [81] Building on Loraux (1997b) 202–21.   [82] Bredekamp (2012).
[83] McCormick (2011); Pedullà (2011); Arum (2020).
[84] Loraux (1997b) 105–6; for *homonoia* (like-minded concord) as *stasis*'s opposite and the paradoxical need to internalize commotion to stop commotion (106–8).
[85] Agamben (2015) 30. When the *oikos* (household) becomes globalized as a form of belonging as, for example, in the metaphor *la maison d'Europe* (the house of Europe), the entire dynamic field of politics – as tension between *oikos* and *polis* – becomes subject to the negotiation that consists of civil war. This is currently called terrorism. The stakes of this redescription are to deconstruct the war

politics, and the cosmic dimension of civil war in Latin literature performs the same gesture through metaphor.[86]

Roman political thought often addresses political theoretical questions not through explicit argumentation, but with story, metaphor, and subtle variations in conventional imagery.[87] Civil war and the establishment of political order share a repertory of tropes in the Roman political imaginary. Although different authors give different accounts of foundation, disruption, and refoundation, the fact that violence within the family and between the sexes marks political strife as well as foundation sets these in an intimate relation and recognizes discord's role in politics. It also signals the priority of familial and sexual ties over citizenship. As gruesome as killing among citizens may be, it pales before brothers killing brothers and violent betrayal in sexual relationships. Livy links political reform or progress to institutional solutions to civic violence. The rape of Lucretia spawns the Republic's foundation; Verginia's killing by her father, to protect her from dishonoring rape, inaugurates the rule of law. Vergil highlights law and imperial expansion as the Augustan solution to cyclical violence in the *Aeneid* but locates the source of breakdown in love and the soul. Despite making different points about the relation of discord to the political order, Livy and Vergil speak the same political idiom.[88] The disputed question is whether Discord is an intrinsic part of the system or a thorn in overarching Concord.[89]

That Rome's foundation is grounded in fratricide and sexual violence and these return as figures for civil war asks a political theoretical question: Will refoundation follow? The answers vary, but the recurrence of traumatic events in mythic times, in archaic Roman history, and in the present voices outrage with the same vocabulary. Romulus' fratricide is repeated in historical accounts of brothers killing brothers, sons their fathers, and vice versa in civil war.[90] Whether or not these stories actually happened, they

---

between democracy and terrorism. Rather, terrorism becomes an essential articulation of democratic politics.

[86] Price (2001) 12, 22–30. Breed, Damon, and Rossi(2010) 9: "civil wars are not simply a bug in the system . . . that can be either fixed or expelled."

[87] Lowrie (forthcoming a).

[88] For different structures of refoundation in Livy and Vergil, Lowrie (2010a) and (2013).

[89] Momigliano (1942) 118–20: Latin *concordia* was calqued on Greek *homonoia*; he stresses Machiavelli's insistence on discord's importance to republican Rome's thriving. Breed, Damon, and Rossi (2010) 7–8: The Romans continued to perceive Concord as a stable force, despite repeatedly making the deity preside over social restoration after breakdown. The system requires Discord to be overcome, a significant departure from *homonoia*, a civic deity charged with maintaining (as opposed to restoring) agreement and harmony. Hellegouarc'h (1963) 127.

[90] Sisenna frg. 132 Cornell; Livy, *Epitome* 79; Valerius Maximus, 5.5.4; Tacitus, *Hist.* 3.51.1–2. Without a literal fratricide, Sallust suggests it in his account of Catiline's defeat: After the battle, many

bear a mythic valence. The figuration communicates civil war's awfulness and demands reform. Romans, matching Greek myth in abjection, analyze their own history with stories that do myth's work.[91]

Where a story ends and the tone of its telling indicate how much an author believes reform is possible. Such literary features therefore require attention to gauge an author's political thinking. Livy has faith in the ability of institutions to contain violence. Rape, or its threat, moves institutions forward: Reconciliation in marriage ensues after the Sabines' violation, the Republic's foundation after Lucretia's, and the law code's establishment after Verginia's. His attitude seems cheerful compared to the gloomy outlook of Sallust, writing in the turbulence following Caesar's assassination, and of Tacitus, who gains confidence only with Trajan. Sallust colors Catiline's revolt in morally condemnatory hues: Murdering his son perverts his new marriage and literalizes the horror ending Catullus 64. Sallust's story, which ends on a note of mourning after Catiline is defeated in battle, imagines no institutional restoration. Given the time of writing (late 40s BCE), his tone unsurprisingly remains dark. In Vergil, Lavinia's marriage to Aeneas, figured as a rape by Turnus, encodes both violence and its institutional containment in the same figure. Vergil's tonality of mourning accords with his understanding of how the solutions to violence succeed in repressing it only temporarily. The sterility – literal and figurative – Lucan depicts in the marriages of Cato, Pompey, and Caesar and the death of Julia, whose block on violence is modeled after the Sabines standing between father- and son-in-law (1.111–19), remove any possible refoundation after civil war. Lucan's tone, which perverts the tragic into the grotesque, indicates how awful a political future he foresees after Caesar. The rapes and chastity killings of the Republic are perverted in Tacitus' version of Nero's perhaps incestuous matricide – small wonder civil war erupted again at his death. Tacitus' twisted style shrouds the history he tells in horror.

Beyond bloodshed, language and representation are civil war's battleground. In Thucydides, perversion in language is symptomatic of *stasis*:

> The ordinary acceptation of words in their relation to deeds was changed as men thought fit. Reckless audacity came to be regarded as courageous loyalty to party, prudent hesitation as specious cowardice, moderation as a cloak for unmanly weakness. Thuc. 3.82.4

"turning over the cadavers of enemies found some of them a friend, others a guest or even a relative" (*Bellum Catilinae* 61). Bannon (1997) 150, Woodman (1983) 116–19, Ash (2009) 92–3.

[91] Archaic history was the Romans' functional equivalent of myth, Beard (1993).

Discord's semantic disruption resides not in the strict meanings of words, but in their transvaluation, that is their perverse realignment with social values and institutions.[92] Thucydides excoriates language's degradation as an obfuscation giving moral sanction to wrong. Lucan repeats this claim of civil war: *iusque datum sceleri* ("legality given to crime," 1.2).[93]

We submit that *bellum civile* itself is a semantic dodge. The concept covers up the abjection of political disorder by restricting it to battles among citizens. By contrast, the tropes of *discordia* tell a greater truth, civil war's perversion of norms and language together, by illustrating all that *bellum civile* veils. Literature at its best restores language to its rightful function. It tells the story through mythic tropes that lend moral clarity and thereby reveals what ideology tries to deny.

The Inner Orient

Civil war, concept and trope together, simultaneously perpetuates and exposes a precise logic: the externalization of an inner divide. The desire not to recognize the foe as one's own likeness is a desire to avert the horror of self-destruction. It motivates an act of alienation, a failed recognition of the self: what is like appears unlike. Such misapprehension engenders one of civil war's primary figurations: the internal enemy orientalized as external. Orientalizing reassures by abjectifying the horrific in the self. It sets a barrier between itself and whatever is expelled from its own body, corporal or politic.[94] In political terms, this hermeneutic move projects internal conflict onto a reassuringly distanced other.

This figuration's original scene is Latin literature's representation of the Roman civil wars. Eastern mercenaries hired by Pompey and Antony and

---

[92] Price (2001) 39–45, 59–67; all "institutions of society – political, legal, religious" and family relations are perverted along with the corruption of language (59). Bartsch (2012) 174–5 analyzes semantic massaging in Aristotle, the *Ad Herennium*, and Quintilian; imperial Latin literature, particularly Lucan and Tacitus, exposes "the loss of meaning suffered by value-terms through their usage in the ideology of the victors," "political language masks its negative counterpart" (186–7). On the confusion of good and evil in civil war and the reversal of words' meaning, Jal (1963) 472–3. On Lucan's difficult language, hyperbole, excess, rhetorical "(dis)figuration," absurdist paradox, violent compressions and inversions as symptoms of civil war, Henderson (1987), especially 135–51 = (1998) 187–95.

[93] O'Gorman (2000) 15–16: Perverted language among Thucydides' *stasiotai* characterizes the style of so-called Silver Latin. No mere metaphor for or symptom of *stasis*, perverted language "induces the very confusion" provoked by the events.

[94] In psychoanalysis, abjection is technically the withdrawal of identification of what exits the body as part of the self, eliciting disgust. Physically, excrement, vomit, and body fluids induce this reaction. Abjection becomes a metaphor for any withdrawal of identification causing disgust. Stallybrass and White (1986), Kristeva (1982).

Octavian's declaration of war against Egyptian Cleopatra enabled the depiction of Roman soldiers opposing the respective Caesarian sides, first as non-Roman and then as decadent and corrupt.[95] This gesture represents civil war as foreign war, as if it were war between East and West and not internal to Rome. Such representation may have no bearing on actual relations with peoples from the East nor even capture all attitudes toward Easterners.[96] However, the pejorative figuration of the other can and has been taken literally, so that Westerners – some[97] – have come to believe "orientals" really are the way the West has figured them.

The inner orient crystallized during Rome's transition from Republic to Empire.[98] Cicero smears Antony in the *Philippics*, written in the wake of Caesar's assassination, as a slavish and debauched drunkard who aspires to tyranny. These smears do not yet target the Eastern other but express the danger of civil war in moral terms. With the battle of Actium, the poets – Horace, Propertius, and Vergil – transfer Cicero's discourse onto an Eastern queen. Cleopatra thereby becomes a screen for Antony: a slavish and debauched drunkard who aspires to tyranny. With this gesture, the East becomes the orient, a shorthand for the perversion of the free, male, autonomous subject, for the overturn of free and equal relations among citizens, for wrong relations between ruler and subject, man and woman. In short, the woman on top tyrannizes the subjected man. Orientalism is a representational strategy of denial. It projects away from the self all it would cast out. Orientalism – a horror-house mirror that veils its act of mirroring – does not describe the other but figures conflict within the self. It becomes a central figuration of civil war from the Romans up to our times.

The bee society in Vergil's *Georgics* is a straightforward case of civil war orientalized.[99] The poem's historical context is civil war, recently quelled at Rome;[100] the bees fight each other when two kings split the loyalties of a single hive; likened to Eastern peoples, including Egyptians, in their devotion to a king, they tear apart their own hive, an act of self-destruction

---

[95] All sides used foreign mercenaries; none had only mercenaries. On Actium, Gurval (1995); Lange (2009) 79–90, (2013) 82–4: although Actium in Augustus' *Res gestae* is recognized as a civil war, "it was as a foreign war against Egypt and Cleopatra that is became eligible for a triumph"; (2016b) 120 (on dehumanizing the enemy to persuade people to kill their fellow citizens), 122–3 (on Actium as both foreign and civil war), 125–53.

[96] For Greek and Roman attitudes toward Egyptians and the origin of prejudicial depiction post Actium, Gruen (2011) 76–114.

[97] E.g., many followers of Marine Le Pen, the *Alternative für Deutschland* party, and Donald Trump.

[98] Gruen (2011) 95–6, Lowrie (2015c).   [99] Lowrie (2015b).

[100] The *Georgics* were published after Actium and likely no later than 28 BCE.

analogous to civil war, when the monarch is dead. The parallels between the Romans and the bee society give a variety of warnings. Excessive devotion to a charismatic leader is dangerous. It not only risks civil war but also makes the Romans oriental. If analogy makes parallels, it also holds the compared elements apart. The distance between the bees and the Romans allows for plausible deniability: No, that exaggerated picture of oriental despotism and self-destruction cannot correspond to us! Critical distance also enables self-examination. We risk becoming oriental if we overinvest in our leader, newly granted sole rule; dependency on him could lead to civil war just as much as when two leaders divided our loyalties.

More complex forms of orientalism occur in the texts we analyze. Integrative and disintegrative modalities engage in orientalism in different ways. A text may represent one or the other modality without endorsing it. The story level of Vergil's *Aeneid* represents the integrative tradition: Empire arises from the defeat of the oriental other and establishes peace in civil war's wake. The shield of Aeneas in *Aeneid* 8 broadcasts this message. Antony, orientalized along with Cleopatra, fights at Actium, and Augustus integrates subjected foes into the Empire at his triple triumph. The figuration of Aeneas himself indicates that the orientalization of the internal foe lacks authorial sanction. Rome's protofounder wears oriental dress. Whether you see it as such depends on your perspective: Iarbas and Numanus Remulus orientalize him; the narrator does not. Juno insists that Trojan culture, including language and dress, be wiped out in Rome's foundation, but Rome's Eastern origins continue to leave traces. The Julian *gens*, the national *penates* (gods of familial lineage), and the *lusus Troiae* maintain a connection to Troy through bloodlines and institutions. The conflict between Italian and Trojan returns in the conflict between Romans and Egyptians: Both appear literally or metaphorically as forms of civil war.

We argue that the *Aeneid* displays the integrative position in one gesture and reveals its mystification in another. The defeated other remains internalized at Rome and retains its power under erasure. Rome's penchant for civil war remains, just as it has throughout Roman history. The empire without end subjects the oriental other, but defeated foes, who become Roman when incorporated into the expanded Empire, may resent the indignity, like the river Araxes (*Aeneid* 8.728) – dignity, as Caesar tells us, is a reason to engage in civil war.[101] The revelation of orientalism's inner workings in the *Aeneid* allows the poem to covertly critique the triumphant

---

[101] *BC* 1.7.

political form as false consciousness. This revelation requires active engagement on the reader's part, to assemble cues scattered across the textual surface that, pieced together, recast the dominant story.

Disintegrationists present a different picture: The oriental spoils of empire refound the Roman Republic as its conquered other. Lucan establishes this structure, in which the winner of civil war loses the Republic. Caesar is synecdoche for Rome; the leader figures the polity.[102] His dalliance with Cleopatra in Egypt is a scene of perverted republican values. The Empire rising from the Republic's ashes, meant to contain civil war, goes to bed with the oriental foe; Rome embraces its own non-Roman opposite and becomes what it embraces. The difference between republican self and oriental opponent recedes into a lost and regretted past. Abjection's self-protective work is undone, and Romans see themselves in the mirror as their own other. Rome become oriental replays on the outside the internal conflict the repression of the abject masks on the surface. Rome in destroying herself becomes her own other. The masculinist, virtuous Republic that defeated itself in civil war turns into the decadent, effeminate, tyrannical Empire. Civil war's tropology becomes the tropology of empire. Incest and rape, decadence, perverted sexuality, and murder within the family run rampant all for the sake of domination.

Like Vergil, Lucan plays a nuanced game. Republican values are defined in contrast to the oriental mode of the coming Empire on the one hand, but on the other, the Republic as represented fails to live up to its own ideology. The marriage bonds of the three primary Roman leaders – not to say heroes – show perversions of different kinds. All reveal fractures in the realization of republican ideology. The improper takes over the proper as Republic gives way to Empire, but the proper never exists in the poem to begin with. Civil war, a war of like against like, results in indistinction, but instead of making the oriental Roman in the integrationist gesture, it turns out that the Roman was perverse all along. Michel Houellebecq replays this structure: The French Republic collapses through civil war, and an oriental Empire takes its place. But it turns out that the Republic was already corrupt in the same terms as the new Empire, which, in a satiric twist, fulfills the Republic's corruption and reveals its values as already undone by taking every aspect of perversion to a clarifying extreme.

Not all integrationists undo integration from within. Augustine firmly believes the *civitas Dei* offers a new paradigm of restoration that leaves behind the corruption of Rome figured as Babylon. God's grace cleanses

---

[102] See Hardie (1993) 4–5, 13 for the synecdochic hero.

the sinner who accepts it. Hugo similarly believes that the republic to come will offer true liberty, equality, fraternity and sorority, now on a new footing that will uphold Christian values against the oriental corruption of monarchy and the Roman church. The grotesque will be integrated into the sublime. Nevertheless, both authors adopt Lucan's strategy and show how the prior paradigm had fallen prey to its own opposite. Civil war shows classical Rome in its worst guise for Augustine: It had always been a second Babylon. For Hugo, the monarchy and church had always been Roman and hence oriental. Civil war discloses as oriental the true nature of what came before.

Sacrifice, Conversion, Perversion

In the Hebrew Bible and New Testament, for Greek and Roman alike, the restoration of the social bond turns on sacrifice. The purpose of this most ambivalent ritual is to cleanse the abject and refound community. It should overcome internal discord across the cosmos: among humans, between men and animals, between gods and men.[103] In Plato's *Menexenus*, only "prayers and sacrifices" (243e–4a) may reconcile a society torn by *stasis* and *oikeios polemos*. In Christian dogma, Jesus' self-sacrifice is the sacrifice to end all sacrifices; in reconciling man to God and men to men, it is to found a new social order in a new covenant. But sacrifice is precarious. In the Hebrew Bible, idolatry, an import from the Babylonian East, threatens its success. Foreign women typically seduce the Jewish people away from the one true God and enamor them of idols.[104] Greek and Roman literature returns repeatedly to the motif of perverted sacrifice, which speaks to the social bond's fragility and the obstacles to restoring it.[105]

In the Roman tradition of civil war literature, sacrificial restoration is threatened by the very abjection it would integrate. Sacrifice's corruption, often through human sacrifice, reinscribes the violence of like on like into the ritual meant to overcome it. Human sacrifice perverts all a proper sacrifice should perform. For the Romans, there is no further recourse when sacrifice tragically fails. From a Christian perspective – specifically in Augustine – the Romans' lack of proper sacrifice means they will remain

---

[103] Girard (1972).   [104] Vinken (2019) 221–45.

[105] Zeitlin (1965): In Aeschylus' *Oresteia*, sacrifice is "corrupted," murder "in sacramental dress, that is, ritual slaughter" (464) corrupts the project of vengeance (507); the motif's abandonment in the *Eumenides* and the return of "healthful ritual" signal the reestablishment of "harmony of family and state" (508). Seaford (1989) stresses the motif's specificity to Greek tragedy: Homer excludes "kin-killing and sacrificial imagery" (87).

entangled in earthly history and, for all history, inescapably wage civil war. The pagan Romans worship the wrong gods, even turning humans into gods; they sacrifice to their gods the wrong way, even sacrificing their own priest in a scene going back to Lucan; their whole religion is idolatry, and idolatry of power at that. In Augustine, the newly founded covenant of Christianity overcomes the logic of Roman history with a different kind of human sacrifice, one to bring all sacrifice to an end and, with it, civil war. But so long as earthly history endures, the *civitas Dei* will continue on her pilgrimage, without closure, through the morass of the *civitas terrena*.

The representation of sacrifice is a sure index of a text's commitments. The interpretive crux of Vergilian "optimism" or "pessimism" rides on one's reading of the *bugonia* in the *Georgics* and the death of Turnus in the *Aeneid*. In the *Georgics*, Egypt is an ambivalent locus of both peril – the abject worship of a monarch, to the point of self-destruction – and potential redemption. Out of Egypt, the *bugonia* comes as a rite that will ostensibly restore the lost society of bees. It has two guises, each an antitype to sacrifice: technological invention and the grotesque adjunct to a sacrifice of atonement. Each depends on bodily abjection and fails to heal the fractured social bond. The perverse ritual fulfills the desired expiation only on the technological, not the spiritual, plane. Although technically the *bugonia* works – a new hive of bees comes to life – the restoration brings back nothing more than a despotic society prone to civil war. The *bugonia* bears within itself the oriental abjection that sacrifice means to overcome and thereby fails. It does not provide a solution to civil war that Roman society would or could adopt.

When Aeneas kills Turnus with the verb *immolare* (sacrifice), the scene resounds with the register of human sacrifice.[106] Rome's foundation also comes in this register. The other verb qualifying Aeneas' act is *condere* (to bury or found): He buries his sword in Turnus's chest in a gesture that metaphorically both founds Rome and undoes its foundation.[107] A palimpsest of identifications, between Aeneas and Turnus, Turnus and Pallas, Aeneas and Pallas, sets the scene additionally under the register of suicide. If human sacrifice were not enough to set Rome's foundation on a precarious footing, suicide additionally marks it with a common trope for civil war. Rome followed the wrong path even before the beginning. The end of civil war through restorative sacrifice will have to wait for Actium. However, as Julia Dyson has shown, Vergil's depiction on the shield of Aeneas calls into question the piety of Octavian's sacrifice. The *caesi iuvenci*

---

[106] Hardie (1993) 19.   [107] James (1995).

("slaughtered oxen," *Aen.* 8.719) allude to other Vergilian scenes, including
the *bugonia* and Octavian's sacrifice of knights and senators, captured in
the civil war battle of Perusia (40 BCE), at the altar of Divus Iulius.[108]
While Vergil consistently undoes sacrifice's salvific potential from within,
the absence in Lucan of an overriding sacrificial register, even failed, stands
out. Individual acts of sacrifice turn in his hands to the grotesque, and none
has even the potential to end civil war. There is no possibility of restoration, much less redemption.

    Vergilian ambivalence pervades the death of Gauvain at the conclusion of
Hugo's *Quatrevingt-treize*, but the aesthetics of Romanticism prove redemptive against failed classical and Christian models. Gauvain surrenders himself
to republican justice for performing an act of mercy in a Christian mode. He
frees his great-uncle and archenemy Lantenac, caught and imprisoned when
himself performing an act of mercy. By freeing Lantenac, Gauvain betrays
the Revolution, but by handing himself over to justice, he sets it on a new
path of redemption under secularized Christian values. His self-sacrifice at
the guillotine, figured as an *imitatio Christi*, occurs simultaneously with the
suicide of his tutor Cimourdain, a former priest turned dogmatic republican,
who finds himself condemning his beloved spiritual son to death to uphold
the rule of law, fundamental to republican ideals. The conflict between
competing commitments is unbearable. Cimourdain consequently shoots
himself through the heart in the register of Roman civil war. Their two souls,
light and dark, Christian and republican (both secular), Roman Catholic
and classical Roman, sublime and grotesque, fly intertwined up to heaven.
The sublime elevates and redeems the grotesque and puts the new republican
order on firm footing – that is, on as sure a footing as Augustine's *civitas Dei*,
continually on its pilgrimage during earthly history. Hugo, who wrote
Quatrevingt-treize in the wake of the slaughter of the Commune, knows
French history will ever stumble into civil war after the Revolution.

    In the Augustinian tradition, Christ's self-sacrifice opens a collective path
for society to leave the earthly city and join the *civitas Dei* on its pilgrimage.
Individuals must take off Paul's "old self" before putting on a new.[109]
Conversion, the trope for this transformation, becomes a means of individual redemption in the postclassical novel. Conversion entails emptying the
old self (*kenosis*) and relinquishing self-love for love of God. It is modeled on
God's emptying himself (*kenosis*) to become man, in order to redeem man
through the sacrifice of Christ.[110] Obedience to God becomes the path of

---

[108] Dyson (1996). For *caesis iuvencis*, Boyle (1986) 74–5, 81, 547.   [109] Ephesians 4.22.
[110] Marion (1977), Henry (1994).

freedom; love is liberation, not submission. Since Augustine's *Confessions*, conversion has become a central paradigm for narrating the self. In the *De civitate Dei*, obedience to God counters the corrupt politics of the *civitas terrena*.

In *Quatrevingt-treize*, Hugo juxtaposes failed conversion and perverted sacrifice in Cimourdin's suicide with successful conversion and self-sacrifice in Gauvain's execution. Which model wins out depends on the novel's final lines: Does France devolve into the Roman curse of inevitable civil war? Or can it advance to a blossoming and prosperous republic to come? As in Hugo, conversion is central in Houellebecq's novel. *Soumission* progresses from the classical trope of perverted sacrifice to pervert in turn the paradigm of Christian conversion. Michel, on the cusp of conversion to Islam at novel's end, embraces no Christian church based on love and obedience to God – nor indeed even any true version of Islam. No new and purified republic emerges, based on virtue, liberty, equality, fraternity, and free love. Rather, the Islam available perverts Christianity under a new empire – modeled on Rome – that emerges from civil war. All the corruption already besetting the French secular and capitalist republic is fulfilled and comes visibly to fruition in a ghastly, orientalized France. She no longer recognizes herself in the new Babylon she has become. Michel perverts obedience to God into submission before an oriental tyrant.

Augustine is the hinge between classical Latin literature and what Hugo, following Hegel, calls Romantic art, namely art in the Christian age.[III] Sacrifice, which has no salvific potential in Lucan and never attains it in Vergil, finds new life under Christianity. Christ founds a new Christian city on earth through the sacrifice to end all sacrifice and launches it on its pilgrimage. Individuals pledge their allegiance to this new city through conversion, although adlection to full citizenship depends on God's grace. In Hugo, then Houellebecq, conversion is as liable to abject failure as sacrifice in Vergil, but the Romantic at least imagines potential success. Houellebecq's Michel rejects the Romantic vision to follow the path of French decadence as he reenacts the life of Huysmans, but where the historical Huysmans turned from decadence to conversion, Houellebecq satirizes history's whole scope, political and salvation history together, as a twisting arabesque of oriental perversion.

[III] For Augustine's role in the transition from classical to Christian, classical to Romantic, Hugo, *Preface to Cromwell*: Thierry and Mélèze (1963) 416–17.

Twisting the Trope

A methodological constant in our book is tropological refiguration.[112] An author reuses a conventional figuration from a prior ideology, undoes its older meaning, and lends it a new one. We take advantage of *trope*'s etymology from Greek *trepo*, "turn," to explicate how the turning of a figure and its re-turn in a new context enacts a dynamic tradition across the contingencies of history. The process is intertextual in the sense of Julia Kristeva's original definition of intertextuality, a word she coined, as a textual relation that operates a transfer from one system to another.[113] Although intertextuality has become a capacious urn for literary imitation of all sorts,[114] we stay true to her original meaning to underscore the conflictual nature of retroping. Talking about civil war is not just a conceptual battleground over the fundamental failures of society and politics. The conflict is waged through figures.

Refiguration works similarly to the semantic redefinition of concepts. Both bear a similarity to the perversion of language or institutions but differ in shifting normative expectations. Thucydides' commentary on language's perversion during *stasis* speaks to words' semantic persistence despite contestants' abuse to justify their actions as they jockey for power. To protest a word's false usage indicates that speaker and audience share an understanding of what the word should mean. Lucan's Nigidius Figulus is Thucydidean in predicting "virtue will be the name given to unspeakable crime" (*scelerique nefando / nomen erit virtus*, 1.667–8). The paradox requires knowing these are antithetical. Similarly, showing that a sacrifice goes wrong, as repeatedly in Vergil, indicates the expectation that it should work. Abuse of meaning differs fundamentally from creating meaning anew.

Lending a word a new meaning may reveal an older as an abuse, even contrary to the intentions of the speakers, because of a shift in values. Lucan's Scaeva appears tragic, unaware of the perverse shift from republican norms, when Lucan comments, *qui nesciret in armis / quam magnum virtus crimen civilibus esset* ("he was of a sort not to know how great a crime virtue was among citizen weapons," 6.147–8). Augustine, however, will declare not just this sort of perversion but even the republican meaning of *virtus* already perverse, in that the Roman Republic was already paradigmatic for civil war. From Augustine's perspective, Lucan laments a perversion that reveals the hidden truth of the word's original meaning: Republican *virtus* was already

---

[112] Haverkamp (2009).   [113] Kristeva (1980b).
[114] Alfaro (1996). Kristeva (1980c) eventually repudiated the term, since it came to mean nothing more than imitation or allusion without the dynamism she had stressed.

a crime. If Lucan operates a single turn (*versio*) – however thorough (*per-*) – in his perversion of the word, Augustine operates a second in retrojecting the perverted meaning back onto the original. To recuperate *virtus* for Christian values requires displacing it from manly militarism, not just to controlling the passions of the soul, its meaning in classical philosophy, but to a new meaning: female chastity – an etymological surprise, given the word's root meaning "manliness" – becomes the word's new norm.[115]

Battles over a concept's semantics parallel its figurations. Suicide conventionally figures civil war, making a parallel between conflict within the self and within the city.[116] Even republican suicide may stand for civil war in diverse ways, either preserving or undoing ideologies. Cato's suicide during the civil wars ostensibly preserves his republican liberty in the face of capture by Caesar and therefore leaves a fundamental value of republicanism intact.[117] The suicide of Vulteius and his men in Lucan (4.402–581), however, reinscribes civil war at a more intimate level. They kill each other in a spectacle of liberty. Citizens kill citizens "on one" ironically plural "side" (*in partibus unis*, 4.548), instead of opposing sides (*cives*, 4.485–6).[118] The internalization of civil war on one side of the conflict screws the trope another turn.

The figuration twists further when Augustine rejects suicide in defense of virtue, since it violates normative ideologies and, furthermore, the law charged with protecting Roman citizens. His analysis of two Roman examples, Lucretia and Cato, takes their suicides as transgressions of the categories they would uphold. Even the suicides the Romans deem noble undermine the social bond. When his appeal to "Roman laws and judges" (1.19; 30) puts Lucretia on trial in a figurative legal scenario, Augustine takes citizenship for granted as the sphere of Roman law. If she is innocent of adultery, she committed homicide; if she was justified in killing herself, then she was not innocent. Either way, she committed an intolerable

[115] Women's bravery or fortitude, as Cloelia's (Livy, 2.13), could be called *virtus* in classical Latin, but chastity was *pudicitia*. Sexual continence comes under *virtus* with Christianity, Orlin (2016) 992 (at *virtus*).

[116] On suicide as a metaphor for the suicide of the state, Ahl (1976) 183 n. 53, 320. Edwards (2007) 40: The metaphor universalizes the guilt; mutual suicides to avoid capture in historical battles reveal the practice's association with civil war.

[117] Hill (2004) 183–212: Political suicide at Rome established "one's status as a moral witness in the community," typically marked by "ostentation, ritualization, political protest, and philosophical allusion" (184); Cato was exemplary for subsequent political suicides (186–8). Edwards (2007) 3: "Cato's death confirms the value, and marks the end, of all that the republic stood for." His sacrificial death, however, cannot save the republic, as he wishes (Lucan, 2.312). In Seneca, his suicide ends not only his own life, but the Republic's, *De tranquillitate animi* 16.1. Ahl (1976) 244, 322.

[118] On Vulteius as a "paradigm of misdirected virtue" and this scene as a "miniature of civil *nefas*," Ahl (1976) 119–20; combined fratricide and suicide, Saylor (1990) 229; civil war's reversals and the theatrical aesthetic, Leigh (1997) 218–19, 259–64; Edwards (2007) 40–5, 67.

violation. Rather than exemplary model, she becomes in Augustine's argument a figure of violation, not just of the norms but of the laws undergirding society. Her model does not uphold but violates the social bond. Cato does the same. If he rightly killed himself to preserve liberty, he should also have killed his son (1.23; 36). His suicide is revealed as another violation of the social bond. Augustine presses suicide to its logical conclusion in light of a standard trope of civil war. Whether in full-blown civil war, as Cato, or in a moment of discord, as Lucretia, their suicides violate the pillars of the right order of Roman society: law, family, generation, and sexual purity. Even without making the shift to Christian norms, Augustine has these Roman suicides reveal their own values' bankruptcy.

Accepting death in the service of higher values is rebranded in Christianity as redemptive self-sacrifice. The fierce debates over whether martyrdom was justified as *imitatio Christi*, whose sacrifice meant to end all sacrifices and therefore should not be imitated literally, is symptomatic of the conflict over terms.[119] Hugo's ideological commitments, and also his understanding of conceptual and salvation history, appear in Gauvain's and Cimourdain's self-imposed deaths: secularized *imitatio Christi* overcomes suicide. Houellebecq winks at suicide's role in this larger story but satirically pulls the rug out from under suicide's refiguration for ideological purposes: Michel in his anomie has no will to live but, in his continual failure to live up to heroic norms, thinks dying would be a "premature decision" ("décision prématurée," 188). Houellebecq turns the trope in a different direction: Michel commits rhetorical patricide, passing immediately from shrugging off a decision not to die to telling of his father's death in the next sentence.

For his story of layered and conflicting ideologies, Houellebecq turns rather to another figuration to pervert: conversion, likewise rooted in turning.

Rome's Eternal Return

> We should not scorn Hellenistic confusion or Roman platitudes, but listen to those things said on the great surface of the empire; we should be attentive to those things that happened in a thousand instances, dispersed on every side: fulgurating battles, assassinated generals, burning triremes, queens poisoning themselves, victories that invariably led to further upheavals, the endlessly exemplary Actium, the eternal event.
>
> Michel Foucault, *Theatrum Philosophicum*

[119] Vinken (2004).

The collapse of the social bond comes to a pitch in civil war. The discourses that tell this story have long roots in the Roman tropology of civil discord, which shows the limits on civil war to be a sham. Recognizing the structure and history of discourses about civil war is one small step toward a deeper understanding of the figurations of recurrent violence, of the fundamental split at the heart of society persisting to this day. Foucault demands we notice recurrent, surface details because they cue us in to networks of discourses in the *longue durée*. In the nineteenth century, knowledge of these codes remained a shared inheritance. They could be alluded to without needing spell out all the steps. This tradition continued to offer the terms for intellectual dispute within twentieth-century French literature in the works of Jean Giraudoux, Jean Giono, Claude Simon, Marguerite Yourcenar, to mention but a few. More recently, it has returned in Jérôme Ferrari and Michel Houellebecq. Scholarship on these authors, however, has failed to appreciate this tradition's consistency and the tenacity of the paradigm. Civil war erupts, is dissimulated, and is unmasked again and again. The rhetoric of "us versus them" still conceals, perhaps more than ever, the pain of the internal divide. Externalizing the familiar and familial enemy is civil war's guilty secret. This rhetoric has returned virulently in discussions of Islamic terrorism. In modernity, we blindly repeat commonplaces propagated for millennia. Such commonplaces are not newly found truths, but prejudices that refuse to die.

Our philological method is an archaeology of recuperation. Many of the texts treating the social bond's collapse have become illegible, whether or not one agrees with their politics. In particular, the standard repertory of figurations used in nineteenth-century French literature has now become obscure. To understand the traditional discourses that stage conflicting interpretations of society over the *longue durée* will help pinpoint where their strategies are self-justificatory and show that to essentialize violence as cultural conflict lends it unfounded legitimacy. Recognizing that justifications of internal violence rest on age-old clichés, we hope, will give pause.

The Roman foundation of these discourses is a *basso continuo* we aim to make audible. A multiplicity of different Romes – Republic, Empire, the Rome of the Catholic Church, Rome as the whore Babylon – figure fundamentally different conceptions of society and its political forms. We privilege representative texts from French literature because they instantiate this dynamic with great clarity. Paris declared itself the new universal imperial capital: the capital of the nineteenth century and a new Rome.[120]

---

[120] Benjamin (1982).

The burning question was which Rome would return and in what form, Republic or Empire, Christian or Babylon, whether as blessing or curse, as reform or abject prostitution. The continual rereading and restaging of the Roman tradition was the discursive fabric through which to articulate conflicting visions of social order.

Despite the difficulty of defining civil war, its boundaries and differences from other sorts of warfare, the tropological representation of civil discord over the *longue durée* has remarkable consistency and clarity. This active tradition of figuration, despite manifold differences, nevertheless maintains coherence in its dissonances. Unity constitutes *Romanitas* through the *translatio litterarum Latinarum.*[121] The continual rewriting of this tradition in the nineteenth, twentieth, and twenty-first centuries has been underestimated, because a new realist ideology has become dominant and commonplace. The ideology goes like this: Literature, now finally realist, should leave myth behind, should overcome history's constricting framework along with its stale and academic figurations; literature should happen in the radical present; it should describe life as we experience it; the shadows of the past, overcome and left behind, should no longer haunt modernity's present, whose self-understanding as its own autarkic origin lies at the basis of a new realist aesthetic and a new politics of the self-made man. The ideology of modernity has rendered the past unreadable, even while we repeat what we cannot see, let alone read. This ideology seriously underestimates the power of tradition. Starting anew, ditching the ugly past – this is what the tropology of civil discord is about. Sadly, civil war keeps rearing its monstrous head. The desired break from the past is an illusion in literature and in politics alike.

---

[121] Kasper and Wild (2015).

CHAPTER 2

Oriental Empire
Vergil, Georgics

The Roman Republic's collapse into civil war and its "solution" in Empire was a traumatic event. Contemporary literature tried obsessively to come to terms with this wound to the political imaginary, and subsequent literature keeps returning to this unresolved scene. The long century of political disturbances from the Gracchi to the Augustan principate turned perpetually renewing moments of crisis into a political normal.[1] Augustus heralds the prosperity attending the end of the civil wars as his signature accomplishment in his *Res gestae*, and historians generally see the early Roman Empire as a period of unprecedented stability interrupted by occasional turmoil, such as the civil war in the year of the four emperors (69 CE). You would never know it from the heightened language of internal conflict saturating Imperial Latin style.[2] Augustan classicism takes a different tack and accords with the age's official style.[3] Any stark opposition between poetry that mouths the ideology of the principate or debunks its pretense is inadequate.[4] We argue that Vergil's classical illusionism enacts the deep structure of civil war and thereby displays the workings of the fundamental ideology that struggles to keep it under wraps.[5] Literature performs its essential function: to speak otherwise unspeakable trauma.

The many giants on whose shoulders we stand have built up a tower of interpretation arguing for a persistent register of civil war in the *Georgics*

[1] Against and for "crisis" as a term for the last hundred years of the Roman Republic, Flower (2010) ix–xi; Maschek (2018) 10–20.
[2] Alston and Spentzou (2011) 1–9.
[3] For classicism, Zanker (1988). For disjunction between style and political commitments, Thomas (2001) 15–19.
[4] Classic are Kennedy (1992), Fowler (1995), Batstone (1997). Henderson (1998) xi: The empire "was *both* legitimized as a paternalistic principate *and* reviled as tyrannical dictatorship." For fluidity in the meaning of "Augustan," Farrell and Nelis (2013) 10–16.
[5] For ambivalent versus Augustan readings of Vergil, Thomas (1990) 64–8 and (2001). On Vergilian reception generally, Kallendorf (1989), Harrison (1990), Ziolkowski (1993), Spence and Lowrie (2006), Farrell and Putnam (2010), Hardie (2014), and Pogorzelski (2016).

and the *Aeneid* that questions any unqualified affirmation of Olympian order or endorsement of political order at Rome. Our readings synthetize this strand in scholarship and aim to set up the reception of Vergil's methods for representing the collapse of the social bond; these were formative for the French realist tradition. We hope our interpretations add insight beyond the sheer accumulation of civil war figurations, which is compelling in itself.

In the Roman political imaginary, the destruction of the Republic stands for an irretrievable loss. So Tacitus, whose "picture of despotism became classic."[6] In the tradition we analyze, the Republic's downfall is a sign of cosmic disorder. A new foundation would be required for healing. A chronological story of health and collapse overlays and encodes the opposition between an ideal world and corrupt decadence. To overcome civil war, Rome transfers warfare to imperial expansion, particularly to the East,[7] which stands for moral and political corruption. The Empire, figured in Latin literature as oriental under cover, has overcome and estranged Rome's properly Roman nature, which resides in a constellation of republican virtues – liberty, courage, honesty, chastity, frugality.[8] The republican ideal lends Rome its value and gives it an exemplary function. Revolution is – particularly the long century of French revolutions – made on the promise of a restoration according to the pattern of the Roman Republic, whose renewal will, apparently, inaugurate a restored age of virtue.[9] The Republic takes on a symbolic mantle: It stands for a regeneration extending beyond the political into the cosmic order, into the realm of morality and the spirit. In Rousseau's words, "a monarchy is fine with subjects, but a republic needs free men."[10] This paradigm of restoration has informed the political imagination up to Montesquieu, Rousseau, Nietzsche, and recently Houellebecq.

Vergil establishes a different model. Known to posterity as the poet of empire, he strikingly has no conception of the Roman Republic as an ideal for restoration.[11] Although multiple republican heroes make cameo

---

[6] Momigliano (1990) 116: "he cannot really see how it is possible to have an Empire without tyranny" (118); O'Gorman (2000) 19; Gowing (2005).

[7] See La Bua (2013) on Horace.

[8] Connolly (2015) xv stresses the persistence of Roman values in modern liberal thought.

[9] Since Syme's (1939) *Roman Revolution*, "revolution" has been retrojected onto the late Roman Republic and Augustan periods; Farrell and Nelis (2013) 6–7. We reserve it for upheavals contemporaries called by that name.

[10] Vinken (1992b).

[11] This is all the more remarkable given the liminality of the "Augustan age," Farrell and Nelis (2013) 1–7, Schwindt (2013). The exemplary figures from Rome's past, e.g., in book 6, do not bear specifically republican markers, *pace* Gowing (2005) 19, despite Vergil's recognized role as a preserver of memory (70–1); Seider (2013). Gowing (2013) 330 emphasizes Augustan poetry's lack of nostalgia for the

appearances, signally in the catalogues in the underworld and on Aeneas' shield, the Roman Republic disappears as a positive model for political organization. Vergil's most common word for Roman political order is neutral, *res Romanae,* or sometimes simply *res* (affairs).[12] Not only does he never say *res publica,* he never uses *publicus* once in his entire corpus.[13] By contrast, *publicus* occurs frequently in his contemporary Horace. Vergil also never utters *civis* (citizen) in his own voice, only in that of others. A fundamental difference between these poets is that Horace fought in the civil wars as a republican military tribune under Brutus, whereas Vergil never entered the fray. Already in the first *Eclogue,* Tityrus worships a savior figure modeled on Hellenistic ruler cult.[14] Where Meliboeus laments civil discord as a misery of citizens (*Ecl.* 1.71–2), Tityrus' successful petition of this savior undermines the republican conception of citizenship: The sovereign grants an exceptional privilege. Vergil's references to *res Romanae* ("Roman affairs," *Georgics* 2.498) have a broader, more politically encompassing scope than the Republic. Augustus' establishment of de facto monarchy under the guise of a restored republic appears not in a contemporary distinction, convenient for modern historians and literary scholars, between Republic and Empire, but in subtle linguistic shifts. Rome began imperial expansion from its first, mythic beginnings and continued to manage *res publicas* under monarchy, but changes in political metaphors, such as the head of state, the savior figure, and the representation of civil war, symptomatically reveal new conceptualizations.[15]

Civil war for Vergil represents a recurrent and general disruption always already present across all stages of Roman history and across the universe. Rather than a single or even recurrent historical event, civil war structures the

---

Republic. The demagogy Peirano (2019) 174–216 analyzes in the *Aeneid* shows republican-style oratory in a poor light.

[12] E.g., *res*: *Romanae* (*Georg.* 2.498); *Italas* (*Aen.* 8.626). Of other peoples, *Ilia* (*Aen.* 1.268), *Asiae* (*Aen.* 3.1), *Troiae* (*Aen.* 8.471), *Phrygiae* (*Aen.* 10.88); universally, *hominum divumque* ("of gods and men," *Aeneid* 1.229). Without geographical identification, *res* can mean conditions for political order, as in *laetae* ("happy/fertile affairs," *Aen.* 2.783); the following word *regnum* makes the political field clear. *res Agamemnonias* (*Aen.* 3.53) unusually names a leader.

[13] The *Georgics* consistently views the people in a dark light: *populus* (people) cues politics, often republican and riven by civil war. The political sphere contrasts with the blessed life: the fortunate man is unaffected by the people's *fasces* (democracy), kingly purple (monarchy), civil discord, or *res Romanae* ("Roman affairs," *Georgics* 2.495); he avoids the insane forum and the people's record-offices (2.502). Plural peoples are allegorically represented through the society of anthropomorphic but dehumanized bees (4.5), which appear as orientalized fanatics (4.211). Peoples are the conquered whom Augustus will subject to Roman law (4.562). The *Aeneid,* about the establishment of a people, has a more conflicted outlook but notably speaks of founding not a politically constituted *populus,* but a race: *Romanam . . . gentem* (1.33).

[14] Clausen (1994) 48 (at *Ecl.* 1.43).   [15] Mebane (2017); Lowrie (forthcoming a and b).

cosmos. History is consistently cyclical in Vergil; discord repeatedly erupts, and Rome requires continual refoundation.[16] No new foundation, however, ever sets Rome on a fundamentally new footing. Civil war remains the condition of Roman history, ever essentially bound to the same cycle. The burning question is whether Augustus can set the world aright and break the cycle – or is his new golden age only a lull when civil war goes dormant? The Augustan refoundation comes under the sign of an empire whose task is to bring civil war to an end and usher in a new era of peace and prosperity. Vergil's poetry warns, however, that empire reencodes all the violence it should end.[17] No new Republic is possible. The question is rather whether a qualitatively new structure of history can emerge.[18]

Jupiter may promise empire without end in the *Aeneid* because Rome has always been and always will be an empire.[19] *Imperium* symbolizes the capacity to command.[20] Jupiter does not promise peace and concord within Rome, but rather domination over other nations. The *pax Romana* externalizes internal violence through imperial expansion. No ideal republic before opposes a decadent empire after, as becomes standard in the Roman tradition.[21] Instead, the republican civil wars are refigured as an already existing and continual internal conflict within the empire Rome has had from its beginnings. The ideal lies not within history, but in a golden age beyond reach, in a time outside history.[22] Conflict for Vergil inhabits the universe's organization, and recent historical events articulate its form.[23] Roman history reveals the structure of a broader, universal struggle, whose tropes are those of civil war.

Augustus' declaration of war against Egypt folded the civil war against Antony into a foreign conflict and thereby obscured the self-directed nature of civil war's violence. This allowed for an orientalist projection.

---

[16] Hardie (1993); Lowrie (2010a) and (2013).

[17] Geue (2018) displaces civil war as the *Georgics'* political framework and replaces it with empire, understood in Marxist terms as the forced extraction of labor, whose wealth is transferred to the extractors. Our reading shows that empire simply continues civil war, only externalized. The two registers work in sync.

[18] For the "end of history" in Augustan poetry, Farrell and Nelis (2013) 16–18; for turning point imagery, Nelis (2013) 255–6.

[19] Endless empire is an aesthetic and moral problem: Nelis (2004) 90–8.

[20] For change in *imperium*'s scope over time in Latin, Richardson (2008).

[21] Hardt and Negri (2000).

[22] The interpretation of Vergil's golden ages is conflicted; possible in the here and now, Reckford (1958) 82–4; dark, Jal (1963) 245–6; distant, Putnam (2008) 154; already violent, Thomas (2001) 2–3. On the end of the world, Star (2021).

[23] Scheid (1990) 715–23; Nelis (2004) 90. The civil war background to the *Georgics* is well recognized, but many assume Vergil's task was commemorative or ideological. This leads to rhetorical juggling, e.g., Wilkinson (1969) 177–82.

Vergil brings to light the intimate relation of orientalism and empire. The stark contrast between self and other, which externalizes internal conflict, comes undone in the structure of denial enacted by civil war's figuration. Unmasking civil war as war against the oriental other reveals the masking as well as the underlying truth. Masking is a double figure that hides and reveals its own hiding in the same gesture. The tiny Egyptian motifs in contemporary wall-painting are iconic for this gesture (Fig. 2.1); the ostensible proclamation of imperial conquest denatures a properly Roman aesthetic with orientalism. The Roman Empire cannot help but display symptomatically in oriental garb the internal conflict it represses as it suppresses its Eastern other. Regardless of intent, Augustus' empire encodes latently within itself the orient that externalizes its own violence.

Figure 2.1 Boscotrecase, Egyptian motifs, Metropolitan Museum of Art, New York

The *Aeneid* makes Roman history the narrative vehicle for this message, but the agricultural world of the *Georgics* encompasses a universal scope. The internal conflict that is the human condition is laid bare under the conditions of history Augustine will name *civitas terrena*. This violence Vergil consistently mourns but does not hide.

Both *Georgics* and *Aeneid* ask the same essential question through a consistent figurative register: Can broken bonds ever heal? Agriculture figures human society's relationship to nature and both of these to the divine in the *Georgics*.[24] All is ripped apart at all levels: natural, political, moral, psychic, and sexual. Civil war figures this rupture.[25] Its tropes underwrite each realm in a riddle calling for decipherment. In the *Aeneid*, foundation poses the question in political terms, but the poem's mythohistorical register frames the political via other spheres – the soul's conditions, relations between sexes, weather conditions run along parallel lines.[26] Lurking violence, which threatens to overturn cosmic order, infuses all Vergilian worlds of potential idealization – pastoral, georgic. The golden age of the Augustan restoration merely whitewashes the domination of its true nature.[27] Throughout his oeuvre, Vergil systematically undoes from within the societal forms that promise to restore the social bond: sacrifice, prophecy, empire, the idyll, the savior, security.

A new set of virtues, dressed up in classicism, ushers in an empire meant to heal the internal divide by imposing peace. When the senate granted Augustus the *clipeus virtutis*, an honorific shield, to mark the First Augustan Settlement in 27 BCE, the declaration of the virtues of the princeps – *virtus, clementia, iustitia, pietas* – redefined imperial order. Inscribed between the generic classics, republican *virtus* – courage combined with self-control – and piety, are clemency, the mark of the sovereign ruler's decision in contradistinction to the decision-making powers of the Roman people, and justice, which transcends Augustus as an individual.[28] His personal qualities extend into and define the whole of empire. All these play central roles throughout Vergil. Although *virtus* occurs only once in

---

[24] Putnam (1979) 15: "one grand trope for life itself."

[25] For the intersection of literal and metaphorical, didactic and aesthetic registers in the *Georgics*, Haarhoff (1960) 102; Putnam (2008) 138; Gale (2000) x, 232–69; Marchetta (2013) viii–x. For the symbolic value of agriculture in Augustan Rome, Scheid (1990) 678; Nelsestuen (2015).

[26] Putnam (1979) 194.   [27] Johnston (1980).

[28] Weinstock (1971) 228–59 surveys the new Caesarian virtues, which replace typical republican *fides* (243), and their origins in civil war. Wallace-Hadrill's (1981) overview shows there was no fixed canon. Clemency is a "monarchic topos" by Augustus' time, Lind (1994) 49. For Hellenistic kingly virtues, Braund (2012) 88–92.

the *Eclogues*,[29] and never in the *Georgics*, its definition becomes fraught in the *Aeneid*; justice informs the death of Eurydice, etymologically "broad justice," in the *Georgics*; *pietas*, Aeneas' signal virtue, unravels when he considers clemency only to deny it. These Augustan virtues consistently come to ruin in Vergil before the onslaught of *furor*, which sparks failures of self-mastery, conspicuously in Aeneas. His spiritual degradation infuses Roman political order from the beginning, the dark shadow of the commensurability between Augustus' virtues and the character of the Empire.

Imperial healing for Vergil reenacts the *pax Romana*: peace imposed through violence. The new Caesar provides the standard solution to civil violence in Augustan poetry by redirecting aggression outward. Yes, there is peace, but its extension, decadent rather than restorative, undermines Roman identity as traditionally understood. Sallust articulates the trope that republican virtue extends empire, but the wealth gained thereby and the loss of salutary fear through Carthage's destruction undermine virtue in a self-consuming gesture.[30] In Vergil, the radical distinction between East and West on the shield of Aeneas represents, in a first gesture, the Empire that emerges out of the civil wars as a validation of Roman identity. Juno's insistence on eradicating the Trojan East, with all its fashion and barbarous language, from Roman identity reassures in its insistence on a purely Italian Rome. The East, which externalizes the internal enemy, however, endures in hiding, as a figure for internal conflict. Empire in Vergil is built on this erasure and the uncanny persistence of the repressed.

In later literature, the erased East bubbles up as the dominant figuration of the Roman Empire in its decadent mode.[31] Within this figuration, Rome *qua* empire adopts the characteristics of the conquered Eastern other. Ruler worship – the mark of Eastern absolutism – is its most conspicuous sign. Although Augustus himself resisted divine honors at Rome, contemporary literature consistently represents him as a savior on a path to divinization. The gesture's apparent panegyric frames the new imperial order in terms of Hellenistic kingship. The East undergoes erasure but cannot be wiped out. Antony goes native in Egypt, and his characteristic style – oriental, Bacchic – lives on. In an irony of history, the Senate's *damnatio memoriae*, proposed by Cicero's son as consul, never wiped Antony's memory entirely out. According to Dio, young Caesar refused the extensive erasure of the name, which encompassed the entire family of the Antonii.[32] Augustus resisted the

---

[29] What the baby should learn in *Ecl.* 4.
[30] Earl (1961) 41–59; Kapust (2011) 38–52; Hammer (2014) 148–55.   [31] Kasper and Wild (2015).
[32] Flower (2006) 116–19.

pressures to take on the Hellenistic mantle, to accept divine honors, to act the tyrant through eradicating the memory of a noble family. That such honors were his to refuse, however, reveals his power.[33] Like Antony, partially erased, the conquered East persists, refigured as Empire's trope.

Vergil establishes a basic structure. Refoundation in empire ostensibly restores society by ending a civil war that had destroyed a prior republic. Figuration, however, reinscribes civil war into the restoration, so that empire appears decadent. This decadence is defined in orientalist terms. Figuration also reveals that history comes always already corrupted: times before and after civil war end up indistinct, the only difference being that corruption now emerges from under cover. This structure, received and reconfigured, had a formative influence on later literature's conceptualization of civil war.

Disruption

In the *Georgics*, a cornucopia of topoi illuminates the bounty and prosperity of a world where man has brought nature to fruition, only to heighten our shock at this luxuriant world's disruption through nature's chaotic violence, passion, plague, and civil war.[34] Fertile fields, vines joined to elms, well-cared-for herds and flocks, and frugal bees (1.1–4) – word pictures organize patriarchal order under Jupiter, where people work the earth peacefully, raise golden corn, tend their orchards and cattle in a well-ordered cosmos, chastely procreate and raise their children, spin and sing in rustic contentment.[35]

> The *Georgics* have always had a peculiar fascination for Englishmen. Written as a practical treatise on agricultural, vineyards and forestry, stock-breeding and bee-keeping, both its subject and its incidental beauties appeal strongly to the Englishman's love of the land, the chase and domestic animals.[36]

So the ideology, such the conventional reading.[37] Vergil's poem builds this beautiful world in song only to tear it apart. The more order appears, the

---

[33] Freudenburg (2014).

[34] Against those defining the poem's theme as "the universal pattern of degeneration and renewal," Miles (1980) 61–2 stresses contradictions.

[35] Putnam (1979) 156: the "paternal state."

[36] The blurb for C. Day Lewis's 1940 translation – by contrast, the book's epigraph comments on contemporary history: *saevit toto Mars impius orbe* ("impious Mars raging over the whole world," 1.511). Claude Simon's novel, *Les géorgiques* (1981), surveys the revolutionary wars of Europe up to World War II under the sign of Vergil's poem.

[37] Putnam (1979) ix critiques Wilkinson (1969) for shying away from delving deeper than the poem's "surface beauties."

more uncanny the failure to achieve resolution. The end result is tyranny styled oriental. This poem's classicizing textual surface glazes over the incongruous irruption of violence into harmony. The abject horror of plague returns inscribed within regeneration; in the poem's central interpretative crux, the restorative *bugonia* requires a calf to be bludgeoned to a pulp.

Hermeneutic conflict explodes and binds this riddle of a poem together. To fully grasp the extraordinary menace to its apparent calm requires a strategy of rereading. Readers must pick up and string together figures scattered across the text in a continuous metaphorical register (*metaphora continua*), whose recurrent tropes layer meaning over their prior instantiations. The poem demands allegorical reading. Its discordant hermeneutics parallel civil war's destabilization of society and symptomatically reproduce the political conditions it addresses. Its own structure replays the repression and displacement of contemporary politics, perfectly capturing the incipient Augustan settlement.[38] Dazzling beauty, relief at the cessation of violence imperfectly smooth over an underlying violence always threatening to erupt again. The *Georgics* exposes this condition through its own contradictions.

Literature does not always work this way. Jean Giono's fable, *L'homme qui plantait des arbres*, revisits georgic topoi with an integrative gesture.[39] Against the backdrop of two world wars – the speaker, like Giono himself, fought as a soldier in the first – a peasant in physical and social isolation single-handedly restores a devastated landscape, allegorizing the torn fabric of human sociability, by planting whole forests of trees over his lifetime, one day at a time. From shepherd, he turns beekeeper, a metaphor of restoration. The trees draw water back to the deserted landscape and, with it, peace, order, and prosperity. Carefully selected Vergilian trees pass from the oak – Jupiter's symbol – to the beech that offers shelter to Tityrus in the *Eclogues*' first and *Georgics*' last line. The fable's conclusion links human effort – if only of a single, isolated individual – to divine order: "malgré tout, la condition humaine est admirable" ("after all, the human condition is admirable"); the peasant "a su mener à bien cette oeuvre digne de Dieu" ("knew how to bring to good this work worthy of God," 33). Such optimism contrasts fundamentally with the classical poem inspiring it: Vergil never

---

[38] Nelis (2013).
[39] Giono (1982). Giono's meditative *Virgile ou les palais de l'Atlantide* (*Vergil or the Palace of Atlantis*) (2001) attests to how avidly he read Vergil. His pacifist commitments, forged in his experience of World War I, brought him twice to prison, allegedly for Nazi sympathies. Although charges were never pressed, his reputation remains clouded.

authorizes an analogous declaration, nor do the human endeavors represented within ever turn out so well.

If one expects to find the Vergil, prophet of empire, of the received European tradition, the *Georgics'* violence shocks. The horizon of expectation established by the poem's opening, where a cosmic order of nurturing care knits the world of nature, man, the gods, politics, and learning into a unity, is unsettled by repeated outbreaks of violence.[40] Under Jupiter's dominion, passion, labor, and anxiety (*cura*) are necessary conditions of bounty that also necessarily inflict violence on the world they should foster. In Vergil's "deliberately ambivalent assessment,"[41] the world of Jupiter, the world of nature under the conditions of history, appears tropologically homologous with the politics of civil war. The one does not illustrate the other – both belong to the nature of things. Civil war's horrors erupt with greater fury for the lush descriptive detail of the poem's dominant modality.

The description of daily life, of how to grow happy fields of grain, where to plant what when, how to graft one branch on another trunk, how to produce wool as white as moonlight – these peaceful and beautiful cares all take a wrong turn. Vergil's commonplaces of abundance, prosperity, and security have resonated into the nineteenth century and beyond. The light cast on rustic landscapes in Millet's paintings instills peasant labor with cosmic – for him, Christian-infused[42] – order in the spirit of Roman sacro-idyllic landscapes (Figs. 2.2, 2.3, 2.4). Blond or amber waves of grain symbolize prosperity to this day.[43] Still pondering which soil to till for which grape by the beautiful Lake Lario, the reader suddenly lands in Noricum – "the lofty Alps, the hill forts of Bavaria, the fields beside Timavo"[44] – surrounded by raging plague. Horses tear their own flesh with bare teeth. Wine, earlier a symbol of "rejoicing concord between man, nature and the country's gods" (3.514),[45] fails as a remedy, making their "madness and self-rending annihilation" even more horrific. The poem enacts furious violence on

---

[40] Schiesaro (1993) 141–3; Gale (2000) 160; Lowrie (forthcoming b).   [41] Hardie (1993) 86.

[42] Murphy (1999) 1, 14, 22–4, 29.

[43] For blondness in the European tradition, Junkerjürgen (2009). In Bavaria, the happy cow – Horace's *tutus bos* ("safe ox," *Odes* 4.5.17) (compare the cow, Fig. 2.5, on the Tellus relief of the Ara Pacis Augustae) – has replaced the wheat tainted with Nazi associations. Imagery from the patriotic song "America the Beautiful" remains prominent in American political advertising.

[44] Day Lewis's choice to translate Bavaria, which corresponded to the Roman province Raetia, was pointed in 1940. Most of Noricum maps rather onto modern Austria and Slovenia.

[45] Boyle (1986) 62. For parallels between disease, love, family, and civil strife, Putnam (1979) 217, 223. Oliensis (1997) 300–1.

Figure 2.2 Boscotrecase, Sacro-idyllic landscape, Museo Archeologico Nazionale di Napoli

the reader, who has been lulled into a false sense of security by the carefully built, standard ideology, where the world of the plow opposes the world of history with all its internal violence. The farmer, the traditional countertype to luxury and tyranny, where oriental purple dyes kingship in the colors of decadence (2.465 and 495), also serves as the wholesome countertype to the fratricide of civil war (2.496),[46] which brings on the oriental tyranny whose register it inhabits. Political chaos

---

[46] Corrupting luxury, a trope developed among republican Roman historians, was fully in play by Vergil's time, Gorman and Gorman (2014).

Figure 2.3 Jean-François Millet, *The Gleaners*, Musée d'Orsay, Paris

disrupts the farmer's life, but furthermore, the poem disrupts the opposition between them.

Brutality repeatedly flares up across all the structural oppositions that
give the world meaning: relations between nations, citizens, classes, within
the family, between generations, the sexes, man and animal, death and life,
culture and nature, man and god. Nature battles herself in clashing winds
(1.318).[47] The crescendo of disruption starts with imperial expansion:
A world war rages at the end of book 1(*saevit toto Mars impius orbe*, 1.511).
Civil war, evoked by fratricide (2.496, 510, 533) with intimations of rape
(2.532), closes book 2. In book 3, passion – lust and fury – drives animals
wild. The mares' boundless desire produces an ooze of sticky bodily fluid
(*hippomanes*) that wicked stepmothers use as poison or for magic potions
(3.280–4). Unbounded female passion does not procreate but undoes
family ties. Atrocious lust drives bulls to fight over a mate. Animal and
human become indistinct; love with all its lust and fury levels all (*amor*

[47] For civil war metaphors in nature, Putnam (1979) 50–1, 71.

Figure 2.4 Jean-François Millet, *The Keeper of the Herd* (1871/4), Art Institute of Chicago

omnibus idem, 3.244). The life drive proves fatal in a decadent inversion. By book's end, all are overwhelmed by plague and abject bodily dissolution. Death comes alive. Here the tropes of civil war overlay the natural disaster in a parallel between *stasis* and plague that goes back to Thucydides.

> Yet there is a key difference: while social institutions, law, pity and family loyalties simply disappeared during the epidemic, leaving chaos, in *stasis* all these elements continue to exist in changed, distorted forms, or are replaced by other similar, but harmful substitutions. ... *stasis* itself is a state of sickness ... which so changes people that they willfully violated those same norms. Price (2001) 29

Vergil's plague, civil war's figure, undoes the difference between natural and political turmoil. Even the animals become perverse: Unnaturally drinking wine – the classic emblem of civilization – they turn on themselves to rip their flesh apart in fury, another inversion of nature through internal destruction (3.509–14). Wool corroded with pus infects humans with the contagion (3.561–2). In plague, as in passion, the distinction between human and animal dissolves.

But the worst is to come. In book 4, the stories surrounding the collapse of Aristaeus' hive pile layer upon metaphorical layer of dysfunction. In modernity, we recognize the importance of bees as pollinators. A quotation, probably apocryphal, attributed to Albert Einstein, avers: "If bees were to disappear from the globe, mankind would only have four years left to live."[48] Markus Imhoof's 2012 documentary, *More Than Honey*, which uses this quotation as an epigraph, follows in the steps of the *Georgics* in making beekeeping and the social lives of bees an allegory of perverse technologies, human greed, moral inadequacy, misalignment with nature, and xenophobia.[49]

In the *Georgics*, the hive fails due to their beekeeper's crime. Aristaeus' attempted rape of Orpheus' beloved Eurydice violates the marriage bond, the institution grounding social order. The bard successfully petitions the underworld, but his eventual inability to bring his beloved wife back from the dead joins poetic failure to the defeat of the "justice far and wide" spelled out in her ironic name.[50] Eurydice's death surpasses the loving couple's tragedy to signal broader societal collapse. For the second time in the poem, justice leaves the world: *extrema per illos / Iustitia excedens terris vestigia fecit* ("Justice, leaving the lands, left her last footprints among those people," 2.473–4).[51] Even the good Italians, the only ones to retain her traces, are eventually corrupted with the Assyrian dyes symbolizing oriental luxury.

Multiple attempts at rebirth similarly derail. Orpheus, who overcomes death only to succumb to passion, figured as a loss of self-control (*victus animi*, 4.491), is himself eventually dismembered in a phantasmagorical suite of poetic and moral failures. In parallel, the *bugonia*, which does succeed in generating new bees from a rotten carcass, upturns nature and ritual through an alienating technology. The interpretation of this rite continues to plague scholarship – even "pessimists" tend to read the rite as successful, despite the disorienting confusion of disrupted registers.[52]

---

[48] www.forbes.com/sites/paulrodgers/2014/09/09/einstein-and-the-bees-should-you-worry/.

[49] www.morethanhoneyfilm.com/.

[50] Aristaeus' pursuit and Orpheus' failure to restore Eurydice are likely Vergilian innovations, Wilkinson (1969) 116–17.

[51] Compare Catullus 64.395, where Rhamnusia Virgo – divine retribution – has fled the contemporary world, along with Iustitia and other gods; Skinner (1984). For incipient civil war tropes in this passage, above 21 (Figures of Discord).

[52] Putnam (1979), Boyle (1986). Perkell (1989) 76–80 stresses ambivalence and unresolvable tensions.

All the ways in which violence disrupts order in the world make a larger statement about the nature of things. Even without allegory, the poem simply describes the periodic dismantling of every realm constituting the cosmos. This catalogue of woes spreads wholesale death and destruction worldwide, across all dimensions, so that cosmos devolves into chaos and all care is brought to naught and ruin. Civil war is the political expression of a violence that subtends the world. The poem's essential interpretive challenge rests on how to read the *bugonia*, the ritual that brings the bees back to life and perverts the global rebirth for which it stands.

Abject Rebirth

Two versions of *bugonia* sit opposed: one an abject and Egyptian marvel, sacrifice's antitype under the sign of technology, the other an equally marvelous sacrificial ritual under the sign of religion.[53] Either way, sacrifice, already the "emblem . . . of postlapsarian man," provides the terms for the only available restoration.[54] A reader, disconcerted by the poem's massive accumulation of dissolution across the world's symbolic tissue, might hope the latter would offer redemption after catastrophe and correct the former, which remains abject. The stakes for which vision of *bugonia* prevails in the end are nothing less than whether this seminal poem offers a way to overcome civil war.

The *Georgics* is paradigmatic for how the Roman tradition comes to grips with catastrophe and reintegration, abjection and redemption. If the fourth Eclogue promises rebirth through a child – a scheme received as an unknowing prophecy of Christmas – the rebirth through *bugonia* in the *Georgics* offers a pagan analogue to Easter.[55] The institutionalization of a restored society, the burden of refoundation in the *Aeneid*, corresponds on the Christian side to the establishment of the Church as the institution that offers a new, ostensibly whole way of belonging to society. The parallel

---

[53] Although spontaneous generation was widely believed in antiquity, Aristotle denies it for bees. For a thorough overview and evaluation of the sources, Keyser (2020) 157–63. The traditional link between bees and the *bos* (ox) – and only that pair when others were available – lets Vergil adapt a trope that makes the regeneration of society arise from a sacrificial animal. Vergil marks both versions as marvels (4.309, 554), a nod to the skeptical tradition and a sign that the practice carries a figurative burden. For debate about sacrifice, Wilkinson (1969) 117–20; Perkell (1989) 74–6; Habinek (1990); Thomas (1991); Gale (2000) 101–12; Feeney (2004) 5–11; Leitao (2004); Stephens (2004) 158–60; Pellegrini (2007).

[54] Boyle (1986) 81; see also 74–5, on *caesis iuvencis* ("slaughtered cattle"), and 547, on Caesar's triumph (2.537, 3.23). Also Dyson (1996).

[55] *Interpretatio christiana* remains strong in Otis (1964), see Miles (1980) 61. Lee (1989) 77–88 makes Eclogue 4 the optimistic response to Catullus 64.

underlying structures of the Roman and Christian schemes make both available to later reception. The question is whether Vergil's scheme brings redemption or has a hollow core, whether the cosmic and social dissolution attending civil strife can ever be overcome, whether Augustus appears as savior or as the embodiment of an intrinsic and pervasive internal violence that resists eradication, much less healing. The *Georgics* is paradigmatic for how traditions informed by Roman political thought take on catastrophe and reintegration, abjection and redemption.

Textual restoration sets the restoration of the *bugonia*, which seems to mend thins, in the traumatic structure of repetition compulsion.[56] The uncannily doubled rebirth goes monstrously wrong. The first description, which promises *certam . . . salutem* ("sure salvation," 4.292) out of Egypt – the land of civil war in the Roman political imagination[57] – is a bloodcurdling act.[58]

> First, a small place is chosen, drawn close for this function. This they press with gutter-tiles on the narrow roof and with tight walls, and they add four windows with light slanting from the four directions of the winds. Then a calf is found, already curving its two horns on its forehead; its twin nostrils and the breath of its mouth are blocked – it fights back greatly – and once snuffed out by blows, its pounded guts turn to jelly under the skin intact. Vergil, *Georgics* 4.295–302[59]

Sentimentality – we imagine curling locks between the calf's horns, just beginning to curve – enhances our shock at the brutality of death through suffocation and liquefaction, our surprise that we should expect rebirth from this smashed calf's putrefying corpse. This Egyptian method inverts Greco-Roman sacrifice with striking precision: A resistant victim would derail a proper Roman sacrifice; there is no shedding of blood; it occurs not in the open at an altar before a temple, but in a specially constructed dark, narrow shed with state-of-the-art ventilation.[60] The technical specificity evokes horror precisely where we expect ritual. The reduction of flesh to formless pulp within an otherwise intact body hides and heightens the internal dissolution on which this procedure depends. A cannily perverse

---

[56] For refoundation as traumatic repetition in the *Aeneid*, compared to other potential models in Roman literature, Lowrie (2013).

[57] Gurval (1995), Lowrie (2015c). For the contrast between fertile Egypt and the Egypt of civil war in Vergil, Tracy (2014) 7. Since other locales are attested as the source of the *bugonia* (Keyser [2020]), Vergil's choice depends not on fact, but on Egypt's symbolic burden.

[58] Vergil's account is a literary event, Feeney (2004); also Stephens (2004).

[59] Unless otherwise noted, Michèle Lowrie supplied all Latin translations.

[60] The ventilation may recall the temple of Janus, depicted on Neronian coinage with a grated window on the long side; further description at Fowler (1998) 159.

golden line illustrates the horror: *tunsa per integram solvuntur viscera pellem* ("its pounded guts turn to jelly under the skin intact," 4.302). The verb "keeps the peace," in Dryden's famous formulation, betwixt the paired adjectives and nouns to either side.[61] Perfect poetic form heightens the ugliness of the calf's internal dissolution within a perfect exterior.

The second description offers an apparent correction. A classic Greco-Roman sacrifice, whose purpose is atonement, succeeds the abject Egyptian method. Cyrene gives instructions for the sacrifice of four bulls and four heifers to appease the Nymphs, outraged at Aristaeus' role in causing Eurydice's death, alongside funeral rites for Orpheus and a placation of Eurydice (*placatam*, 4.547).

> "But I will first tell you in order the means of supplication: Choose four outstanding bulls of exceptional physique, that now graze the heights of verdant Lycaeus for you, and as many heifers, necks untouched. Set up four altars for these at the high shrines of the goddesses and send the sacred blood down from their necks and abandon the very bodies of the cattle in the leafy grove. Then, when the ninth Dawn shows her rising, you will send Lethe's poppies as funeral offerings for Orpheus, and you will sacrifice a black ewe and you will revisit the grove. You will worship Eurydice placated with a slaughtered heifer."
>
> No hesitation. He immediately performs his mother's commands. He comes to the shrines, he erects the altars as directed. He leads four outstanding bulls of exceptional physique and as many heifers, necks untouched. Then, when the ninth Dawn had shown her rising, he sends Lethe's poppies as funeral offerings for Orpheus and revisits the grove. Vergil, *Georgics* 4.530–58

Aristaeus follows her instructions to the letter – almost. The lines and phrases repeat with minor, but decisive variations (4.538–47, 550–3). Formal precision highlights all the more Aristaeus' hermeneutic and ritual failure.[62] He does not fulfill all the detailed instructions – crucial in Roman understanding for success in religious and magical formulas as well as scientific recipes[63] – and neglects precisely the essential placation of Eurydice, namely the "broad justice" carried in her name, whose return could theoretically repair the world.[64] It is his attempted rape of her that sets the sorry story in motion, and the omission of this crucial element

---

[61] Wilkinson (1963) 215–16.   [62] Putnam (1979) 318.

[63] For the complexity and variety of Roman sacrifice, Scheid (2003) 79–110. On the importance of accuracy and the danger of omission in medicine, von Staden (1997); Totelin (2012) 312.

[64] The etymology of Eurydice's name is rarely noted, e.g., by Haarhoff (1960) 107–8 ("wide rule"); Lee (1996) 7, 10. Similarly, the omission of her placation is overlooked or underplayed in the scholarship, e.g., Perkell (1978) and (1989), Putnam (1979), Conte (1986) 134–5, Morgan (1999). Johnston

undoes the expected restoration. Failure to restore justice cuts to the heart of the social order. Cicero's Scipio declares that "without justice" no republic "can in any way exist" (*sine iustitia nullo pacto esse potest*, *De re publica* 2.69; cited by Augustine, *De civitate Dei* 2.21). Sacrifice, the institution that performs the social bond, is here perverted.[65] Roman rites, which should correct the Egyptian, technological *bugonia*, turn out to be defective. There is no commensality, no sharing of the meat, which is left to rot.[66] The social practice that ostensibly unifies, recreates, and knits society together is omitted; instead, decomposed cattle's entrails (*liquefacta boum per viscera*, 4.555) bring back the bees.[67] Rather than overcoming the Egyptian model, this infelicitous sacrifice undoes sacrifice's essential function.[68]

The abject version of *bugonia*, where the calf is beaten to pulp, resonates within the sacrificial *bugonia*: Abjection is not overcome but sealed. The putrefaction of nine sacrificed animals undoes proper sacrifice, namely ritual cleansing consequent on bloodletting and the shared meal that reconstitute the social bond. Structurally speaking, if redemption's condition is that sacrifice contain and redeem abjection, the second *bugonia* reinscribes what it should supplant and heal.

Even the cornucopian imagery conveying the bees' rebirth as a society encodes inescapable violence. The clouds evoke Jupiter, the rain god responsible for withholding earth's bounty and imposing the iron age.[69] The grapes, a classic emblem of civilization, recall wine's failure as a healing draft during the plague, where it drives animals to self-destructive fury.[70] If Orpheus' wife Eurydice dies from an attempted rape, which is therefore sterile, the Latin literary tradition records another story of another Eurudica, another rape from her lineage, that is fertile. In Ennius' *Annales*, "Broad Justice" is the name of Ilia's mother. Telling her dream

---

(1977) 171 notes the lack of repetition. Horne (2018) addresses justice's failure throughout the *Georgics*.

[65] Scheid's (1984) seminal analysis of the distribution of sacrificial meat in Roman ritual underscores sacrifice's communal function. For public sacrifices uniting the Roman people, Scheid (2003) 90–91.

[66] Thomas (1991) 213.

[67] For "incomplete," even "perverted" sacrifice, Habinek (1990) 215, 219; "sacrifices which are not real sacrifices," Thomas (1991) 216.

[68] For infelicity in speech acts, Austin (1962). Reading the scene as failed sacrifice attributes more closure – that is, determined meaning – to the poem's ending than interpretations espousing indeterminacy: Fowler (2000) 286–7; Feeney (2004) 8, 10, 18–20.

[69] Bad weather ascribed to Jupiter at 1.328 – *imber* ("rain") and *nubes* ("clouds") a few lines before (1.323–4) recur here (4.312). Putnam (1979) 51–2, 138: Jupiter attacks the natural landscape indiscriminately and "must be feared" (*metuendus*, 2.419).

[70] Batstone (1997) 128: The poem circles back to storms and grapes. Lowrie (forthcoming b).

of being raped to her sister, Ilia emphasizes their lineage: *Eurudica prognata pater quam noster amavit, . . . germana soror* ("born of Eurydice, whom our father loved, . . . full sister," Skutsch [1985] frg. 36). Raped by Mars, Ilia bears Romulus and Remus, Rome's founders and first fratricidal pair. The joyous restoration of the bees is a monstrous birth from the putrefied flesh of the oxen's entrails (*boum per viscera*, 4.555), a metaphorical "uterus" (4.556) in a rotting corpse.[71] It is consequent on a rape that recalls an earlier foundational rape. It encodes universal suffering together with a specifically Roman story of civil war. Monstrous birth recurs in the *Aeneid*, where the womb's fruit is again civil war, overlain with empire.[72]

The apparently joyous rebirth, as often in Vergil, is suffused with an underlying disquiet.[73] Vergil returns to central georgic topics in condensed form. Rather than rewriting them as restoration, he reinscribes the essentially torn nature of the social bond.

Restoration as Collapse

The rebirth succeeds, but what is reborn? From *bugonia*'s monstrous birth comes no human society, healed from civil war, to answer our hopes, but a society of bees in an oriental and tyrannical mode that belies any renewal under Augustus Caesar. A full restoration within the historical order entails still living under Jupiter's dispensation: Law still belongs to the iron age (*ferrea iura*, 2.501), upheld by a state monopoly on violence (*fasces*, 2.495); avarice (2.506) and class struggle (2.509) persist. The internal abject is an icon of Rome's social destructuring during civil war; humanity has died and been reborn into the Rome of Empire. Restoration comes soaked in abject blood. With the bees' rebirth, cosmic disorder becomes a permanent condition concretized into a political form.

The *Georgics'* sacrificial ending does not solve the pressing problem it raises, namely how to restore the social bond between Romans who have torn themselves apart in fury. The Roman civil wars were about who would rule. The language of kingship of the bees beset by the discord of civil war reveals the reason behind the conflicts between Marius and Sulla, Caesar and Pompey, Antony and Octavian, namely desire for domination – not even over others, but over their very selves. *Rex* codes the antitype of republican values: The word "king" exposes the Roman Republic's collapse as a struggle for rule.

[71] Rimell (2013) 114, (2015) 237–40.   [72] Below, 104, 135.   [73] Johnson (1976).

The bee society that returns looks at first like an ideal state modeled on Rome.[74] Their "citizens" are even *Quirites* (4.201). C. Day Lewis, however, misleads when he translates their society's listed elements as "Republic."[75]

> admiranda tibi levium spectacula rerum
> magnanimosque duces totiusque ordine gentis
> mores et studia et populos et proelia dicam.   *Georgics* 4.3–5

> I'll tell of a tiny
> Republic that makes a show well worth your admiration –
> great-hearted leaders, a whole nation whose work is planned,
> Their morals, groups, defenses.

Day Lewis' terms presuppose a republic existed to begin with, and the translation reveals its absence. Vergil goes further: The bees have always been under a kingship. The implication for the Roman analogue is that the Republic as an ideal is always already erased.

The totalizing communitarianism of the *Georgics'* bee society inverts republican values. The bees thrive in a system that would crush the human spirit. They lack subjectivity, liberty, individuality, free will, any love besides a utilitarian commitment to subsistence and economic gain (*amor ... habendi*, "love of possessing," 4.177; *amor florum*, "love of flowers," 4.205).[76] They devolve into civil war.[77] Divided into factions following two kings (4.67–70), they figure slavish and docile peoples in an orientalizing mode. When their leader is destroyed, they engage in an autodestruction marked as Eastern, with Egypt leading the pack (4.210–12).

> Praeterea regem non sic Aegyptus et ingens
> Lydia nec populi Parthorum aut Medus Hydaspes
> observant. rege incolumi mens omnibus una est;
> amisso rupere fidem, constructaque mella
> diripuere ipsae et cratis soluere fauorum.
> ille operum custos, illum admirantur et omnes
> circumstant fremitu denso stipantque frequentes,
> et saepe attollunt umeris et corpora bello
> obiectant pulchramque petunt per vulnera mortem.   4.210–18

Furthermore not to this extent does Egypt or extensive Lydia, not thus do the peoples of Parthia or the Median Hydaspes pay court to a king. When the king is safe, all hold to the same purpose; when he has been lost, they

---

[74] Dahlmann (1954); Lowrie (2015a) 324 nn. 3 and 4.   [75] *Pace* Nelis (2013) 247.
[76] At *Aeneid* 8.327, *amor habendi* ("love of gain"), along with rage for war, marks the decline from the Saturnian age; Putnam (1965) 134.
[77] Morley (2007).

break faith and themselves rip apart the hives they have built and dissolve the framework of the honeycomb. He is the guardian of works, him they admire, and all stand around him with thick buzzing and crowd him in a dense throng. Often they raise him on their shoulders and shield him with their bodies in war and seek a death glorious through wounds.

Destroying *fides*, the normative word for the social bond, they dismantle the physical hive, which, in the *Georgics'* register, stands for their world. The bees' adulation and self-sacrifice for their king is anything but republican. Rather, in putting their lives under the *fasces* (4.204) and destroying the hive, they parody military discipline and the virtuous suicide for liberty's sake that characterizes republican values. Furthermore, they lack imperial virtues: The clemency, justice, and *pietas* that would appear on Augustus' shield in 27 BCE make no appearance here. Their perversion of the Republic offers no alternative. The poem projects onto the abject other what the Romans cannot hear: their potential descent into an oriental kingship – that Republican taboo – with the advent of a new Caesar, the only available savior.[78]

Later literature turns monarchy's establishment as the solution to civil war into a cliché. In Victor Hugo's *Cromwell*, a tragicomedy where the Lord Protector toys with kingship, an orator argues, with Augustus as precedent, that kingship inevitably follows on civil war.

> On voit, en méditant Gabaon, Actium,
> Que, lorsqu'au sein d'un people une lutte s'élève,
> C'est un nœud gordien que toujours tranche un glaive.
> Ce glaive devient sceptre, et démontre à la foi
> Que toute question se résout par un roi.　　*Cromwell*, 3.14.3465–9

We see, meditating on Gabaon, Actium, that when struggle arises in the breast of a people, the knot the sword cuts is Gordian. The sword become scepter and shows at the same time, that a king is the solution to every question.

The critique of this solution is to expose the orientalist nature of kingship. Carr, a stern Protestant Republican, denounces to Cromwell the royalist plot to assassinate him and put a Stuart back on the throne.

> Ils disaient : – Profitons de leurs sanglants débats;
> Nous ferons succéder Babylone à Gomorrhe.　　2.10.1597–8

They said: let's profit from their bloody debates. We'll make Babylon succeed Gommorah.

---

[78] Lowrie (2015a). For orientalist projection, Said (1978), Vinken (2015b), Lowrie (2015c). For Augustus' adoption of the role of chief sacrificer, Feeney (2004) 8.

He himself reproves Cromwell with acting too much like a king: "Dieu de Jacob! / Entends-tu ce Nemrod qui prend des airs de Job?" ("God of Jacob! Do you hear this Nimrod, putting on airs as if Job?" 2.10.1660–1). Vergil's bee king offers early traces of this trope and presents a subtle warning to Augustus about the dangers of kingship: This political form would turn the Romans into orientals.

The king bee, whose intact body guarantees social order, overlays and clarifies the figure of the savior that first appears at the end of book 1. Vergil's prayer to the gods for succor in a world overwhelmed by war conjures up a youth as a bearer of aid. As in Eclogue 1, the youth is traditionally identified as the future Augustus.[79] The mix of the Roman foundational gods Romulus and Vesta with the native Italian gods, of the Roman cityscape with the Italian landscape hits the essence of Roman identity. At issue is not merely an end to war but society's restoration.

> di patrii Indigetes et Romule Vestaeque mater,
> quae Tuscum Tiberim et Romana Palatia servas,
> hunc saltem everso iuvenem succurrere saeclo
> ne prohibete.   1.499–501

> Paternal gods, the Indigenous ones and Romulus, and mother Vesta, you who preserve the Etruscan Tiber and Roman Palatine, at least do not prevent this youth from succoring the overturned world.

To this hope for restoration, the allegory of the bees comes as a chilling answer. Rome's rebirth figured in the *bugonia* becomes readable as a potentially oriental tyranny. The call for Rome's restoration under Caesar's name threatens a terrifying healing where social cohesion would depend, as in Egypt, on Augustus' own intact body. That Empire would turn out to be oriental tyranny (4.210–18) makes Vergil's vision devastating.[80] The joyous rebirth works – but uncannily, as horror under erasure. Projection onto an oriental other is a quick fix. The poem warns that all the internal dissolution denied may well return.

The successful rebirth of the *bugonia* is the only option available. What it brings back, however, is domination, whose highest expression is empire.

---

[79] Boyle (1986) 76–84: the expectation that Caesar will "make the darkness into light" (76) founders on the impossibility of salvation.

[80] Morgan's (1999) positive dialectic, which recuperates death as integral to life (185, 207) approximates classic right-wing Hegelianism (*Rechtshegelianisch*). His interpretation follows Pauline *kenosis*, Henry (1994). Ancient mystery cults provide the scheme the Western tradition will fold into and identify with Christianity, Creuzer (1837). Although Morgan finds so-called pessimistic readings of Vergil anachronistic, his own redemptive reading depends on Christian hermeneutics; see Thomas (1998) 275 and (2001) xiii.

Caesar does what he should: push the borders back, especially in the East. However, we have known since Sallust the danger of empire. It is the source of luxury, which corrupts and undermines the republican virtues that have enabled it: Success cannibalizes itself.[81] But if we think that turning domination outward is the solution to violence within, as often in Augustan poetry, closer examination reveals that Vergil's poem is informed throughout by Sallust's devastating analysis of empire's corrupting influence. Imperial expansion imports into Rome the East with all its luxury, all its decadence. The solution to internal dissolution inescapably undermines the restoration it is meant to perform.

Triumph and Civil War

The ostensibly celebratory panegyric to Caesar opening the third book of the *Georgics* reveals the nature of empire. Conventionally associated with the future Augustus' triple triumph over Egypt, Actium, and Illyricum in 29 BCE,[82] the ecphrasis of a phantasmagorical triumph inscribes orientalism into Rome's apparent victory.[83] This strategy demonstrates that externalizing violence onto others cannot heal the internal division that is civil war. Caesar, Rome's triumph over the world, the poet himself – all get caught up in an Asiatic frenzy. Taking Horace's dictum a step further, by conquering the other, Rome becomes the other it has conquered.[84] This overblown fantasy, planted in the heart of Mantua, Vergil's own homeland, offers no escape even within the self, even within the poet's own poetic voice.

The temple built for Caesar in Vergil's imagination will sit alongside the green grass of the River Mincius. At first, we see a lovely pastoral locale: The Mincius wanders lazily and weaves together the banks with tender reed (3.13–15). But *ingens*, Vergil's characteristic adjective for the hyperbolic, mysterious, and awe-inspiring, overlays the blander meaning of "inborn."[85] The river "weaves" the reeds on its shore, so technological imagery

---

[81] Sallust, *Cat.* 11: "For prosperous affairs wear out in fact the spirits of the wise – still less would those of corrupt morals temper their victory."

[82] E.g., Nelis (2004) 84. On the "multimedia extravaganza," Lowrie (2009) 150–7.

[83] Whether the proem to book 3 refers to Vergil's future project the *Aeneid* or to the *Georgics*' own performance is immaterial to our argument, which analyzes the symbolic register, rather than the referential. On this philological chestnut, Citroni (2015).

[84] Horace, *Epist.* 2.1.156: *Graecia capta ferum victorum cepit* ("Captured Greece caught its fierce victor").

[85] Thomas (1988) *ad loc.* collects Vergil's references to the Mincius, only here called *ingens*. Analyzing this word's etymology and usage in Vergil, Quartarone (2011) restricts its meaning here to "natural,"

infuses natural beauty in a metaphor from poetics. It meanders – like the famous Asian river – in the vocabulary of error (*errat*).[86] The line-end -*ine ripas* anticipates the line-end -*ine ripae* (4.527) of the Hebrus that carries off Orpheus' head in book 4. The Italian landscape is already underwritten with orientalist touches revealing the congruence of politics with style. Furthermore, Vergil's native river, which first appears in a pastoral mode, turns into a monstrous Asiatic river under its clear surface for a stylistic point. In register, the muddy Euphrates along which Caesar thunders (4.561) spills into the Mincius.[87] The "sources" of the river name the rhetorical influence behind the passage's Asiatic panegyric. The oriental underwrites the rustic with its opposite in poetics just as in politics.

The pomp and circumstance of the festival celebrating Roman victory over the world comes in oriental garb. The highlight of imperial expansion is the East: the Nile, the "subdued cities of Asia" (*urbes Asiae domitas*, 3.30), the beaten Niphates, the Parthians. The wealth of Asia converts into monuments celebrating its conquest. The ecphrasis of the temple doors displays the vanquished world through luxurious materials, gold and ivory. The theatrical show opens with a crimson curtain embroidered with conquered Britons who seem to open it in an artful, illusionistic marvel. The bronze columns built of ship beaks proclaim victory. The accumulation of Parian marbles, of statues so realistic you think they breathe – all this luxury, this perfect technology of the arts, is the fruit of empire.

The poem stages the enervating effect of imperial expansion not simply by putting Caesar into a temple as a virtual god – a hint of Eastern emperor worship – but by internalizing all this pomp in the poetic voice. The poet himself appears in the guise of the victor. He dons the crimson robe of the triumphator, whipping up one hundred hyperbolic four-horse chariots, celebrating Caesar, the actual victor, in a grandiloquent triumph. The poet will bring Idumaean palms back from Palestine (3.12). The denaturing of the poet himself, out of place in his beloved homeland Mantua, drives the grandiosity home. The empire has consumed all, including the poet conventionally viewed as its most laudatory voice. By himself donning empire's most seductive mask, Vergil unmasks the ideology. It is the reader's task to see through the illusionistic display. As beautiful as it

---

from "in-born" (20); her point about its flat meaning, however, pertains here as well. Our interpretation matches the passage's hyperbole. For civil war associations of the word in later reception, Ginsberg (2011); comments on Vergilian usage (359).

[86] Strabo (Augustan period), *Geography* 12.8.15: "from it all wanderings are called meanders." Putnam (1979) 167: "the Mincius meanders"; orientalist elements (167–70).

[87] For the Euphrates' Callimachean associations, Scodel and Thomas (1984).

appears in its making, Vergil's poem unravels its own world-making abilities. It is as hard on him as he is on Caesar, as he is on the Romans who have failed to build the world they aspire to. Success in art, as in politics, undoes itself from within. The displacement of civil war into imperial expansion is a solution that bears the seeds of a return to civil war within itself. The *Georgics* both proclaims this solution and exposes it.

The poem's center, typically the locus of programmatic definition in Augustan poetry, is a diptych spanning the end of book 2 and beginning of book 3.[88] In each passage, a contrasting register, civil war and orientalist empire respectively, puts pressure on the life and landscape of the farmer. Before the book divide, georgic life, presented in its blessed modality, is defined by its antitype, the urban space of the political, which devolves into civil war; after it, the orientalist extravaganza of the imagined triumph denatures the native, Italian landscape. While these registers from internal and external politics are themselves antithetical, they merge in planting seeds of violence in the georgic world.

At the end of book 2, metaphors of civil war contrast systematically with the blessed life of the farmer. In a first move, georgic life is idealized as lacking all the elements of civil war, namely political discord whether in republican or kingly guise. The autarkic farmer lives in cosmic harmony; he tills a land superlatively just (2.460); neither external nor internal Roman politics subjects him, nor do the disturbances of the soul such as avarice, that paradigmatically imperial vice (3. 496–9). The farmer offers a model for an idealized society before politics. The relations between the sexes and the generations, among men, between man and god, man and animal, all lack violence. It is a life of liberty from discord and from the envy driving class struggle, a life of equality among classes and fraternity among the men, of chastity and patriarchy, of family first (2.473), of mooing cows (2.470) and fat and happy pigs (2.520), of staying in one's homeland of plenty, and of rustic celebration. These rustic people, living in a "most just" earth (2.460), are the ones personified Justice abandons last (2.474).

Such prepolitical life, however, is defined through the negation of a specifically Roman politics that reinscribes all that is denied. The Sabines' idealized life in close proximity to the harmony between Remus and his unnamed brother recalls the rape and fratricide that together founded Rome (2.532–3);[89] the golden Saturnian life before Jupiter's

---

[88] For proems in the middle, Conte (1992); in this passage, Gale (2000) 18; on Augustus' tendency to occupy the middle of otherwise linear narratives in Vergil, Nelis (2004) 85–90.

[89] The substitution of *frater* for Romulus' name evokes fratricide and hence civil war: Marchetta (2013) 438–40 builds on Putnam (1979) 159–60.

postlapsarian rule (2.536) recalls the arts that came with it (1.133). The luxuries negated – tortoise marquetry, gold brocade, spices disguising clean and basic olive oil, Assyrian *venenum* dying pure-white georgic wool – appear in markedly orientalizing terms (2.464–5, 506). Rome and the East, then and now: Oppositions of space and time define this idealized life of purity *ex negativo*. The lack entailed in personified Justice's departure (2.474) is revealed as definitive at the poem's end, when the broad justice embodied in Eurydice fails to return from the dead. Warfare negated (2.539–40) turns out to have been already anticipated in the before times, when Rome surrounded her seven citadels with a wall (2.535).

Eastern corruption brought by empire brings to fruition the civil discord that lies latent in the idealized times. Negation of discordant arms and imperial luxury first define the just life of the farmer in parallel (2.459, 463–6).[90] The causal link between them then appears: The worry and rush of trade, war, and politics serve a purpose, "that a man may drink from jeweled cups and sleep on scarlet linen from Tyre" (*ut bibat ... et ... dormiat*, 2.506). Imperial expansion leads next to the public theater of rhetoric, class warfare, joy in the blood of brothers (*gaudent perfusi sanguine fratrum*), and exile far from the Italian homeland (2.508–12). If the juxtaposition of political to the georgic life of the farmer, moving land with his curved plow (2.513), lulls us into thinking civil war has been left behind, a virtually identical line (1.494) in the previous book already shows future farmers digging up the bones of Roman soldiers killed on the battlefields of Philippi, a recurrent site of civil war (*iterum*, 1.490). Civil war at the end of book 2 builds on its treatment at the end of book 1 and identifies its cause. The drive to acquire luxury through empire, the insanity of politics (*insanumque forum*, 2.502), and fratricide – civil war's own trope – all unite in the same register for the same purpose.

This link between empire and civil war in book 2 exposes the consequences of the orientalist triumphal festival beginning book 3. The terms defining the farmer's freedom from disturbance are realized in the elements of the festival and reveal its true nature as the antitype to georgic life in its idealized form. The farmer does not marvel before the orator's speeches at the rostra (2.508), namely the space at Rome where the columns of ships' beaks rose, as on the temple doors at 3.29. He does not indulge in the oratorical spectacle of the *contio* before the people, of speeches in the senate, or of the theater (2.508–10),[91]

---

[90] Putnam (1979) 144.

[91] *Cunei* (2.509) are the seating divisions in a theater; a theater audience is often depicted as consisting of various political classes, Lowrie (2014).

a space that anticipates the *scaena* of 3.24–5. The theatricality that perverts the propriety of sober and effective Republican oratory returns in the festival.[92] The description of georgic life closing book 2 keeps empire, civil war, and the whole political order under wraps through negation, but the celebration of empire that descends on the pastoral landscape of Mantua encodes civil war as empire's other orientation.

Violence Generalized

Beyond politics, internal violence infuses Vergil's entire georgic universe. In Jupiter's historical world, labor's law subjects all life in the register of conquest (*labor omnia vicit / improbus* (1.145–6)). *Improbus* calls labor violent, shameless, and unjust.[93] The georgic world encodes the world of history.

Under Jupiter's harsh and patriarchal rule (*pater ipse*, 1.121), the earth may not freely give her bounty of her own accord as before (1.127–8) but lies subjected, divided, and marked with signs (1.125–6). Mother Earth, violated with furrows, the veins of her rocks pounded to release their fire (1.133–5), is forced to bear the fruit she previously gave unasked (*nullo poscente*, 1.128), much less through subjection. Violent undertones evoke warfare: The thistle bristles – like spears (1.151); the crops die – like soldiers in battle; the harsh woods sneak up (*subit*, 1.152), as in ambush; the weeds dominate the crops (*dominantur*, 1.154); the armed farmer will pursue (*insectabere*, 1.155) them as enemies. The metaphors become explicit in the simile for the quincunx, a geometric planting optimizing space between trees:

> ut saepe ingenti bello cum longa cohortis
> explicuit legio et campo stetit agmen aperto,
> derectaeque acies ac late fluctuat omnis
> aere rinidenti tellus, necdum horrida miscent
> proelia, sed dubius mediis Mars errat in armis.   2.279–83

> As often in awe-inspiring war when the long legion of the cohort unfurls and the marching ranks stand on the open plain, and the straight fronts and the whole land far and wide undulates with shining bronze, nor yet do they mix the bristling battles, but Mars wanders ambivalent in the midst of arms.

Georgic space allegorically tells history as universal warfare.

---

[92] For the theatricality of Roman political space, Bartsch (1994), Beacham (1999), Lowrie (2014).

[93] Thomas (1988) and Mynors (1990) deny redeeming virtue to *labor* at 1.145–6, contrary to the tradition of "honest toil."

Warfare images peak in successive evocations of internal violence. The lunar calendar brings back monthly the fifth day as a memorial of Gigantomachy (1.277–83). While this can be avoided, even if one works on the seventeenth, the labor to be done entails domination (*domitare*, 1.285). The story of Nisus and Scylla offers a familial analogue to the cosmic revolt of the Giants against the Olympian order. The eternally repeated assault of the metamorphosed father-bird on the metamorphosed daughter-bird perpetuates the trope of intrafamilial violence and inscribes it into the natural order. Her wings "cut" the air (*secat*), just as she cut her father's purple lock of hair, their city's protective talisman. Her treachery against family and state, as Ovid tells it (*Metamorphoses* 8.1–151), was motivated by her passion for Minos, the enemy commander. The story encapsulates Vergil's obsessive themes: destruction wrought by love; the parallel between family and state; internecine violence and the inversion of proper relations between family members; such tropes spill over from the human into the natural world. The verbatim repetition describing Scylla's repeated attempts and inevitable failure to break with violence's cyclical structure illustrates a universal truth.

> quacumque *illa levem fugiens secat aethera pennis,*
> ecce inimicus atrox magno stridore per *auras*
> insequitur *Nisus* ; qua se fert *Nisus* ad *auras,*
> *illa levem fugiens* raptim *secat aethera pennis.*   1.404–9

> Wherever she cuts the light air with her wings in flight, behold comes Nisus a harsh enemy with a great screech through the breezes; where Nisus brings himself through the breezes, she cuts the light air snatching rapidly with her wings in flight.

Such stories, imported and naturalized on Italian soil, tell Rome's recent history allegorically. The praise of Italy (*laudes Italiae*, 2.136) likewise embeds an oriental strain into the idyllic homeland; comparison keeps the suppressed terms in play.[94] Insisting no foreign land may compete with Italy, the poem conjures up Persia and India, the locus of Greece's Persian Wars and the furthest reaches of Alexander's conquest, both paradigmatic for East / West conflict. The contrast between native and alien prepares for another trope of civil war. The detailed description of the earthborn, sown from the teeth of the hydra, and their harvest of weapons plants in the Latin language a conventional image of civil war negated of Italy (2.140–2). Knowledge of Apollonius' *Argonautica*, one of the *Aeneid*'s most influential

---

[94] For Italy's paradoxes, where "armed men [are] mothered by a land of golden peace," Boyle (1986) 83.

models, lets Vergil's learned reader supply that they mow themselves down, a trope of self-destruction. If idyllic Italy keeps civil war under negation, it is because Rome has exported it to the battlefields of Greece, Egypt, and around the Mediterranean basin. Such containment reassures: Julius Caesar's port at the Lucrine lake has gated even the entrance to the Underworld (2.161–4). But this boundary, enforced by Jupiter's technology, will be transgressed by Orpheus in this poem and repeatedly in the *Aeneid*, when the Sibyl escorts Aeneas to and from the underworld, then explosively when Juno raises Allecto from hell's depths.

The inevitability of civil war underwrites Vergil's cosmos. Cosmic order, political order, the order of nature and of the family break down repeatedly and in parallel. Just as Nisus and Scylla attack and flee forever in a paradigm of familial and natural violence (father against daughter, bird against bird), history also repeats. Philippi sees Roman civil war twice: *Romanas acies iterum videre Philippi* (1.490). Future farmers will exhume the detritus of battle and marvel – the bones of civil war cannot rest in peace. Fraternal discord occurs twice in short succession (2.495, 510). A cyclical link between civil war and empire binds history. After Philippi, the poem moves from civil war to imperial expansion in a familiar metonymic progression.[95] World war breaks out as Mars rages across the limits of the Roman Empire, from the cradle of civilization to the barbaric North.

> hinc mouet Euphrates, illinc Germania bellum;
> vicinae ruptis inter se legibus urbes
> arma ferunt; saevit toto Mars impius orbe,   1.509–11

> The Euphrates on this side, on that Germany are on the move to war; neighboring cities bear arms against each other, the treaties broken; impious Mars rages over the whole world.

This repetition goes back to Rome's mythic perjury at Troy. Vergil's prayer for an end to self-slaughter, by which Rome has already paid enough for its original sin in Laomedon's Troy (*iam satis pridem sanguine nostro / Laomedonteae luimus periuria Troiae*, 1.501–2), finds no realization; hope in Augustus Caesar to save the world remains suspended.

The cosmos retains order not materially, but paradoxically in representing its own destruction. Omens tell civil war as a tale of the distinctions ordering nature breaking down.[96] The moon commemorates the Gigantomachy, figuring civil war (1.277–83). With the sun's eclipse at

---

[95] Putnam (1979) 78, 80, 82.   [96] Jal (1963) 242. Schiesaro (1997) 76.

Julius Caesar's assassination (1.464–8), actual civil war catalyzes from latency. This murder's omens not only signal but also enact collapse: Aetna erupts, the Alps quake, rivers either halt or flood, land gapes apart, flocks speak (*locutae*, 1.478) in an ironically unspeakable act (*infandum*, 1.479). Language fails to capture the inversion of nature's laws, because language is structured as the cosmos it represents. In a quintessential emblem of Vergil's eloquent grace, the perfect form of the cosmos figures its own internal collapse. The semiotic form remains intact even against its message, encrypted because it cannot be signified.

Art's Promise Withheld

Art alone has the potential to imagine a space immune from violence. The *Georgics* offers a single idyll from which civil war is banned, a sweet homeland, a "world apart,"[97] over against a global, bitter world of exile. The garden of the old Corycian man comes in a marked genre, the pastoral idyll. There is no strife (4.125–48), seasons keep order but lack winter's harshness, the only light disharmony is domesticated: the man scolds (*increpitans*) the summer, late in coming, like a child. For him, the mild winter is foil to the gentle weather that brings first the rose of spring, then autumn's apple. Lush description holds up an image of a nostalgic world that surpasses the peace of Vergil's usual ambivalent Saturnian age. No technology, no economy, no luxury sullies this autarkic world; the old man enjoys nature's cornucopia without exercising or submitting to domination.

This idyll floats in the poem like the illusionistic paintings in *trompe l'oeil* frames of third-style Roman fresco, depicting pastoral idyllic landscapes in miniature, enchanting works of art. Vivid description frames the garden's reality as a product of art's labor (*sub fine laborum*, 4.116). This idyll interrupts Vergil's account of the society of bees and, if excerpted from the poem, would leave no trace. Consecutive frames heighten and reveal the idyll's illusion in a *mise en abyme*. *Praeteritio* – if time would permit, Vergil would tell of gardens – signals rhetorical construction; the figure goes by its own name (*praetereo*, 4.148). Despite claiming otherwise, *praeteritio* introduces another rhetorical construction: ecphrasis or *phantasia*, which puts what is absent vividly before the eyes.

A framing garden (4.120–4), depicting a greater and harsher reality outside the idyll, heightens by contrast the artistic construction of the

Figure 2.5 Ara Pacis Augustae, Tellus relief, Ara Pacis Museum, Rome

old man's world. Metaphorical plants subtly call out natural warfare: endive, whose bitter roots elsewhere do harm (1.120); cucumber, twisting through the grass with swelling belly, evokes a snake; narcissus and shore-loving myrtle – Venus' plant, in Venus' own gesture – remind us that in Vergil passion is always unhappy; the ivy, here sacred to Bacchus, was earlier identified, along with pitch and noxious yew, as an indicator of criminally cold soil (2.258). Like the snake, soon to devour nestlings in the framing frieze of the Ara Pacis, which reveals the artifice of the peaceful image of prosperity of the Tellus relief (Figs. 2.5 and 2.6), Vergil's georgic garden encodes the natural violence that disappears from within the frame. The historical context suggests the old man is a former pirate settled by Pompey. Persuaded to give up his lawless ways, he transforms "into a paradigm of peace and fecundating, nourishing *labor*."[98] The layered violence shows up all the more its lack within the peaceful garden and highlights that it is an imagined creation crafted by rhetoric's techniques.

---

[98] Servius (4.127). Wilkinson (1969) 174–5; Boyle (1986) 65; Geue (2018) 129 stresses the imperialism behind the aestheticization of the old man and his extraction of apian labor.

As a powerful act of rhetoric, ecphrasis creates a representation so vivid that what is absent appears present.[99] The poet lets us view this paradise, only to foreclose it to himself and to us. Its artificial, poetically constructed peace and beauty heightens longing for what is withheld. His theme, however, excludes him from this *locus amoenus* and redirects him to textual and actual spaces characterized as unfair (4.148). The pleasure garden is a space of memory (4.125) located in a past time, accessible only through a mediating act of imagination.

Orpheus' art cuts deeper into the poem's fundamental questions. Orphic poetics promises to heal, even undo death through resurrection, but Orpheus' art is exposed as phantasmagorical illusion. Orpheus moreover falls prey to the same weaknesses that destroy the world to begin with. The madness, subjection of spirit, passionate love, and furor (4.464, 488, 491, 495) that beset Orpheus are all the more heartrending because of the tantalizing promise he would be able to win his lost wife back from the dead. His failure of self-control with his backward glance falls short of

Figure 2.6 Ara Pacis Augustae, detail from the acanthus frieze, snakes eating chicks, Ara Pacis Museum, Rome; photo by Ralph Lieberman.

[99] Webb (1997). Bartsch and Elsner (2007).

republican and imperial norms alike; his deficient *virtus* is also a failure
before the gods' mercy.[100]

The love story of Orpheus and his cherished wife overlays the story of
social rupture of the *Georgics'* continuous metaphorical bassline. As mentioned above (pp. 63–5), Eurydice carries in her name the "broad justice"
that repeatedly dematerializes in the poem and, as one of the virtues on
Augustus' *clipeus virtutis*, evokes contemporary political language. In flight
from the sexual violence of Aristaeus' attempted rape, she dies from the
natural violence of snakebite. Rape in the Roman political imaginary is
a foundational figure that has inscribed civil strife into the family and
between the sexes ever since the rape of the Sabines. As the rape fails to be
consummated, even a perverse foundation does not arise. The fatal venom
of the snake comes into the world through the intervention of Jupiter
(1.129), who is responsible for the whole mess of the world's internal split to
begin with.

Orpheus' poetics devolves into fruitless elegiac lament, where language's
order and its order-giving potential fall into the meaningless repetition of
mere mechanical echo. This poetics cannot restore; its impotence brings
collapse into language itself. In a senseless distortion of language's com-
municative burden, the poem's echo of Orpheus' echo underscores futility:
Orpheus laments Eurydice's death with a fourfold repetition of "you" (*te*,
4.465–6), then laments her second death by repeating her name (4.525–7).
A signifier whose signified – both name and etymology – has been lost fills
the world in the voice of a poet himself dead. The nightingale simile
reinscribes this echoing grief (*maerens, maestis*, 4.511, 515); her inhumanly
beautiful voice can neither restore her lost young, "pests" destroyed by the
hard farmer, nor communicate any semantic sense.

Love fails along with poetry. The trauma of love lost renders Orpheus
incapable of loving again – Ovid adds a new, homoerotic reorientation as
the sterile fruit of his trauma (*Metamorphoses* 10.83–5). The violent dismemberment of his body in an orgiastic perversion of Bacchic rites cleaves
in two the body poetic along with the body politic. The decapitated head
cannot bear the republican rights *caput* stands for. Orpheus' cold tongue
and voice embody poetry's failure to reconstruct the world through resurrection, or even to complete the essentially Roman task of commemor-
ation. Orpheus' words build no tomb but rather resound along the
riverbank, swept away in Catullus' image for futile language: the oaths of
lovers written on water (poem 70). There is no rebuilding the world in

---

[100] On parallels between politics and poetics in Vergil's backward glances, Gale (2003).

a worldly sense or even in poetry. Lament in all its heartbreaking beauty comes to naught. As with the georgic world, shown in all its comfort and quotidian splendor only to be ripped apart, so with Vergil's poetics: An image of restoration only sets up its failure.

Orpheus' inability to retrieve Eurydice mirrors within poetics the ritual perversion of the *bugonia*. The negation of forgiveness adds to the parallel of attempted resurrection. Orpheus' weakness, paradoxically love itself, which should reunite lovers and thereby reknit the frayed social bond, "should be forgiven, if only the shades knew how to forgive" (*ignoscenda quidem, scirent si ignoscere Manes*, 4.489). But just as Orpheus is not forgiven, so does Aristaeus fail to supplicate the angry Nymphs and placate the shades, as instructed by Cyrene. He omits the very task of winning pardon (*veniam*, 4.536) and, as we saw above (pp. 63–4), precisely the rite that would placate Eurydice (*placatam Eurydicen*, 4.547). The forgiveness denied Orpheus hints that the same is denied Aristaeus. His success in regenerating the bees may bring back animal life, but it is sterile: all meaning-giving spheres – poetry, politics, ritual – have become either impotent or monstrous.

The *Georgics'* final lines create a final parallel, between politics and poetics in the names of Caesar and Vergil, that brings to a head the poem's constituent frames of reference to tell the same story of empire substituting for and fulfilling civil war.[101] The political register erases republican values under the new language of empire, and the poetic register conveys its impotence to do anything but reveal the new reality through poetry's canonical means of speaking without saying, namely, via figuration.

For politics, Justice herself does not return; instead, Augustus establishes law's rule through conquest. In the *pax Augusta*, willing peoples are not citizens but docile subjects. By extending empire to the Euphrates, Augustus acts the oriental king. Thundering like Jupiter, he does god's work and wins his way to Olympus, all the while encoding Gigantomachy, civil war's cosmic trope. The imagery sets a rift between the nameless masses below and the absolute ruler as lord above. Jupiter has filled the world with labors and cares, technology and economy, so modeling Caesar on him hardly offers a method for community restoration.[102] Rather than refounding any social bond within Roman society, Augustus turns absolutely outward and upward.

---

[101] Gale (2003) 324–33.
[102] For a similar parallel between Jupiter and Aeneas, Thomas (1998) 295–7, (2000) 405.

For poetics, Vergil in his own name parallels the ruler as his opposite, precisely in terms of the social bond. Against the backdrop of Caesar's glorious Olympus, a patriarchal male world of domination, the poet appears an inglorious and playful youth – small wonder his own name was etymologized as "the virgin." The shelter of Epicurean Naples, called by the virginal name of Parthenope, its Greek nymph, offers a space where the bonds of friendship establish an alternative *civitas* of political withdrawal, embracing peace and pleasure in a pastoral world. In this alternative landscape, the poet's own chaste love of his subject matter – the only love imagined as sublimating passion and violence – may thrive, sharing in the labor of its world (3.284–94). But Parthenope was also a seductive and deadly Siren, and the poet's love also snatches him with a violence that anticipates Eurydice's rape (*raptat*, 3.292; *raptam*, 4.519). Where the political world is overtly violent, even poetic retreat reencodes violence. Vergil himself glances backward, to the first line of the *Eclogues*: Its signature trope of the sheltering tree sets his name on his earlier work as telling the same story. He invites us to reread Eclogue 1, where the *Georgics'* themes are already adumbrated: Caesar appears as a savior worshipped in absolutist mode; liberty has been won only to be immediately lost; the poetic voice mourns but does not heal. Between the conquered Euphrates and apolitical Naples, between Olympus and the idealized landscape, no public sphere remains, even in poetry. In the end, no proper Rome reemerges.

CHAPTER 3

Empire without End
Vergil, Aeneid, *and Lucan,* De bello civili

Lucan is often called anti-Vergilian.[1] His poem on civil war discloses the hollowness of Jupiter's promise of eternal empire in Vergil's *Aeneid*. The *pax Augusta* has produced an Empire without end without the fruits of peace, much less liberty's restoration. If Lucan promotes civil war's horrors as worth their consequences – Nero as a new super-Augustus – he does so without representing the new Empire's glory, rather indulging his shocked reader with the gory details of the Republic's demise. We argue that Lucan condenses and makes explicit on his textual surface the implicit and scattered tropes of civil discord troubling Vergil's apparently hopeful message of a new golden age to come. He heightens the disturbance and tips the tone from tragic lament to grotesque horror. Far from upending the *Aeneid*, Lucan is a faithful reader whose apparent perversity arises from a strong reading of his influential predecessor. *De bello civili* exposes the *Aeneid*'s underlying truth: Empire completes the structure of civil war without overcoming it; the cessation of civil discord's cyclical violence makes visible politics' underlying premise.[2] History ends not in a golden age of revival, but in a static, unchanging state of domination.

The *Georgics'* universal scope lays bare the internal conflict of the human condition; the *Aeneid* speaks the language of Roman history. Rome, a specific instantiation of political order, becomes paradigmatic for universal history. Rome's repeated dissolution into civic strife and refoundation declare history a repetitious cycle of violence, only ever

---

[1] Zwierlein (1974) 65–6 n. 79 traces the scholarly topos; Bramble (1983) 37; Reggiani (2005) 114. Quint (1993) 133: He fathers an "anti-Virgilian" epic tradition that embraces "the cause of the politically defeated." Henderson (1998) 166 skewers the commonplace: "post-Virgilian, and (so) propter-Virgilian." Retrospectively stabilizing the earlier text enables a subversion narrative, Thomas (2001) 19–20, 83–4. Narducci (2002) 75–87.

[2] Boyle (1993c) 86: Nothing like the *Aeneid*'s use of myth for moral and political scrutiny, which later became a central feature of the genre, exists in prior epic. Lucan "removed Virgil's veil of myth to make his critique unambiguous."

temporarily quelled.[3] Sigmund Freud exposes civil war as Rome's unconscious by making Juno's resolve – "if I cannot bend the gods above, I will stir up Hell below" (*flectere si nequeo superos, Acheronta movebo*, 7.312) – the epitaph to *The Interpretation of Dreams*.[4] From earliest history, Evander in mythic times, Saturn before human history, foundation at the site of Rome in the *Aeneid* entails discord's signature tropes. Before Romulus, before Aeneas, Evander fled from domestic violence into exile (*pulsum patria*, 8.333); Saturn fled from threatening patricide into exile at the same spot (*arma Iovis fugiens*, "fleeing the arms of Jupiter," 8.320). Doubleness inheres in Rome's foundation from the beginning: Saturn and Janus both founded cities on the hills of Rome (*duo oppida*, 8.355), presaging the double founders Romulus and Remus.[5]

Civil discord underlies the *Aeneid*'s foundation narrative as a subtext for a discerning reader to uncover. The techniques for its representation include many standard literary strategies: indirect expression through allusion, displacement, projection, substitution, asymmetry, pointed omission, hyperbole with or without anticlimax, various metaphors for the body politic (severed heads, dismemberment, marriage and procreation, dehumanization), the violation of the sacred, spectacle, regime change, inability, indistinction or hyperdistinction between self and other, traumatic repetition, failed closure, as well as the canonical series of tropes for civil discord that take the violence of same on same progressively inward, from citizens into the family, into the self in suicide, and into the soul through madness, fury, and indecision. These speak out a story the poem does not narrate. Scholarship on Latin literature frequently calls civil war traumatic and understands its representation as revealing the unspoken wound symptomatically.[6] The inability to narrate typically attributed to victims of trauma is a response to a wound externally imposed. The Vergilian strand of representing civil war, however, externalizes through fragmentation an internal, self-generated split too painful to reckon with straight on.

---

[3] Johnson (1976) 137–8 emphasizes that Vergil lived his young life "under the constant reality, or the constant threat of civil war."

[4] Oliensis (2001) 39; she also cites Harold Bloom's assessment of Vergil's originality in contrast to Homer as residing in "Juno's dark resolve to rouse the underworld."

[5] Lowrie (2013) 85–6.

[6] Quint (2018) locates the original trauma at Troy (13 n. 11, 16). He sets a new standard for tropological reading and interprets Vergil more "pessimistically" as debunking empire even than the so-called Harvard school.

If civil war is traumatic, its direct narration should theoretically be impossible. It becomes legible, however, in retrospect.[7] Where the *Aeneid*'s contemporary, backward-looking perspective reveals the future meaning of mythic events in terms of recent history – the hindsight as foresight Auden declares makes no sense in "Secondary epic" – Lucan's later poem discloses in its plot what the prior text encodes as its metaphorical substrate. *De bello civili*'s relationship to the *Aeneid* is paradigmatic for the hermeneutic clarity that emerges from retrospective reading.[8] Our subsequent chapters analyze the cumulative effect of the repeated rereadings of the Roman civil wars in the constitution of *Romanitas* as a tradition. In this chapter, the *Aeneid* and *De bello civili* taken together establish these poems' interdependent relation as a model for our subsequent readings of their reception, with greater or lesser degrees of authorial awareness, in Augustine's *De civitate Dei*, Hugo's *Quatrevingt-treize*, and Houellebecq's *Soumission*. This tradition's consistency legitimates recent scholarly emphasis on civil war's persistent metaphorical register throughout Vergil's works, whether interpretation stresses the poems' hope civil war may be overcome or, as does ours, their insistence that empire contains civil war without fully eradicating its threat.[9] Recent scholarship on Vergilian ambivalence subsumes the previous dichotomy between optimism and pessimism. While individual readers may emphasize either the moments tilting toward a brighter future or those mourning empire as peace's tragic price, the poem nevertheless sets moral dilemmas or encodes tensions the straightforward Augustan reading is blind to.[10] We argue that the *Aeneid*'s hermeneutic structure maps civil war's political containment. Not given in the plot, civil war's repression leaves traces in the poem's schemes and figurations. Always threatening to erupt, it must be read out, but cannot be denied.

---

[7] For retrospective rebranding, Armitage (2017a) 156. Joseph's (2012) analysis of Tacitus' *Histories* as "epic successor" to Vergil and Lucan – a phrase taken from Hardie (1993) – shows how later allusion retrospectively constructs the *Aeneid* as a poem about civil discord.

[8] For growing clarity in civil war narratives, Lowrie (2008): *Enargeia* increases as the Catilinarian conspiracy is renarrated in Latin and French literature. On the hermeneutics of rereading, Jauss (1978), De Man (1979), Felman (1981), Edmunds (1992), Haverkamp (2004).

[9] Johnson's (1976) 111 comment on the dialectical process in the *Aeneid* similarly looks forward to the next stage of reception: "Vergil thus creates by art and political mediation a pattern that – alternatively affirming and denying the healing powers of poetry and of history – underscores the dialectical process of both imagery (art) and of human behavior in time (history). This stern dialectical process issues in no synthesis, which is at once a reason for bafflement and for the renewal of belief, for a kind of negative affirmation that is eminently suited to, say, the Christian temper."

[10] Thomas (2001); Tarrant (2012) 16–17. Fowler (1995) 266, speaking of Horace, finds it "dull and cowardly" to remain with ambivalence in tension. However, we take his interpretation of the Gates of War in the *Aeneid*, which burst open when closed, as an allegory of reading; Fowler (2000) 173–92.

Civil war flares up again in Lucan. The republican civil wars appear as a self-inflicted wound. For him, writing under Nero, a history he never experienced becomes fully nameable and narratable. Over a century of historical distance separates his death in 65 CE from the battle of Pharsalus in 48 BCE. The story of his historical epic is told directly: the literal civil war of the past. What is figured through this history – what cannot be directly narrated – is the traumatic collapse of the social bond under Nero.[11] Vergil's coded oriental empire has become Lucan's lived reality, one he cannot tell directly any more than Vergil could his own times. The told past is a metaphor for the untold present. Civil war on the battlefield becomes a metaphor for civil discord in society, rather than vice versa. Any hope for a better politics has vanished. All the republican fears of tyranny have been realized with the Julio-Claudians. Discord becomes literal again in history. Lucan's participation in the Pisonian conspiracy against Nero and subsequent forced suicide realizes civil discord. He undergoes in person one of his predominant tropes for internal conflict: suicide. Once Nero himself commits the suicide he imposed on so many others, including Lucan's uncle Seneca, Nero's own teacher and advisor, literal civil war erupts on the battlefield during the year of the four emperors (69 CE).

Vergil and Lucan's shared dark outlook becomes manifest through radically different styles. The *Aeneid*'s Augustan classicism lends a deceptive coherence whose beauty and pathos show contained horror through cracks in its surface.[12] Ostensible coherence allows less exacting readers to gloss over how everything the political order should and fails to contain persists through figuration – witness the conventional European strand of Vergilian reception, which views the *Aeneid* as a Bible of empire and an Augustan apology.[13] Lucan, by contrast, overtly narrates the atrocity of the republican civil war in the register of the grotesque but cannot tell directly the hideousness of his own present, which his narration of the past encodes. His poem's form embodies the fracture of his reality. Broken syntax, relentless hyperbole, episodic narration that resists narrative unity and teleology, the descent into detailed description of abject and broken bodies symptomatically enact discord on language.[14] Whereas the *Aeneid*

---

[11] Narducci (2002) 92–3 notes *enargeia* (vividness) at 7.212–13, where future readers will marvel at "fated events as if not past, but coming" (*velut venientia fata, / non transmissa*).

[12] Johnson (1976) analyzes Vergilian pathos, where surface coherence blurs toward a mood picture, against Homer's realistic and rational tragic mode, which tends toward redemption.

[13] Thomas (2001) 223: "the dominant European reception of Virgil is always inextricably involved with the reception of Augustus"; "much of the European reception of Virgil has always been a function of elitist, particularly scholarly, communities supporting the interests of the state, be it a monarchy or a tyranny."

[14] Quint (1993) 134–7; Masters (1992) 87–90; Bartsch (1997) 6–7; Henderson (1998) 165–211; Narducci (2002) 84–5.

finishes with a disquieting, nonclosural end,[15] *De bello civili* lacks any ending at all. Although scholarly consensus currently tends to view the transmitted end of the *Aeneid* as intentional, the dispute as to whether Lucan finished the poem or not, whether its ending was staged as incomplete – literary history's first intentional fragment – or the sad consequence of his forced suicide, still often takes a positivistic tack.[16] Either way, the incomplete ending responds to and encapsulates the problematic relationship of *De bello civili*'s representational form to the represented world.

Vergil and Lucan together establish basic literary paradigms for the conceptualization and narration of the Roman civil wars. Each in different ways entails indirection, occlusion, displacement, and the tropological representation of what cannot be spoken overtly. The differences in style, however, are different symptoms, at different times, of the same underlying cause: The Roman Empire has gone oriental. No bright future will dawn.

Typology

Methodologically, teasing out answers to the *Aeneid*'s puzzles depends on typological reading. Is Augustus' new golden age imagined as definitively ending civil war and establishing a new world order, or as perpetuating an endless cycle despite higher aspirations? Typology comes itself in two types, which in turn ramify.

Within classical terms, exemplarity creates similarity across time and suggests similar outcomes with no intimation of teleology. One may see Augustus in the simple model of semidivine culture heroes who stamp out evil, for example, Hercules exterminating Cacus in his lair.[17] Alternatively, but equally classical, Augustus could achieve success along the repetitive model of Saturn, Evander, Aeneas, Romulus, Julius Caesar – his father by adoption – and of the founders depicted on Aeneas' shield. Each of these mythohistorical figures refounds peace after civil discord, whether experienced as victim or agent.[18] This model leaves the fundamentally cyclical order of history intact as a stable system.[19] However, the remarkable recurrence of similar events from the same mold challenges the finality of the most recent historical instantiation.

Both models obey the typological principle that history teaches: in Cicero's trenchant phrase, *historia magistra vitae* ("history is the

---

[15] Johnson (1976) 122; Lowrie (2013).   [16] E.g., Stover (2008) versus Masters (1992) 216–59.
[17] Hardie (1986) 110–18 aligns Cacus with Gigantomachy, but Feeney (1991) 159–62 shows that Hercules evokes the Giants too.
[18] For civil discord on the shield, Rossi (2010).   [19] Gransden (1976) 14–20.

schoolmistress of life," *De oratore* 2.9.36).[20] Although Roman exemplarity demands critical engagement from readers, who must read out unexpressed moral lessons from stories and translate partially similar, partially dissimilar situations into a course of action, it relies on the comparability of historical actors and actions over time.[21] Those following in time aspire to live up to their predecessors and may even surpass them, but the fundamental assumption is that they function within the same historical system. How that system works, however, is disputed. The two exemplary models outlined in the preceding paragraph conflict within the *Aeneid*. The latter, cyclical refoundation after civil war, jeopardizes the full realization of the former, violence finally suppressed by a culture-hero.

Another model operates by analogy to Christian typology and would interpret Vergil's Augustus in Messianic terms as bringing an end to history.[22] This Augustus not only surpasses culture heroes and exemplary historical Romans, he also finally realizes their promise. He overcomes the obstacles to their incomplete foundations and changes the structure of the entire historical order. This thinking obeys a different logic from the assumptions underlying Roman exemplarity, which imagines nothing more than regime change and the restoration of existing values. This model is based on Jesus's overcoming Adam's original sin in substance and the New Testament's realization of the promise of the Old in medium. As opposed to *imitatio* and *aemulatio*, whose highest achievement is to surpass the *exempla* of the ancestors, Christian typology realizes and fulfills prefigurations and overcomes obstacles to fulfillment.

The importation of overcoming and fulfillment, structures inherent in Christian typology, into Vergilian criticism has a long, contested tradition.[23] This model, which well illuminates Vergil's later reception, is nevertheless anachronistic. If Augustus can end the endless cycle of civil war as savior – however much precedents in Roman history query this goal's complete realization – we emphasize that Vergil conceptualizes such a putative end to history in strictly historical and geographical terms. The

---

[20] Chaplin (2000); Levene (2000); Roller (2004), (2009), (2018); Lowrie (2007).

[21] Langlands (2011), (2015), and (2018).

[22] Griffin (1985) 186 nicely summarizes Knauer's (1964) 352 Christian typology and frames the debate between positing a "single pattern and meaning" and the pattern where "the Christ fulfilled and replaced the Biblical models" (190); he feels the Greco-Roman tradition is sufficient for understanding how Vergil's characters, story, and history are multilayered (193) and rejects the Christian typological approach (196–7). Hardie (2018) 167–9 analogizes classical "historical mirroring" (167), e.g., the death of Turnus, which "prefigures Romulus' killing of Remus" (165), to Christian typology, with the caveat that pagan antiquity lacked a "Christian teleological view of history" (167).

[23] For an overview, Horsfall (1995) 162–7.

political solution to the violence of the civil discord threatening home and homeland – the *patria*, Italy, loudly proclaimed in the poem's second line – is the externalization of civil war into empire.[24] Vergil's poetry never articulates a fully successful model for politics or cosmic order. Rome's foundation in fury on the human sacrifice of Turnus sets Roman history on a path of discord. Augustus may contain civil war but never eradicates it. War will be redirected away from Roman citizens, not as an end to global violence among men, but into ever-expanding conquest under the guise of the Augustan peace. As the border encompasses more and more territory, redefined as Roman, internal violence fills the cosmos. Jupiter's prediction – *imperium sine fine* ("empire without end," 1.279)[25] – expands the turf of what appears in retrospect to have always been civil war.[26] The moral renewal of the Augustan program depended not only on legal reform, but also on a formal religious revival. Vergil's stresses strictly political terms and neglects the religious in Augustus' golden age. He heralds no renewal of spirit.

What makes Vergil an *anima naturaliter Christiana* is the strong intimation that some spiritual renewal is necessary beyond what Augustus supplies – beyond even Roman exemplary history.[27] The problem resides in the soul, and Epicurean rationalism is insufficient to meet its needs beyond personal contentment.[28] A faith that changes the potential of human social relations as well as within individual souls still lies over the horizon. But in the tradition of Rome's reception, Augustus models the historical realization of a new foundation's promise, and the *Aeneid* becomes a Bible of empire, the New Testament's secular analogue. *Pax augusta* within the unified Empire becomes a necessary vehicle for the spread of glad tidings through the institution of the all-embracing – that is, Catholic – Church. This entails a translation from Roman exemplarity

---

[24] The intimate links between the Social Wars – Rome's conflict with Italian neighbors (early first century BCE) – and the civil wars proper, waged between prominent Roman generals from Sulla to young Caesar, implicate civil war with empire long before Vergil. Toll (1997).

[25] For the "terrible price one must pay for this glory," Parry (1963) 78.

[26] Pogorzelski (2016) 68–90 argues in a positive Hegelian dialectic that the representation of the conflict between Italians and Trojans as civil war (*Aeneid* 7–12) retrospectively unifies Italy in accord with Augustan ideology. He locates present unity in overcoming past disunity; retrojecting a nation, rent by civil war, before the state's existence creates an imagined community – as in Anderson (1983) – brought together in shared mourning. Fowler (1998) demonstrates the insufficiency of the repeated closural gesture: The Gates of War, as of interpretation, remain ever prone to burst open.

[27] Haecker (1931) 140 is the first to apply Tertullian's phrase to Vergil; Hardie (2014) 92, 143–7. Hermann Broch's *Der Tod des Vergil* (*The Death of Vergil*), published in 1945, plays out the difference in perspective between Augustus and Vergil as one between historical and spiritual horizons.

[28] Johnson (1976) 141–54.

into Christian typology. Augustine precludes Augustus and his prophet Vergil from changing world order but keeps the *Aeneid*'s fundamental question in play by making civil war, defined in Roman terms, emblematic of what needs overcoming on the path to renewal. He ups the structural ante by correcting Roman exemplarity with Christian typology and, with it, correcting Roman institutions, that is, the whole Roman system of spiritual and political thought. Hugo, who understands himself as a new Vergil, reinfuses the purported end of history with a Christian structure. Augustus may have failed to realize the promise of ending civil war permanently, but surely the new republic of his own fertile imagination will fulfill this promise and change the ground rules. Houellebecq's subversion of this model in *Soumission* depends on its credibility in the tradition.

The *Aeneid*'s Christian reception furthers the structure immanent in Vergil's conception of history through universalization and salvation history, and by emphasizing spirit, but its transformative misreading nevertheless preserves a fundamental Vergilian hope. It is not only the fourth Eclogue, where a child's birth affords a new start, that makes Vergil an *umbra* for Christian conceptions. Most clearly in Dante, the Vergil of the *Aeneid* establishes basic structures for understanding civil war his Christian reception sees itself as overcoming.[29]

Twinned Cities

The *Aeneid* and *De bello civili* establish alternative cities as registers against which to define, if not the ideal city, at least the antitypes to what Rome should be. Troy, Carthage, and Alexandria are oriental cities that uncannily double Rome.[30] But, no foil to the new foundation's virtues for Vergil or to the city lost to civil war for Lucan, these cities mirror Rome's true nature.[31]

The earliest chronological events in Aeneas' story (book 2) find him in a city midcollapse. Troy must burn for Rome to be born, but the question is whether the monstrous death in birth, perverted sacrifices, doublings and indistinctions between Greek enemy and Trojan self, the self-inflicted

---

[29] Auerbach (2016), Mazzotta (1979), Freccero (1986).

[30] Tacitus, who repeatedly alludes to *Aeneid* 2 in his account of Rome's successive captures in the year of the four emperors, literalizes civil war as the underlying link between Troy and Rome; Keitel (2010) 349–51. Jerome's equation of Troy's fall in *Aeneid* 2 with Rome's in his own times (*Ep.* 60.16 and 127.12) recognizes the layering of cities in the text; Joseph (2012) 1.

[31] Henderson (1998) 165: Epic should tell of a city's foundation or defense and "the *other* city's defeat or *un*making." Hardie (2013) tracks historical overlays between Troy and Rome, their sacking and rebirth in *Aeneid* 2 and 8: "positive and negative versions of the same place."

violence besetting proto-Romans and their enemies alike will ever cease. Only in this way can a new patriarchal order be established, where marriage is chaste and children are born who resemble their fathers. The same questions arise of Carthage, emblematic foreign imperial enemy, then again of Italy, exemplary precedent of the internal enemy. Vergil's lament questioning the divine politics behind the violence within a future single people is reserved until the poem's climactic book: *tanton placuit concurrere motu, / Iuppiter, aeterna gentis in pace futuras?* ("Was it ratified, Jupiter that peoples who would exist in eternal peace clash in such great commotion?" 12.503–4). This closes the circle on his opening challenge to theodicy, *tantaene animis caelestibus irae?* ("Were the divine spirits' angers so very great?" 1.11).[32] But parallels with the previous cities show the homology between internal and external violence, between events in Italy, Carthage, and Troy. Each locale activates the recurrent question, whether discord can be left behind and how: through political solutions? religious?

The earliest chronology in *De bello civili* (also book 2) is set in Rome, in collapse like Troy in the *Aeneid*. Now the mirror is Rome itself. Romans recollect the violence between Marius and Sulla in horror as civil war returns. As far back as anyone can remember, history repeats; the Republic offers no space free of discord. As with Vergil's Troy, abjection articulates the city's space. In neither can sacrifice remake the social bond – there is no social bond to restore. Instead of expiation, perverted sacrifice brings back the abjection it should heal. The difference in narrative strategy, however, is marked. Vergil allegorizes civil war by encoding figures of discord, where self and other blur and the self destroys itself by destroying its likeness. Lucan narrates civil war, bringing Vergil's hidden story into view, by using variants of the same repertory of figurations to tell Rome's own history. Once the principals reach Alexandria, however, he remakes a strategy in the *Aeneid*: The foreign city reveals even more clearly the abjection within the self.

Troy: Raped and Raping

Sex and religion lie at the heart of Augustus' program of reform. His restoration of the temples, vaunted in his *Res gestae*, and marriage legislation aimed to put the patriarchal order back on its feet.[33] For Vergil,

---

[32] Johnson (1976) 167 dismisses attempts since antiquity to harmonize the oxymoron created by the juxtaposition of *futuras* and *aeterna*.

[33] Treggiari (1991) 277–98; Edwards (1993) 37–42; Milnor (2005) 140–1.

desecration – of religious ritual, of chaste procreation within marriage – is a central trope that highlights the horror of social collapse. Repeated rapes and monstrous births in *Aeneid* 2 figure Troy's fall as the desecration of chaste procreation's enclosed spaces.[34] The perverse birth of soldiers from the Trojan horse's hollow womb is the most conspicuous symbolic undoing of marriage and procreation, the institutions that found and guarantee patriarchal order. Worse, however, than foreign foes, the Trojans undo patriarchy from within.

First, the external threat: The Greeks metaphorically rape Troy's innermost spaces. Phallic snakes – with necks erect, bloodstained crests, and measureless tails, licking their lips with vibrating tongues (2.206–11) – tower over Laocoon and his sons, encircling them in a deathly embrace before gulping them down (*amplexus ... morsu*, 2.214–15; *amplexi*, 2.218). The Trojan horse crosses the city's threshold with choirs of unmarried boys and girls, as if a wedding procession that brings not life but death (2.238–9). Gates are breached, entries forced (2.32, 204, 234, 237, 243, 266, 478–84, 491–6). Pyrrhus, another snake, tumescent with slippery tail (2.473), plunges over the threshold into the intimate, protected rooms (*penetralia*, 2.469, 484, 508) of Priam's house.[35] Hollow spaces within Troy figure the city as fertile mother. The Greek war on Troy is fought in and over space; their penetration of the inner sanctum of home and city, hidden from view, is a metaphor less of the heart than of the womb. Priam's home is a femininely encoded place of incredible fertility. He and Hecuba have spawned one hundred children, fifty daughters and fifty sons. In desecration, this hidden space is ripped open, laid bare to weapons and to the gaze. Aeneas describes what he ought not to have seen to Dido and to us. Even worse, the Greeks crawl back into the huge horse's belly (2.400–1), violating the incest taboo.[36] Such superimposed images of violent penetration depict a city being raped, and with it social order.

This rape, an attack on fertile Troy by an external foe, arises perversely from a huge, phallic horse bearing a crafted womb that inverts nature with artifice, birth with death, male with female. Minerva's creation is paradoxically bereft of femininity. Sexless, not born of a woman, she makes an artificial and destructive womb. The poem insists repeatedly on the female

---

[34] For siege as rape in *Aeneid* 2, Lewis (1974); Oliensis (2001) 43. In Seneca's *Phoenissae*, Ginsberg (2017b).

[35] Whittaker (2009).

[36] The horse is, as often, *ingens*. For the uncanny and birth in Vergil's favorite word, Quartarone (2011). *Aeneid* 2 plays out Freud's theory of the *Unheimliche* ("uncanny," from *Heim*, "home"): the innermost familiar space, which should be hidden, is penetrated by violence, even laid bare to view.

organ of the consistently male horse (*equus*, 2.15, 32, 48; *uterus*, 2.20, 38, 53).[37] Sinon, a treacherous and male midwife, loosens the closed passages of this womb (2.258–9). Out of it comes not life but the monstrous birth of a Greek triumph (*parto . . . triumph*, 2.578). Such birth paradoxically rapes. The enemy breach the middle of the city in the middle of the night to cut Troy down in a gang.

> ac veluit summis antiquam in montibus ornum
> cum ferro accisam crebrisque bipennibus instant
> eruere agricolae certatim, illa usque minatur
> et tremefacta comam concusso vertice nutat,
> vulneribus donec paulatim evicta supremum
> congemuit traxitque iugis avuulsa ruinam.   2.624–31

> like an ancient ash on the peaks of the mountains, when the farmers press and compete to overthrow it, cut with iron and pounding ax-blows, she continually threatens to fall and, made to quiver, nods her hair, her crown shaken, until gradually overcome by wounds she groans and having been uprooted she drags ruin down the ridge.

The womanly tree groans in orgasm, hewn with the violence of rape.[38] Men and women groan without distinction (Hector, 2.288; Panthus, 2.323; Cassandra dragged from the inner spaces of Minerva's temple, 2.413; distraught mothers as the Greeks break into Priam's innermost house, 2.486; Creusa, 2.680). Birth, rape, male, female – death comes as sexual violence.

Patriarchy, fatherly authority, and male lineage fall to ruin at Troy. Again and again, sons are slain before their fathers' eyes: Laocoon's sons, Polites before Priam. The metaphorical disfigurement of fatherhood supplements the literal. Impotence and castration cut down the fathers in turn. Laocoon's spear fails to penetrate the horse – the Trojans reject boring through the "hollow hiding places of the womb" (*cavas uteri . . . latebras*, 2.38), even as the image evokes intercourse; the womb is shaken, the caverns groan (2.51–2). Priam's spear hangs impotently from Pyrrhus' shield (2.546), penetrating neither armor nor body. His wife Hecuba effeminizes him; Priam must crouch with his daughters and wife like doves under the altar (2.516). Neoptolemus, revolting against Priam's accusation that he lies about his father and, "degenerate" (2.549), does not live up to Achilles (2.540–1), ruthlessly tells the man who reminded Achilles of his own father in the *Iliad* to die (2.550). At every turn,

---

[37] Paschalis (1998) 104–5; Rimell (2015) 23, 33–4.
[38] Hardie (2013) 120–23: Allusion intimates possible rebirth from the tree, cut down but not uprooted; Rome will sprout as the shoot of felled Troy.

fatherhood is cut off. Priam's headless trunk, lying dismembered and nameless on the shore, figures patriarchy's undoing. The name of the father is erased, the head of the body politic ripped off. In the traditional interpretation, this trunk alludes to Pompey's death on the shores of Egypt, a reference to the civil wars.

Rape imagery is not merely external. The Trojans metaphorically rape themselves, dissolving any distinction between friend and enemy, self and other in civil warfare's classic figuration. Patriarchy unravels from within. In Vergil's house of mirrors, the Trojans breach their own protecting walls, which guaranteed the impenetrability of their city, to receive the monstrous horse, a fatal womb, into their inner sanctum (2.234). In their encounter with Androgeos, who mistakes them fatally for his own side, they morph into a very phallic snake, its sea-blue neck swelling (2.381) – the very image representing their rape. They reify his misperception by dressing in his and his companions' plundered armor to fool the enemy, before falling impotent before friendly fire (2.410–11, 429). They destroy their own tower in an autoimmune attempt to destroy their enemy (2.445). A war between clear-cut enemies becomes a monstrous war of blurred distinctions: between friend and foe; animal and human; slaughter, sacrifice, and warfare; men and women; human and gods. Greeks and Trojans, ostensible opponents, unite against each other to rape together the legitimate patriarchal order.

In the *Aeneid*, rape concerns women's lives less than it does their role as pillars of family and city. The violation of the twinned, reciprocal, and chaste goddesses Vesta and Minerva figures patriarchy's defilement most intimately. These national tutelary goddesses protect the city's safe spaces of hearth and home and its citadel respectively. Vesta's loyalty and Minerva's female devotion to masculine principles, her abstention from any identification with her sex, together map Trojan social space as patriarchal. Untouched by sex, birthed without sex, virgin Minerva keeps the city intact from military assault. Vesta presides over marital chastity, patriarchy's guarantee in every father's home. The goddesses' violation figures the collapse of the city along with Priam's line. They, however, succumb not just to foreign invaders; their defilement reinscribes the violation the Trojans wreck on themselves. The Greeks' violation of them and the Trojans' participation overturns political order both externally and from within.

Vesta unites politics and family, nation and home. In Aeneas' dream, Hector consigns her ribbons and fire to him (2.296–7): not Anchises' household gods, but "the State-gods of Troy and the holy fire of Troy."[39]

---

[39] Austin (1964) at 2.297: The Penates "were sometimes known as the *di penetrales*."

The gesture subsumes the individual house into national patriarchy. Hector gives Aeneas a mission: to extract the Penates from the "innermost recesses" (*adytis . . . penetralibus*, 2.297) and seek out other walls. The new city will convert the monstrous birth of Troy's destruction, embodied in Hector – no newborn, but a corpse covered in matted hair and wounds – into a proper renaissance. Hector, whose line is failing, creates a restoring succession narrative in Aeneas' new patriarchal line (Anchises – Aeneas – Ascanius), to replace the Trojan kings of Asia (Priam – Hector – Astyanax). The substitution displaces Rome's origins away from an oriental kingdom, an association that nevertheless remains available for reactivation.

Transfer to Rome purifies Vesta with a new line. At Troy, her pure space had been polluted. The Helen episode shows the icon of female desire lurking at the threshold of Vesta's shrine, "in the secret seat," as an avenging "Fury common to both Troy and her original fatherland" (*secreta in sede . . . Troiae et patriae communis Erinys*, 2.568, 573).[40] She is the sign that the Trojans raped first. Neither side may claim innocence. Even after Paris' death, the Trojans kept her. Her second Trojan husband Deiphobus – repetition underscores the irony of his name, "God-fearing," when Aeneas encounters him in the underworld (6.495, 500, 510, 544) – receives his just reward in the figurative castration of his hands, ears, and nose. Helen, who betrayed her first husband, also betrays her third. Aeneas, however, forgets the male and Trojan agency of her original rape. His blame of Helen, an internalized foreigner, externalizes internal responsibility. He imagines her restoration in patriarchal terms that highlight what he is losing: She will see "paternal Mycenae" and "her marriage and the house of her father and her children" again (*patriasque Mycenas . . . coniugiumque domumue patris natos-que videbit*, 2.577–9). She is the pollution Aeneas would avenge at Vesta's shrine, but wreaking vengeance on her would only defile Vesta all the more and reenact war's logic – sex is murder, penetration rape. Venus' intervention saves Aeneas by redirecting him to his own family. She names Aeneas' father first (2.597–8) and promises to set him on his father's threshold (2.620). Restoration will require a new Trojan family line and a new foundation to reestablish patriarchy.

Both violated and violator, Trojan Minerva, with her Greek double Pallas, similarly figures the self-violence of Troy's destruction. The Greeks steal her statue; defiled by bloody hands, the Palladium becomes an

---

[40] We read the disputed Helen passage as transmitted, with the assumption that, if authentic, Vergil would have revised it. The passage sets up Aeneas' propensity to rage when exacting vengeance. Overviews at Gransden (1985) 69–70; Conte (1986) 196–207.

uncanny portent, soaked in another abject bodily fluid, salty sweat (2.168, 173–4).[41] Her temple – another interior space (*adytis*), here coded in enemy language – witnesses Cassandra's rape (2.404), which replays the Palladium's own in the blazing eyes of both.

But Minerva also inflicts destruction on the very city over whose citadel she presides. The Greeks built the horse with Pallas' own art (2.15) to send against her own city – ostensibly as expiation for her statue's violation, stolen from her temple at Troy's innermost interior on the citadel. Pallas Athena, phallic goddess immune to feminine vulnerability, not of woman born, who has never known a man and cannot become a mother, helps the Greeks carefully craft this man-made, artificial womb. Repetition underscores Minerva's agency of this deathly gift (2.31, 189). Taking refuge at her feet (2.225–7), the snakes that devour Laocoon spark ambivalence. Do they desecrate a virginal space, or are they sacred to her? The indistinction captures the problematic. As Venus reveals, she, among other gods, aids in Troy's destruction (2.615–16). Helen and Paris, mere individuals, stand for a larger principle. The gods' inclemency (2.601–2) raises the autoimmune self-destruction to a cosmic plane.

The Trojans are not the only ones to wreak havoc on themselves. In the epic cycle, Troy's destruction reverts on its destroyers. The *Iliad*'s Achilles figuratively kills himself when he kills Hector, who is wearing Achilles' own armor, a metaphorical suicide that haunts the *Aeneid*'s ending. By raping Troy, the Greeks blur with the rapists they would avenge, with the degenerate bastards Pyrrhus vaunts he is not. The distinction between friend and foe collapses, between Trojans and Greeks, but also each on their own side. Venus cannot save Troy from self-inflicted destruction. She saves her own lineage by transferring it elsewhere. However, the curse of Laomedon, who defrauded Neptune and Apollo of their wages for building Troy's walls, becomes a recurrent theme in Latin literature: Rome's ancestral sin, ever in need of expiation, goes back before its own foundation to Troy and keeps bringing its abjection home.[42] As the children of Laomedon, called such in the voice of characters, focalized, and even in the poet's own voice, the Trojans appear untrustworthy and incapable of leaving the past behind.[43]

Sacrifice at Troy fails to expiate rape. If animal offerings should reconstitute the bonds between gods and men, here indistinction between

---

[41] If the Helen passage is authentic, sweat and blood are linked at 2.582. For the symbolic rape, Fowler (1987) 194.

[42] E.g., Vergil, *Georgics* 1.502, Horace, *Odes* 3.3.22.

[43] E.g., *Aeneid* 3.248, 4.542, 7.105, 8.18, 8.158, 8.162.

human and animal sacrifice, human and divine destruction, tears Troy's world apart. Again and again, from Iphigenia, to Sinon, to Laocoon, to Priam, sacrifice leads only to further desecration. The horse is a false idol, destruction masquerading as salvation. Priam is slaughtered in a perverse sacrifice, his blood mingling at the altar with his son's, desecrating the institutions of family and religion together. Sinon's faked sacrificial crisis presages a real one. Distinctions break down even further. Laocoon, sacrificing a bull at Neptune's altar (2.202), is himself metaphorically sacrificed by snakes rising from Neptune's realm.

> clamores simul horrendos ad sidera tollit:
> qualis mugitus, fugit cum saucius aram
> taurus et incertam excussit cervice securim.   2.222–4

> At the same time, he raises horrific cries to the stars: such is the roar, when a bull, wounded, flees the altar and shakes off the ax sticking uncertainly from his neck.

If man and animal become indistinct, the gods act just like the Greeks. In Venus' revelation, the gods' actions magnify Greek destruction to a cosmic scale and eradicate the city: *totamque ab sedibus urbem / eruit* ("he unearths the whole city from its seat," 2.611–12). When man, animal, and god become indistinct, cosmos devolves into chaos.

Any restoration requires leaving this mess of violence, desecration, and indistinction behind. Aeneas is saved by the gods to establish a new race, a new city, a new legitimate patriarchy in a right relation to the gods, which will guarantee its purity by protecting its women – or rather, protecting male lineage through policing women's wombs. What Aeneas fears is the repetition in his own house of what he saw in Priam's, the "enemy in the middle of the intimate familial spaces" (of Priam's: *medium in penetralibus hostem*, 2.508; of his own: *mediis hostem in penetralibus*, 2.665). The metaphorical rape of the city and all the enclosed spaces threatens to come home; Pyrrhus will be there soon, "he who truncates a son before his father's eyes, the father at the altar" (*natum ante ora patris, patrem qui obtruncat ad aras*, 2.663), unless Aeneas can persuade his father to leave Troy behind with him.

But if we think what is at stake is the unified nuclear family represented when Aeneas addressed his father (*genitor*, 2.657) and mother (*alma parens*, 2.664) in the same speech as he names his son, father, and wife (*Ascanium patremque meum iuxtaque Creusam*, 2.666), the gods have other plans. Roman Venus has no interest in women except as tools for her own male line – Jupiter even less so. The sign that persuades Anchises to leave recalls the *sidus Iulium*, a sign of the future glory of his own line. The comet that indicated Julius Caesar's divinization guarantees its future return. Anchises' assent comes in paternalist terms: "I follow and am present where you lead, paternal gods; preserve my house, preserve my grandson" (*sequor et qua ducitis adsum, di patrii; servate domum, servate nepotem*, 2.701–2). Creusa must stay behind in her homeland to free Aeneas for another lineage. However, she must not be harmed, and Cybele will protect her from rape and slavery in an immaculate female space (2.784–9).[44] But the actual home, the *domus* secured by the woman, yields to empire's collective house. While Troy's houses collapse in destruction along with her dominion (2.363–5), what will rise to take her place is another empire, another set of masters, the "masters of things and the toga-clad people" (*rerum dominos gentemque togatam*, 1.282). The apparent universalization, however, retains the familial as metaphor for political order: Blood relations assert their primacy in the Julian line; the household of emperors becomes synecdoche for empire's capacious house.

Rome's lineage, along with the Julian, will also arise from a stolen bride, from a marriage perceived as rape, from mixed Eastern and Western peoples. The poem's second half spells this out. The oriental, however, is already inscribed into the Western land in Creusa's prophecy: "and you will come to Hesperia [the land of twilight], where the Lydian Tiber flows among the rich fields of men with a gentle march" (*et terram Hesperiam venies, ubi Lydius arva / inter opima virum leni fluit agmine Thybris*, 2.781–2). The Tuscan Tiber's Lydian roots and Hellenized spelling bring oriental elements from the lands of the rising into that of the setting sun. The river's military march metaphorically stomps violence into the landscape. Fluids from abroad – literal foreign influence – infuse the fertile fields belonging to presumably native men. The desire to keep the womb of family and city pure and immune from violence, specifically from violence wrought by others, appears as a patriarchal fantasy, undone already before the beginning.

Unfortunately for this fantasy, Troy haunts Rome as its evil twin, as the city against which it differentiates itself and which therefore defines it. Even at Troy, the Trojans are already like Roman wolves, not just predators, but plunderers (*lupi ceu / raptores*, 2.355). The word for plunderer and ravisher, *raptor*, unites the objects of rapine: women and property. The doorposts of Priam's palace display Troy's wealth and show it up as a barbarian empire that despoiled its enemies with pride (*superbi*, 2.504),

---

[44] Johnson (1976) 142–3: The *Aeneid* unusually deorientalizes Cybele.

a signal in Latin of tyranny. This alienating perspective bubbles up in Aeneas' voice. This gesture inscribes the impossibility of separating self from other within the protofounder whose departure should allow Rome to leave Troy behind. The oriental city's luxury repeatedly tars Aeneas and his companions as the foreign rapists they leave Troy to escape. Iarbas in North Africa sees Aeneas through an orientalizing lens, as a new, bonnet-wearing Paris with perfumed hair who "takes possession of what he has plundered" (*rapto potitur*, 4.2170), specifically Dido, who spurned Iarbas' offer of marriage. The same perspective returns voiced through Numanus Remulus: Effeminate, ever-bonneted Phrygians seek marriage with their women (9.600, 616–17). But if Numanus Remulus articulates a hard and rustic Italian virtue as Eastern corruption's opposite, he reinscribes plunder and rapine into the values the Romans will adopt as their own: Even as old men "we press our white hair with a helmet and it is always pleasing to amass new plunder and to live on rapine" (*canitiem galea premimus semperque recentis / comportare iuvat praedas et vivere rapto*, 9.613).[45] The "proud doorposts" (*superbis / postibus*, 8.721–2) of Priam's palace recur of the temple of Palatine Apollo on Aeneas' shield and figure Augustus as Priam's heir.[46] The Trojan line apparently supplanted by that of Aeneas, all that would be purged keeps returning.

Uncanny echoes, horror-house mirrors across the textual surface undo the fundamental contrast between the old and oriental empire of Troy and the new, reformed Roman Empire. Twinning – the serpents attacking Laocoon, Romulus and Remus – keeps blurring the clear distinctions apparently made by separating self from other. Rome's heartland at Troy must be abandoned, but the more Romans attempt to eradicate their origins, the more these operate under cover. Vergil's poetic language reveals the structure of Roman ideology as a split within the same, indistinction within difference. Figuration reveals internal conflict as Rome's essential nature.

Carthage: Seduction and Suicide

Carthage is another anti-Rome.[47] The future archenemy yet again uncannily figures home as alien (*unheimlich*), enemy as self. Dido and Aeneas, who personify their respective cities, are a perfect pair, loving fraternal

---

[45] For ethnographic stereotypes here, anticipating a "flawed element" to the future Roman state, Thomas (1982) 98–100.

[46] Fowler (2000) 40–63 on point of view and *superbus* ("proud"); this passage (54).

[47] For Carthage's importance to Rome's conceptualization as an empire in the *Aeneid*, Starks (1999) 259–60, Syed (2005) 143–93, Feeney (2017), Giusti (2018).

twins parallel to Diana and Apollo, to whom each is compared (4.143–9, 1.498–502).[48] Yet one twin ends up dead. Not even murdered, like Remus, Dido commits suicide in a figure that internalizes conflict even more. Her suicide paradoxically externalizes her personal enmity to a national level, to conflict between Carthage and Rome. Through love gone wrong, the enemy who defines the blossoming of Roman imperialism in the Punic wars is born. Of course it is the woman who dies. Her foundation cannot equal Rome's male, patriarchal founding line. By fraternizing with Dido, Aeneas risks not only diverting Rome's foundation to the enemy city, but also establishing an alternative effeminate and oriental foundation, where male is subordinate to female, contrary to patriarchal order.[49] Dido/Carthage must be destroyed. The personal is political indeed.

The conflict enacts the incompatibility of erotic love with love of nation: Aeneas leaves a beloved woman to found Rome. But the difference dissolves, so that another clash of same on same engenders another externalization of internal conflict into imperial expansion. The twinned cities are rivals in foundation. Juno knows Rome will destroy her favorite city and therefore plots to capture its foundation by marrying Aeneas to Dido. In an autoimmune gesture, her matchmaking ironically spawns the very enmity she would avert. Her attempt to erase political difference through union founders historically, but the poem erases the cities' difference figuratively. Their founders would be a perfect match, had they only not fallen in love. Both exiles from Eastern lands, effectively widowed, founders – by joining forces, they would be unbeatable if they could remain in a chaste, fraternal relation, like Apollo and Diana.

A model of collaboration and equality between the sexes glimmers briefly as a thought experiment before going up in flames. Dido, before even seeing Aeneas, is remarkably open, hospitable, and egalitarian given the fragility of her young and otherwise vigilant security state. The temporary suspension of her Carthaginian cruelty by divine intervention lets another politics appear.[50] Generous, she welcomes the Trojans as refugees; cool, she entertains giving them resources to go on their way, or to share power equally (*pariter*) and make her city theirs: *mi casa es su casa* (1.573–4).

---

[48] On parallels and disjunctions, Syed (2005) 158; "specularity," Hardie (2013) 108–9; incestuous Oedipal parallels, Mac Góráin (2018) 144.

[49] Gransden (1976) 29: Aeneas reverts to "Asiatic" origins in Dido's bed, "Paris not Hector, the type of Antony not Augustus," but then rises refreshed from sleeping in Evander's primitive hut, now a θεῖος ἀνήρ (divine man), "'Iliadic' victor and Roman *triumphator*," a stoic and "Christian hero." Boyle (1999) 155. In its reception, the Dido episode repeatedly reestablishes patriarchy's victory, Leopold (2014) 62–76.

[50] Dido's representation is conflicted regarding Carthaginian stereotypes, Starks (1999).

Her plan entails equality and furthermore indistinction between the two peoples: *Tros Tyriusque mihi nullo discrimine agetur* ("Trojan and Tyrian will be treated by me with no distinction," 1.574). Aeneas joins Dido as founder (4.260), as partner of her rule (4.374). Such openness founders on two overwhelming forces: fiery passion imposed by Juno's and Venus' stereotypically female conniving; patriarchy imposed by male Jupiter, with Mercury as his mediator. The goddesses, driven by self-interest, show no intrinsic loyalty to their sex but make Dido their tool, squabbling over Aeneas, who bears a patriarchy each wants to capture for herself. Gender hierarchies in the cosmic order make Dido's vision of equality unworkable. Indistinction becomes as destructive a motor of civil war as division.

Mercury swoops down from heaven to reestablish difference, order, and hierarchy.[51] The masculinist fear is that man will become subordinate to woman: Aeneas will become Hercules in drag, subordinate to Omphale.[52] Divine intervention on the male side spins Dido's egalitarian plan as a monstrous inversion of hierarchical order among the sexes.[53] The gifts Dido gives Aeneas show he does not in fact – from a Roman perspective – join an ideal partnership but goes oriental.[54] Decked out in jasper, Tyrian purple, and gold (4.261–4), subject to a woman he calls queen (4.334),[55] Aeneas inverts the values of his mission. The weave of Aeneas' robe reintroduces through Dido's own handiwork the distinctions she tried to overcome (*discreverat*, 4.264). He himself internalizes division and distinction in his mind: *atque animum nunc huc celerem nunc diuidit illuc / in partisque rapit varias perque omnia versat* ("and he divides his spirit quickly, now this way, now that, and snatches it in various directions and keeps turning it over everything," 4.285–6). His reorientation toward Rome is painful, but necessary.

Jupiter, patriarchal ruler par excellence, reimposes hierarchy, distinction between the sexes, and a concomitantly violent sexuality: Aeneas must impregnate with empire a feminine land, whose shores are identified with a woman early on (*Italiam ... Laviniaque ... / ora*, 1.2).[56] He is to make

---

[51] Oliensis (1997) 303: In the *Aeneid*, "women make trouble and men restore order"; women prove their virtue by submitting "to the masculine plot of history."
[52] Thomas (2001) 156: "An Augustan reading will always attempt to subordinate Dido to Aeneas."
[53] Syed (2005) 184–92: Dido and her analogue Cleopatra pose a threat to patriarchy.
[54] Thomas (2001) 166; Syed (2005) 197.   [55] Ahl's (2007) 87 translates "my ruler."
[56] For the link between Lavinia and the land, and the eroticism of colonial conquest, Syed (2005) 137–9, 142–3.

Italy growl, like a beast, with war. The bloodline comes with the mandate
to spill blood.

> sed fore qui gravidam imperiis belloque frementem
> Italiam regeret, genus alto a sanguine Teucri
> proderet, ac totum sub leges mitteret orbem.   4.229–31

> But he will be of the sort to rule Italy, pregnant with empire and growling
> with war, to bring forth a race from the deep-rooted blood of Teucer, and
> put the whole world under the rule of law.

Aeneas will neither impregnate Dido (4.328–30) nor be ruled by her. The
vision of love and equality in marriage conjured up through Dido falls to
love's erasure in subjection. Jupiter reasserts an animalistic and violent
male sexuality that subjugates and exploits. The relationship is not egalitarian, but hierarchical, and it bears the name of empire.[57]

Dido's sad fate exemplifies the destructive force of sexuality and passion
untamed, outside the patriarchal hierarchies that make sense of the Roman
world. Instead of a child to put her future on a sure footing, what
abandoned Dido conceives is the madness that, throughout the *Aeneid*,
destroys relations, loving or legal (4.474). With either conception, her
relation to public space goes wrong, paradoxically in divergent directions.
The sexual woman must go indoors. Contrary to her sovereign first
appearance, to her place leading the hunt, once Dido mingles with
Aeneas in the cave, she loses her public capacity and is relegated to private
spaces deep within her palace. She sets her pyre in its "innermost seat"
(*penetrali sede*, 4.504). The mad woman, however, cannot be contained
indoors. Dido hears the call of the wild, whose symbol, Cithaeron, is the
mountain where Evadne dismembers her son Pentheus.[58] She rages over
the city, unsovereign in her failure of self-mastery and failure to master the
spaces she built (4.300–3). Dido's nightmarish tragic analogues (4.469–73),
Pentheus and Orestes – who killed his mother deep within his ancestral
home and is beset by mad *Dirae* at its liminal threshold – blur the outdoors
with the recesses of Dido's psyche.

The absolute divide between the vision conjured up from Dido's love
and its Roman antitype rests on the distinction between free love and legal
contract. Law and foundation – Rome's genius according to Hannah
Arendt[59] – inflict pain on wretched Dido. If the root of the social bond

---

[57] Fowler (1987) 197: "If there are 'two voices' in the *Aeneid*, there is a sense in which the voice of
triumph and domination is male, the voice of suffering and defeat female."
[58] The Theban myth figures civil war here, Mac Góráin (2018) 133.   [59] Arendt (1958) 195.

resides in the relation between a man and a woman, Roman ideology insists society is grounded not on love, but on marriage before the law. The antithetical systems structuring the *controversia* between Dido and Aeneas over their relationship's legitimacy are irreconcilable. For her, marriage depends on love, for him, on contract. Cut out from legal marriage, unable to enjoy the uncivilized life of a wild animal without legal culpability (4.550–1), Dido is doubly excluded and cannot live.

Justice would require a different divine order for the different imagined political order crushed by the necessity of Rome's foundation. Dido, in desperation, prays to no known god, but to one, if there be such, who cares for "lovers joined in an unequal treaty" (*non aequo foedere amantis*). This imagined god would be "just and mindful" (*iustumque memorque*, 4.520–1). Ahl's translation joins the registers of legality and love intertwined in god's *cura*: "whose jurisdiction embraces all lovers with one-sided contracts" (2007: 93). But there are always contracts, and equality is impossible. This is a fantasy Dido imagines in her misery, only as foil to the poem's actual gods. Indeed, they not only fail to meet this ideal but actively oppose it. "Cruel" Juno is "mindful" only of the causes of her anger (*saevae memorem Iunonis ob iram*, 1.4). Never does she appear just. Rather, Jupiter's perspective wins: The Romans subject the whole world to the law's loveless rule.[60] In revenge, Dido's curse bases the future enmity between Carthage and Rome on the equal impossibility of both terms: *nullus amor populis nec foedera sunto* ("let there be no love nor treaties between the peoples," 4.624). Since Aristophanes' *Lysistrata*, updated in Spike Lee's *Chiraq*, the only solution to the erosion of treaties that make peace within communities and between nations is to make love.

If Jupiter reasserts distinctions, the poem undoes them. Aeneas acts in the tropes of the Carthaginian antitype to Rome and comes as a Trojan horse, violating the innermost feminine spaces of Carthage as another Troy.[61] Aeneas is the structural analogue to Sinon, the seductive speech-maker who leads the lady – city or woman – astray, so that she brings on her own destruction.[62] Sinon aims to deceive, while Aeneas is, as usual, clueless about what he does and is to do. Paradigmatically *nescius* or *inscius*, he knows not what he narrates when telling of Troy's downfall in

---

[60] Feeney (1991): Jupiter defines the Roman Empire without end as slavery (1.285; 140–1); "institutionalized violence" (150); the dilemma of divine violence undergirding harmony remains unresolved (153).

[61] Not just Trojan, but stereotypically Carthaginian, Starks (1999). For Aeneas as Trojan horse, Spence (1999) 87, Hardie (2013) 118.

[62] For parallels to Sinon, Bartsch (2021) xxxiii–xxxviii.

sexualized terms, nor that he is the vehicle for sexualizing the downfall of Carthage.[63] Artifice, deception, lying despite his best intentions – Greek arts and Carthaginian stereotypes show Rome's protofounder internalizing the enemies it will conquer.

Troy and Carthage both fall to ruin through self-destruction figured as rape. The Roman sword comes not as a weapon of heroic virtue, but a metaphorical male member. Aeneas and Dido both draw his sword from its sheath, he to cut his ship's ropes fleeing union (4.580), she to inflict a deadly metaphorical rape on herself (4.664–5). The two acts merge. She literalizes in her suicide the rape Aeneas' lovemaking has been. Lying on the marriage bed she has placed on her pyre, alongside the effigy substituting for her absent lover's body and the infamous "arms of the man" (*arma viri*, 4.495),[64] Dido's passion sends her up in flames.[65] Her declaration *quo perii* ("where I died," 4.497), of the bed where she has already died, mingles *la grande* with *la petite mort*. Her death, the death of Carthage, results from letting the enemy in: *immissis . . . hostibus* (4.669).[66] Anna spells out the metonymies linking family and state.

> exstinxti te meque, soror, populumque patresque
> Sidonios urbemque tuam.   4.682–3

> You have killed me and you, sister, and the people and fathers of Sidon, and your city.

Dido has waged destruction on herself, her family, the people and fathers of Sidon (SPQS), and her physical city in the tropes of civil war.

Dido's self-rape is a dead end, literally for herself, but also for her lineage and city. If childbearing is the means and sign of a city's prosperity, her death is a perverse impregnation. Her love for Aeneas spawns not life-bringing union, but destruction unto death. Cupid's sitting on her lap prefigures her desired child. He fills her not with life, but the wound, poison, and flames of passion: Dido is *infelix* – agriculturally infertile above and beyond her unhappiness. She falls not chastely for Aeneas's son, but perversely for his brother, an incestuous tinge parallel to the incest implied in the fraternal analogy to Diana and Apollo (1.498–502; 4.143–6).[67] The magic rites

---

[63] Aeneas is clueless, about foundation, art, his role in history, his own feelings, Johnson (1976) 99–108; Barchiesi (1994) 119–24; Chew (2002) 620; Feldherr (2014) 292.

[64] The transfer of the *Aeneid*'s first words into Dido's bed was noted in antiquity: *ille tuae Aeneidos auctor / contulit in Tyrios arma virumque toros* ("that famous author of your [Augustus'] *Aeneid* conferred arms and the man into a Tyrian bed," Ovid, *Tristia* 2.533–4).

[65] For tragic parallels behind Dido's wedding as funeral, Mac Góráin (2018) 138.

[66] Syed (2005) 130.   [67] For incest in Aeneas' relationship with his mother, Oliensis (2001) 52–3.

shrouding her death scene, as if in expiation (4.636), anticipate Dido's perverted fertilization by the penetrating sword: "herbs pubescent with the milk of black venom" (*pubentes herbae nigri cum lacte veneni*, 4.514); the love charm "twisted off the forehead of a horse being born," a "love stolen from the mother" whose natural right it is (*nascentis equi de fronte revulsus / et matri praereptus amor*, 4.515–16). The waters from Avernus do not purify or bring life and renewal, but rather death. In a further twist, they are fake (*latices simulatos fontis Averni*, 4.512). The sword she drives into her belly foams not with semen, but with gore: *ensemque cruore / spumantem* (4.664–5). Her pregnancy births her own death then engenders not a bloodline, but a bloody avenger. He will rise from her bones to drive an ancestral curse of love turned to hatred (*odiis*) onto the "stock and whole future race" (*stirpem et genus omne futurum*, 4.622–5) that will come in a child's stead.[68] A "self-styled revenant,"[69] Dido will haunt Rome as Hannibal, bringing destruction in the Punic wars. While victory gave these wars to Rome as an imagined site of conquering virtue, their prize, empire, nevertheless bred civil war, in Sallust's analysis, as the wages of imperial luxury and hence corruption (*Bellum Catilinae* 10–12).

Dido's destructive love affair with Aeneas is hardly the beginning of the cycle of civil war tropes in their story. Troy's self-destruction on Aeneas' side encodes one set, but Dido herself encodes another. She had already suffered from fraternal strife, when her brother killed her husband. Even her relationship with her loving sister goes wrong. Anna's advice to love Aeneas proves fateful to Dido, and the open intimacy they had before her affair degrades into deception and doublespeak as Dido hides her intentions. Dido becomes the lying Carthaginian of the Roman trope, doing what she blames Aeneas for doing to her. Just as he inflicts on her what he tells of suffering, so does she reenact the internal divide; she wreaks on her own nearest and dearest, including herself, the destruction wrought on her by others.

The same tropes continue after death, even into other texts. Her sister Anna reenacts the same structures of internal, sexual-political violence, within the family and the state (Ovid, *Fasti* 3.543–54, March 15). Pursued by her brother – the same Pygmalion who killed Dido's first husband Sychaeus – she eventually takes refuge with Aeneas, rousing jealousy in Lavinia. The cycle finally ends with her flight and transformation into

---

[68] Oliensis (2001) 60: With psychoanalytic precision, the sword compresses phallus and baby, *parvulus ... Aeneas* ("little baby Aeneas," 4.338–9), as Aeneas' synecdochic replacement. Also Oliensis (1997) 307.

[69] Oliensis (2001) 47. Mac Góráin (2018) 139 supplements the picture with intertexual ghosts.

a water nymph. Her festival on the Ides of March, the date of Julius Caesar's assassination, returns annually. Ovid marks the date by commemorating the vengeance his successor takes against the assassins in the civil war battle at Philippi (*Fasti* 3.705–10).[70]

Vergil wages civil war on Carthage through his unhappy story of Dido and Aeneas.[71] Their two cities, governed by Jupiter Optimus Maximus and his consort Juno respectively, are bound in the intimate enmity of an impossible marriage. The Punic wars that found Rome's empire turn out to originate in an internal conflict. For Vergil, passion is war by other means. Here, the social bond's collapse appears in the conflict between gods – Juno and Jupiter, Juno and Venus – and in the destruction they wreak on humankind. Given that the social order arises from marriage, making Juno the center and source of Aeneas' travails is a devastating poetic choice. The destruction wrought by the gods on humans rips apart social foundations, whose collapse structures unhappy relations between the sexes, beyond legality, beyond marriage, down even into love. Jupiter's stern commands pervert nature's fertility, a decadent degradation of life into death.

Rome: Unhappy Marriages

Vergil's tropes of discord return in Lucan: Marriage splits in civil war, and sexuality tracks the collapse of normative Roman values. If marriage stands for the social bond, then the deathly undoing of marriage, the institution that binds woman to man, men to men, and produces the next generation, reveals the truth of civil war as always more than civil war. With Lucan's rent marriages, civil war surpasses awful bloodletting among citizens on the battlefield to become more pervasive social collapse.[72] *De bello civili* negates any potential for happy and fertile union. Tombs are warm, not the marriage bed. Marcia, Julia, and Cornelia all end up married – dead, alive, in a living death – to civil war. Not just death, but also splitting and doubling undo even apparently warm and passionate love from within. No one succeeds in making love, even in the bedroom[73] – then Caesar sleeps with the

---

[70] Ovid distances himself from narrating the assassination by putting it in the mouth of Vesta, but it is unclear whether the final lines on Philippi, which call the vengeance just, are in her voice or his, Heyworth (2019) at lines 3.703–8.

[71] Giusti (2018).

[72] Lowrie and Vinken (2019) previews this section. Fertik (2018) shows how the fantasy of warm relations with the emperor substitute for broken familial bonds in Lucan – we emphasize the perversity of this substitution.

[73] "L'unica scena di amore" (5.722–815) – Sannicando (2010) 43 – is a tearful scene of separation.

enemy.[74] From Cato to Pompey to Caesar, their paradigmatic relations with their wives represent progressive alienation from Rome. Each wife stands for a different aspect of social and therefore political failure.

Marcia's remarriage to Cato figures the Republic's sterility.[75] Greek tragedy's trope of wedding as funeral frames Marcia's return to her first husband Cato. Frequently, killing the young woman before her social role's consummation in marriage (Antigone, Iphigenia, Polyxena) shows what is wrong with society.[76] In the *Aeneid*, a funereal wedding cuts down a mature, still-fertile woman in her prime. The nymphs' wailing in the cave scene presages Dido's suicide. In these stories, society cannot advance. In *De bello civili*, Marcia, worn down from childbearing and grief, remarries her former husband Cato after the death of Hortensius, to whom Cato regifted her to bear children. Her exhaustion stands for a Roman social bond past its prime.

Defined *ex negativo*, Marcia's wedding is the antitype of happy, joyous fertility, of any future for society. As the embodiment of a stern and Stoic republicanism,[77] this couple's sterile reunion rings a death knell for the Republic and challenges the desirability of its return. Bride and bridegroom wear mourning – the most inappropriate wedding dress. Marcia's request for "the empty name of marriage" (*nomen inane / conubii*, 2.342–3) and for Cato's name on her tomb sets empty signifiers under the sign of death. Lucan's luxuriant description of a Roman wedding, one poignant *non* (2.354) negating the whole rite, shows what could be but is not,[78] thereby figuratively negating the Republic's future.

Cato's remarriage to Marcia scandalized Romans for different reasons than it does moderns.[79] We find oppressive a wife's objectification as a womb, a *venter*. In other accounts, Cato created controversy, but not by lending her to Hortensius. This patriotic gesture created an alliance

---

[74] Ahl (1976) 177, 181: Lucan's women allegorize Roman society. Mulhern (2017): Cato and Pompey's chaste and loving wives define Caesar's transgression of Roman values by contrast; while the wives further link their husbands to Rome, Caesar abandons personified Rome when he crosses the Rubicon and loses his Romanness when he takes Cleopatra as his lover. We, by contrast, read all of Lucan's wives and lovers as figures of social relations gone wrong in civil war.

[75] On Cato's embodiment of the Republic's ideals and Marcia's personification of the Patria, Ahl (1976) 249; Reggiani (2005) 113.

[76] Rehm (1994).

[77] Johnson (1987) 37 and Sklenár (2003) 72, 76, but see Sannicandro (2010) 83–4.

[78] On negation in Lucan, Bramble (1983) 48–58, 543; Johnson (1987) 43.

[79] Cantarella (1995) analyzes the legal and cultural aspects of this episode in Roman history: *locatio ventris* (renting the belly) was practiced not just among elites or Stoics; shared children forged lateral links between families.

through shared sons; using a fertile woman to the breaking point bolsters paternalism. Bearing children and winning the privilege of the *ius trium liberorum* for their husbands brought honor to Roman wives, whatever their actual desires. This is not to say Roman marriages lacked love, but the husband of the so-called *laudatio Turiae* appears exceptional. He praises his wife for suggesting he marry another in the face of her sterility; their mutual affection shines through the inscription, and he cannot imagine taking anyone else as wife (2.31–43).[80] The scandal was not passing Marcia on, but taking her back. Roman youth debated in declamation whether Cato was venal in remarrying his wealthy former wife.

Against this backdrop, the civil war tropes in Lucan's version stand out. All parties become overly entangled, and distinction fails.[81] As both "husband and father to the city" (*urbi pater est urbique maritus*, 2.388), Cato commits political incest.[82] The fruitlessness of Cato and Marcia's union occupies front and center. As fertile as Marcia has been, she falls paradoxically under the sign of sterility. Cato will not make love to her; for him Venus serves only for procreation (*unicus usus*, 2.387–8), a misunderstanding of her erotic power as of her role as founding goddess of the Roman race. Venus' descendent, Caesar, will make no such mistake in enjoying Cleopatra. Furthermore, Cato's and Hortensius' houses are bound in terms that set the Republic on a course of civil war. Doubling, splitting, and indistinction mark this arrangement as perverse. Marcia's passage to Hortensius comes not as divorce, which would set the dissolution of their first marriage on firm legal ground, but in a transfer with undertones of betrayal (*tradita*, 2.345). Her "maternal blood" unifies not a single family, but the "twin houses" (*geminas . . . domos*, 2.331–3) of "twin husbands" (*geminos . . . maritos*, 2.339). Twinning, slyly doubled, evokes Romulus' fratricide, one of civil war's central tropes ever since it became conventional for discord in the triumviral period (e.g., Horace, *Epodes* 7). Cato and Marcia fail to make either a proper break or a proper join. Their separation and remarriage paradoxically enact both the internal split and the doubling characteristic of civil war simultaneously.

Cato's Rome, already sterile in his excessively cold Stoic virtue, has no future besides civil war. Where the husband of the *laudatio Turiae* loves his wife, not least because she saved him from proscription during the triumvirate, Marcia's loveless marriage saves neither Cato nor the Republic but

---

[80] Osgood (2006) 72 and (2014) 70–1.

[81] Fertik (2019) 21–38: Lucan's military commanders usurp roles properly belonging to family members.

[82] Fertik (2018) 464 stresses the autocratic associations of this incestuous figuration.

comes as a death wish emblematic of Rome itself. Her climactic request, made in jealousy not of her husband but of the perverted political order, is that Cornelia be no closer to civil war's embrace than she (2.349).[83] She rejoins her husband to join disunion.

Against the procreative and emotional sterility of Marcia's reunion with Cato, Cornelia offers a contrasting overabundance of love.[84] She plunges just as much into civil war and away from normative Roman values. At every turn, Cornelia is thwarted from acting the proper Roman wife she aspires to be. Despite her best intentions, she plays the mistress in the Hellenized tones of the demimonde of Augustan elegy.[85] If Cato and Marcia embody a lifeless form of Roman virtue, Cornelia and Pompey would live out free love, if only they could. Pompey somehow never enjoys this (or any) love, and it weakens him.[86] Even had things worked out, their marriage could hardly represent the restoration of Roman society. Aestheticized eroticism evokes Roman elegy in its celebration of an alternative to procreation and love as duty, a genre in resistance to Augustan marriage legislation. Not only do they have no children, wanting them does not even come up. Pompey's sterile marriage to Cornelia matches the dead end of his politics. Doubling, inversion, splitting, and deathly union couch their marriage, like every other, in civil war's signature tropes.

Civil war is the vehicle of familial discord not only between male in-laws, but also between Pompey's double wives, who compete for him across the divide that should separate life from death. As her twin and rival, Cornelia supplants Julia, who in life had been a "latter-day Sabine" joining her father Caesar to her husband Pompey (1.118), but whose death is one cause of rupture.[87] Cornelia also joins the houses of two of the three political allies who made up an informal triumvirate. She links Crassus and Pompey not through life but in death, not as a daughter-in-law in the proper sequence of generations, but laterally. As the ghostly Julia comments to Pompey in a dream, she led him to triumph, while Cornelia led Crassus to defeat and death (3.20–2). This unhappy story repeats of Pompey in a further doubling. Cornelia upends Julia's role as Sabine. Instead of joining peoples in peace, her marriages follow a downward spiral

---

[83] Sklenár (2003) 74.

[84] *Amor* attaches most often to Cornelia (five times), once to Marcia, thrice to Cleopatra, where it rages; Tucker (1990) 43–4.

[85] Bruère (1951); Ahl (1976) 183–9; Narducci (2002) 294–8; Reggiani (2005) 103–6; Sannicandro (2010) 9–11, 43–81.

[86] Ahl (1976) 173–83.

[87] Chiu (2010) 345. Reggiani (2005) 102: Since Julia had been dead since 54 BCE, the figuration surpasses historical fact.

from Crassus' foreign war against the Parthians to Pompey's civil war against Caesar.

As with Marcia, neither Julia's nor Cornelia's marriage can be fully broken or fulfilled. Julia's speech combines elements from both Dido and Creusa, mixing illicit lover and wife.[88] Civil war's deleterious effects on marriage reach into the underworld, beyond the putative division between life and death. Julia herself becomes Fury-like (*furialis*, 3.11), driven from Elysium by civil war to keep company with the chthonic goddesses of fate and revenge (2.12–19). She foments civil war to bring Pompey paradoxically back to her side: "civil war will make you mine" (*bellum / te faciet civile meum*, 3.33–4). Her marriage cannot be dissolved after death; rather death will ratify their bond. Julia is happy to let Cornelia accompany Pompey to war and even to share Pompey – just not with his new wife: "but let Caesar occupy your days and Julia your nights" (*sed teneat Caesarque dies et Iulia noctes*, 3.27). The two Julians will get in Cornelia's way, "so there may be no time free" for the new couple's "love" (*nullum vestro vacuum sit tempus amori*, 3.26). Pompey's dream embrace of his haunting dead wife can neither hold her nor dispel her. Lucan's women cleave to civil war, cementing their marriage bonds in a perversion of life and death.

Not even hot elegiac passion can break civil war's deathly entanglements to attain either proper union or division. Cornelia, degraded by Julia as a mistress (*paelex*, 3.23), never consummates her love for Pompey in the text. Separation with overtones of divorce haunts their marriage. Crassus' funeral pyre remains warm (3.23), not her bed. In an unhappy bedroom scene, Cornelia initiates lovemaking – already a normative inversion – but her husband turns away. Venus unmans Pompey and makes him "uncertain and trembling for battles" (*dubium trepidumque ad proelia*, 5.728–9), but love also makes him incapable of loving: "Not now," he begins. He might as well have a headache. To save her, he sends her away perversely in the language of divorce (*dimissa*, 5.765). Cornelia's feeling his empty side of the bed (5.808–13) searingly depicts their failure to join. The couple's logic acts out the logic of civil war: He tears the two of them apart because he cannot imagine she could endure watching warfare between citizens (*civilia bella*, 5.748–9), but he accepts the necessity of yielding to civil war because his most fundamental partner is not his wife, but Caesar: *iam totus adest in proelia Caesar. / cedendum est bellis* ("now Caesar is present entirely for battles; we must yield to wars," 5.742–3). Lucan perverts Gallus' speech in Vergil's *Eclogues*, distraught because his beloved Lycoris has followed a rival

---

[88] Narducci (2002) 287–8.

abroad to face war and hardship: *omnia vincit Amor: et nos cedamus Amori* ("Love conquers all: let us also yield to Love," 10.69). Pompey yields to the wrong force and acts rather like Gallus' rival than the loving elegiac poet Cornelia deserves. Going off to fight, he leaves discord in the bedroom.

By hiding Cornelia on Lesbos, Sappho's island, Pompey sets her in the Greek heart of Latin love elegy. He consigns himself to the role of the emasculated lover who can neither fulfill the republican, virile ideal of the military man nor take full possession of his beloved. The elegiac lover inverts the ideal Roman patriarch and degrades into impotent and Greek countercultural softness[89] – a rejection of Cato's hard and Stoic perversion and a step closer to the orientalist debauchery of Caesar and Cleopatra's embrace. Cornelia herself plays the abandoned heroine, the typological female mate to the elegiac poet; neither achieves normative union. Like Ariadne on the beach in Catullus 64, watching Theseus' ship leaving from afar, like Sappho on the Leucadian cliffs in Ovid's epistle, seeking to cure her love at Actium, another theater of civil war,[90] Cornelia nervously paces seaside cliffs (8.45–8). Hints of civil war overlay the heartbreak on Lesbos, locus of discord.

Doubling, indistinction, and medial spaces between life and death prevent Cornelia from realizing felicity in marriage. Always fainting, Cornelia neither enjoys love's swoon nor suffers death's collapse. The parallel scenes between Pompey's leaving her for safety's sake in Lesbos (*labitur infelix*, "she faints, unfortunate," 5.799) and his retrieving her there in defeat (*membra ... labant*, "her limbs slip," 8.60; *semianimem*, "half-living," 8.66; *infelix*, "unfortunate," 8.89) set her in unfortunate Dido's mold, always *infelix* (*Aeneid*, 4.68, 450, 539, 596).[91] But Dido at least experienced love and – a plus in Lucan's perverse logic – was capable of suicide. Cornelia, stuck between life and death, keeps repeating the impasse of her incapacity.

Cornelia rhetorically undoes even her own marriage. Adopting the prognosis of her husband's former wife, she turns herself into his mistress.

> ubicumque iaces civilibus armis
> nostros ulta toros, ades huc atque exige poenas,
> Iulia crudelis, placataque paelice caesa
> Magno parce tuo.   8.102–5

---

[89] Narducci (2002) 296: Pompey is a "condottiero indebolito" and "addolcito" (weakened and sweetened military man), which explains his military "*defaillances*" (failures).

[90] *Actiacum populi Leucadiumque vocant* ("peoples call it Actian and Leucadian," Ovid, *Heroides*, 15.166; also 185–8; *Actia bella ... Leucaten* ("Actian wars ... Leucates," Vergil, *Aen.* 8.675, 677).

[91] Johnson (1987) 84: Dido is a model for Cornelia's fainting; on its historicity, Bruère (1951) 227 n. 86.

Wherever you lie – you've avenged our bed with civil arms – be present and exact your punishment, cruel Julia. And spare your Magnus, appeased when his mistress is slain.

Even if her love is great enough for her to give up life and marriage to save him, all will still be in vain. Cornelia will witness what Pompey tried to spare her: his death, in similarly repetitive limbo. Difficulty severing his head renders him also "half-living" (*semianimis Magni*, 8.670); his truncated corpse also ends up on the shore (2.685, 8.708, 712, 720). Incapable of full separation or full union, they unite in their failure to unite.

Even after Pompey's death, civil war impedes Cornelia's performance of wifely duties. Incapacity besets her all around. Separation from Pompey's burial (8.739, 9.55–68) violates her wifely role. Her receipt of Pompey's actual ashes is deferred (8.769), parallel to Crassus' missing funeral (8.394). She goes through the motions with an empty pyre heaped with his clothes, replaying Dido's heaping her pyre with whatever Aeneas left behind (*exuvias*, *Aen.* 4.507; *De bello civ.* 9.177). But unlike Dido, she lacks capacity: She cannot carry out her intended suicide. The sailors prevent her (8.647, 653–6); she condemns herself for not simply dying of grief (9.106–8). All she can do is transmit Pompey's inheritance – civil war – to his sons. She ventriloquizes his haunting words: "Take up civil war, O my sons" (*excipite, o nati, bellum civile*, 9.88); "there are no peoples to whom my heir will not bring war" (*noster nullis non gentibus heres / bella dabit*, 9.94–5). She has nothing left but to die and cannot manage even that.

Lucan's second model of a Republican marriage is no more viable than Cato's with Marcia. Pompey's marriage to Cornelia channels elegiac incapacity, the genre of elite postcivil war disenfranchisement under Augustus. If Cato is Rome's father and husband, Pompey becomes Rome's lover by equating Cornelia with Rome.[92]

> tenuit nostros hac obside Lesbos
> adfectus; hic sacra domus carique penates,
> hic mihi Roma fuit.   8.131–3

With this hostage [Cornelia] Lesbos held my affections; here was my sacred house and dear household gods, here was Rome for me.

Neither father nor lover is a proper husband for Rome. Furthermore, Cornelia as Rome has moved to Lesbos, so the *penates* Aeneas so

---

[92] Ahl (1976) 181: "For Pompey is, in Lucan's terms, the lover of Rome as surely as Cato is the city's father or husband."

painstakingly brought from Asia Minor to Italy have migrated back to the Ionian coast. Adopted as virtual citizen of Lesbos (8.152) for her purity and virtue (*pudor, probitas, modestia,* 8.155–8), Cornelia abandons Rome. Although it is for modesty that she lives as if Pompey were already conquered while still standing (8.158), the figuration blurs the distinction between victory and defeat in yet another disastrous mix of categories.

Rome at Lesbos loses its nature and takes a step toward Egypt, where yet another couple's sexual politics becomes paradigmatic. The new Rome, conceived at Alexandria, is no longer republican, but imperial in a raging orientalist mode.

Alexandria: Emasculation

> This Rome cannot decide whether it has become Alexandria, it just feels that way temporarily, it manages to hide the fact from itself, or it must never think any such thing.
>
> Henderson (1998) 265[93]

Civil war's victor sets society on no path to restoration. Instead, sexuality defines postrepublican Rome as going headlong to ruin. Caesar establishes no marriage legislation, as will Augustus, with the aim of tamping down on adultery and regulating the birth of legitimate children. Instead, Caesar's indulgence in political and sexual degradation at Alexandria flouts Roman norms and establishes empire as a regime of oriental degeneration.[94] The late attestation of any historical dalliance between Caesar and Cleopatra underscores the figurative burden of Lucan's narrative.[95]

Julius Caesar's heir, Augustus, mentioned once in the epic (*Caesar,* 10.65), does not rectify his behavior but rather repeats it. Cleopatra provides a hinge of disgraceful continuity. Lucan imagines an alternative history, where the woman comes out on top. His work fills the textual blank spot that is Augustus, perversely realizing the fears caused by Dido's fleeting vision of peace and egalitarian love and politics in the *Aeneid* and articulated in Horace's Cleopatra Ode (1.37). In it, Cleopatra prevails at Actium: She terrified the Capitoline and would have led the new Caesar in

---

[93] Henderson diagnoses shifts in power to women and freedmen under Nero in Tacitus' *Annales* in terms familiar from Lucan.

[94] Sannicandro (2010) 115: The juxtaposition of Romanness and the oriental world makes Caesar and Cleopatra's union an original sin. Tracy (2014) 7: Rome's refoundation by Augustus rejects Egypt's "alien ways."

[95] Zwierlein (1974) 56–8 questions the historicity of the affair; Lucan transfers Augustan propaganda against Antony onto Caesar.

triumph, were it divinely sanctioned; at Leucadia, it was unclear whether a "matron – not even one of our own – would rule the world" (*an mundum ne nostra quidem matrona teneret*, 10.67). The outrage ratchets up; Cleopatra is not just a woman, but a wife, not just a wife, but one not ours. The contrafactual represents the reality of empire as Lucan sees it. Actium is reimagined as placing Rome under a woman's thumb. Contrary to historical fact, the image reveals a deeper truth. Julius Caesar, soon to be succeeded in Cleopatra's bed by Antony (10.69–72), initiates this history as a template for imperial Rome. Any difference between Augustus and Antony, winner and loser, friend and foe is erased.[96] Caesar's relations with Cleopatra in Alexandria infuse Rome's newest twin city with indeterminate marriage, adultery, incest, unmanning, and a bastard son's mixed blood.

Cleopatra and Caesar realize the sexual degradation Pompey averts when he chooses Egypt over Parthia, his first plan for refuge. The barbarian lust and perversion of marriage Lentulus describes among the Parthians set the scene for Alexandria. Harems of a thousand daughters-in-law, lawless bestial couplings, fully conscious incest with sisters and mothers – putting Oedipus' inadvertent transgressions to shame – and mixed-blood sons afford compelling reasons not to expose Cornelia to potential rape (8.396–409). These reasons overwhelm Pompey's misguided thought of avenging his defeat in civil war with the help of his old Parthians foes, who, in a familial twist, killed his wife's first husband Crassus (8.321–4). Pompey entertains entering the land of the Roman enemy par excellence as a friend in a position of weakness.[97] Lucan's hypothetical history, as often, reveals actual history's greater truth: Pompey would bring Parthian troops against Rome – another act worse than civil war. But even Pompey has limits. He may have lost his shame as a general, but he still would prevent his wife, who feared capture by Caesar (5.783–4), from becoming the spoils of unburied Crassus' defeat (8.394, 416). For all the incapacity marking their marriage, Pompey still adheres to basic Roman norms. These Caesar violates in Alexandria.

Cleopatra surpasses every other Roman heroine who figures the body politic – Marcia in mourning, Julia as Fury (3.11; 10.59), Cornelia as lover – to define the Julian line and, with it, the Roman Empire. Both go headlong on a course to full-blown orientalism. She perverts mourning's

---

[96] Stephens (2004) 158: "Augustus after the death of Cleopatra – albeit in absentia – became de facto the new pharaoh of Egypt."

[97] Pompey's triumph over Mithridates VI did not actually include the territory of Parthia in 61 BCE, Vervaet (2014) 141–2.

dishevelment as a ploy to seduction, coming to Caesar with beguiling bedroom hair to lament her exile and her brother's subjugation to his servant Pothinus (10.82–104). Eros' power play brings destruction. Piled-on language of disgrace and lust turn her into a new Helen, who brings not foreign but civil war; her Emathian house recalls the plains of Pharsalus (10.56–62). She even arrives in a two-oared boat (*biremi*, 10.56) that punningly evokes twinning and Remus, signs of civil war. The overlay of female figures, all of whom personify some failure in marriage, culminates in Cleopatra, who embodies Rome's normative collapse.

Aeneas' past returns as Caesar's present. Numerous parallels to *Aeneid* 4 set Rome on a course of repeated dalliance with Eastern queens. She now wins with a vengeance; sexual conquest is political conquest, and Roman values lose out. Where Dido obeys a tragic paradigm of chastity violated, Cleopatra has no inhibitions. She shows her true colors in a display of oriental luxury – precious materials detailed at length (10.111–35) – at a feast that eclipses the banquet Dido offers the Trojans in the *Aeneid*.[98] Her dress, whose open needlework reveals breasts normally covered in cloth, recalls Dido with "Sidonian thread" (10.141), but without the Carthaginian queen's decorum and shame.[99] Iopas' learned song (*Aen.* 4.742–6) becomes didactic grotesquery in Acoreus' long disquisition on the Nile (10.195–331), Lucan's parody of Alexandrian scientism on steroids. More monstrous than the Euphrates, measure of bombast in Augustan poetry,[100] here the Egyptian river swells out of proportion. The repetition of pouring (*infundere*, 10.155, 166) cues us to watch for literal as for metaphorical influence.[101] Wine becomes a liquid symbol of Roman subjection: The "unconquered Falernian" becomes denatured when Meroe "forces" it to foam prematurely (*indomitam Meroe cogens spumare Falernum*, 10.163). Horace's dictum *Graecia capta ferum victorem cepit* ("captured Greece captured its fierce victor," *Epist.* 2.1.156) now applies of Egypt. Cleopatra's luxury has "not yet been translated to the Roman ages" (*nondum translatos Romana in saecula luxus*, 10.110), but the implication is it will be soon.

Incest, polygamy, and indistinction between male and female rule chart Rome's moral and political degeneration. Bastard births pollute the body

---

[98] Zwierlein (1974) 55, 58, 61–3; Ahl (1976) 227–8; Tucker (1975); Schmidt (1986) 218; Gagliardi (1987); Bettenworth (2004) 178–213; Reggiani (2005) 107–12; Sannicandro (2010) 101. Tracy (2014) 55: "the Egypt of Cleopatra's banquet offers a disturbing glimpse into Rome's decadent future."

[99] Lucan retrojects a Roman topos of luxury back onto Alexandria; see Schmidt (1986) 222.

[100] Scodel and Thomas (1984).

[101] Pichon (1912) 44–7 details the sources of Lucan's Nile. See Tracy (2014) 144–80 for Acoreus' rhetorical and cosmic mystification.

politic's bloodline. Like Cornelia, Cleopatra marries two Roman generals. Sequential marriages supplement an incestuous and concurrent marriage to her brother (*fratre marito*, 10.138).[102] Pothinus' phantasm of her "running back and forth between husbands" reveals her true motivation as consolidating power: *interque maritos / discurrens Aegypton habet Romamque meretur* ("she holds Egypt and earns Rome," 10. 358–9). This double marriage, however, adulterates her marriage to Caesar: *rex hinc coniunx, hinc Caesar adulter* ("the king her husband on one side, Caesar the adulterer on the other," 10.367). She, in her plenipotency, infantilizes the one (*puero*, 10.361) and unmans the other, who appears, like Pompey, an "old man" before his time (*senem*, 10.360–1). Egyptian "indifference to the sex" of the ruler (*nullo discrimine sexus*, 10.91) lets them tolerate a queen, a normative inversion on two counts at Rome: monarchy and sex.

Egyptian transgression of Roman norms would be immaterial had it no influence on Rome, but Cleopatra bears brothers (the plural nods to Caesar and Antony as fathers) to Julia out of wedlock (*adulter*, 10.74: *fratres ... non ex coniuge partus*, 76–7). Caesar's adding Venus to his cares (10.75) ironically perverts the Julian line. Indecision about whether Cleopatra and Caesar actually marry undermines the institution's grounding function.[103] Along with Roman institutions, the poem subverts Rome's synecdochic representative in the man himself. Egypt reduces Caesar to holing up in a "degenerate hiding-place" (*degeneres ... latebras*, 10.441). The subsequent similes undo his Roman, male, normative nature: "like an unwarlike boy or woman in captive walls" (*ceu puer inbellis vel captis femina muris*, 10.458). Worse, he is compared to Medea, a barbarian woman and fratricide: *sic barbara Colchis ... fratrisque simul cervice parata* ("thus the barbarian Colchian woman ... with her brother's neck at the same time prepared," 10.464–7).[104] Medea's famed infanticide, needing no mention, cuts off the future represented by children. Winning civil war denatures Caesar even more than civil war itself. As the symbolic embodiment of Roman power, he has become no manlier than the eunuchs he admires in Cleopatra's court (10.133–5). Caesarion, his only natural son, is not fully Roman, a hybrid Egypto-Macedonian-Roman with a name diminutive and Greek. And Lucan's reader surely knows the rumor that tarnishes Caesar's legal but

---

[102] See Sannicandro (2010) 125–7 on politics in Cleopatra's bedroom.
[103] Propertius 3.11.31 and Vergil, *Aen.* 8.688 decisively call her *coniunx*.
[104] On the insult, Ahl (1976) 225–6.

unnatural successor, his posthumously adopted great-nephew, with civil war's common trope: Augustus will do away with Caesar's rival heir in fratricide.[105]

The Augustan marriage legislation literalizes the trope of marriage as the bedrock of social norms and makes sexual regeneration central to restoring a society rent by civil war. The fertility of the bare-breasted mother with twins on the so-called Tellus relief of the Ara Pacis (Fig. 2.5) vividly illustrates how children symbolize a peaceful future. Fidelity and fertility convey the Augustan program at Horace, *Carm.* 4.5.21–4, *Carm. Saec.* 18–20,[106] and at Velleius, 2.103.5. Lucan accepts the trope's logic but turns its meaning around. The sterility, literal and figurative, of the legitimate marriages in his poem proclaims the Republic's end. Caesar not only fails to restore marriage but also perverts it. His sexual depravity condemns the Empire.

That Rome's path from civil war to empire furthermore runs through Egypt is another signal of Rome's alienation from good republican values. In the final book's opening, civil war persists from one leader to the next and spreads abroad:[107] The upshot is its perpetuation within empire, civil war's apparent solution. Repeated tropes of discord tarnish the coming empire. Pompey's cut neck in the first line yields to indistinction between the "head of victor and conquered" (*uictoris uictique caput*, 10.6) – civil war rages on despite the opponent's death. Speculation on whether the Egyptians will also murder Caesar (another hypothetical history) fore-shadows his eventual assassination and projects civil war beyond the scope of the poem. Roman discord, theoretically at rest after Pharsalus, bubbles up in the *discordia pectora* ("discordant hearts," 10.12) meeting Caesar in Alexandria. Receiving a less-than-warm welcome from the mob, which anticipates domination and the imposition of Roman fasces and laws (10.11–12), Caesar seals their fears by visiting the tomb of Alexander, paragon of empire. *Cupide* ("desirously," 10.19) shows Caesar's real lust is for power.

Alexander casts an exemplary shadow over Caesar and thereby the regime he ushers in.[108] Lucan's evaluation is clear. Alexander is the "crazed scion of

---

[105] Ahl (1976) 227. Zwierlein (1974) 56–7 reviews these stories' dubious historicity and suggests Caesar's erotic relations with Cleopatra derive from Aeneas' with Dido (63–7). Reggiani (2005) 107–9: Lucan's Alexandria is a metaphor for Nero's court and the Republic's moral collapse.

[106] Their antonyms convey civil war in *Carm.* 3.6; Lowrie (2018).

[107] Masters (1992) 216–59 reads the poem's ending according to civil war's "endlessness."

[108] Ahl (1976) 225; Fantham (1985) 126–31; Reggiani (2005) 87–8; Kimmerle (2015) 50–9. For the transfer of the motif of visiting Alexander's tomb from Augustus to Caesar, Schmidt (1986) 34. For Augustus, among other Romans, modeling himself on Alexander, Kienast (1969) analyzes the visit to the tomb, the complex valence of orientalism associated with him, and later abandonment of the

Pellaean Philip" and "crazed king" (*Pellaei proles uaesana Philippi*, 10.20; *vaesano regi*, 10.42). His father's name evokes the civil war battle, Philippi, where Caesar's assassins lost to his heir. He himself exercises no self-mastery; his disordered soul maps disorder in the body politic. Despite the noxious nature of Alexander's example, Rome nevertheless follows it to its ruin.

> nam sibi libertas umquam si redderet orbem
> ludibrio servatus erat, non utile mundo
> editus exemplum, terras tot posse sub uno
> esse viro.   10.25–8

> For if freedom ever restored the world to itself, he would be preserved to mock it, who was given as an exemplum not useful to the world, that so many lands could be under one man.

Republican freedom will not be restored and the world will be united in disharmony under the rule of one man. Rome's emperor will not be fully Roman but will follow in the wake of Alexander, conqueror of Babylon and founder of Alexandria. The future Augustus will divinize Caesar as a star upon assassination, but, according to Lucan, Cleopatra gets there first. She makes him a "star favorable to our peoples" (*gentibus nostris / sidus . . . nostris*, 10.89–90). The benevolent star of the Roman Empire is orientalized in advance.

Rome: Always Already Discordant

The tropes of Rome's degeneration, so evident in Lucan, cast Cleopatra's cameo appearance on Aeneas' shield retrospectively in a clearer light. Her dalliance with Caesar in the imperial poem reveals distinctly what the *Aeneid* hides in plain sight. Vulcan's construction of the shield in return for sexual favors from Venus perverts not just any marital relation as if it were prostitution, but the marriage of Venus *genetrix* ("mother," 8.383) herself. The founder of the Julian line was himself conceived through her lust for Anchises outside marriage.[109] The battle of Actium itself, ostensibly a battle of degenerate Cleopatra against normative Augustus, is of course a civil war battle.[110] Augustus emerges from it, like Lucan's Caesar, in the

---

model (451–4); Griffin (1985) 189. In later traditions, Augustus and his age succeed Alexander and his in glory, e.g., in Voltaire, Briant (2012) 485.

[109] Oliensis (1997) 299. Boyle (1999). Venus' seduction of her husband to bring war and fury inverts her adulterous seduction of Mars in Lucretius to bring peace.

[110] Wyke (1992), Gruen (2011) 108–9, and Lowrie (2015c). Syed (2005) 177–93 ultimately views the gender and ethnic tropes slurring Cleopatra as foil to the successful definition of Roman identity.

guise of an Eastern imperial potentate, with strong resonances of Priam. Rome has, by implication, reverted to Troy.

Whereas Augustus aimed to restore patriarchy in the wake of civil war's devastation with marriage legislation, promoted long before its passage the year after Vergil's death, the scenes leading up to and on Aeneas' shield show that adultery, rape, and civil discord mark Rome from the beginning. The Roman history depicted on the shield rings the changes on the tropes of civil discord. As a result, top-down attempts to impose normative values will face an uphill battle. Venus' seduction of Vulcan, to persuade him to forge arms for a son not his, is all the more scandalous for her being his wife and the *progenetrix* of the Julian line. As with Lucan's Cleopatra, feminine seduction is a power play that surpasses sexuality and spills into politics. Her calling the shots diminishes male force and corrupts the Empire in advance.

Venus' seduction scene ironically hammers home the scandalous nature of her ties with multiple words for family relations. She requests arms from Vulcan as a "mother for her son" (*mater*, 8.370; *genetrix nato*, 8.383): the words' proximity evokes her cult epithet as founder of the Julian line and reveals its bastard lineage. Vulcan may be her "husband" (8.372, 377), but he is "father" (*pater*, 8.394) because he is venerable – not because he engendered Aeneas. Thetis and Dawn, explicitly identified as others' daughters and wives (8.383–4), succeeded in their petitions to Vulcan to make armor for their sons – one of whom (Achilles) in fact killed the other (Memnon) – so why should his own wife (*coniunx*, 8.393) not prevail?[III] He is "chained" (*devinctus*, 8.394), after all, in the same sort of bonds, as we recall, he himself crafted to catch her with Mars (*Od.* 8.266–366). It is not the righteousness of her petition or persuasive words that win his consent, but rather her fondling, fleshly embrace, which arouses in him the "accustomed flame" (*solitam flammam*, 8.389). He thereby turns into a Dido figure, overcome by "traces of the old flame" (*veteris vestigia flammae*, 4.23) against her better judgment. The simile comparing him to a wife who rises early, forced (*impositum*, 8.409) to ply Minerva's craft, emasculates him, once more like a woman, with spinning, a metaphor for domestic chastity from Penelope to Lucretia (8.408–15). The image of this woman, who also rouses literal sleeping fires, stresses the purpose of marital chastity: to rear legitimate children in direct contrast to Vulcan's home life (*Volcani domus*,

---

[III] Ahl (2007) 403 suggests why not: Vulcan's necklace for Harmonia, another child Venus bore Mars out of wedlock, brought destruction on its wearers. For the necklace's civil war overtones, Keith (2018).

8.422); *castum ut servare cubile / coniugis et possit parvos educere natos* ("so as to preserve the bedchamber of her husband chaste and be able to bring up little children," 8.412–13). Vulcan, who sinks into sleep after pouring himself into his wife's lap (8.405–6) and rises "from soft bedcovers" (*mollibus e stratis*, 8.415) in his "golden bedchamber" (*thalamo ... aureo*, 8.372) to go to work, is orientalized through sex, luxury, and effeminacy. The simile reveals the patriarchy lacking in the shield's production and demotes its craftsman from master to mistress when an overwhelming feminine force subjects him.

The analogues to the shield Vulcan forges put it on a wrong path one way or the other. Either it resembles the simile's spun wool, a soft, womanly production, or, if at all like his workshop's other artefacts, will partake of terrifying lightning, noise, fear, and anger, which, together with yet more flames, mix into Jupiter's thunderbolt (8.431–2). The shield becomes a horrific weapon of war imprinted with the anger that besets Aeneas at the death of Pallas. Either way, the flames of lust and fires of the forge (8.421) hone a weapon borne of a marriage figured as prostitution.[112] The gift's granting further dwells on familial dysfunctional. In bestowing the shield on Aeneas, Venus identifies its author as her husband (*coniugis*), addresses her son as such (*nate*), and – the coup de grace – seeks her son's embrace (*amplexus nati*, 8.612–15). She comes on to Vulcan with the same word (*amplexu*, 8.388; *amplexus*, 8.405). Otherwise, she studiously avoids giving her son so much as a chaste maternal hug.

The shield itself details stories from Roman history that highlight civil discord explicitly, through imagery, or allusion: adultery, rape, fratricide, and political turbulence set Rome on a path of foundational self-destruction.[113] The idyllic scene of the she-wolf licking Romulus and Remus in Mars's green grotto encodes sexual transgression. The archaic form of Mars's name (Mavors) recurs from Lucretius, as does his *tereti cervice reposta* ("with rounded neck placed back," *DRN* 1.35); the phrase characterizing Venus, gazing up at her adulterous lover Mars, recurs of the wolf, *tereti cervice reflexa* ("with rounded neck bent back," 8.633). Allusion to one of the war god's sexual peccadillos implies another, the rape of the Vestal Virgin Ilia that spawns the twins. "She-wolf" is famously slang for prostitute (Livy, 1.4). Her licking the twins' "bodies into shape with her tongue" (*corpora fingere lingua*, 8.634) forms Rome's founders in her image.

---

[112] Prostitution within marriage is also sign and symptom of civil war at Horace, *Odes* 3.6, Lowrie (2018).
[113] Mac Góráin (2018) 148.

The motif's transfer from the typical mother bear alerts the reader to pay attention: The message is that Rome has been wolf-like from inception.[114]

Tropes of discord pile up. Rape is named as such: *raptas sine more Sabinas* ("the Sabines raped in defiance of custom," 8.635). Mettius Fufetius' exemplary dismemberment by four-horse chariots apparently teaches allies to keep their word, but the gruesome image of brambles dripping with the gore of limbs rent asunder lingers (8.642–5). Aeneas' descendants fight for liberty against Porsenna's attempt to reinstate the exiled tyrant Tarquinius; the pair Cocles and Cloelia – whose patriotism comes with a perhaps-suspect gender equality – similarly enjoys a brief moment of republican heroism. But Manlius saves the Capitoline from the Gauls in language colored with Tarpeia's treachery and his own eventual end, flung from "the Tarpeian citadel" (*Tarpeiae … arcis*, 8.652) for aspiring to tyranny. The repetition of "Gallos" in "Galli" (8.656–7) recalls Cybele's castrated priests; their hair (*caesaries*, 8.659) conjures up their conqueror Caesar right before the image of the Salii and the Luperci – ostensibly a moment of fertility, where the "chaste mothers led a sacred procession" (*castae ducebant sacra … matres*, 8.666–7) – recalls the Lupercalia, where Antony tried three times to crown Caesar king. Luxury tars even the mothers who travel in "soft carts" (*pilentis … in mollibus*, 8.666). The contrast in the underworld fates between Catiline as conspiratorial sinner and Cato, rewarded as law-giver, belies a similarity: Both died in civil war.

We stress Vergil's shocking choice. He did not have to describe the shield or its creation this way. Images of civil discord, encoded to a greater or lesser degree, shape his narrative of Roman history and identify its core. The climactic battle of Actium sets civil war in the shield's very center. Unlike the indirect ways the epic colors Roman history and prehistory as civil war, here a civil war battle receives direct narration. The shield could contrast peaceful and warring cities, as in Homer, or describe fertility and beauty spreading out from peaceful Italy. Any number of options were available, but the shield represents civil war.

Before treating the poem's last mention of Augustus – we argue his image on the shield orientalizes him as a tyrant in Priam's mold – we step back to consider a fraught question. Does the poem, in the other two passages that depict Augustus and prepare for his depiction on the shield ecphrasis, show him as successful in bringing civil war to an end?

---

[114] The tradition about bears goes back to Aristotle, Bömer (1986) at *Met.* 15.379–81.

Civil War Externalized

In Vergil, governance finds its highest legitimacy in ending civil war, but civil war's erasure reinscribes it discursively at every level – even where it should never have been present from the beginning. The Saturnian age defines the new age's mythic template, but, in a first gesture, the promised new golden age of empire fails to live up to the model because it entails domination. In a second gesture, hints of civil war and domination turn out to inhabit even the apparently pristine, idealized model.[115] Jupiter's prophecy to Venus in *Aeneid* 1 may promise Fury's imprisonment within the Gates of War,[116] but the new laws ushering in an age of peace will be written under the aegis of the divinized Romulus and Remus, whose fratricide stands as the paradigmatic trope of civil war. Although their reconciliation ostensibly brings it to an end, reconciliation cannot be named except through the repetition of civil war's tropes. The *Aeneid*'s various proclamations of civil war's demise break the heart all the more for their failure. The more fervent the promise, the closer the ideal world comes within reach, the more rabidly civil war breaks out.[117] Literature from Roman times to the present shows that civil war's underlying logic remains potent despite ideological declarations of its cessation. Violence reasserts civil war's claim repeatedly across history under the cover of some reign of golden peace.

The three great predictions about Augustus define him in terms of civil war, which comes increasingly closer to him as the poem progresses until we see him as a full-blown civil warrior at Actium.[118] He appears as a figure not of peace and prosperity in any absolute sense,[119] but of disturbance externalized. He stands for Empire as civil war's solution. The question is whether the Roman Empire can inaugurate a better order.[120] The poem answers a feeble yes, if this means no more than directing civil war away from Rome, but a resounding no, if empire means anything beyond transferring domination from the self onto others. Even this transfer appears hollow, as the self reenacts the otherness it would subject.

---

[115] Thomas (2001) 2–3; Star (2021).

[116] On fury as a metonym for civil war, Jal (1963) 421–2. Harris (2001) surveys conflicting attitudes to anger. This period disapproved of its expression, particularly by rulers (201–63).

[117] Putnam (1965) 163–4 makes a similar point about the violent outbreak after the truce between Aeneas and Latinus.

[118] The interpretation here parallels Lowrie (forthcoming b).

[119] *Pax* developed an absolute sense starting in the Augustan period, Cornwell (2017).

[120] Putnam (1965) xiv answers no: "Aeneas – and through him Augustus – can never fulfill in fact the ideal conditions of empire, where force and freedom must be fused into a fortunate amalgam."

Paradigmatic elements from the alternative cities Aeneas' quest for a new homeland should put behind him reappear within Rome's figuration. The new foundation ends civil war at a price: becoming an oriental empire, Troy reestablished as Rome.

Civil war defines Augustus across all his appearances in the *Aeneid*. In book 1, Jupiter predicts to Venus that Augustus will extend Empire to the Ocean and that she will receive him in heaven bearing the spoils of the conquered orient.

> nascetur pulchra Troianus origine Caesar
> imperium Oceano, famam qui termine astris,
> Iulius, a magno demissum nomen Iulo.
> hunc tu olim caelo spoliis Orientis onustum
> accipies secura; vocabitur hic quoque votis.
> aspera tum positis mitescunt saecula bellis:
> cana Fides et Vesta, Remo cum fratre Quirinus
> iura dabunt; dirae ferro et compagibus artis
> claudentur Belli portae; Furor impius intus
> saeva sedens super arma et centum vinctus aënis
> post tergum nodis fremet horridus ore cruento.   1.286–96

There will be born a Trojan Caesar from a beautiful origin to bring Empire's bounds to Ocean, his reputation to the stars, Iulius, a name sent down from great Iulus. Him you will one day receive in heaven – don't worry – laden with the spoils of the orient. He will also receive prayer. White-haired Faith and Vesta, Quirinus with his brother Remus, will give the laws; the dire Gates of War will be closed with iron and tight fastenings; impious Furor within sitting on cruel arms and bound behind his back with a hundred bronze knots will roar, horrid with bloody mouth.

Empire is the political form required to end civil war. The closing of the Gates of War and imprisonment of personified Furor seal the new era as containing, not overcoming civil war's passion.[121] When Juno later breaks the bonds of the "Gates of War" (*Belli portae*, 7.607), allusion to Ennius aligns her with personified Discord, Vergil's most common word for civil war.[122]

---

[121] Hershkowitz (1998) 106 n. 124. Fowler (1998) 165. Oliensis (2001) 42: Repressed drives yearn to break out from bondage.

[122] Personification transfers from Discord in Ennius to War in Vergil. *Postquam Discordia taetra / belli ferratos postes portasque refregit* ("After harsh Discord broke open the iron doorposts and gates of war," *Annales* frgs. 225–6 Skutsch). Fowler's (1998) reading of this passage's rich allusive texture notes that Augustus will open the gates for the foreign wars of empire, thereby binding empire to civil war (162, 169).

Cracks mar the foundation even here. Jupiter's speech, for all its imperial triumphalism, nevertheless encodes civil war. The divinized Romulus exists in the timelessness of divinity shared with the personified virtue Fides and Vesta, guardian goddess of the Penates and chastity. Rome's origin in historical time nevertheless raises its ugly head with the otherwise unmotivated reference to Remus – he could simply have been left out. Fratricide generally, and Romulus' murder of Remus in particular, is a civil war trope in this period.[123] Whereas in the *Georgics*, reference to accord between Remus and his brother sets the Saturnian age before the advent of Roman history (2.533), here the fratricidal pair, presumably reconciled, become law-givers in the Augustan age.[124] Their harmony connotes a new golden age.[125] If the first foundation was based on fratricide, the refoundation rests on successfully putting civil war to rest. The brothers' reconciliation, however, is not named in so many words. The establishment of peace, harmony, or concord could receive mention instead.[126] Civil war's traces resonate through the inclusion of its standard tropes despite its ostensible historical end. Furor has been contained, but not destroyed, and continues to rage, threatening to burst his bonds.

The characterization of Augustus as Trojan while bearing the spoils of oriental conquest makes a further point about the nature of the empire that contains civil war. This empire, like Augustus himself, is not Roman, despite the fact that *Romanus* would scan just as well as *Troianus*. The cultural transformation that supposedly lifts the lineage from Troy to Rome to a higher plane – the eradication of Eastern identity for Italian Juno insists on in book 12 – does not occur. Troy persists in the Julian clan's identity, which symbolically encodes Roman identity. The ages that grow mild through setting war aside entail paradox. How to win those Eastern spoils if not through war? Can Romans maintain their belligerent identity if they grow soft through peace? Softening would make them like those they conquer.

---

[123] Jal (1963) 408.

[124] On reconciliation, Austin (1971) at 1.292. The presence of Remus here, however, is "extraordinary," Wiseman (1995) 145, who nevertheless accepts the reconciliation narrative (146) and traces associations of Remus with Agrippa as Augustus' right-hand man. Such whitewashing dissolves by the time of Ovid (146–50). Servius notes how Vergil "dissimulates here about the parricide, because he conjoins them, and calls him not Romulus, but Quirinus." Perkell (1999) 43; Putnam (1999) 212.

[125] Ambivalence inhabits the question of whether law obtained during the golden age; Latinus' (7.202–4) and Evander's versions (8.319–22) are inconsistent, Lowrie (2005) 951.

[126] Lange (2009) 89–90. To his remark that "either civil war is mentioned or it is not," we counter by stressing the *Aeneid*'s complex representational processes, which mask and reveal simultaneously. Servius' interpretation at 1.294 attests that Furor was taken in antiquity to refer to civil war.

In Anchises' speech in the underworld, the most overt declaration that Augustus will "found golden centuries" (*aurea condet / saecula*, 6.792–3) replays on a larger scale the structure established in book 1: civil war contained but not eradicated.[127] Disjunction between history's chronological order and the narrative order initially glorifies Augustus by seating him centrally next to Romulus.[128] But Roman history's reassuring beginning quickly devolves into civil war. Like the fratricide shadowing the conjunction of Augustus with Quirinus in book 1, intrafamilial violence is paradigmatic for Roman history in the parade of heroes. Brutus slays his sons who moved "new wars" (*nova bella*, 6.820) in their plot to restore the Tarquins[129] – counterrevolution perverts the Republic's foundational revolution; filicide further couches the sorry mess in a trope of civil discord. Brutus' misplaced "love for country and immeasurable lust for praise" (*amor patriae laudumque immensa cupido*, 6.823) destroys near and dear – Venus and her son Cupid – that is, Desire – make yet another Roman devoted to his country "unhappy" (*infelix*, 6.822). The momentary concord between Pompey and Caesar, soon to break into discord, drives home the theme of familial strife. Reference to them only by their marriage bond, "father-in-law" and "son-in-law" (6.826–40), highlights the civil war figuration. Anchises' asking them not to "drive their vigorous strength into the guts of the fatherland" (*neu patriae validas in viscera vertite viris*, 6.833) twists the trope a notch further.[130] Internal violence passes from family to country, as already in Horace (*ut . . . urbs haec periret dextera*, "so that the city perish by her own right hand," *Epodes* 7.9–10), whose poem ends with the curse of Remus' spilled blood. Lucan similarly makes civil war a metaphorical suicide: The people "turned on its own guts with victorious right hand" (*in sua victrici conversum viscera dextra*, 1.3), surpassing the implication of familial violence in *bella . . . plus quam civilia* ("wars more than civil," 1.1).[131] If any doubt clouds the value of pardon, Anchises asks Caesar, his own descendant, to eschew violence and spare first: *tuque prior,*

---

[127] Lefèvre (1998): Civil war notes in this speech cast the Caesarian line in a disadvantageous light. Thomas (2001) 3–14: Ambiguity in the meaning of *saecula condere* cautions against triumphalism. Kennedy (1992) deconstructs pro- and anti-Augustan positions in scholarship.

[128] Johnson (1976) 108.

[129] *Res novae* is a standard phrase for constitutional change through upheaval, see *Oxford Latin Dictionary, novus* 10.

[130] Against Servius' encomiastic reading of an allusion to Caesarian clemency, Gale (2013) 291 argues that emphasis falls on the "tragedy of civil war" rather than "Caesar's greatness."

[131] For the familial interpretation, Bern scholia: *ut . . . inter generum et socerum gesta. ubi et filii cum parentibus et fratres dimicauere cum fratribus* ("As it was waged between son-in-law and father-in-law. Since even sons fought with parents and brothers with brothers," Usener [1967] 9). See Della Corte (1984–91), *guerre civili*, for the ancient distinction between *bellum civile* and *bellum plus quam*

tu parce . . . proice tela manu, sanguis meus ("you first, you spare . . . throw the arms from your hand, my blood," 6.834–5). The civil war context of his injunction matches and balances the imperial context of his famous *parcere subiectis et debellare superbos* ("to spare the subjected and war down the proud," 6.853).[132] Aeneas will conspicuously fail to obey his father in slaughtering Turnus.

Although Augustus' position adjacent to Romulus may initially shield him from the civil discord that follows, the centuries to be ushered in by his rule hardly return Rome to a period of Saturnian tranquility or a Hesiodic-style golden age of peace.[133] Mention of Saturn's age implies a parallel, but it could just as well establish contrast.[134]

> Hic vir, hic est, tibi quem promitti saepius audis,
> Augustus Caesar, divi genus, aurea condet
> saecula qui rursus Latio regnata per arva
> Saturno quondam, super et Garamantas et Indos
> proferet imperium.   6.791–5

> This man, this one, whom you often hear promised to you, Augustus Caesar, the race of the divinized, who will found golden centuries again in Latium through lands ruled once by Saturn, and will extend empire over Garamantes and Indians.

Augustus presides over an expansion of empire, which looms large in the future imagined by Anchises (*imperium*, 6.682, 795, 812, 819, 851). Domination is lacking in descriptions of the mythical golden age. At *Georgics* 2, for instance, life under Saturn is incompatible with war (2.539–40). Furthermore, empire in the Roman political imaginary brings in corrupting wealth, which in turn leads to civil war.[135] If Augustus' sole reign puts an end to civil war and redirects Roman military might toward external enemies, known conventions suggest Empire will bring it back. Egypt, which awaits Augustus' arrival with trepidation (*turbant*, 6.800), is the site of his eventual conquest over Antony and Cleopatra after Actium. The new golden centuries may bring prosperity, but civil war infuses

---

civile; in the latter, the principals' relationship extends beyond citizenship to family. Also, Jal (1963) 35–7; Ahl (1976) 313; Conte (1988) 17–20; Lowrie and Vinken (2018). Compare Seneca, *Phoenissae* 354–5: *non satis est adhuc / civile bellum: frater in fratrem ruat* ("civil war is not enough so far: let brother rush against brother"). Henderson (1998) 187 assembles the range of excesses; his leitmotif *plus quam* enacts Lucan's hyperbole *passim*.

[132] The latter is often linked to the death of Turnus, e.g., Tarrant (2012) 16–19, but not the former.

[133] For darkness in the golden age, Boyle (1993b) 98; Thomas (2001) 2–3; Star (2021).

[134] Horsfall (2013) at 6.793: "The problem has been discussed with notable ill-feeling."

[135] The commonplace has Greek roots, Gorman and Gorman (2014).

Anchises' speech: Instead of ushering in generalized peace,[136] the Augustan age keeps the lid on civil war.

The scene of Augustus' third appearance, on Aeneas' shield, is the climactic civil war battle of the first century BCE at Actium. We have become so inured to this central passage of Augustan literature that its celebration of victory in civil war, however obscured, has ceased to shock. The Romans themselves normalized civil war and had no hesitation to celebrate triumphs over Roman opponents, provided they came mingled with foreign triumphs, as represented here.[137] But what Roman politicians may have gotten away with in public conflicts with the horror expressed toward civil war in the *Eclogues*, the *Georgics*, and Anchises' speech only two books previously. Anchises begs his own lineage to spare first in civil war. The context supplies Julius Caesar, but equivocation between the Caesars at 6.769 suggests an analogy: like great-uncle, like great-nephew.[138] Now Augustus, proximate to civil war in Jupiter's prophecy and Anchises' speech, actually wages it. No sparing of the subjected civil war enemy happens, however. The scene of celebration in the triple triumph shifts the focus away from defeated Romans. The image of Augustus reviewing pacified foreign enemies recodes civil war as imperial expansion.

Pro-Augustan readers see the depiction of Actium on the shield as declaring an end to civil war and validating empire. Critics of Augustus also perforce critique Vergil on the grounds that masking the civil nature of the war as a foreign war supports the regime and whitewashes the ideology. Those who would save the poet from the ideology take his sympathy for Egypt, embracing her defeated in mourning, and for the Araxes, chafing at being bridged, as an undertone of lament that questions the passage's dominant triumphalism.[139] But the clarity of the East/West dichotomy dissolves under closer scrutiny: "it is precisely the tendency of the *Aeneid* to install in the epic a partisanship that pits evil against good, yet at the same time radically to problematize that opposition."[140] The shield's orientalism displays how the orientalist projection of abjection within onto a demonized foreign enemy makes self-inflicted trauma bearable by externalizing it.

---

[136] Such a definition of *pax* began in the Augustan period, Cornwell (2017).

[137] See above, Chapter 1, p. 35.   [138] Horsfall (2013) at 6.789.

[139] Parry (1963) contrasts the poem's "public voice of triumph" and "private voice of regret" (79). Lyne (1987) 2 characterizes the "further voices" that work against the "epic voice" as discrete, but persistent.

[140] Hardie (1993) 74. Johnson (1976) 116 is scathing of readers who turn the characters in the *Aeneid* into "good guys" and "bad guys." Reed (2007): "moving boundaries between Greek, Oriental, and Italian" make Roman identity a synthetic construction against "a series of foils" (2); (2010).

Nevertheless, such externalization replays all it would repress.[141] Vergil's own method demonstrates how ideological representation contains civil war without eradicating it. Beyond the emphasis on discord in Roman history, allusion to civil war – particularly to the *Georgics* – and other coded references frame Augustus' appearance on the shield, tarnishing the otherwise-dominant triumphant image. Twin radiant lights projecting from Augustus' and Aeneas' heads establish the closest textual link between them.

> hinc Augustus agens Italos in proelia Caesar
> cum patribus populoque, penatibus et magnis dis,
> stans celsa in puppi, geminas cui tempora flammas
> laeta vomunt patriumque aperitur vertice sidus.   8.678–81

> On this side is Augustus Caesar, driving Italians into battle with senators and people, with domestic and great gods, standing on the high stern, whose felicitous temples spew out twin flames and his father's star opens from his peak.

Augustus unifies the Roman state (SPQ with *Romanus* elided) with divine and cosmic order, conveyed by the ranks of gods and the star. The comet of his adopted father "Julian star" (*sidus Iulium*) confirms the succession of his line and folds the Julian lineage into state and cosmos.

The radiant light projecting from his head, combined with the *sidus Iulium*, encodes civil war but also hides it at the same time. The light links Augustus to the Julian line; light and flames shed from the top of Iulus' head likewise portend his line to come (2.682–4); Romulus' head, like Augustus', gives off "twin crests" (*geminae cristae*, 6.779). The leader's iconic representation is repeated when Aeneas returns to camp from his embassy to Evander, leading the Tuscan allies in book 10, holding the gleaming shield on which Augustus looks like Aeneas himself in a *mise en abyme*.[142] Verbal repetition marks Aeneas' position "standing on the high stern" (*stans celsa in puppi* 10.261) and the description of the light streaming from his head: *ardet apex capiti cristisque a vertice flamma / funditur* ("the crown of his head shines and flame pours from summit in crests," 10.270). This parallel grounds the claim that Aeneas functions as the contemporary leader's mythic analogue in the poem, but the parallel to the crests on Romulus' head also reinscribes civil war: The two Julians who actually

---

[141] Lowrie (2015c).
[142] For this famous parallel and the *sidus Iulium* (Julian star), Binder (1971) 224–30; here 226.

engaged in civil disorder – Romulus, who killed his twin (8.631), and Augustus at Actium – are distinguished with twin lights.[143]

The ensuing simile, comparing the light emanating from Aeneas' head to comets, corresponds to the *sidus Iulium* above Augustus. Rather than indicating renewal and divine sanction, the blood-red comets are ominous. Furthermore, continued comparison to Sirius specifies the star's baleful influence.[144]

> non secus ac liquida si quando nocte cometae
> sanguinei lugubre rubent, aut Sirius ardor
> ille sitim morbosque ferens mortalibus aegris
> nascitur et laevo contristat lumine caelum.   10.272–5

> Not otherwise than if at some point in the limpid sky bloody comets redden in mourning or the famous ardor of Sirius is born, bringing drought and illnesses to sick mortals, saddens the sky with ill-omened light.

Metaphorically, the celestial portents target body and soul, bringing drought and illness, mourning and sadness. The only other Vergilian comets portend civil war (*Georgics* 1.488): The twin battles of Pharsalus and Philippi come two lines later.[145] A portent of civil war shines over Augustus as he rides the ship of state into Actium. Discord lurks in this image of Augustus. To all appearances, the shield tells a story of "violence ultimately leading to peace."[146] The heartbreak of civil war emerges only through an archaeology of reading, forward to book 10 and backward to the *Georgics*.

The image of Augustus sacrificing and receiving tribute from conquered nations, after riding into Rome in the triple triumph (8.714), evokes civil war specifically and the collapse of the social bond generally. The "slaughtered bullocks" (*caesi iuvenci*, 8.719) here recall the *Georgics'* first, abject description of *bugonia*, where perverted sacrifice mars the slaughter of bullocks (*caesis . . . iuvencis*, 4.284) in Egypt.[147] As we argue in Chapter 2, *bugonia* fails to placate broad justice, encoded in Eurydice's name. The bullocks of the *bugonia* in turn recall the impious slaughter and consumption of oxen in the fall from the Saturnian age (*caesis . . . iuvencis*, *Georgics* 2.537). If Augustus is inaugurating a new golden age, this one does not include a vegetarian diet and fully embraces the militarism excluded from Saturn's reign (*Georgics* 2.539–40).

---

[143] Servius at 1.292 records an ancient interpretation that Romulus tried to placate the shades of the brother he slew by making everything twinned, hence his twin crests at 6.779.

[144] Boyle (1986) 92–3.

[145] For comets as signs of civil war, Tracy (2014) 256–7; for ambivalence, Pandey (2018) 35–82.

[146] Putnam (1965) 150. The rest of the book takes us back to violence.

[147] For impiety in the sacrifice of oxen as a leitmotif, Boyle (1986) 81, Dyson (1996), Keith (2018).

The shield stresses sacrifice, which shatters the bond between animals and humans at the fall into history, and the imperial domination of other peoples. These stand generally for the societal rifts characterizing post-Saturnian history. Reference to three hundred temples evokes a civil war battle more specifically. The number is inflated, consolidating all the temples consecrated by Augustus during his reign – by contrast Augustus' *Res gestae* identifies twelve. Three hundred, however, was the traditional number of knights and senators young Caesar slaughtered at Perusia.[148]

The image of Augustus receiving tribute encodes civil war's solution as empire in the guise of oriental tyranny. He appears as a new Priam, that is, an oriental king. He fixes the gifts of conquered peoples on his "proud door-posts" (*superbis postibus*, 8.721–2), just like the "doorposts, proud with barbarian gold and spoils" (*barbarico postes auro spoliisque superbi*, 2.504) of Priam's palace.[149] Pride marks tyranny at Rome since Tarquinius Superbus. The Araxes' chafing at being bridged (*indignatus*, 8.728) looks back to Fury's containment in the Gates of War and forward to Turnus' soul, descending indignant to the underworld (*indignata*, 12.952). The battle of Actium has brought Roman history full circle, back to Troy, back to the early kingship that had to be exiled for the Republic to be founded. History repeats, as foretold in *Eclogue* 4, before the golden age may return.

Augustus has no mate in the *Aeneid* to indicate his relationship to the body politic. In overcoming Cleopatra at Actium, he presumably sets marriage right. Her illicit marriage to Antony violates divine law: *(nefas) Aegyptia coniunx* ("execrable! his Egyptian wife," 8.688). By defeating the pair, Augustus eradicates a bad model for marriage. Nevertheless, doing so wages discord in the family. In the received story, he kills Caesarion, Caesar's illegitimate male scion. Therefore, fighting Cleopatra (his posthumously adopted stepmother-out-of-law?) was as much a family affair as fighting Antony, his erstwhile brother-in-law, before he left Augustus' sister Octavia for Cleopatra.[150] These entanglements, silent in the poem, were widely known.

Augustus' mythic progenitor also figures civil discord subtly through deficient family ties. Aeneas never has a happy marriage himself. However much he grieves for Creusa, he neglected her – patrilineage took priority,

---

[148] Dyson (1996) 284–5. Lange (2019) argues that Augustus' autobiography mentioned this event with a focus on clemency, as in Appian (*B Civ.* 5.48–49); Cassius Dio (48.14.3–6), by contrast, emphasizes slaughter.

[149] Fowler (1990) 50–2 explores "deviant focalization" in these passages. The text, however, gives the figuration to read regardless of point of view; Oliensis (2001) 44–5 and (2009).

[150] Boyle (1999) 158: Naming Antony risks disintegrating the shield's conceptual framework (civilized versus barbaric, etc.).

so Creusa found refuge with the Magna Mater. His affair with Dido comes in the guise of a marriage both perverted and rejected. His eventual wife Lavinia is a cipher. She blushes at Turnus' declaration of passion, but the poem withholds her feelings and depicts no love on her part.[151] The blush, however, reveals more than emotion.

> Indum sanguineo veluti violaverit ostro
> si quis ebur, aut mixta rubent ubi lilia multa
> alba rosa, talis virgo dabat ore colores.   12.67–9

> As if someone stained Indian ivory with blood-colored crimson or white lilies mixed with many a rose grew red, such colors did the maiden give in her face.

Double similes convey excessive meaning. A red-and-white contrast conventionally signals eroticism in Latin poetry.[152] Additionally, an orientalist and imperial touch marks the young woman who plants Aeneas' line in Italian soil. The Roman race sprung of this marriage will shed much blood, whose luxurious crimson color infuses exotic Indian ivory in the language of violation. The intimation of a virgin's defloration, never touched by her first fiancé, pales in perversion before her mother's passionate declaration she cannot live without him. When Amata – who bears a "strange love" (*miro amore*, 7.57) for Turnus[153] – commits suicide, because she thinks he cannot survive, the love story turns incestuous.[154] Whether orientalized Lavinia or the fully Trojan Iulus becomes the ancestor of the Julian line, orientalism will stain Rome's future either way.

On Aeneas' shield, this civil war battle is waged between East and West, between Cleopatra and Augustus. Stress on Egypt and Antony's eastern allies underscores the clear antithesis: "Egypt and the strength of the orient, and furthest Bactra" (*Aegyptum virisque Orientis et ultima . . . Bactra*, 8.687–8).[155] Similar antitheses elsewhere stress the divide. The Trojan war, emblem of conflict between Europe and Asia (*Europae atque Asiae*, 7.224), is the type replayed on Italian soil in the poem's second half and replayed again at Actium on the shield. These antitheses reinforce Rome's Western identity. If the intention behind presenting Actium as a battle between Rome and the East

---

[151] On the indeterminacy of Lavinia's feelings, Johnson (1976) 56–8. Fowler (1987) 190–1; virgin – male and female – blood, spilt in death, frequently replaces marriage in the *Aeneid* (193–8). Thomas (1998) 294–5: Turnus, whom love disturbs, focalizes her blush; passion unambiguously directed at Turnus belongs to her mother.

[152] Oliensis (1997) 308: "a symbolic deflowering."   [153] Mitchell (1991) 223.

[154] Fantham (1989) compares Amata to Hecuba, whose plea to her son Hector lacks the eroticism of Amata's plea to her preferred son-in-law.

[155] Gurval (1995); Lange (2009) 79–93.

was to hide the reality of conflict between Romans, the obfuscation is turned on its head as both sides are colored Asian. Augustus was first identified as "Trojan" (1.286), so that the antithesis between him and his civil enemy appears less than Antony's Bacchic associations would suggest.[156]

A similar dynamic plays out in Juno's insistence on the eradication of Trojan traces within Roman identity. This structurally puts Rome's ostensibly Eastern origins under erasure, so that a purely Western Rome emerges – at least in theory. Oriental language and dress, the marks of Trojan culture, are to disappear at Rome, and so they do. Their elision in myth allows the East/West divide, as in the shield's depiction of Actium, to appear in more antithetical terms than warranted. But Rome's Trojan origins are anyway a historical phantasm. We interpret their creation and erasure as a joint figuration that first recognizes, then externalizes the abject within the self. In Vergil, the presentation of civil war as if it were a foreign conflict masks the crime, but in a further twist, unmasks the gesture of masking. This is the paradoxical gesture of the inner orient.[157] Like all repressions, Rome's (fictive) oriental origins return symptomatically: in institutions – the *lusus Troiae* (5.596–603) and the *penates'* establishment in Vesta's temple – and in the bloodline the same *penates* represent.[158]

Just as Rome must continually erase its oriental nature, so must it overcome discord again and again. Passion in the *Aeneid* only temporarily abates. Juno, whose demonic anger drives the plot and stands for the collapse of the social bond, is only temporarily reconciled to Rome in book 12. The literary history of her reconciliation suggests she must be appeased over and over again.[159] She is signally absent among the Olympians fighting on the Roman side against Cleopatra. Where does she stand: with Antony or with Augustus? or against Rome in its entirety, yet again?

Rome Ever Imperial

Rome in Lucan's *De bello civili* is already imperial, but still, no end to civil war lies in sight. The poem notoriously ends without completion or closure.[160] Although scholars have tried to reconstruct the poem's narrative

---

[156] Mac Góráin (2013) 143–4.   [157] Vinken (2015b).   [158] Lowrie (2005) 971–6.

[159] Feeney (1984): Juno must be reconciled to Rome repeatedly across Latin literature, here when the Trojans are assimilated into Italy; in Horace 3.3 at the time of Quirinus' apotheosis; and in Ennius, according to his reconstruction, again during the Punic wars.

[160] Masters (1992) 216–59: Lucan's poem ends at the same point as Caesar's commentary, a remarkable coincidence that suggests the poem's incompletion mirrors its major source; the poem's ending reflects civil war's "endlessness."

scope, asking when and if Lucan planned to stop his civil war, the existing poem does not anticipate either historical or poetic resolution. A Pompeian soldier's question to Cato, *nam quis erit finis, si nec Pharsalia pugnae, nec Pompeius erit* ("For what end will there be to the fight, if there is neither Pharsalus nor Pompey," 9.232–3), pertains as much to the poem as to civil war itself.[161] Whatever Lucan's plan, the last act in the poem is Caesar's backward glance to Scaeva, and Pompey's name returns to get the last word: *Magnum* ("Magnus," 10.546).[162] These gestures refer the reader back into the poem, preventing any motion forward to resolution. The lack of closure means civil war is not imagined as ever being overcome. We are skeptical the poem's putatively missing conclusion would say anything not already well expressed in the extant text.

The poet's invocation to Nero as Muse and declaration that the civil wars were all worth it, if Nero could come no other way, proclaim the value of empire (1.33–66), but this passage's interpretation is fraught. The standard way of evading the panegyric, which counters the poem's hyperbolically pessimistic tone, is to take it ironically.[163] However, if Lucan wanted to praise Nero for keeping civil war at bay, he could have said so directly. Instead, civil war remains in view. Irony is not needed. The words' literal meaning argues against any imputation of a lasting, Augustan peace. Nero's reign does nothing but continue Roman history as before. The poem details Pharsalus and the civil war battles, down to Actium, that occur after the poem's conclusion, but the last two items listed reverse their historical order. Reference to Actium (31 BCE) precedes battle with Sextus Pompey, armed by slaves in Sicily (36 BCE): *quas premit aspera classes / Leucas et ardenti servilia bella sub Aetna* ("fleets which harsh Leucas defeated and the slave wars under burning Aetna," 1.42–3). Even in word order, history goes backward. No intervening Julio-Claudian history is mentioned. The poem pivots to Nero's future apotheosis.[164] Only at that point – emphatically after Nero's death – is the hope voiced that peace may break out on Earth.

> tum genus humanum positis sibi consulat armis
> inque vicem gens omnis amet; pax missa per orbem
> ferrea belligeri conpescat limina Iani.   1.60–2

---

[161] Stover (2008) 571; he endorses Cato's suicide as the intended end to civil war and poem together.
[162] Lowrie (2015d).   [163] Tarrant (2012) 24–5, but see Konstan (2018).
[164] Schrempp (1964): Lucan covers no historical events between Actium and Nero and refers the Julian house back to the originators of civil war (87). Although Actium was the last civil war battle, it marked the end of Rome as the Romans knew it; after it came either iteration or reversion (56).

Then may the human race look to its advantage and lay down arms, and every people love mutually; may peace, spread across the world, close the iron threshold of warmongering Janus.

The temporal adverb *tum* sets peace after Nero's future ascent to heaven; the subjunctive sets it outside historical reality; the wish for the gates of Janus to close indicates that their closing by Augustus was only provisional.[165] After the call for Rome to direct her love of war to foreign theaters before turning a hand on herself (1.21–23), the distinction between internal and external warfare blurs in Lucan's dream of world peace. The mutual love among peoples is ambiguous: love for other peoples or among themselves? The Latin *invicem* (1.62) splits iconically in two – some divide within love ever remains. Indistinction gives plausible deniability, but the lack of an assertion that civil war ended at Actium contrasts with the explicit language available – for example, Augustus' own claim, *bella civilia extinxeram* ("I had extinguished the civil wars," *Res gestae* 34.1);[166] Tiberius' similar claim, *omnibus civilis belli sepultis malis* ("when all the evils of civil war had been buried," *Senatus consultum de Cn. Pisone patre* 47); and their echoes in Velleius Paterculus, *finita . . . bella civilia* ("the civil wars were finished," 2.89.3).[167] Ending war and, with it, civil war is only ever a wish projected into the future.[168] The end of war of any sort must await Nero's death. History in its irony brought civil war back, of course, in 69 CE.

Sacrifice/Suicide

If sacrifice heals the relations of gods and men and suicide upholds republican liberty, their degradation in Vergil and Lucan shows Rome unraveling. Perverted sacrifice inscribes civil war tropes into Rome's foundation. Suicide makes manifest the devastating consequences of civil war's eruption. Worse, suicide infuses sacrifice with its register and undoes its promise. Sacrifice's failure indicates more than mere human weakness or depravity before the sacred; civil war resides in the corruption of divine order itself. In Vergil, the gods do not merely fight among themselves over Rome's foundation, Jupiter prolongs battle among men without cause. Letting Fate find its way (10.105–13), he abdicates divine responsibility. In Lucan, theodicy goes downhill: The gods themselves demand our slaughter as their holocaust.

---

[165] Lange (2009) 156–7. [166] Cooley (2009) 98–9, 256–7. [167] Woodman (1983) 251.
[168] *Pax* shifts in meaning from pacification of foreign enemies to general stability regarding civil strife in the 40s BCE and becomes an Augustan mandate, Cornwell (2017).

Several strands unite to color Rome's foundation in the death of Turnus not only as a perverted sacrifice, as has been well established, but also as a metaphorical suicide. These tropes inscribe civil war into Rome's very foundation. Vergil's technique is to build up detailed type-scenes earlier in the poem, so that economical reference backward compresses and layers meaning. The result is a consistent tropological register. Dido's death sets up sacrifice's perversion through suicide, a motif that keeps returning in the text. The magical ceremony to expiate love, "strange rites" (*novis ... sacris*, 4.500), screens Dido's suicide at the plot level and figures it as a ritual act bringing not the restoration of sacrifice, but abject and deathly birth (above, pp. 103–5). These rites have their own priestess who inverts life into death: The dragon-feeding, deadly-herb-collecting witch comes in the guise of Medea. The love story of a powerful girl who kills nearest and dearest, brother and children, informs both Dido and the priestess.[169] Her black magic symbolically reverses creation with de-creation. The gods worshipped invert life with death. Diana, goddess of childbirth, appears in her triple aspect as Luna and Hecate (4.511). Dido's vengeance is figured as a child of night and death. The magic rites are an oxymoron: What should restore and give new life instead spawns death and destruction, "Erebus and Chaos" (4.510).

Dido's suicide lands on Italian soil in Amata.[170] Leitmotifs from book 4 return of a second queen to reinforce the structural parallel: Line-initial *at regina* ("but the queen," 4.1, 296, 504; 12.54); *moritura* ("soon to die," 4.308, 415, 519, 604; 12.55); *infelix* ("unhappy/infertile," 4.68, 450, 529, 596; 12.598).[171] Amata also is subject to Juno's plots: Cupid was sent to Dido, Allecto to Amata. Allecto's phallic sexuality engenders another perverse pregnancy. The "deathly, raging venom of the snake," plucked from the Fury's hair, which slithers under her clothes, between her smooth breasts, and all over her body (7.349–53), "penetrates deep into her innards" (*penitusque in viscera lapsum / serpentis furiale malum*, 7.374–5). The mania she conceives drives her in a Bacchic register, like Dido, all over her city (*per urbem*, 4.300; 12.377). Both dissimulate rites: Dido hides her preparations for suicide under a magical ritual; Amata pretends her madness is inspired by Bacchus. The latter's frenzy sets off a chain of events that do not lead her to rip off her own son's head, like her analogue Agave, but prove just as deadly to the young man she adores. Her fierce love, of a potential son-in-law, has incestuous undertones. Where Dido and

---

[169] Spence (1999) 87–8.   [170] Dido's avatars are legion: Oliensis (2001) 47.
[171] Fantham (1989) 140, 144. Tarrant (2012) at 12.598.

Aeneas pervert Diana's and Apollo's fraternal love, Amata's passion violates a relation whose perversion has connoted civil war since Pompey and Caesar. Amata and Dido both die "overcome by pain" (*evicta dolore*, 4.474; *turbata dolore*, 12.599; both line-end). Although neither's city falls in the moment, the text imagines enemies let in, roofs burning, at both women's suicides (4.669–70; 12.595–6).

Dido and Amata add a heterosexual layer to the typological lead-up to Turnus' death. They complement the series of beautiful young men, whose death before their time prepares for the climactic scene's homoerotic valence.[172] Turnus' figurative defloration, which substitutes for Lavinia's wedding night, colors the foundational act as rape. Overtones of sacrifice and suicide further stain the scene. Pallas' baldric, *infelix* like Dido and Amata ("unhappy/infertile," 12.941), which Turnus wears as the strange fruit of his own paradoxically "penetrable weapon" (*penetrabile telum*, 10.481),[173] depicts the Greek Danaids, who kill their husbands, the sons of Aegyptus, on their wedding night.[174] The ecphrasis makes an analogy between Turnus and the tragic slaughter of the ephebe before marriage. Turnus's homoerotic rape surpasses such horror. Aeneas drives his sword into his chest, penetrating Pallas' baldric, which lies across his shoulder. Wearing Pallas' armor, Turnus substitutes for him. Aeneas' love for Pallas is perverted into a deadly rape. Turnus' "limbs melt," not with the heat of passion, but the "coldness" of death (*solvuntur frigore membra*, 12.951); he groans, not in pleasure but in pain (*gemitu*, 12.952).[175] If the ephebe's slaughter turns life into death, if the homosexual register suggests sterility, heterosexual allusion to Dido intimates the monstrous fertility of a deadly birth.[176] A *balteus* was worn not just by soldiers, but women.[177] Rome is born from this fruitless rape as monstrous abjection. If Dido's suicide spawns the enmity on which Rome built an empire, then Turnus' death, following on Amata's, figuratively engenders civil war. Empire, in Sallust's analysis, plants the seeds of civil war, but civil war yields empire as its fruit.

---

[172] For the intersection of murder, sacrifice, and defloration and the connection between marriage and politics here, Mitchell (1991). Male fury has a feminine hue, Syed (2005) 116–35. Quint (2018) presses typological reading systematically.

[173] Servius notes the reversal from the expected *penetrale* (penetrating). Mac Góráin (2016) 410–11.

[174] Spence (1991); Putnam (1994) and (1998) 169–207.

[175] Parallel to Aeneas, whose "limbs dissolve from cold" (*solvuntur frigore membra*, 1.92) in the storm. Contrast the pleasing sleep Vulcan seeks and finds "through his limbs" upon "pouring himself" into his wife's lap (*placidum petivit / coniugis infusus gremio per membra soporem*, 8.405–6).

[176] Oliensis (1997) traces gender indistinction and crossed homo- and heterosexual roles in Vergil.

[177] Ovid, *Met.* 9.189 (Amazons); Lucan, 2.362 (Cato's wife); Mart. 14.207 (Venus). The cutting of soldiers' baldrics results in abject civil slaughter, Tac. *Hist.* 2.88.

Yet again, the Egyptian other, in the ecphrasis of the baldric, encodes the internal enemy.

Perverted sacrifice in the poem's climactic scene stresses on another register the impossibility of overcoming civil war. As with the sexual and Egyptian overtones, human sacrifice returns, compressed from earlier scenes. Aeneas took human captives to sacrifice in honor of Pallas (*immolet*, 10.519); in short order, his sacrificing a priest heaps on perversion (*immolat*, 10.541). Aeneas kills Turnus, next in the procession of victims, with the same verb: *immolat* ("immolate," 12.949).[178] The figure comes as traumatic repetition compulsion not just in the poem, but also in history. The slaughter of *equites* and senators at Perusia sets the figuration of civil war as perverted sacrifice on a recent historical basis.[179]

Suicide further corrupts the already perverted sacrifice, heaping on yet another civil war figuration. Numerous parallels make Turnus Aeneas' metaphorical twin, not least in that both play Achilles.[180] When he kills his twin, Aeneas enacts *avant la lettre* Romulus' foundational murder of Remus. But suicide also overlays fratricide in the text. Both Aeneas and Turnus appear as Pallas.[181] Turnus wears his baldric and suffers in turn a similar fate from another penetrating weapon. In his rage, an internal division within the soul, Aeneas channels Pallas, whom he declares the agent of this vengeful sacrifice. In striking the blow, Pallas strikes his own baldric, namely his own image. Pallas, the native son from the site of Rome, returns in Aeneas, only to die all over again, this time at his own hand. Underscoring his simultaneous active and passive positions, Pallas' name resounds three times in succession, as victim and as perpetrator of violence (12.943, 12.948 twice).

This metaphorical suicide has many resonances with the Iliadic scene where Achilles, who kills the image of himself when he kills Hector wearing his armor, exacts vengeance on himself for Patroclus' death. The homoerotic love of Achilles for Patroclus echoes in the man crush Pallas feels for Aeneas, which replays the crush Pallas' father Evander

---

[178] For perverted sacrifice in this foundational scene and throughout the *Aeneid*: Bandera (1981); O'Hara (1990); Hardie (1993) 19–35; Dyson (2001) 112–24, 191–2, 226–7; Tarrant (2012) 21–2, 26, and at 12.947–9. Contemporary Romans found human sacrifice horrific, so the argument that sacrificial language here sanctifies the death neglects the human victim.

[179] Thomas (2000) 404–5: Aeneas' human sacrifices evoke Perusia.

[180] Thomas (1998). Quint (2011) = (2018) 1–27: "The exchange of identities between Aeneas and Turnus, the sense that Aeneas defeats and kills a version of himself, evokes again Virgil's experience of a barely finished, *if* finished, civil war" (288; 18).

[181] Mac Góráin (2016) 419 examines homoerotic narcissism here; also (2018) 150, with overlays of Pentheus (2013) 142.

once felt for Aeneas' father Anchises. Erotic language colors Pallas' corpse as Aeneas gazes on it and weeps.[182] Love and responsibility fuel Aeneas' rage. But where Achilles' vengeance on himself recognizes his personal responsibility for the death of the one he held most dear and catalyzes the fall of Troy, the *Aeneid* inscribes Aeneas' psychic disturbance and the internal division of his soul into Rome's own foundation. The reverberations of his act bring down not an enemy city, but Rome itself.[183] Even his hesitation, which redeems him in Servius' eyes, splits his soul.[184] The external fire and fury that destroys Troy in book 2 is internalized in Aeneas and the city he founds.

Aeneas buries his sword in Turnus' breast with the verb *condere*, providing ring composition with the epic's beginning: *tantae molis erat Romanam condere gentem* ("such a labor it was to found the Roman race," 1.33); *ferrum adverso sub pectore condit* ("he buried his sword in the breast against him," 12.950).[185] The patriarchal, war-loving Roman race is birthed here. Multiple registers layer civil war tropes over each other. These tropes derive from Rome's history of civil war, but the poem, set in the mythic past, projects them forward to be literalized in the history from which they derive. Lucan takes Vergil's foundational suicide out from under cover and declares openly that the Roman people enacted suicide on their own body politic: *populum ... / in sua victrici conversum viscera dextra* ("a people turned on its own bowels with victorious right hand," 1.3). This image conjoins the same set of metaphors as in Vergil: perverse love, the unholy, and empire's intimate entanglement with civil war.

> Tum, si tantus amor belli tibi, Roma, nefandi
> totum sub Latias leges cum miseris orbem,
> in te verte manus: nondum tibi defuit hostis.   1.21–3

If you have so great a love of unholy war, Rome, turn your hand against yourself only then when you have put the whole world under Latin laws: you had not yet run out of enemies.

Paradoxically, Lucan's wish that civil war follow on the exhaustion of imperial foes valorizes Rome's suicide, despite warding it off. He suggests civil war was premature but acknowledges its inevitability. Vergil already shows it was endemic to Rome.

---

[182] Parallels with Dido reinforce the eroticism. Gillis (1983); Putnam (1985) 5–14; Mitchell (1991) 221; Reed (2007).
[183] For the political psychology of Aeneas' fury, Lowrie (forthcoming b).   [184] Boyle (1999) 156.
[185] James (1995).

De bello civili makes the *Aeneid*'s tropes readable by separating out historical layers and metaphorical registers. The old man's speech in book 2 spells out civil war's eternal return. Exemplary history (*exempla*, 2.67) entails repetition. The horrors of Marius and Sulla now return again: "these things remain to be suffered again" (*haec rursus patienda manent*, 2.223).[186] Discrete images make the breakdown of social and bodily order vivid and easily readable. They bear a symbolic weight apart from any narrative determination; social rank inverts when senators lay down the purple to disguise themselves in plebeian mufti (2.18–19); bodily integrity dissolves through *sparagmos* (2.119–21); laying a cut head on festive banquet tables undoes social and ritual order (2.123). These details come in rapid succession without any organization according to the plot. The different standard civil war tropes separate out, each distinct, in a list: fratricide and familial inversion (2.148–51); the inversion of life and death, humans and beasts (2.152–3); suicide (2.154–9); indistinction (2.166–8); human sacrifice, exacerbated by repetition (2.126–8), by dismemberment and torture (2.173–80). The pinnacle is Pompey's headless corpse on the shore, which stands for civil war already in Vergil: *informes veniunt ad litora trunci / qui medio periere freto* ("shapeless trunks of those who perished in the channel come to shore," 2.189–90).[187] Lucan spells out and rhetorically pumps up each Vergilian image and register one by one. The disfiguration of Deiphobus in *Aeneid* 6, succinctly described in two lines (496–7), returns of Marius Gratidianus, now expanded to eight with hyperbolically gruesome detail (2.177–85). Gender is also marked out in women's and men's separate laments (2.38–42, 45–63). A fully elaborated, nearly conceptual clarity pulls apart the terse and dense compression of Turnus' death, where the overlay of multiple figurations on his broken body politic creates a depth of discomfort whose full impact requires time to sink in. The elements of Lucan's horror hit the reader individually, in marching order.

The old man's speech provides a didactic introduction to a host of civil war's tropes in *De bello civili*, book 2. Lucan furthermore uses a Vergilian overlay of suicide and sacrifice to subtle effect. In the suicide of Vulteius and his men, a sacrificial register shows suicide to be a perversion of *pietas*. Authorial commentary marks suicide as a trope for civil war: "They enacted the unspeakable unholiness of warfare on one side" (*totumque in partibus unis / bellorum fecere nefas*, 4.548–9). The plural of "one" wittily inscribes internal division. A simile comparing their force to that with which brothers kill brothers and a son his father, where holy duty (*pietas*) requires

---

[186] Henderson (1998) 177: Sulla is "(a) Caesar *avant la lettre.*"   [187] Mebane (2016).

a single swift blow (2.562–5), piles on the fratricide/parenticide trope overtly, and their perverted love of Caesar yet another (*amoris*, 4.502). The scene additionally intimates human sacrifice. The soldiers show not only *fides* but *pietas* to Caesar by falling on their swords *pro te* ("for you," 4.497–501), as if he were a god. If the object of *pietas* is family, country, and gods, then Caesar usurps the latter two positions.

Multiple perversions of sacrifice foreshadow Cato's suicide, which looms over the poem, despite not being narrated. No other suicide figures the death of the Republic's body politic to such a degree. Cato joins the civil war in defense of personified Libertas, already an "empty shadow" (*inanem umbram*, 2.303) of her full republican self, so that his absent suicide turns out to be additionally futile. With no possibility of escaping guilt, the only freedom remaining is to wage civil war – which crowds out the entire public sphere – or to hate (*data libertas odiis*, 2.145). Cato's wish to die in a *devotio* like the Decii's salvific self-sacrifice in battle confronts the reader's knowledge that his actual death in suicide marks the end of republican liberty. It furthermore fails to save the state from devolving once again (and then some) into civil war. His thwarted desire for expiation instead reveals the breakdown of relations between gods and Romans. The logic of sacrificial substitution, of giving *unum pro toto*, falls before the total dedication of all Roman blood to war, his own included. Expiation by death in battle, as in suicide, purges nothing, but only gluts the gods' appetite for slaughter.

> sic eat: inmites Romana piacula divi
> plena ferant, nullo fraudemus sanguine bellum.   2.304–5

> So may it go: may the harsh gods take Rome's propitiatory sacrifices to repletion; let us defraud the war of no blood.

Like Turnus' death, Cato's layers civil war tropes over each other. Where the *Aeneid* predicts inevitable and recurrent civil war with its inscription into a perverted sacrifice, the futility of sacrifice in *De bello civili* proclaims civil war's pervasive nature. No longer, as in Vergil, a ritual tragically undone, that brings on what it would avert, sacrificial suicide in Lucan is nothing more than a figure of despair. No hope for salvation exists to begin with, such that sacrifice makes sense as a ritual to be perverted.

Corrupted sacrifice in Vergil and Lucan alike shows there is something rotten in the relations between gods and mortals and, worse, in the divine order itself. The gods in the *Aeneid* themselves wage civil war against each other; Jupiter frames their dissention as civil discord when he fails to persuade Venus and Juno to resolve their enmity in divine council (*discordia*, 10.9, 106). Their championship inflicts pain on their own: Aeneas suffers in love from Venus' machinations; Allecto, roused by Juno, wreaks psychic havoc on Juno's own favorites, Amata and Turnus.[188] Whatever the collateral damage, the goddesses aim at least for one or the other people to prevail. To that extent, their discord mirrors human discord. The terrifying Dira – yet another twin[189] – Jupiter sends against Turnus at least serves as a horrific means to an apparently justified end.

By contrast, the disturbance of nature in Lucan is generalized tumult. It assaults cosmic order without partisanship. If the gods protect one side – not divine favor but anger shields Marius (2.85–6) – they do so without *fides* (2.17), only to exact further damage. The gods work as a collective rather than act as individual characters. Their wrath thereby stirs the plot not by taking sides, but by universal disruption. The legal terms marking the signs of disruption expand human politics into the cosmos.

> iamque irae patuere deum manifestaque belli
> signa dedit mundus legesque et foedera rerum
> praescia monstrifero vertit natura tumultu
> indixitque nefas.   2.1–4

> And now the wrath of the gods was manifest and the world gave open signs of war and foreknowing nature overturned the laws and treaties of things with monster-bearing tumult and declared unspeakable unholiness.

Whether the "parent of things" fixes causes for eternity or "chance holds mortal affairs" (2.7–14), no guiding providence oversees the destiny of the world, much less of Rome.

In Lucan, structuring contrasts, which maintain norms in the *Aeneid* as the standards by which to judge violation, dissolve. The result is a sense that no norms ever existed to pervert – everything, everywhere has always already been perverted. In Vergil's poem, the Punic wars are paradigmatic for just warfare and contrast with the forbidden wars waged on Latin soil (10.11–15). In Lucan, the geographical span of the Empire's hostile borders reorients the conventional solution to civil war – directing inevitable violence outward – from the Augustan mission of bringing peace and the rule of law to conquered peoples (*Georgics* 4.562; *Aeneid* 1.293) toward generalized warfare throughout the globe. In a topsy-turvy prayer, Roman men voice the gods' perversity (2.45–63). They beg for the only mercy imaginable, from a divine "parent" assumed

---

[188] For Allecto as a figure of discord, not just madness, Heinze (1993) 148–50; Fantham (1989) 138.
[189] Johnson (1976) 129.

to be "cruel" (*saeve parens*, 2.59). The only way to prevent parochial civil war is universal enmity – *omnibus hostes / reddite nos populis: civile avertite bellum* ("make us rightly the enemies to all peoples: avert civil war," 2.52–3). The prayer undoes any distinction between leaders; neither (*neuter*) should achieve dominion. Even the object of imperial rule is perverted here; whoever wins would "command the city" (*imperet urbi*, 2.61), not the world (*orbi*). Since the gods are bent on destroying Hesperia, they should exercise agency and do it the right way, by Stoic *ekpyrosis* (2.56–60), rather than deploy civil war with men as their tools. The gods themselves pervert the right relation of ends and means, so that the norms presumed can rest on no stable locus.

Cosmic collapse in *De bello civili* surpasses even Ovid's gigantomachy, where the gods fight humankind.[190] Lucan envisions a cruel divine order bent on a holocaust of self-destruction. Human worship does no better: women in throngs accost the gods' ears, which expect prayer, with violence equaling what they would avert (*feriunt*, 2.32–3); gore fouls the temples (2.103); exacting vengeance violates justice (2.110). Every twist of phrase highlights perversity in every relation and inscribes civil war's corruption into every act. His own prayer for *salus* (safety) and Concordia, for the rectification of the "world's sacred love" (4.190–1) is merely foil to heartbreak when the temporary peace fails once more. Small wonder then that Augustine condemns Roman religion and sweeps Rome's gods together with Babylon's. Instead of protecting humanity, the city, and the world with love, they achieve total destruction through civil war.

The Poetics of Empire

Vergil imagines his epic's immortality as depending on the Roman Empire's longevity.[191] He and Lucan link their poems inextricably to their respective Julian protagonist.

> Fortunati ambo! si quid mea carmina possunt,
> nulla dies umquam memori vos eximet aevo,
> dum domus Aeneae Capitoli immobile saxum
> accolet imperiumque pater Romanus habebit.   *Aeneid* 9.446–9

> Fortunate both! If my songs have any power, no day will ever remove you from a mindful age, while the house of Aeneas will dwell on the immovable rock of the Capitoline and the Roman father will hold empire.[192]

---

[190] Johnson (2008).
[191] Quint (2018) 105 n. 49 notes the conditional eternity of Vergil's Roman Empire.
[192] Syed (2005) 215: Romanness expands here from blood descent to symbolic identification.

o sacer et magnus vatum labor! omnia fato
eripis et populis donas mortalibus aevum.
invidia sacrae, Caesar, ne tangere famae;
nam, siquid Latiis fas est promittere Musis,
quantum Zmyrnaei durabunt vatis honores,
venturi me teque legent; Pharsalia nostra
vivet, et a nullo tenebris damnabimur aevo.

De bello civili 9.980–6

O holy and great labor of bards! You snatch everything from death and give longevity to mortal peoples. Do not be touched, Caesar, by envy for your holy fame; for, if the gods give the right to promise anything for the Latin Muses, those to come will read me and you as long as the honors of the bard of Smyrna endure; our Pharsalia will live and we will be condemned to the shadows in no age.

Given the harsh assessment of the Roman Empire we have argued for in both poems and their ambivalence, if not downright hostility, toward their leading men, hitching their poems to the star of what they abhor seems surprising at best. They could have made their poems' aesthetic or moral worth the vehicle for immortality, but both actively choose a politically compromised bond.

In an earlier mode, Vergil deflects the political register, emphasizing rather how his future reader, "captivated by love," will hear his honorand's name sung out by the *Eclogues'* tamarisks and groves as he reads (*captus amore leget*, 6.10–11). By implication, the loveliness of his poetry suffices to attract readers. However, his love of his subject matter in the *Georgics* (3.285, 292) suggests even his poetry is as compromised by destructive passion as everything else in the world. A different choice operates here: The lovers, Nisus and Euryalus, are destroyed and he defines his poetry no longer in terms of love. Lucan, by calling Homer "the bard of Smyrna," evokes Catullus 95, a poem honoring his fellow poet, Cinna, for his epyllion *Zmyrna*: The centuries, gray with age, will read this poem because of its aesthetic beauty, in contrast to Volusius' *Annales*, slammed elsewhere for rusticity and coarseness (36). The citation highlights a contrast: Lucan chooses to define his poetics politically.

Why do both poets embrace what they apparently despise? No order exists outside the Roman Empire, set on its way by Aeneas and brought to ghastly fruition by Caesar. Vergil cannot imagine time outside the imperial and patriarchal rule of the Roman father. It would mean the end of history. In space, the citadel of Rome stands immovable. That his own poetic immortality depends on the time–space continuum of the political system in which he dwells implies he cannot sing his way out of it, nor even deflect its horror through poetry's beauty, as he thought when younger.

Vergil crowns with this statement one of his most pathos-laden episodes, the deaths of Nisus and Euryalus, where all values, imperial and loving alike, tragically backfire.[193] Their dutiful mission to bring back Aeneas and to win praise founders on an unnecessary detour, to slaughter, unheroically, the sleeping soldiers of a Latin camp. Euryalus does not obey orders to hold back but joins in the fray. Their shared love, remarkable and unique in this poem, unifies them in mutuality (*his amor unus erat pariterque in bella ruebant,* "to them there was one love and they rushed into battle as a pair," 9.182–3). Their sphere of mutuality is battle, a hint that love will destroy them. When Euryalus insists on joining the mission, overtones of Dido foreshadow impending doom: *mene ... fugis?* ("Do you flee me?" 9.199–200; 4.314). Nisus risks himself to save his love in a suicide mission that saves neither. When the poet declares the pair's good fortune because their names will live as long as his poem, he reveals the limits of good fortune in the Roman world. This empire, where love brings no hope, is one of perverse values. The lament of Euryalus' mother, following hard on this declaration's heels, gives the lie to their good fortune. The *Aeneid* itself is not immune from this devastating world. The poetry preserving the lament is underwritten by the very empire whose foundation cost life and love.

Lucan goes further in self-implication. His language joins him closely with Caesar. Both will be read (*me teque*); the poet's labor and Caesar's fame are both "holy" (*sacer, sacrae*); Pharsalia belongs to them together (*Pharsalia nostra,* 9.985–6). They are partners in crime. If Lucan has been created by the system established by Caesar, then his Caesar has likewise been created by him. Conjoined, they may not be condemned to obscurity's shadows, but the poem nevertheless sheds no light. Condemnation furthermore awaits both. Lucan condemns Caesar and, unbeknownst to him, will be in turn condemned by Caesar's heir.

For all the beauty and energy of their verse, Vergil and Lucan embrace a poetics that excoriates themselves as much as it does Rome.

---

[193] Reed (2007) 16–73.

CHAPTER 4

The Eternal City
Augustine, De civitate Dei

quod cuncta mala praecidit, bella illa civilia
... a thing which surpasses all evils, those Civil Wars

Augustine, De civitate Dei[1]

tristius ac perniciosius urbi Romae nihil umquam fuisse quam bella civilia satis notum est.

It is well known that nothing sadder or more destructive ever happened to the city of Rome than the civil wars.

Orosius, Historiae adversus paganos

In *De civitate Dei* (*CD*), Augustine lambasts pagan Rome with furious energy. If love is a positive criterion distinguishing the *civitas Dei*, based on love of God, from the *civitas terrena*, based on self-love, the negative criterion differentiating actual earthly cities – Rome, Babylon, Jerusalem – in their respective relations to the heavenly city is civil discord. Civil war occupies a central place in Augustine's hermeneutics of history.[2] In order to safeguard God's heavenly city from its logic, Augustine must better Vergil in several respects. If the Augustan peace sits on the cusp of a real future, the city of God is a real possibility in the present, although its full realization is deferred to the end of history. If the Augustan peace comes at the cost of an oriental empire, God's *civitas* must rest on a foundation of love. The traces of Rome, of civil war, however, are hard to eradicate. In his integrative mission, Augustine walks a tightrope. Like Vergil, he acknowledges the inevitability of civil war within history. His

---

[1] Citations in this chapter are marked as follows: book.chapter for Latin; page numbers from Dyson's (1998) English translation of *CD*. Translations are slightly revised for greater fidelity to the Latin.

[2] Brown (1972) 319: Augustine's political theory assumes political activity is "merely symptomatic," merely one way for men to express "orientations that lie far deeper in themselves." For love's centrality in Augustine's political thought, Cary (2005) 3–8, Weithman (2014) 232–3.

innovation is to imagine a better world that can be realized at least partially in the present.

The political genius of the Romans was to posit their city's exemplary status for universal imitation.[3] Augustine, rarely lacking sarcasm in tarnishing Roman splendor, systematically discredits the historical basis of Roman normativity.[4] He redirects our gaze from historical Rome, the city that was, to heavenly Jerusalem, the city to come.[5] The heavenly city is a parallel city, built in the heart, to which he makes a confession of faith. His description shifts Roman exemplarity to Christian typology.[6] The *CD* demotes Rome to an *ektypon*: against its shadow, the heavenly city shines as the *archetypon*.[7]

Retelling Roman history as a history saturated with civil war, Augustine overturns its exemplary status. He argues against two sets of adversaries with different agendas.[8] The pagans he calls *adversarii* saw Rome as preeminent in virtue; his fellow Christians have misunderstood Rome's role in God's plan.[9] History unfolds as it does because it is governed by God's providence, but the reasons ultimately remain "hidden for us" (18.22).[10] Augustine therefore reaches for the hermeneutic principles developed to make sense of scripture to make sense of history. Old Testament figurations are understood to be realized in the New Testament. An analogous structure informs his rewriting of Roman history and rewriting of Rome's place in history. His method, however, cannot eradicate Rome but depends on the fruits of its earthly glory to define what must be overcome. He needs Rome's horrors, and he needs Latin literature as the medium of their transmission. While his hermeneutics discards Rome as

---

[3] Cicero's *De re publica* 1.33–4: The Roman Republic has the best realizable constitution; Livy, *Pref.*: The greatest, most reverent, and richest in good examples.

[4] Also *Epistles* 154–5 to Macedonius, Dodaro (2012) 386–90. "A highly polemical version of Roman history," Weithman (2014) 239.

[5] Abandoning paganism compelled Augustine to enlarge his historical horizon and think in terms of universal history, Momigliano (1977 [1963]) 110.

[6] Cameron's (1999) 81–8 analysis of Augustine's Biblical exegesis shows how his thought shifted from the Roman model of exemplarity to a Christian model of transfiguration over time. Christology affects his theory of signs (90).

[7] Schürmann (1996) 290–306.

[8] For Augustine, the "real enemy" was not contemporary pagan historians; he therefore attacked the sources of contemporary antiquarianism, e.g., Varro, to undermine the "idealization of the Roman past," Momigliano (1977 [1963]) 123.

[9] A. Cameron (1977) 11–12 doubts Augustine and Orosius were writing against sustained pagan historical works. Augustine's contribution to the debate was to refute paganism through their own history. His narrative reveals his "deeply personal and sometimes eccentric reflections on Roman history." A letter from the aristocratic pagan Volusianus prompted immediate response and sustained answer in *CD* (*Epistles* 135, 137, 138), M. Cameron (2012) 3–5.

[10] Weithman (2014) 244.

an instrument to bring about God's will, his *De civitate Dei* depends on its traditions for his own language, his own rhetoric. Small wonder then that he wages verbal war so fiercely against it.

In *CD*, Rome, complete with its civil wars, occupies a special place in God's plan as the historical city most exemplary of love's failure. Within the *civitas terrena*, Rome's *libido dominandi* (lust for domination) perverts the right kind of love and, with it, the right kind of politics. Retelling its history this way – perennial civil war, based on a misguided conception of virtue – discloses Rome's true nature from a Christian perspective. This first gesture belongs to the diatribe against the pagans. A second gesture, directed toward the debate among Christians, dramatically redefines Rome's providential purpose. The Roman Empire is denied its typical role as the vehicle for disseminating Christianity. Rome fits into God's plan not as means to an end, but rather as the *civitas Dei*'s negative antitype. If Jerusalem prefigures the heavenly city in a typological relation of *figura* and *implementum*, Rome comes not as a *figura*, but a dark *umbra* that systematically perverts all right relations and institutions.[11] Rome has a place in the world, but not one the Romans imagined; it sustains the divine plan, but not as other Christians understood.

Augustine admired Latin literature and loved to hate it: He emulated it to overcome its shortcomings and strove to replace it with something new and better.[12] Emphatically within the Roman tradition,[13] Augustine attacks Rome's virtues as perverse on their own terms, before demonstrating their inadequacy as precursors to Christian love. Classical Rome stands for him as the preeminent model of everything wrong with the world; retelling its history as a history of civil war globalizes this model for all secular history. His debate with Eusebius about Rome's role in God's plan defines the parameters for *translatio Romae* henceforth. Is Rome a blind, but

---

[11] On the mutuality of promise and fulfillment in *figura* and *implementum*, Cameron (1999) 94; *Contra Faustum* extends figurative interpretation to any text (95). For Rome as *umbra*, Hawkins (1975) 100.

[12] Earl (1967) 126–7: Augustine starts from "traditional Roman definitions" then, by importing a "theological consideration," turns the definition "on the Romans' heads," in an attempt "not to destroy the Roman tradition but to convert it." His terminology builds on Roman political and social terms, "hence the violence of his redefinitions." Stock (1996) 4. O'Donnell (2000) 227: Ambrose and Augustine both Christianized Cicero; *CD*'s style and range of reference are "deliberately traditionalist" (n. 39).

[13] For the Latin sources of *CD*, Marrou (1958 [1938]) 418; generally, Hagendahl (1967); O'Donnell (1980): Augustine undertook "a fresh program of classical readings" for writing *CD* (147), but his research among the historians was sketchy (172); MacCormack (1999); Shanzer (2012); on Augustine's remarkable classical and Christian education within its broader context, Kaster (1988) 32–96; contemporary book culture, O'Donnell (2005) 113–45, Stroumsa (2012); Latinity and styles, Burton (2012); his relation to Vergil, MacCormack (1998).

providential and therefore ultimately beneficent vehicle for what it does not know, or a negative antitype to be overcome?

Augustine's influence was formative for subsequent political thought and continues to reverberate today.[14] *CD* is a decisive hinge between classical Latin and modern French letters and has lately had a conspicuous comeback:[15] Jérôme Ferrari analyzes contemporary France under an explicitly Augustinian aegis. His novel's title *Sermon sur la chute de Rome* translates *De excidio urbis Romae sermo.* Jacques Derrida's "democracy to come" takes inspiration from Augustine's city to come.[16] The novels analyzed in our subsequent chapters exemplify the continued power of this conflicted tradition.[17]

Augustine's deconstruction becomes paradigmatic for *Romanitas.* Rome must be overcome, but its overcoming continually preserves its traces and brings back under cover everything the *civitas Dei* would surpass. A central question for salvation is the status of the traces left by deconstructed structures. Where civil war remains latent in Vergil, though its traces maintain its potential to erupt again, Augustine is convinced salvation history will finally extinguish it. But Augustine is Vergilian despite himself. The Augustan peace is predicted but never realized in the *Aeneid.* The city of God is present on earth, but so long as the earthly city remains in effect, civil war will rage. Its full overcoming, as in Vergil, must await a future still to be realized.

In the modern novels we examine, individual characters become types that exemplify Augustine's different cities. Hugo's Gauvain is the only character we treat whose soul becomes a citizen of anything like the heavenly city. The rest wage civil war within themselves, on nearest and dearest, according to ideological commitments and blindnesses that become layered as the tradition advances in time. The plots and characters of *Quatrevingt-treize* and *Soumission* enact the relations between typological figurations their respective authors understand to structure world

---

[14] For Flaubert's *translatio Romae* in Augustine's wake, Vinken (2009a). Overviews of Augustine reception in: Funkenstein (1965) 36; Beyer de Ryke (1999); von Heyking (2001) 9–12; Caputo and Scanlon (2005); Vessey (2012) 429–515; Harich-Schwarzbauer and Pollmann (2013); Pollmann and Otten (2013). O'Donnell (1991) 22–3: His controversial authority as bishop and writer began during his lifetime and became entrenched in the centuries immediately following his death; his modern preeminence surpasses his contributions to theology.

[15] Augustine plays a special role in French scholarship and literature. Augustine scholars of all nationalities tend to be Catholic, but the systematic commentaries and translations published in France beginning in the 1950s have solidified French "prestige" in the field. O'Donnell (2001) 11.

[16] *Specters of Marx* (1993). Derrida's *Circonfession* (1990) plays on the title of Augustine's widely read work. Caputo and Scanlon (2005); Caputo (2012) 498–502.

[17] On Oedipal struggles – modern and postmodern – against the church father, O'Donnell (1991) 23.

history. While the *Confessions'* formative role in the development of the representation of interiority is widely recognized, scholarship on *CD* tends to focus on theology, political theology, or the culture of Late Antiquity. Our reading of the role of civil war in this seminal book attempts to recuperate, first, how Augustine defines its role in salvation history, but also how he paves the way for later representations of character and plot in civil war's terms. As stressed in Chapter 1, "Figures of Discord," his representational procedure has lost currency in favor of realism's focus on psychology. Readers schooled in its assumptions find themselves at sea in works where characterization aims not to depict a well-rounded and convincing person but to exemplify ideologies.

Rewriting Rome

The parallel *CD* establishes between Judea, a tiny Roman province in Asia, and an empire that spanned the world would have seemed absurd, judging by their disproportionate worldly power. Hundreds of pages, setting classical authors and Old Testament alike as foil to the New Testament, spell out the comparison. For both, antithesis structures the parallel.[18] Unlike the Old Testament, however, Roman history and literature together neither prefigure (*figura*) nor foreshadow (*umbra*) God's city or Christian scripture in the traditional sense.[19] *Umbra* is redefined in its full literal meaning: darkness in contrast to brightly shining light. The Romans offer, with few apparent and no real exceptions, a perverse model of everything to be overcome.

   CD brings onto a historical and universal plane the structure behind the conversion story of Augustine's singular, paradigmatic self in the *Confessions.*[20] The distortions, sins, and errors of his "I" become clear retrospectively in light of conversion. The perverse figurations of the Roman tradition similarly appear fully in revelation's light. Augustine's strong readings, themselves canonical, end up canonizing the classical authors he would depose.[21] As his price of inclusion, they must be read against the grain from now on. Literal and ironic quotation undermines.

---

[18] Ratzinger (1961 [1954]) 62 argues against the conflation in political theology of the *civitas Dei* with a Christian state, such as monarchy based on the divine right of kings; Augustine subsumes any historical state, including a Christian state, *qua* state under the "*civitas terrena* or *diaboli.*" For an overview, Ratzinger (1954) 276; Kölmel (1970); Thraede (1983) 93: "eine hinreichend stimmige 'Staatslehre' liefert Augustinus daher so wenig wie eine . . . Kirchentheorie" ("Augustine forwards an adequate, meaningful political science as little as he does a theory of the church").

[19] For the fourfold sense of scripture, Auerbach (2016), Ohly (1977 [1958]) 195.

[20] Freccero (1975) and (1986).   [21] He is a strong reader in Bloom's (1973) sense.

Their recontextualized meaning overturns any original intention. Augustine twists the words of canonical Latin authors in their mouths to set them straight.

This move is paradoxically integrative despite the disintegrating gesture. The structure includes the pagan Roman city and its letters within God's plan and gives them a significant place in the figural schema of typology.[22] Parallel to the prophetic Old Testament, made fully readable in the New Testament's Christian fulfillment, Latin literature now becomes fully readable through Christian hermeneutics. Whereas the Old Testament comes to light as prefiguration, the hidden sense of Latin letters, only hinted at, is revealed as perversion in the etymological sense: They twist the truth. Their inclusion requires subsuming the Roman mission of empire without end in time or space within salvation history. The stones and letters of Rome, read as a precise inversion of what their unenlightened authors could not see, translate into Christian typology through an ironic emptying of their semantics. Their role in salvation history and the place Augustine assigns them was opaque to them. But for him, whereas the Old Testament, read in light of the New, is shown to be a prefiguration of the heavenly city, the total darkness of Latin letters is enlightened as its ironic perversion.

Augustine's intervention – an ostensible untwisting that charges what he twists as already twisted – offers a new take on Rome's place in divine providence and also innovates in hermeneutic method. No instrumentality is granted the negated term or even the process of negation. The negative antitype forwards nothing. Its role is rather illustrative, that is, rhetorical or poetic: to lend greater clarity to the light that overcomes it. Rome's perversity highlights the truth of the *civitas Dei* by contrast. Latin literature displays Rome's ugliness and therefore plays an important role. But once Rome and its literature have done their revelatory work, an operation Augustine performs in arguing against them, they must be discarded for a new city and a new scripture. *CD* retropes Latin literature's conventional figurations and redefines Roman categories through Christian hermeneutics.[23] Its rhetorical process is a figural transfiguration that

---

[22] Blumenberg (1988 [1959]) 160.

[23] Kopperschmidt (1990). For the "counterintuitive" preference for the nonliteral in allegorical readings of scripture, O'Donnell (2005) 133–5. King (2014) 306: In scriptural exegesis, the Holy Spirit was assumed to work through the writer, therefore Augustine endorsed interpretations he took to express a truth, even counter to authorial intention. Cameron (1999): Augustine synthesizes Christian allegorical and typological approaches; Cameron (2012): His method combines Paul's "prophecy-fulfillment structure" (10) with the language of classical rhetoric; he eventually settled on

mirrors and enacts on the textual, argumentative plane the same structure as salvation history's salvific transfiguration.[24] Augustine's great insight is that he cannot erase Roman history or Latin letters. So he appropriates and transfigures the good and gives new meaning to the bad by doubling down on their literal signification.

CD retropes Roman categories and tropes systematically. Some terms are rejected outright, but many are retained, now suffused with new meaning.[25] The choice to describe the world of human relations as a *civitas*, for instance, is not obvious.[26] Augustine defines the basic structure of the world as two *civitates* based on two different kinds of love:

> And so two loves have made two cities: that is, love of self, extending even to contempt of God, has made the earthly, and love of God, extending to contempt of self, has made the heavenly. 14.28; 632

The *civitas terrena*'s self-love is essentially carnal lust for power, while the ardent love of God within the *civitas Dei* motivates human love of others. Basing the *civitas Dei* on love is an entirely novel foundational gesture – this cannot be overemphasized. It is the Christian gesture par excellence. But why *civitas* and not *regnum*? God's city is not yet a kingdom. *CD* does in fact conceptualize God's *civitas* as kingship when the Bible and its kings set the stage, and as empire (2.29; 92) to counter the *Aeneid*'s famous dictum, *imperium sine fine* ("empire without end," 1.278–9). God is the Lord and, if you want empire without end, His will be the one – but Augustine focalizes such conceptions. They appear as if in quotation marks, and when he speaks in his own voice, the *civitas Dei* stands against these terms as a fellowship among men united by love of God.[27]

In the Roman tradition, republic stands as the alternative to empire: *res publica* stresses citizenship and participation, aspects central to the

---

figura (15, 17–18). Paul's method allowed Augustine to overcome his initial resistance to the Bible: La Bonnardière (1999); Van Fleteren (2001) 4; for Augustine's access to Paul, Bastiaensen (2001).

[24] Cameron (1999) 76: Augustine took both history and prophecy to contain "a literal and a figurative sense"; he eventually collapsed the terms and spoke of "prophetic history" (97). Bochet (2004) argues for scriptural hermeneutics as the "fundamental matrix" (506) of Augustine's thinking beyond any history.

[25] Leupin (1993) 10 follows Kojève in speaking of a Christian epistemological break and quotes Jean-Claude Milner, who reformulates Kojève's theorem: "There is never any synonymy between a notion belonging to the pagan system of thought and a Christian, that is, modern notion."

[26] Pépin (1976 [1958]) 85–92 and (1987) 279–85.

[27] Citizenship depends on eschatological rather than political belonging; citizens in the *civitas Dei* are those destined for eternal life. Augustine is uninterested in constitutional forms per se. Weithman (2014) 234–5.

republican imaginary, over against the subjection written into *imperium*, with its derivation from "command." Augustine finds *res publica* attractive, but not the historical Roman Republic with its bloody virtues. Instead, the *civitas Dei* will be an inchoate *res publica* of the heart, with Christ as its founder.[28] Its citizens congregate under the sign of love, faith, and hope.

Civitas, however, is Augustine's primary category rather than *res publica*, because he prioritizes the social bond over political participation and political forms. Neither a physical city (*urbs*), nor a political entity (*res publica*), *civitas* in Latin, like Plato's *politeia* in Greek, depends on basic relations among people. The idea comes from Paul ("our city is in heaven," Philippians 3.20), but Augustine, writing in Latin, redefined words originally forged to mean something else. His definition highlights the social bond within a multitude: *Civitas, quae nihil aliud est quam hominum multitudo aliquo societatis vinculo conligata* ("For a city is nothing other than a multitude of men bound together by some tie of fellowship," 15.8; 649).[29] His textual procedure mirrors his conceptual overwriting and correction: Translation and transformation of the failed and wrong promise of the Roman *civitas*, both republic and Empire, through God's new order of love cross it out, elevate it, and establish it on a higher plane. The metaphor derives from Cicero's *De re publica*: *cum lex sit civilis societatis vinculum* ("since civil law is the bond of alliance"), *quid est enim civitas nisi iuris societas civium?* ("For what is a city if not an alliance of citizens before the law?" 1.49). Augustine overwrites Cicero's *De re publica* radically and systematically in book 2.[30] By book 15, the social bond has become a Christian idiom.

While the Roman political theorist bases his *civitas* on custom, law, and the will of the people, the Christian counters term for term with love, justice, and the will of God. In the passage cited above, Cicero identifies the bonds holding a *civitas* together as equality before the law. He quotes Ennius for the Roman conceptualization of their state as founded on custom: *moribus antiquis res stat Romana virisque* ("the Roman state stands

---

[28] Schürmann (1996) 307. God founds the eternal city in the Preface (also 5.18; 223), but Christ is the founder elsewhere. Inglebert (2016) surveys Christian reinterpretations of Roman citizenship; Augustine approved of the Roman extension of citizenship, but not the militarism (109).

[29] *Vinculum sociale* also at 15.16; 666. For the Roman background to Augustine's definition of *civitas*, Earl (1967) 123–7, who stresses the shift from justice and the rule of law to love as unifying principles (124). Augustine adopts the classical definition of a *civitas*, not a physical city, but a citizen body, Inglebert (1996) 423.

[30] For *Quellenforschung*, Testard (1958) and Hagendahl (1967). On Augustine's engagement with Cicero, O'Donnell (1980) 151–7: He read *Rep.* "with care and attention" at the outset of *CD*; Dodaro (2004), Weithman (2014) 238–44.

on ancient customs and men," Ennius, *Annales* frg. 156 Skutsch; *De re publica* 5.1.1). Augustine cites Cicero citing Ennius (2.21) to dismiss earthly law and human customs together, relying on Cicero's own authority: "the republic was long ago lost in fact" (2.21; 79; *De re publica* 5.1). It was, for Augustine, always already lost: "no such commonwealth ever existed" (2.21; 80); it was "never a true republic" (2.21; 83). Instead, a corresponding Christian term replaces each criterion on which to base a *civitas*: love, justice, and a more radical equality. He overwrites Cicero's theory, which he cites at length, and transfigures its terms: The only true and real *res publica* is one based on the law that is God's will and justice.[31] Cicero's definition of *res publica* as *res populi* (*De re publica*, 1.39) seems comparatively acceptable in the limited sense of "property of the people," but in the end is rejected as inadequate. It never had any true justice in it; that rather dwells in the *civitas Dei* of scripture, whose founder is Christ (2.21; 80); no people is sovereign before the sovereignty of Christ. Cicero's equality before the law yields, as Susanna Elm has argued, to a vision of universal equality for its citizens, justice for everyone, the abolishment of slavery, and equality among the sexes.[32] Augustine's conception of God's new city undermines classical hierarchical patriarchy, the privileges of the reigning sex and the ruling classes. With *societas* (alliance), lateral relations between men gain emphasis in a gesture that anticipates the equality of the French Revolution; the affirmation of women's agency returns in Hugo.

For Augustine, Cicero's model sets up a form to be emptied and reinfused with new meaning. Its traces remain in the tightly corresponding elevated terms. Augustine offers the hope of a new social bond in Ciceronian language to replace Cicero's *civitas*, that is, Augustine's *civitas Dei* in his *De civitate Dei* politically and textually supersedes the *res publica* of Cicero's *De re publica*. He likewise erases Varro's *Antiquitates rerum romanarum et divinarum* so as to replace Roman civic religion with a new *religio*.[33] But his extensive quotation of both texts preserves on his own page the views he cancels in his argument. *CD* is not only a major source of their remaining fragments, but, in an irony of philology, its figural overwriting comes materially true in the transmission of Cicero's text. Major sections of *De re publica* are known to us only because a manuscript copy was erased so one of Augustine's *Expositions of the Psalms* could be written over it on the very same paper. The palimpsest bears in its ink the traces of the formative

---

[31] Law: *Caelestique re publica, ubi Dei voluntas lex est* ("the heavenly republic, where God's will is law," 2.19; 75); God's justice (2.21; 76–80).
[32] Elm (1996).   [33] For Augustine's use of Varro, MacRae (2016).

tradition that was made to disappear and preserves it in the act of cancellation.[34]

Roman concepts, erased and supplanted, are reborn in *CD*. The tropes of Latin literature similarly gain new life for a new use: to reveal a fundamental truth about Rome against the grain of any triumphalist narrative. The Christian city of God supersedes Vergil's *imperium sine fine*, just as it supersedes Cicero's republic – their ideologies and their texts. But why argue directly with a poet as with Cicero and Varro? Instead, Roman history told in a grotesque Lucanian vein overwrites the classical empire of the *Aeneid*.

Vergil is the author closest to Augustine's heart.[35] For him, Vergil is "the most noble of the Roman poets" (15.9; 615) and therefore the most in need of overturning.[36] *CD* is yet another anti-*Aeneid*, with Lucan enlisted as Augustine's closest ally.[37] Christian overwriting retrospectively constructs the *Aeneid* as a Bible of Empire that gets everything wrong: love and politics, relations between the sexes and within the soul. Vergil and Augustine both tell stories of foundation, and their books are themselves foundational; for both, politics comes in the register of love, but where in Augustine, love of God wins over politics, Aeneas' tragic and earthly loves are crushed before the overwhelming pressure of earthly politics. Love, earthly or heavenly, becomes impossible within the Roman project. For Vergil, political order requires the taming of passion. Augustine sees only lust for domination at Rome, in need of correction in all its terms: from lust to love, domination to obedience, Rome to the city of God. Love, earthly or divine, in its success, failure, degradation, displacement, or sublimation, becomes a central figuration – after Vergil for Lucan, Augustine, Hugo, and Houellebecq alike – through which to represent the travails of the bond within the city. In answer to the destructive passion that breaks out for Vergil within the soul, between self and beloved, self and enemy – the self's intimate mirror – Augustine redefines love.

In Augustine, Latin literature's own categories overturn Roman ideology. Cicero and Varro in his hands turn the Republic against itself. For

---

[34] Fuhrer (2004) 146; Shanzer (2012) 167.

[35] Hagendahl (1967) 384–463; more *testimonia* of Vergil than of any other Latin author, "151 in *D.C.D.* [*CD*] for polemical effect," most likely from memory, O'Donnell (1980) 166; MacCormack (1998).

[36] Westra (2007) argues that Augustine "settles for a willful literalist reading of Vergil" (16), rejecting the allegorical strategies that redeem the Old Testament, that Servius and Macrobius used for Vergil, and that Augustine at times seems to countenance for classical literature (22–3). Our argument that the Romans are a dark *umbra* for Augustine instead of an enlightening *figura* gives classical Latin literature – read literally and rejected – a role within Christian hermeneutics.

[37] On Vergil's "epic successors," Hardie (1993).

Empire, Jupiter's declaration that he gives Rome empire without end in the *Aeneid* becomes paradigmatic for what Augustine combats. This empire fails at love and breaks out both literally and metaphorically in civil war. Latin elegy tries hard to subordinate war and politics to love but reinscribes violence in the *militia amoris* nevertheless. Augustine does one better by accusing Rome of a wrong relation to love and politics alike.[38] He cites with approval Sallust's diagnosis of "lust for domination" (*libido dominandi*, 3.14; III; *lubidinem dominandi, Bellum Catilinae* 2.2) as the greed underlying Rome's expansion into empire, eventual decline, and devolution into civil discord during the late Republic (*Cat.* 5.2).[39] Lucan, however, brings Rome's true nature to light: Augustine names him, cites him verbatim, and retells his gruesome stories.[40] *De bello civili* debunks the possibility of a united Republic and undoes any attempt to legitimate the Roman Empire as eternal and world-encompassing or the Romans as the universe's masters. Lucan's vision of Rome brings to the surface the civil war encoded in the *Aeneid*; the marriages in his poem institutionalize the failed love Vergil tells with such pathos. But while Augustine's Lucan could see and depict openly the truth of the Roman Republic's self-implosion, he could not see beyond it. Augustine turns Lucan's tropes to reveal the truth latent in Vergil's story of foundation, so he may set a new foundation in Rome's place, his new text in the place of classical Latin literature altogether. God's love supplants erotic passion and his city the earthly city rent in civil war; his *civitas Dei*, founded on the right kind of love, defounds classical Rome; Augustine's *CD*, written in the right kind of Latin, deconstructs Rome's literature by setting it against itself.

In *CD*, Rome becomes the preeminent historical model for a universal earthly condition. Augustine diagnoses civil war as the earthly city's

---

[38] Lepelley in Mayer (1986–), 1.942–57 outlines the Roman civic ideal for Augustine's contemporaries: Life in a *civitas*, the only imaginable form of civil existence, is conceptualized against both uncivilized barbarism and overcivilized oriental tyrannies, which revert to barbarism through brutal subjugation. By contrast, the ideal *civitas* is a self-governing autonomous republic. Education and culture can blossom only in a *civitas* (944), which guarantees social peace, order, and prosperity and provides the necessary pleasures of life, including entertainment and hygiene – theaters and the baths. The *civitas* attracted passionate attachment. Rich citizens, who benefited the city (euergetism), were to share the star-like immortality of the gods (see Scipio's dream in Cicero's *De re publica*; 945). Against Mommsen, who argued that Christianity supplanted Rome's dying civic religion, Lepelley maintains that North African imperial cities were thriving and committed to their traditional *religio*. Augustine structures his *civitas*, founded on "cooperation for well-being" (947; also, Marrou 1958 [1938]), by exposing the perversion of the Roman ideal and offering an alternative.

[39] Sallust's *Bellum Catilinae* occupies pride of place; references are concentrated in *CD*, O'Donnell (1980) 163–4.

[40] E.g., 3.13; 108 (Lucan named); 3.14; 110; 15.5; 640. O'Donnell (1980) 161: The bulk of Lucan citations come in the early 410s.

inescapable ontological condition, and he identifies Roman history as its most vivid instantiation. Strife governs the structure of self and community alike in the earthly city. It poisons the bonds between men, between generations and sexes, between man and god. The most extreme rupture within the human bond is civil war. Like his Latin predecessors, who develop an analogy going back to Plato, Augustine describes the structure of the self and all interrelations in a political register. He quotes, for instance, a simile from Cicero's discussion of different governmental types in the *De re publica*, which compares an individual's body and soul to structures of governance (14.23; 623–4). Augustine elaborates: The soul maintains command (*imperium*) more easily over the body than over itself. Strife (*rixa*) within the soul comes in the structure and register of civil unrest. To rise above it requires the soul to conquer (*vincere*) its passions in an orderly way (*ordinate*) that depends on reason's subordination (*subdari*) to God. The metaphors of civil discord extend to internal strife across spheres.

In Augustine, just as in his Latin predecessors, the right kind of sacrifice is required to overcome these deadly structures. For him as for them, Rome has failed to perform it; instead, human sacrifice has perverted sacrifice even on Rome's own terms. Augustine, however, is certain he has a solution, while they do not: Setting the right city on the right path requires accepting the right God and the right human sacrifice. The Roman terms are transfigured, so that being a citizen of the *civitas Dei* is no mere institutional affiliation, but a condition of the right kind of love: of God, not of self. Citizenship in the heavenly city means having right relations with oneself – body and soul – with others, and with God. Civil war is the perversion of right relations, just as human sacrifice is the perversion of salvific sacrifice. Such perversions arise from idolatry, that is, worship of the wrong gods or the self. Having the wrong gods or the wrong relation to God sets the individual on a path to internal strife and the *civitas* on a path to civil war. Love of the one true God, for Augustine, allows the city to perform the one true sacrifice.

> But the other, the heavenly, a pilgrim in this world, does not make false gods. Rather, that city is itself made by the true God, whose sacrifice it is itself to be. 18.54; 907[41]

---

[41] Translation lightly altered. Augustine transfers and reverses the pilgrim metaphor from Tertullian, who applies it to Christians within the *civitas terrena*. For Tertullian, they are foreigners in the world, but at home in the Church (*De corona* 13.1–4), while Augustine sets the whole *civitas Dei* on a pilgrimage toward a heavenly home but denies the reality of any institutional home for it on earth. Lepelley in Mayer (1986–) 1.943.

In Augustine's scheme, a new human sacrifice cancels the Romans' false and failed sacrifice and replaces and elevates it with a true and effective one. The self-sacrifice of the Passion is to bring strife in the soul and civil war in the city to an end; it will allow humanity to heal the internal divide that produces strife and to escape history's carnage; contrary to the sacrificial perversion at the heart of civil war, Christ's self-sacrifice will heal the social bond among humans and the religious bond in their relations to God. This sacrifice is to be imitated by believers without being repeated. It is enacted by the heavenly city as a collective in *imitatio Christi*. Among mortals henceforth, citizenship in the *civitas Dei* requires conversion and obedience to God.

Because he understands Rome's position in salvation history as a historical antitype to the heavenly city – it is the earthly city's preeminent historical instantiation – rather than as a necessary vehicle to it, Rome's sack is immaterial to Augustine. It cannot signal the end of history because it has no causal relation to the heavenly city. Neither the duration of the Roman Catholic Church nor the *civitas Dei* depends materially on an endless Roman Empire, universal Roman citizenship, or the *pax Augusta*. Augustine's city breaks with Rome, just as his appropriated citizenship breaks with Roman citizenship. Both are less transformed than transfigured into a new republic of the heart.

Augustine argues against a view best represented by his contemporary Orosius (c. 375–418), who wrote his *Histories against the Pagans* while Augustine was writing *CD*. In Orosius' apology of Roman history as guided by God's providence, citizenship in the Church is consequent upon Roman citizenship: Christ's inscription in Augustus' census paves the way (6.22).[42] For Augustine, citizenship in the *civitas Dei* cancels that of its earthly precursor; it transforms Roman citizenship by breaking with it. Every Roman, every human being should aspire to become a citizen rather of this new *civitas*, whose promise cancels and elevates the Roman model into a better world.

Augustine sacks Rome rhetorically and rails against the revival of neo-paganism by citing, inverting, and surpassing Rome's own exemplary authors.[43] Classical Romans could not help their idolatry, because, coming

---

[42] Inglebert (2016) 104, on Christian interpretations of the census story in Luke (100–5).

[43] Brown (1967) 312: "a deliberate confrontation with paganism." For Augustine's use of Roman *exempla* for his own purposes, Inglebert (1996) 414–15: Roman history does not interest Augustine in itself, but because it reviews his theses in advance, history in its classical sense is reinterpreted in a Christian sense. Augustine omits the original arguments of his sources that contradict his own and quotes out of context (417).

as they did before Christ, they were unable to recognize the one true God. They do, however, have a place – reviled, but nevertheless a place – in salvation history as an *exemplum* for what is wrong in the *civitas terrena* and as its antitype. After Christ, Romans who do not accept the message can be blamed for their blindness, and these are Augustine's *adversarii*. These neopagans cling to the classical order without recognizing that a turning point in history has given new meaning to the shared inheritance of the past.

Augustine dismantles the Roman Empire and transforms Roman ideals – liberty, citizenship, virtue – whose realization at Rome he declares a failure, by translating and elevating them onto a Christian plane and transfiguring them into a new *civitas* of love. The universal belonging promised by Roman citizenship becomes a new way of belonging. Retaining citizenship as the proper category makes a strong political intervention that proclaims the failure of earthly politics. Hardly apolitical, his is a politics against politics. The substitution retains, but radically redefines the given categories. History is subsumed in politics, itself rooted in *libido dominandi*, and becomes a story of recurrent strife. A new politics must take its place, one that can be realized on earth, although never fully. Not ruled by desire for domination, these new citizens serve each other; even the ruler serves his subjects.[44] Where citizenship may have been Rome's promise, civil war – war between citizens – is its curse. Rome comes to stand for a transhistorical logic of politics whose dynamics pervade and pervert human relations contrary to God's *civitas*, which creates a new social bond, grounded in love, a commonwealth, as Paul puts it, of the heart.[45]

Roma aeterna?

Shortly after the sack of Rome, Augustine wrote a laconic letter to the monks of Hadrumetum, *De excidio urbis Romae* (410 CE), to counter an interpretation of Jerome.[46] The latter, following the earth-shattering events from a safe distance in Bethlehem, believes the end of mankind is near, which for him would coincide with the completion of the Vulgate.[47]

---

[44] This idea still lives in the Italian greeting, *ciao*, derived from the Latin *servus* (slave), itself a Bavarian greeting meaning "at your service."
[45] Cho (1998).   [46] Augustine, *De excidio urbis Romae sermo*, 8.1–4.
[47] Hieronymus, *Epistolae* 125, in Migne (1865) 12. Inglebert (1996) 421: Eusebianism foundered during three days in 410.

By contrast, Augustine stays cool.[48] Reactions to Rome's sack are a litmus test for conceptualizations of the Roman Empire's place in salvation history. Those who saw it as a vehicle for the spread of Christianity through the Roman Catholic Church thought they were seeing the end of time.[49] For Augustine, Rome is one empire among others, exemplary yes, but no means to an end.[50] He does not consider the city's fall a unique, let alone apocalyptic event. Instead, he ranks it among the long lineage of destroyed and punished cities of the Old Testament: Rome's demise is one more variant of Sodom and Gomorrah. In contrast to the Vergilian prophecy, which promises the city eternity with its empire (2.29; 92; Vergil, *Aen.* 1.278–9), Augustine considers Rome an emblem of *vanitas*, another illustration of instability and the transitory, of the deceit of the earthly. In *CD*, Rome's fall is the archetype of *sic transit gloria mundi*, but still, only one example among many. If, for Augustine, Rome remains the city of cities, it is only an ironic illustration of the ways of all earthly things: Rome embodies the *civitas terrena* as a body politic torn apart by *concupiscentia*.[51]

The civil wars that plagued Rome's history, depicted so brutally in Lucan, motivate Augustine's break with Eusebian salvation history.[52] According to Eusebius, who offers an *interpretatio christiana* of Vergil, the earthly Roman Empire is the condition for the spread of the Christian faith (*praeparatio evangelica*) and prepares for the heavenly empire's realization through the *pax Romana*.[53] The *Aeneid*'s bold prophecies promise

---

[48] For the sociological pragmatics of Augustine's sermon *On the sack of Rome*, Elm (2017). Also de Bruyn (1993), Piccaluga (1995), Salzman (2013) and (2015).

[49] Orosius in Arnaud-Lindet (1990) 291, 296, 297.

[50] The reception of Augustine, so-called "Augustinism," goes curiously against the grain of his writing. Whereas Augustine opposes Eusebius, Orosius, and Jerome, who interpret historical events in the frame of salvation history as a *Reichstheologie* and see the Roman Empire as God-willed, Augustine understands secular history as indifferent to salvation history. Augustine has been misread as advocating the realization of the *civitas Dei* in a Christian Empire, the divine right of kings, Caesaropapism, and the secular power of the Church. He has therefore been used to legitimate exactly what he argues against: no earthly kingdom, empire, or republic can be instrumental within salvation history. The politics of those he refutes, namely Eusebius and Orosius, was misattributed to Augustine during the Middle Ages, Arquillière (1934), Cary (2005) 24–5. The conflation of the earthly *civitas* with the *civitas Dei* produces political theology, which he sees as a misguided perversion. This controversy acquired special momentum in France at the moment of secularization and the separation of church and state. For this history, Inglebert (1996); Jerphagnon (1998) preface.

[51] Strife and dissension are part and parcel of the life of the flesh (14.1–2; 581–4).

[52] For Eusebius' new historiography of a Christian nation, Momigliano (1977 [1963]) 115–17.

[53] For the Roman Empire as vehicle for the Church, Salin (1926). His theory is a theological politics: The heavenly city continues earthly politics. This inverts political theology, in which, according to Schmitt's (1985) 36 definition, "all significant concepts of the modern theory of the state are secularized theological concepts." Augustine's break between earthly and divine cities rebuts theological politics and political theology alike, however much the two mix in daily life. Von Heyking (2001) argues Augustine is a "right-by-nature" political thinker. Although political life is

an everlasting empire of divine predestination. This empire is the pre-requisite for the all-embracing catholicity of the Roman Church, which will legitimate a new political order.[54] By contrast, Augustine puts a decisive hermeneutic break between the *civitas terrena*, with Rome as its most exemplary embodiment, and the *civitas Dei*. He constructs world history not as the divine city's necessary prototype, but as its negative antitype, with the result that the heavenly city needs the earthly city only for illustration and nothing more.

The structure of providential history in *CD* turns on the analysis of a series of historical cities, each structured by an internal divide.[55] This story is told in a logical, not chronological order.[56] Each orientation within a historical community has a different figurative relation to the *civitas Dei*. Stressing the figural averts any misleading notion of progress or historical causation implied by chronological organization.[57] Rome comes in two guises: the Rome of civil war and the Rome of virtue. The former comes first because it establishes Rome's nature, grounded in pure abject blood-shed, a grotesque perversion of salvific sacrifice. The heavenly city's anti-type shows human history in its most despicable form. The Rome of virtue, although admirable in part, nevertheless also founders. The virtue of the classical Roman heroes belongs to the earthly city just as much as their civil

---

insufficient for human happiness, which depends on an orientation toward God, we are nevertheless political by nature and political life is a positive good; Christianity reforms politics and redirects it toward justice, but church and state serve different ends. The "enlightenment, romantic, and Hegelian symbolizations of historical progress and human agency" (1–2) that secularize Augustinian paradigms write out basic human needs, while the fusion of church and state exemplified by Charlemagne mistakenly ascribes "salvational meaning to political life" (6). The relation of church to the *civitas Dei*, as of Rome to the earthly city, is by symbol rather than identity, Barr (1962) 223–7; on the Holy Roman Empire as a "mistaken desire to clothe the mystical Christian community with flesh" (227–9). For Augustine's political "pessimism" or "realism," Niemeyer (1983), Doody, Hughes, and Paffenroth (2005).

[54] For the standard reading, which legitimates the political through the theological, Arquillière (1934). Augustine does not aim to replace the classical political order with a Christian political order. The metaphor of *civitas* may come in the language of Ciceronian republicanism, but the idea is from Paul ("our city is in heaven," *Phil.* 3.20). Augustine counters Tertullian (*De corona* 13.1–4) and Origen (*contra Celsum* 3.29), who proposed the Church should supplant the classical *civitas* as a worldly institution. The Church according to Augustine belongs to the *civitas permixta*, while the heavenly *civitas* is spiritual and cannot be instantiated in any political order, Lubac (1984); Lepelley in Mayer (1986–) 1.942–57; Fuhrer (2004) 137–44; Hollingworth (2010) 1–17. Antoine (2003) challenges any strict separation of the secular from the religious in Augustine and underscores his interest in the political form of the *res publica* over against *regnum* and *imperium*.

[55] The two *civitates*, earthly and heavenly, set the criteria for judging the different orientations of historical cities, Hawkins (1975).

[56] Existing Christian chronology, which emphasized Jews' temporal priority before pagans, made "the scheme of redemption" easy to perceive, Momigliano (1977 [1963]) 110.

[57] We avoid calling the *civitates'* progress a "negative dialectic." This anachronistic term implies the need for something to cancel to move forward.

wars because their motivations were misguided. According to the Romans' own categories, such virtue was exemplary. However, Augustine stresses it was to be corrected at best and avoided at worst. Roman devotion to country offers a lesson in humility to Christians rather than providing a model to be imitated *tout court*.

Universal history, as told in the Bible, starts with Cain and Abel and similarly divides in two. Unlike the split internal to Rome, this division into two cities advances in salvation history.[58] Cain founds the earthly city, while Abel, a citizen of the city of God in its pilgrimage on earth, prefigures Christ, the founder of the city of God. With the birth of the bearer of redemption, a new potential emerges in the Biblical conception of history, which is absent from the Roman model. Rome's negative example, good and bad, abject and admirable, taken together illustrates all that is wrong with the universal earthly city. It, in its entirety, fulfills Cain's foundation.[59] This negative example is repeatable: Rome itself is a second Babylon and numerous cities replay its history. Only within history as told in the Old Testament do two cities emerge wherein one prefigures the heavenly city.

Rome: Universal Civil War

Rome remains for Augustine the city of cities.[60] He tells universal earthly history under its sign not because it is unique, but because it is extreme. Rome exemplifies "the gravest evils suffered by other nations everywhere" (3.1; 94). If its civil wars show the worst of humanity, Rome simultaneously offers the paradigm of the highest earthly *virtus*. Instantiating worldly goodness and evil in contrary extremes, Roman history paints a complete picture of the *civitas terrena* in two parts. The Roman civil wars illustrate the earthly city's horrors in book 3; in book 5, Roman *virtus* shows it at its awful best. Augustine carefully retails Roman distinctions, only to flatten them into a salient negative example before a greater truth.

Augustine's recasting of Roman history means to expose the corruption beneath Rome's ostensible glory. He reserves metaphors of "revelation" for his hermeneutical reading of the Old Testament as prefiguration (*velata*

---

[58] Van Fleteren (2001) 21: Abel and Cain, members of the two "mystical cities," are archetypes whose historical instantiations, Jerusalem and Babylon, arise later.

[59] On Rome's rhetorical, ideological, and symbolic example, Inglebert (1996) 415–16.

[60] Earl (1967) 123: "The great model was, of course, the Roman empire. If in his completed work Augustine was not primarily concerned with Rome, it was from Rome and Roman definitions that he began."

tegminibus, "veiled in coverings," 16.1; 694) but uses a brutal metaphor of uncovering for the Romans:

> Why do our adversaries plead the words "praise" and "victory" to me? Take off the cloak of vain opinion (*remotis obstaculis insanae opinionis*) and let such evil deeds be examined naked. Let them be weighed naked and judged naked. . . . Away, then, with concealments and deceitful whitewashings! 3.14; 111

The stories the Romans tell themselves about their history and their gods turn out to be lies clothed in, like a false rubric recently in vogue, "truthful hyperbole."[61] Romulus' apotheosis is a "flattering fiction" (*adulatio fabulosa*, 3.15; 113) or "polite fiction" (*benivole iactatum diffamatumque*, 114).

Augustine's ironic inversion, a forceful act of hermeneutic violence, not only exposes Rome's nature as a city of civil war but also sets Roman categories at odds. A plethora of hyperbolic and sarcastic degradations takes energy from the transvaluation of terms. But if glory or virtue now mean something else, Augustine nevertheless speaks the language of Rome's own rhetoric, to uncanny effect. Latin literature's tropes of civil war convert the praise Roman historians had lavished on their city into invective almost on their own. All he need do to uncover the grotesque truth is repeat their own words:

> The writers of Rome's history, therefore, judged that an honourable freedom of speech required them not to pass over in silence the ills of the city whose praises they had in so many other places been compelled to proclaim . . . we say nothing more dreadful against the gods of the Romans than their own authors – the authors whom they read and commend – say again and again. Indeed, all that we have said we have derived from them; although we are by no means able to speak as well [as] they do or say as much as they say. 3.17; 199

Augustine ironizes the paradigm of emulation: his derivative account shows the truth Rome's most famous authors were telling against their own grain and gleefully sets their words against their authors.

Augustine claims to read the tropes straight and often does. Rape is rape. Fratricide is fratricide. If they undergird Rome's foundation, as the Romans freely admitted, then their city's foundation is *ipso facto* corrupt. The Romans, in their blindness, despite their best intentions, says Augustine, display their society's, their gods' true nature. He shows

---

[61] Trump (1987) 58.

repeatedly that, from the perspective of Christian revelation, Roman institutions are wrongheaded to begin with; furthermore, ineffectual on their own terms, they encode self-destruction. Augustine turns many Roman civil war tropes a notch further. This reading of Rome, allegedly a straight retelling, launches a gesture characteristic of *Romanitas*; stretching conventions beyond their original context turns them against themselves.

Augustine's ironic inversion of Rome's glory in book 3 depends in part on recoded values. Roman religion appears often as bloody sacrilege even to the Romans themselves, but revelation's new light doubles the horror. Roman religion inverts salvific sacrifice. The wrong gods attend the wrong values; they are empty, because they cannot save their people from external disaster, much less from civil war; they are worshipped only for earthly felicity and glory; even for this, they founder miserably; Romans sacrifice in the wrong way, for the wrong reasons, and it does not even work. Augustine debunks the Roman gods step by step in pagan, Hebrew, and Christian registers: These gods have no *fides*; they are man-made, fictitious idols; not only do they not prevent civil war, but they also lust for the spectacle of destruction. The idolatry and human sacrifice the Hebrews strove hard to eradicate rage with these gods in Augustine's rhetorical torrent. Internal disturbances move onto a cosmic plane in his description of domestic animals going wild (3.23; 132) – a gesture reminiscent of the *Georgics*. He derides classical signs and makes evil a sufficient portent in itself. The classical opposition between chaos and cosmos comes in a Biblical register. Rome does not master the universe: Chaos visits the city "within the very walls" under the sign of the Old Testament God's signature punishment, fire and flood (3.18; 124).

Much of Augustine's diatribe aims to show that internal political and semiological breakdown inhabits Roman history from within. His relentless retelling, in excruciating detail, redefines and undoes every structure through which the Romans make sense of their world. In his hands, all oppositions that give meaning and legitimacy to Roman history dissolve systematically into indistinction: humanity and barbarity, ally and foe, human and animal, sacred and profane. Roman history, for Augustine, tells a story of the perversion of all bonds: between allies, master and slave, within the family, between the sexes and the generations, between human and gods, and finally the bonds that keep the body politic together. The very body politic, figured in the corporeal body of the Republic or Empire (3.1; 94; 3.10; 103), is no unity obeying a hierarchical order but devolves into rabid, dehumanizing self-destruction.

In Augustine, the Roman world has always already been topsy-turvy. Winners are losers, triumph is ruin, the glory of imperial expansion results in further internal violence. In good Roman fashion, he gives examples of each. Those who would save the Republic end up slain, Cicero, who hoped to restore it, and Caesar, who at least exercised clemency, alike (3.30; 139–40). Augustine generalizes even Roman victory as failure: the "same wars" were fought "again and again"; war flared again despite treaties of peace; the gates of war were never closed until after the Punic wars (3.14; 112–13); even then, "the victor was more like the vanquished" (Florus, *Epitome* 2.6; 3.19; 125); the overthrow of Carthage "harmed Rome more than did its prolonged enmity" (3.21; 130). Even foreign acts of aggression turn Romans against each other. When Mithridates ordered all Roman citizens, happily living in Asia, to be put to death, they were forced to witness the slaughter "in their own houses" and even "participate in it themselves." The wounds belong as much to soul as to body: "All . . . were wounded together: the smitten in body and the smiters in soul" (3.22; 131). Even when the violence is not self-inflicted, there is nothing, according to Augustine, but a sequence of catastrophes (3.17; 118–23; 3.31; 141). The worst victories, however, are internal:

> What rage displayed by foreign nations, what ferocity of the barbarians, can match the horror of this victory of citizens over citizens? 3.29; 138

Roman civil war appears in Augustine's retelling as the political manifestation of the larger disorder that inhabits their world. Augustine undoes Roman categories step by step from the political to the cosmic. In a sweeping gesture, he conflates the careful distinctions that structure Rome's violent world. The polarity of peace and war collapses in the proscription of thousands following Sulla's victory, "even crueler" (*crudelius*, 3.28; 136) than the war; the following peace rages (*pace saeviente*, 3.28; 137). Social hierarchy breaks down, as senators and equestrians are targeted. The license to cut throats indiscriminately (*licentia iugulandi*, 3.28; 137) inverts Republican *libertas*, which should have protected the high-born against the grotesque tortures described. Men, torn apart alive and cut to pieces, are forced to witness their own death. Distinctions between life and death, viewer and viewed, license and liberty falter. Instead of "felicity and glory" (3.20; 128), Rome's is a story of unfolding strife. For Augustine, the Romans snatch defeat out of the mouth of apparent victory. The peace the Romans, "lords of the world, the nation of the toga" (Vergil, *Aen.* 1.281; 3.13; 107), have imposed is revealed as nothing more than the cruel horror of *libido dominandi* (3.14; 111). Categories of internal strife pile on in a crescendo of Roman terms, only to be leveled as all the same bloody devastation: sedition, urban warfare, *bella socialia, bella servilia, bella civilia* (3.23; 132; 3.26; 135). Where Cicero coolly evaluated Pompey's excellence in civil war as one kind among others in a similar list (*De imperio Cn. Pompei* 28, above p. 26 in Chapter 3), here *bella civilia* climactically crown the lot (3.26; 135).

Retelling Rome's story from its mythic beginnings in its own tropes underscores the consistency of corruption. In classical political theory, sex and family establish the foundations of society; here, they reappear as central categories of perversion. Rome's divine origins are no cause for glory but pervert their lineage with adultery and rape. Venus and Mars, myth's notorious adulterers, each procreated separately, through further adultery with a different mortal, producing a double lineage for Rome: one from Aeneas on Venus' side and one from Romulus on Mars's (3.3; 97). Were that not enough, Romulus was born from sacrilegious offence, Mars's rape of a Vestal Virgin (3.3–5; 97–8). Beginning with Romulus' fratricide, all Roman history replays ad nauseam the original scene of rape and familial slaughter. Fratricide extends into patricide: Responsibility for Remus' death exceeds Romulus; the whole city is indicted for murdering one of their two paternal founders (3.6; 99). Furthermore, Augustine lends credence to the story that the senate murdered Romulus – the Romans murdered both founders (3.15; 113). Roman social order, normatively grounded in marriage, is perverted from the beginning: The rape of the Sabine women is told here as sexual *mésalliance* and warfare within the family:

> The Romans, therefore, conquered so that they might with hands imbued with the blood of fathers wrest embraces from their sorrowing daughters. . . . It was not Venus but Bellona who bestowed such marriages on the Romans. 3.13; 108

The Sabines' rape shows that procreation at Rome arises paradigmatically not from love, but from sexual violence, which generates war. The story's shift in meaning, from reconciliation to Rome's original act of war, twists the Romans' own trope for ending civil war. Therefore, civil war inhabits Rome from the beginning and can be overcome only with conversion to a new world order.

From mythic origins to Republican history, Augustine's Rome is a broken record, continually rehearsing the same fatal plot. With arch sarcasm, Augustine dwells on choice horrors, mythic and historic, found in Vergil and Lucan.[62] He asks if Juno's help granted Allecto more license to

---

[62] Brown (1967) 309: sarcasm is "Augustine's most formidable weapon."

harm; the goddess of marriage no less sent the Fury to disrupt Lavinia's engagement to Aeneas (Vergil, *Aen.* 7.323–405; 3.14; 108). Pompey and Caesar, conventional civil war opponents, are rhetorically demoted: "only one father-in-law and one son-in-law" (3.14; 107–8) – yet Lucan lamented their strife as "worse than civil war." Parallels between mythic and republican history generalize civil war as Rome's foundational structure. Earthly history's theme and variation produces nothing new under the sun.

As if the Roman tropes were not extreme enough, Augustine rhetorically surpasses them through various heightening techniques. He continues the tradition by doing to Lucan what Lucan does to Vergil. He magnifies familial division further as the condition of Rome *qua* city: She killed not only her founding fathers, but even her own mother, Alba Longa.

> a mother city, was still destroyed by her own daughter. 3.14; 112

> For when daughter city fought with mother city, this was indeed a state of affairs "worse than civil war." 3.14; 110

Against Alba Longa, there was only the perennial motivation, *libido dominandi* (lust for domination, 3.14; 111). In these passages, Augustine repeatedly cites Lucan's opening phrase, "worse than civil wars" (3.14; 108, 110), traditionally taken to mean that war within the family made the fight between Pompey and Caesar worse than civil. Even within the house of Atreus, the classical tragic paradigm for incest and familial slaughter, no daughter ever kills her mother with her own hands. Rhetorical amplification denies Rome any escape, any catharsis, much less redemption.

Relentlessly systematic, Augustine shows all Roman solutions fail. Their relation to their gods perverts what even Romans saw as religion's function. Their gods honor no loyalty or bond, the binding etymologized in religion (*religio*).[63] They forsake those who worship them, moving randomly from city to city, from Troy to Lavinium to Alba Longa, without providence, as Augustine cruelly insists: "They departed indeed, and from a third dwelling place, so that Rome, you see, might be thought all the more provident in becoming their fourth" (3.14; 112). They abandon the Saguntines to utter ruin at the hands of the enemy in return for their loyalty (3.20; 126–9); they turn on themselves in cannibalism. The Roman gods are recast as the flesh-eating gods of Babylon: "here at any rate the gods should have done something: those gluttons and wastrels who long for the fat of sacrifices" (3.20; 127).

---

[63] Maltby (1991) collects ancient, perhaps erroneous, etymologies under *religio*.

Beyond perverting cultic norms per se, Rome's gods are even tarnished with civil war. A multiplicity of paradoxes stresses Roman religion's systemic flaw. The temple of Jupiter Optimus Maximus was built by Tarquinius Superbus, who came to power by "parricide" (3.15; 115), one of civil war's central tropes. Internal destruction threatens the Vestal Virgins. Their own fires, raging out of control, nearly consume those who keep the fire alive; destruction inverts protection, along with the cult of the national goddess of the hearth (3.18; 124). The deluded Romans founded temples on the hallowed grounds of internal strife. Augustine satirizes the building of a temple to Concord on the very site of "the dreadful tumult" where Caius Gracchus was destroyed and Marcus Fulvius "was put to death with his children" (3.24–5; 133) – the goddess was clearly out of town. Discord should have received the temple instead.[64] Repeated inscription of internal division into Roman cult amasses cumulative evidence their gods are incapable of overcoming civil war, which saturates Roman politics and religion.

Roman moral discourse against their own perversion recurs intensified. Augustine turns Roman fascination with and high-minded distaste for spectacle against them. Where Lucan's hyperbole makes the civil wars the ultimate show, Augustine rhetorically escalates their lust for spectacles of cruelty even further by comparing the gods themselves to "theatrical spectators" watching these struggles (3.14; 112).[65] Game and spectacle – condemned by Roman philosophers – tar Roman religion. Augustine mocks the Secular Games – renewed during the Punic wars and after to refound Rome every century – as a mistaken attempt to ensure the happy continuance of their society through ritual. He elides the Olympian gods' role in the rites, added by Augustus, in an act of singular inaccuracy, mentioning only the infernal gods, who delight in watching suffering (3.18; 124). These Roman gods not only lack compassion, but they also behave worse than the lustful Roman mob that savors the spectacle of the arena.

The description of Alba Longa's destruction, an unbearable exhibition of matricide, recodes Roman spectacle in Christian norms to increase the shock value.

> Gladiators also fight and they also conquer. This cruelty has its reward of praise . . . But if two gladiators were in the arena to fight, one a son and the other his father, who could endure such a spectacle? Who would not shun it?

---

[64] Augustine repeats the Romans' own criticism. Graffiti proclaimed "A work of discord produces a Temple of Concord" (Plutarch, *C. Gracchus* 17.6), Breed, Damon, and Rossi (2010) 3.

[65] For the Roman imperial culture of spectacle, Beacham (1999). Augustine's disapproval ranges from "reluctant forbearance" to "stern opposition" depending on his audience, Lim (2012) 146.

How, then, could the clash of arms between two cities be glorious when one of the cities was a mother and the other her daughter? 3.14; 111

Killing the mother, even worse than patricide, shifts the operative value from paternity, the Romans' highest principle, to holy motherhood, embodied in Mary.

Topping Lucanian hyperbole, Augustine describes how perverted viewing corrupts public space. The spectacle of civil war is bad enough. That perpetrators and victims become viewers corrupts the act of witnessing: "the two Crassi, father and son, were put to death in one another's sight"; "those whose salutation Marius refused to accept" were "cut down before his very eyes" (3.27; 136). Rome is a society of spectacle, and the spectacle is death. So much Lucan already says. *CD* internalizes such viewing into the body politic, which attacks itself in self-butchery. The distinctions between victim and perpetrator, violence and viewing elide.

> What rage displayed by foreign nations, what ferocity of the barbarians, can match the horror of this victory of citizens over citizens? Which of the attacks that Rome witnessed was more destructive, more foul, more bitter: the Gallic invasion of long ago and the more recent invasion of the Goths, or the ferocity of Marius and Sulla and of the other men of great renown who supported them – a ferocity as if of their own eyes against their own limbs? 3.29; 138

This extraordinary image of ferocious eyes unites lust for viewing with lust for violence.[66] All public spaces blur in the bloodbath. These spaces are listed in ascending order of civic and religious purpose: "streets, squares, markets, theatres and temples were ... filled with the bodies of the dead" (3.27; 136). The climax is the preeminent pagan pair, theater and temple, the Christian Church's abject and sacrilegious antitypes.[67]

The pinnacle of horror is the return of the absolute taboo: human sacrifice. In the violence of civil war, *religio* dissolves and reverts to the unthinkable barbarism of the archaic past. Human sacrifice was thought to have been long resolved among Jews and Romans alike.[68] Surpassing the sacrilege of the Greeks, who kill Trojan Priam at refuge on the altar (Vergil, *Aen.* 2.550–8), the Romans sacrifice themselves at their own altars.

---

[66] On curiosity and cruelty in Augustine, Blumenberg (1973), Vinken (1991a) 20–2.
[67] For the juxtaposition of church and theater, Thirouin (1998) 282; church and spectacle, Lim (2012). During intense controversy in the Port Royal, Bossuet (1694) reverses the opposition and praises the church as a better spectacle.
[68] Girard (1972). For nineteenth-century understanding, de Maistre (1884) vol. 5, 283–360.

Augustine quotes Lucan precisely, down to the detail of blood sparing Vesta's flames (*flammisque pepercit*, 2.126–8):

> Mucius Scaevola, the pontiff, was slain even though he clung to the very altar of the temple of Vesta, the most sacred of all shrines in the estimation of the Romans. With his blood, he almost extinguished that fire which ever burned under the perpetual care of the virgins. 3.28; 137

Criminal, human bloodshed does not cleanse like sacrificial animal blood, with which early Hebrews and Romans alike honored their God(s). The altar is systematically deconsecrated, at Rome as at Troy. Catulus may escape his enemies through suicide – this figuration of civil war reaches its apogee in Lucan – but Augustine does one better: Merula lays hands on his own body in perverted sacrifice as he becomes sacrifice and sacrificer at the same time.

> Merula, the flamen of Jupiter, cut his veins and so poured out a libation of his own blood to Jupiter. 3.27; 136

The Romans are degraded as sacrificial animals not for the betterment, but, in a perfect normative inversion, the ruin of the commonwealth. As with Vergil, who inscribes sacrificial language in the foundational gesture of Aeneas' killing Turnus (*immolat, condit, Aen.* 12.949–50), the taboo of human sacrifice continually returns in Augustine's account of Roman political disorder. His simultaneously Biblical register condemns Rome as a second Babylon, for human sacrifice no less (e.g., 18.2; 824).[69]

In Augustine, the proper distinctions guaranteeing meaning are restored by the human self-sacrifice to end all sacrifices. Civil war's abject bloodshed, all the catastrophes of the *civitas terrena* exemplified in Roman history amass as negative foil for Christ's salvific blood. Only a new foundation, new salvation can end such perverse self-destruction by shifting to a new plane. Augustus, the agent, in the Roman conception, of ending civil war and purveyor of the *pax Augusta*, is condemned as just another agent of civil war. He may have restored "liberty to the commonwealth," but he nevertheless authorized the slaughter of Cicero, who had supported him. The Augustan refoundation simply repeats, one more time, Rome's original flawed foundation. Augustine cites Lucan's precise characterization of the first foundation in one of civil war's primary tropes: *primi fraterno maduerunt sanguine muri* ("The first walls were wet with

---

[69] Siegert (2006) 15: John's apocalypse is a prominent grounding passage for the opposition of Babylon and Jerusalem, in which Augustine inscribes the mythical identity of Rome as Babylon; at the beginning of all *translatio* theories, he makes the *translatio imperii Babyloniae* first.

a brother's blood," *BC* 1.95; 15.5; 640). Augustus' Empire reenacts the bloody beginning all over again.

Augustine stops telling Roman history at this historical turning point. Christ, born during the time when "Caesar Augustus had become emperor, and had brought peace to the whole world" (18.46; 891), is now "king and founder" (*rex et conditor*) of the *civitas Dei* (14.13; 609; 17.4; 771; 18.29; 858). The accident of history, however, is not instrumental, but figurative. Unlike the Hebrews, who had both *civitates* from the start, the Romans could not help but mistake the true ruler. Their historians could do no better than to praise their carnage: "After all, they had no other and truer City: that City whose citizens are to be chosen for eternity" (3.17; 119).

Exemplary History: Roman *Virtus*

If Augustine exposes Roman history as drenched in civil bloodshed simply by magnifying its self-condemnation, his procedure with Roman virtue is more insidious. The civil war he inflicts on them cuts more deeply because it turns their deepest values against them.

Rome is not all bad (they were good men according to the light of the earthly city, 5.19; 225), and God put it on earth for a purpose. The civil wars may be the worst of the *civitas terrena*, but Romans also offer examples of extreme virtue "for our necessary admonition" (5.18; 223).[70] As "magnificent" as their successes, as "wondrous" (5.12; 208) as their accomplishments may be, their virtues are completely misdirected.[71] Augustine subtly transvalues Roman *virtus* by shifting from pagan to Christian norms. Even the Romans condemned civil war, but since *virtus* was their highest political motivation, Augustine must delineate finely between what Christians may learn from the Romans and their destructive politics of *virtus*.[72]

The argument runs like this. Some of the great *exempla* of Roman virtue teach a valuable lesson to Christians (5.16; 216–17; 5.18; 218–22): to

---

[70] Roman greatness depends on providence, Hawkins (1975). "The reprobate dominion is, in fact, 'something of a model' for the redeemed. Not only do sheep and goats pasture in the same field; the sheep are given an image of themselves as they ought to be in none other than their capric opposites!" (97).

[71] Earl (1967) 127–9: Augustine summarizes aristocratic, republican ideals fairly, then condemns them because even their noblest "lacked the smallest qualification for salvation." Also Morrissey (2010) 28–32. Augustine's method is a "process of rejection, selection and reinterpretation." Brown (2012) 57–8: Roman discourse on avarice gave Augustine a language with which to critique Roman virtue from within.

[72] Brown (1967) 311–12: Virtues the Romans ascribed to their heroes "would be realized only in the citizens of this other city"; "Cicero's noble definition of the essence of the Roman Republic could be achieved" only in heavenly Jerusalem (*CD* 2.21; 116–23). Also, Brown (1972) 318.

relinquish what you cherish most for the sake of your *civitas*, to sacrifice self-interest for the common interest. However, the marvelous deed separates out from the wrong motivation. The Romans' astonishing heroism, driven by lust for glory and praise, can be dismissed. Christians must redirect Roman obedience to the state toward obedience to the city of God. All virtuous action must be done for God's sake alone, as He possesses the only glory, and not for one's own renown or even the renown of one's earthly city. Augustine scolds Christians for their pride in renunciation and self-sacrifice in the face of Roman fortitude and courage: glorying in martyrdom undoes its testimony; no one enters the city of God by earning it and pride bars the way. He cuts Romans and weak-minded Christians alike down a notch for mistaken pride and glory. Rather than models for imitation in full, the traditional Roman heroes afford only further occasion for driving home the Christian message of humility.

The model Augustine appropriates, overcomes, and leaves behind is Roman exemplary history, best expressed in the preface to Livy:[73]

> This is especially healthy and fruitful in thinking about things, for you to look at the records of every *exemplum* that have been placed on an illustrious monument and from there to take for yourself and your country (*rei publicae*) what you should imitate, from there to determine what you should avoid as foul in its beginning, foul in its end. *praef.* 10

In Livy's conception, the events of history are to be analyzed for their moral burden and imitated or avoided accordingly. His actual history offers *exempla* containing positive and negative lessons mixed together – no single *exemplum* can be taken whole.[74] History teaches deliberation and moral reasoning beyond mere facts. Roman exemplarity is therefore educative in method as well as content.[75]

Like a good Livian reader, Augustine separates the wheat from the chaff. Roman virtue, admirable in its extreme devotion to serving the *civitas*, teaches that Christians should direct their all toward the *civitas Dei*. His a fortiori argument typifies Roman exemplary reasoning.[76] After recounting how Brutus and Torquatus had their own sons killed for the *res publica*'s benefit, Augustine asks why Christians should boast merely about "holding in contempt all the good things of earth: things which

---

[73] Augustine extensively recontextualized Livy, one of his primary sources for Roman history. His treatment of Camillus may represent his general approach. He focuses on "the episodes that helped highlight Rome's inner division, the corrupt nature of Roman public life, and the suffering wrought by Rome's many wars . . . to the exclusion of positive moments," MacCormack (1999) 204–5.

[74] Chaplin (2000).   [75] Langlands (2011), (2015), (2018).   [76] Lowrie (1997) 47–8.

are surely loved far less than sons?" (5.18; 219–20). The comparative marks the argumentative structure: Romans give up possessions of greater value than Christians do, therefore Christians should feel humility before their model. The principle of Roman exemplarity is not just imitation, but emulation; each generation should attempt to meet and surpass their ancestors' deeds.[77] Augustine preserves the model but inverts the message: Christians should be ashamed if they do not match, much less surpass the "same virtues" as the Romans (5.19; 223).[78] But rather than just substituting Christian humility as the operative term, Augustine deploys a more complex and agonistic dialectical logic.

Augustine's argument advances systematically. First, he corrects pagan values with their own categories, only to leave them behind. He shows that Romans make vice the motor for virtue: *laudis aviditas et gloriae cupido* ("avidity for praise and passion for glory," 5.12; 208). Although he differentiates between "the desire for human glory and the lust for mastery" (5.19; 223), in the end, both are condemned. Even Roman virtue is based in desire and lust. Therefore, the direction of motivation, from glory to virtue, should be reversed: glory, honor, and power should serve virtue, not vice versa (5.12; 210). As often, Augustine enlists the Romans against their own values. A quotation from Horace shows even they thought "love of praise" (*amorem laudis*) was a vice needing remedy (5.13; 213). In Augustine, their burning metaphorically with a "huge desire" for glory and empty pride leads pointlessly to warfare's literal burning, merely for glory's sake – the Romans could have accomplished the same ends more effectively by peaceful means (5.17; 217).

Next, Christian categories surpass and substitute for Roman. Accepting "Christ's poor as our sons" for the sake of a true liberty that will set one free from the "dominion of iniquity and death and the devil" has advantages. These are also structured by comparison, the essential move of the a fortiori: it is more humane, less monstrous, and even easier than killing one's sons for the liberty of the *res publica* (5.18; 219). Virtue serving human glory pales before the "first and least virtue of the saints, who have placed their hope in the grace and mercy of the true God" (5.19; 226). Augustine

---

[77] Roller (2018) 1–31. Inglebert (1996): Augustine's conception of decline among the Romans is structural; they are now less virtuous than their ancestors, because they have succumbed to *libido dominandi* (lust for domination), which brought on Empire and civil war. His temporal opposition is more moral than political (425).

[78] Augustine comments explicitly on exemplarity and its limits: sound reason is preferable to examples (1.22; 34–5); the good in Rome's "admirable example," e.g., the establishment of asylum, "has now been followed in honour of Christ" (1.34; 48).

sets "true virtue" in the place of the "imperfect ... virtue" that serves the earthly city (5.19; 225). This lets him chastise Christian pride in martyrdom as yet another manifestation of empty glory (5.18; 221). Eternal felicity trumps glory of any kind; it entails offering the "true God the sacrifices of humility and contrition and prayer" (5.24; 232). One must serve the city of God without any guarantee of citizenship. *Felicitas*, whom the Romans worshipped along with *Virtus*, is sufficient in that she is everything one should desire; furthermore, she is a godsend (4.21; 167).

Rome offers negative foil to the *civitas Dei* even in its virtues. These are misguided: prudence, justice, fortitude, and temperance are corrupted because they serve glory, whose personification as a "voluptuous woman" Augustine disparages, only to further deny the figuration's truth (5.21; 227). He rejects all chances to make Rome the precursor of a Christian paradigm. Roman filicide does not foreshadow God's sacrifice of his only son for the redemption of sin. The Roman universal extension of citizenship (5.17; 217) does not prefigure the inclusive citizenship of the *civitas Dei*. Only Romulus' Asylum is a dark *umbra* for the remission of sins (5.17; 218).[79] This "shadow" does not rise to the level of a shining *figura*.

In the end, the apparent distinction between Roman glory and civil war collapses in Augustine's analysis. The Romans have been honored for their glory.[80] They have received their reward on this earth (5.15; 216; cf. Matthew 6.2). They neither wanted nor deserve anything more. Felicity for them is one goddess among others. Their mistake is tragic because adoration of glory brought them to civil war, that "great infelicity" (*magna bellorum civilium infelicitas*, 4.23; 170). The Romans turn out not to have two cities, but only one, riven throughout by civil war.

Two Earthly Romes in Milton

The two cities on the shield of Achilles in the *Iliad* create the expectation that whenever we encounter two cities, one will be bad, one good – or at least better. Conflict may not disappear, but, instead of resulting in warfare, it will be mediated through law. The Rome of the Augustan Empire advances over the civil wars of recent history in Vergil in that it brings the rule of law, but it nevertheless exports war to foster peace at home. The alternative cities, Troy and Carthage, are not only defeated, but

---

[79] Hawkins (1975) 101: Romulus is a "pagan image" of Cain, his "biblical archetype"; his asylum "is also 'a sort of image cast ahead,' into the shadows of history" that darkly prefigures "the constitutive principle of God's kingdom."
[80] Hollingworth (2010) 75 n. 24.

oriental empires. Augustine's two Romes split into an abject city of civil war and a better city of misguided virtue, but the whole – whose analogue is Babylon – belongs firmly on the terrestrial side of the allegory. This structure, bad versus better, but still fatally flawed, becomes a central figuration within the Roman tradition.

The Archangel Michael's account of human history in Milton's *Paradise Lost* offers a signal instance of this structure and attests to its power in the *longue durée*. Two terrestrial cities are modeled, once again, on Rome. Here, a contrast between Republic and Empire articulates the split. Both, however, are riven by civil strife. Augustine's model of Rome divided returns here as the earthly city par excellence. In Milton, the Christian father's account of Rome overlays and corrects Vergil's optimistic model of the Augustan peace as at least some form of advance. It shows Rome, as in Vergil's pessimistic model, as an oriental Empire that does not even keep civil war at bay. Such layered allusion is a Vergilian technique; the message accords with Augustine.

The Judaic figure of the promised land and the Christian heavenly Jerusalem divide the world into historical actuality and transcendent aspirations. Milton's two cities likewise both remain bound to earthly history. The two cities in *Paradise Lost* differ, but only in style. Like Augustine's two Romes, both are corrupt; unlike his earthly and heavenly cities, they do not organize around a meaningful distinction.[81] One represents a masculinist and Roman republicanism, where oratory dissolves into "fractious opposition."[82] "Sword-law" reigns; the virtuous orator, modeled on the authoritative statesman of the *Aeneid*'s first simile, has to be saved, like Romulus, in epic mode.

> till at last
> Of middle Age one rising eminent
> in wise deport, spake much of Right and Wrong,
> of Justice, of Religion, Truth and Peace,
> And Judgment from above: him old and young
> exploded, and had seized with violent hands,
> had not a Cloud descending snatched him thence
> unseen amid the throng.
>
> *Paradise Lost* 11.664–71

The other comes in the form of the effeminate luxury and lewdness of Babylon that at first glance corrects republican faction with peace.

---

[81] For contemporary debate about the "first and second Romes," Lim (2010) 126–47.
[82] For Milton's view of oratory, Walker (2009) 137–8; right reason, merit, and virtue legitimate governance, not a particular political form (166–88).

He look'd, and saw the face of things quite chang'd
The brazen Throat of War had ceast to roar,
All now was turn'd to jollity and game,
To luxury and riot, feast and dance,
Marrying or prostituting, as befell,
Rape or Adultery, where passing fair
Allur'd them; thence from Cups to civil Broils.   11.712–18

Rather than a saving distinction, the difference between the earthly cities dissolves. Civil strife besets both. The first evokes the wise orator from *Aeneid* 1.148–53, but instead of assuaging the crowd, his audience turns on him so that the model shifts to Romulus' murder by the Roman senate. In the second, sexual depravity, signal of a rent social bond, reignites "civil" discord. "Rome" returns as "Babylon," differing only in style. As in Augustine, only acceptance of God's city will overcome civil war. Anonymous, the cities represent two sides of universal paradigm.

Providential History: Jerusalem Divided

The terrestrial city's inescapable condition is civil war. Its worst manifestation is instantiated at Rome, but civil war is no mere condition of individual historical cities, among which Rome stands preeminent. Its figurative inscription into Biblical history through fratricide, starting with Cain and Abel, universalizes the internal divide as the paradigm of all earthly history.[83] As with the Romans, the Jewish people is split between right and wrong. Some of them at least love God. As such, they offer a different hermeneutical model: Unlike the virtuous among the Romans, Jews exempt from civil war prefigure the *civitas Dei* founded by Christ. The position of the Jews marks an advance over the Romans and toward the Christians who have heard the good news. Although Christians inhabit a *civitas permixta* always threatened by civil war, whose definitive downfall will arrive only at the end of time, with this move, the *civitas Dei* makes a step forward on its pilgrimage.

---

[83] MacCormack (1999) 205: contrary to Sallust's view that Rome enjoyed primeval innocence (*CD* 2.21), Augustine dwelt on Livy's story of Rome's foundation by Romulus and Remus, which was immediately followed by fratricide (3.6). Hardly alone in finding this story grounds for criticizing Rome, Augustine forwarded a novel interpretation in juxtaposing it with the fratricide of Abel by Cain recounted in Genesis (15.5; 639–41). Rome's foundation legend thereby transforms into an archetypal account of the flawed nature of political power, not just in Rome but universally. MacCormack's survey of late-antique commentators' attempts to square Vergil's apparent story of reconciliation between brothers with the standard story attests to the text's interpretive challenges; she accepts the reconciliation narrative (1998: 7–10).

This is a new intervention: Augustine breaks decisively with the paradigm of history transmitted by the Romans. Henceforth, Rome's return, figuring humanity's inevitable subjection to civil war, comes as backdrop to the promise of its overcoming. With Augustine' *civitas Dei*, founded on love, a new conception enters the tradition – the promise of a real alternative in the establishment of a radically different order. The republic to come becomes a new figure that counters classical pessimism, instantiated in Vergil and Lucan, whose only solution to civil war is an oriental, Egyptianizing empire. Hugo's embrace of the republic to come is paradigmatic for the nineteenth century's happier strand. But the darker classical model remains potent. Houellebecq skewers the possibility of any republican restoration and resurrects the old Roman story modernized: Civil war may be suppressed only under the auspices of an oriental, Islamic empire.

Augustine's scheme moves forward by regressing in time. Biblical history counters the Romans. It is similarly divided, with the fundamental difference that there are two social orders, what Augustine, "speaking allegorically," calls two cities, one that lives "according to man" and one that lives "according to God" (15.1; 634). His parallel surprises: A small sect, which happened to leave behind one of the most influential books of all time, counters the greatest empire of recent years. As in his usual method, the parallel serves a greater antithesis.

Human history begins for Augustine with Cain and Abel. Their story mirrors central elements in the Roman foundation: two brothers, fratricide, the first foundation of an actual city. The difference is that the two Biblical brothers now define the two allegorical cities. Structurally, fratricide supplements the Fall as the original scene of earthly history, which develops and replays this "first example – or as the Greeks call it, archetype" (15.5; 640) until the advent of Christ, which is world-changing. It allows the foundation of a different order, the city of God in pilgrimage in this world. Abel, although already a pilgrim of this city, was not its founder (15.1; 635) – that had to wait for Christ. The foundation of the first earthly city in fratricide is "mirrored by a kind of image of itself" in Rome's foundation, which Augustine characterizes with a quotation from Lucan: "the first walls were wet with a brother's blood" (*BC* 1.95; *CD* 15.5; 640). That is, Rome fully instantiates Cain's foundation; its violence surpassed even that of the other great empire, the Assyrian kingdom.[84] Founded "as a kind of second Babylon" (18.22; 848–9), Rome presents the extremes of good and bad within the limits of the earthly. While Biblical

---

[84] Brown (1967) 309 adopts Augustine's mirror imagery to describe the parallel he makes between Roman pagans and the "aggressive Empire of the Assyrians."

history advances in a providential teleology, captured by the typological hermeneutics of *figura* and *implementum*, earthly history's trope is the mirror, an emblem of vanity and infinite repetition.[85] Like the two brothers, who kill their peer, like the split in the self, which the mirror illustrates so beautifully, earthly history pursues a course of self-division and self-destruction. The difference between Cain and Abel and Romulus and Remus is that the Biblical pair figures the difference between the two cities, whereas the Roman twins figure Roman history entirely within the *civitas terrena*.[86]

Rome, completely earthly, and Jerusalem, which points toward the heavenly city (15.2; 636), offer two paradigms of strife that, like the two allegorical cities themselves, extend throughout all history, "the whole of this time," defined as the age of dying and birth (15.1; 634). Rome's strife is structured as internal division within the same, whether good or bad, while that of the figurative Jerusalem sets the good against the bad. Only in the fully realized *civitas Dei* will strife vanish. Even the good may strive among themselves in a qualified way before attaining perfection. Social strife externalizes strife within the soul.

> Thus the strife that arose between Remus and Romulus showed the extent to which the earthly city is divided against itself (*adversus se ipsam terrena civitas dividatur*), whereas that which arose between Cain and Abel demonstrated the hostility (*inter duas ipsas civitates . . . inimicitias*) between the two cities themselves, the City of God and the city of men. The wicked, therefore, strive among themselves (*inter se*); and likewise, the wicked strive against the good and the good against the wicked (*inter se*). But the good, if they have achieved perfection, cannot strive among themselves (*inter se*). While they are making their way towards perfection, however, and have not yet attained it, there can be strife among them inasmuch as any good man may strive against another (*contra alterum*) because of the part of him with which he also strives against himself (*contra semet ipsum*). Even within one man, "the flesh lusteth against the Spirit, and the Spirit against the flesh."

---

[85] Mirror imagery: Hugedé (1957), Cramer (2005).

[86] Augustine uses fratricide, which clearly shows the city "divided against itself," to denounce paganism, Wiseman (1995) 15. Dante's *Inferno*, with a systematic parallel between the Bible and Rome, follows the Augustinian pattern of history. The descent into Hell follows the standard figurations of civil war. Mahomet's bodily split visualizes schism (Canto 28). Nimrod, the author of Babel's division into multiple languages and a hunter against God (also *CD* 16.4; 702–4), accompanies Ephialtes, an earthborn Giant who rebelled against Jove (Canto 31). The Giants are the classical figuration of civil war as rebellion against heavenly order. In the frozen lake of Cocytus, the space devoted to violence within the family and against God is called after Cain: Caina. In the final Canto (34), Satan, rebel against God, is compared to a giant. He chews on Brutus and Cassius along with Judas: the perpetrators of civil war parallel the betrayer of Christ. Against the traditional interpretation of these sinners as traitors to Church and Empire, we suggest their common sin is the internal split.

Thus, the spiritual desire of one man can strive against the fleshly desires of another (*contra alterius . . . carnalem* [*concupiscentiam*]), or fleshly desire can strive against another's spiritual desire (*contra alterius spiritualem*), just as the good and the wicked strive against one another (*inter se*). Or even the carnal desires of two good men, who have, however, not yet achieved perfection, may strive, just as the wicked strive among themselves (*inter se*), until those who are being healed are finally brought to victorious health (*ad ultimam victoriam sanitas perducatur*). 15.5; 640–1

A similar structure extends through the cities, in relations between individuals, and within the soul.

All human history before the end of time takes place in the *civitas permixta*. The citizens of the two cities "swim together without separation" in the same net (18.49; 896). But not every mixture is the same. The question is what kind of relationship structures one's interactions with others, hence Augustine's repetition of *inter se* in the passage above. The history of actual cities instantiates the differences between mixtures, rendering them vivid. Even though there were good and bad Romans – Regulus is the exceptional example of a virtue even Christians could aspire to[87] – Rome, with her history of extreme virtue and extreme civil war, amounts to a single figuration for the earthly city divided against herself.[88] Jerusalem, however, is divided into two figurations: the earthly and the heavenly. The one is "in servitude with her children" and the other is the "free mother of us all, eternal in heaven" (20.21; 1015). The history of the Jewish people plays out these two figurations. It is not just that the Hebrews endured servitude at the hands of others, they also themselves engaged in civil war. To that extent, the worst of Biblical history matches the Romans.

> Also, they were afflicted not only by external wars, but also by civil wars with each other, in order that the mercy or anger of God might appear through the coming into being of certain causes. 17.23; 819

Jewish civil war follows the model of the wicked striving against the wicked, but in another Hebrew paradigm, the good and wicked strive against each other. Israel was divided in two: one part is the "enemy of Christ" and one "cleaves to Christ" (17.7; 788). This division is "eternal and

---

[87] Augustine uses Regulus to redefine glory as secondary to virtue rather than its aim, von Heyking (2001) 150–71. His recognition of glory as a political good, if short of God's true glory, is a prime instance of his general rhetorical strategy, wherein he "evacuates certain words of their meaning . . . then resuscitates them and redeems them within his own conceptual framework" (151).

[88] Weithman (2014) 240: "Augustine is at his most shocking and effective when he impugns the virtues of venerable figures of Roman history." He grants the Romans "civil virtue" in *Epist.* 138 (241–2), although he never grants them true virtue.

immutable" (789). But Biblical history also establishes a model where the good who have not yet achieved perfection strive against each other. In an advance over the Romans, people can be divided without fighting against each other. Augustine recounts the division, after Solomon, between Judah and Israel: because of Solomon's offences, they were "divided by God's vengeance." Nevertheless, "the people were forbidden by God to fight with their brethren," because "it was not their religion which had been divided but only their kingdom" (17.21; 816–17). The separation of Abraham and Lot shows that division does not necessarily lead to "strife and discord"; "brethren" may separate in peace (16.21; 727). Division does not necessarily spark civil war. Only Christians, once they have reached perfection in the city to come, will not strive against each other at all.

All earthly cities illustrate the city of God, but just as they stand for different mixtures in society, they also enact different types of figuration. While Jerusalem is the type,[89] Rome and Babylon are negative antitypes of the city of God, and hence equivalent. Rome was "founded as a kind of second Babylon" (17.22; 848).

> Thus, we must give the names of Assyrian kings where necessary, in order to show how Babylon, the first Rome, as it were, pursues its course alongside the city of God on pilgrimage in the world: but the things which we must insert into this work for the sake of comparing the two cities, that is, the earthly and the heavenly, must be derived rather from Greek and Latin history, in which Rome herself is like a second Babylon. 18.2; 824

Rome and Babylon replay each other's history in a distorted mirror of Christian history. Such figurations are sprinkled evocatively over Augustine's text.

The detailed story of Semiramis, founder of Babylon, which follows the passage above, as if by the way, illustrates the perversion of Rome's parallel city with familiar tropes. The Babylonian mother's slaying by her son Ninus, "because she, his mother, had dared to defile him by incestuous intercourse" (18.2; 824), reverses Mary and Jesus, mother and son, who figure the Church and the sacrifice that heralds the kingdom of heaven. The inversions are systematic but must be inferred. Mary, immaculate Virgin, gave birth undefiled to a king, not of this earth, who sacrificed himself. She was pierced not by him in passion, but by the seven swords of sorrows in his Passion. The incest of a maculate mother, who succumbed to unholy violence at the hands of her son, matches his lust for imperial

---

[89] Inglebert (1996) 415, 417 for Rome and Babylon as archetypes.

domination (4.6; 149). The parallel between Rome and Babylon intimates Agrippina and Nero as a comparable couple; rumor hinted at another incestuous matricide by an emperor son.[90] Rome and Babylon together precisely reverse the heavenly city as its antitype. Augustine does not flag the point, nor draw a moral. One known category flips places with another: Incest inverts chastity, revenge murder inverts self-sacrifice. The accumulation of horrific stories sets Babylon and Rome on par.

By contrast, the earthly Jerusalem, called the "Holy City," signifies the heavenly city without being "the exact likeness of the truth which is yet to come" (15.2; 636). A difference in figuration separates the earthly Rome, which has no heavenly equivalent, from the earthly Jerusalem. Although both have a role in salvation history, the pagan cities invert, while the city of the chosen people prefigures the heavenly city through a "sign-making image" (*significantis imaginis*, ibid.).

> One part of the earthly city [Jerusalem], by symbolizing something other than itself (*non se significando, sed alteram*),[91] has been made into an image of the Heavenly City; and so it is in bondage (*ideo serviens*), because it was established not for its own sake, but in order to serve as a symbol (*propter aliam significandam*) of another City. . . .
>
> We find, therefore, that the earthly city has two aspects. Under the one, it displays its own presence (*suam praesentiam demonstrantem*); under the other, it serves by its presence to point towards the heavenly city (*caelesti ciuitati significandae sua praesentia servientem*). 15.2; 636–7

Augustine presents even the figurative Jerusalem as split, but this split differs fundamentally from the split dividing Rome. The split in Jerusalem is analogous to the sons of Sarah and Hagar: Ishmael, born in slavery, points to the heavenly city, while Isaac, born free, displays the heavenly city. Augustine describes the task of prefiguration as a division in which one part displays in itself (*sensus literalis*) and the other points to what it serves (*sensus allegoricus*). Just as the chosen people were enslaved politically, so is figuration a kind of servitude. The difference is between literal slavery and the liberation of serving God. The very structure of language, split into proper and figurative meanings, obeys *CD*'s politicized theology. As with the progression from Rome to Jerusalem, language in Augustine passes through analogous semiotic stages.

---

[90] Barrett (1999) 182–3. While Augustine does not endorse the association of Nero with the Antichrist (20.19; 1008), the figure nevertheless circulated.
[91] The figure here, contrary to the translation, is not symbolism, but allegory.

Rome is cut off from the city to come doubly, through figuration and, unlike standard Eusebian doctrine, in *not* serving as the material vehicle for Christianity's dissemination. Instead, the diaspora of the Jews disseminates the word through books prophesying Christ's advent (18.46; 892). Augustine's Jews play a role similar to Dante's Statius, who carries the light behind him, namely to bear a truth they are themselves incapable of understanding. They go before, but "read with darkened eyes" (ibid.). Again, political and semiotics functions align. Political scattering and linguistic division share their origin in God's punishment for the hybris of Babel – ironically, since the aim of building the tower was to prevent people's being "scattered abroad upon the face of the whole earth" (16.4; 702). Although the Roman Empire has imposed a common language on subject nations "as a bond of peace and society," this solution to the problem of Babel backfires. The extension of empire produced wars "of a worse kind, that is, social and civil war" (19.8; 928–9).

History, mythic and actual, in Augustine must always be read figuratively. The different nations stand for different stages in his schema and articulate the structure of his typology. We cannot generalize a person's status as a citizen of the earthly or the heavenly city on the basis of nationality or of belonging to a particular religious institution. This is a universal story, where Rome and Jerusalem embody different figurations, and citizenship in the heavenly city is figured by the Jews, not as a particular people, but as representatives, "in a shadowy and mysterious sense," of "all mankind" (16.3; 700). The example of Job shows that non-Jews may also belong to the "true Israelites, the citizens of the supernal fatherland" (18.47; 893). True Israelites may be found among all nations. The chosen may be found outside the chosen people and not all among the chosen people will be chosen.

Everything depends on an individual's relation to God. No classical Roman, no matter how virtuous, is identified as belonging to the heavenly city, because none of them ever recognizes or can recognize the one true God. Even Regulus, a positive example of fidelity to his city, proves the pagan gods' impotence (1.15; 24–5). He is limited to an exemplary function short of prefiguration. Nevertheless, even in the horror that was Rome, one Roman institution foreshadows the remission of sins, namely Romulus' Asylum (5.17; 218). Some Jews, however, may be citizens of the heavenly city: belief in the one true God is necessary but not sufficient for citizenship. Abel is the supernal city's first citizen, but his brother Cain did not have the right relationship to God. For Augustine, the Jews prefigure the fully realization of Christianity. After the advent of Christ, anyone could potentially embrace the catholic faith, since prefiguration has been ful-filled. The encompassing nature of the universal religion is not linked to any unifying empire but to diaspora. The city of God, spread throughout the world, is not identical to the Catholic Church.[92] Its unification into a kingdom cannot happen within human history: "the unity of the Supernal City . . . is not yet completed," but will be "in time to come" (15.21; 678).

Division within the Soul

Ever since Plato's analogy between city and soul in the *Republic* (*Politeia*), it has been available to political thought.[93] In Augustine, the structure of the two cities maps the internal structure of every human: "in the first man, who was created in the beginning, there arose . . . the two societies or cities (*societates tamquam civitates*) to which the human race belongs" (12.28; 540). "For Augustine, the life of a human being merely retold on a smaller scale the story of all human history."[94]

Civil strife provides the metaphors that articulate the soul's internal structure in *CD*. Sexual desire is as much part of its metaphorics as war. The soul's struggle against itself is "warfare" (19.28; 964); the flesh "lusteth" against the spirit and vice versa in Pauline language (*concupiscit*, 19.4; 920–1; 21.15; 1074; Galatians 5.17). Internal division, which becomes the human condition after the Fall, is a wrong internal hierarchy, which tracks one's relation to God. Postlapsarian misery arises from one's own disobedience to one's self, the result of disobedience to God and a kind of slavery (*servitutem*, 14.15; 612). In Augustine, internal division is the universal structure not only of earthly history, but also of every individual.

Just as the earthly city is the city according to man and the heavenly city is the city according to God, so among citizens of this world, self-love dominates over love of God. Love defines politics as well as the self. Classical conceptions join with Christian to express the workings of the soul. Pauline categories define divergent states of soul – living for the flesh (*concupiscentia*) or for the spirit (*caritas*). For structure, Augustine trans-lates the soul's classical division into three parts, most forcefully expressed by Plato in his *Republic* and mediated by Cicero (14.18–19; 617–18; 14.23;

---

[92] Hofmann (1933) 506; Ratzinger (1954) and (1961).
[93] Lear (1997); Williams (1997); Ferrari (2005); Blössner (2007).
[94] O'Donnell (2005) 303. Sibling rivalry between Abel and Cain marks the two communities to which all belong; people may go "from the city of Abel to the city of Cain by their own free will, back the other way only by divine intervention" (304).

623–4), into a Christian *ars amatoria*. For politics and psychology together, a Christian vision surpasses and supplants Plato's views about the ideal *polis* and Cicero's about the real *res publica*. When the *civitas terrena* eventually yields at the end of history to the eternal *civitas Dei*, the soul's healing will make all politics otiose.

The parallel between city and soul allows psychological conflict to be figured as internal warfare.

> how, or in what sense, is the final state of the wicked to be understood as being one of war? Anyone who asks this question, then, should pay attention to what it is that is so harmful and destructive in war; and he will see that it is nothing other than the mutual opposition and conflict of things. What war, then, can be imagined more grievous and bitter than one in which the will is so much at odds with the passions, and the passions with the will, that their hostility cannot be ended by the victory of either? 19.28; 964

Because Roman civil war stands as the paradigm of earthly history, this metaphorics translates well into the soul. The lust of flesh against spirit (and vice versa) is a kind of warfare, specifically *bellum intestinum* (19.4; 921), a Latin expression for civil war since at least Cicero (*Cat.* 2.13.28).[95] *Intestinum* refers to the guts, the most internal and abject part of the body, where sin is imagined to reside. Adam and Eve's shame at their nakedness results when "the law of sin warred against their mind" (14.18; 616). The passions, anger and lust, are "turbulent and disorderly," Latin metaphors for civil strife; they need to be ruled by the mind and reason, which resides in a "kind of citadel" in the soul, a metaphor encompassing the material city and its political organization; overcoming them requires "compulsion and struggle" (14.19; 618). Lust, in a kind of *mise en abyme*, is divided even against itself, since impotence may happen when "desire grows cold in the body even while burning in the mind" (14.16; 614–15). *Libido dominandi* is the climax of a list of lusts, and civil war provides evidence for its sway over the minds of tyrants – classic instances of failed self-control (14.15; 614).[96] Even when actual sedition and civil war are absent from the city, turbulence infests the courts with lawsuits; even the home is beset with "injuries, suspicions, hostilities and war" (19.5; 925–6). These metaphors consistently span psychic, social, and political orders.

The parallel holds for overcoming turbulence. Civil war is the vicious manifestation of internal warfare within the city, but a better struggle is possible, of the good against the good (15.5; 640–1; cited above pp. 176–7).

---

[95] *In Catilinam* 2.13.28; Sallust, *Bellum Catilinum* 5.2.
[96] White (2008) 49–50; lack of self-control is effeminate.

A better psychic struggle is also possible, where the "soul is conquered only by itself" in an "orderly" fashion (14.23; 624). The soul must conquer the body and its own passions, since it "is at odds with itself," but this is the right kind of victory. Its full realization (*ultimam victoriam*) will come only when the good have themselves reached perfection in the full realization of the city of God (15.5; 640–1). Meanwhile, the prophetic admonition to "flee from the midst of Babylon" should be understood "in a spiritual sense, as meaning that we should flee from the city of this world" (18.18; 842). The progression from old to new covenant allows history to develop, and the soul likewise: the succession of covenants is fit to preserve, "just as it is preserved in the progress of each individual man towards God" (18.11; 834).

As in politics, peace is the desired aim in the soul. Total peace dwells only in the fully realized heavenly city. Over against warfare within the soul and within the *civitas terrena*, Augustine's "Final Good" is "'peace in life eternal' or 'life eternal in peace'" (19.11; 933). Until it is realized, peace is worth fighting for in a structure that recalls the Augustan peace. It will come about through subjugation, but internalized as subjugation of self, that is, obedience to God. Even within the earthly city, war is waged for the sake of "peace with glory" – the wrong aim, but peace nevertheless (19.12; 933–4). Before the full realization of the heavenly city, the "kingdom militant" remains, in which "conflict is still carried on against the enemy" (20.9; 989). In the warfare of the struggle of flesh and spirit, "it is better, I say, to wage war in the hope of eternal peace than to suffer captivity without any thought of release" (21.15; 1074).

It would be tempting to understand such warfare between the two cities as civil war. But this would discredit legitimate warfare as unjust, and Augustine carefully sidesteps such language. Rather, the war of spirit on flesh corresponds to the war of the good against the bad (15.5; 640–1).[97] The future state will be one in which there will be no enemy against whom to fight, a "most peaceful kingdom in which we shall reign without an enemy" (20.9; 989). Augustine enlists Ezekiel's prophecy in support: In the future, there will be "one King" who will rule over all, and "they shall no more be two nations, neither shall they be divided any more into two kingdoms" (18.34; 870). The "present conflict" and "present condition of misery" where the righteous struggle against their vices will yield to a "togetherness" or "harmony" where humankind's spirit will be perfected in "unalloyed peace and virtue" (22.23–4; 1157–8, 1163–5). Spiritual and

[97] Cary (2005) 18–19.

social peace will come together. Humanity will not win the internal battle whose worst manifestation is literal or figurative *bellum intestinum*, but rather will leave conflict behind.

The political register coloring the *civitates* could mislead if taken literally. The heavenly city is no political entity, but a state of being. Until politics is overcome at the heavenly city's full realization, the language of politics will inform humanity's ability to conceptualize it.

Suicide: Rome's Exemplary Sin

Augustine fulminates against suicide, a central trope for civil war in Latin literature, as a normative perversion. This trope tells an unspoken story about the wrong foundation of the wrong city that runs in tandem with his argument. Vergil's metaphorical register tells an unhappy story against the dominant narrative and inscribes civil war into Rome's foundation. In Lucan, virtue and civil war turn out to be paradoxically equivalent, so that history becomes a monotonous horror. Augustine consistently uses Rome's miserable figurations to bolster the differences between the cities. Any further story supplements what he says overtly without contradiction.

The prominent condemnation of suicide in *CD* book 1 indicates the urgency of a contemporary issue. During the sack of Rome, some women who had been raped killed themselves, leaving others, who had not, open to reproach. Lives were at stake, and the values behind the decision to kill oneself or not articulate essential criteria for the definition of the heavenly city against its earthly shadow. Compassionate toward victims, but a fierce defender of survivors, Augustine uses the occasion to excoriate the classic Roman gesture as misplaced pride, perversion of justice, and a misevaluation of purity in body and soul. His argument is that suicide rests on the wrong values; his figurations condemn it as part of civil war.

Augustine's denunciation of suicide – an abomination the Romans cloaked in virtue[98] – unmoors both Christian and Roman assumptions about two subjects central to the right relation of body to soul, soul to God: chastity and freedom. He condemns Lucretia's suicide for the former and Cato's for the latter. Sexuality again parallels politics. Consistent with his usual method, conventional Roman examples show the inadequacy of their standards. These complementary female and male exemplars of Republican sexual and political virtue both also conventionally figure political discord. Suicide, in Augustine's view, neither defends chastity nor brings liberation. Lucretia exemplifies

---

[98] For Roman suicide, Hill (2004), Edwards (2007).

a misunderstanding of the legal order and Cato a mistake in principle. The ostensible virtue in this Roman practice turns out to be, from a Christian perspective, not merely tragedy, but sin. These figurations imply that republican Rome rested on a wrong foundation.

Not all Romans show suicide in the same light. While normative Roman ideology makes Lucretia and Cato paragons of virtue, however lamentable their unnecessary deaths, in Lucan's conflicted depiction, suicide, simultaneously gruesome and virtuous, is paradigmatic of civil war in its paradoxes.[99] Augustine eliminates the paradox by redefining virtue, leaving suicide entirely gruesome and perverse. As such, it retains its function as a trope for civil war. An anecdote in book 2, a traditional Roman story,[100] sets suicide fully within civil war's self-destructive logic. A brother did away with himself upon discovering he had killed his own brother in battle: "He cursed the civil wars and then slew himself, uniting his own body with that of his brother" (2.25; 87). Heaping suicide onto fratricide offers no remedy but only intensifies the slaughter. The brother's remorse turns grotesquely on himself and hardly heals the body politic. His curse does not end civil war but perpetuates it in a further figuration.

Augustine defends women who refrained from suicide on the grounds of corporeal purity's moral indifference: bodily holiness is not destroyed provided the will (*voluntas*) to chastity persists (1.18; 28). He argues it is only one's own – not another's – lust that corrupts; what it corrupts is not the body but the soul. Suicide, the ultimate sin, takes pride in misplaced virtue. Pride arises from love of self, as opposed to humble love of God, and therefore marks the earthly city. Purity of volition eclipses bodily integrity. Suicide touches on will and self-regulation, the intimate relation of body to soul, and the orientation of desire. It paradoxically destroys the self for the ultimate glorification of self. The right relation of will to body, the basis of salvation, saves one specifically from the internal divide, where body and soul fight one another and the soul fights itself. The figurative culmination of this divide is suicide, which maps the structure of the earthly city. No woman, therefore, should act according to Roman values that support suicide, Christian women least of all.

In the first great Roman story, Augustine's "rape of Lucretia" puts her exemplary suicide on trial. He turns the law, a characteristically Roman institution, against their own values to prove that an event that catalyzed

---

[99] Above, pp. 43, 138–9.
[100] Sisenna frg. 129 Peter = frg. 132 Cornell; Livy, *Epitome* 79; Plutarch, *Marius* 39; Velleius Paterculus, *Hist. Rom.* 2.19; Valerius Maximus, 5.5.4; Tacitus, *Histories* 3.51.2. Bannon (1997) 150.

the Roman Republic's foundation was self-contradictory.[101] Argumentatively, the "case" reduces to a "dilemma": "For if she is acquitted of murder, she is charged with adultery; if acquitted of adultery, she is charged with murder" (1.18; 30). Rhetorically, doubling Lucretia's victimization shows she reperforms the problem instead of rectifying it: "She slew the innocent and chaste Lucretia, who had moreover suffered violence" (1.19; 30–1). A logical and legal dilemma, a moral abomination, Lucretia's traditional exemplarity furthermore figures the city's foundation. In Livy, her blood motivates and justifies Brutus' expulsion of the tyrannical Tarquins. Reference to her within the *CD*'s larger framework, about the right foundation of the right city, activates the latent context of her foundational rape. Only values that deplore rape, suicide, and tyranny can put a city on the right foundation; therefore, the foundation of the Roman Republic was perverse from the beginning.

Lucretia's male partner in crime is Cato, equally exemplary of republican virtue. Their suicides frame the beginning and end of the Roman Republic; they conventionally figure its foundation in strife and its collapse into civil war respectively. On *CD*'s figurative level, they demonstrate republican Rome's moral perversion. In addition to suicide, filicide, another of civil war's tropes, overlays Augustine's account of Cato: If he killed himself rightfully, he should not have spared his son but killed him too (1.23; 36). Instead, Cato evinces pride: "For Cato had never conquered Caesar, but, conquered by him, disdained being subjected and, lest he be subjected, chose to be killed by himself" (1.24; 36). Accumulated figures of civil war complement Cato's wrong spiritual disposition.

In parallel to rape, Augustine condemns Cato's concern for subjection as a wrong relation between body and soul. Regulus' counterexample is a better model, even among Romans, for citizens of the heavenly city. The Carthaginians sent Regulus, captured with his men, back to Rome under oath to negotiate for the release of the soldiers. He argued against ransom and returned to the enemy to face torture and certain death. Augustine's favorite Roman exemplar of virtue showed the right values within the limited pagan parameters available. He not only directed love toward the right object in putting his city before his life, but he also disdained death for the right reasons; he was "constant in his love of the Romans, neither stealing away his conquered body from his foes nor his unconquered spirit from his countrymen" (1.24; 37). The right direction of love, the right relation of body to soul make Regulus Augustine's only

[101] Fögen (2002), Koschorke et al. (2007).

consistently positive Roman *exemplum*. But even Regulus shows the insufficiencies of Roman virtue in loving the wrong city. As Regulus surpasses Cato, so do Christians surpass Regulus (1.24; 36). Likewise, Christian women, unsullied even by rape, surpass Lucretia in their humility before divine law.

Lucretia is a countermodel for personal virtue. Cato is paradigmatic for wrong relations of power. Together, they instantiate wrong citizenship. Among other sins, suicide is a problem of pride. Both are vainglorious and unwilling to submit to worldly constraint.[102] This is a double vice for Augustine. Lucretia was "excessively eager for praise" (1.19; 31), and what she wanted to protect, her reputation, was first of all worthless before true humility and secondly could not be assailed if her heart was chaste. Cato blushed "to give Caesar the glory of pardoning himself" (1.24; 36) and disdained subjection to Caesar (1.25; 36). This is again a double error: pride and resistance to worldly domination, which should be indifferent. The only *dominus* is the Lord, whose love is rejected in suicide. Targeting the vainglory of Stoic self-mastery and self-reliance in Cato takes down Roman Stoicism. Debunking the central heroic *exempla* of Roman republican virtue figuratively undoes the foundational values of the Roman Republic: its internal split offered no real change from the tyranny Lucretia's example served to overthrow. The exemplary virtue attributed to suicide by the Roman tradition appears as nothing more than internal violence. Instead of bringing liberation, suicide perversely reenacts civil war. To kill oneself is not to escape from domination, but to pull down all of civil war's horror onto oneself.

CD puts traditional Roman *exempla* to new use: to unravel Roman ideology. Augustine's rhetorical, argumentative, and figural procedure shows up Roman conceptualizations as self-contradictory and misdirected. The *civitas terrena* stands and falls according to whether its institutions and virtues rest on a right foundation. By arguing away Stoic virtue and putting Lucretia on trial, Augustine shows the republican foundation rested instead on internal division. The foundation myth of the Roman Republic, whose catalyst was Lucretia's dead body – raped and self-slain – crumbles when her gesture is deprived of heroism. Reading the rape and suicide of Lucretia thus is an aggressive defoundation of the Roman Republic. In its place, Augustine offers an alternative. He aims to correct and heal Roman folly by redirecting

---

[102] Brown (1967) 309 on Lucretia: "the flamboyant 'set piece,' the *controversia*, in which he piles on innuendoes against the chastity of Lucretia, would have appeared in singularly bad taste."

all that is admirable in their mistaken virtues from the earthly toward the spiritual and substituting in their place salvific Christian values.

God's *pulcherrimum carmen*

Although Augustine's hermeneutics make Rome a mere *umbra* to the heavenly city in substance, his text needs the Romans rhetorically. To overcome their categories, their model, he must undo the media that circulate exemplary stories about Lucretia, Cato, and their ilk. Correcting the means of transmission powerfully corrects ideologies. Therefore, he must overturn the imperial order's founding book, Vergil's *Aeneid*, which announces Augustus' misguided mission of overcoming civil war in the *pax Augusta*. This must be replaced with a new founder of a new city with a new mission. Correct reading for the right ends means supplanting Latin literature with scripture, theater with the Church. The ultimate literary work, however, belongs to God. Latin literature, however, leaves its mark even on His poetics.

Augustine's famous analysis of misreading in the *Confessions* illustrates literature's spiritual power. His account of reading *Aeneid* 4 prior to conversion tells how Dido's passion and suicide evoked in him, still pagan, a pity that foreshadowed Christian compassion but still got it wrong. Dido's suicide already advances over Lucretia's: she killed herself not for glory, but for love. Nevertheless, she dies the wrong way, for erotic, not spiritual love. She is furthermore the wrong object of compassion.

> What is more pitiful than a piteous man not pitying himself and weeping over Dido's death, which came about from her loving Aeneas, not weeping over his own death, which came about from not loving you? ... I did not love you and I was fornicating away from you and around me as I fornicated resounded everywhere "bravo, bravo!" *Confessions* 1.13

All are homologous: suicide for the wrong reason; death of the soul in the wrong kind of reading; vainglory from the approval of spectators, who watch the wrong reading, as in a theater. The passage compresses overlapping elements that occur separately in *CD*, book 1. The theater foreshadows the Church, where self-love is abandoned for the right kind of passion, namely compassion for the true Passion.[103]

CD's first of many citations from Roman authors pointedly corrects Anchises' slogan, a foundational ideological topos, from his speech to

---

[103] Freccero (1986), Vinken (1992b). Scipio Africanus provides a comparatively positive pagan example of resistance to bad politics (destroying Carthage would leave Romans with nothing to fear) and bad institutions (the establishment of a permanent theater, a vehicle for luxury, 1.30–1; 44–6).

Aeneas in *Aeneid* 6. Transfer from a political to a spiritual register opposes the Bible of the heavenly Jerusalem to the Bible of the Roman Empire. "'*Your*' Vergil is now deliberately juxtaposed, at every turn, with '*Our*' scriptures."[104]

> For the King and Founder of this City of which we are resolved to speak has revealed a maxim of the divine law in the Scriptures of His people, where it is said, "God resisteth the proud but giveth grace unto the humble."[105] But the swollen fancy of the proud-spirited envies even this utterance, which belongs to God, and loves to hear the following words spoken in its own praise, "To spare the humble and subdue the proud."[106] I *pref*, 3

The chiasmus of "proud" and "humble" inverts Vergil's categories and elevates them into Christian terms. The spiritually humble replace those subjected militarily; God as king and founder resists the proud, instead of warring them down, like imperial Rome, and gives the gift of grace, rather than sparing the lowly with merely political clemency. Salvation supersedes clemency, the antidote to civic strife; the spiritual supersedes the temporal. Because God's law is prior, Vergil's line becomes a derivative mistranslation, despite the chronology of the citations.

In Augustine, the internal divide is a universal structuring principle. His own writings, like scripture, move the hermeneutic needle forward. As the Old Testament figures the New, Christian writings figure the true word, which belongs to God. This structure can be tamed, it can be deconstructed, but there is no getting around it. Even the metaphorical poem of God's creation divides into light and darkness, itself divided into primary darkness, which enhances the world's beauty, and another darkness of angelic revolt that cannot win approval.

Augustine attributes to God a poetics surprisingly contrary to the usual understanding of providential history. The Romans understood their own literary contribution as offering an edifying history for emulation or avoidance. This is a model not to follow but to overcome. But if we expect God's poetics to offer pure light, Augustine's solution astounds. Aspects of classical rhetoric are folded into a vision that anticipates Romanticism: The contrast between shadow and light is necessary to highlight light itself.[107]

---

[104] Brown (1967) 306.
[105] *Deus superbis resistit, humilibus autem dat gratiam,* James 4.6; 1 Peter 5.5.
[106] *Parcere subiectis et debellare superbos, Aen.* 6.853.
[107] Roberts (1989) 54–5 surveys light images in the *Rhetorica ad Herennium*, Cicero, and Quintilian as background to Augustine's poetics in the *Confessions* and *De doctrina Christiana*. Human learning and style must not self-advertise but rather turn the mind to God (125–31). Chiaroscuro, which lends a role to darkness, is lacking in these passages, but can be found in Pliny: "for in painting, no other thing recommends light so much as shadow" (*nam ut in pictura non alia res magis quam umbra commendat, Epist.* 3.13.4).

Augustine's hermeneutics follows the structure of the cosmos, and his book translates God's creation, "as if a most beautiful poem" (*tamquam pulcherrimum carmen*, 11.18; 472), into Latin. Like God's creation, "set out with antitheses" (*ex quibusdam quasi antithetis*), which are "among the most elegant figures of speech" (*in ornamentis sunt decentissimis*, ibid.) and shared universally by the languages of all nations, his work sets up a series of structural oppositions – or, in language taken from Quintilian, "contrapositions" (9.3.81, quoted in 11.18; 472) – that juxtapose light with darkness. God structures the world according to the figures of classical rhetoric, elevated into Christian hermeneutics.[108] Rome, an *umbra* of darkness, contrasts with earthly Jerusalem, a *figura* of heavenly Jerusalem's light. This contrast replays cosmological order. Antitheses rhetorically shadow the contraries with which God adorned the universe, primary among which is separation of light from darkness (11.19; 472–3).

> Just as the opposition of contraries bestows beauty upon language, then, so is the beauty of this world enhanced by the opposition of contraries, composed, as it were, by an eloquence not of words, but of things. 11.18; 472

Although the universe is prior and rhetoric derives from it, Augustine must explicate its structure by analogy with rhetoric because our all-too-human access to understanding is mediated through language.[109] We come to understand this structure first through book-learning, which illuminates our experience of the world. Much as Augustine tries to escape the tradition that formed him, he cannot shake it off. He therefore redeems what he can and neutralizes the rest.

The darkness of God's word is a means of enlightenment. It "is beneficial in this respect: it causes many views of the truth to appear and to be brought into the light of knowledge, as one reader understands a passage in one way and another in another" (11.19; 472). Since God declared his separation of darkness from light good at the Creation, the primary darkness cannot in itself be bad. Nevertheless, the later angelic darkness that opposed God's light was not approved by him (11.20; 474). This division into good and evil darkness corresponds to Augustine's salvation history, where classical Rome illustrates *ex negativo* the light of the heavenly Jerusalem and has an indispensable hermeneutical function. It nevertheless cannot win God's approval – or indeed Augustine's.

---

[108] Van Fleteren (2001) 13: "Curiously, Augustine's semiotics stem from grammar and rhetoric, not the Bible."
[109] von Heyking (2001) 18.

This illustrative function explains how Augustine justifies telling the story of the earthly city despite its ghastliness, despite his admission he does not match the Roman historians in style or facility (*otium*). All he need do is let them tell their own history in their own words (3.17; 119): They condemn themselves. But if he did nothing but tell their history he would himself be nothing more than another Roman historian (3.18; 123). More than a historian, he is also the exegete of the poem that is the *civitas Dei*. He is the literary critic who analyzes the figurations in the world and the orator who makes the case for the heavenly city. The role Roman history plays in revealing the earthly city is to illustrate at best misguided virtue and at worst nothing more than civil war. This role warrants its inclusion within Augustine's own *magnum opus et arduum* ("a work large and difficult," 1 pref.; 3).[110]

Once again, Rome leaves its traces, however erased. The phrase Augustine uses of his own task comes from Cicero (*Orator* 23.75). The orator, philosopher, rhetorician, and poet whom Augustine acknowledges, citing Lucan's assessment, as *Romani maximus auctor eloquii* ("the greatest author of Roman eloquence," 14.18; 617) speaks of the difficulty of matching style to subject, that is, of decorum. Augustine obeys the principles of classical decorum in giving a scathing account of Roman scoundrels so as to highlight the beauty of the heavenly city in his apology for it. Mirroring God's creation, his rhetorical strategy nevertheless takes a page from the Romans.

***

Shadow and light, the grotesque and the sublime, become foundational tropes for Hugo's Romantic poetics.[111] At the end of the day, Hugo, in his *Preface to Cromwell*, elaborates on Augustine's poetics of opposition. He cites Longinus and Augustine as the authors who bring a new poetics into being.

> Thus, we see born together, and as if holding hands, the genius of melancholy and meditation, the demon of analysis and controversy. At one end of this transitional era sits Longinus, at the other Saint Augustine. We must resist casting disdain on this era where the seed has since borne fruit, on this

---

[110] Brown (1967) 303 translates "a giant of a book" (22.30; 149).

[111] Augustine's light and dark are aesthetic as well as ethical categories, Barr (1962) 222 with n. 1. Brown (1972) 325: "In substituting for the classical ideal of an available self-perfection, the idea of a man placed as a stranger in an uncomprehending land, a man whose virtue lies in a tension towards something else, in hope, in faith, in an ardent yearning for a country that is always distant, but made ever-present by the quality of his love, that 'groans' for it, Augustine could well be called the first Romantic."

time when the least of writers – to use a trivial but frank expression – provided manure for the harvest to follow. The middle ages came on the heels of the late Empire.

Here therefore a new religion, a new society. On this double basis, we must recognize a new poetics has grown. *Preface to Cromwell,* Purnal, Thierry, and Mélèze (1963) 415–16 (our translation)

Paul's second Epistle to the Corinthians is Augustine's illustrative example (11.18; 472). His conversion provides Hugo with shorthand for his own poetics: "chute transfiguration" (fall transfiguration).[112]

---

[112] From Hugo's *William Shakespeare,* Rey (2008) 27.

CHAPTER 5

The Republic to Come
Hugo, Quatrevingt-treize

Quels bonhommes en pains d'épice, que ces bonhommes! Tous parlent comme des acteurs.

All these fellows in gingerbread – what fellows! They all speak like actors.

Gustave Flaubert to Mme Roger des Genettes, upon
reading Quatrevingt-treize (May 1, 1874)[1]

Nineteenth-century literature thinks through the recurrent upheavals that ravaged Europe during its long century with the help of Roman terms. Just as Rome became exemplary of inclusive citizenship as well as earthly history in antiquity, the rights of man established in the French Revolution became universal principles. Victor Hugo embodies the history of the age in his politics, as engaged activist, and in his writings. He represents the hopeful strand of interpreting the conflicts, and his solution provides the next stage in our narrative. Neither the advent of the *civitas Dei* nor the earthly institution of the Church has overcome the Roman curse of civil war. Rather, history will correct Rome with Rome by bringing back its political forms: first republic, then empire. Rome, however, first needs reform.[2] Hugo envisions a new republic, still to come, based on secularized Christian values. With hope comes a fragrant bouquet of Romantic kitsch; both substance and style put him out of sync with the despairing irony of our own troubled times. We hope to make Hugo readable again by clarifying his role in the tradition.

---

[1] For Hugo's interest not "in the psychology of his wooden or stone characters" but their "symbolic value," Eco (2006) 291. Translations of *Quatrevingt-treize* in this chapter are lightly revised from Hugo (1889). The first number is from Boudout (1957), the second from the translation, according to the respective volume number. References given in the form X.Y.Z are to part, book, and chapter number.

[2] Lowrie and Vinken (2018).

Synecdochic Author

First royalist, then admirer of Napoleon, later ardent republican, Hugo is the man of the century; his political commitments track French history as it unfolds. Promoting equality of the sexes and opposing the death penalty, he forwards the values of humanist Romanticism the Revolution of '48 came to stand for. Like many of his compatriots, he writes the history of Paris by rewriting the history of Rome.[3] The allusions to Roman literature and history pervading his writings, however, still need the systematic analysis they deserve. Typical is his citation of Lucan (*bella per Emathios plus quam civilia campos / canimus*, "We sing of wars more than civil waged over Emathian plains," 1.1) in his chapter heading *plus quam civilia bella* (3.2.1). Although scholars duly note the allusion, the plot's enactment of the traditional interpretation of the phrase "more than civil war" as war within the family goes unmentioned. Nineteenth-century scholarship reads the century as self-enclosed, but Hugo knew Vergil and Lucan better than he knew Gustave Flaubert or George Sand.[4]

Rome's long century of civil war, the failure of the Roman Republic, and its replacement by Empire provided a lens for nineteenth-century authors to confront their own successive multitude of political forms.[5] After absolutist monarchy came the 1789 Revolution, foreign wars with Britain, Russia, Austria, and Prussia, among others, the Commune of the Revolution, then the First Republic, the Napoleonic Empire, the restoration of monarchy with Louis XVIII, the 1830 Revolution, the constitutional monarchy of Louis Philippe, the 1848 Revolution, the Second Republic, the Second Empire of Louis Napoleon, war again with Prussia, the Commune, and the Third Republic. Each change allegedly brought the French Revolution to its ultimate conclusion, only to start all over again. Tocqueville is skeptical.[6] After a list of regimes, he exclaims:

> After each of these successive changes it was said that the French Revolution, having achieved what was presumptuously called its work, was finished; men had said that and they believed it. Under the Restoration, I, too, alas! hoped for that, and I continue to hope after the Restoration government

---

[3] Vinken (2009a) and (2011).

[4] Translating Vergil and Lucan at the age of fifteen taught him French prosody, Josephson (1942) 44.

[5] On revolution's creative energy, Ferguson (1994) 3.

[6] Braudel (1978) 117–18; Campion (2004) 104. Brombert (1984) 207: "It is as though Hugo could not come to terms with the mystery of a historical event that was to usher in a redemptive era of indefinite progress, but that instead, by some inexplicable irony, led to the farcical relapses of Louis Bonaparte's tyranny, then to the horrors of the Commune and its repression. The great revolution seemed forgotten, betrayed."

had fallen; and here was the French Revolution starting again, for it was always the same. As we go on, its end seems ever farther off and darker. *Recollections*[7]

Would these upheavals ever cease? Do they serve some end? Is history doomed to repeat nightmarish calamities, or can it advance to salvation? Roman models offered a medium for addressing such questions. Just as civil war was a persistent obsession for Rome, so was its counterpart, revolution, for Europe. France looked back to Rome for historical parallels, but also a model for understanding its long century of tumult. If revolution was truly civil war, that would discredit its ideals and suggest a never-ending cycle. The figuration of contemporary history through Roman tropes is no mere display of learning or humanistic platitudes. The meaning of the present hung in the balance. If Rome had returned, which one, Republic or Empire? Rome torn by civil war? Rome as terrestrial city or as prefiguration of the city to come? Was the Revolution a moment of Vergilian foundation, a Lucanian outbreak of perennial civil war, or could Paris be the site of history's transfiguration into a *civitas Dei*?

Victor Hugo styles himself a new Vergil throughout his literary career, but Lucan always haunts him.[8] In the end, he chooses the Augustinian paradigm. While in *Arc de triomphe* (1837) he declared Napoleonic Paris a better Rome, lacking the stains of founding fratricide, "c'est qu'on n'a pas caché de crime dans ta base, ni dans tes fondements de sang qui s'extravase!" ("The crime in your foundation has not been hid, nor in the extravagant outpour of blood"),[9] thirty-five years later he lost confidence. In 1872, he began *Quatrevingt-treize* (published 1874), the third volume of a projected trilogy on French history conceived in 1862. After *L'homme qui rit* (*The Laughing Man*, 1869), he skipped the second volume on the French monarchy and, prompted by the upheaval of the Commune (1870–1), passed directly to the Revolution.[10] Hugo retreated into voluntary exile in 1872 to write *Quatrevingt-treize* in Hauteville House on Guernsey and finished in 1873. This was his second exile; he had previously withdrawn to Jersey before settling in Guernesey in '1851 to protest the coup of Louis Bonaparte – Napoléon le Petit. He remained there until the Empire fell during the Franco-Prussian War in 1870, when he returned to Paris and

---

[7] Mayer and Kerr (1970) 66.   [8] Josephson (1942) 44. Albouy (1964) 98–9. Vinken (1991b).
[9] "A l'arc de triomphe, Les voix intérieures" ("At the Arch of Triumph, Internal Voices") in Albouy (1964) 945.
[10] Prompted by the Revolution of '48, Michelet interrupted his history of the monarchy (*Histoire de France 1837–1867*, vol. 6 [Louis Onze et le Téméraire]) and turned to writing his *History of the French Revolution*.

was elected to the Assemblée nationale as a patriotic republican for the second time, having already served in 1848. When the French army slaughtered the Commune in Paris, which was protesting the surrender to Prussia and supported workers' rights, he withdrew to Brussels and offered asylum in his own house to the persecuted Communards. For this, the Belgian government expelled him, and he returned to Guernsey. His support of amnesty for the Communards lost him his bid to win reelection to the Assembly in 1872. The Communards, if they escaped slaughter, had meanwhile been sentenced to deadly exile. Hugo actively opposed civil war and firmly identified with resistance: "J'ai cru devoir être présent à la guerre étrangère et absent à la guerre civile" ("I believed I was obliged to be present for external war and absent to civil war").[11] In principled withdrawal, Hugo absents himself from politics to write his novel on civil war. Its original title was *Quatrevingt-treize. Premier recit: La guerre civile* (*Ninety-three. First Story: Civil War*).[12]

Hugo's melodramatic page-turner was an immediate success, selling 200,000 copies in short order. Its subject is the counterrevolutionary upheaval in the Vendée, which opposed the new French republic of the Revolution. Against the background of the Terror in Paris, a symbolic conflict between characters outlines divergent moral and ideological commitments. Lantenac represents the old monarchy, grounded in the divine right of kings, whereas Gauvain and Cimourdain exemplify the clement and unforgiving dimensions of republicanism respectively. Cimourdain represents the historical French revolutionary republic and is condemned, whereas Gauvain embodies Hugo's Romantic ideal and voices his politics. All three are related: Gauvain is Lantenac's great-nephew and heir, as well as the spiritual son of his tutor Cimourdain, who loves him with maternal tenderness. Their conflict revolves around the fate of three innocent children who figure France's future. Their mother, Michelle Fléchard, represents an apolitical and primal maternity set against the patriarchal order of the *ancien régime* and the new republican Terror alike. The novel's climax puts each of the three main male characters in a structural double-bind that pits their own lives and deepest values against these values' institutionalization. Lantenac, who had taken the children hostage and left them to burn as he escaped capture, jeopardizes his cause by putting his own life at risk in answer to their mother's cry when she sees their

---

[11] *Carnets de la guerre et de la Commune* ("Notebooks on war and the Commune"). Carnet du 12 février 1871 au 31 mai 1871, p. 1141. Spiquel (2002) 227.
[12] First edition with Michel Lévy Frères, Paris 1874, volume 2.

imminent horrific death. Lantenac's saving the children puts Gauvain in conflict with himself: to save the institutionalized republic against Lantenac's counterrevolution or to adhere to its universalizing values and grant clemency to his enemy, who has come to embody ideal republican values. Gauvain escapes this impasse by sacrificing himself: He saves the enemy and faces the republican tribunal. Cimourdain, who presides over the tribunal, faces the choice of giving up either his republican commitment to the terror of law or his humanity, whose highest expression resides in his love for Gauvain. He cannot in the end grant clemency, nor can he survive his choice. He commits suicide at the moment the guillotine's blade severs the neck of his spiritual son. The double-bind besetting all the combatants obeys the logic of the Terror and enacts the problematics of civil war.[13] It goes beyond the moral and political dilemma and reveals structural disorder in the order of the world.

Quatrevingt-treize juxtaposes paired paradigms that retrace French history in a dialectic with strong Hegelian overtones.[14] The characters personify clashing worldviews that struggle for ideological dominance. The novel asks whether the new world order envisioned by Hugo can overcome civil war's recurring cycle of violence.[15] The Terror had reduced the Revolution's promise of republican fraternity to fratricide, a familiar classical paradigm. The Commune's violent repression, which spurred Hugo to write, made overcoming civil war urgent again. His hope for an ideal republic, which would enshrine maternal love as its highest virtue, upends the Roman inheritance of masculinist republican values and replaces them with a vision inspired by the Sermon on the Mount: the meek shall inherit the earth; mercy toward women, children, and the weak shall prevail over Roman *virtus*. He conceives of his novel as a secular New Testament that points the way, like Christianity, to those with ears to hear; it offers a promise of charity and chivalry. The living word of literature may not prevent violence but is for Hugo a sacred calling.[16] The novel's climactic ending sets a redemptive self-sacrifice, on the model of Christ's crucifixion, against a suicide that reinstantiates civil war. The novel's interpretation hangs on this final scene.[17]

---

[13] On foundational violence in the ambivalent and structural double-bind of the Terror, Wahnich (2002) 911.

[14] Brombert (1984) 205–30, Ferguson (1998), Catani (2011).

[15] Zard (2009) outlines the novel's three irreconcilable paradigms: history as progress, catastrophe, and genealogical narrative.

[16] Bénichou (1973).

[17] Brombert (1984), the most trenchant analysis of the novel to date, analyzes Hugo's affirmation of the messianic myth of revolution.

Hugo's last novel represents the culmination of his thinking. Various characters, stages, and symbolic positions retrace his political evolution from a stout royalist to a pillar of the French Republican faith and also retail his own family drama. His father, who had fought on the side of the republican Blues, met Sophie Trébuchet on campaign. A *vendéenne* sympathetic to the royalist Whites, she would become Hugo's mother. He tells an early version of this story in *Les contemplations* 5.3.2 (1846): He wept when his mother saved twelve priests, he wept over Louis XVI, over the heroism of the counterrevolutionaries, and he asks if his misreading of history condemns him to "imbécillité" ("foolishness").[18]

The year 1793 was no new date for Hugo when he wrote the novel bearing this title. It was the critical year for the interpretation of the Revolution, for its possible justification and legitimacy, and with it the fate of a republic.[19] The question is whether the Terror of '93 undid the Revolution of '89, whether the Revolution revealed itself in truth to have been civil war. Within Hugo's oeuvre, 1793 first figures civil war as an inadmissible political catastrophe; he later revises his understanding of it in a Hegelian vein, as a stage in a dialectical process through which one must pass to reach a better future. Whereas he condemned the Terror in 1842 as "le flamboiement hideux de ces quatre chiffres sinistres: 1793" ("the hideous blaze of these four numerals: 1793"),[20] in *Les Châtiments* (*Punishments*), written in 1853 in the aftermath of the coup of 1851, '93 becomes the logical and necessary consequence of one thousand years of monarchy, which he condemns as severely as Michelet.[21] The fateful year appears at the end of history as a Titan, "égal par la stature au colosse romain" ("equal in stature to the Roman colossus"), a son of monarchy, nourished on bad examples, that saves liberty with terror and resembles what it overthrows: "Et jetant bas tyrans, parlements, rois, Capets, / Tu te levais contre eux et comme eux tu frappais" ("Overthrowing tyrants, parliaments, kings, Capets, your raised yourself against them and, like them, you struck").[22] The necessity attributed to '93 is the correlate of Lucan's claim that if – a big if – civil war was necessary to bring the reign of Nero, then he has no complaint (1.33–7). We argue in Chapter 3, however,

---

[18] Albouy (1967) 675.
[19] White (2008) 113: 1793 "incarnates the Revolution in an act of self-sacrifice that redeems France from the law of the ancient régime ... the novel's redemptive role (like the Revolution's) can never be disentangled from its sanguinary implications."
[20] *Le Rhin* ("The Rhine"), political conclusion 1842, Seebacher and Rosa (1987), vol. "Voyages": 421.
[21] Vinken (2007).   [22] *Les châtiments*, "Nox" ("Punishments: Night") viii, Albouy (1967) 17.

that Lucan undermines this utterance and, in this chapter, that Hugo progresses from such an understanding.

In the 1850s, Hugo makes '93 the daughter of monarchy. The revolutionaries continue the monarchical reign of hatred and death as if its dutiful children. Having learned nothing better, they obey the *lex talionis*. At stake is whether a new birth can ever make a break. Hugo continues the metaphor of paternity in *Les quatre vents de l'esprit* (*The Four Winds of Spirit*, written on Christmas 1857, not published until 1881), where Louis XVII appears in a vision, and the murdered child identifies his ancestors as responsible for the guillotine. In a fictional dialogue, when asked who built the guillotine, he answers, "O mes pères c'est vous!" ("O my fathers, it's you!"). Hugo consistently sees monarchy and the Terror as trapped within the same murderous logic of filiation:

> Les révolutions, ces grandes affranchies,
> Sont terribles, étant filles des monarchies;
> "Le Verso de la page" ("The Other Side of the Page") 21–2 (1857–8; *Oeuvres complètes* 10, 251–8; Paris: Le Club Français du Livre, 1969)

> Revolutions, those great freedmen, are fearsome, being the daughters of monarchies.

Contrary to the kings stuck in cyclical vengeance, the revolutionaries at least repeat their inexorable violence for the sake of producing a new regime of mercy. The Terror in '93 continues and fulfills the monarchy by bringing it to an end. Itself civil war – the metaphor of "titans" and "giants" persistently recurs – the heir of a regime of civil war, its task is to overcome its own bloody logic, its own Roman inheritance, once and for all. Hugo translates into a political framework the Christian hermeneutics of *figura* (figure) and *implementum* (fulfillment), the trope whereby the New Testament overcomes and fulfills the Old. In Hugo's vision, the giant will purge republican fraternity under Christ's saintly law to become "la fraternité pure" ("pure fraternity," *Châtiments*, "Nox" viii, Albouy [1967] 17).

Henceforth, Hugo adheres to the interpretation he shares with Michelet. A New Revelation, the beginning of a new era, a turn as radical as the birth of Christ, the Revolution provides the conditions for a new reign of love and sacrifice in a republic always just over the horizon. The republic of "liberty, equality, fraternity" has to give way to a republic of "equality, liberty, charity."[23] The adherents of this new faith form a humanitarian apostolate that, in

---

[23] *Préface de Cromwell*, Purnal, Thierry, and Mélèze (1963) 409–54: 415.

a republican reversal, gives even bishops their benediction. In *Les Misérables* (*The Miserable*), it is G., a member of the Convention, who blesses the dying Monseigneur Bienvenu Myriel, rather than vice versa. He explains that the Revolution is "le plus puissant pas du genre humain depuis l'avènement du Christ. Incomplète, soit; mais sublime" ("the most powerful step of the human race since the coming of Christ – incomplete, yes, but sublime").[24]

Quatrevingt-treize discards the paradigm of inevitable filiation – paternity's curse. Hugo is also skeptical of the republican paradigm of fraternal equality. He forwards an ideal republicanism under the sign of the feminine; sisterhood and maternal sacrifice overcome fraternity and patriarchy.[25] Gauvain's program toward the novel's end voices Hugo's own social vision. Sounding like Louise Michel, it includes equality between the sexes,[26] female emancipation, the right to work, guaranteed compensation, the rights of children, and a then forward-looking energy policy that harnesses nature for the betterment of mankind. Hugo secularizes Christ in the figure of the mother, both biological and spiritual.[27] As in the *familia in Christo*, Hugo extends the capacity for maternal care also to men.

In a Hegelian dialectical mode, Hugo gives civil war a necessary role within human history. In Augustine, the light of love revealed illuminates the darkest darkness of Roman history as its negative antitype. Rome's ruinous foreshadowing can therefore, by retrospective rereading, be understood as part of salvation history. Gruesome perversion before the fact highlights all the more history's eventual love and truth. For Augustine, however, Rome, with all its civil war, can never be redeemed. For Hugo, the revelatory light of the Revolution extends redemption retrospectively to all history. In the novel's grand finale, the murderous Terror turns against its own mother, murderous feudalism – for Augustine, the worst of the worst. The mutual cancellation of two evils results in a potentially positive new order to rise from the ashes.[28] Darkness is now fully redeemed. Nobody, even Satan himself, is left behind. In theology, enlightenment's birth from deepest darkness is *apokatastasis*; in philosophy, this is dialectics; and for hermeneutics, the structure is Pauline. There is no escaping civil war's foundational role in earthly history, a lesson Hugo takes from Vergil. Furthermore, the end of history is nowhere in sight.[29]

---

[24] Seebacher and Rosa (1987), vol. "Roman 2": 34.   [25] Derrida (1994).

[26] Grossman (2012) 236–7: In Gauvain's republic, equity takes the place of strict equality so that reciprocity underwrites the political order. His incantatory rhetoric prioritizes poetics over politics.

[27] Bynum (1984).

[28] Karl Marx, read in a messianic way, develops the same structure in the *Eighteenth Brumaire*: the bourgeois revolution finishes off the bourgeois régime.

[29] Gohin (2002) 173: He insisted, more than before 1870, on the impossibility of an absolute end to history.

Nevertheless, there still exists the possibility of founding the right kind of community among men. Like Augustine's *civitas Dei*, already a pilgrim on this earth, Hugo's republic can begin here and now. Its full realization nevertheless remains to come.

Hugo turns to the institution of Latin literature to found his *civitas Dei* in the sphere of letters. He corrects the *translatio imperii* (transfer of empire) with a *translatio litterarum* (transfer of letters). In the spirit of Lucan, who revisits civil war between Caesar and Pompey a century before to indict empire during his own times, Hugo reverts to the French Revolution and the Terror to comment on contemporary politics. Hugo judges 1793 "in the light of (February) 1848 in the wake of 1871."[30] Both disclose horror in the foundational changes of the new order. For each, traumatic, unresolved, and repetitive origins threaten the possibility of a new republican order. Lucan is pessimistic, but Hugo's last novel cleaves to the promise realized in itself.[31] If, in Augustine, classical Rome figures a negative antitype, fulfilled for Hugo in feudalism and absolutism, Hugo turns to a literary work, Vergil's bible of empire, as a perverse foreshadowing to be sublated into his new republic of letters.[32] Roman polemical allusion is subsumed into the Christian hermeneutic schema of *figura* and *implementum*.[33] Hugo fulfills and redeems the Roman literary tradition as the New Testament does the Old.

In Augustine, scripture forwards the right kind of love, which grounds the social bond on earth as in heaven. For Hugo, the right literature, instantiated in his writing, makes available a new mode of being, which grounds the new republican bond. This new, Romantic literature subsumes and displaces both religion and politics. Hugo's novel, offering an alternative politics, an alternative *to* politics, ostensibly escapes from civil war's foundational and bloody structure to enact the new order. Augustine fervently opposes literature as an institution, with Vergil as its preeminent representative.[34] Having used Latin letters to illustrate false reading, in antithesis to the right reading of the true word in scripture, he discards literature once it has served its purpose. The Church Father's own writings aim to convert via the exegesis of scripture. Hugo shares the project but rehabilitates literature as his institutional medium. He sees his vast corpus

---

[30] Mehlman (1977) 46.
[31] Dickens' *A Tale of Two Cities* is an important intertext for *Quatrevingt-treize*, Grossman (2012). Brooks (1984) reads Dickens's novel typologically, according to Augustinian categories.
[32] Grossman (2012).   [33] For polemical allusion, Thomas (1982a), Conte (1986).
[34] *Confessions* 1.13.

as a Romantic New Testament to the republic to come, with himself as its incarnation: "Je suis une chose publique" ("I am a *res publica*").[35]

Hugo voices Paris, which speaks for all Europe: "Écoutez, je suis la ville de Paris / En temps de paix, je suis l'Europe, / En temps de guerre je suis la France, / Moi Paris je stipule pour la France" ("Listen, I am the city of Paris. In times of peace, I am Europe. In times of war, I am France. I, Paris, wager for France").[36] Holding up an idealized Europe, escaped from civil war, as a latter-day *civitas Dei*, Hugo will transfigure the recent catastrophes through poetry and fiction: "L'Année terrible" ("Annus horribilis") tackles the history of the Franco-Prussian War and the Commune; *Quatrevingt-treize* the civil war of the Terror.[37] In *Paris* (1867), prefatory to *Quatrevingt-treize*, Paris even appears as a new Jerusalem.[38] Hugo's literary republic, in his own conception, is not of the prose of this earth but founds the republic to come; it resides in the here and now in the transfiguring body poetic of Victor Hugo. In the face of unspeakable disaster, from the midst of history's catastrophe, Hugo draws his "prophétie de lumière" ("enlightened prophecy") up out from deepest darkness.[39]

In the preface to *Cromwell*, a drama on the English civil wars, Hugo maps out literature's historical stages leading to his own Romantic poetics. Lyric, epic, and drama correspond to primitive, ancient, and modern eras, where each era, although containing all genres, nevertheless has one dominant modality. Like Hegel, Hugo puts the decisive break between ancient and modern in the advent of Christianity, whose celebration of the unification of body and soul discloses a poetics whose highest value is not the beautiful, as in classical antiquity, but rather the heightened conjunction of the sublime with the grotesque, light with shadow, in the hallmark of Romantic aesthetics. For the "muse moderne" ("modern muse"), led by Christianity, in creation,

> le laid y existe à côté du beau, que le difforme près du gracieux, le grotesque au revers du sublime, le mal avec le bien, l'ombre avec la lumière. *Préface de Cromwell*, Purnal, Thierry, and Mélèze (1963) 416

> In it, the ugly subsists beside the beautiful, the deformed near the gracious, the grotesque on the underside of the sublime, evil with good, shadow with light.

[35] Carnet, le 7 novembre 1871, "Voyages," p. 1068. Rosa (1985) 184. Spiquel (2002) 238.
[36] Carnet du 15 août 1870 au 12 février, date unknown, p. 1098; Spiquel (2002) 242.
[37] Mehlman (1977) 46: "If Hugo is imaginable for the nineteenth century as Literature incarnate, that century enters the literature of Hugo with maximal density in his final novel *Quatrevingt-treize*, or 1793 judged in the light of (February) 1848 in the wake of 1871."
[38] Hugo (1867) 26, 326; Spiquel (2002) 244.
[39] Letter to Paul Meurice, June 19, 1871, Spiquel (2002) 234.

While crediting Latin literature in its death throes with the birth of the grotesque, particularly in imperial satire (Juvenal) and the Roman novel (Petronius), he situates Longinus among classical authors and Augustine among Christian at the turning point (333–5). The two stand respectively for the sublime and for Christianity's redemptive message. The former anchors his style, the latter the template for bringing his new good news.

Hugo in fact became the lion of nineteenth-century European literature, despite or perhaps because of his overblown excess, which was and remains for moderns as difficult to stomach as his message.[40] His dominance has forced writers of modernity and its fragmentation to define themselves in his shadow.[41] In revolt, they repeatedly savage with epigram the father they would kill. Jean Cocteau: "Victor Hugo était un fou qui se croyait Victor Hugo" ("VH was a crazy man who took himself for VH"). André Gide, asked to name France's greatest poet: "Victor Hugo, hélas" ("VH, alas"). Umberto Eco: "a single cliché produces kitsch; a hundred clichés, scattered around aimlessly, become epic."[42] Henry James: "Certainly France occasionally produces individuals who express the national conceit with a transcendent fatuity which is not elsewhere to be matched."[43] The Romantic father may have gone into hiding, but he must still be slain and surpassed. His latest son, Michel Houellebecq, adopts many Hugolian techniques: characters symbolizing political positions and the long weight of European history since Roman times; speaking monuments that encode this history in France's landscape and Paris's cityscape; the French habit, taken from the Romans, of universalizing their history as world history; retelling French history in Roman dress. In revenge, Houellebecq completely overturns Hugo's message together with his style.

Children of the Republic

Quatrevingt-treize begins with an act of mercy programmatic for the novel's symbolic registers and their interaction. Upon encountering maternal nourishment, masculine violence transforms into benevolent paternity, the best of republicanism to date. In the forest of Saudraie in Brittany, the republican forces have been cut down from 12,000 to 4,000 in a metaphorical hunt. The battalion of the Bonnet Rouge (the Red Caps) fears ambush at every corner and is prepared to fire at will. Their sutler

---

[40] For Hugo's bathos and sentimentalism, Denby (1997) 7. [41] Mehlman (1977) 24–60.
[42] Cocteau (1950) 21; Gide (2002); Eco (2006) 275.
[43] Henry James, *Parisian Sketches*, ed. Isle Dusoir Lind, New York (1957): 66, quoted in Brooks (2008) 543.

(*vivandière*) stumbles upon a mother seeking refuge in the woods with her three children and nips any violence against them in the bud. Two maternal registers confront a male register. The bread and milk of life oppose the blood of death. The life-giving *vivandière* nourishes the troops and mediates between soldiers and mother.

The mother and children form a touching genre scene in the spirit of the nativity, huddled in a mossy, pastoral alcove among the branches. The sentimentality matches contemporary ideologies that find Christian types among the lower classes. In Millet's *The Keeper of the Herd*, golden lights similarly transfigure a virginal peasant into an icon of the Virgin Mary (Fig. 2.4). Hugo's mother, one babe at the breast, two blond heads sleeping at her feet, becomes the novel's first paradigm of maternity: self-sacrificing motherhood ignorant of politics.[44] Her trinity of children surpasses the Roman twins representing fertility on the Augustan Ara Pacis (Fig. 2.5). All she knows is her name, Michelle Fléchard, her children's, René-Jean, Gros-Alain, and Georgette, and her village, Siscoignard. Her family is dead. Her husband, a soldier for king and church – the monarchical Whites – has died at the hands of she knows not whom. She has fled. Her incomprehension is matched by her devotion to her children. She still nurses her youngest, otherwise too old, because she has nothing else to give. Starving, she feeds her children her last piece of bread. Compassion, needing no knowledge, comes in the gesture of a Christian sacrament.

The tableau of maternal love melts the soldiers' hearts. In the first of the novel's many conversion scenes, saving the refugees transforms them from killers to nurturing fathers. The "Arcadian scene" contrasts sharply with the vocabulary of penetration and violence; in these surroundings, "history and politics appear as obscene intrusions."[45] By adopting the trio of children, the battalion turns them figuratively into children of the republic. They christen the mother "citizen" in the chapter's last word (21; 16). Radoub, the battalion's leader, becomes a loving surrogate father. Phallic, killing masculinity converts into loving nurturing parenthood. Hope for a better future, a republic of charity, emerges from civil war through a secularized conversion.

The children's figurative burden as the futurity of the republic becomes explicit in a later scene. Street-urchins in Paris stammer out the republican motto, *Ça ira* ("it will work"). The narrator spells out, "Ces petits enfants,

[44] Roulin (2001) 197. Chamarat-Malandain (1991) 150: Taught French by nuns and raised in the old faith, Fléchard is ignorant of new, secular republican vocabulary (*patrie*, "fatherland," *parti*, "party," *les Bleus*, "the Blues," *les Blancs*, "the Whites"). She swears by the Virgin: *Dame* ("Lady").
[45] Brombert (1984) 210.

c'était l'immense avenir" (130; "These children, they were the immeasurable future," 128).

Lantenac: Heartless Sovereignty

With Lantenac, monarchy is redescribed in shocking terms. The republican compassion seen in the first book puts Lantenac's exercise of cruel and ruthless justice in a bad light. The aristocratic hero's initial anonymity signals his symbolic role. Rome and the monarchy condense into a single figuration: The counterrevolutionary Lantenac unites Caesar and Pompey, the two opponents of Lucan's *De bello civili*, in boat scenes that evoke and transform challenges facing each Roman hero. Surpassed together, the two enemies merge into a single figuration of Roman civil war. Even more condensed, Lantenac figures monarchy as a *translatio* not only of Rome but also of Hebrew, that is, pre-Christian Jerusalem. Sovereignty rests not on the Christian divine right of kings but on a tyrannical application of law without compassion. Contrary to the monarchic ideal of a merciful king in Christ's image, Lantenac pursues the vengeful justice of the Old Testament's God.[46] Up to the Revolution, for Hugo, as for Michelet, neither Rome nor the Old Testament has been overcome. Together they stand for antiquity without redemption. Where Christian hermeneutics holds that the good news of the New Testament fulfills the words and story of the Old Testament, in Hugo both Rome and the Hebrew Bible turn into negative antitypes.[47] His republic to come makes the New Testament's story in turn a figure to be fulfilled by the Revolution's promise – the Middle Ages missed the opportunity offered by Christianity. Lantenac remains in a feudal, pre-Christian modality, marked as Roman and Hebrew. His medieval politics lacks all grace.

Formally, *Quatrevingt-treize* alludes to Lucan to make symbolic points. A standard civil war trope marks Lantenac's departure from Jersey. He receives good wishes from two aristocrats who call him respectively "general" and "cousin," greetings combining warfare with family relations. Boarding the *Claymore* incognito in peasant garb, Lantenac recalls Caesar, also in disguise (*plebeio ... amictu*, "plebeian cloak," 5.538) when he tries to slip across the Adriatic to rally his fleet, becalmed in Brundisium.[48] Lantenac

---

[46] Michelet (1952), Kantorowicz (1957), Lefort (1986).

[47] The nineteenth-century oriental renaissance thought the Semitic needed overcoming, Olender (2002).

[48] Zard (2009) 31: In the insurrection of the Commune (1871), the gunboats were named *Claymore* and *Carronade*.

himself is the weapon that must cross the English Channel to bring new energy to the French counterrevolution in Brittany, eliding the border between inside and outside. He sets forth from Jersey – besides Guernsey, the other great Channel Island, where Hugo had gone into voluntary exile after the failed '48 Revolution and the coup d'état that established the Second Empire. Both ships meet disaster, Caesar's a storm thwarting his passage, Lantenac's a loose cannon, which his bravery and cunning manage to stop. Lucan redeploys a Vergilian image, civil war figured as cosmic disorder:[49] A simile makes the storm waves as high as Leucas (5.638–40), the cliffs overlooking Actium, where the future Augustus beat Antony in the last battle of the civil wars (31 BCE). Hugo's plot surpasses its Roman forebears. Caesar cannot achieve his attempted passage and must turn back. Lucan's scene meditates on Caesar's characteristic good fortune and allegorizes history's inability to move forward. By contrast, Lantenac overcomes obstacles in ways suggesting human agency. The following scene advances from pagan Fortuna and establishes a different relation to God.

As a blocking device, Hugo's loose cannon reduces Lucan's natural and cosmic disorder to human technology's demonic potential and elevates Lantenac, who masters the monstrous engine of war through calculation. At risk of getting crushed, he inserts a stick between its wheels. Authorial comment interprets his success in one of the novel's many figurations of the letter as the old order: He could not have done better if he had practiced all the exercises in the manual. Lantenac masters the situation, as it were, by the book. A sailor, who irresponsibly failed to secure the cannon from the beginning, can now upend and leash the bronze "monster" (47; 40). The monstrous in Lucan is the visible manifestation of civil war; here, mastering the monster puts only the dead letter on display.

The scene progresses beyond the Romans to the next historical stage with a critique of monarchy. Its symbol, Lantenac, appears as the executor of the Old Testament's merciless law. The captain respects his authority as general – hierarchy is obeyed. Lantenac steps into the role of judge; he decides the fate of the irresponsible sailor, who nevertheless showed heroism by tethering the cannon. Like punishing God, Lantenac first decorates him with a medal for saving the ship, then has him shot and his corpse tossed overboard. His negligence had endangered not just the ship but the whole mission; the entire sea is an ambush, and any fault committed before the enemy merits death (51; 42–3). Lantenac's position appears sovereign

---

[49] Hardie (1986) 103 n. 48, 381–2.

when one sailor remarks to the other that the Vendée has a head, an ancient trope for the executive in the body politic (51; 44).[50]

The threat to this head in the next scene evokes Lucan again: Pompey is decapitated on a little boat by Septimius, a Roman soldier now obedient to the Egyptians (8.597). With heightened drama, the *Claymore*, which had wasted time fighting the cannon, is now threatened by a hostile fleet on one side and shipwreck on the other; while it delays the enemy on a suicide mission, a man comes forward to escort Lantenac to safety on a little boat; he turns out to be the brother of the man who was shot and wants blood vengeance (67; 61). Whereas Pompey, a Roman general, succumbs to a soldier who owes him allegiance in a "civil crime" (*facinus civile*, 8.604), Lantenac talks Halmalo, the brother, into preserving his life on the basis of the divine right of kings. Just as the cannon scene surpasses Lucan's Caesar, so this one surpasses his Pompey. Lantenac reestablishes the medieval order but nevertheless embodies civil war by unifying in his person the two classical opponents. He does not leave civil war behind but only intensifies its feudal incarnation. With him, truth about the monarchy appears: It was not legitimated by the divine right of kings, but rather combined the worst of Rome with Old Testament justice.

The exchange between lord and subject articulates a feudal argument in favor of sovereignty (69–70; 66). If Halmalo truly believes in the cause of God and king, he must acknowledge his brother risked this cause; God now suffers from the assaults on the Church and the imprisoned king, his son just like baby Jesus (71; 67); by killing Lantenac, Halmalo will endanger the cause and align with Satan, just like his brother. Halmalo cannot withstand the reasoning, falls at his feet, and asks for grace, which the marquis accords. In acknowledging the fealty owed his lord, Halmalo voices the chain of analogy of king to God and lord to king according to the medieval conception.[51] A ray of light hits his face, a leitmotif in the novel for moments of conversion.

Lantenac's argument presents the divine logic of sovereignty in the cold legalism of the dead letter. Parricide furthermore reinscribes a paradigm of civil war. Lantenac would not only condemn Halmalo's brother to death again. Saying he would do the same to his own son (72; 68) evokes the exemplary story of Brutus, who killed his sons for conspiring against the

---

[50] E.g., Catiline's statement, reported by Cicero (*Pro Murena* 51), that there were two bodies of the republic, one feeble, with a weak head, the other strong, without a head; and that the latter, as it had been deserving of him, would not lack a head while he was alive. These are conventionally taken as referring to the Senate and the Roman people respectively. Mebane (2017).

[51] Kantorowicz (1957).

newly established republic. Jacques-Louis David's famous painting made him an icon of the French Revolution (Fig. 5.1).[52] Monarchy and republic both appear in the guise of civil war. The plot realizes Lantenac's affirmation of political commitment over family on both sides; he and his heir Gauvain each set a death warrant on the other. Lantenac, advocate of a legalistic sovereignty, embodies Roman civil war as a more powerful unification of Caesar and Pompey; his expressed willingness to kill his own son drives the message unmistakably home. Lantenac undermines the Christian tenet of the divine right of kings, revealing its cold politics as nothing more than civil war continued.

History in Hugo's story has not moved forward. Roman civil war and the divine right of kings turn out to be equally violent and lacking in mercy, as if Christ had never come.

Figure 5.1 Jacques-Louis David, *The Lictors Bring to Brutus the Bodies of His Sons*, Musée du Louvre, Paris

[52] Roulin (2001) 184: this painting is symptomatic of revolutionary patriarchy. Tauber (2016).

Tellmarch: Charity versus the Law

Tellmarch is the novel's first alternative to perpetual civil war. His model of charity casts Lantenac's cruel and legalistic sovereignty in a new light. Meticulous parallels divulge a vast chasm between what they represent. Once Lantenac comes to land, he discovers he has been proscribed as the leader of the uprising in the Vendée. He encounters his double in the man who takes him in: Tellmarch the beggar corresponds to but also inverts his lord. A chthonic and virginal figure of maternity, he joins the novel's other figures of nurturing care apart from or beyond sexual reproduction.[53] Lantenac, who in the previous section enforced a merciless justice, now rises to new levels of savagery with his military strategy of shock and retaliation. Tellmarch, by contrast, exercises a charity indifferent to politics.[54] He saves anyone in need, friend or foe, whereas his lord exterminates all enemies, even women. But the feudal relation linking the two figures yields to a much deeper dependence arising from their precarious humanity. By saving the outcast Lantenac, Tellmarch equalizes lord and vassal, overcoming the hierarchical structure of worldly domination through the practice of charity.

Feudalism, affirmed by Halmalo in the previous section, returns in the figure of the beggar subject to his lord. Now rewritten in a charitable register, Tellmarch's feudalism also rewrites Roman hierarchies. Like Amyclas, the poor soldier Caesar asks to ferry him to Brundisium (Lucan, *De bello civili* 5.504–95), Tellmarch sits beyond politics. While Amyclas, "unconcerned about war" (*securus belli*, 5.526), knows that humble shacks are no booty and his social status guarantees not only safety but also tranquility, for Tellmarch, to be at risk but carefree is rather a state of being. By contrast, Lantenac transgresses the horror of Roman civil war by destroying even the huts of the humble. Total war allows for no sphere of safety beyond the political. On the spiritual plane, his roller-coaster of feelings when facing risk and escaping danger mark him as lacking even Roman virtues (90 and 93; 1.89 and 1.91),[55] while Tellmarch's caring and carefree spiritual disposition points the way to a new realm.

---

[53] Gohin (1979) 520; Tellmarch's name combines earth (*tellus*) with mother (*mater*) (287 n.).

[54] Denby (1997) 10.

[55] By contrast, Augustine admires Regulus' stalwart virtue (above pp. 186–7), however misdirected. In the Roman political imaginary, *securitas* is not simply an objective state of safety, but an affective orientation attending its expectation. Hamilton (2013) 51–67. It is intimately tied to the preservation of social hierarchies and to the reciprocal responsibilities that link citizen, leader, and state. It articulates the emotions attending politics. By contrast, Christian *salvatio* is a spiritual orientation that escapes the political. Lowrie (2015a), (2015b), and (forthcoming b).

Tellmarch advances over Amyclas by reconfiguring social hierarchies. He saves politics from itself by disclosing a space beyond the political. While Amyclas does what Caesar orders (*iussa*, 5.559), Tellmarch saves Lantenac not because he is in fact his lord, but simply as another vulnerable human being. For Lantenac, being outlawed is a temporary and circumstantial parenthesis for a man accustomed to institutional dominance and safety. By contrast, Tellmarch lives always on the edge of starvation, but his actual persistent danger nevertheless fails to undermine a deeper sense of security. He maintains the carefree inattention of the dreamer (114; 1.112). Whereas the Roman and feudal models establish hierarchies of dominance, the Christian figure of the beggar throws domination off balance with his compassion. This radical politics upsets the various received orders. Charity equalizes all as human beings. A Christian register infuses the classical convention of the rich and powerful receiving hospitality or aid from the humble and intensifies, inverts, and overcomes Roman hierarchical discourses.

Parallels between Lantenac and Tellmarch sustain the contrast between them. Their different degrees and kinds of knowledge reveal their opposing natures. Once he leaves the refuge of Tellmarch's underground lair, Lantenac becomes aware of a battle nearby. He exposes himself on a hill out of a special desire for knowledge Augustine chastised as vice: "la curiosité est plus forte que le danger" (106; "curiosity is stronger than a sense of peril," 1.103). From the mayhem, Lantenac infers the republicans have burned down disobedient farmholdings to set an example (106; 1.103). But it is his own men who have taken the republican flag. Being wrong is not merely a failure of knowledge but of self-knowledge. He projects the worst part of his self onto his enemy. In a parallel scene, Tellmarch will also experience "desire to know what was going on" ("il voulait savoir ce que c'était," 115; 1.115) and will also reach the top of a hill. The hamlet has now really burned down, on Lantenac's orders. Tellmarch comes thereby to know Lantenac's true nature.

The revelation of Lantenac's name, dramatically shrouded in mystery, alternately suppressed and revealed at moments of danger and release, indicates not just his individual vulnerability but also his symbolic relationship to knowledge and power. Lantenac's name first joins his person when he reads his own proscription notice. Tellmarch immediately finds him and calls him by name. Exposed in identity as in ideology, Lantenac expects the destitute Tellmarch to betray him and claim the bounty on his head. But informing on him never occurs to Tellmarch. Lacking self-interest, he sees Lantenac as poorer than himself, someone another could

profit from. Tellmarch's charity has no political commitments. Neither
royalist nor republican, he would save anyone in this position (98–9; 1.98).
Having read the proscription, he knows Lantenac is *hors la loi* (an outlaw),
but the law means as little to him as politics. What matters is Lantenac's
absolute status as outcast, his humanity, not his rank.

Circumstances have put the lord at his beggar's mercy. Their dialogue
contrasts feudal hierarchy with humane recognition. Tellmarch outlines
a Christian perspective: The order of charity is a reciprocal relation.
Lantenac gave him daily alms that warded off starvation and saved his
very life. It is now his turn to return the favor. He accordingly shelters him
overnight and shares a humble meal in his underground lair – a chthonic
space of hospitality apart from the world. In Ovid's story of Baucis and
Philemon, they do not recognize the gods they take in and offer them
hospitality as they would anyone. Tellmarch, however, knows and recognizes Lantenac, not merely in his status as lord but fully as a human being.
By contrast, he himself passed in unseen anonymity before Lantenac's eyes
(103; 1.101). Lantenac saw only the rank, not the person, and therefore fails
to recognize him literally, but Tellmarch gives recognition in a broader,
humane sense.[56] Whereas Lantenac's charity was conventional and hierarchical, Tellmarch's is extraordinary. He refuses to profit from their
inverted rank. Whereas Lantenac's few pennies cost him nothing,
Tellmarch, destitute, forgoes a huge fortune.

Naming marks both characters' place in society. Tellmarch's nickname,
"le Caïman," is a native American loanword, meaning alligator, coming to
French from Spanish as a colloquialism for the brigand or glutton who
transgresses legal or social norms. In an ironic twist, his name inverts
perception and reality. This paradigm of charity stands for a postpolitical
politics.

Acclamation by name heralds Lantenac's accession into his full role as
a figure of civil war. His temporary state of suspension – exile in England,
sea voyage, proscription – heightens his reentry onto the political stage.
Observed on the hill, he prepares to hand himself over, but, in a dramatic
inversion, instead of being seized by the enemy, he is hailed. The troops are
royalists who had captured the republican flag, a misleading sign masking
their identity.[57] Once again, Lantenac undergoes peripeteia: Thinking
himself at risk, he is saved. The scene foreshadows his later spiritual

---

[56] Markell (2009).
[57] Mistaking sides characterizes civil war, e.g., Trojans, dressed as Greeks, fight their own men (*Aeneid* 2.372–412).

salvation, when he risks his life to save the children. A simile announces a new way to exist outside society; over against Tellmarch's apolitical modality, Lantenac comes into an idolatrous and charismatic sovereignty.

> La légende raconte qu'il y avait dans les vieilles forêts thuringiennes des êtres étranges, race des géants, plus et moins qu'hommes, qui étaient considérés par les Romains comme des animaux horribles et par les Germains comme des incarnations divines, et qui, selon la rencontre, couraient la chance d'être exterminés ou adorés.
> Le marquis éprouva quelque chose de pareil à ce que devait ressentir un de ces êtres quand, s'attendant à être traité comme un monstre, il était brusquement traité comme un dieu. 109

> Old legends tell of strange beings that were found in ancient Thuringian forests – a race of giants, more or less than men, who were regarded by the Romans as horrible monsters, by the Germans as divine incarnations and who, according to the encounter, ran the risk of being exterminated or adored.
> The marquis felt something of a sentiment which must have shaken one of those creatures when, expecting to be treated like a monster, he suddenly found himself worshipped as a god. 1.108

Aristotle defines the political as the human: The autonomous have no part in the city, as either beast or god (*Politics* 1253a27–9). Lantenac regains his political life with a triumphalist drumroll. This mythic formulation in a German Romantic vein evokes Caesar's perpetual contrast between *Romani* and *Germani* and the classical trope of gigantomachy as civil war. The royalists call for him by name, he announces himself by name and rank, he is named by his troops: "Vive Lantenac! Vive monseigneur! Vive le général!"(109; "Long live Lantenac! Long live monseigneur! Long live the general," 1.107). With emphatic naming, he reemerges from hiding to reclaim his life and his sovereign position, above the law, no member of humanity, but a new divinized Caesar.

Saved by Tellmarch, Lantenac comes into his true nature. He pursues total war in a partisan vein without comprehending any higher duty to humanity, any obligation to pass on his fellow's compassion. He neither understands nor follows Tellmarch's charitable example. Tellmarch saves Lantenac on the condition he do no harm (103; 1.101). Lantenac, who accepts, radically misunderstands the message. Viewing the good through victory's lens, he violates the principles of human charity. He orders the hamlet, which he thought destroyed by republicans, to be burned and all to be shot – soldiers and women alike. Taking children as hostages, he becomes worse than his republican enemy, who had saved a mother with her children.

The conflict between modes of being climaxes in the autoimmune backfiring of Tellmarch's charity.[58] He is aghast to find two women shot on Lantenac's orders; his own mercy has enabled atrocity (120; 1.120). According to his consistent principles, he rescues the one still breathing (Michelle Fléchard). These principles set up Lantenac's eventual transformation, but for now, Lantenac's deafness of heart marks his unrealized potential for conversion. The title of the section's second chapter alludes to Psalm 115.6, where idolatrous statues are rejected as lifeless: *Aures habet et non audiet* ("he has ears and will not hear," 1.4.2). The New Testament (Matthew 11.15) adopts the metaphor of hearing for conversion from Isaiah 6.9–10. Lantenac's literal inability to hear church bells sounding the alarm figures his inability to hear the good news of Tellmarch's charity.

In Hugo, Roman history and feudalism alike are saturated with civil war. The medieval monarchy betrayed the charitable order inaugurated by Christianity. However, it became possible to at least imagine an alternative, more loving polity, which, although unrealized, could exist *extra muros*. Tellmarch, who figures humane charity outside law, politics, economy, and self-interest, discloses the possibility of compassion realized at the novel's climax. Healing the broken bond, he prefigures Gauvain, who imagines a republic of charity in the world. The Revolution's republican mantra, liberty, equality, and fraternity, falls short of the principle of charity. Furthermore, it perverts its own ideals and perpetuates monarchic vices. The new republic falters and falls back into civil war.

This section's last chapter title, "Pas de grace (mot d'ordre de la commune), pas de quartier (mot d'ordre des princes)" ("No mercy! [Watchword of the commune] – 'No quarter!' [Watchword of the princes]," 1.4.7), layers the insurrection against the Assemblée nationale in 1871, the events that prompted the novel's composition, over the original Commune, the name of the revolutionary republican government of 1792. Interlocking word order highlights the symmetry between republican and monarchic opponents, equally inexorable. Obeying a hard principle of retribution that devolves into retaliation, both share the same violence, despite conflicting ideologies.

The *Convention*: Revolution as Civil War

In Part 11, the shift from Brittany to Paris plunges into the grotesque. The Revolution's leaders appear in two guises: high-style Lucanian monstrosity and the low-style perversion of Juvenal. Cimourdain, a former Catholic

---

[58] For protection measures that turn on the self, Esposito (2011); Hamilton (2013).

priest, embodies the Republic's harsh side as a sublime monster, while the unholy trinity of Robespierre, Danton, and Marat embodies the revolution in a satiric mode. For all Cimourdain's awful and hard republicanism, his nobility is denied the leaders of the Terror.

The trope of the republic as substitute family governs Cimourdain. Traditionally, the monarch married the state as a symbolic husband; in Lucan, Cato's is the Republic's husband (above, p. 107). Cimourdain keeps his vows, though not his faith, on leaving the priesthood. He finds a substitute for the bodily family and wife he had foresworn by adopting his fatherland and marrying humanity instead (133–4; 1.132). Natural love's frustration drives him to a saintly devotion to the people in their misery and a passionate hatred of oppression. He exhibits at the same time "tendresse redoutable" ("formidable tenderness") and inexorable rationality that forecloses tenderness ("Le logique ne s'attendrit pas"). Like other republican intellectuals of the nineteenth century, Hugo found chastity monstrous. Cimourdain embodies a sinister virginity in sublime isolation (134, 140–1; 1.132, 1.138). The trope of perverted sexuality critiques the Catholic Church and monarchy together: the monstrous chastity of the one matches the cruel libertinage of the other.[59]

Cimourdain has one love, the young aristocrat he tutored as his spiritual son (142; 1.140). His love for Gauvain, his only redeeming virtue, humanizes his republican ardor. He secularizes the cloister as a family *in Christo* with a masculinist republicanism. Uniting tender male roles (*père, frère, ami, créateur,* 141–2; 1.139), his love nevertheless opens Cimourdain to the maternal. As tutor, as nurse, Cimourdain substitutes for the ideal parent. Educating Gauvain into the life of letters, Cimourdain also nurses him back to health during a life-threatening illness; he gives bodily and spiritual nourishment as father and mother combined (143; 1.140). In this figuration, republican spiritual parenthood adopts Bernard de Clairvaux's model of the Church as maternity and paternity united.[60]

Cimourdain's republican program stands under the double signs of pagan antiquity: rationality and horror. The former priest embraces revolutionary renewal (134; 133) with zeal for logic and science. Eager for regeneration even at the price of revolution, Cimourdain justifies civil bloodshed among nearest and dearest to Marat: "Oui, c'est plus que la guerre dans la patrie, c'est la guerre dans la famille. Il le faut, et c'est bien. Les grands rajeunissements des peuples sont à ce prix" (247; "Yes; this is more than war in the country – it is war in families. It is necessary, and it is

---

[59] Vinken (2007) analyzes these tropes in Michelet.   [60] Bynum (1984).

well. The grand restoration of the people must be bought at this price," 2.2). Although the Revolution has right and reason on its side, he fears it will abort. He adds Pallas' terrifying shield, emblazoned with Medusa's snaky head, to the revolution's bright future as star-crowned Minerva (135; 1.134). To classical reason, he adds classical terror as retribution ("terreur pour terreur"); to Roman republicanism, he adds a more primitive and Greek justice ("la Thémis d'Homère," 137; 1.136). His conception of the republic takes inspiration from Sparta and Athens, and from Draco as well as Plato (134; 1.133). Cimourdain belongs to the Évéché, whose members include men worthy of Sparta (138; 1.136). As a Stoic (129; 1.127), he is styled in Greek roles: philosopher, athlete (134; 1.133), and hero. His love of Gauvain is his Achilles' heel, not bathed in the Styx (141; 1.139). The Revolution's aftermath, when Europe attacks France and France attacks Paris, comes in Aristotle's canonical high-style genres: epic and tragedy (135; 1.134).

The pagan underworld stamps the Terror's leaders as hellish in a fanfare of classical allusions. The chapter "Minos, Éaque, et Rhadamante" (145; "Minos, Aeacus, and Rhadamathus," 1.145) introduces Robespierre, Danton, and Marat as the judges of Hades.[61] Citation of the *Aeneid*'s *katabasis* (*magna testantur voce per umbras,* "they give witness through the shades with loud voice") puts in the plural a Vergilian phrase: Theseus reprimands the sinners of the underworld and enjoins them to learn justice (6.619).[62] Parricides, perpetrators of incest and fraud – their actions figure the social bond's rupture. Marat announces himself and his compatriots as the three heads of Cerberus (159; 1.158). He prophesies in an ancient mode, predicting to their faces that Robespierre will send Danton to the guillotine (158; 1.157). The rational Roman model of republicanism crumbles before this infernal trio. Antiquity returns as pure horror.

In revolutionary Paris (1.1.1), contemporary history comes in a jumble of ancient genres. Heroism and orgies, tragedy and parody mingle in the topsy-turvy world of the carnivalesque (132; 1.131). A jumble of high and low, classical, biblical, and oriental sets a tone of upheaval and mixes exuberance with fear. Stoicism, upstart freedmen like Trimalchio, orientalized suppers, bare feet adorned with diamonds, a fashion for Latin and Greek, the Peloponnesian war, Thermopylae, Gomorrah – all mixed together satirize the Revolution in a pastiche of orientalized antiquity. In the *Eighteenth Brumaire of Napoleon Bonaparte*, Marx identifies the French

---

[61] Peyrache-Leborgne (1996) 59: epic register.   [62] Chamarat-Malandain (1991) 147: allusion.

Revolution of '89 with tragedy and that of '48 with farce. *Quatrevingt-treize* puts parody in the Revolution from the start.[63]

The deformed bodies of the Terror's unholy leaders are caricatured in the spirit of Daumier (146; 1.145–7): Robespierre has a tic; Danton is a dandy marred by smallpox; Marat is yellow and twisted. Disfiguring the Revolution's ideals, they dismember and distort the body politic. Marat proposes dictatorship (158; 1.157). Already in republican Rome, this legitimate magistracy, meant for short moments of crisis, was perverted by Caesar's perpetual dictatorship. Here, it heralds tyranny. The French three, disunified from the beginning, turn each against the others to win dominance for himself.

The Terror's triumvirate is riven by dissension. Their disagreement, down even to the enemy's identity, formally reenacts civil war.[64] Danton thinks the greatest threat is external, coming from Prussia; for Robespierre, foreign war comes home when Brittany joins Britain (150, 152; 1.150, 1.151); Marat shows both are fools: While they correctly identify individual sites of conflict, they miss the war of all against all (149; 149). For him, the worst threat is faction in Paris among the multifarious parties meeting in cafés: "Il est dans l'absence d'unité, ... dans l'anarchie des volontés" (156; "It consists in the absence of unity; ... in the anarchy of wills," 1.155). Each level of conflict intensifies the closer it comes to home (159; 1.158). In Lucan, internal violence spans citizens and family members; friendly fire destroys allies; suicide takes division within the individual. Danton picks up the concentric circles of progressive interiorization as a central trope of civil war; fratricide is the overarching category of his denunciation of, in order, foreign, civil, and domestic war (163; 1.163–4). Robespierre pulls the metaphor within the body: Civil war is an ulcer (150; 1.150). Danton even reproaches Marat by calling him Cain, the archetypical fratricide, a toad petrified by hatred who returns after six thousand years (166; 1.166).[65]

Sexualized language figures civil war's monstrosity as internal and abject. Marat has spies everywhere and knows everything: who was with whom and where, down to the bed of each petty whore. When his spies know what Robespierre's spies have been up to, a sign of internal mistrust, it is not clear who conspires against whom: "on conspire, on conspire, on conspire" (157; "conspiracies – conspiracies – conspiracies," 1.156). In Roman conspiracy stories, a woman nudges a man from behind or

[63] Marx (1960).
[64] External, civil, religious, and familial warfare intertwine in this scene, Campion (2004) 108. Danton's fixation on Prussia anticipates 1870–1 (109).
[65] Laurent (2002) 156, Zard (2009) 36.

transmits information.[66] Marat views his fellows through the lens of sexual politics: Robespierre becomes a vain and girly dandy, scheming to advance through marriage (161; 162), Danton and prostitute and client simultaneously; revolutionary acts have all served profit (164; 1.164–5). Even the guillotine sexualizes death. With the nickname *Louisette* (165; 1.165), Marat puns on, belittles, and feminizes the Bourbon monarchy. Danton and Marat spar over whether it is widow or virgin, whether they can impregnate it or not (163; 1.164). If Rome is a monstrous mother in Joachim Du Bellay, who in decadent fertility gives birth only to death, Paris, in civil war, is figured as a monstrous mother who births a stillborn nation. The scene foreshadows the imminent death of Marat, murdered by Charlotte Corday, an unheroic death in a bathtub, by a woman, with a kitchen knife, a woman's weapon. Seneca's suicide, forced by the tyrannical Nero, also in a bath, appears noble in comparison (214; 1.229). Republican male public space, already perverted under the Roman Empire, is further degraded through feminization indoors. Roman *virtus*, republican manliness, dissolves here into effeminate lasciviousness and debased animality. Marat, in Danton's view, leads a secret, reptilian life, like vermin in the basement ("cloporte," 164; "wood louse," 1.164). Like pests, the internal enemy must be "exterminated" (149; 1.149), the monarchy "eliminated" (152; 1.151).

The three charge Cimourdain with a surveillance mission. Spying not on the enemy, but their own side, fosters internal division. Ironically, they instigate division under the sign of unity: RÉPUBLIQUE FRANÇAISE, UNE ET INDIVISIBLE (171; "THE FRENCH REPUBLIC, ONE AND INDIVISIBLE," 1.171). Cimourdain's charge, to oversee none other than Gauvain, the Vendéean leader on the republican side, brings the conflict into his own spiritual family, pitching father against son. The Terror's leaders promote the same inexorability as their enemy Lantenac. By giving Cimourdain full power over life and death if Gauvain pardons Lantenac – evident foreshadowing – they wage war even more insidiously than their opponent. Father must mistrust son; they mistrust Cimourdain and enforce proscription. In a literal sign of distrust, Marat posts a decree throughout the Vendée: Republican leaders who let a monarchic prisoner escape will be executed (175, 214–15; 1.174, 1.229–30). The plot's engine is now fired for a war of all against all.

[66] Pagán (2004) and (2008).

Plus quam civilia bella: All in the Family

That family maps the ideological terrain of civil war was not an inevitable choice. In Balzac's *Les Chouans*, on the 1799 revolt in Brittany, erotic love probes whether civil war can be overcome. Love interest, however, is banned from Hugo's novel – an extraordinary move for the genre. In *Quatrevingt-treize*, where eroticism tarnishes aristocracy and Terror alike,[67] Roman paternity and Christian maternity supplant sexual love as vehicles for ending civil war. The first is rejected and the second reformed. A French novel on republicanism could well turn on fraternity. Hugo draws on Vergil instead, who makes paternity the primary relationship between male family members.[68] But, rather than grounding refoundation, all fatherhood simply reenacts civil war.[69] On the Christian side, the positive model of maternal self-sacrifice splits in two. Spiritual maternity naturalizes in a fertile biological mother, who sacrifices herself for her children. Gauvain spiritualizes virginity. These are civil war's only humane alternatives.

Family relations between the three male protagonists in *Quatrevingt-treize* enact the familiar Roman trope for civil war.[70] The triangulation between Lantenac, Cimourdain, and Gauvain sets a hermeneutic riddle. Progressive revelations underscore that the three, one royalist against two republicans in the Vendée, belong symbolically to the same family. Lantenac and Cimourdain are both father substitutes for Gauvain. Allusion to the traditional interpretation of Lucan's first line (*bella plus quam . . . civilia*) with the title of the chapter (*plus quam civilia bella*, 3.2.1)[71] evokes the war between Pompey and Caesar, apparently "more than civil" because the two were related by marriage. In Latin literature, they often appear as father-in-law and son-in-law. Pompey had married Caesar's daughter Julia (Vergil, *Aeneid* 6.830–1), and Lucan cites her death as a reason for their alliance's dissolution (1.113). Violation of the marriage bond figures civil war at Rome just as much as killing blood relations, but Hugo banishes marriage along with eroticism. Allusion to another famous Roman pair bound by paternity, by inheritance rather than heredity, sets Gauvain, an orphan and Lantenac's great-nephew and heir, in the model of Octavian, great-nephew of Julius Caesar, adopted as heir in his will.

---

[67] A constant topic for Hugo, e.g., *Le Roi s'amuse* and *L'Homme qui rit*.

[68] Lee (1979), Lloyd (1999).

[69] Hamilton (1994) and Roulin (2001) explore motherhood and fatherhood in the novel.

[70] Grossman (2012) 183, 190–1, links civil war and familial conflict in Hugo, touching on his references to Cain, Manlius, and Greek *stasis*.

[71] Campion (2004) 110 notes the allusion.

Mystery heightens the shock of their enmity. As with Lantenac, the dramatic revelation of Gauvain's name discloses the character's structural role. In the twilight, Lantenac cannot at first decipher the signature authorizing his proscription (95; 1.92). At daybreak, he discovers it is Gauvain. He becomes pensive and repeats the name four times in bafflement. The first mention of Gauvain's name in the novel, Lantenac's recognition alerts the reader that more than conventional enmity links them, although their relation and Gauvain's identity remain opaque.

Repetition drives the point home. Cimourdain had tutored Gauvain and raised him in the new doctrine of republicanism. The formal parallel between fathers is strong. When Cimourdain is sent to oversee Gauvain by the Terror's leaders, the full gut-punch of his mission in this *bellum intestinum* is dramatized when Robespierre, who does not know Gauvain's name, rifles through his papers, heightening the suspense. Cimourdain grows pale when he realizes he must surveil none other than his spiritual son (176; 1.175). En route to Dol, he hears an innkeeper recount the recent battle between Lantenac and Gauvain first anonymously, then through a series of symmetrical oppositions:

> –L'un est jeune, l'autre est vieux; C'est le petit-neveu qui se bat contre le grand-oncle. L'oncle est royaliste, le neveu est patriote. L'oncle commande les blancs, le neveu commande les bleus. Ah! ils ne se feront pas quartier, allez. C'est une guerre à mort. 246

> One is young, the other old. It is the grand-nephew who fights the great-uncle. The uncle is a Royalist, the nephew a patriot. The uncle commands the Whites, the nephew commands the Blues. Ah, they will show no quarter, I'll warrant you. It is a war to the death. 2.4

The names emerge climactically on paired, symmetrical placards: Cimourdain reads that Lantenac and Gauvain each threatens the other with death (247; 2.4).

The Roman model now transforms. In Lucan, the apparent balance between Pompey and Caesar, the main civil war opponents, is upset when a third leader, Cato, joins the alleged republican side. A noble Stoic, he calls Pompey's bluff. As a republican fighting for *libertas*, he shows that Pompey fights for domination no less than Caesar. Once Pompey is gone, civil war, however, does not rest. His split spirit occupies both Brutus and Cato, who return to the fight. In Hugo, Lucan's divisions and asymmetries transfer onto a higher plane. The symmetrical paternity between Gauvain's two surrogate fathers is disrupted with the shift from a masculinist and Roman paradigm to a new figuration: self-sacrifice under maternity's sign.

Whereas even Stoicism fails to overcome civil war in Lucan, the resurrected high medieval ideal of spiritual motherhood points beyond it in Hugo. If any male character acts nobly, it is within this new paradigm.

Each of the protagonists engages in a self-sacrifice that leaves Rome behind to a greater or lesser degree. The character most in the Roman model is Lantenac. Ever committed to paternalism, his masculinity never challenged, he falls short of both literal and symbolic paternity. Never fathering a child, even out of wedlock, he figures monarchy as decadent, sterile, and cruel. He abandons Gauvain orphaned at home and departs for frivolous Versailles (142; 1.140). He appears as a man of pleasure; a *libertin*, who wages war on the weaker sex before becoming a warrior – he is "terrible" (170; 1.170). Because he never comprehends the revolutionary, world-changing implications of risking his life to save the mother's children, he cannot break from a Roman mode. Like Vergil's Aeneas, "ignorant" of the empire to come (*ignarus, Aen.* 8.730), and Dante's Statius, who carries the light behind him, he enlightens others but cannot see his own truth (*Purgatorio* 21).

Cimourdain takes a step in the right direction; nursing Gauvain as a young child graces him with a maternal touch. At a fork, unlike Hercules, who hesitated before fixing on the high road, he automatically and without reflection chooses the dangerous path to Dol. Throwing his body between a saber and his spiritual son, he saves Gauvain's life yet again (269–70; 2.27–8). Nevertheless, Cimourdain remains monstrous; his sacrifice falls short of a second coming. With blood obscuring his face, Gauvain reads his name off the papers in his wallet – another recognition by reading – according to the conventions of classical *anagnorisis* (271; 2.29). Rage, not love, motivates Cimourdain's political fervor. His love for Gauvain never escapes narcissism; he has formed his pupil as Pygmalion formed his statue (143; 1.140). He cannot live beyond the earthly life of his beloved and his suicide follows classical models: Lucanian suicide as civil war and Cato's Stoic suicide. The republican *libertas* he kills himself to save is insufficient for Christian liberation. Whereas Lantenac represents a decadent Rome and perverts the divine right of kings, Cimourdain represents a cold republicanism and perverts Christian spirituality through dearth of charity.

Michelle Fléchard and Gauvain together rise to the spiritual maternity of the Virgin Mary and Christ's self-sacrifice. The mother quests to find her lost children along the "Stations of the Cross" ("la Voie Douloureuse," 365). *Dolorosa* (chapter title, 3.2.8) evokes the *stabat mater*; *Vox in deserto* (chapter title, 3.4.5) overlays the image with the voice of John the Baptist.[72] Christ-like, she becomes a slave (365; Paul, Philippians 2.7; 2.132) and cries forsaken in her solitude (366; 2.131). Radoub, finally seeing her again after long separation, casually, somewhat jocularly remarks she has been resurrected (423; 2.197). The figuration is complete. Love brings this mother, who lives only for her children, back from death in an *imitatio Christi*.

Gauvain's self-sacrifice at the guillotine transforms him into the virginal mother of the ideal republic in the fullest sense. His innocent femininity, purged of masculine features, looks to Galahad rather than Gawain, after whom he is named. Critics have tirelessly hunted for biographical clues in Hugo's life. He bears the name of his most prominent lover, Juliette Drouet (born Gauvain), and is modeled on Hugo's last love. In sharp contrast to the French monarchy, the Republic's future depends not on legitimate sexual procreation but, like Roman Catholicism, on spiritual children.[73] French monarchy, which relied on patriarchal filiation, specifically excluded female succession according to Salic law. Hugo's republic anxiously avoids anything male or patriarchal. His republic to come secularizes the highest values of the Catholic Church: Both exclude patriarchal filiation and sexual procreation; both purge and redeem masculinity with a maternal model; both bear and raise spiritual children with motherly, not paternal love.

No single man mentioned in the novel procreates sexually. Whereas Lantenac and Cimourdain are both monstrous within a sexual paradigm, one promiscuously active without issue, the other obeying an awful abstinence, Gauvain adheres to the chaste love of Late Antiquity. In Hugo, spiritual maternity is the measure against which both sexes' humanity is revealed.[74] Gauvain, transfigured in the luminous sublime of the virginal maternal, overcomes biological motherhood to fully combine Mary with Christ.

Quatrevingt-treize makes sexuality and family violent and perverse. The social bond as historically realized from Greece, through Rome, up to the present has been unable to escape internal violence. All history sweeps into the bin of civil war: "Les guerres entre parents sont tout l'histoire du moyen âge; les Étéocles et le Polynices sont gothiques aussi bien que grecs, et Hamlet fait dans Elseneur ce qu'Oreste a fait dans Argos" (317; "Wars between kinsmen make up the history of the Middle Ages: Eteocles and Polynices are Gothic as well as Grecian, and Hamlet does at Elsinore what Orestes did in Argos," 2.75). Christianity's revolution, the substitution of

---

[72] Gohin (1979) 520.   [73] Gohin (1979) 519.   [74] Grossman (2012) 198–9.

spiritual motherhood for paternalistic and biological families, families in Christ for families tied by blood, sex, and property, has failed. The family remains fallen throughout history, the coming of Christ ineffective. Hugo must renew the faith with another politics, finally humane.

La Tourgue: A Spectral History

The violence of universal history turns to stone in a fortress (2.2.9). The fictional tower, bridge, and library are an allegory of history. The description of each part of the Gauvain family's ancestral home falls into subchapters. The only section of the book to undergo such formal segmentation, it is emblematic of Hugo's periodic conception of history. The rubric, "Une bastille de province" ("a provincial Bastille") makes the complex an icon of tyranny waiting to be overthrown.

The chapter traces a historical arc from antiquity to the Revolution. With the etymology of the Romanesque from the Roman, fallen empire inserts itself into the tower's medieval origins. Begun in the ninth century, it is completed in the twelfth after the third Crusade (293; 2.53). Like the eighty-foot tower Caesar builds to besiege Marseilles (Caesar, *Bellum civile* 2.1), described by Lucan as an immense labor (3.374–82), the Tourgue is a monstrous technology of civil war. The dungeon, shaped as an oubliette (296; 2.55), a hatch in the ceiling for an exit, resembles Sallust's description of the horrific Tullianum, into which the Catilinarian conspirators were lowered and where they were strangled (*Bellum Catilinae* 55). Allusion to Horace signals the fortress's Roman aspect, making the civil war context and its repetition clear:

> Cette tour, droite sur un bloc de roche à pic, avait presque l'aspect romain tant elle était correcte et solide, et tant dans cette masse robuste l'idée de la *puissance* était mêlée à l'idée de la *chute*. 292–3

> This tower, rising from a perpendicular rock, was so severe and solid that it looked almost like a bit of Roman architecture, and the frowning mass gave the idea of strength even amid its ruin. 2.53

> Altera iam teritur bellis civilibus aetas,
> suis et ipsa Roma *viribus ruit*.   *Epodes* 16.1–2

> Now another age is worn down with civil war and Rome rushes to ruin under her own force.

It is as if the (ancient) Titans had thrown (revolutionary) paving stones at each other's heads (299; 2.58). Its doors resemble those of the twelve cities that in Biblical Judea escaped the earthquake under Tiberius – yet other cataclysmic events representing civil war (294; 2.54).

The tower ecphrasis presents all history as repetition. The name of Alain Barbe-Torte (301; 2.59) evokes an episode of medieval history as a blueprint for civil war in the Vendée. A ninth-century duke who had been exiled in England, Alain restored the power of Brittany against the Normans with the help of the English and of his ally, the abbot Jean de Landévennec. The primary geographical sites of this conflict (Dol, Nantes, St. Brieuc, the Loire) recur here, as well as the union of throne and altar. Lantenac's name, otherwise unattested, is phonic shorthand for the historical Landévennec.

The apparent contrast between dark dungeon and elegant library, bridging the ravine, offers no fundamental opposition; the *trompe l'oeil* masks essential sameness. The dark Middle Ages are only apparently overcome by the civilized splendor of the Renaissance. The library on the bridge quotes Chenonceau (300; 2.58), also the site of power struggles. The hyperfeminine chateau was a token in the rivalry between women who strove for courtly dominance between the king's sheets. Catherine de' Medici and Diane de Poitiers fought to influence Henri II, the latter famously the mistress not just of Henri but additionally his father, François I – since the Theban cycle, incest has engendered civil strife. The library's prized possession, the manuscript of St. Bartholomew, evokes the epitome of civil war in France, the massacre of Protestants under the regency of Catherine de' Medici.

Altogether, the architectural complex allegorizes civil war. Stylistic dissonance splits and fiercely binds the whole in civil war's fundamental figuration, conflict within the same.

> Les deux édifices, l'un abrupt, l'autre poli, se choquaient plus qu'ils ne s'accostaient. Les deux styles n'étaient point d'accord; bien que deux demi-cercles semblent devoir être identiques, rien ne ressemble moins à un plein-cintre roman qu'une archivolte classique. Cette tour digne des forêts était une étrange voisine pour ce pont digne de Versailles. Qu'on se figure Alain Barbe-Torte donnant le bras à Louis XIV. L'ensemble terrifiait. Des deux majestés mêlées sortait on ne sait quoi de féroce. 300–1

> The two edifices, the one rude, the other elegant, clashed rather than contrasted. The two styles had no agreement. Although it should seem that two semicircles ought to be identical, nothing can less resemble a Romanesque arch than a classical archivolt. That tower, in keeping with the forests, made a strange neighbor for that bridge, worthy of Versailles. Imagine Alain Barbe-Torte giving his arm to Louis XIV. The juxtaposition was sinister. These two majesties thus mingled made up a whole which had something inexpressibly menacing in it. 2.58–9

All evoked history summons up internal bloodshed. The traditional under-standing of the *translatio Romae* in French history goes backward. Rather than providing a model for enlightenment that comes to fruition in the rebirth of the French Renaissance and the glory of Louis XIV, Rome returns only as civil war. The tower, prison and tomb, represents the bloody horror that culminates in French history and reveals its glories as a sham.

Up to the Revolution, French history, according to Hugo, has been caught in a repetitive cycle that replays all the horrors of Old Testament retribution and Roman civil war. Christ's coming has not changed this history; instead, it is the Revolution that has brought the tower along with its history to an end. Already in ruin forty years ago, the fortress's dis-appearance by the time of narration stands for the end of history (292; 2.53). History had already become the object of antiquarian research. A famous archaeologist and historian, August Le Prévost, who bore the nickname "Pausanias normand" excavated the crypt at a precise date, 1835. The crypt has been emptied of what it was hiding. The oubliette has consigned history to oblivion. Leaving no trace, the fortress has devolved from ruin into mere shadow ("ombre," 299; 2.57), a pun on its figurative function. Like the birth of Christ, the French Revolution was interpreted by the republicans as a turning point for deliverance from history's terrors. The question remains whether history has the potential for redemption. As shadow, the tower anticipates the novel's last lines. As ghost, it haunts.

The Word Made Flesh: St. Bartholomew

J'ai lu, j'ai comparé l'aube avec la nuit noire,
Et les quatrevingt-treize aux Saint-Barthélemy;
Car ce quatrevingt-treize où vous avez frémi
Qui dut être, et que rien ne peut plus faire éclore,
C'est la lueur de sang qui se mêle à l'aurore.

Letter to Coriolis d'Espinousse, 1846[75]

I've read, I've compared daybreak to the dark night, '93 to the Saint Bartholomew's Day Massacre; for that '93 that made you shiver, which had to be and which nothing can make disclose any more, it is the gleam of blood that mingles with the dawn.

---

[75] Comparison of the St. Bartholomew's Day massacre with 1793 becomes a topos for the critique of tyranny in Voltaire, Balzac, Hugo, and Flaubert. Gohin (1979) 522.

At the heart of *Quatrevingt-treize*, a poetics of life resists the dead letter. Lush and vivid description, a technique from Virgilian pastoral and georgic, revives the New Testament mission of renewal, which has foundered on fossilized institutions.[76] The novel wages its own war on the book through Georgette, bearing the *Georgics* in her name, who brings to life a new and innocent figuration of language as natural as it is Adamic. The scene makes Hugo a new Vergil and a new evangelist, who resurrects the life in both traditions in his ambition to sublate civil war. He fulfills and redeems Vergil with a New and living Testament of universal access. *Vates* and Christian prophet, he proclaims the good news that the split inhabiting civil war may be healed.[77] Whereas Augustan literature imagines the golden age's return at a moment of refoundation after civil war,[78] Christian hermeneutics sets a model for performatively enacting a better future through the word. In Hugo's hands, literature, as much a Roman inheritance as civil war,[79] is converted from its vatic function into a sacrament that performs what classical religion was understood to do – one etymology of *religio* was *religare* (to bind) – but never accomplished: It binds what is torn in Romanticism's central project.[80]

The unique copy of an illustrated, printed, and apocryphal gospel according to St. Bartholomew in the library (305; 2.61) alludes to the French Wars of Religion. Catherine de' Medici ordered the massacre of French Protestants on the August 24, 1572. Two thousand Huguenots were slaughtered overnight on the feast day of St. Bartholomew. Agrippa d'Aubigny had already characterized the Wars of Religion as civil wars in his seventeenth-century epic *Les Tragiques*.[81] The title of *Quatrevingt-treize*'s third book, "Le massacre de St. Barthélemy," adjusts the massacre's conventional name (*le massacre de la Saint-Barthélemy*), shifting from the feast day to the body saintly on which internal strife is waged. The allusion suggests the revolutionary events replay the old civil wars of French history, but the children, whose systematic shredding of the book destroys the old regime, clear the slate in all innocence, so a new one may emerge.

---

[76] Petrey (1980).
[77] Bénichou (1977). For the *vates* in Latin literature, Newman (1967); Feeney (1998).
[78] Star (2021).   [79] Lowrie (2001).
[80] For language and the word in *Quatrevingt-treize*, Chamarat-Malandain (2005) 289. She notes that chapter 1.3.1, "La parole, c'est le Verbe" ("The word is the Word") uses "Verbe" (Word) in a similar sense as in John and recalls *Les Contemplations* 1.8 (Albouy [1967] 271): "Oui, tout puissant ! tel est le mot … / Car le mot c'est le Verbe et le Verbe, c'est Dieu" ("Yes, almighty! Such is the word … / Since the word is the Word and the Word is God").
[81] Frisch (2018).

This story superimposes registers: Vergilian and Biblical, Old and New Testaments. The poetic competition maps onto a hermeneutic problem. Whose vision will prevail? Of the children eating blackberries, authorial commentary suggests the three little seraphim's transformation into three little fauns would have shocked Dante and charmed Vergil (339; 2.99). The names of two canonical poets, classical and Christian, layer incommensurate poetics onto the scene. A Christian would read eating the fruit as a fall from grace in preparation for the saint's massacre, while the pagan would see a bucolic paradise. If Dante is the new and Christian Vergil who leaves his predecessor behind, Hugo takes Dante's place in turn. The secularized New Testament of his novel reinscribes Vergil with a view to his transfiguration.

The hermeneutics of Old and New Testaments restructure Hugo's relationship to his classical predecessor. Both registers mark a new beginning.[82] The children's awakening recalls the Fourth Eclogue, regularly read in postclassical times as foreshadowing Christ's birth.[83] The library, a place of the letter, becomes a surprisingly living and pastoral space. Morning casts its rays on Georgette's cradle, and the metaphorical flowers clustered around it echo the bower embracing the newborn boy of the Eclogue: *ipsa tibi blandos fundent incunabula flores*, ("the very cradle will pour out pleasing flowers," *Ecl.* 4.23). René-Jean appears as a new Hercules, whose heroic apotheosis is intimated of Vergil's baby: At poem's end, the poet prods him to smile at his mother – Christianizing interpretation would invoke Madonna and child – so he may join the gods' feasts and marry a goddess (*Ecl.* 4.60–3). The labors of Hercules, another prefiguration of Christ, correspond to the Passion; his final agony purges him of mortal flesh before he ascends to heaven to marry Hebe.

The ray of light gracing Georgette's cradle is a recurrent motif signaling moments of mystical enlightenment in the novel. Eden overlies the classical pastoral. Language emerges from prelinguistic sound (birdsong) through a natural religious impulse of a babbled, indistinct hymn uniting pagan song with medieval *cantique* ("cantica," 328–9; 2.88). Georgette learns the names of the animals in an Adamic scene where her brothers teach her in all innocence about nature (334–5; 2.94–5). The children make no hierarchical distinctions. Vermin, swallows, and bees are all objects of

---

[82] White (2008) II, 120–1 traces parallels between *Quatrevingt-treize* and Hugo's poems of *L'Année terrible* in Arendtian terms: Natality guarantees the possibility of a new, revolutionary beginning; Arendt (1963) 28 and (1958) 9, 178.

[83] Hugo translated Eclogue 4 over the Christmas season in 1816–17, Albouy (1964) 72–4. Peyrache-Leborgne (1996) 61 notes the pastoral register. Heil (2007).

innocent curiosity. Lacking any sense of abjection, they approach a beetle, called by the same name as Marat ("cloporte," "wood louse," 164; 1.164), merely as a natural phenomenon. As innocent as Adam and Eve and knowing as little shame, they cannot discover the beetle's sex in their ignorance and mistake a bee for a fly (335; 2.92).

History, however, infuses Hugo's Eden, as it does Vergil's golden age. The scene unfolds against the background of warfare's recurrent soundscape. Vergil's luscious idyll still bears the "traces of ancient fraud" (*priscae vestigia fraudis*, *Ecl.* 4.31) and history must be relived backward to reach the desired golden age. In Hugo, language emerges within a temporal framework that delivers a Romantic manifesto, fusing opposites into unity.[84]

> Ce bégaiement se compose de ce que l'enfant disait quand il était ange et de ce qu'il dira quand il sera homme; le berceau a un Hier de même que la tombe a un Demain; ce demain et cet hier amalgament dans ce gazouillement obscur leur double inconnu; et rien ne prouve Dieu, l'éternité, la responsabilité, la dualité du destin, comme cette ombre formidable dans cette âme rose. 329

> These lispings are the echo of what the child said when he was an angel, and what he will say when he enters eternity. The cradle has a Yes-terday, just as the grave has a To-morrow; this morrow and this yesterday join their double mystery in that incomprehensible warbling, and there is no such proof of God, of eternity, and the duality of destiny, as in this awe-inspiring shadow flung across that flower-like soul. 2.88

History's linearity collapses into synchronicity. There is no time before the Fall; the cross already inhabits Eden; shadow occupies the soul from the beginning; tomb and cradle are entwined.[85]

A reenactment of the Fall advances to the next Biblical stage: the cross appears in the eating of fruit, like death in the evocation of Eden. The children gorge on blackberries, a symbolic unification of the forbidden fruit, the crown of thorns, and the purple of robe of Christ mocked during the Passion.

> Ils s'en grisèrent et s'en barbouillèrent, et, tout vermeils de cette pourpre de la ronce, ces trois petits séraphins finirent par être trois petits faunes, ce qui

---

[84] Following Hegel, Hugo's preface to *Cromwell* (Purnal, Thierry, and Mélèze 1963) expounds the Romantic program as a quarrel between ancients and moderns: The Christian paradigm integrates opposing principles of flesh and spirit, grotesque and sublime, which the classical paradigm keeps apart. His *William Shakespeare* identifies '93 with Romanticism's birth (*Oeuvres complètes* 1985, *Critique* 432); White (2008) 113.

[85] Gohin (2002) 164: The Fall, instantiated in the children's appetite for destruction, however innocent, has always already taken place.

eût choqué Dante et charmé Virgile. . . . Georgette tendit à René-Jean son doigt où perlait une petite goutte de sang. 339

They stained their faces and hands with the purple juice till the trio of little seraphs was changed into a knot of little fauns, which would have shocked Dante and charmed Vergil. . . . Georgette held out her finger to René-Jean, on which showed a tiny drop of blood. 2.99

The species of blackberry, identified as a "mûrier de renard" (339; "fox blackberry," 2.98), insinuates a fox, a metaphor for cleverness, into the library – a substitute for the temptation of the crafty snake in the garden. The children's stained mouths recall Milton's Eve. Vergil can be charmed because he cannot see the Christian figuration behind the pastoral fauns, but Dante would have understood the symbolics and been appalled. The children debate whether the thorn that drew blood is a vicious beast that stings or a stick (340; 2.99). In their childishness, they judge the stick mean, but eating the fruit meanwhile has caused harm, like the beating of Christ during the Passion, like the wood of the cross.[86] The salvation of the novel's climax is foreshadowed here, as the Fall prefigures the Passion.

The scenes of Eden, the Fall, and the Passion, merged into a synchronic hermeneutic, set up the children's destruction of the book, a metaphorical act combining civil war with martyrdom that wipes the slate clean: The *tabula rasa* gives history a chance to begin again on a new footing. The book is already a dead letter; a catalogue of international dignitaries of the Church and their relations, one more obscure than the other, unfurl within the fictitious book (342; 2.104). Despite living in a library, the children encounter the book only after eating of the fruit. But the fruit brings them no knowledge whatsoever, let alone of good and evil. They do not read the book but destroy it. The materiality of the printed book, a precious, venerable, and gorgeous artifact, monumentalizes world know-ledge (340; 2.100). Like the stones of the Tourgue, the letter of the book figures history. A product of technologies of knowledge, the long intellec-tual tradition of commentary, geography, science, jumbled together with sacred rites, superstitions, and mysteries (343; 2.104), the book contains but does not transmit learning. Like Aeneas' incomprehension of the weight of history borne on his shield, which brings him aesthetic joy (*Aen.* 8.729–31), Hugo's children see the book but do not understand. Instead, they perform its meaning. Already sterile, a mere object of curiosity (305; 2.61), an orientalized letter in Arabian paper (340; 2.100), in their hands it ends up

---

[86] Seidel and Landau (1983) for the Augustinian cloister of St. Florian near Lenz.

in fragments, bits of text and image in the skeleton of its binding (345; 2.105). Instead of the living word becoming flesh, the dead letter ends up a corpse. The inversion of Annunciation and Resurrection illustrates the failure of the Church to live up to the promise of its institution.

Christian martyrdom comes overlain with Roman civil war. René-Jean tears the saint's image in two, leaving the eye on the page and giving Georgette the skin. The ripped-out eye figures civil war in Lucan, and the skin replays the flaying of the saint.[87] The picture of St. Bartholomew is halved; the saint was flayed in Armenia, "quartered" in Brittany ("écartelé," 342; 2.103). Flaying and quartering were Roman methods of torture, used against pagans and Christians alike. With the skin of parchment, the book's material, the saint is killed both as living flesh and as dead letter. The children displace "extermination" from a mouse, who scurries by unseen, onto the book (345; 2.105) and enact "massacre" (346; 2.106–7) on the saint whose feast day is shorthand for the worst bloodbath of the French Wars of Religion.

Ascension follows martyrdom. These innocents' massacre is no crime, but liberation. The tragic and literal fall of the majestic book off its pedestal (343; 2.104) inverts into an ascension.[88] The children throw history in fragments to the breezes. Like the Platonic soul freed from the prison of the body rising to its celestial home, the little shreds of white paper metamorphose into figurative butterflies that disperse into the blue of the sky (346; 2.106). The children go to bed in a repastoralized scene of angelic, paradisiacal bliss. These "malefactors" are revealed as true innocents, whose erasure of history allows for potential recreation.[89] Cosmic harmony is restored.

At the same time, however, history is and has always already been present; sounds of civil war continue to break the peace. The poetics of Romanticism integrates the monstrous into a harmony that thereby becomes sublime. Cosmic order appears not as measured beauty, but in the union of sublime immensity with humble smallness. Contrasting extremes merge in Romanticism's signature gesture. The sweetness

---

[87] Scaeva pulls out and treads on his own eye, stuck with an arrow (6.218–19). His body, a massive wound held together only by the countless arrows piercing it, embodies the paradox of civil war, where virtue becomes crime (6.147–8).

[88] For Hugo's figure, "chute transfiguration" ("fall transfiguration"), based on the example of Paul's conversion, below p. 244.

[89] On the scene's erasure of history, Rosa (1974); Peyrache-Leborgne (1996) 62. Eco (2006) 291–2 counters the interpretation of the book's destruction as a "negative imitation of the night of St. Bartholomew": it is the "tragedy of an actant who may not have been redemptive but was at least benevolent: Innocence."

engulfing the children is colossal, their innocence venerable despite their combined ages not reaching nine years (347; 2.107–8).

> il semblait que le vaste monde étoilé retînt sa respiration pour ne point troubler ces trois humbles dormeurs angéliques, et rien n'était sublime comme l'immense respect de la nature autour de cette petitesse. 347

> It seemed as if the vast starry world held its breath for fear of disturbing these three humble angelic sleepers, and nothing could have been so sublime as that reverent respect of nature in presence of this littleness. 2.108

The cannon blast waking Georgette is simultaneously history's irruption into bliss and the repetition of an always present condition. History reasserts its cruel imperative with metaphorical lightning, followed by thunder, Jupiter's own sign. In Vergil's *Georgics*, his intervention removes the Saturnian Age of natural abundance and ease for a world of labor and insecurity, doubly blessed with technology and art (1.121–59).[90] Civil war is the political condition of Jupiter's dispensation, and Vergil's conception echoes in the sounds of battle. When discord splits the bees' allegiance between two kings, they buzz "imitating the sounds of martial trumpets" (*fractos sonitus imitata tubarum*, 4.72). Before the climactic cannon, the French combatants communicate their intentions, to attack and defend, to the sound of bugles and trumpets (331; 2.91). Each time the children discern civil war's monstrous sounds, they hear the *fracas* (336; 2.96, from the Latin *fractus,* derived from breaking) as comforting harmony: music (332; 2.91), God's harmony reminding them of their mother (336; 2.97), a mere *poum!* (348; "Boom!," 2.108). Hugo's Romanticism integrates the awful into the cosmos with a sentimental touch.

Symbolic time organizes narrative time. The siege of La Tourgue takes place in August, the same month of the St. Bartholomew's Day massacre (308; 2.64). The feast day itself is the day on which preparations for Christmas begin. The scene is a double new beginning that invokes the beginning of the creation and the second beginning of the birth of Christ alike. Georgette's awakening in the cradle, touched by a ray of light, points to the novel's last chapter, "Cependant le soleil se lève" ("Meanwhile the sun rises") and unites in one traditional image the rise of Son and sun. When their mother arrives, the three appear as baby Jesuses in a grotto, confidently asleep while hellish fire rages around them (416; 2.191). The

---

[90] Vergilian history follows the same logic. Despite an initial contrast between the Golden Age and Jupiter's dispensation, the former is revealed to have always had agriculture – a traditional sign of falling away from nature's abundant self-sufficiency – inscribed within. Johnston (1980) 62–89.

meteor above merges Caesar's comet with the star of Bethlehem. Salvation is born from horror, like the birth of Christ with Augustus' census and the massacre of the innocents as its backdrop. Just as the New Testament figures spiritual awakening as a change in medium from letter to flesh, so here, the children embody a newly innocent world against the torn book, dead paper killed again and turned definitively into dead letter. The book's destruction turns a page in history so that this war might become the massacre to end all massacres.

Foreshadowing the novel's conclusion, shadow mixes with light. When the children fall back asleep, the landscape undulates in a luxurious play of flickering light.

> Le paysage, ineffablement assoupi, avait cette moire magnifique que font sur les prairies et sur les rivières les déplacements de l'ombre et de la clarté. 347

> The landscape that seemed asleep had those lovely hazy effects which the changings of light and shadow produce on the fields and rivers. 2.107

This scene maintains a consistent register: grandiosity interwoven with sentimentality. The lowly pulls at the heartstrings. Aiming for the New Testament's sublime humility,[91] Hugo rewrites Vergil's lush and vivid descriptions of nature to infuse with new life a letter that has, in his view, become dead. Whereas Dante overcomes Vergil by embracing the letter of the Scriptures, Hugo leaves the dead letter behind by incarnating a new Vergil, whose words become flesh in Georgette. He brings to life a poetics of annunciation, which he thinks the institutionalization of the New Testament in the earthly Church has brought to failure. He redeems the classical and the Biblical alike by affirming the life within each tradition and renouncing their killing politics and dead monuments. As in the readings of the Scriptures, esoteric allegory underlies the easily accessible surface meaning. This procedure is common in the nineteenth century. Its most obvious illustration are the paintings of Millet (Figs. 2.3, 2.4), which infuse everyday labors with a divine light and elevate the farmers as incarnation revealed.

This scene sets up the novel's paradoxical representation of the dual structure of the persistence of history on the one hand and its continual erasure and reerasure before a new paradigm on the other. Each human being replays individually the whole of the Christological narrative in a hermeneutical sublation, which parallels a similar structure in poetics. The *rota Vergiliana*, the progression from pastoral, to georgic, to epic,

---

[91] Auerbach (1965).

marches through the hierarchy of genres, which matches a shift in political conception from the individual to the social to the national. This classical paradigm balances the Pauline understanding of the progression from Old to New Testaments as *figura* and *implementum*, a structure that overcomes history through fulfillment.[92] The integration of poetics and hermeneutics, begun here, comes to a head in the novel's dramatic climax. It is poetry, in Hugo's understanding, that lifts disharmony into the sublime.

Lantenac and a Higher Sovereignty

The didactic plot's lockstep forward march literalizes Hegel's canonical history of philosophy. Paradigmatic figures mark each stage. Some span stages, enabling the transition from one to the next. First, the prephilosophical: Lantenac's sergeant Imânus and the mother mobilize ancient and carnal forces arising from blood and passion in destructive and constructive modalities respectively. Both are eventually surpassed. Next, classical philosophy: Imânus and Lantenac appear as the two faces of Stoicism, one monstrous, the other noble. Then, Lantenac takes the first step toward a spiritualization that prefigures Christian possibility without enacting it in full – this must await Gauvain.

Lantenac represents the divine right of kings in its heartless legal dimension, up to the point when the children risk being burned alive. When he takes the children of the Republic hostage, the principle of living maternity confronts cruel adoptive paternity. The decision to murder the children as hostages is made coolly by his sergeant Imânus, characterized as perversely Stoic. His name evokes bestial monstrosity. It is a Norman word derived from the Latin *immanis*, "monstrous" – a Vergilian favorite.[93] His "epic" ferocity announces the classical register in a cruel vein (258; 2.13). Wounded in the battle of La Tourgue, his intestines spilling out of his belly, Imânus suffers the simultaneously grotesque and noble death of Cato.[94] In holding the attackers back, so Lantenac and the others can escape, he plays the hero who devotes himself to save the army.[95] However, setting the fuse on fire, to incinerate the library and the children along with it, precipitates his tragic fall – underscored by authorial comment – from hero to assassin (258; 2.13). Combining monstrous Catonian Stoicism with the medieval monstrous "ogre" (258; 2.12), Imânus evokes a horror that is processed and tamed through Hugo's Romantic poetics: Georgette

---

[92] Rey (2008) 27.   [93] E.g., in *Aeneid* 1 alone at 110, 139, 347, 428, 616.
[94] Plutarch, *Cato Minor* 70.6.   [95] Vinken (2007).

phatically recalls the ogre by answering "Orgette" (425; 2.201) when Lantenac asks her name. The transformative *figura verborum* (figure of speech) leaves no remainder: The monstrous is redeemed as cute.

Parallels between Imânus and Lantenac lend the former Stoicism's grotesque face and the latter its noble. Lantenac's stature is huge, but, no ogre, he has the magisterial agility of an ancient athlete (424; 2.198). The two embody the monstrous and heroic sides of the powerful, classical body. Lantenac is Stoic in the nobler vein of emotional self-mastery.[96] When he first escapes from La Tourgue, in a miraculous turn of plot, he quickly quells a brief hint of joy. His near-death experience has been a shock (407; 2.179). His full *securité* is not just physical safety, but the emotional tranquility (*securitas*) prized by all ancient philosophical sects.[97]

The mother, who arrives at the siege just in time to witness her trapped children going up in flames, rouses a force both more primitive and higher. Dramatic touches heighten the effect: She views the fire creeping inexorably up the dried ivy on the building – Imânus had arranged the combustibles for maximum efficiency. There is little time to save the children, and she sees no one even trying. Readers know the ladder Gauvain had ordered to save them has been destroyed in an ambush. The contingency of history turns into an act of fate serving Hugo's plot. Royalists, trying to capture and destroy the guillotine, were puzzled that what they thought was a machine of destruction was merely a farm implement. Not knowing it was intended as an instrument of rescue, they destroy it for its utility in a siege. The mother sees only the imminent death of her children, and her cry of anguish stops Lantenac in his tracks. He immediately and without thinking abandons his war plans and selflessly puts his life – and with it his cause – at risk. His change, just short of conversion, is the first step towards spiritual love.

The mother's cry is a rhetorical tour de force. Tellmarch's earlier rescue of both Lantenac and the mother sets up their confrontation. Returned from the dead, she appears as a she-wolf, Hecuba, the Gorgon, the Eumenides (414; 2.187). Her voice rings out as the archaic cry of chthonic maternity. She allegorizes sublimity rooted in ancient figurations of monstrosity.

> Cette mère, c'était la maternité; tout ce qui résume l'humanité est surhumain; elle se dressait là, au bord de ce ravin, devant cet embrasement, devant ce crime, comme une puissance sépulcrale; elle avait le cri de la bête et le

---

[96] Gauvain, for instance, recognizes Lantenac's abnegation as Stoic (513; 2.216).
[97] E.g., Cicero, *De finibus* 5.8.23.

geste de la déesse; sa face, d'où tombaient des imprécations, semblait un masque de flamboiement. Rien de souverain comme l'éclair de ces yeux noyés de larmes; son regard foudroyait l'incendie. 414

This mother was no longer a simple mother – all maternity's voice cried out through hers; whatever sums up and becomes a type of humanity grows superhuman. There she towered on the edge of that ravine, in front of that conflagration, in the presence of that crime, like a power beyond the grave; she moaned like a wild beast, but her attitude was that of a goddess; the mouth, which uttered imprecations, was set in a flaming mask. Nothing could have been more sovereign than her eyes shooting lightning through her tears. Her look blasted the conflagration. 2.188

A mythical personification from the venerable tradition of classical antiquity, she embodies the poetics of the romantic sublime. In her, Mary at the Cross and Hecuba unite. Pure phatic emotion finds expression through rhetorical convention, deployed in a rushing stream of kitsch.

A higher sovereignty inhabits the mother's anguish. She resumes humanity from above and below, like Lantenac (109; 1.108), simultaneously beast and goddess. While Aristotle makes a creature outside the polis either god or beast (*Politics* 1253a27–9), and therefore apolitical, the Romantic aesthetic surpasses Aristotle's conception to encompass what is above and below the human, synthesizing it into the larger humanity of motherhood. Her eyes unite incompatibles, fire and water, and the metaphorical lightning of her glance sets Jupiter's punishing sovereignty against the abject criminality of the literal fire. Her cry, falling on Lantenac's head, continues the metaphor of the lightning bolt. Lantenac recognizes this higher sovereignty, which he obeys immediately without thinking.[98] He takes the key to the library's impregnable door out of his pocket, returns to the burning tower, and risks his life to save the children, all with a sense of inevitable calm. This tranquility is no longer Stoic, but something new.

In a sentimental set piece thick with Christian images, Lantenac transforms. In a moment of compassionate emotion, he leaves behind Stoic impassiveness and progresses from the old order (*ancien régime*) of the law to a higher and humane sovereignty. He passes through stages, from physical "safety" ("sûreté," 405; 2.176), to the emotional tranquility offered by ancient philosophy ("sécurité," 407; 2.179), to salvation. Instead of facing death, besieged in his own stony tower, his petrified heart comes alive; by sacrificing his physical safety, he finds new life. He is freed from

---

[98] *Pace* Chamarat-Malandain (1991) 151, Lantenac does not listen, but merely hears; he does not recognize others' rights but instinctively obeys a higher sovereignty.

the dungeon of his own monarchic past to obey the higher calling of the mother's cry in agony. He no longer pursues the cause of death but is free to risk his life and his cause, free to become fully human. He enters the library, sets the emergency ladder – a "safety ladder" ("échelle de sauve-tage," 424; 2.198) – out the window, and rescues the children one by one. Gros-Alain and René-Jean are afraid, cry, and resist, but Georgette's smile of dazzling innocence outshines their tears. Carrying Georgette down the ladder arouses in Lantenac for the first time an unfamiliar feeling: a parent's love, sealed with a tear and a kiss. Lantenac has no understand-ing – words for what he undergoes fail him – but he feels it. He hands the children down to Radoub, a male figure for motherly love. The mother herself waits below, at the foot of the ladder, like Mary by the Cross. Christological imagery binds the scene's elements into a unity. When Radoub first sees her, he greets her on the model of resurrection: "Tiens, dit-il, la fusillée! vous êtes donc ressuscitée?" (423; "'Well!'" cried he. 'The woman who was shot! So you have come to life again?'," 2.197). Receiving her children, she ascends without transition from hell to paradise. A great shout sets the terms.

> – Tous sont sauvés!
> Tous étaient sauvés, en effet, excepté le vieillard.   425

> "They are all saved!"
> All indeed were saved, except the old man.   2.201

Lantenac has traded in his own safety for a better prize: salvation.

Lantenac's release comes under two signs: feudalism and Christian self-sacrifice. His salvation in a Christian mode, however, is short-lived. He passes in and out of death both literally and figuratively. Every act of rescue builds in a forward dialectical movement. He is saved miraculously twice in one night, once by Halmalo and once again by Gauvain, a doubling that recalls his paired rescue at the beginning of the novel, by Halmalo, who abandons his plan of vengeance, and by Tellmarch, whose charity saves him. His loyal subject Halmalo rescues him from the tower out of feudal devotion, just as he released him in the boat. Verbal parallels align the two double scenes of rescue (Halmalo and Tellmarch; Halmalo and Gauvain). The word *carnichot*, used of Tellmarch's underground lair, foreshadows the tower's underground secret passageway (100; 98). Whereas Tellmarch's charity was chthonic, Gauvain's is spiritual. When Gauvain takes his great-uncle's place in the dungeon, a higher self-sacrifice that moves history forward substitutes for Lantenac's temporary salvation. Coming down off the ladder, Lantenac is arrested and imprisoned. Pale as marble, like the statue of the *commandeur* from *Don Juan*, he returns to the sepulcher (426; 2.201). The sacred horror that attaches to him here may be the noble correlate of the semi-divine horror that marks Imânus as a monster (258; 2.13), but Lantenac nevertheless descends again into the realm of death from which he had come. In the end, he remains mired in an aristocratic, deadening view of the world.

The insufficiency of Lantenac's worldview is revealed in his rant to Gauvain in the dungeon. Aristocracy and republicanism matter to him most for their aesthetic value. He contrasts polite courtesy and heroic chivalry with the revolutionaries' moral and aesthetic lowness. He misses an opportunity to lift spirit over the letter by railing against republican writings in terms that value noble blood over ink's criminal blackness (452–3; 2.226–7). His praise of the deed over the mere word comes in a classical antithesis. He accuses the revolutionaries of being incapable of heroism, chivalry, or sacrifice (456; 2.228). All this appears empty and witty rhetorical flourish when Gauvain, hitherto silent, declares Lantenac's liberty in three words, an economical and effective speech act, and pushes him, astounded, out the door. Gauvain takes his place literally in the dungeon and as a figure in the plot. Lantenac's sacrifice sets up Gauvain's. Lantenac's uncomprehending moment of salvation was temporary, whereas Gauvain thinks through and embraces a higher self-sacrifice. True nobility does turn out to pass through the bloodline after all, but it rises into a salvific register that surpasses genealogy. The blood of inheritance is purged and fulfilled by the blood of sacrifice.

Just as Tellmarch's chthonic charity is surpassed by Gauvain's spiritual charity, so is the mother's chthonic sovereignty surpassed and fulfilled by a sovereignty of the spirit. A simile comparing her to the Eumenides alludes to their transformation from the Erinyes, who enforced maternal blood vengeance, into the guardian spirits of Apollo's law, newly founded at Athens in Aeschylus' *Oresteia*. Comparison to the she-wolf evokes Roman foundation. The similes mark the place of the chthonic maternal, which is then written out of the novel's schema. All ancient orders are overcome in turn by a purified spiritual motherhood, whose chaste and male guise adumbrates the republic to come as the realization of heavenly Jerusalem.

In good realist technique, humble quotidian objects symbolize the forward march of successive ages. When first released from the tower, Lantenac checks his watch. He carefully notices that the key to the iron door into the library is in one pocket and therefore puts his watch back into the other to protect the crystal. The radical break in the temporal order from antiquity to Christianity appears in his gesture and foreshadows the radical break inaugurated with Hugo's secular New Testament. Lantenac unknowingly points to the future temporal break through the key, Peter's traditional attribute, which symbolizes the Church. A change in genre accompanies the change in the ages: Ancient tragedy yields to Romantic comedy, whose low-style register bears an evangelic humility.

Noble Gauvain in Crisis

Lantenac's saving the children puts Gauvain in a crisis in its etymological sense. He decides to save Lantenac and sacrifice himself to redeem the Revolution from civil war and the logic of terror. Gauvain has been profoundly shaken; an inverted Aeneas, who cleaves Stoically to Jupiter's command, like a buffeted oak before Dido's moving call to fleshy love (*Aen.* 4.441–9), Gauvain has perceived a human absolute that deracinates his commitment to the revolutionary absolute like a tree uprooted (431; 2.209). The love he embraces is spiritual. Hugo's signature contrast of shadow with light rises above the literal: Gauvain cannot escape the light once he has seen it (431; 2.208).

Didacticism invites the reader to an *imitatio Gauvain*. Gauvain's internal deliberations spell out the message of Hugo's book and the meaning of the Revolution. Lantenac's arrest by Cimourdain means he must come before the law. He now faces certain death by guillotine. The trial is a mere formality. Cimourdain has already decided on the outcome as the officer of the Comité du salut publique (Committee on public safety). He has stacked the decks with judges whose decision he already knows. Nevertheless, delay before the trial and execution opens narrative space for the novel's climactic decision, which belongs to Gauvain. His deliberations expound the events in all their symbolic clarity: "Cimourdain, c'est à dire 93, tenait Lantenac, c'est à dire la monarchie" (440; "Cimourdain, that is to say 93, held Lantenac, that is to say Monarchy," 2.214). In Hugo's paradigmatic technique, interpretation follows illustration.

At stake in Gauvain's decision is how to overcome civil war. Lantenac has momentarily transcended its logic in an act Gauvain calls sacrifice (443; 2.216). Transfigured, he is no longer a tiger (442; 2.216) – Vergil's icon of heartlessness (*Aen.* 4.366–7) and Lucan's of bestiality in civil war (1.328) – but has become humane. From monster and killer has arisen a savior and hero – more than that, even a man! (437; 2.212). This radical transformation shakes Gauvain's sense of a republican absolute and discloses for him the possibility of a humane absolute superior to that of the revolution (431; 2.209). These, which should accord, have now become disaligned. The resulting paradox is that, if the Revolution now kills Lantenac, it, not the monarchy, will bear responsibility for civil war's inexorable logic.

> Tandis que l'homme des préjugés et des servitudes, subitement transformé, rentrait dans l'humanité, eux, les hommes de la délivrance et de l'affranchissement, ils resteraient dans la guerre civile, dans la routine du sang, dans le fratricide! 435–6

> As this man of prejudice and servitude, suddenly transformed, returned into the circle of humanity, the men who strove for deliverance and freedom elected to cling to the horrors of civil war, to the routine of blood, to fratricide! 2.211

If the monarchy saves children, then the Republic loses stature if it in turn puts old men to death. The contest of magnanimity puts the war on a moral footing. The very legitimacy of the Republic hangs in the balance. The family ties between Gauvain and Lantenac double the problematic by making the civil war a parricide, its own traditional figuration.

Roman exemplarity structures the logic, but, as in Augustine, elevation to a higher purpose reforms it. Furthermore, the contestation between paradigmatic figures dramatizes a struggle between worldviews grounded in conflicting values. The civil war in French history wages a cosmic struggle for the world's historical order. Cimourdain's literal application of the law of the Terror would undo the Revolution in the face of Lantenac's self-sacrifice. To refound the Revolution on higher values, Gauvain, who embodies clemency, must aspire not just to emulate but to surpass Lantenac's example. If Lantenac were put to death, this would reinstate through parricide the civil war he has ended. Gauvain – fully aware that an escaped Lantenac might betray France to foreign enemies – cares more about the Republic's moral compass than about winning the literal war. His own self-sacrifice sets in motion a logic of love that should purify the Revolution from the taint of civil war, whatever the practical outcome.

Gauvain's cloaking his head has both narrative and symbolic functions. It allows him to enter Lantenac's prison and give him a disguise so he can escape, but it also looks back to both Caesar and Pompey, who, in the literary tradition, covered their heads at the moment of assassination to signal their acceptance of inevitable death.[99] Head-covering in Roman

---

[99] Suetonius, *Julius Caesar* 82; Lucan 8.613–15.

iconography takes two forms. With the face exposed, it is the costume of the officiant of sacrifice (*Gabino cinctu*); with the head fully obscured, it indicates death. Gauvain, who already envelops his head in the cloak before his deliberations, symbolically shows his acceptance of death. His gesture transforms pagan sacrifice into self-sacrifice in a Christian mode. While Lantenac, by saving his life, surpasses Pompey and Caesar in the boat scenes toward the novel's beginning, Gauvain surpasses Lantenac, along with the two Roman heroes, by sacrificing himself. Lantenac may best the Romans in civil war, but Gauvain does better by ending the Roman curse through a Christian gesture.

This gesture, one among others, advances over Rome. Three supreme values stand for Rome's highest ideals: the canon of *pietas* comprises devotion to gods, family, and country. A new canon, which articulates Gauvain's deliberations, replaces Roman idolatry by putting humanity in the place of the pagan gods: "humanity, family, fatherland" (444; 2.217). This new value overwrites even Republican fraternity.

Although it looks initially as though Gauvain and Lantenac parallel each other in sacrificing themselves to a new order, in fact, only Gauvain fully instantiates Hugo's vision. He is the only one to understand what Lantenac has done and what he himself is about to do. Lantenac remains grounded in the prior order. Once released by Gauvain, he pauses while pondering his new freedom. His hesitation recalls two signal features of Aeneas: his incomprehension of the world he himself is in the process of founding and his famous hesitation before killing Turnus. When Aeneas looks at his future people, his own offspring, depicted on his shield, he is uncomprehending (*ignarus*, 8.730). From a Christian point of view, choosing vengeance over clemency is a definite error, despite Servius' interpretation of his hesitation as redeeming his character. Lantenac fails to understand his transformative role: Gauvain saves him precisely because he has redeemed barbarity by an act of sacrifice. By accepting a death warrant, he has signed his own pardon: "ce n'était pas un monstre l'homme qui venait d'illuminer de la clarté d'une action divine le précipice des guerres civiles! Le porte-glaive s'était métamorphosé en porte-lumière" (443; "The man who had just illuminated the abyss of civil war by the light of a divine action was not a monster. The sword-bearer was metamorphosed into the angel of day," 2.216). Hugo's leitmotif, light, once again transfigures the darkness.

The darkness of monarchic faith in blood ties is manifest in Lantenac's blindness. His speech before deliverance exposes the benighted viewpoint of his class and the world he represents. For him, the Revolution simply reverses the single right and natural order. That he himself is held in the dungeon of his own castle, where he formerly put his own prisoners, exemplifies the Revolution's topsy-turvy inversions. He fails to understand that he put his own life and his cause on the line for peasant children to whom he was not at all related and that this act changes history: he has unwittingly undone patriarchal inheritance and made humanity his family. His stupefaction at Gauvain's saving him, which matches his incomprehension of the significance of his own act, signals his world is a dead end (456; 2.229). Like Vergil's Aeneas, repeatedly unknowing (*inscius, Aen.* 1.207, 6.711, 10.249; *nescius*, 4.72; *ignarus*, 8.730), he cannot see what his own story means. He perceives only the paradox – "The native son returns as the liberating enemy"[100] – not its higher resolution. Beyond classical knowledge, he lacks faith. His interjection "Ma foi!" (457; "'My faith!',", 2.229) reduces transcendence to a colloquialism. His instantiation of the dead letter is revealed in a pun.

Gauvain and Cimourdain: Earthly and Divine Republics

The political visions of Cimourdain and Gauvain outlined in 3.2.7, "Les deux pôles du vrai" (281–9; "The two poles of truth," 2.40–7), are programmatically opposed.[101] The opposition anticipates the conceptual and structural conflict that peaks in crisis at the novel's denouement. After years of separation, they meet again dramatically when Cimourdain takes a head wound to save Gauvain (271–4; 2.30–2). They expound their conceptions of republicanism in the subsequent scenes. According to Cimourdain's feverish imagination, Rome in its imperialist guise returns in the French Republic, while Gauvain's principle of grace overcomes this model. Structurally, intimate opposition, a classical trope for civil war, yields to the possibility that history could finally be brought to an end.

Classicizing imagery grounds Cimourdain in antiquity. He himself resembles Achilles' tutor, the centaur Chiron, a monster only half human, who adores his "disciple" with narcissistic and idolatrous fervor (272; 2.30). He has aggrandizing visions, of himself as the almighty, of making his creature, Gauvain, into France's preeminent general, who will expand empire in the four cardinal directions – a Roman imperial trope – so Rome will rise again (273; 2.31). The ambitions of the Ultramontane faction of the French Catholic Church are fit wittily into a classical mold. To the extent that Cimourdain's conceptions fall within Christian categories, they come under the sign of the sword; in his imagination, Gauvain

---

[100] Brombert (1984) 215.   [101] Gohin (2002) 164.

magnifies into an exterminating angel. Like the archangel Michael, he will crush the shadows under his feet; like Augustus, with the rays of Caesar's comet shining above his brow (*Aen.* 8.680–1), a meteor will hover over his forehead. Whereas Gauvain's pardon of the man who tried to kill him is *grâce*, Cimourdain reclassicizes Christian grace as Roman *clémence*. Clemency, Julius Caesar's signal virtue, became the inheritance of sovereign absolutism (274; 2.32).[102]

Split unity figures the two men, symmetrical opposites ("l'un était l'opposé de l'autre," "the one was the other's opposite"), in one of civil war's basic tropes. Each represents the Republic respectively in one of its two forms: terror and clemency (281; 2.40). They disagree in metaphorical warfare:

> L'amitié était entre les deux hommes, mais la haine était entre les deux principes; c'était comme une âme coupée en deux, et partagée; Gauvain, en effet, avait reçu une moitié de l'âme de Cimourdain, mais la moitié douce. Il semblait que Gauvain avait eu le rayon blanc, et que Cimourdain avait gardé pour lui ce qu'on pourrait appeler le rayon noir. De là un désaccord intime. Cette sourde guerre ne pouvait pas ne point éclater. Un matin la bataille commença. 283–4

> There was friendship between the two men, but hatred between the two principles; It was like a soul divided in two and shared. It seemed that Gauvain had received the white ray and that Cimourdian had kept what one could call a black ray for himself. From there, an intimate disagreement. This hidden war could not fail to burst forth. One morning the battle began. 2.41

They disagree about pardon itself, the principle of sovereignty and the hinge on which the finale turns. Gauvain voices chivalric principles: You cannot kill unless you put your own life at risk; you must therefore spare women, children, the old, and the weak. Chivalry is the one positive element the Romantic paradigm accords the Middle Ages – exactly what the actual Revolution was accused of eradicating.[103] Furthermore, Gauvain elevates clemency with a Christian valence: The war is a contest of *grâce*. If royalists spare Republican prisoners, he matches them to better the Republic's name (286; 2.45).

---

[102] Caesar's grant of clemency to Domitius shows it as a sovereign virtue, contrary to republican norms (Lucan, 2.512–18). In Seneca's *De clementia*, clemency is the highest kingly virtue. Cromwell, in Hugo's play of the same name, is denounced most absolutely as a tyrant, despite refusing kingship, when granting clemency to all he had condemned to death for plotting against him (*Cromwell* 5.14).

[103] Vinken (2013).

In Hugo, overcoming civil war is impossible in the political realm. Gauvain, who disavows politics ("je ne suis pas un homme politique," 285; "I am not a political man," 2.42) even while making war, is the novel's icon of its insufficiency. Contrary to Cimourdain and the Terror, he refuses total war. His vision, to confront enemies as enemies, but to become their brothers after conquest (289; 2.47), emulates and surpasses the Vergilian ideal, "to spare the subjected and war down the proud,"[104] in accord with the opening of Augustine's *De civitate Dei*. Instead of folding the vanquished into empire by granting them citizenship, as the Romans did, Gauvain's category of integration is fraternity, a republican value that stresses apolitical bonds.

Gauvain's vision of the republic to come outlines Hugo's script for transcending civil war. The new order requires no new foundation on the Roman model, but a new covenant. Cimourdain and Gauvain's last supper in the dungeon prepares for this new covenant's performative enactment out from the crypt.[105] Gauvain's death follows as an *imitatio Christi*. It is the last moment Cimourdain shows maternal affection for Gauvain, whom he finds asleep. In one of many reversals, he becomes the child, who rubs his eyes (470; 2.242). The pupil does not so much teach his former tutor as outshine the lapsed priest with visionary prophecy.[106]

The humanistic republic of love articulated by Gauvain fulfills and surpasses the patriarchal republic of strict justice and inexorable law Cimourdain stands for (472; 2.246). This republic of progress does not reject but builds on and transcends the past (472; 2.245). Whereas Cimourdain would found a republic on the sword, Gauvain's foundation rests on *esprits* – both intellect and spirit (478; 2.249). The opposition of sword to spirit first recapitulates that between Rome and Christianity and, second, that between Old and New Testaments. The political subla-tion results in transfiguration: "Plus d'homme reptile. Je veux la transfig-uration de la larve en lépidoptère" (480; "'No more reptilian man. I wish the transfiguration of the larva into a butterfly'," 2.250). The Christian trope supersedes classical metamorphosis. Various villains throughout the novel have been called reptiles or insects – Marat conspicuously a "cloporte" (wood louse," 164; 1.164), a "couleuvre" ("snake") who turns into a dragon (165; 1.165). Gauvain transfigures them into butterflies, symbols of the soul's liberation from its bodily weight, like the torn

---

[104] *parcere subiectis et debellare superbos*, Aen. 6.853.
[105] The dungeon is categorized as a "crypt" earlier in the description of La Tourgue, Boudout (1957) 296.
[106] Gohin (2002) 167.

fragments of the book Georgette throws to the wind (345; 2.105). Gauvain points the way, like John the Baptist, to the new republic: from underground he seems to see the stars above in a transformational cosmic vision (479; 2.249).

Romanticism's Republican Testament: *Gauvain en gloire*

He has made us competent as ministers of a new covenant – not of the letter but of the Spirit; for the letter kills, but the Spirit gives life.

Paul, Corinthians 3.6

At the novel's close, two simultaneous deaths bring its ideological conflict to a head. Gauvain's self-sacrifice in the name of a charitable, maternal republic to come is modeled on Christ's crucifixion. The suicide of Cimourdain, Gauvain's spiritual father and metaphorical creator, figures the civil war into which the masculinist republic devolves and thereby gives the lie to its high aspirations. Which wins out? Does civil war overwrite self-sacrifice and damn history to an eternal repetition of woe? Or does self-sacrifice finally overcome civil war, not through victory but through redemption?

In the end, the deaths, metaphorical twinned sisters, are unequal. In Hugo's conception, Romantic poetics, based on the principle of uniting and elevating contraries, will finally heal the absolute split they stand for. These juxtaposed deaths map onto the hermeneutic structures of biblical exegesis, in which the Old Testament prefigures the New, which transfigures the Old. Always a Romantic optimist in a Christian vein, Hugo elevates the structure of conversion into a principle of history. The novel's appropriation and fulfillment of New Testament hermeneutics retrospectively politicizes Augustine's *civitas Dei* by making it a blueprint for a republican politics. Hugo's republic to come depends, like Augustine's, on self-sacrifice, namely, the right kind of love, for its realization. In both, the new city can be realized on earth, but will always be deferred. Unlike Augustine, however, Hugo outlines a specific political program.[107]

While the novel, up to its denouement, tells of history step by step from Rome, through Hebrew, then Christian paradigms, in its climactic moment, these layers all overlie one another in an extravaganza of civil war redeemed. Transfiguration subsumes prefiguration. The Tourgue surveys and encompasses all the miseries of history in its lifeless stones.

---

[107] For the politization of Augustine, Antoine (2003).

The killing republic of the Terror brings these to an end under the sign of the guillotine, but it itself is saved, transfigured into a living republic. Gauvain's self-sacrifice redeems Cimourdain's suicide. Gauvain's republic redeems Cimourdain's just as spirit gives the dead letter life. Supplanting the deadening end of the *pax Romana* with a new republic of charity, Hugo can now definitively enlighten Vergil, traditionally Christianity's dark, foreshadowing *umbra*.

The nineteenth century often generalized Paul's conversion on the road to Damascus as a providential model of history.[108] Nearly a decade earlier than *Quatrevingt-treize*, Hugo's *William Shakespeare* (1864) names a new trope: "chute transfiguration" ("fall transfiguration"). The story of one man's paradigmatic conversion becomes Hugo's leading metaphor of history as a story not of progress, a continuous march forward and upward, but of repeated falls transfigured, of light overcoming darkness.

> Le chemin de Damas est nécessaire à la marche du progrès. Tomber dans la vérité et se relever homme juste, une chute transfiguration, cela est sublime. C'est l'histoire de saint Paul. À partir de saint Paul, ce sera l'histoire de l'humanité ...
>
> Paul, après sa chute auguste, s'est redressé armé, contre les vieilles erreurs, de ce glaive fulgurant, le christianisme; et deux mille ans après, la France, terrassée de lumière, se relèvera, elle aussi, tenant à la main cette flamme épée, la Révolution. *William Shakespeare*, Part 1, 2.10

> The road to Damascus is necessary for the march of progress. To fall into truth and arise a just man – a fall transfiguration – is sublime. It's the story of St. Paul. Starting with him, it will be the history of humanity ... Paul, after his august fall, arose armed, against the old errors, with Christianity's lightning sword; two millennia later, France, floored by enlightenment, will stand again, she too, holding in her hand the sword enflamed of the Revolution.

All history, born of the deepest fall, becomes for Hugo an ever-improving series of progressive enlightenments. Paul's conversion was itself modeled on the abjection of the crucified Christ, who after total abasement will be exalted; human history, instantiated in the French Revolution, will finally see the light in an *imitatio* of Paul's conversion. In a theory of progress modeled on conversion, things necessarily take a turn for the worse before getting better.

---

[108] Rey (2008) 27; on Hugo, 30–1. Vinken (1993).

Between *William Shakespeare* and *Quatrevingt-treize*, the slaughter of the Commune shook Hugo's confidence, not in the structure per se, but in history's direction. In *L'année terrible* (1872), he sees current disturbances as a double war: "the war" against Prussia, that is, "among Europeans, is a civil war" ("Une guerre entre européens est une guerre civile").[109] Unlike Marx, who hoped a permanent revolution would realize messianic history in the here and now, Hugo sees the horror of history as a necessary, providential means, a precondition for transfiguration. Hugo gives history, structured by civil war up to the Terror, a different function from Augustine.[110] No mere negative antitype, enlightened in retrospect as a negative prefiguration of redemption, Hugo grants history an active, productive function. It forces salvation out, it makes redemption happen, and it is totally transfigured by the salvation to come. *Quatrevingt-treize* answers the need for refoundation in the face of civil war's horrific eternal return with a showdown for all time. The novel itself refounds a new republic on the back of the failed Revolution, on better principles than have hitherto been achieved, through its climactic *chute transfiguration*. As in the crucifixion, a tree of death will burst into bloom as a tree of life.

Two paradigms are consistently inscribed in this sinister fulfillment: Roman civil war, via Latin literature, and the biblical story, through the Old Testament. Both negative antitypes, fully realized in history, come under the sign of civil war and deadening letter, both are instrumental to the new order that will transfigure them. Only from the abyss, salvation's precondition, will heavenly Jerusalem arise. As evil is instrumental for the good's manifestation, it too will be included in salvation; in a sweeping *apokatastasis* (restoration), everyone and everything, even Satan, will be redeemed.[111]

In the final chapter of Hugo's Romantic, republican testament, another paradigm supersedes the over-layering of the Old Testament with Latin letters. With remarkable ambition, *Quatrevingt-treize*, whose reigning tropes are Pauline, succeeds not only classical epic, but even the New Testament itself. It confidently steps into the role of a Newer Testament. As the New Testament resumes and succeeds the Old with its promise of a new world order, Romanticism subsumes all of history in its promise of a republic to come by succeeding the whole of its own literary tradition.

---

[109] "Carnets de la guerre et de la Commune" 15 août 1870–12 février 1871, in Seebacher and Rosa (1987), vol. "Voyages": 1102. Also: "la guerre civile ferait les affaires de la guerre étrangère" ("Civil war would arrange matters for foreign war," 1051).

[110] Peyrache-Leborgne (1996) 51. [111] For *apokatastasis*, Kittsteiner (1991).

Literature takes up the promise of a new covenant institutionalized but never realized by the Church.

A densely allusive cluster of intertexts dramatizes Gauvain's self-sacrifice in the name of love. His crucifixion confronts the catastrophe of history. The novel's final chapter opens with paired and monstrous constructions that equate the monarchy with the Terror in symbolic and tragic equilibrium: "La Tourgue, c'était la monarchie; la guillotine, c'était la revolution" (483; "La Tourgue was Monarchy; the guillotine was Revolution," 2.252). Their showdown drives home an allegorical point: "Un monstre de pierre faisant pendant au monstre de bois ... un édifice est un dogme, une machine est une idée" (483; "A monster of stone rising up to hold companionship with the monster of wood ... an edifice is a dogma; a machine an idea," 2.252). The dead and killing letter is literalized in the guillotine: the engine of death appears as a Hebrew letter or Egyptian hieroglyph (481; 2.251) and takes the geometric form of a capital "E" (487; 2.254). The heavy and harsh angularity of these letters conveys the horror of law, history, and death under the sign of Semitic and Egyptian cultures.[112] The stony Tourgue, icon of the stony heart unmoved by the unspeakable tortures inflicted within, sits in a desert symbolizing darkness of spirit. Personified, it watches the guillotine that emerges from the fateful ground as a sinister tree, a metaphor for the cross (485; 2.253).[113] Equally personified, the revolutionary guillotine declares its filiation from the monarchy: "je suis ta fille" (485; "'I am thy daughter'," 2.253). Horror and terror, mother and daughter, they eye each other as the living dead: "et le phantôme regardait le spectre" (486; "the phantom stared at the spectre," 2.253). As Augustine figures the unsurpassable horror of Roman civil wars in the daughter's killing her mother, the guillotine will finish off her monstrous mother, the Tourgue ("tué par elle," "killed by her"), as the Terror finishes off the monarchy, in an act of civil war.

In this Augustinian structure, a new order advances over these death-bearing human constructions. While the two are matched and the guillotine's victory over the Tourgue brings only further death, nature also comes in a stark antithesis, death with life, whose second element at last marks an advance. While in man-made history, death wrecks death on death, in God's natural order, life emerges triumphant in its struggle against death

---

[112] Whereas Mehlman (1977) 66 explains the hieroglyphic as a symbol of differentiation before the holistic unity and presence of the voice, we interpret it within Pauline hermeneutics.

[113] The cross replaces the gibbet in the 1832 preface of *Le dernier jour d'un condamné* (*The Last Day of a Man Condemned to Capital Punishment*), Brooks (2008) 543. He reads the novel's denouement in light of Hugo's lifelong opposition to the death penalty.

with life. Gauvain's Calvary, soaked in the bloody motifs of Old Testament and Roman civil war, plays out the barbarity of history once again under the sign of a tree. A living landscape of exuberant nature is foil to the dead wood of the new Cross: the guillotine sits, useless, amid the blooming heather. Fertile flowers, birdsong, and rich perfumes chasten mankind with the contrast between divine beauty and human ugliness (486; 2.253–4). The "earth" – six times – is the ground from which the tree of the guillotine grows allegorically as a new Cross, soaked with the blood, sweat, and tears (Luke 22.44) of the people, who have suffered under feudal and absolutist monarchy (485; 2.253).[114] This chthonic space births civil war: the earth shelters the Bretons in underground lairs (3.1.3–4); these "giants" (231; 1.251) evoke the monstrous fertility of the earthborn that conventionally figure civil war.[115] In one chapter title, two cosmic battles come compressed: "Titans against Giants" (3.4.9; 146). The difference between monsters that both fight against the Olympian gods is elided in a battle of like against like. Against the backdrop of symmetrical conflict without resolution, a tree of death is transfigured into a new tree of life.

Two scenes foreshadow this transfiguration. In the midst of deadly war, the Republicans find the mother in a thicket of living branches, and Tellmarch, another figurative mother, lives under the earth in the roots of a living tree.[116] These life-bringing trees foreshadow the salvific tree of the cross, into which even the fatal guillotine will finally be transfigured. Gauvain's martyrdom furthermore transfigures the dead tree of the church's cross, which has, in Hugo's view, devolved into a deadening letter, into the living cross of the republic to come. The guillotine, as a new cross, is the "redeeming price to pay for the original sin of fratricidal violence and oppression."[117] Gauvain surpasses even Christ in his *imitatio Christi*: He gives himself of his own free will into the hands of his murderers and not only suffers but fully embraces the law. He saves his father, who has inflicted this law upon him. The republican soldiers also live up to the challenge and surpass their model. Unlike the Jews who called for Jesus' death, they fall to their knees and cry out for "Grâce!" a total of four times (490; "'Mercy!'," 2.256). The novel overlays the historical event of the Terror with the liturgical year in scenes spanning from Christmas to Easter. Successive conversions, from stone to flesh, letter to spirit, begin with a nativity scene – the mother amongst the branches melts hearts of stone

---

[114] For the people, not the king, taking the role of Christ in the Passion, Lefort (1981).
[115] For the exotic otherness of Brittany, Grossman (2012) 180–1. Lowrie (2015c) 26–7.
[116] Gohin (1979) 503 underscores Tellmarch's tellurgic aspect.   [117] Brombert (1984) 208.

with love – and lead up to the Golgotha and Easter of Gauvain's *imitatio Christi*. His martyrdom testifies to the new republic of charity and redeems civil war with purifying blood. Hugo's renewed covenant surpasses the New Testament's new covenant by fulfilling its promise. Love finally overcomes hate. Redemption finally makes progress.

The Roman register of civil war maintains its drumbeat through to the climactic ending. Roman exemplarity colors Gauvain's death sentence: Captain Guéchamp, the voice of legal formalism in the vote against Gauvain, cites Manlius, who in 414 BCE put his son to death for infringing military discipline. War in the family means fathers tragically kill their sons, and Cimourdain follows dutifully in Manlius' footsteps. Cimourdain not only wages civil war with this act, he figures it. He shoots himself at the moment the guillotine's blade falls. His suicide opposes and parallels Gauvain's purifying self-sacrifice.[118] Lucan's signature trope for civil war comes in his own grotesque style – blood flows from Cimourdain's mouth (491; 2.257). But contrary to the Roman fathers who Stoically outlived the sons they killed, however great their grief, putting to death his beloved spiritual son breaks Cimourdain's heart.

A Biblical framework yet again overlies the Roman model. Upon Cimourdain's actual devastating decision, his ghastly smile of triumph is compared to Jacob's when he asked for and received the blessing of the angel he had wrestled down (467; 2.238–9). Jacob, newly named Israel, becomes a founding father of the Jewish people. His analogue Cimourdain becomes a perverse founder of the republic to come by his suicide. Like Vergil's Aeneas, he kills a young man at the same time as avenging another; unlike him, these are one and the same. Like Aeneas, his new foundation comes in the tropes of civil war: clemency forgone for vengeance underwritten by suicide. Each element is his republic's root and the seed: "Rien ne vient sans racine; la second époque est toujours en germe dans la première" ("Nothing comes rootless; the second era always germinates in the first," *Préface de Cromwell*, Purnal, Thierry, and Mélèze [1963] 417). If Cimourdain were the new republic's sole founder, the old paradigms of Hebrew law and Roman civil war would return.

As ideological figures, Cimourdain and Gauvain incarnate the Pauline antithesis of letter to spirit; as literary, their physical appearance embodies respectively the contrast between death and life. The former priest, who has converted to the harsh republicanism of the Terror, repeatedly turns

---

[118] Eco (2006) 278: "What do you call a ferocious, death-sowing monster that promises a better life? An oxymoron."

increasingly pale. He figures death alive. When first given his commission to oversee Gauvain by Robespierre, he grows pales, then livid in death's own color (176; 176). When Gauvain emerges in Lantenac's place, Cimourdain looks like he himself he had been guillotined; his breath fails in yet another foreshadowing of the death to come: "pâle comme une tête coupée ... Il semblait ne plus respirer" (461; "pale as a severed head ... He no longer seemed to breathe," 2.234). Casting his vote against his beloved spiritual son, he metamorphoses into the "stone" that represents his heart: "rocher" (462; 2.235), then earth and marble (466–7; 2.238–9). The bullet through his heart literalizes the death of a heart he has already killed.

On the tribunal of judgment, under a *faisceau* (from the Latin *fasces*) on the platform atop the Tourgue and looking across the ravine, Cimourdain sits on the side of deadening history under the sign of Rome and the law. The French Republic for which he speaks and whose tricolor hat he wears is revealed thereby as the heir of the debunked Roman Republic. On the other side of the ravine stands the guillotine, to which Gauvain is brought. The gulf between them can be bridged by words only. This gulf reenacts the chasm that irrevocably separates the damned and the saved in the parable of Lazarus. A rich man lifts up his eyes from the netherworld and appeals to Abraham in heaven, whom he sees from a great distance. Abraham responds, "between us and you there a great chasm has been fixed, in order that those who would pass from here to you may not be able, and none may cross from there to us" (Luke 16.26). The gulf may not be crossed in the Bible, but it will be crossed in Hugo: Gauvain will not leave Cimourdain behind, he does not lose sight of him while going to his beheading, their eyes remain locked until the moment of death, when, finally united, their souls soar united into the heavens.

The setting drives home both the absolute difference and the parallelism between Gauvain and Cimourdain. Before their twin deaths, both declare their respective commitment to the order each represents. Cimourdain cries out "Force à la loi!"(490; "'Fulfill the law!'," 2.256). Even lions, who evoke martyrdom's arena, would have been moved, but not Cimourdain. His call for the killing letter of the law under the sign of force counteracts the soldiers' call for grace – the executioner therefore hesitates, another evocation of Aeneas killing Turnus. By contrast, Gauvain's redemptive republic looks to life and the future: his last words are "Avenir" and "Vive la République" (481, 491; "'Future'," 2.250 "'Long live the Republic!'," 2.256).

The layering of world orders is not limited to Hebrew, Roman, and Christian. Even within the Christian story, time inverts, so that the final scene superposes the crucifixion onto the second coming. Just before his head falls, Gauvain appears as a vision of living beauty (490; 2.255–6), modeled on the iconography of Christ in glory. The later mosaic by Olivier Merson, H. M. Magne, and R. Martin in the apse of the Sacré-Coeur on Montmartre (Fig. 5.2) shows the medieval image's continued currency. The turning point of time, of a time after time, is prepared by the incarnation and fulfilled in the second coming, when Christ returns in glory, his body transfigured after the last judgment at the end of time. Lantenac's care not to break his watch has already foreshadowed this "turning point," but rather than tragic *katastrophe*, there will be transfiguration, realized in Gauvain. Cleansed of deadening, violent, ugly masculinity, he overcomes in his body the opposition between female and male. The wind in his flowing hair is the breath of spirit.[119] The sun behind him sets him "as if in a mandorla" ("comme dans une gloire," 490; 2.256). The eschatological representation of the glorious Christ fulfills the terrestrial scenes – nativity or crucifixion – of Jesus's life. In its *sensus anagogigus* (from Greek ἀναγωγή, *anagoge*, upward leading), which, of the fourfold

Figure 5.2 Olivier Merson, *Christ en gloire*, mosaic (1923), Sacré-Coeur, Montmartre, Paris

---

[119] Grossman (2012) 228: The natural world metaphorically redescribes "how history should operate."

senses of scripture, reads history as fulfilling God's plan in its eschatological meaning, Gauvain's Republic to come is Hugo's heavenly Jerusalem.[120]

In Hugo's Romantic eschatology, all layers of providential history unite in a massive figuration that subsumes the horrors of civil war and the darkness of deepest abjection into an integration from which light shines out as humanity's divine nature is fully realized at last. Roman civil war, instantiated in killing the beloved and in suicide, inscribes itself into the climactic scene, not, as in the *Aeneid*, in an act of foundation that sets Rome on a perpetual course of civil war, but in an act of transfiguration to redeem it ostensibly once and for all.[121] The choice between enforcing the law's violence and charity translates Aeneas' dilemma, to exact vengeance or exercise clemency, precisely into Christian terms.

Upon death, the souls of Gauvain and Cimourdain rise to heaven with language that recalls but inverts Turnus' soul, which goes complaining down to the underworld. Hugo emulates Virgil, only to redeem him.

> Et ces deux âmes, sœurs tragiques, s'envolèrent ensemble, l'ombre de l'une mêlée à la lumière de l'autre. 491

> And those two souls, united still in that tragic death, soared away together, the shadow of one mingled with the radiance of the other. 2.257

> ast illi solvuntur frigore membra
> vitaque cum gemitu fugit indignata sub umbras.
> Vergil, Aeneid 12.951–2
> But his limbs are loosened with cold, and his life flees with a groan, full of resentment, down to the shades.

Hugo's souls rise, while Vergil's descend; Gauvain and Cimourdain embrace as sister souls, while Turnus is alone and resentful; the Romantic souls mix shadow with light, while the Roman shades wait below;[122] the united, loving souls soar to the heavens, while mere limbs, bereft of life, flee to the underworld. With their embrace, the two souls finally heal the internal divide of their "single soul cut in two" ("une âme coupée en deux," 284). This healing overcomes not only Rome but the republic based on it. Sisterly love takes the place of the Revolution's

---

[120] Bloch (1994) examines the renewed interest in patristic hermeneutics in the nineteenth century.

[121] Peyrache-Leborgne (1996) 64: The ending is a "theatrical return of the catastrophe in a redemptive and anti-tragic vision"; the registers of tragedy and transfiguration remain in tension until close to the end.

[122] Ending all his works with shadow, Vergil inscribes his signature poetic darkness into Turnus' death. Boyle (1986) 12, 32, 34, 164–5, 175–6.

bloody fraternity, while enacting liberty and sublating equality into a sublime unity. Sisterly mingling purifies the monstrous fertility of tower and guillotine and elevates maternity as a feminine principle through chastity.

The upward rising of the entwined souls to heaven not only reverses and redeems the downward motion of Turnus' soul in the *Aeneid* but also sets the book of Revelation straight. Gauvain consistently overcomes and redeems, in addition to Rome and the Old Testament, all deadly violence in the Christian avenging spirit. The archangel Michael's gesture, shoving Satan down to Hell, inverts – the scene is a stone's throw from the Mont St. Michel. Cimourdain had envisaged Gauvain as an "exterminating angel" who would exact vengeance. Instead, he pardons the man who attacked him. Cimourdain misinterprets his clemency as Caesarian sovereignty. Rather, it is charity. A "shadow" ("ombre") of consternation passes over Cimourdain's face (274; 2.32). No, an angel passes. With a free "gesture of farewell," Gauvain commends Cimourdain to God ("un geste d'adieu," 491; 2.256) and testifies to his living republican faith, shouting "Vive la République." In excusing himself to the executioner for a moment with "pardon," he colloquially grants the pardon he has not received. Gauvin replays the martyrdom of Stephen: As he gazes into heaven and sees the glory of God, Stephen, on the verge of being stoned, calls out, "Lord Jesus, receive my spirit" (Acts 7.59) and forgives his executioners.[123] Likewise, Cimourdain, become pure shadow, is lifted up instead of being shoved down. In Gauvain's thought, Lantenac had transformed from Satan to Lucifer by saving the children: "L'infernal Satan était redevenu le Lucifer céleste" (443; "The infernal Satan had again become the celestial Lucifer," 2.216).[124] Cimourdain realizes this transformation as Gauvain is revealed as an archangel, not of vengeance but of redemption.

Gauvain's self-sacrifice redeems the tropes of civil war and brings the dead letter to life. Hugo translates and sublates the letters of antiquity, of Latin literature, of Old and New Testament into his novel testament. All fallen history, all fallen literature is transfigured into Romantic unity; the dead and deadening letter comes alive in Hugo's *chute transfiguration*.[125]

---

[123] We thank Paul Keyser for several Biblical allusions, including the lions of martyrdom.

[124] Gohin (2002) 167.

[125] Mehlman (1977) makes a heroic attempt to rescue Hugo from his self-totalization with a reading in which the novel itself undoes its hermeneutic, teleological, idealist drive; particularly 57–63.

Le sacre de la littérature

Le livre prendera la place de la cathédrale.

The book will take the place of the cathedral. *Notre Dame de Paris*, chapter "Ceci tuera cela" ("This will kill that")

For Hugo, literature is a holy sacrament.[126] In the scene where Gauvain and Cimourdain share their contrasting visions of republicanism, Gauvain's republic embraces love above the law and harmony above mathematical calculation: He avows Homer as his model where Cimourdain avows Euclid (472; 2.246). Beyond the scales of justice, there is the lyre. Poetry nourishes inspiration: "penser, c'est manger" (473; "'To think is to eat'," 2.246). Man, after all, does not live on bread alone (Matthew 4.4). This is the last supper of Gauvain and Cimourdain, a prisoner's meal of black bread and water shared the night before their shared deaths. Hugo's novel hereby steps into its role as the testament for his new evangelism.

God authors the book of history, whose events are signed by historical agents as their clerks.

> Les événements dictent, les hommes signent . . . mais Desmoulins, Danton, Marat, Grégoire et Robespierre ne sont que des greffiers. Le rédacteur énorme et sinistre de ces grandes pages a un nom, Dieu, et un masque, Destin. 208

> Events dictate; men sign . . . but Desmoulins, Danton, Marat, Grégoire, and Robespierre are mere scribes. The great and mysterious writer of these grand pages has a name – God; and a mask – Destiny. 1.223

But God's book can also be read out of nature; the cosmic glides over the tempests of history.

> Au-dessus des révolutions la vérité et la justice demeurent comme le ciel étoilé au-dessus des tempêtes. 208

> Above revolutions Truth and Justice remain as the starry sky lies above and beyond tempests. 1.224

Hugo's own role is the exegete who rightly interprets God's book.[127] Subsuming all prior Testaments, *Quatrevingt-treize* fills the void left by the children's destruction of the *St. Bartholomew* (3.3).[128] Rising into

---

[126] Bénichou (1973).
[127] Campion (2004) 111–12: Cimourdain's adherence to the law lacks imagination.
[128] Chamarat-Malandain (1991) 147 refers to the novel as *Reliquat de Quatrevingt-treize* (*Oeuvres complètes*, ed. Jean Massin, vol. 15).

heaven's azure in torn fragments (346; 2.106), the dead letters of the printed book show the way to Gauvain's republic, which lifts mankind up in harmony (472; 2.246) out from history's abysmal horror. Obeying the structure of Christian hermeneutics, his book embraces eschatological love and hope; it springs from the total despair of stony hearts and dead letters. Christianity, most paradoxically, has shown the way to a new, Romantic aesthetics in literature.[129] Hugo's new testament, which fulfills the New Testament just as the New fulfills the Old, is the newest edition of God's book.[130]

Hugo's corpus – his body, his oeuvre – incarnates the promise of the republic to come. He writes this body of work in exile as an alternative to the politics of worldly Paris, a *civitas terrena* torn apart in the Commune's *semaine sanglante* (week of bloodshed) by war imperial and civil. In this all too real Paris, like Augustine's Rome, the *res publica* figures only as grotesque. The true Paris, "*sa* Ville éternelle" ("*his* eternal City"),[131] not as in Marx a new Rome, but a heavenly Jerusalem, is realized in this corpus, the *chose publique* incarnate *res publica* in its most sublime form.

Even in his own times, realism had ripped Hugo's poetics to shreds before *Quatrevingt-treize*. Gustave Flaubert wrote *L'Éducation sentimentale* as a *dysangelium* to counter Hugo's rosy republicanism.[132] His revolution of '48 undoes Hugo's new republic of '74 *avant la lettre*. Flaubert's Paris is a New Rome that turns out to be, still in Augustinian terms, a new Babylon. It is precisely the hope and promise of salvation in a republic of love that feeds the *civitas diaboli* (city of the devil). Already a decade beforehand, in reaction to Hugo's earlier writings, Flaubert had undone the Pauline antithesis between living heart and dead letter so fundamental for Hugo. He showed it up as a sentimental cliché of bourgeois idealism. He skewers *Les Misérables*: "Ce livre est fait pour la crapule catholico-socialiste, pour toute la vermine philosophico-évangélique" ("This book was written for all those catholico-socialist bull-shitters, for all the philo-sophical-puritanical vermin").[133] The same goes, all the more so, for *Quatrevingt-treize*. For Flaubert, the Revolution was no messianic over-coming of history, but the lamentable return of the same old dreck.[134] He insists that literature's function, hardly redemptive, is to bring this truth to

---

[129] Brombert (1984) 205–30, Ferguson (1998), Catani (2011).
[130] Gohin (1979) 520 calls the novel an "évangile apocryphe" ("apocryphal gospel").
[131] Spiquel (2002) 242.
[132] For Flaubert as a *contre-Hugo* ("anti-Hugo"), Scepi (2017), Séginger (2017) 284.
[133] Flaubert, letter to Edma Roger des Genettes, "Correspondance juillet 1862," in Bruneau (1991), 236.
[134] Vinken (2009a).

light in a dark, Babylonian poetics, whose dissolved sentences reveal the world's dissolution. Realism, that is, modern literature, came into its own by undoing Romanticism in ideology as in poetics.

In our day and age, Michel Houellebecq, the baddest boy of French letters, has adopted Flaubert's project, but with an accessible realism as easy to consume as Hugo's page-turners. Still, just as Flaubert could never have written his protest without Hugo to counter, Houellebecq is steeped in the tradition he writes against. His *Soumission* drives another stake in the heart of a father who refuses again and again to be killed.

CHAPTER 6

The Empire to Come
Houellebecq, Soumission

Among other authors, the gentle Virgil, he whom school ushers name the Swan of Mantua, presumably because he was *not* born in that city, appeared to him as one of the most terrible of pedants, one of the most dismal twaddlers Antiquity ever produced; his sheperd swains, all washed and beribboned, taking turn and turn about to empty over the unfortunate reader's head their slops of sententious, chilly verses, his Orpheus whom he compares with a weeping nightingale, his Aristæus blubbering over bees, his Æneas, that weak-kneed, fluent personage who stalks, like a shadow figure at a show, with wooden gestures behind the ill-fitted and badly oiled screen of the poem, set him beside himself with exasperation.

Huysmans, *A Rebours*

Some coincidences of history become allegorical. Michel Houellebecq's satiric novel *Soumission* (*Submission*) was published on January 7, 2015, the day of the attacks on *Charlie Hebdo* by domestic terrorists, internal enemies acting in the name of Islam. That day's issue featured the novel, with the author in prophetic mode on the cover. The headline read "Prévisions du mage Houellebecq" ("Predictions of Houellebecq the Mage"). As a Cassandra figure, denouncing civil war, he himself suffered when its violence struck Bernard Maris, a dear friend who was visiting the editorial staff that day. The magazine played on his own words.[1]

> Pendant plusieurs années, et sans doute même plusieurs dizaines d'années, *Le Monde*, ainsi plus généralement que tous les journaux de centre-gauche, c'est-à-dire en réalité tous les journaux, avaient régulièrement dénoncé les "Cassandres," qui prévoyaient une guerre civile entre les immigrés musulmans et les populations autochtones d'Europe occidentale. 55

---

[1] Unmarked quotations are from Houellebecq (2015a). The first number refers to the page of the French text, the second to the Stein translation (Houellebecq [2015b]). We lightly adapt the translation in places and translate any other French ourselves.

For years now, probably decades, *Le Monde* and all the other center-left newspapers, which is to say every newspaper, had been denouncing the "Cassandras" who predicted civil war between Muslim immigrants and the indigenous populations of Western Europe. 41

Cassandra's predictions always come true, however misunderstood, and her most horrific prophecies in Aeschylus' *Agamemnon,* canonical for tragic violence within the family, are those predicting her own demise. Houellebecq became a sorry Cassandra despite himself, but the prediction and its realization are at odds.[2]

Soumission tells in a palimpsestic filigree the collapse of France's Fifth Republic into an oriental tyranny. This dystopian story of political catastrophe, predicted for the French election scheduled in 2022, follows the model of the collapse of the Roman Republic, which, ravaged by civil war, emerged transformed into empire under Augustus.[3] In the first round of voting, no one receives a majority: the National Front is in the lead, with the Socialists and Muslim Brotherhood appearing neck and neck (75; 59). When the Socialists drop behind, the remaining parties proceed to a runoff (77; 60). A leader, it is hinted, among the radical French *identitaires* (nativists), the aptly named Lempereur tips off the narrator François to their plans: to set off a civil war – in all caps, just in case we miss it: *PREPARER LA GUERRE CIVILE* (69; civil war also at 70, 73, 116, 125, 128, 142; 53, also 54, 57, 92, 101, 103, 115).[4] Civil violence breaks out between radical branches, the nativist French racist and Islamophobic nationalists and the French Muslim jihadists, who disrupt the runoff's first round and mar the democratic process equally on both sides (143; 114). Each fears the other will win because they are polling, like twins, at exactly 50–50 (83; 143; 65, 114). Their perfectly mirrored opposition erases the distinction between them in a primary trope of civil war. In a gesture sure to enrage both sides, nativists are equated with jihadists.

In the second round of voting, with polling sites under military guard, the traditional centrists align to confer legitimacy on Mohammed Ben Abbes, the candidate representing the Muslim Brotherhood. Since Jacques

---

[2] Houellebecq has identified what the novel depicts: not murderous Islamist terrorism, like that on *Charlie Hebdo,* but rather anti-Islamic, racist white mobilization, instantiated in the terrorist attack committed by Anders Breivik in Norway. Should right-wing, nativist terrorism occur in France, it would fulfill the civil breakdown depicted in the novel. Nonnenmacher (2016) 187.

[3] Parallels between European and Roman history have come back into vogue: Engels (2013). For the novel's first reception in reviews, Komorowska (2016).

[4] Threatening civil war has become an international gesture within rightwing discourses: www .nytimes.com/2019/09/30/opinion/trump-civil-war.html?smid=nytcore-ios-share.

Chirac's election, the story has become well known: French parties, right and left across the spectrum, regularly hold their noses and vote for their standard opponent to prevent the National Front from coming to power. Ben Abbes founds an empire on the example of the *imperium Romanum*. He aims to unite under one religion Europe and the Mediterranean countries spanning from Turkey to the Maghreb, including Egypt. While Rome waged many a war of expansion to build its empire and France many a colonial war, the fictive Ben Abbes is expected to manage everything in a few years through peaceful diplomacy. The seat of the European Commission is transferred to Rome; the European Parliament will sit in Greece. His ambition is to usher in a new golden age of peace, a new union of restored moral values modeled explicitly on Augustan Rome.

The novel touches on such a *translatio Romae* twice, first in the voice of a republican secret-service man. Tanneur, charged with protecting the French Republic from a hostile takeover, sums up Ben Abbes, whose new regime will immediately dismiss him:

> "Mais sa grande référence, ça saute aux yeux, c'est l'Empire romain – et la construction européenne n'est pour lui qu'un moyen de réaliser cette ambition millénaire." 157

> "The first thing you notice is that he's always going on about the Roman Empire. For him, European integration is just a means to this millennial end." 126

> "Ben Abbes lui aussi croit à l'Europe, il y croit même plus que tous les autres, mais lui c'est différent, il a une idée de l'Europe, un véritable projet de civilisation. Son modèle ultime, au fond, c'est l'empereur Auguste; ce n'est pas un modèle médiocre. On a conservé les discours d'Auguste au Sénat, vous savez, et je suis certain qu'il les a étudiés avec attention." 160

> "Ben Abbes believes in Europe, too, more than anyone, but in his case it's different. For him Europe is truly a product of civilisation. Ultimately, he models himself on the emperor Augustus – and that's some model. We still have the speeches Augustus made to the Senate, you know, and you can bet he read them closely." 128–9

Soumission surveys European history as Roman history replayed but tells it against the grain of the canonical tale parroted here: that civil war ended in the *pax augusta* (Augustan peace) under the guise of a restored republic.

Tanneur's mistaken claim that Augustus' speeches to the Senate were preserved – an error particularly blatant from a man who, François suspects, subscribes to the ancient-history journal *Historia* (147; 119) – indicates he misunderstands Augustan politics, even if he retails the Augustan program's correct purpose. The reader who knows Suetonius' life of Augustus will find a *mise en abyme* of exemplarity. Augustus is said to have recited to the senate speeches, already ancient, by Quintus Metellus "on increasing the birth rate" and by Rutilius "on the manner of building." He wanted to show he had precedent for his marriage legislation, which was meant to encourage child-bearing and bring the punishment of adultery into the legal sphere, and his building program, which resulted in the city's adornment (89) – he boasts he found a city of brick and left it made of marble (28).[5] The biopolitics lurking in the allusion to the Augustan program erupts in the novel in the guise of extremist right-wing fears that the immigrant population will outbreed and replace the *français de souche* (French stock).[6] We argue that the novel is no echo chamber for those discourses, nor even merely ambivalent. It certainly does not subscribe to them but leaves them in the lurch.[7] Their proponents are shown to collude with their worst enemy. The classical, apparently civilizing precedent is revealed as oriental horror in the program of Ben Abbes. We show that this horror follows the logic of the inner orient, where the apparently external other turns out to be none other than the self.

Tanneur's errors in interpretation, of which his misinformation about Augustus' speeches is symptomatic, show how secular republican dis-courses (*laïcité*), of which he is a proponent, are in fact complicit with the new politics that emerge from under cover in the Islamic republic. This complicity is mirrored in Tanneur's marriage. The couple acts out, with no little irony, the new order of the sexes. His wife Marie-Françoise, François' colleague at the Sorbonne, is fired by the new regime because she is a woman. Her role immediately switches without much ado. Let go as a professor, she abandons any claim to intellectual participation. While the men discuss the state of the nation, she retires to the kitchen. Her talents in the cuisine of *la France profonde* (French heartland) obey the dictates of the new regime.

---

[5] Milnor (2005) 140–54: The Augustan marriage legislation brings the domestic sphere for the first time into the state's legal purview and accords women a new "legal subjectivity" (151); Tacitus criticizes the laws as overreach. Bhatt (2017) approaches the marriage legislation and sovereignty within the Augustan principate through a biopolitical lens. For the link between literary form and biopolitics, particularly the latter's alleged role, since Augustus, in overcoming civil war through marriage legislation, Auer (2019) 35–50.

[6] As unanimously acknowledged, *Soumission* mobilizes extreme right-wing discourses. The writings of Renaud Camus, *Le grand remplacement* (*The Great Replacement*, 2011), and Éric Zemmour, *Le suicide français* (*French Suicide*, 2014), have set the agenda of extremist racism. Their Islamophobic, antifeminist nostalgia for virile and authoritarian masculinity – ostensibly lost in an effeminate and emasculated Europe – has obvious antisemitic overtones.

[7] Knobloch (2016) 251–63 also reads *Soumission* as a critical analysis of these discourses. McAleer (2020): He is a "false friend" to conservatives.

The republican Tanneur's role as expounder of the Roman analogy is superseded by Rediger, another aptly named leader in the novel's second half. Playing the part of careful thinker and statesman in a dazzling piece of stagecraft, the new president of the Sorbonne has a bright future as the foreign minister to be. As ideologue and mastermind of the new regime, he drafts (i.e., *rédiger*) their political program. The repetition of the analogy between Augustus and Ben Abbes underscores its importance. Rediger expatiates on its meaning and sets it within world history.[8]

> Je me souvins alors de Tanneur, du rapprochement qu'il avait fait avec l'empereur Auguste, [...] la comparaison parut intéresser Rediger, lui donner à penser. [...] "Rares sont les bâtisseurs d'empire ... " ajouta pensivement Rediger. "C'est un art difficile que de faire tenir ensemble des nations séparées par la religion et par la langue, de les faire adhérer à un projet politique commun. À part l'Empire romain je ne vois guère que l'Empire ottoman, sur une échelle plus restreinte. Napoléon aurait sans doute eu les qualités nécessaires – sa gestion du dossier israélite est remarquable, et il a montré au cours de l'expédition d'Égypte qu'il était parfaitement capable, aussi, de traiter avec l'islam. Ben Abbes, oui ... Il se peut que Ben Abbes soit de la même trempe ... " 289

> I thought of Tanneur and what he'd said about Augustus [...] The comparison seemed to interest Rediger. [...] "Rare are the builders of empire," Rediger mused. "It is a difficult thing to hold nations together, when they're separated by religion and language, and to unite them in a common political project. Aside from the Roman Empire, only the Ottomans really managed it, on a smaller scale. Napoleon could have done it. His handling of the Israelite question was remarkable, and during his Egyptian expedition he showed he could negotiate with Islam, too. Ben Abbes, yes ... you could say he was cut from the same cloth." 237–8

Soumission reveals a very different *translatio Romae* from the project of civilization under Augustus' name articulated by Tanneur. The novel unmasks as a sham the standard narrative of peace, union, and moral restoration that became empire's calling card for all the empires in Augustus' shadow. The summary of European history in the wake of the Romans comes with a twist. The restored republic that ended civil war and reformed

---

[8] Aside from the pun, "Rediger" also twists the name of Redeker, a philosopher of the extreme right who published a virulent manifesto against Islam in 2006. For Redeker as a nativist fundamentalist, Asholt (2016) 128–9. Similarly, Farouk Ben Abbes is the name of a militant jihadist who allegedly told the French Central Directorate of Internal Intelligence in 2011 that he planned an attack on the Bataclan on the grounds that its owners are Jews. Götze (2016) 247. These and other names in *Soumission* blur the line between fact and fiction; as signifiers, their specific literary function is to echo, often ironically or uncannily, within the collective, ideological imaginary.

sexual morals under the reign of universal peace is exposed as an advertising strategy, a gambit for legitimation cloaked in a benevolent but naïve humanism that masks brutal subjection in a biopolitical vein. Tanneur's exemplary interpretation of Augustan Rome's civilizing mission yields to Rediger's, who overwrites the Roman Empire with the Ottoman. *Soumission,* an updated and oriental Bible of Empire, supersedes the canonical function of Vergil's *Aeneid* and likewise deconstructs the ideologies it has been made to espouse.

Soumission vehemently satirizes French history as a less-than-edifying repetition of Roman history. The novel operates in the rhetorical mode the Greeks called *hyponoia,* a precursor of allegory. In this discourse of doublespeak, the obvious and public meaning also conveys a different, cryptic message to be deciphered via insider knowledge.[9] The novel points to its rhetorical secret: Those to whom François turns to make sense of this "civil war" tell secrets, that is, stories not made for public consumption. Much is conveyed through innuendo. On the republican side is Tanneur, in the "secret service" and charged with the surveillance of extremist groups (80, 140–1; 62, 114). On the other, Lempereur, a shadowy "éminence grise," a "leader politique dans un movement plus ou moins clandestin" (87–9; "éminence grise," a "political leader, in a clandestine movement," 68–70), plots behind the scenes. Both give obscure hints to François. From behind the curtain emerges a takeover that ends the Fifth Republic under the guise of restoration.

In France's dystopian future, the Fifth Republic will reenact the collapse of the Roman Republic into civil war and its refoundation as Empire, now as then figured via orientalist tropes. French history is Roman history always already *déjà vu.* What is new is that the Fifth Republic had already gone oriental under the radar. In a satiric smash, the great French arts, eroticism and gastronomy, had already degenerated into service industries before the new empire's establishment. Pornography, prostitution, and cheap oriental take-out, all awash in excessive consumption of alcohol, are rife before as after. Food, drink, illicit sex – these are the tropes of satire.[10] With them, *Soumission* paints a complete picture of social, spiritual, and institutional collapse. Its Islam comes not at all from outside; its new Islamic Empire fulfills the Roman Empire's true nature as the Babylon already latent in the Fifth Republic.

---

[9] Haverkamp (2000) 55: "The probable precursor to allegory and a temporarily concurrent term, the Greek *hyponoia* or 'deep meaning,' stresses the learned, esoteric character of allegory. The composition of *allos* and *agoreuein* in *allegoria,* on the other hand, points to speaking differently from public, political discourse, in which to 'talk differently' also implies a 'different way to negotiate.' There is a 'secret' understanding of what is said that depends on 'elitist' knowledge."

[10] Xuan (2015) 129: That Houellebecq counts on such a self-dismantling lets us read *Soumission* throughout as a comedic novel.

The oriental Empire to come, here in the guise of Islam, continues the Fifth Republic, only to finish it off effectively by perverting its already corrupted values. By no means France's first empire, it is the successor to the First and the Second Empires. All are informed by the same Augustan matrix.[11] With the analogy between the Roman Empire and the Islamic empire to come, *Soumission* takes a page from Latin literature and twists the orientalizing trope several further turns. The new empire parallels those of Napoleon I and III respectively, equally established through coups d'état, equally modeled theatrically on Roman history.[12] Both Napoleons masked civil war as a war against an external enemy and allied with the foreign foe to crush internal opponents. Empire follows inevitably on civil war, first as tragedy, then as farce in Marx's famous assessment – the umpteenth time as satire.[13] In *Soumission*, electoral legitimation, in the runoff's second round, allows the incipient empire to present itself draped – to use Marx's metaphor (*drapiert*) – in the guise of yet another republican restoration. Like the Augustan renewal, like both Napoleonic renewals, Ben Abbes restores the alliance of throne and altar in yet another empire masquerading as a republic.

These are not the novel's only historical layers, which multiply reference points in a dizzyingly finite regression. Vichy and the Third Reich are equal partners to Rome.[14] This new regime wages its program in the thoroughly familiar tropes of civil war: family and sexual politics; the demonization of the other, now defined via religion and race. Vergil's Egyptians are updated as Jews, the West's long-standing stereotype for the externalized internal enemy.[15] The regime's values are modeled on a Vichy-inspired and antisemitic patriarchy whose mantra was "travaille, famille, patrie" ("work, family, fatherland"). In an ironic inversion, the only characters who actually balance work with life, have a happy family, and love France as their native land, are a Jewish family. François's inability to love and marry Myriam, his lover and their daughter, indicts French society's incapacity to become a home to Jewish people. The parents, prescient, flee from France and immigrate to Israel along with their daughter. The Third Reich offers another direct model for the new regime's gender politics: By banning women from public service, this empire of the Muslim Brotherhood instantiates a law from the

---

[11] Vinken (2015b).

[12] Huet (1999). Morrissey (2010): The motor for emulating the ancients and surpassing them in the context of the Revolution was an ideology of glory, inherited from antiquity, which allowed for the reconciliation, incarnated in Napoleon, of conflicting imperatives, personal ambition and collective purpose (especially 110–11).

[13] Marx (1960) 115.   [14] For Vichy, Mathy (2017) 259.   [15] Nirenberg (2013).

national-socialist regime.[16] The term *rééduqué* also points ironically to Nazism: "elle allait certainement disparaître, ou du moins être sérieusement rééduquée" (90; "she *would* disappear, or at least she'd be in for some serious reeducation," 71). Americans "reeducated" defeated Germany; here a young Jewish woman risks it.

With the advent of this new Islamic Empire, *Soumission* tells an all-too-familiar tale. There is no clash of cultures after all, only global internal war. The novel exposes the classic strategy of Western denial: The orient has been a projection from antiquity to the nineteenth and now the twenty-first century. The fight for absolute dominion of all against all, of near with dear, brother with brother, men on women through the unholy trinity of power, money, and sex is projected onto some oriental foe, first Egyptian, usually Jewish, now Muslim. In the nineteenth-century realist novel, oriental topoi and tropes reach prominence as vehicles for the analysis and critique of the decadent and corrupt societies that identify themselves as the West. We call this strategy the inner orient.[17]

"Islam," however, has been a cipher for the inner orient in French literature since at least the Enlightenment. In Montesquieu's *Lettres persanes* and Voltaire's *Mahomet*, the orient denotes a political system, tyranny and the idolatry of power, which strives lecherously for total subjugation. From within a regime of censorship, Montesquieu and Voltaire caricature the subjugating monarchy's idolatry through an oriental register: "Mohamed" stands for French absolutism, and "harem" alludes to the sexual mores of the French court.[18] These figurations gained force when European nation states embarked on the large-scale project of colonizing "the Orient" in the nineteenth century. Realist and naturalist fiction respond by exposing Paris as a new Rome, that is, in Augustine's figuration, always already an old Babylon.

Soumission's satire follows in the steps of Flaubert, Zola, and Maupassant, who analyze the rotten contemporary world as the return, once more, of the oriental idolatry at the heart of European imperial politics. This new inner

---

[16] Much scholarship stresses the parallels with Paris occupied in World War II, collaboration, and national-socialist ideology. For allusions to Nazism, Weitzmann (2015); the victory of the Muslim Brotherhood evokes France's capitulation to Pétain in 1940. Morrey's (2018) title, "The Banality of Monstrosity: On Michel Houellebecq's *Soumission*" obviously alludes to Hannah Arendt, *Eichmann in Jerusalem: The Banality of Evil.* The measures taken by this new republic – women evicted from the labor market, "the de facto control of women's dress in public, and the explicit Islamicisation of that most secular of institutions, the French education system" (203), Jews driven out of the country – have all the more shock value for coming under the veil of the ordinary. Armus (2017), after noting "we are in Occupied Paris" (209) and the "culturicide" and collective suicide of secular France, curiously then gives a neo-Zionist reading of the novel.
[17] Vinken (2015b) and (2019).   [18] Montesquieu (1949), Voltaire (1762).

orient, cannily called Islam, provokes a referential fallacy. Houellebecq mobilizes European fears and prejudices and rides the wave of Islamophobia: the loss of European identity when "they" outbreed "us"; foreigners overrunning Fortress Europe by violating borders and women; hordes flooding our welfare system and leading our *Leitkultur* (dominant culture) astray; the *banlieues* (suburbs) aflame in terrorist, Islamist warfare. The fear of such an external takeover goes back at least to the Crusades and the foundational text of French literature, *La Chanson de Roland* (*The Song of Roland*), which retails, in the words of Tanneur, how "Charles Martel a battu les Arabes à Poitiers en 732, donnant un coup d'arrêt à l'expansion musulmane vers le Nord" (148; "Charles Martel – Charles the Hammer – beat the Arabs at Poitiers in 732, ending Muslim expansion to the north," 119). This conflict with actual Muslims resulted in continuing "batailles entre la chrétienté et l'islam" ("battles between Christianity and Islam"). *Soumission* restages this ur-scene in the village of Martel, named after the king who established a church there to commemorate one of his victories (148; 119). Tanneur literalizes the current conflict in historic terms. He thinks what is at stake in this "Islamic" takeover is indeed the age-old conflict between Christianity and Islam on French territory, namely what Martel is shorthand for.

The text, however, suggests otherwise. François runs into Tanneur in this village. They down a good number of beers at the "place des Consuls" ("Consuls Square") looking out at the "hôtel de la Ramondie" (147; 119). The Roman touch, followed by reference to a hotel founded by the king's collector of the *taille* (tax) in 1280, suggests a layered history. Tanneur reads history all over again as external conflict. But the consuls, always two, indicate the internal doubling of civil conflict. The gorgeous phrasing that conveys the sunset's light and the context of hospitality between two men, one driven out by civil unrest (Tanneur, Meliboeus), the other who will enrich himself, collaborating with the new regime (François, Tityrus), recalls the most famous line from Vergil's *Eclogues*.[19]

> maioresque cadunt altis de montibus umbrae   *Eclogues* 1.83
>
> And the shadows fall greater from the high mountains
>
> le soleil couchant teintait la pierre blonde de lueurs fauves 147
>
> Evening fell on the Place des Consuls, the yellow stones glowed gently in the setting sun. 119

[19] Lowrie (2018) 215.

If the Roman register were not enough, the hotel evokes the Middle Ages, again nodding to internal conflict. The monarchic taxes imposed on bourgeois, clergy, and nobility were universally unpopular.[20] Tanneur cannot see that the new regime repeats an old story about internal conflict. He holds the place for the standard literal interpretation.

Soumission, contrary to all appearances, is not about Islam taking over the "West." It tells an altogether different story against this backdrop. The corruption of the French republic, paradigmatic like Rome for all republics, comes to the surface under the name of Islam. It is not about submission to a foreign enemy, to another religion, to another culture. The Islamist characters are all converts. They become their own worst enemy. The novel reveals how the Fifth Republic goes oriental, the perennial gesture of European history – in the tradition we trace – since Roman times. It is about French collaboration with imperial structures, be they economic or ideological, American, German, or Saudi, which overthrow the republic.

Houellebecq has been charged with Islamophobia. In response to these accusations, scholars have pointed out that what is staged in *Soumission* is an age-old inner French conflict, namely that of the "two Frances": "the daughter of the Church"[21] and "secular republic." Kai Nonnenmacher stresses that, in *Soumission,* the politics of 2022 repeat the culture wars of the French separation of Church and state; the religious discourses alluded to provocatively superimpose contemporary debates about the role of Islam over those concerning the role of the Catholic Church around 1900, with both taken as political religions.[22] At stake is a complex play on the history and anxieties of the French Republic, more concerned with its own history than with Islam itself. David Spieser-Landes likewise analyzes *Soumission* as staging an inner French conflict and reads Houellebecq through the lens of the contemporary religious crisis outlined by Emanuel Todd in *Qui est Charlie? (Who is Charlie?).*[23]

Todd argues that, in the wake of World War II and accelerated by the massive loss of faith during the 1960s, France, which had remained Catholic within the secularized Republic, has finally achieved secularization (*laïcité*). While the first secularization, an

---

[20] Favier (1971), Gauvard, de Libera, and Zink (2004), Paris and Buchon (1827).
[21] Pope John Paul II used this phrase in speech, given in 1980, questioning France's continued faith.
[22] Nonnenmacher (2016) 172.   [23] Spieser-Landes (2017) 43; Todd (2015).

outcome of the Revolution, defined itself against the Church and produced the separation of Church and state with the *loi Combes* in 1905, this new secularization, likewise the result of spiritual crisis, has produced what he calls a kind of zombie Catholicism – dictatorial, fundamentalist, and Islamophobic. The degradation of the Catholic Church also reduced its most loyal opponent, the secular Republic. The new secularism is not the old but breaks away from the classical, secular values inherited from the Revolution. The forces that lay claim to laicity today in the French Republic are not republican. A "zombie secularism" parallels "zombie Catholicism." This new antiegalitarian, orthodox laicity defines itself, not like the first, against the Church, but against Islam. It finds a scapegoat in the most powerless, impoverished, and marginalized population, Muslim immigrants. In the name of "freedom" and in the guise of secular republicanism, the new secularism, in fact antirepublican, because antiegalitarian, functions as a secularized religion. Although Todd locates Houellebecq on the side of Islamophobia, we argue that his analysis in fact parallels what is staged in the novel. In a superironic twist, the new, orthodox laicity goes by the name of Islam, the very enemy secularism identifies for itself.

Soumission, however, is no mere presentist critique. It frames the contemporary crisis in discourses it traces, layer by historical layer, back to ancient Rome. The newest repetition of the age-old story upends, once again, the canonical narrative about the Augustan restoration of the Roman Republic post-civil war. The novel replays the problematics of civil war on the narrative level, but the plotline is the least subtle of its literary techniques. *Soumission* enacts civil war as a hermeneutic crisis through its processes of representation. The first-person narrator, François, witnesses the extraordinary political crisis only through mediation – from a distance, after the fact, through television, through hearsay. He tries to put the puzzle together by consulting others with more insight. His attempts at understanding set the procedure required of the reader in a *mise en abyme*. Beyond the ken of its uncomprehending main character, whose alert eye for detail sees without understanding, the *satura* of *Soumission* is stuffed with hermeneutic clues. This other story, which must be deciphered, is told through reference to the stones, streets, and monuments of Paris, to the monuments of France, through speaking names, through literary history and historical allusions, through appearances, clothes, interiors, and consumer culture.

Satura tota nostra est

Il souriait de plus belle, je me demandai un instant s'il ironisait, mais en fait non, je ne crois pas.

He gave me his most beautiful smile. For a second I thought maybe he was being ironic, but no, I don't think he was.

Soumission 294; 242

URANIE – Ne voyez-vous pas que c'est un ridicule
    qu'il fait parler?

Urania: "Don't you see it's an idiot he has speak?" Molière, *La critique de l'école des femmes*, scene 6

Satire is the only genre the Romans claimed for themselves: *satura tota nostra est* ("satire is all ours," 10.1.93), Quintilian vaunts.[24] Satire is not just any genre but the "generically encoded story of Rome's lost, and much lionized Republican identity."[25] Its founder, Lucilius, exists now only in fragments, but the Romans made him emblematic of freedom of speech:

> [E]xpectations of aggressive and uncompromised speech are not just built into the genre as its defining, "Lucilian," hallmark, they are a key defining feature of the elite, male self.

Extant Roman satire from Horace through Juvenal, however, never quite lives up to the ideal of the intact, male, republican self. Starting with Horace, writing in the 30s BCE, satire was composed when civil war had already undermined the Republic or in its imperial aftermath. Roman satire from Horace on presents itself as impotent. It never attacks its targets directly but avails itself of all the strategies of indirection characteristic of literature. If extant Roman satire's point is the failure of the imperial self to live up to the longed-for ideal, *Soumission* adopts the genre to show that the ideal was always already a mirage.

In a tradition starting with Horace, the speaking voice is the ultimate satiric target.[26] One typical error in reading Houellebecq, shared by the press and academic scholarship alike, is to conflate the author with his narrators' voices.[27] Many of Houellebecq's narrators are racist, sexist, and

---

[24] On the tendentious claim, Freudenburg (2005) 1.

[25] Freudenburg (2001) 3; also of quotation below.

[26] The fragments of his predecessors Ennius and Lucilius are insufficiently well preserved for us to determine how much they satirize themselves. Personal voice is a consistent feature of the genre from its Roman beginnings. Muecke (2005).

[27] Trüstedt (2018) critiques the latest crude misreading in the German movie adaption.

fascist, and he has been read as affirming his characters' views.[28] He exposes these views, and the *persona* (mask) has been forgotten. Speaking through a *persona* is specific to satire as a genre, as is the carefully staged collapse of the difference between author and first-person narrator.[29] The critical backlash against the intentional fallacy has resulted not in an expansive view of destabilizing discourses but in a new and widespread literalism.[30] Houellebecq's public performance as a decadent *provocateur*, his autobiographical inscription into his fiction, down to the smoke that rings his narrators' heads, does everything to play on, prey on this peculiarly modern mistake, the cult of authenticity.[31] He flags this mistake in his benighted character François's reading of Huysmans: "une formule simple, éprouvée: adopter un personnage central, porte-parole de l'auteur" (49; "a tried-and-true strategy: he adopts a main character, an authorial stand-in," 36). Houellebecq's role-playing cultivates notoriety by shoving the bodily decay that presages inevitable death before our eyes, in the ugliness of an old man chasing young skirts.[32] Even the prurient interest manifest on the internet in his loss of teeth (a pun on *décadence*) enacts a generic reference to satire's bite and its failure. Like Horace, who presents himself in the *Epodes* as an impotent would-be canine in the invective tradition of Archilochus, but whose society no longer tolerates the republican liberty of open criticism, Houellebecq plays both the rabid dog and the impotent *littérateur*. He stages himself as a Cassandra everyone is invested in not understanding.

[28] E.g., Govrin (2016).

[29] For the history of the critical shift from understanding the figure of the satirist as a moral commentator and agent to how satire "functions as an explosive force routinely applied to a culture's big, regulatory myths" and satirists' performative "self-victimization," Freudenburg (2005) 26–30. He calls for going beyond formalist persona theory, which can make a case for, e.g., Juvenal's "not necessarily 'being' an overblown xenophobe, but of [his] 'playing' one to good effect" (28), to confronting how "the satiric act on the page floats a set of judgments that oblige us to commit ourselves as judges, critics, and fellow performers" (29). For individual Roman satirists, Oliensis (1998) disentangles Horace's layered voices; Uden (2015) challenges the traditional reading of Juvenal's persona as bitterly ironic by showing that the poems' plurality of voices dissipates any central message, conveying instead the sense of rootlessness and loss of identity in cosmopolitan Imperial Rome.

[30] Pushback against literalism begins in antiquity. Selden (1992) disentangles layers of sexual and verbal assault in Catullus 16.

[31] For the distinction between author and narrating voice in Houellebecq, Baggesgaard (2006) insists on this fundamental literary critical principle. For the unreliable narrator also in Baudelaire's *Au lecteur*, with which *Soumission* engages in sustained allusion, Koppenfels (2012). Dilmac (2014) analyzes Houellebecq's carefully staged self-fashioning, which deliberately confuses character and author, as a constant of his oeuvre.

[32] Magazine *Palais* 23, Palais de Tokyo (2016) covers the exhibit where Houellebecq staged his decaying body as the embodiment of a decadent society.

Houellebecq's strategy of scandal sells.[33] He replays the very strategies of the right-wing rhetoric he exposes.[34] He is complicit in repeating this rhetoric in that exposure requires the existence of what it exposes. He takes the risk of exposing himself as well and embraces the danger of being misread, just like Vergil. The potential for misreading is the price of the scandal that ensures his phenomenal sales. His very success depends on this risk. Houellebecq's satire of right-wing discourses presents no way out. There is no redemption available, no possible return to healed republican values. *Soumission* twists the tropes of social collapse and civil war in a dizzying spiral that poses a difficult hermeneutic challenge. Its deliberate provocation forces readers to take a stand, but the politically correct implied reader constructed by the text finds their ideological grounding cut out from under them. To resist each twist puts you back at another level of perversion with no ideal left intact. The scholarly imperative is to uncover the history of these discourses, of the critiques of them, and to show how the novel undoes each, layer by satiric layer. The capacity of undoing such ideologies – by displaying them together with their contradictions, their ideological counterdiscourses, their mutual erasures – belongs to the sphere of art.

Houellebecq's staged bodily decay and the self-destruction of his characters are central tropes of civil war; combined, they manifest the dissolution of the body politic as a self-inflicted wound. Like the horses in the *Georgics* that enact war on themselves by ripping their flesh with their own teeth, the first-person narrator of *Soumission*, François, also tears himself apart when he cannot stop scratching. An awful skin condition, *dyshidose*, attacks his emasculated toes (205–6; 167–8). He further suffers from hemorrhoids (208; 169), metaphorical plumbing failures (272; 223), and fears jaw cancer on the *exempla* of Huysmans and Freud (263; 214). Horace paves the way for the trope in his satire on the voyage to Brundisium. He accompanies Octavian, along with Maecenas and Vergil, to a meeting where Caesar's heir reconciles with Antony in an uneasy alliance (40 BCE). The political background recedes in the poem in favor of keeping bodily fragility in focus. The two poets withdraw from sport, Horace felled by an eye infection that mars his vision, while Vergil gets a stomachache (*Satires* 1.49).

---

[33] For its economic payoff, Mecke (2003), Spiller (2004). Authenticity, carefully staged as intentional fallacy, is a bestseller: Meizoz (2007) and Weiser (2013).

[34] Noiriel (2019) compares the polemical strategy of Zemmour's (2014) Islamophobia to the anti-semitic strategy displayed by Drumont (1886).

Houellebecq plays the *décadent* in a long tradition of life imitating art, whose preeminent modern example is Oscar Wilde and salient contemporary genre is rap.[35] Michel Houellebecq works hard to conflate narrator and author: Like Marcel Proust's narrator "Marcel" and Horace's satiric *ego* "Horatius" or the limp "Flaccus," he often names his first-person speaker "Michel." In *Soumission*, he furthermore inscribes his own editorial history obliquely in a scene played in Jean Paulhan's house (242, 260; 197, 212). For many years, Paulhan was the editor of Gallimard, Houellebecq's own publishing house. It is also in this house, the novel tells us, that the paradigmatic erotic novel of submission was written by Dominique Aury: *L'Histoire d'O* (260; 212). In *Soumission*, free female submission will be perverted into masculinist subjection. Rediger has himself written a book, *Dix questions sur l'islam* (259, 264, 268; "Ten Questions about Islam," 211, 215, 219), that expounds his theory of polygamy, natural selection, and inequality as truths recognized and put into practice in Islam. The subject matter of both books reveals the ideology of the fake religion, while the three million copies sold by Rediger (259; 211), the fictive owner of Paulhan's house, winks at Houellebecq's own position: As France's best-selling author, he gets the biggest advances.

The care with which Houellebecq inscribes his work into the literary canon has not attracted the attention it deserves compared to the commentary on his contemporaneity.[36] Like many heroes in the realist novel, François is a jerk whose human failures put the reader off. He is a sellout, a sloth who collaborates out of vapid self-interest. Lacking in self-understanding, he is seduced by his lowest lusts: sex and drugs. But even these do not inspire passion. He couldn't care less; his cardinal sin is acedia. Like Flaubert's Frédéric in *L'éducation sentimentale* (*Sentimental Education*), he hardly even manages to be despicable. He inspires no mourning, as when Vergil's Aeneas succumbs to the forces of violence and irrationality,[37] no sublime and therefore redemptive hatred like that elicited by Hugo's grotesque or Balzac's realist antiheroes. Unlike their great figures of evil incarnate, he is banal. Blind to his own sexism, François is not overtly misogynistic or racist. He gradually comes around to conversion to an alien religion, not through conviction, but through indifference

---

[35] On the authenticity myth in rap, its effects on art, the spiral of artist, persona, and alias, and how shock sells, Christgau (2006) on Marshall Mathers, Eminem, and Slim Shady; Coates (2013) and Fagen (2017) on Kendrick Lamar; Abdurraqib (2017) on the Migos, compared to Johnny Cash.

[36] On Houellebecq and canonicity, Schober (2002). For a new realism and hence canon, Steigerwald and Komorowska (2011).

[37] Putnam (1965) 192 calls Aeneas' yielding to passion a "complete submission."

to anything but the pleasures of sex and comfort – even the vainglory of ambition is only moderately tempting.

Literature's way to *plaire et instruire* (please and instruct), to join *l'utile et l'agréable* (the useful and the pleasant) – we nod at Horace (*Ars poetica* 343–4), mediated through Boileau (*Art poétique* 3) – is to elicit the reader's identification with a work of fiction, most economically through the speaking voice. Contemporary readers often identify the degraded voices of Houellebecq's speakers with the author and therefore understand the fascist, misogynist, and racist political program represented in his fiction as the author's own agenda, a misunderstanding that has given his oeuvre a *succès de scandale*. But fiction also operates through repulsion, which can equally mobilize a form of literalism. In this case, readers identify their felt repulsion toward the sexist, fascist, and racist regime represented and draw the inference that the author embraces Islamophobia, since this horrific regime, as represented in the novel, overturns fundamental republican values, including respect and equality among the sexes and races. Even based on a literalistic reading, the author, however, must logically either be sexist, fascist, and racist or hate Islam because it allegedly empowers such antirepublican ideologies. He must endorse either intolerance or Islamophobia; he cannot do both, at least not at the same time. This contradiction, however, is endemic to the right-wing discourses the novel exposes.[38] It therefore becomes vulnerable to being judged for what it so carefully represents.

Satire's denunciatory mode, however, is more encompassing and operates with greater subtlety. *Soumission* shows up the ugliness of misogyny, racism, fascism, and other internal splits by projecting them onto Islam but also demonstrates the hypocrisy of this externalization, which in any event provides no relief. The novel's perhaps most provocative irritation is to call out the reader's hypocrisy in thinking we are any better than the despicable nullity that is François. The novel's satiric target is not the Muslim other, but the collaborator François, the French everyman who bears *français* in his name. As a collaborator, he gives the lie to his name and that of the French nation: Francus, denoting those who lived and the territory of the Franks, means "free man." Up to the seventeenth century, the French, *les français*, were spelled like the first name of *Soumission*'s protagonist: *les françois*. If we do not resist collaboration, if we do not approach human relations with active engagement, with love and compassion, if we do not make more than a half-hearted effort to understand that the world is going down in flames around us, Houellebecq denounces us. He turns this denunciation onto himself, in satire's central gesture, through the self-hating spectacle of his own inadequacies, represented in his first-person narrator. This gesture is central to the French tradition: Flaubert inscribes himself in his character Frédéric, as does Maupassant in his Bel-Ami. We give a detailed reading of *Soumission*'s sustained allusion to Baudelaire's "hypocrite lecteur" ("hypocritical reader") below.

Roma temporalis

Soumission gives a resounding "no" to the perennial question, whether Rome's decadent, tyrannical, in short, Babylonian heritage can ever be overcome. The end of civil war brings on empire, which provides no real solution to civil war but only puts it under erasure. The reinscription of civil war's tropes announces an eternal return. Like Flaubert, like Maupassant, Houellebecq's dark "realistic" outlook upends Victor Hugo's bright Romantic vision all the while adhering closely to his allusive methods. Hugo aims to overcome Rome's corruption and hopes to replace it with a new republican order, in fact, a secular retroping of Roman Catholic institutions and values called *laïcité* ("secularism").[39] Rather than separating Church and state and leaving religion behind, laicity replaces the Church, an institution figured as perverse and whose political instantiation is the divine right of kings, and substitutes for it a reformed institution, the republic, which thereby becomes the secular Church one and indivisible. The republic of the Romantics is a product of the Reformation. It is an institution that claims it has overcome the Roman Catholic Church, which it condemns as perverse, sterile, adulterous, effeminate, and idolatrous – in short, decadent. This new republic aims finally to realize the promise of the glad tidings the Catholic Church has failed to keep. Hugo shares his optimistic republicanism with Quinet, Michelet, Zola, to name only a few.

Houellebecq joins a countertradition – whose preeminent mouthpiece is Flaubert – to declare that this vision has clearly not managed to save modernity. *Soumission* tells history via literary history, among other vehicles. The central institutionalization of the republican promise is the university. Humanistic study, with *lettres modernes* (modern literature) in pride of place within it, serves as dartboard for *Soumission*'s satiric barbs.

---

[39] Lefort (1986) 265, Krulic (2011); for Michelet, Vinken (2007).

The novel articulates the problematic of civil war on the battleground of French literature, where the secular faith of the republic is proclaimed.

François teaches nineteenth-century French literature as a professor at the Sorbonne. He is a specialist of Huysmans, who converted to Catholicism after writing his novel *A rebours* (*Against the Grain*; Huysmans [1977 (1884)]), the bible of decadence. The Sorbonne nominally brings the secular good news of the republic's founding fathers, buried in the hallowed halls of the Pantheon, the Republic's new church: *les grands hommes de la patrie* (the great men of the fatherland) become the new church fathers, each with his own special exegete *ex cathedra* (in office).[40] Opposite the classic curriculum of republican greats – Rousseau, Condorcet, Michelet, Jules Ferry, Hugo, and Zola – *Soumission* stages an oppositionalist antirepublican canon of Catholic renegades. This canon opposes modernity: The antimoderns have taken over *lettres modernes*.[41] In addition to Huysmans, whose turn-of-the-century conversion was breathtakingly spectacular, the voices of Léon Bloy and Charles Péguy echo through allusion and quotation. Marginalized Catholic authors have taken over the curriculum and undermine the creed of secular republicanism. In a sarcastic commentary on the state of the canon, Rimbaud is represented by the hapless Steve, who yields to the bribes of the new regime at the price of presenting Rimbaud's own Islamic conversion as dogma (180; 148). Houellebecq kills and outdoes his literary, Romantic fathers in the same gesture; he reinscribes the Roman decadence that Hugo and the republicans attempt to overcome by redeploying and inverting a now familiar set of tropes. History returns, neither tragedy nor farce, but a careful and exact perversion of the republican tradition.

The novel challenges two central narratives of French history by turning both republican and Catholic resistance around. In the first, *Soumission* restages the collapse of the Third Republic into a Fourth Reich à la Vichy. Collaboration supplants resistance. In the second, the novel tells an alternative narrative of the conflict between republic and Church that structured the nineteenth century. The Church, in a consistent tradition ranging from Huysmans to Léon Bloy, Péguy, and the *renouveau catholique* (Catholic renewal), is seen as the victim of and legitimate source of resistance to the Terror, then the Nazi regime. The tradition of Catholic resistance was particularly strong in Belgium, which never became a secular republic but remained a Catholic monarchy. In *Soumission*, via Huysmans, via Baudelaire, all ways lead to Brussels, capital of the European Union, the

---

[40] For this function of literature, Bénichou (1973) and (1977).   [41] Compagnon (2005).

newest of the new Romes. The scholars who work on Catholic authors end up collaborating with the newest in a long line of usurpers.

Soumission sees the return of religion in a different light. This is the light in which Zola, and most strikingly Maupassant, saw the relation of Church and state.[42] Empire, to wit, restores the alliance of throne and altar only apparently undone by the Revolution and the republicanism it ushered in. The bankruptcy of French history, for Maupassant, is that the Third Republic turns out to be a corrupt mock-monarchy that kept the unholy alliance of throne and altar intact: The idolatrous Church and corrupt political sphere got back into bed together once again.[43] This Church has abandoned everything Christian. In Houellebecq's novel, the Roman Catholic Church paves the way for unconditional submission to the totalitarian power of the new regime. The Church is no resisting force, nor is it a force outside this world. Betraying its message and mission, it is implicated in the internal collapse that eases collaboration, only to be dismissed for a different conversion. Absolutist power triumphs and brings about total subjection in the name of religion by surpassing the Church in corruption. Along with it, everything Christian must be overcome and left behind.

Lempereur and Rediger, the two central characters who exercise real power, whether behind the scenes or in the open, pass figuratively or actually through the Catholic Church as they make their way up the ladder. But the Church is for them only a way station. Lempereur, a literary scholar whose specialty is the Catholic, monarchic Léon Bloy, lives on rue Cardinal Mercier – literally and figuratively "une impasse" ("cul-de-sac," 65; 50). The Belgian Cardinal Mercier (1851–1926), a Thomist philosopher at the Catholic University of Leuven, stands for an educational system in the hands of the Church and, even more important, for a possible realization of the *civitas Dei* in Christianity on earth. He resisted the Germans' burning of the Leuven library during World War I and therefore figures resistance to fascism. His Christian hope, however, is marked as an "impasse," a dead end, just as much as Huysmans's decadent novel before his conversion (38; 25). Neither decadence nor Catholic conversion has done the trick. Only the new Islamic regime will have the power to end the French republican and secular school system and turn the university into a sectarian institution. Laicity, the core value of the French Republic, crumbles before a Nietzschean, fascist racism via a narrative detour through the Catholic Church in Belgium.

---

[42] Rieser (2018).   [43] Vinken (2020).

The Brussels-born Rediger, a former nativist who, as a long-standing convert to Islam, rises to prominence in the new regime, was first tempted by Catholicism before turning to Nietzsche. His dissertation, from Louvain-la-Neuve, Francophone as well as Catholic, was called "René Guénon, lecteur de Nietzsche" (245; "René Guénon, reader of Nietzsche," 199).[44] Like Rediger, François attempts first to convert to Catholicism on the model of Huysmans, the object of his research. The parallelism is striking: François is forty-four, like Huysmans, when he tries to follow his example.[45] François's conversion, however, does not succeed. His defeat is emblematic for Catholicism's failure. Narratively, the novel then brings him to the brink of conversion to another religion bound in an unholy alliance to politics that also fails to meet the promise of the *civitas Dei*. It masquerades under the name of Islam.

In Rediger's eyes, Catholicism is insufficient: Religion creates no new covenant and government no social bond. Rather, religion and government should do what Catholic Church and Republic alike see as a perversion of their respective pastoral and representative roles, namely, to subject their subjects into submission. The new regime consequently turns to more potent forms of subjugation. What circulates under Islam in the novel turns out in fact to be a mishmash of Nietzsche's *Herrenmensch* (superman) and social Darwinism's survival of the fittest. France submits to a racist German and Anglo-American ideology under the cover of a falsely accused Islam. When laicity is overthrown, together with Republic and Catholic Church, the old alliance of throne and altar, namely, worldly and spiritual power, triumphs in a new totalitarianism. Only the name is republican in the Islamic Republic of Mohammed Ben Abbes. This dynamic accounts for the centrality of Huysmans and Péguy, for François's failure to be moved by the Black Virgin of Rocamadour, for his failed Catholic conversion at the abbey of Ligugé. Catholicism, which initially seems a promising venue for subjection – at least from Rediger's perverse perspective – does not in the end provide a powerful enough form

---

[44] René Guénon did not, in fact, read Nietzsche. One of the most elusive figures of the period between the wars, he played a signal role in the oriental renaissance. A convert to Islam, he started out as a "traditionalist" who saw the occident in decline since the Middle Ages. This decline could be overcome only by a genuinely new orientation toward the East. Guénon converted to Islam and died in Cairo. Guénon's nostalgia for the traditional societies of the Middle Ages marks Lempereur's first name, Godefroy, and the historicizing medieval touches of the décor of Rediger's house. Houellebecq's Rediger reorients Guénon toward Germany, contrary to his commitment to an eastern revival, toward the "Indogermanic studies" of a country then called the "India of the Occident." For Guénon, Compagnon (2005).

[45] For Huysmans and *Soumission*, Ritte (2016); Roloff (2016).

of submission. The trope of failed conversion to Catholicism tells a story of the Church's impotence before worldly and spiritual powers unified in the singular, potent institutionalization of empire.

In *Soumission*, stereotypes about Islam are a literary device for representing decay within European institutions. The novel is not about Islam, the complexity of its history, its theology and institutions, or even its fraught relations with the West. Houellebecq's notorious statement "la religion la plus con c'est quand-même l'Islam" ("the most asinine religion is Islam, after all") is often cited without his broader hit at all monotheisms: "Je me suis dit que le fait de croire à un seul Dieu était le fait d'un crétin" ("I am of the opinion that believing in a single God was the invention of a moron").[46] He does not target Islam per se as an external enemy that has taken over France.[47] Rather, the new Muslim Brotherhood regime externalizes internal French resistance to the universal promise of inclusion through German and Anglo-American ideologies. The paradox is manifest in that sworn enemies, French nativists and all Muslim factions, unite against secularism. *Soumission* targets all who sell out to tyranny, instantiated lately in the Third Reich and now in the Saudi monarchies. The Islamic conversion that takes place in fact turns away from both republic and Church toward the authoritarian, racist, misogynistic, and neoliberal fascism that comes under its name.

The novel targets the central Western, Christian institutional problem: the relation between spiritual and secular powers. The text knowingly speaks its own blindness to Islam through François's voice. His confusion about the prohibition against consuming alcohol is symptomatic of the novel's indifference towards Islam proper: "au fond c'est une religion que je connaissais mal" (245; "it wasn't a religion I knew much about," 199). Rediger, Islam's false prophet, is well aware his Muslim coreligionists would find his program "peut-être blasphématoire" (260; "perhaps sacrilegious," 212). Rediger's central tenet is submission: As woman should submit to man, so should man submit to God (260; 212). The submission of women in his Islam provides the chance for the moral and familial rearmament of Europe in a New Golden Age, Augustus' own slogan (276; 226). According to Rediger, Christianity has lost its way in becoming too liberal and renouncing its will to domination. Woman no longer submits to man; the Church has "renounced submitting temporal power to itself" ("renoncer à se soumettre le pouvoir temporal," 276; 226). The epigraph to the book's tragic fifth act is a citation from Ayatollah Khomeini: "*Si l'islam*

---

[46] www.lexpress.fr/culture/livre/michel-houellebecq_804761.html.   [47] Lilla (2015).

n'est pas politique, il n'est rien" (223; "*If Islam is not political, it is nothing,*" 181). Political Islam, which began with the Iranian Revolution, comes around here to the views of Carl Schmitt. Even François notices Rediger's "religion" always returns to the "champ politique" (270; "political field," 221). It is no surprise when Rediger is named Secretary of State to the Universities and will later become the Minister of Foreign Affairs. His "*orientation*" after all, has always tended toward a political career – religion has been just a means to domination ("*s'orientait,*" 298, our emphasis; 245).[48] Rediger's Islam is not Islam but the Western sin par excellence: political theology. All tend in the same direction: toward the submission of others to oneself and the attending pseudolegitimations.

Soumission is a contemporary period novel about Europe.[49] None of the developed characters is originally Muslim. They are European converts who forsake Christianity and humanism alike in their will to power. They abandon Republic and Church to collaborate with Islam, the latest stand-in for the orientalism that covers up the trauma of inner corruption. Civil war in the novel figures self-imposed collapse, within society and within the self. *Soumission* targets the bankruptcy of the West, its much-touted values, and its dominant and exemplary *Leitkultur* (dominant culture). Houellebecq's novel belongs to the tradition of the nineteenth-century realist novel, in which the inner orient figures moral, political, spiritual bankruptcy.

Babel: Narrative Blackout

The political events in *Soumission* come focalized through François, the first-person narrator. His increasing blindness leaves us in a world of Babel. The true story, inscribed in topoi, intertexts, and names, and available to the discerning reader, plays as dramatic irony. We decipher it behind the perfectly clueless François's back. He does not see the light at the end of the tunnel – his dissertation's title is *Joris-Karl Huysmans, ou la sortie du tunnel* (11; "Joris-Karl Huysmans: Out of the Tunnel," 3), and Rediger's assessment attributes little clarity to it (246; 200). The more he discovers, the more he loses himself in Babylonian darkness.

François's editorial procedure for the Pléiade edition of Huysmans cues us on how to read this novel. His notes will not explicate the "innombrables auteurs, musiciens et peintres cités par Huysmans" (230; "innumerable writers, musicians, and painters mentioned by Huysmans," 187–8) –

---

[48] The pun does not come through in translation.   [49] Pornschlegel (2015) 619.

the curious may look up information about Lactantius, Angela de Foligno, or Grünewald on their own. His choice is a hermeneutic flag: Really, we had better look up the references to all the innumerable authors, musicians, and painters cited, if we want to understand. We also have another task. François's job for the Pléiade edition is to write the preface, which should explain the links between Huysmans and contemporary authors: Zola, Maupassant, Barbey d'Aurevilly, Gourmont, or Bloy. What we need to understand is the novel's own links to these authors.

François's flight from Paris during the runoff election's two rounds of voting, numerous and variegated failures of the media (blackout, 61, 66; 46, 51; static, 128, 130; 103, 105; need to listen to the BBC, 135–6; 109), and indirect narration and political analysis by other characters create a narrative black hole. Like François, the reader must reconstruct events from a position of literal or hermeneutic distance. Whereas François, who has never paid attention to politics, is a slow and unreliable learner, *Soumission* makes available to the alert reader an allegorical apparatus that invites us to interpret whatever happens during the election not as a unique historical event, but one that replays the age-old story: Civil war destroys a republic that returns, seemingly restored, but effectively erased, as an oriental empire. Houellebecq joins Flaubert and Maupassant in declaring French Republicanism, in all its layered manifestations, the same history all over again. A new empire oriental-style reveals that the republic never realized its own ideals, never fully existed to begin with. *Soumission*'s oriental empire replays France's repetitive replay of Roman history, a succession of republics yielding to empire or Reich since the Revolution. In parallel to history, his novel reiterates a French literary strategy in the tradition of Romanitas, which repeatedly unmasks history as a broken record. In a gesture of irony in its etymological sense, François does not know the tragedy he cannot help but reenact in his blindness.

The violence resists interpretation. Leading up to the election's various stages, riots, street violence, and hate crimes break out. Each time, understanding escapes François. Right-wing extremists clash with apolitical Africans, but the nativist website's alleged high death rate conflicts with the government account, making the truth unknowable (54; 41). Turbulence happens within earshot and is witnessed by François at a distance, after the fact, but the media fall silent (61; 46). He happens upon the aftermath of an altercation at a gas station when fleeing to the southwest during the second electoral round. Opposition appears in a schema, but no narrative makes sense of the events. The cashier's dead body is symbolically Christian: She lies as a *gisant* with arms crossed on her chest, like a tombstone in a church; by contrast, the corpses of two young Maghrebians wear the "uniforme typique des banlieues" (129–30; "typical uniform of the banlieus," 105). Smashed glass evokes Kristallnacht, another historical stratum. Is the conflict religious, nativist, economic, random? Static on the radio gives no clue. François joins the locals at a sports bar for news of the runoff, but they watch foreign coverage. He follows the English of the BBC with difficulty; anyhow, they miss the scoop of violence at the polling stations (136; 109–10). François, and therefore the reader, remains in the dark.

The tropology we trace throughout this book structures the convoluted crisscrossing of relations and events. It declares that what gives birth to the new regime is civil war. Figured disorder accompanies actual violence. Allies split, deepest enemies turn into the most intimate friends in a topsy-turvy world of doubling and indistinction. Nativists and jihadists, structural enemies, are revealed as structural twins enmeshed in an uncanny resemblance. From the extremes, they fight equally against the centrists – worn-out parties as well as the Muslim Brotherhood – who remain committed to moderation (51; 38–9). They paradoxically unite in their antagonism to the democratic order precisely when each is convinced their opponent will win.

> les identitaires européens, comme les musulmans djihadistes se sont persuadés, chacun de leur côté, que le parti adverse allait l'emporter – qu'il n'avait pas d'autres choix que d'interrompre le processus électoral en cours. 143

> The nativist Europeans, like the Muslim jihadists, each on their own, decided that the other was about to win, that they had no choice but to disrupt the electoral process. 115

Faced with perfectly balanced 50–50 polls, both foster violence that disrupts the first run-off.

> Les identitaires, oui, pour une part. Et, aussi, de jeunes musulmans djhadistes: pour une part, à peu près égale d'ailleurs. 142

> The nativists, yes, partly. And partly young Muslim jihadists – it was roughly half and half. 114

The extremists mirror each other in disrupting the standard left/right opposition whose mutual balance allies them in stabilizing the Fifth Republic. It turns out, moreover, that moderates are extremists in disguise and vice versa. The National Front and the apparently moderate Muslim Brotherhood are twins running neck and neck (83; 65). The nativists and the Muslim Brotherhood could not agree more in perfectly balanced disharmony ("parfait accord," 275; "perfect agreement," 225). The government suspends the electoral process (136; 110) and seems to prefer it that way (141; 114), but it cannot stop electoral disaster. The nativists sleep with the enemy and embrace the same subjecting, imperial, patriarchal, masculinist order. To assure domination, the indigenous go oriental.

In *Soumission*, all parties split internally among themselves. The nativists themselves have no coherent identity. They are a ragtag assemblage of racists, nationalists, Catholics, royalists, nostalgics, Romantics, alcoholics, neopagans, and secularists, "divisé en multiples fractions" (68; "divided into multiple factions," 52). They break with their natural allies, the National Front, and prepare for civil war. Muslim intellectuals (273; 223–4), Flemish and Walloon in Belgium (278; 228), Ben Abbes and the Saudis (237; 193) – all fracture into faction. Civil discord's internal division cleaves all political parties. In spite of or because of this factionalism, the most antithetical parties end up fundamentally the same. If the nativists espouse the same tactics as the jihadists, the Union for a Popular Movement (UMP) cozies up to its traditional centrist opponent, the Socialists, like an old couple united in struggle (145; 117). The UMP is much closer to the Muslim Brotherhood to begin with. The Socialists give up secularism to preserve their antiracism but succumb to another pressure point in the culture wars when they are punningly sodomized in the process: "acculés ... au fond du trou" (146; "buggered up the wazoo," 118). The centrist parties unite against the National Front in a punning "front républicain" (145; "republican front," 117) to give electoral legitimation to the Muslim Brotherhood. Before winning the election, Ben Abbes looks to be the moderate candidate, so the centrists breathe a sigh of relief. But the new empire, brought in under the mantle of republican moderation and integration, makes Marine Le Pen look moderate in retrospect.

From an oversaturated hermeneutic of allusion and conventional tropes, the familiar story can be read out from the negotiations behind closed doors. When the centrists align around a "front républicain élargi" (150, 163; "broad republican front," 121, 131), an alternative republican regime rises from the ashes of civil war. But the legitimation is a front. The metaphoric register reveals that what hides in the narrative blackout is civil war, that Ben Abbes's careful politicking (154; 124) masks a coup d'état. The phoenix, always oriental, is reborn as an imperial eagle. The figuration replays the accession of Augustus, Napoleon, Louis Napoleon, and the Third Republic after the Commune as eternal return. The new emperor ends civil war in the name of the republic; he is a savior who unifies and brings peace. Mohammad Ben Abbes carries unification and concord in his name – the three monotheisms are all represented through the Islamic prophet, the beloved son of Jacob, and the monastery. The new president of the republic comes triply in the name of religion, an arch commentary on the collapse of laicity, the principle on which the republic no longer stands.

Historia magistra vitae

Manifold strata in *Soumission*'s historical palimpsest make French history readable as eternal, catastrophic return: A corrupt republic, in an outbreak of civil war, yields to an empire from Augustus to Napoleon I, on to Napoleon III, to the Third Reich and now, in 2022, to a Muslim Brotherhood whose religion is de facto Anglo-German, neoliberal fascism, disguised as Islam. The geography of Paris, the very clothes of the characters, their choices in interior decorating inscribe the eighteenth- and nineteenth-century revolutions as forerunners to the corrupted Fifth Republic's collapse. Marine Le Pen's call for insurrection at the place de la Concorde alludes to the Revolution of 1789; everything about Lempereur conjures up the second Empire from 1851 to 1871; events play out on the sites of revolutionary battles.

After witnessing tumult at the place de Clichy, which evokes the end of the first Napoleonic Empire, François accompanies Lempereur to his house. A time warp sets them in the age of Napoleon III.

> nous nous trouvions exactement à l'époque de nos écrivains préférés, fis-je observer à Lempereur; presque tous les immeubles, remarquablement conservés, dataient du Second empire ou du début de la Troisième république. 62

> we stepped back into the precise era of our favorite writers, a fact I point out to Lempereur. Nearly all the buildings dated from the Second Empire or the start of the Third and were unusually well preserved. 48

The architecture's remarkable preservation brings history vividly back in layers. The '48 Revolution, which Marx and Flaubert both depict as civil war,[50] conjures up the ephemeral Second Republic, which itself soon collapses with Louis Napoleon's coup d'état in 1851. When the Prussians vanquished the Second Empire in 1870, another civil war was raging simultaneously between the Commune and bourgeois republicans. The

---

[50] Vinken (2015a) 202.

Commune was vanquished, the Third Republic followed. The history evoked in the novel replays the history in the plot.

Napoleonic history, where civil war overtook conflict with a foreign enemy, returns in two sites of unrest François witnesses in Paris: Montfermeil and the place de Clichy. These loom large in the French political imaginary. After the Battle of the Nations against Napoleon at Leipzig in 1813, the allies marched on Paris, with Russians and Prussians approaching from the north. They first saw the city from Montfermeil, the site of the last skirmish before the barricade at Clichy, the only place where the French National Guard succeeded in stopping the foreign incursion.[51] The *Barricade of the rue de Clichy* (1820; Fig. 6.1), a famous painting by Horace Vernet, depicts Maréchal Moncey holding off the world united against Napoleon on March 30, 1814. Despite this heroic defense, Paris was taken that night by the P/russians. An armistice, marking the end of the

Figure 6.1 Horace Vernet, *Barricade de la rue de Clichy* (1820), Musée du Louvre, Paris

---

[51] Rau and Cronenthal (1826) 219.

first Empire and inaugurating a new European order at the Congress of Vienna, stopped the slaughter. The absolutist Bourbon monarchy was restored and, with it, a firm alliance of throne and altar under the auspices of the divine right of kings. Allusion to Clichy figures France's future as a military takeover. Backed by Russian funding, the regime change ushers in neoliberal Americo-German protofascist ideology, with Muslims as the new Prussians.

Allegedly subsidized by Russian oligarchs, Lempereur evokes old enemies. He plays the Republic's internal enemy, leading racist, misogynistic nativists behind the scenes – implausible deniability keeps his political power under wraps (85, 87; 67, 69). He foreshadows Rediger in a perverse prefiguration; the shift from republic to empire brings already-imperial power structures into the open. At that moment, the clandestine puppeteer shifts to the open operator. Lempereur fittingly carries the empire to come in his name. The civil war he announces to François with great fanfare (69; 53) is on the verge of overstepping the bounds of metaphor – the nativists could quickly infiltrate the French army; while he expects the political branch to retain control in France, the army could exercise ideological control; the countries where literal outbreak of civil war, "émeutes sérieuses" ("serious disturbances") and an "insurrection générale" ("general uprising"), is more likely to occur include the novel's leitmotif Belgium (71; 55); there could be a European financial crisis (87–8; 69). Lempereur's civil war resonates with a historical mix of internal and external turmoil evoked by the city's geography.

The protests that broke out in Montfermeil in 2005 put the suburb back on the map. Protestors demonstrated against the police's excessive use of force against two young men, French citizens identified as Muslim. In the novel, this suburb becomes once again a theater of conflict, now between the extreme right and young North Africans (54; 41). Several strands of French history overlay this unrest, which returns when a mosque's desecration incites sporadic violence throughout this community. The phrase "le territoire de la commune" ("the township's territory") echoes the Commune. In another multiple layering of history, the name applied first to the government from 1789–92, next to the second Commune of Terror from 1792–5, and again to the short-lived "communist" regime slaughtered in 1871.

The last is particularly relevant for the dates depicted in the novel, which start on May 15 and extend to May 31. This is the only timespan identified: Most chapters have no temporal markers. The first date corresponds to the first election night, which ends in the announcement of a runoff. Its first round is disrupted on May 29. On the last date, the centrists announce their deal with Ben Abbes, making the electoral results a foregone conclusion. The same date range frames the violence when the Commune of 1871 was brought down. Both the army and Republican guards had fought united against the Prussians but now turned in defeat against each other. A "semaine sanglante" ("week of bloodshed") was announced on May 16 in the journal *Le Cri du people* (*Cry of the People*), when the *communards* (communists) threaten to burn Paris if the Thiers government attacked. The government troops marched from Versailles, symbol of monarchy, against the Republican guards, who had taken power in Paris, during the week of the May 21 and 28, 1871. The Commune was most brutally crushed, its members executed or deported. The governmental forces fittingly retreated to Versailles as the National Assembly came to power in the Third Republic. They were able to defeat their inner enemy only with the help of the foreign foe they had surrendered to: The Prussians helped Thiers against the *communards* who had refused to surrender and lay down their arms. The Prussians allowed the Versailles army to cross the neutral zone in the north of Paris so that they could take Paris from the rear. The battles between *communards* and government also took place around the place de Clichy.

The name Clichy resonates. In *Soumission*, rioting and government intervention erupts near the place de Clichy, within earshot of a reception François attends for the *Journal des dix-neuvièmistes* ("Journal of Nineteenth-Century Studies"), the century whose violence the text replays. All the guests hear explosions and gunshots not far off: "Cela devait venir à peu près de la place de Clichy" (61; "It must have been coming from somewhere near Place de Clichy," 46). François, however, is not afraid: "J'étais sans grande raison persuadé que les affrontements s'arrêteraient au boulevard de Clichy" (62; "I don't know why, I was convinced the fighting would go no farther than the boulevard de Clichy," 47). When François and his new colleague Lempereur retreat to the latter's house, they pass through the rue Ballu, named after the architect who restored the Hôtel de Ville after the Commune burned it down. On their way, they pass by "la place de Clichy . . . complètement envahi par les flames" (63; "Place de Clichy was completely enveloped in flames," 48). Lempereur gives a history lesson about the statue that stands out from the fire: "Le maréchal Moncey? . . . C'était un soldat de Napoléon. Il s'est illustré en défendant la barriére de Clichy contre les envahisseurs russes en 1814" ("Maréchal Moncey? . . . He served under Napoleon. He won distinction defending the Clichy barrier against the Russians in 1814," 48). This allusion to history has dramatic irony: François thinks the violence will stop on the boulevard de Clichy. Why should it? It never has before.

The literary precedents for Lempereur come from the same period. Maupassant's *Bel-ami* (1885) presents the Third Republic as a full-blown orientalized Empire, whose main metaphors are effeminacy and prostitution. Its title character Georges Duroy fittingly carries this corrupt mock-monarchy in his name, just as Lempereur carries the name of the empire to come. Another model for Lempereur is Zola's pretty boy Fougerolles. In *L'oeuvre* (*The Work*, 1886), this second-rate painter tarts up his art – prostituted saccharine kitsch sells. Fougerolles is in turn modeled on a mix of Bouguereau and Cabanel, two influential academic painters who catered to the court, as well as French and American nouveaux riches.[52] Lempereur himself owns a Bouguereau, which hangs over the mantlepiece (67; 51). Like the great Second Empire courtesans, Lempereur lives in a "maison particulière" ("private mansion"), splendidly equipped with effeminate, over-decorated silk-covered ottomans and intarsias. Like them, he is luxuriously kept. "Ce n'était certainement pas son traitement de maître de conférences au premier échelon qui lui permettait d'habiter un endroit pareil; alors, quoi?" (65; "There was no way he lived here on a teacher's salary. How did he do it?" 50), muses François. The insinuation of Russian financing makes him a treasonous puppet (85; 67), a mafia don who enjoys tight security (65; 50), in thrall to yet another overlord.[53]

Lempereur tells the truth of the emergent politics with his name, his neighborhood, and his décor, even with his looks and clothes. He is a decadent Marianne, the French Republic personified, whose most famous portrait had already taken a prostitute for its model.[54] Superwhite skin, blue blazer, bright red sneakers – body and clothes turn the tricolor Republican flag into a fashion statement. Mascara tops off the look (58; 43–4). His PSG (Paris Saint-Germain) t-shirt sports a heraldic crest, the *fleur de lys*, sign of the absolutist Bourbon monarchy, under the Tour Eiffel – this most French soccer club is in fact owned by Qatar Sports Investments. Saint Germain-en-Laye is also nineteenth-century French literature's premier aristocratic quartier, named after Saint Germanicus –

---

[52] Zola on Bouguereau: "c'est le comble du pommadé et de l'élégance lustrée" ("he's the utmost in pomade and glossy elegance"): Leduc-Adine (1991) 297.

[53] Houellebecq's focus, already in 2015, on Russian financing for nativist politics appears prescient. It has since then threatened elections in Europe and the Americas.

[54] Marianne was already tainted by prostitution in the most famous painting of the French Revolution, by Delacroix. Ubl (2010).

whose imperial cognomen is, of course, germane. Lempereur figures the collapse of a prostituted republic into an oriental empire. His prostitution is told via signifiers: his use of "passerelle" ("back channels") to mediate between nativists and radical Islamists (67; 51) calls to mind the idiom "faire une passe" ("to have intercourse with a prostitute").

As events unfold, *Soumission* simultaneously goes back in time. For all its national-identity politics, despite claiming France's Catholic tradition, the National Front now, ironically, becomes the prime representative of republican values. Marine Le Pen's speech has, according to François, a striking "caractère républicain" (110; "republican ... tenor," 87). Her republicanism reinscribes the violence of the French Revolution and the Terror. Le Pen cites the article sanctioning "insurrection" as a sacred right of the people from the *Declaration of the Rights of Man*, which, as under- scored, was added to the earlier set of declarations in 1793, namely, the year of the Terror (115; 91). This article legitimated the overthrow of the monarchy on the grounds of tyranny. Her republicanism, in the guise of revolutionary civil war, tars Ben Abbes as a tyrant. Her call for protest under the banner of insurrection rouses François Hollande, who makes a risible claim to be "le dernier rampart de l'ordre républicain" (115; "last bastion of the republican order," 92). However, his declaration that those who put themselves on the margins of "légalité démocratique" ("demo- cratic legality") will be treated as outlaws in fact shows he would willingly suspend republican values in a state of emergency against the internal foe.

The protest Marine Le Pen calls for is to take place on the "place de la Concorde," another telling location. The original square was built by Louis XV and called both "place Royale" and "place Louis XV." The revolution- aries replaced an equestrian statue of Louis XV with a monumental statue of liberty and renamed it the "place de la Révolution" in 1792. This square sported the guillotine that executed Louis XVI and Marie Antoinette, Robespierre, Danton, and up to 1,200 people over the course of two-and -a-half years. In 1795, the Directoire renamed it "place de la Concorde" in allusion to Cicero's notion of *concordia* as the solution to the conflict of the orders. We recall Augustine's sarcastic comment: the Romans should have put up a temple to Discord instead (above, p. 166). Louis Philippe later erected a more "neutral" statue: Mohammad Ali Pasha, founder of modern Egypt, had promised to send some obelisks to Paris, but only one arrived. Still there, it is supposed to symbolize the difficult achievement of concord. An oriental token of empire, it replays the obelisks Augustus imported to Rome to broadcast his victory over Egypt after Actium. The obelisks Napoleon brought back to Paris in an intermediary conquest put a modern signature on the Roman gesture.[55] The monuments of Paris reveal the same history, always replayed behind the actors' backs.

Now, in 2022, violence is again civil. The external enemy has been internalized. Russian oligarchs finance the republic's undermining. The repressive monarchy of Saudi Arabia buys out humanism and Christianity. The rumor that Lempereur is subsidized by the Russians reinscribes Napoleonic-era foes (85; 67). His own comment that the ethnic confrontations now happen *intra-muros* similarly reinscribes the phrase Cicero uses for the Catilinarians: they are the enemy "within the walls" (*intra moenia, In Cat.* 2.1). They pass not far from the "rue de Rome," where Mallarmé held his Tuesday salons (63; 48).[56] A Latin pun further layers Napoleonic over Roman history. François and Lempereur see on the very rue de Clichy the modern successor to the old National Guard, the CRS, which stands for *compagnies républicaines de sécurité* ("Republican Security Forces"), a branch of the national police.

> À ce moment j'aperçus avec stupéfaction deux CRS, mitraillette en bandoulière, vêtus de combinaison de kevlar, qui descendaient tranquillement la rue de Clichy . . .
> "Ils sont . . . " j'étais tellement ahuri que j'avais du mal à parler, "ils font absolument comme si de rien n'était." 63–4

> At that moment I was amazed to see two riot police in Kevlar, machine guns slung over their shoulders, walking calmly down the rue de Clichy toward Gare Saint-Lazare. . . .
> "They . . . " I was dumbstruck. "They're acting as if nothing's going on." 49

These "republican companies" have abandoned the Republic whose job it is to defend. When the "companies of security" walk by tranquilly in unconcern, the Latin behind their acronym resonates. Tranquility, one meaning of *securitas*, abuts another from post-Augustan Latin: indifference.[57] Many in the novel remain unconscionably calm: colleagues at the Sorbonne (79; 61), journalists and the public reassured by Ben

---

[55] The appropriation of Egyptian obelisks and their transfer to Rome has been an object of fascination since the Renaissance, Mercati (1981), originally published in 1589 and still cited; on the Augustan obelisks (209–13, 221–6), also Zadro (2007) 127–34: deracinated from their religious context in Egypt, they become symbols of victory and power at Rome (122). This speaks to theology's politicization in Houellebecq. For individual obelisks, D'Onofrio (1967) charts their subsequent history. He recounts an amusing anecdote: Answering Napoleon's question, whether they could plant trees in Rome, Canova quipped that in Rome they plant obelisks (7). Brier (2016).

[56] Mallarmé's *Hérodiade* and *L'après-midi d'un faune* (*Herodias* and *Afternoon of a Faun*) are read by des Esseintes in *A rebours*.

[57] *Oxford Latin Dictionary*, *securitas* 1 and 2.

Abbes's apparent moderation (109; 87), even the weather (128; 103). François loses his worry over his failed love Myriam (164; 132). Such calm signals imperial depoliticization:[58] Huysmans attributes to des Esseintes "un imperieux besoin de rester tranquille" (138; "an imperious need to remain calm," 112) that keeps him from travel. The erasure of cares is the erasure of liberty, responsibility, and autonomy. As François relinquishes his intellectual life, he exclaims, "fuck autonomy" (227; 185). Pacification is the fruit of empire.

By taking us back in time, the novel brings us closer to empire. The cobblestones of Paris encode foreign war as civil violence. Constitutive of the change from republic to empire is the destruction of the values of both republic and Church, of enlightened humanism and Christianity. This is achieved, in the advent of Napoleon III, by bringing the backbone of the secular republic, the schools and the universities, under the control of the Empire and Church. In the tradition of the French realist novel, such sacralization of worldly power on the model of the absolutist monarchy is criticized as corruption, as an oriental idolatry, as the return of blind myth. Nothing Christian remains in this Church, which serves worldly power and subjection. This is the central event of *Soumission*. Only now, the place of Catholicism is taken by another, allegedly more fitting religion: Islam. But only the name is religious. No social bond is restored, no union of love is founded, but an undercover war rages over the very subject of love, the birth rate, and its aim is brutal subjection.

Some Sex and No Love

Bad sex and bad love yet again figure civil discord. Scholarship has analyzed *Soumission*'s generic affiliation within the comparative framework of the realist and naturalist novel.[59] Failed love serves as a metaphor for failed politics within this novelistic tradition, but it is hardly exclusive to the genre. We show its longer tradition in our earlier chapters. From Dido and Aeneas in Vergil to the marriages in Lucan, the foundation – or dissolution – of the social bond passes through the bonds of love. Augustine finds hope for the passage from the *civitas terrena* to the *civitas Dei* through the enlightened discovery of love, where love of one's fellow leads to a more enlightened love of God. That progression here reverses course; in a pointed reversal of the injunction of the Gospel to love your neighbor as yourself, François hates his fellow humans as he hates himself. Step by

[58] Lowrie (forthcoming b).   [59] Schober (2002).

step, François's failure to love any man in friendship, any woman as anything but a source of sex and food, sets him in a position of impotence. He cannot even recognize how he is bought and seduced into a system of domination where, himself dominated, he will get to role-play a dominator. All alone, he degrades into collaboration, so he may join in degrading his fellows and subjecting women.

François is shown to have always already been oriental before the political takeover. At the novel's beginning, he was already eating cheap Eastern take-out – Indian, sushi, Chinese – instead of the cuisine of *la France profonde* (the French heartland). He was already at a dead-end for love: Serial monogamy with his students, with a fresh face every academic year, eventually came to naught. Under the Empire, all liberty has vanished, even to choose a love that will fail. Now, instead, three wives will be arranged (293; 240); the students – sexual prey before as after regime change – he imagines, will be happy, proud, and honored to share his bed (299; 246). Sex, drink, food, intellectual life, political liberty all fall backward, against the grain, in the spirit of *A rebours*. The new reality simply literalizes the old. In François, the oriental other already resides within the conflicted self. Western society incarnate, he appears incapable of forging any unreified bond. Sardonic self-despair rather than Islamophobia lies at the heart of *Soumission*'s critique. It presents the past and future European catastrophe as revealing that the perversion of its central values and promises already resides within. The inner orient is outed under the name of Islam.

From republic to empire, *Soumission* is pessimistic about family. The one happy family, Myriam's, goes into exile. Their solidarity, however, is less about love than the tribe, that is, a primordial social structure typically assigned to Judaism: "C'était une tribu, une tribu familiale soudée" (111; "a tribe, a close-knit family tribe," 89). There is no single happy erotic union. François fails to love Myriam, who returns to him despite his inability to connect (44, 96; 31, 76).[60] The republican ideals of free love and sexual liberation shrink to Pavlovian conditioning. The sex scenes in *Soumission* show men responding mechanically to physical signals. Women come objectified in an indifferent, generic seriality. The pinnacle is prostitution.

---

[60] Morrey (2018) 205 sees Myriam as a stereotypical pornographic fantasy "of a sexy teenage goth whose greatest wish is to give sexual pleasure to a man twice her age." He draws the literalist conclusion that "the novel is thus complicit with the most unreconstructed orientalist fantasies of 'eastern' sexuality, imagining both potent young men and submissive yet devilishly accomplished young women" (206). We repeat that the novel deploys the tropes of orientalism to expose them as such.

Even the escort girls think of nothing but busily earning their square meters. The only marriage depicted among François's "friends" comes as a disaster, soon to end, probably, in divorce (94; 74).

These relations play against the background of failed republican sexual ideology. Equality between the sexes and female emancipation are republican goals, which have actually been achieved with remarkable success in France. The autonomous woman who can support herself without financial dependence on marriage is its ideal. Emancipation entails erotic choices not just for men, but for women. This includes desires outside marriage. The singular French republican equality is articulated for women in terms of love, career, and income. Women would not have to choose between marriage, motherhood, and a career but could have it all – a side effect has been that France has one of the highest birth rates in Europe. Having a career without having to pay the outrageous price of motherhood, love, and femininity has been one of the hallmarks of French society since the end of the War.[61]

If the layering of history shows that *historia magistra vitae* only ever teaches the same lesson, the layered systems shift gears: Sociology supplants Roman exemplarity and Christian typology. The novel is obsessed with models and sociological normativity.[62] In *Soumission*, the ideal of the equal marriage, where even mothers have careers, is a republican dream turned nightmare. With marriage again figuring society, the French ideal is shown here beset on all sides even before the Islamic takeover. Its failure is symptomatic of a society that cannot live up to its promise. American capitalism has infiltrated and corrupted the republican ideal; everybody is already subjected and alienated. The supremacy of German ideology, which, under Nietzsche's name, will design the masterplan for the new Islamic republic, is hinted at in the unmistakably Germanic names of a paradigmatic spousal pair, Bruno and Annelise (94; 74). American and

---

[61] This achievement has recently come under attack. Badinter (2010) sounded the alarm with her defense of liberal feminism in *Le conflit. La mère et la femme* (*Conflict: Mother and Woman*). Berest (2015) offers a coded attack on Badinter with *Recherche femme parfaite* (*Looking for the Perfect Woman*): She names the perfect woman who goes to pieces Émilienne, after one of Badinter's books, *Emilie, Emilie* (1997), where she outlines the republican ideal. Slimani (2016) points out that there is a price to pay: the ideal is unlivable.

[62] *Schema* (12, 19–22, 41; 4, 9–12, 28); *modèle*, of Augustus (160; 129), of society (203; 165); *normalité* (25; 14); *scénarios identiques* (26; 15); *analogue* (27; 16); *prototype* (32; 20); *typologie* (42; 29); *exemple* (55; 42); the reproduction of relationships from French authors in their scholars (59; 44–5); *femmes*, every Western (93; 74), *normale* (194; 158); *existence individuelle*, burden of (99; 79), illusion of (127; 103), dissolves (167; 134); *contre-exemple* (104; 83); *catalogué* (164; 132); *type* (229; 187). We leave out the English, since the 2015 translation by Stein rightly elides some of these and uses different vocabulary for the same terms according to context.

German ideologies about "mother," "couple," and "sexuality" undermine the French republican model from both sides, Allied and Axis, alike.[63] France appears not to have won the War. Post-War peace has become a battleground over cultural, economic, and ideological hegemony, in which France continues to collaborate with the Third Reich and American-brand neoliberalism under the cover of its native, republican achievements.

François's failure to imagine any grown woman happily fulfilled is paradigmatic for the masculinist erasure of female agency already under the Republic. He systematically dismisses random thoughts about pursuing women that pop into his head (Alice, 62; 47; Annelise, 94; 74). Women – as opposed to girls – have no erotic interest for him. He cannot imagine anyone desiring them, certainly not their husbands, if they are lucky enough to have one. Various scenes show their professional success brings nothing but sexless loneliness; having children brings not happiness, but more stress and less sex. The sexual revolution, supposed to offer fulfillment along with erotic freedom, has left women without sex, let alone love. France's greatest feminist success, women's equality supported by generous childcare, here falters in a whirl of reactionary clichés, the stuff of social scientific research and women's magazines made in the USA: Equality between the sexes means less sex. It is presumed to be self-evident that no one would want *that*.

A barbecue, the ur-scene of suburbia, puts the social bond's collapse under capitalism's rubric. Its mode blends typically American and German ideologies. The citizen degrades into the consumer. Houellebecq's assessment of capitalist republicanism's inherent decadence maps onto Augustine's evaluation of the *civitas terrena*. In Maris's analysis of Houellebecq's critique of the neoliberal economy, "it is a state of permanent warfare, a permanent battle that can never come to an end. ... The violent world in the end turns against itself and destroys itself from within."[64] Maris enlists the structure of civil war. *Soumission* plays out social collapse most symptomatically as failures of love and sex, analyzed in a sociological register.

Mediated through memory's screen, François's description of a ruinous visit to a former graduate student pal, Bruno Deslandes, and his wife Annelise sets up a dystopian paradigm. Bruno's speaking last name makes him an icon of how *la France profonde* is already teutonic. He and his wife live a lifestyle coded as American (lawn) and sprinkled with

[63] Vinken (2001).   [64] Maris (2014) 121.

Anglicized loan words: *barbecue, guacamole*, blow-dried hair (called *brushing* in faux English), the *living* room, *marketing, jogging, sexy* (92–4). Core republican values wear a *sweat-shirt* that puts the ideological squeeze on the fortunate couple who aspire to the Martha Stewart lifestyle and have everything but love.

Annelise represents the ideal of the emancipated woman whose salary surpasses her husband's and who still fulfills the roles of wife and mother. That is *the* French achievement par excellence, and it is much admired and envied within the framework of European feminism. Her husband even splits the chores, specifically childcare – a typically American or German ideal of gender equality. The model derails according to typical patriarchal critique. Annelise loses her equilibrium juggling the double burden of work and family. Both spouses lose their sex appeal and with it their sex life to the tune of an American right-wing refrain: Equality kills good sex. By subjecting Annelise to the demands of work–life balance, the system cashes out her femininity as a status symbol in the labor market and crushes it in the bedroom – a typical German argument against the neoliberal misuse of women's labor. It never occurs to the emasculated Bruno, already sloshed on rosé, to attempt to perform the suburban male role par excellence: master of the barbecue. Like the cooking-show-inspired *"dîner presque parfait"* (92; *Come Dine with Me*, 73), her dinner fails in her overreach. This almost-perfect French couple just about meets the demographic rate of reproduction with their two children. However, achieving economic autonomy without job satisfaction and at the price of sex heads them toward divorce (94; 74). *Soumission*'s send-up is graced with oriental notes; lamb chops with a side of tabbouleh globalize the whole capitalist system.

This system erupts in chaos. Farcical figuration in the weather elevates the scene to a cosmic level – a Lucanian gesture modernized.[65] The butane threatens to explode; a storm disrupts the party with glacial and slanting rain. As in the *Georgics*, the commensality that should establish the social bond falters. In a recurring motif, meat is perverted. Butchery, sacrifice's abject other, infuses the scene: the child begins to scream, the mother "s'abattait" ("succumbs," with a pun on the slaughterhouse) on the couch, and the sacrificial lamb chops come in a charred mound (93; 73). The burnt meat is carcinogenic; consuming it, already inedible, would kill you. The cold buffet chills the social landscape. Suburbia is the sarcastic inverse of a pastoral paradise. A brief opening to human warmth is foil to all that goes

---

[65] For the figure of the weather in European modernity, Ungelenk (2018).

wrong in the earthly city. When François tries (and fails) to help with the gas grill, his rare gesture of compassion goes nowhere, despite Annelise's gratitude. His indifference to a potential affair blocks what would anyway be no loving relation. His solidarity's vanity hollows it out from within (94; 74).

These are, it is worth stressing, not the problems of the French Republic, but rather of countries like the United States and Germany. The low birth rate, women's failed careers, the obsessive idea that all can be fixed if fathers would only take a more active part in managing the household and educating children – these are specifically German discourses. In all these countries, right-wing discourses obsess about the "great replacement," whose solution is enslaving white women as breeding machines. Margaret Atwood's *The Handmaid's Tale* exposes the logical consequences of this fear.

The sexual bond, already under assault in *Soumission*'s republic, implodes under its empire. Polygamy is but legalized adultery, the marriage market but human trafficking. The French embrace of "Islamic" – in fact, Anglo-American-German – submission is exposed as sexual perversity in an oriental bathrobe. Sodomy, prostitution, and polygamy, which could appear, for instance, under the banner of a joyous and liberated diversification of practices, join pedophilia under the sign of male privilege. Worse, they are coupled with female reification and enslavement. The Romantic ideal of love as irreducible singularity – "Parce que c'était lui, parce que c'était moi" ("Because he was the one, because I was the one")[66] – is perverted through the seriality, indistinction, and interchangeability of the marriage object. If it were not enough that beauty lies no longer in the eye of the beholder, the girls' – not women's – objectification is further degraded through the perversion even of the free market. Since every man makes the same choice, freedom is an illusion; marriage brokers measure and systematize girls' attractions in a difference-erasing norm and correlate them to the status of their future husbands (293; 241).

Under the empire, Woman must be erased to bolster Man. Whereas the novel's men live in blind denial of female power and female desire in the republican *ancien régime*, they turn to aggressive subjugation in the restoration. Sexuality and emancipation – women's institutional and economic power – are the vehicles to show how the dysfunction of the republic is replayed in the Islamic regime's ostensible societal renewal, now with greater shock value. The Empire to come is a masculinist war against

[66] Montaigne (2007 [1580])189.

women and children and a war of strong against weak men. Money and power give men access to women, who are totally subjected. No trace is left of either republican freedom or the Christian promise, whose classic articulation is Paul's formulation, "without love, I am nothing" (1 Corinthians 13.3).

The self *Soumission* satirizes is representative of modern capitalist society. All relations unravel, all institutions, all forms of *religio* fail to bind. The Fifth Republic is already incapable of fostering love, family, friendship, or community. François's inability to keep it going with Myriam shows he cannot recognize love, much less accept it, still less himself love anyone but himself, and not even that. Unable to desire women his equal, he cannot imagine married colleagues his age as even former objects of desire (Marie-Françoise, 79; 62). The successful independent woman is always condemned to a lonely, love- and sexless life (Alice, 62; 47); she cannot arouse desire even in the old lover she picks up for a one-night stand (Aurélie, Sandra, 21–2; 11–12). François consistently views relations between men and women through a lens that deprives the female sex of potency, sexual or institutional. He cannot imagine authority and femininity together in a woman: If sexually desirable, she's a girl; if she has power, she's unattractive. Female desire is as unthinkable to the republican male as to the Islamic convert. François, trying his level, inadequate best to think through the consequences of the new subjugation of women, represses his own fleeting recognition that women may indeed have desires. He brings up "l'impulsion érotique chez les femmes," only to dismiss its details as *hors sujet* (280; "for women erotic stimuli . . . I didn't have time to go into that right now"), literally off topic, punningly outside any imaginable subjectivity. Male repression is simply too strong.

The background metaphor for the social bond's perversion in the Islamic empire to come is sodomy, a sexual practice associated closely with the orient in the Western imagination.[67] Like no other sexual pose, sodomy is made to stand for the subjugation of the penetrated in the hierarchy of the sexes: the male "fucker" over the effeminate, boyish "fuckee."[68] Through this sexual trope, the novel figures the fight of all against all and for absolute dominion. Women are dominated; the dominant male dominates women and men. Women's degradation redounds onto the men who degrade them. The text is explicit. To borrow

---

[67] Hampton (1993).

[68] For the pornographic terminology and how hierarchies of power structure sexual relations, Dworkin (1981); MacKinnon (1989) and (1996).

a colloquialism in tune with *Soumission*'s tonal register, François is fucked, he fucks himself. He internalizes his own degradation in a syntactically impossible arabesque that reveals his blindness. He imagines opening himself up to the cosmic order in orientalism's signature sex act: a paradoxically masturbatory, self-sodomy with delusions of grandeur that furthermore codes the male obsession with size ("Je me pénétrerais de la grandeur de l'ordre cosmique," 298; "I would penetrate myself with the grandeur of the cosmic order," 244).[69] The arabesque of tortured syntax exposes the cosmic disorder.

Liberté, égalité, fraternité

Social order in *Soumission* devolves in progressive steps: inadequacy, imagistic perversion, then perversion's full-blown realization. The universal, all-inclusive republican promise – liberty, equality, fraternity – is already inadequate for life: it offers neither love nor fulfillment. In this dystopian Fifth Republic, people are isolated like monads in their apartments, lacking the connection of family or religion. Nobody loves, nobody is loved. Everyone is *free* to partake only of their toxin of choice. Their *freedom*, already a metaphorical death, is fully realized in perversion under the empire: François, freed from any obligation to love or work, enters a limbo of worldlessness when pushed into retirement unless he converts. Asking if he should die, but finding it premature (188; 153), he lives a life of disengagement, neither life nor death, that simply literalizes his republican life.[70] But even the republican promise is already perverted. "Freedom, equality, and fraternity" are all shown to be already hollow. The empire will fulfill their perversion, as with Augustus, under the hypocritical mantle of moral renewal. The Augustan program aimed to restore family ties with marriage legislation and the religious bond by restoring temples. The imperial renewal in *Soumission* puts the nail in the coffin of the republican trio.

The effective *equality* of sexes in the Republic – a woman is president of the Sorbonne – is undermined as libertine perversion through conventional images of the *ancien régime*. The president of the university, a woman named Delouze specializing in gender studies, is into lap dogs.[71] Already symbolically emasculated despite being on top, François

---

[69] Stein (2015) regularizes the syntax with "I would penetrate ... "
[70] Suicide plays an equivalent role to conversion in Houellebecq's latest novel, *Serotonine*.
[71] Diderot (1800) has the female sex discuss this preference of theirs.

thinks she is a hardcore "lesbienne 100% brut de béton" (29; "lesbian, one hundred percent raw concrete," 17). His colleague Marie-Françoise undermines her authority with pornographic innuendo. Steve, a male colleague with fine girly curls, plays the poodle to the aristocratic lady. This standard French image of aristocratic decadence is best illustrated by Fragonard's painting (Fig. 6.2), which intimates canine cunnilingus. François ruminates over Marie-Françoise's declaration that "il broutait le minou de la mère Delouze" (29; "*eating Mother Delouze's pussy*," 17), imagining her "fantasmes dominateurs" (29; "fantasies of domination," 18). A horrific mother, a monstrous gender-bending contradiction, she abuses her power, doling out favors like a corrupt feudal lord in return for sexual services. Everybody is officially *equal* only in a vainglorious, exploitative fight for money and sex, symbolic and real capital. *Soumission*'s Republic is already

Figure 6.2 Jean-Honoré Fragonard, *Jeune fille et son chien / La Gimblette*, Alte Pinakothek, Munich

indistinct from the *ancien régime* – the "old regime" tarred by revolutionary calumny.

Republican *fraternity* comes in a perverse figuration as homosocial male bonding. It is induced by women, disposable go-betweens among men since time immemorial. François first meets Lempereur when conversing with Alice at a university reception. She is quickly eclipsed.

> Alice posait sur nous ce regard à la fois affectueux et légèrement moqueur des femmes qui suivent une conversation entre hommes, cette chose curieuse qui semble toujours hésiter entre la pédérastie et le duel. 58

> Alice watched us with the affectionate, slightly mocking look women get when they witness a conversation between men – that oddity, not quite buggery, or duel, but something in between. 44

When Alice tries to speak, her intervention goes unheard (59; 45). Greek love jockeys for power within the aristocratic honor code before a female audience excluded from the game.

The Fifth Republic already perverts the values of "liberty, equality, and fraternity." In the empire masquerading as a republic, these values return as empty letters. Men and women are now officially not equal, neither in work nor in marriage. The survival of the fittest demands women's absolute subjugation, achieved through ending coeducation and curtailed schooling for girls. They finish at age thirteen or fourteen so they may enter the marriage market and take up the labor of sex and child-bearing. The republican school system totters, its budget slashed in a shocking contrast to the actual state of affairs. France's current support for public education surpasses every other line in the national budget.[72] *Soumission*'s imperial parents, their eyes on their children's future, will send them to well-endowed Muslim schools – an echo of the enduring commitment among French parents to Catholic private schools, despite a historically robust public-school system. In the novel's topsy-turvy universe, private becomes public. Empire spells the end of the Republic's backbone, secular education: obligatory, free, coeducational. Again, the conflict plays out not in a clash of cultures, but in French issues on French territory. Who had the authority to raise children was the dominant conflict between Church and republic during the entire nineteenth century and well into the twentieth. The Sorbonne will

---

[72] In 2018, France allocated 14% of its budget to national education (99.3 billion euros), the highest single investment. By comparison, in the USA, education and research fall somewhere down the list at 3%, and in Germany at 5.2%.

become, in a hostile Saudi takeover, a French Harvard: the richest university of the world. All its professors will be male and Muslim.

In a precise inversion of the *freedoms* won by feminism, women's effective expulsion from the workplace has an ostensibly marvelous effect on the unemployment statistics. Slashing the budget for education frees up resources for child allowances, which depend on women not working; only husbands of stay-at-home moms will get the allowance:

> Un autre succès immédiat était le chômage, dont les courbes étaient en chute libre. C'était dû sans nul doute à la sortie massive des femmes du marché du travail – elle-même liée à la révalorisation considérable des allocutions familiales, la première mesure présentés, symboliquement, par le nouveau gouvernement. Le fait que le versement soit conditionné à la cessation de toute activité professionelle avait un peu fait grincer les dents, au début, à gauche; mais au vu des chiffres de chomage, le grincement avait rapidement cessé. 199

> He'd had another instant success with unemployment, which had plummeted. This was clearly due to women leaving the workforce en masse – due, in turn, to the hugely symbolic first measure passed by the new government: a large new subsidy for families. At first there had been some squirming on the left, since the subsidy was reserved for women who gave up working. The new unemployment figures put an end to that. 163

In short, the left sells out women's *liberties* for the sake of economics. With hardly a blink, they betray core republican values won over decades of struggle. But the left is not alone. The women themselves collude in their rush to take advantage of family subsidies. The only liberty left is the ironic "free fall" in the statistics, which holds the place of erased freedoms.

Even men are not *equal* in the new empire, but strictly ranked. Actual inequality comes perversely under the mandate of distributive justice. The number of females they may marry, their earning power, their apartments' square meters correlate exactly to their position in the hierarchy. According to natural selection, only the genes of the fittest racial elite, the alphas, will reproduce. The crass inequality between men in polygamy is not a perverse effect, but the system's goal: "si certains se voyaient accorder la jouissance de plusieurs femelles, d'autres devraient nécessairement en être privés" (268; "If some males enjoyed access to several females, other would necessarily have none," 220). In this unnatural selection, it is the race's fate according to Darwinian principles, not the word of the Lord, be it Allah, that is fulfilled: "C'est ainsi que s'accomplissait le destin de l'espèce" (269; "It was how the species achieved its destiny," 220). This polygamy smacks of Nazi *Lebensborn* (Fount of Life): The empire carries out the racial politics of the Third Reich. The so-called *fraternité* of the Muslim Brotherhood here perverts religion as a vehicle of biopolitics. But this perversion, neither new nor foreign, is already familiar from European history.

Women in polygamous marriages will be *equal* among themselves, only in submission to a husband who will reify them without distinction (292; 240). They will, however, be ranked from the world's top women on down and assigned a husband whose earning power matches their physical allure. Whereas men in the republic freely chose their lovers and prostitutes, the new regime's marriage market leaves no need for freedom. Matchmakers rationalize the girls as commodities, subject to expert evaluation of their naked bodies and married off as slaves to sex and procreation. Since all men in fact want the same thing without distinction, freedom of choice turns out to be unnecessary. François's astounded silence at the news marks not only the eradication of liberty's presumed last frontier, the individuality of erotic choice, but his own loss of freedom of speech (293–4; 241).

The exclusion of women under the new regime of the *Fraternité Musulmane* recreates the frat house. Not even disposable go-betweens, women are nothing but conversion bait for men, lures so they will join the fraternity. This structure, however, is nothing new but replays familiar Western exclusions. As in the Third Reich, non-Muslims (read Jews) and women are barred from public service: Rediger replaces Chantal Delouze as president of the university; François's colleague Marie-Françoise is forced from her post. As under Vichy, as in the Nazi regime, a woman's place is that of mother, wife – or prostitute. Republican fraternity had already elided the sister.[73] Men now completely occupy not only the workplace, but all social space. It finally dawns on François why the ambience of a university reception falls short of success: There are no women (235; 192). Rather, men come with male companions, with slicked-back hair and seductive three-piece power suits (236; 193). Men's seduction by men recreates the homoeroticism of Greek life, the social bond now in the guise of social bondage.

The Islamic empire not only inverts the values of the republic, *liberté, égalité, fraternité*, but also perverts the monastic *forma vitae* (form of life): obedience, humility, and chastity. Women are subjugated in the name of modesty and religion. Obedience is perverted into subjection, the absolute will to power triumphs over humility, chastity is perverted into pedophilia.

---

[73] How to include the sister in republican fraternity is a leitmotif of Derrida (1994), e.g., 13, 118, and *passim*.

Whereas in the republic, men's lovers were the same age as their daughters, if they had any, in the new regime their multiple wives are the age of their granddaughters: Rediger, a sixty-year-old man, marries Aïsha, a fifteen-year-old girl (243; 198). Generations are incestuously distorted. Women never mature, let alone become independent – witness the girl wives François observes on a train (225–6; 183–4). Perfectly subjected, the sexual objects of the Muslim converts remain children. Lacking agency of any kind, they age out of sexual slavery to enter into another form of subjection. Equally unthreatening, women, like Rediger's first wife Malika (247; 201), now serve comfort food, domestic slaves one way or another. If such subjugation shocks the reader's presumed liberal values, male desire to subject women is neither new nor external to the West. Huysmans voices the fantasy of the "femme pot-au-feu" ("pot-roast woman"), who can transform herself at set times into a girl (97; 77). The decadent fantasy is realized pragmatically in the new empire by splitting women's functions. The error, a trace of humanism even in decadence, was to assume the ideal of singular love realized in marriage. Polygamy offers a coldly logical solution.

Soumission shocks not because of the brutality of the empire's perversion of core republican values, but because their perversion turns out to be nothing new. The new order takes the destruction of these values, already destroyed, to its logical conclusion. The heartless solutions to social problems, to alienation expose republican ideals as false consciousness before the imperatives of neoliberalism, the economic ideology undergirding republicanism itself. You want to reduce unemployment? Remove women from labor. You want comfort and excitement from a woman? Take two. The shock shakes us into putting on the brake. Satiric disfiguration reveals in its grimace these ideals' true value *ex negativo* (from negation). Liberty does not mean subjection. Equality does not mean distributive commodification. Fraternity should not exclude the sister through homosocial fraternization. Their positive meaning is not spelled out. But, if we want to find even negative redemption in *Soumission*, another satiric layer undermines what we, the implied readers, hold dear. You want liberty, equality, and fraternity? These cannot hold a candle to the higher value republicanism cannot meet, namely love.

L'homme régénéré

The same structure of preservation *ex negativo*, which passes through perversion's exposing lens, targets Christianity. While Flaubert and Maupassant, among others, denounce the unchristian politics of the church, the new neoliberal, fascist, masculinist politics of year 2022 turns traditional critique on its head. Instead of calling for reform, the new empire asks for the revocation and abolition of Christianity period, not on the grounds that it has failed to live up to its values, but, in a twist played for shock value, because it is not fascist enough. The antifascist reader – again, read out negatively from the text – is manipulated into defending Christianity, whose institutionalization in the church they might, under other circumstances, charge with corruption, in an attempt to undo this imperial critique. As with *Soumission*'s assault on republicanism, the satiric inversions pile up in layers. To resist it catches the reader in a double bind.

The imperial critique is masculinist, that is, it layers sexual politics over religion. Jesus, in Rediger's view, simply loved human beings too much. To sacrifice yourself for love is, to say the least, a "faute de goût," as Nietzsche would have said (272–3; "mistake in taste," 223). Incarnation, for Rediger, is an effeminate love of humanity leading to the bullshit of human rights. Now, he avers, clear hierarchies are needed: Absolute subjection to a god who certainly would not have become human and in whose name the adulteress is to be stoned, women and the poor subjected to superrich alpha males – his version of the Nietzschean *Herrenmensch* (superman). Christianity, with its feminization, bears the blame, according to Rediger, for a Spenglerian *Untergang des Abendlandes* (Decline of the West).

If we object, we ostensibly enlightened readers end up defending a monolithic West we do not even believe in. The politically correct reader would prefer to critique the West – but not like this. The attempt to roll back the ideological twists layer by layer entangles readers in contradiction with deeply held beliefs. To resist, to say, no, Christianity is not effeminate, spins readers around, so that secular republicans find themselves defending the religion they would separate from the state, Catholic readers find themselves endorsing the masculinist values condemning their religion, at whose heart lies worship of Mary (162; 131).[74] To insist that Christianity is charitable, charity is a strength, and there should still be separation of Church and state requires standing back from *Soumission*'s entire fictional universe. Each layer of perversion corresponds to actual ideologies and their histories. The novel shows the awful result of accumulated ideological entailments.

Combined sexual and religious registers undergird the perverted polit-ical order. Christianity as construed by Lempereur and the Nietzchean

---

[74] For the effeminization of the Catholic Church, Borrutta (2010); for the French republicans, Vinken (2007).

Rediger simply cannot, in their view, foster the right biopolitics. Their answer to the European crisis is demographic. The nativists have pushed the crisis to the point of civil war. The war effort once again requires breeding. To reject this solution as an alien misunderstanding, however, must confront the fact that this age-old formula for restoration is a quintessential part of the tradition since ancient Rome. The Augustan program, especially the *leges Iuliae* (Julian laws), promoted literal birth as social rebirth. Patriarchal marriage, biopolitical restrictions on women, and the legal containment of their sexuality were the solution to the social bond's dissolution in civil war. It brought the age-old concern with legitimate paternity into state purview. The birth rate, as much as the clash of armies, is the field on which every war between France and Germany has been fought. These hereditary enemies agree at least on this. As in Vichy France and the Third Reich, the putative regeneration in *Soumission* depends on bedroom politics.

Just as old as the solution is resistance to it, with art the primary opposing institution. In Augustan Rome, love elegy rejects marriage, rejects breeding, and looks instead to erotic love and the genre's own poetic power as alternative loci of value.[75] But the resistance is caught. It in turn metaphorically internalizes what it rejects: The *militia amoris* figures love as war between the sheets; the disavowed term, warfare, revisits what love would overcome. *Soumission* forwards not even a futile possibility of resistance through art or love. The incorporation of the hostile field is not merely metaphorical; the republic has already lived the perversion the empire brings to light. Intellectuals, who might be expected to defend women from assault, were already indifferent – how can they be expected to stand up in protest against an all-out war on the so-called weaker sex?

The novel reenacts social dissolution, the signature of Augustine's earthly city, in the civil war tropes of the long Roman tradition. The relations between man and woman represent once again society's primary bond. Since the Augustan marriage legislation, since Jesus's defense of the adulteress against stoning in the New Testament, adultery has stood as the exemplary case for the dynamics of civil and social discord. If the great novels of the nineteenth century are about adultery – *Madame Bovary, Effi Briest, Anna Karenina, Bel-ami* – to name four, it is not because they are about morals, but about the

---

[75] The *militia amoris* reencodes, within ideologically peaceful elegy, the violence it rejects, Drinkwater (2013): Propertius' declaration there would be no civil strife, if sex were the battleground for warfare (2.15.41–6) is small consolation for the battered beloved (200); the metaphor undercuts his resistance to the Augustan marriage legislation (201). Vacillation between critique and complicity leaves Ovid in an ideological double bind (202–3).

social bond. Society's response to adultery in these texts is a litmus test: Is it Christian and enlightened or barbaric and decadent? In the New Testament, how to treat the adulteress is determinative of the New Covenant. With it comes the equality of the sexes. Is adultery a male privilege? If so, should the adulteress be stoned or forgiven? Jesus tells the male accusers of a female adulteress that he who is without sin should throw the first stone. All depart. As Augustine puts it, adulterers rage against adulterers.[76]

Availing itself of this tradition, *Soumission* makes adultery the site for revealing imperial social order. Adultery has indeed become an all-male privilege, now legalized in polygamy. Revocation of the Christian good news of forgiveness sweeps away sexual equality in its wake. Blood vengeance holds this society together. In Rediger's writings, Jesus lacked discernment, as usual, in pardoning the adulteress; she should rather be justly punished through stoning.[77] He directly contradicts Jesus's injunction that he who is blameless should cast the first stone: The obvious solution is to have a seven-year-old child throw it. François's editorial comment, "putain de gosse" (273; "fucking kid," 223), only apparently opposes the horror of stoning. The phrase not only alludes to Guy Bedos's famous quip about the unwanted results of love-making but also evokes the Babylonian signifier par excellence, the great whore.

Suicide – one of civil war's most intimate figurations – again brings back ancient Rome. Rediger exploits the trope to denounce European decadence: "l'Europe avait déjà accompli son suicide" (255–7; "Europe had already accomplished suicide," 208–9). He makes fifth-century Rome its analogue in repugnant decomposition.

> parvenus à un degré de décomposition répugnant, l'Europe occidentale n'était plus en état de se sauver elle-même – pas davantage que ne l'avait été la Rome antique au Ve siècle de notre ère. 276

> Europe had reached a point of such putridness that it could no longer save itself, any more than fifth-century Rome could have done. 225

The analogy links decadence to suicide:

> Certainement les Romains avaient eu la sensation d'être une civilisation éternelle, immédiatement avant la chute de leur empire; s'étaient-ils, eux aussi, suicidés? 258

---

[76] Augustine, *Ad Pollentium de adulterinis coniugiis* II, VII, 6, 388.

[77] The Augustan marriage legislation innovated in restricting the punishment of the adulterous woman; the barriers were high for either husband or father to kill her. By requiring her exposure and punishment through trial, the legislation captured sexual morality as the state's purview, a biopolitical move. Milnor (2005) 140–54.

> No doubt the Romans had felt that theirs was an eternal civilization, right up to the moment their empire fell apart. Were they suicides, too? 210

The solution to internal dissolution is therefore to return analogically to Rome's solution to the civil wars: a golden age of renewal. Rediger's martial call for the "réarmement moral et familial de l'Europe" ("moral and familial rearmament of Europe"), so that decadence can be overcome in a "nouvel âge d'or" (276; "new golden age," 226), brings back the conventional moniker for Augustus' inauguration of a new Empire and restoration of values. The ideology of individual liberty and atheism, he avers, has promoted moral decadence and corrupted the family, the basis of the state. Regeneration is called for. *Soumission* shows how, by claiming moral restoration, the new empire perversely imposes immoral subjugation.

In Rediger's version of Islam, a right-wing perversion of Nietzscheanism, the European male stands in greatest need of restoration – a pun on *l'homme régénéré* (regenerated man) of the Revolution, which aimed at restoring not masculinity, but humankind.[78] Rediger sees Islam as the proper means: "L'islam a des *hommes* pour condition première" (272; "Islam at least assumes that it is dealing with *men*," 222). All the restorations of the new ostensible Islamic order attempt to rectify the assaults masculinity has undergone at Christianity's hands.

> Nietzschéenne aussi était son hostilité sarcastique et blessante á l'égard du christianisme, qui reposait uniquement selon lui sur la personalité décadente, marginale de Jésus. Le fondateur du christianisme s'était plu dans la compagnie des femmes, et *cela se sentait*, écrivait-il. 272

> He was similarly Nietzschean in his sarcastic, withering hostility toward Christianity, which according to him was based on the decadent, antisocial personality of Jesus. The founder of Christianity enjoyed the company of women, he wrote, *and you could whiff it out.* 222

Beyond Christian fraternizing with women, male dominance has, in his view, been emasculated by republican egalitarianism, with equality of the sexes its most intolerable instantiation. If the French Revolution aimed to regenerate humanity by overthrowing tyranny, in 2022 regeneration subjects anew: The restored, dominant male puts woman under the yoke. Rediger himself plays the role of the new savior. He first appears as a metaphorical Messiah who saves a reception gone wrong (237; 194).

---

[78] For the ideology of the Revolution, Ozouf (1989), entitled *L'homme régénéré: Essai sur la Révolution française* (*Regenerated Man: Essay on the French Revolution*). We take our section title from her.

Once again, religion means breeding. *Soumission* overlays these right-wing discourses with Nietzsche and Darwin. Religion becomes, in a perversion of Christian dogma, a vehicle for natural selection. Faith, miraculously transmitted through genes, no less, is degraded to preserve the race. Lempereur, who summarizes a statistical study on the birth rate published by nativists, reduces transcendence to survival of the fittest:

> "La transcendence est un avantage sélectif: les couples qui se reconnaissent dans l'une des trois religions du Livre, chez lesquels les valeurs patriarcales se sont maintenues, ont d'advantage d'enfants que les couples athées ou agnostiques; les femmes y sont moins éduquées, l'hédonisme et l'individualisme moins prégnants. La transcendence est par ailleurs un caractère génétiquement transmissible." 69–70

> " . . . transcendence conveys an advantage in selection: couples who follow one of the three religions of the Book, and maintain patriarchal values have more children than atheists or agnostics. You see less education among women, less hedonism and individualism. And to a large degree, this belief in transcendence can be passed on genetically." 53–4

Rediger, Lempereur's correlate, takes social Darwinism to its logical conclusion, not survival but domination. His totalitarian critique spells out, with heavy didacticism, that Christianity, retroped in republican humanism and the Declaration of the Rights of Man – including women – has erased the hierarchies that sustain society: Egalitarianism's ridiculous weakness corrupts from within. Hierarchical subjugation – of the average man to the superman, man to God, woman to man – can be guaranteed through religion alone, but certainly not through the Christian faith: "seule une religion, essayait de démontrer l'article [de Rediger], pouvait créer, entre les individus, une relation totale" (274; "Only one religion, the article tried to show, could create a total relationship between individuals," 224). Rediger's solution, "Islam," is masculinist totalitarianism – even he recognizes his coreligionists would accuse him of blasphemy (260; 212).

The new imperial ideology is a confused jumble, each strand a degraded version of what it espouses, whether Nietzsche, Darwin, political theology, sociology, or scientism. The novel lampoons Rediger's didacticism, and by extension contemporary nativist dogma, with his garbling of incompatible theories. In one of the most absurd, he reaches for yet another legitimating discourse – he passes the definition of absolutist monarchy through the prism of mathematical analogy (the only point that may link all points on a plane lies in a sovereign position outside the plane). His imperial political theology puts the king above the law (274; 224). For once, even François is dubious – a narrative wink to the reader. Bad math equals bad politics, not to mention bad logic.

Soumission's blurring of ideologies sticks a satiric barb in its nativist characters. They are incoherent as well as self-serving. From their mouths, nevertheless, arises a fundamental truth about discord in French society. Shared resistance to the secular promise of universalism binds nativists and Islamists together, nominally bitter foes. In Tanneur's analysis, "Et, surtout, le véritable ennemi des musulmans, ce qu'ils craignent et haïssent par-dessus tout, ce n'est pas le catholicisme: c'est le sécularisme, la laïcité, le matérialisme athée" (156; "For these Muslims, the real enemy – the thing they fear and hate – isn't Catholicism. It's secularism. It's laicism. It's atheist materialism," 125). The inverse also holds. The nativists are in bed with those they imagine to be their worst enemy. Rediger instantiates the otherwise-surprising passage from nativist to Islam, the movement's apparent foe. The dystopian future of 2022 reveals a truth about contemporary discourses, still relevant since the novel's release in 2015: Nativists most resemble what they most revile. This equivalence slams the right. But the novel's most trenchant critique targets lukewarm republicans, impotent, with their secular catholic – and Catholic – values, before the combined onslaught.

Something derails in this masculinist regeneration. Ironic inversion reinscribes the decadence it purports to erase. Lemperer and Rediger, the two characters who most embody the new regime, exemplify the unity of style and politics. Both are former nativists gone oriental. Feminine notes grace both hypermasculinists. *Soumission* unravels the differences they would police and sticks them with the effeminacy their masculinist politics would condemn. A topsy-turvy, satiric romp overturns the distinction between masculinity and effeminacy. All the macho men mince like the paradoxically homophobic dandies of Nazi fame. The new court's courtiers are courtesans after all: Domination comes as prostitution.

Masculinity's inversion gives the lie to the gender identity on which male domination asserts its legitimacy. Muslim converts and nativists alike are strangely effeminate in their brotherhood. The elaborate description of their clothing is symptomatic. As we know from Proust, attention lavished on male dress is effete.[79] Elaborate descriptions spritz these men – who themselves catch the "womanly scent" wafting from Jesus (272; 222) – with an *odor di femmina*. Their regenerated manhood brings back the decadence the new political order means to clean up. The bourgeois suit, republican

---

[79] Schuhen (2007).

dress par excellence, works best when it attracts no attention.[80] The business suit leaves the scene along with the civil equality for which it stands. In its stead, the Saudis will instate their white robes, whose skirts are a retro update of the manly toga (299; 245). The oriental perversion of the symbol of the male Roman citizen connotes tyranny.

Such play on homophilia cannily ridicules right-wing gender suprem-acy. Their own fears turn back to bite them. To those who say, *j'accuse* (I accuse), *Soumission* accuses right back. As with Islamophobia, those calling for restored masculinity are mocked with the same terms they use to accuse others of decadence. Those who hate foreigners are the ones who are truly "oriental," more effeminate than the women they would subject.

But if we expect effeminacy to undermine totalitarian power – look! the *Herrenmenschen* are hypocritical pansies! – *Soumission* turns the tables yet again. The feminine register of decadence coyly bolsters the new leaders' hegemonic position. Ben Abbes's last name inscribes not the Abbot, but the Mother who heads the Abbey. In the tyrannical power play of subjec-tion, the weapons are as homophilic as effeminate. Rediger calls Nietzsche, the philosopher of male regeneration, "la vieille pétasse" ("that old queen," 272–3; 223). Christianity's arch-critic is less tarnished by the homoerotic slur than claimed in fondness by his follower. First seen in black jeans and a black paramilitary aviator jacket, Rediger shows his true colors: Mussolini's brigades in the *camicia nera* (black shirt). This supermuscular giant in black – a pendant to Zola's "white giant" Bismarck? – who evokes a rugby player more than a university professor, pulls out a tiny shell-like cell phone, "presque feminin" in the very emblem of Venus (238; "almost feminine," 194). Phallic ostentation tips over into effeminacy.[81]

The new regime is all about men loving men. François, emblem of republican indifference, is seduced. The luxurious dress of the regenerated men has allure. His editor Lacoue appears with a Saudi courtier as his companion. François lusts to touch his magnificent three-piece silk suit. His description of the fabric swells with poetic effusion: "bleu nuit parcouru verticalement d'imperceptibles rayures blanches, le tissue légèrement brilliant paraissait d'une douceur extrême" (236; "midnight-blue fabric with nearly invisible white stripes. It had a light sheen and looked immensely soft," 193). French or Arab (235; 192), the distinction no longer matters. Schrameck in any case embodies the Arabian knight.[82] François's restraint puts a transparent

---

[80] Hollander (1994).   [81] Vinken (2014a).
[82] In the end, the man codes Jewish: Schrameck bears the name of the real director of Lionel Jospin's cabinet and great-nephew of Abraham Schrameck, the minister of the interior who voted in Pétain's

mask over homophilia. From the silken courtesans of the *ancien régime*, courting each other like *mignons* (minions), up to the supermasculinist, fascist, fetishistic dandies, Houellebecq emasculates the new Supermen with sardonic humor, dressing them in catsuits. The joke is not even on them, but on the secular humanist, lapsed Christians who fall for them.

La sacrée littérature

François and, with him, modern French culture falter across the board. Hugo's sacred rite (*sacre*) degrades into an expletive (*sacrée*) that picks up the ambivalence of the Latin *sacer*, both sacred and accursed. Literature, François's only meaningful bond, surpasses friendship. It is the sole venue for a profound, durable relationship (13–15; 5–6). Others named as friends, like Alice (73; 57), are forgotten and forsaken. In the novel's first phrase, he calls Huysmans a friend – his only true friend in the entire book.

> Pendant toutes les années de ma triste jeunesse, Huysmans demeura pour moi un compagnon, un ami fidèle; jamais je n'éprouvai de doute, jamais je ne fus tenté d'abandonner, ni de m'orienter vers un autre sujet; puis, une après-midi de juin 2007, après avoir longtemps attendu, après avoir tergiversé autant et même un peu plus qu'il n'était admissible, je soutins devant le jury de l'université Paris IV – Sorbonne ma thèse de doctorat: *Joris-Karl Huysmans, ou la sortie du tunnel*. Dès le lendemain matin (ou peut-être dès le soir même, je ne peux pas l'assurer, le soir de ma soutenance fut solitaire, et très alcoolisé), je compris qu'une partie de ma vie venait de s'achever, et que c'était probablement la meilleure. 11

> Through all the years of my sad youth Huysmans remained a companion, a faithful friend; never once did I doubt him, never once was I tempted to drop him or reorient myself toward another subject; then, one afternoon in June 2007, after waiting and putting it off as long as I could, even slightly longer than was allowed, I defended my dissertation, "Joris-Karl Huysmans: Out of the Tunnel," before the jury of the University of Paris IV-Sorbonne. The next morning (or maybe that evening, I don't remember: I spent the night of my defense alone and drunk) I realized that part of my life, probably the best part, was behind me. 3

These lines set up François's conversion to Islam, which replays every term: Doubt returns in his inability to be moved by the Black Virgin of Rocamadour; he yields to temptation; he abandons his only friend Huysmans; re-*orientation* erases not only his choice of subject, but himself

---

plenipotentiary powers. François's initial inability to distinguish his name (236; 193) marks a gap. The literary strategy invites curiosity.

as a subject; procrastination – conversion's deferral most trenchantly expressed in Augustine's prayer "O Lord, make me chaste but not yet" (*Confessions* 8.7) – etymologically has him "turn his back" on the past ("tergiversé"); conversion's sublime, salvific light is reduced and secularized with the banal "light at the end of the tunnel." Not finding inspiration in the companionship of a divine Spirit, François indulges in earthly spirits alone. *Soumission*'s constitutive contrasts structure his conversion as perverse.

Literature plays a double role in this story. The field thematizes conversion as a topos and alerts the reader to the allusions through which François' con/perversion plays out. The book joins a long tradition, from Augustine, through Dante, to Rousseau, and on to Huysmans.[83] The shift from the original title, *Conversion*, to *Soumission* stresses the layering of an Islamophobic discourse over the standard Christian conversion narrative. Whereas Islam means peace in the sense of submission to God, Islamophobia translates such devotion as subjection. Islam becomes understood as a subjecting threat to Western identity and freedom, adding one more layer onto the numerous perversions that turn François's conversion the wrong way.

From the beginning, François looks back on the best part of his life, understood long ago as already over, in an inversion of conversion's new and elevating life. Conversion within Christian topology is a singular event, happening independent of autonomous will, a gift of grace. You cannot count on it. Its telling in the conditional, with modal verbs (296–9; 243–6), as a planned ceremony in the future, undoes the basic concept. No unpremeditated turn-around, the decisive beginning of a new life and a new "me," it appears here as a cyclical – and cynical – version of the eternal return. Like his father before him, Francois thinks he will gain not a new, true life, but a second life, with little in common with the first. The novel's second-to-last line is "Chance d'une deuxième vie, sans grand rapport avec la précédente" (299; "chance at a second life, with very little connection to the old one," 246). Arbitrary discontinuity substitutes for conversion's opening, to comprehension of the sinful orientation of one's past life, to the capacity to regret this orientation and atone for it. François's having nothing to regret after conversion, stated in the novel's last line (300; 246), points to his opportunistic management of an advantage, in perfect continuity with his life up to now. As successful as he is selfish, he will get more symbolic capital, more money, multiple wives,

<hr/>

[83] Freccero (1986).

more prestigious square footage.[84] But the most enticing lure turns on literature.

François's foreseen conversion comes in two steps: Baptism in the *sacre de la littérature* (the sacrament of literature) prepares him for conversion to Islam. Both entail inversions that institutionalize a dead letter, one deadlier than the other. Literature's secularization of the living spirit is followed by abject Babylonian perversion. The pseudo-Muslim authorities know exactly how to seduce François. In a scene of consecration in a consistently Christian register, they bribe him with the currency he recognizes: They entrust him with editing the Pléiade edition of Huysmans, to rectify an "inexplicable omission" (229; "inexplicable oversight," 186) in the series.[85] The Pléiade canonizes literature as a living letter in the eternity of shared humanist values. This institution of the literary canon, named after the Renaissance revival of classical letters, refers to a starry cluster of nymphs divinized in compensation for rape. This venerable temple of humanism substitutes for the New Testament in a familiar gesture. The name of François's book, *"Vertiges des néologismes"* (*"Vertiginous Neologisms,"* 188), puns on the "new word" of God, which brings the good news. The fictitious editor, Bastien Lacoue, who replaces the historical Hugues Pradier, encodes Christian martyrdom and Roman sovereignty. His speaking name alludes to St. Sebastian, a Roman Christian soldier, whose name in turn recalls the Greek for Augustus, *Sebastos*. His surname, which evokes the necks cut in the French Revolution, perverts martyrdom and sovereignty together. His *nomen* (name) is an ill *omen* for what awaits François.

In a parody of liturgy, Lacoue and François seal the deal with ritual gestures. François raises his right hand, indicating reserve, and Lacoue raises his left, solemnly appeasing him. The iconography of the Salvator Mundi appears in a mirror image. François will labor for eternity – no spiritual eternity, however, but Thucydides' *ktema eis aei* ("possession for all time," 1.22), the classical topos for a work that endures for all posterity. The rhetorical unction (*onction*) that invests him into the cenacle of literary fathers anoints him as sacrificial victim with a metaphorical chrism: The edition will swim in oil (231; 188). But this consecration is a lure. Lacoue is Rediger's intermediary and brings his message: He has taken every professor's departure from the Sorbonne as a personal wound. If the Pléiade is literature's New Testament, the Sorbonne is its church; Rediger's wounds

---

[84] Nonnenmacher (2016) and Wodianka (2018) 305.
[85] This omission has been rectified with the edition's publication in 2019.

are on the body of this church's Christ ("comme . . . le Messie," 237; "like the Messiah," 194).

François, inducted into the Pléiade, receives his catechism for joining the converted Church of the Islamic Sorbonne. His anointing marks him doubly as a father of the new church and as its victim. He exits from the office through a "labyrinth" ("dédale," 232; 189) that takes him on a tortuous path not from darkness into light, as do the labyrinths in the cathedrals of Chartres or Reims among others, but into the amphitheater of the lecture hall (248; 202). His conversion will reinstitute a Babylonian sacrifice, namely a human sacrifice, but not as sacred restitution through martyrdom. François's conversion takes us to the spectacle of the Roman arena, transferred to Paris. What plays at the "arènes de Lutèce" ("arena of Lutèce") is no gladiatorial game, but the sad sacrifice of the liberty François never had after his student days (15; 6), of the remnants of his one true love, literature, and of his one companion and faithful friend, Huysmans. The offer to edit the Pléiade of Huysmans is the bait. Once François has completed his task, he is not to be reborn to a new life but finished forever.

> c'était vraiment la fin de ma vie intellectuelle; et que c'était aussi la fin de ma longue, très longue relation avec Joris-Karl Huysmans. 283

> this time my intellectual life really was over; and that so was my long, very long relationship with Joris-Karl Huysmans. 232

> Que ma vie intellectuelle soit terminée, c'était de plus en plus une évidence. 295

> Yes, my intellectual life was finished. 242

Nothing remains to prevent François from submitting. Islamic conversion is a renaissance, a new birth that, like all Renaissances, brings back ancient Rome, not now in its humanist guise, but rather as empire in oriental garb. This conversion inverts the foundational principles of the French Republic, inaugurated in the Revolution. François imagines announcing his incipient conversion to Rediger, who will pretend to be surprised, to leave him the impression of free will ("libre arbitre," 296; "free agent," 243), the fetish object of the enlightened, autonomous, independent subject. His actual freedom in tatters, François reveals the vapidity of the maxim that "Absolute submission can be a form of freedom," as effectively as Jenny Holzer, whose inclusion of it in her *Truisms* series ironizes its truth – in Houellebecq and in Holzer, we pause, wondering if our withdrawal of assent to the formulation means no freedom is available at all.[86] François will join his Muslim brothers, equal only before God (297; 244).

Con/Perversion

Conversion in *Soumission* plays the same role as sacrifice in the tradition we have examined so far. From Vergil through Hugo, sacrifice means restoration. Whereas Greco-Roman sacrifice remakes the social bond by restoring relations between men and gods, and therefore with each other, in Christian dogma, conversion makes whole the bond between God and a single human being, by restoring an individual's relation to self. Two scenes of conversion set up a third. The first two are Christian, modeled on the conversion of Huysmans. François fails spectacularly and twice to realize the model of decadence redeemed: before the sovereignty of the Black Virgin of Rocamadour and in the fraternity of monks at the abbey of Liguge. The third is an Islamic conversion, couched in satire's generic trappings: food, drink, and seduction. Like Rediger, François passes through Catholicism, the novel's most symptomatic dead end, on the way to political Islam. Each scene analyzes a different problematic in the relation of Church, community, and state: sovereignty, fraternity, and sex.

The Black Virgin of Rocamadour

At Rocamadour, Christian conversion is debased in a series of precise and satiric inversions, laced with Roman undertones. Tourism (164; 132), often gastronomic (168; 135), replaces pilgrimage (160, 166; 129, 133). Nevertheless, François enters a sacred space: His perception of historical time disappears (164; 132), his individuality dissolves, a first step to joining the Christian people "uni et solidaire" (167; "unified, in solidarity," 134). He feels ready to lose himself before the Virgin, who seems to rise up magnified (169; 136). Being ripe for transcendence sets in relief his inability to be touched by any holy spirit. He visits the Black Virgin every day for two weeks, but, neither mounting the sacred steps on his knees (he rather descends them to the parking lot, 170; 137) nor kneeling before her like the kings of old, he sits for a few minutes just like any tourist or art student (161, 166; 129, 133). The Virgin, not otherworldly, appears extraterrestrial (166; 133); she rises not into heaven, but into the atmosphere (169; 136).

---

[86] https://twitter.com/jennyholzer/status/970391525036142592; https://www.cs.utexas.edu/~field/holzer/truisms.txt.

François sadly loses the connection to her, as he loses the connection to all human beings (170;137).

The Virgin's sovereignty becomes a contested site for political theology. Two sets of citations from Charles Péguy invert the Augustinian paradigm. In the first, Tanneur's recitation makes the Virgin of Rocamadour an emblem of European civilization in the face of dying French patriotism. He articulates Ben Abbes's project of restoration on the model of Augustus here. The context politicizes religious renewal in a militaristic vein.

> *Heureux ceux qui sont morts pour des cités charnelles*
> *Car elles sont le corps de la cité de Dieu.*
> *Heureux ceux qui sont morts pour leur âtre et leur feu,*
> *Et les pauvres honneurs des maisons paternelles.*   162

> *Happy are they who died for the carnal cities,*
> *For these are the body of the city of God.*
> *Happy are they who died for their hearths and fires*
> *And the meager honors of their native homes.*

> 130; italics in originals

The refrain, "blessed are those who," a *makarismos* taken from the Sermon on the Mount, replaces the meek and the poor who will attain the kingdom of heaven with the classical Roman valorization of death in battle, as in Horace's line, *dulce et decorum est pro patria mori* ("it is sweet and beautiful to die for one's fatherland," *Odes* 3.2.13) and Aeneas' cry, *o terque quaterque beati, / quis ante ora patrum Troiae sub moenibus altis / contigit oppetere* ("o thrice and four times blessed, who could die under the high walls of Troy before the faces of their fathers," Vergil, *Aen.* 1.94–6). The atrium, Penates' fire, and paternal houses in Péguy mark the ideology as Roman. At Rocamadour, François chances upon the same author again. The openness and fraternity of the young Catholic humanitarians who listen to an actor's dramatic reading are foil to Péguy's violent patriotism (168–9; 135–6). Stanzas beginning "Mère voici vos fils" ("Mother, behold your sons") introduce no annunciation or *pietà*, but a mother receiving the corpses of her sons killed in war. Republican patriotism is undercut as leading to an "uninterrupted succession of stupid wars" (163; 131). The blasphemy of such a nonprayer in a church, which has turned into not just any theater, but a very particularly *Comédie française* (168; 135), conjures up one of Augustine's *bêtes noires*, the need for an absolute separation of Church and theater, its uncanny double.

François, for all his obtuseness, at least suspects Péguy gets the proper relation of Church and state wrong. Tanneur, however, rightly declares that, for all he was "républicain, laïc, dreyfusard" (162; "republican, secular, a supporter of Dreyfus," 131), Péguy understood that the living heart of the Middle Ages was devotion not to the Father, nor even to the Son, but to the Virgin Mary. With François's third conversion scene, it becomes clear that Rediger abandons Christianity for this reason: He leaves this feminine orientation for a masculinist (pseudo-)Islam. Nevertheless Péguy, like Huysmans, turns out to be a bad introduction to Catholicism. The statue of the Virgin has "quelque chose de mystérieux, de sacerdotal et de royal" ("something mysterious, priestly, and royal") that surpasses attachment to fatherland or even childlike desire for a mother. She has "suzeraineté" ("sovereignty"), and the infant Jesus in her arms could raise his right hand to destroy pagans and idolaters (169–70; 137). Her power, inflected in medieval diction, bears an absoluteness incompatible with any link to political power. It casts Péguy's hybrid of medieval Christianity with republicanism in the same light as the failed republic and perverse empire that comes. Political Islam makes evident what is already wrong with patriotic Catholicism. The Roman register shows up all available systems as political theological mistakes. The transience of François's access to mystery, the reduction of his vision to a hypoglycemic crisis easily resolved with some pornographic duck thighs, his feeling of desertion by the Spirit, his reduction to corporeality, cast even this glimmer of higher sovereignty into another dead end, ripe for satire.[87] He gets even the diction wrong. The Virgin is not, as standard, *immaculata* but *immarcescible* (170; "timeless," 137), a rare Latinate word that reduces her spiritual purity into fleshly resistance to rot.[88]

The Abbey of Ligugé

After sovereignty's failure, François's attempted conversion at the Benedictine Abbaye de Ligugé stages a parallel failure of fraternity. This republican ideal falters also in its religious dimension. The oldest abbey of Europe encodes the conflict between republic and Church, Church and infidel in its history. Originally founded in 361 by Martin of Tours, it was destroyed in the Arab invasion of 732 and eventually became Benedictine. Secularized in the French Revolution, in 1852 it was bought by the bishop

---

[87] Similar satiric degradation figures the assumption of the Virgin as sexual climax (26; 15).

[88] Google ngram, which tracks usage in printed materials, shows a spike in usage during the Second World War. Pope Martin V in 1425 published a Papal bull, *sapientiae immarcescibilis* ("of timeless wisdom"), to grant the establishment of a *studium generale* in Leuven. The overlay of the university with the Virgin unites the novel's deepest themes.

of Poitiers and refounded. Combes's laws separating church from state in 1905 resulted in the expulsion of the Benedictines, who left for Belgium, then returned in 1923. It was a shelter for members of the French Resistance during the Second World War. François is interested in the place because Huysmans served as an oblate there.

Sustained allusion to Baudelaire's *Au lecteur* ("To the reader"), which opens the *Fleurs du mal*, adds a poetic dimension to François's crisis. The poem celebrates and denounces our attachment to folly, error, sin, and avarice. Its catalogue of sins, lovingly detailed, climaxes in *ennui*.

> C'est l'Ennui! L'oeil chargé d'un pleur involontaire,
> Il rêve d'échafauds en fumant son houka.
> Tu le connais, lecteur, ce monstre délicat,
> – Hypocrite lecteur, – mon semblable, – mon frère! 36–40

> It was *Boredom!* Its eye laden with an involuntary tear, it dreams of scaffolds smoking its hookah. You know him, reader, this delicate monster, – hypocrite reader, – my fellow – my brother!

François's obsessive smoking at the abbey and involuntary tears evoke the poem's last stanza. Echoes from Baudelaire frame his visit.

> L'humanité ne m'intéressait pas, elle me dégoûtait même, je ne considérais nullement les humains comme mes frères, et c'était encore moins le cas si je considérais une fraction plus restreinte de l'humanité, celle par exemple constituée par mes compatriotes, ou par mes anciens collègues. Pourtant, en un sens déplaisant, je devais bien le reconnaître, ces humains étaient mes semblables, mais c'était justement cette ressemblance qui me faisait les fuir. 207

> Humanity didn't interest me – it disgusted me, actually. I didn't think of human beings as my brothers, especially not when I looked at some particular subset of human beings, such as the French, or my former colleagues. And yet, in an unpleasant way, I couldn't help seeing that these human beings were just like me, and it was this very resemblance that made me avoid them. 169

François cannot love humanity in itself, much less in the image of God, because he cannot love himself. Close to suicide without good reason (206; 168), François in his isolation lacks the will to live, but also the initiative required to do himself in. Even civil war's most desperate gesture fizzles. The leitmotif of *semblable* (fellow) and *frère* (brother) drives the allusion home. On François's arrival at Ligugé, his taxi driver wishes him well, and François realizes the man is a rare *brave homme* ("a *nice guy*," italics in original) who takes joy in the "bonheur de leurs semblables" (212; "pleasure in the happiness of their fellow men," 173). At his departure, he enters the "Bar de l'Amitié" ("Friendship Bar"), but he not only discovers no friends but feels no satisfaction at finding himself again among his "semblables" (220; "people like myself," 180). The scene's insistence on naming the monks "frère" (213; "brother," 174–5), with or without their proper name, underscores the expectation that fraternity will foster a sense of shared humanity through the recognition of likeness.

The allusion reveals François's failure to convert as a failure of community, what the abbey's brotherhood stands for. He came to Ligugé when he found himself completely alone – unlike past scant happy New Year's wishes, he now receives not even a single email. A "crise de larmes" (208; "unexpected tears," 170), a potential opening onto grace met with incomprehension, provokes the trip. But this community, like all others, lies beyond reach. He cuts his visit short. The only fraternity he can access – and this not consciously – is Baudelaire's literary club, but even Huysmans, his closest friend in the republic of letters, loses his hold on him. The episode reveals acedia as François's cardinal sin, a deadening indifference of spirit named once he returns home to find not the sublime boredom of the symbolist poet, but a mess of quotidian annoyances ("ennuyeuse," "ennuis," 228; "dull," "irritations," 186). François's "disgust" frames the passage ("dégoûtait," 207; 169; "dégoûté," 228; 186). His apartment, no home, is a place where "personne ne s'aimait, et que personne n'aimait" (228; "no one loved each other, and that no one loved," 186). Baudelaire's line, "Nos péchés sont têtus, nos repentirs sont lâches" ("our sins are stubborn, our repentance cowardly," 5), sums up François as the poem's delicate monster in a nutshell.

The episode at Ligugé replays the traditional Pauline opposition between living spirit and dead letter, encoded in a wealth of realist detail. François's deadening perception systematically converts the place into a cold cipher. His calculations whether he may ring the bell without disrupting services are emblematic. Rather than the grand *Très riches heures du Duc de Berry*, a sumptuous, ducal book of hours for reliving the Holy Story, a little sign announces the hours. For François, these services are hollowed out by fatal ennui: Nothing, minute by minute, hour by hour, but meaningless numbers of absurd routine (217–18; 178). The welcoming monks have speaking names. Joel, who greets him, means "the Lord is God," and Pierre, in charge of hospitality, stands for the foundation of the Church on the rock of Peter's name. In François's deadening imagination, the latter recalls a minister of finance or the budget (214; 175); he sees only a resemblance to Pierre Moscovici, a Zionist finance minister of the

European Union (219; 180), who – according to internet rumor – is also a member of the Freemasons of the Grand Orient of France. The lens of economics obscures hospitality. François flees, not even from the Rock of the Christian Church, which he cannot see, but from the Promised Land degraded by its fall into politics, a united Europe layered over Israel. The coldness in François's body – his gray cell has no hot water, and the chapel no heat (214–18; 175–9) – conveys the frigidity of his unfeeling heart.

Killing cigarette smoke, which, in Baudelaire's words, brings only "la mort dans les poumons" ("death in the lungs"), usurps the place of any salvific *pneuma* of the Holy Spirit. Instead of accepting the spirit of the order, François breaks the letter of the monastic rules: He evades the smoke detector. He cares only about creature comforts. Already Huysmans doubted his capacity to tolerate a smokeless existence. Curling up alone in bed with a pile of books and a packet of tobacco was for him one of life's pure joys. The phrase, "une pile de bons bouquins" ("stack of good books") contrasts in both content (dead literature versus living scripture) and colloquial tone with the books provided: the Bible and Jean-Pierre Longeat's slender tome on monastic life (215; 176). Flying into an addict's rage, François contrasts Huysmans's diagnosis of his own hardened heart, "racorni et fumé par les noces" ("hardened and smoked dry with dissipation") with his own hardened lungs, "racornis et fumés par le tabac" ("hardened and smoked dry by tobacco," 219; 179). Baudelaire's hookah clues us in to the oriental origin of this fatal spirit.

François's citation of the novel's epigraph from Huysmans indicates we have reached the heart of *Soumission*. Whereas Huysmans eventually overcomes his resistance to conversion, François has no heart to be hard. With the descent from heart to the lungs' abject materiality, monastic sublimity falls into filth. Instead of following the "chemin de lumière" (219; "journey of light," 180) announced by the Renaissance buildings (213–14; 174), François sinks into furor and fulmination – a bathetic lowering of Aeneas' rage and Jupiter's divine vengeance – against Longeat, whose treatise invites him to knock on love's door. He abuses this poor monk as "Ducon," evoking female genitalia in vulgar terms (218–19; "fucking wellspring," 179). Lust and anger, two of the seven deadly sins, foreclose any possibility of joining the monastic community of love. The only abstinence he affirms is refraining from attending offices on his first day (215; 176).

The interplay of literal light and darkness, of Roman and medieval institutions, encodes François's spiritual failure as a victory for pagan Rome over the church. Seeing no light, François, on his benighted trip – no spiritual journey this – does not even reach the darkest night in which the mystic tradition, from Jean de la Croix to Thérèse de Lisieux, sets hope for reemergence. At Ligugé, he misses the Vigils, his favorite service from his prior visit. At the deepest darkness of two in the morning, this office brings "attente pure, d'espérance ultime sans raison d'éspérer" ("pure expectation, of ultimate hope without reason to hope"). It precedes the promise of a new dawn brought by morning Lauds (216; 176). This office is distanced doubly: through memory and literal displacement to ten in the evening. Allusion to the paradoxical topos of mysticism highlights François's contrasting incapacity. He is dazzled by the "soleil éblouissant" ("dazzling sun") of the brightest part of the afternoon instead of any spiritual light. He cuts short his visit in a dense fog caused by a climatic "zone dépressionaire" (219; "low-pressure system," 180) that reflects the condition of his soul and sets the stage for the next scene of conversion.

Nietzschean Islam

In its fifth act, the satire ends in the *catastrophe* of a perverse conversion. A full show of seven deadly sins troops onto the topsy-turvy tragic stage.[89] Instead of heavenly Jerusalem, François heads to Babylon via a detour through Rome. Although the stones of Paris tell the true story, François remains clueless. References to the allegorical cities drop in as François makes his way to visit Rediger. The scene, where gladiatorial games, Christian martyrdom, and abject sacrifice mix, colors his conversion as anything but salvific.

Rediger has invited him to "tea" at his home on the rue des Arènes. Butchery along the way announces his true end. The neighborhood's charm – grace's worldly analogue – reassures with earthly attractions, including butcher shops (241; 196). François, full of misguided security, is not led by grace to salvation, from the earthly to the heavenly city, but lured to his own butchering in the Roman arena of the street's name. Puns on mouths and butchery met François exiting from the Metro (*bouch*eries, je dé*bouch*ais, je dé*bouch*ai, *bouche* de métro).

> Au métro place Monge, j'eus la mauvaise idée de prendre la sortie Arènes de Lutèce. Certes, sur le plan topographique, c'était justifié, je dé*bouch*ais directement rue des Arènes; mais j'avais oublié que cette sortie n'avait pas

---

[89] The novel has five sections that formally enact a "dramatic five-act structure," Schneider (2016), who sees François' final conversion as wavering ambivalently between a happy ending and catastrophe. Rather, following the rules of tragedy, the novel's full-blown catastrophe ends in farce.

d'ascenseur et que le métro place Monge se situait cinquante mètres en dessous du niveau de la rue, j'étais complètement épuisé et hors d'haleine lorsque je dé*bouch*ai de cette curieuse *bouche* de métro, creusée dans les murs d'enceinte du jardin, avec ses colonnades épaisses et sa typographie d'inspiration cubiste, dont l'apparence générale néo-babylonienne était parfaitement incongrue à Paris – et l'aurait été d'ailleurs, à peu près n'importe où en Europe. 242

At the Place Monge metro station, I made the mistake of going out the Arènes de Lutèce exit. Geographically, I wasn't wrong – the exit *disgorged* me straight on the rue des Arènes – but I'd forgotten that there wasn't an escalator, and that the Place Monge metro station was fifty meters below street level. I was exhausted and out of breath by the time I *popped out* from the curious *mouth* of the metro, a hollow carved out of the walls of the parks, its thick columns, cubist typography, and generally neo-Babylonian appearance all completely out of place in Paris – as they would have been pretty much anywhere else in Europe. 197; our emphasis and revised translation

François – no Hercules, but at a fork in the road – takes a wrong turn as he emerges from a labyrinthine hell: Cubist fragmentation styles Babylonian decadence. He exits the mouth of the Metro – like a bottle uncorked – to face a lion in his den. The repetition of "boucherie" (257; "butchery," 210) later in the scene cues us to its meaning. Rediger, then François review history in its terms: World War I, 1870–1, the Romans, the most enlightened civilizations have committed suicide through self-slaughter. François, paradigmatic Frenchman, inevitably follows suit.

Spiritual twilight descends on him in the guise of a Roman spectacle. Neither a Daniel, whose faith preserved him, nor a martyr, saved by self-sacrifice, François enters the gladiatorial arena at the Gallo-Roman site of ancient Lutèce as a scapegoat unarmed for the fight. His remarkable view of the whole auditorium sets him figuratively on the sands (245; 199). The site looms large when his potential for Islamic conversion comes up: "il était étonnant de penser que des combats de gladiateurs et de fauves avaient réellement eu lieu ici, quelque deux mille ans auparavant" (250; "It was amazing to think that fights between gladiators and wild beasts had actually taken place here, two thousand years before," 203). His conversion brings him to the site of antiquity's greatest barbarity, described in the standard trope of their "civilisation brutale" ("brutal civilization"), "civilization cruelle" ("cruel civilization"), whose entertainment was battle to the death among men, between men and beasts (258; 210). Seduced by Rediger, he observes the sinking sun and invasion of night: "Le soleil disparut derrière les gredins, la nuit envahit les arènes" (250; "The sun vanished behind the terraced steps; night washed over the arena," 203). Repetition frames the scene: "La nuit était tombée sur le square des Arènes de Lutèce" (258; "Night had fallen on the square ... on the steps of the arena," 210). But the rising of the sun from the orient brings no illumination. Rather it eclipses the occident's sun as it sets. Incapable of either fighting or bearing witness, François allows himself to be seduced though acedia's indifference. The Roman setting renders his dystopian conversion out of place in France, here an explicit synecdoche for Europe. But the text's secret is that with Rome, it is Babylon that returns. François now reaches Europe's most penetrating figuration, *translatio Babylonis*.

All conversion scenes twist spirit into flesh. The worn topoi of seduction pad the Islamic conversion. A slick salesman, Rediger aims to entice François back to the university at the price of conversion. He lures François, as naïve as any girl who falls for the promise of etchings, to his house with an irresistible smile. His library stages the scene. Since Abélard and Héloise, the Nouvelle Héloise, and Julien and Mathilde in Stendhal's *Le rouge et le noir* (*The Red and the Black*), the library is the classic site of seduction. François, for once, feels desired during his audience: "il ne m'était jamais arrivé, je pense, de me sentir à ce point *désirable*" (249, emphasis in text; "It occurred to me that I had never felt so *desirable*," 202). The seducer objectifies his object of desire with a violence couched in politeness: "Et, pardonnez-moi d'être brutal, vous êtes quelque chose que je veux" (247; "And if you'll forgive me for being blunt, you are something I want," 201). When François leaves, he declares that the afternoon had been "passionate." Rediger avers he had also spent "un très bon moment" (262; "a great pleasure," 213), as if answering the postcoital commonplace: "was it good for you?" The two are "sincere"; sincerity also marks Huysmans's conversion (264; 215). The tropes of seduction and conversion merge.

The living Spirit as *pneuma* is perverted in cigarette smoke and alcohol, fatal breath and fatal spirits. The quantities of alcohol – an Arabic word – consumed in the novel are astounding. Here François downs a whole bottle of Meursault, a great Burgundy, but also a name in the so-called conflict of civilizations, first as the famous and bloody name of the *pied noir* (French colonizer) who shoots "the Arab" on the beach in Camus' *L'étranger* (*The Stranger*), and now in Kamel Daoud, *Meursault, contre-enquête* (*The Meursault Investigation*, 2013), which rewrites the classic novel from the perspective of Camus's nameless Arab's brother. François has a predilection for Augustinian flavors on his path to conversion: Lempereur serves him a whole bottle of pear brandy in an earlier paired scene (66; 50); here he indulges, beyond the Meursault, in Tunisian *boukha* (254; 207), a distillation of figs meaning "alcohol vapor," that is, "spirit" in the Judeo-Arabic dialect of Tunisia. Augustine provides the model for conversion up to Rousseau perverted here. The pear tree stages young Augustine's original sin (*Confessions* 2.4–8), and he converted under a fig tree. What he famously picked up and read was a passage from the Bible.[90]

> Not in rioting and drunkenness, not in bedchambers and wantonness, not in strife and envying; but put on the Lord Jesus Christ, and make not provision for the flesh, in concupiscence. No further would I read; nor needed I: for instantly at the end of this sentence, by a light as it were of serenity infused into my heart, all the darkness of doubt vanished away. *Confessions* 8.12.28

François corrupts Augustine's model with his sins: drunkenness, gluttony for Rediger's pastries – Eastern baklava and Moroccan *briouat* (254; 207) – lust for sex and money, vainglory and sloth. The promise of three wives entices, plus triple the salary, luxurious apartments, and access to society's better circles. Rediger pampers his vanity and flatters him with the cheap flowers of rhetoric: he declares François's flatly entitled dissertation, *Joris-Karl Huysmans, ou la sortie du tunnel* ("Joris-Karl Huysmans: Out of the Tunnel"), as brilliant as Nietzsche's *Birth of Tragedy*.[91] The philosopher's title underscores tragedy throughout this fifth act, at number 5, rue des Arènes. Instead of light at the end of the tunnel, let alone any spiritual illumination, Nietzsche's famous thesis on the origin of tragedy conjures up the goat's song, lamenting in sacrifice. François's conversion perverts the sacrifice and perverts illumination: Satire overturns the lament, and tragedy plays as satyr play.

Not touched by any living spirit, shrouded in cigarette smoke, François's conversion literalizes the dead and deadening letter. Bringing his Pléiade edition of Huysmans to completion enables his final turn. Writing the preface has been a stumbling block; François simply cannot fathom Huysmans's conversion. He realizes he must visit Brussels to make progress without any inkling why (277; 227). The text reveals to us what remains opaque to him. As Europe's capital, yet another new Rome, Brussels emerges as *the* locus of "civil war": "guerre civile" (278; 228) is named

---

[90] Freccero (1975).
[91] Bodo Kirchhoff's novel, *Schundroman* (Frankfurt, 2002), comments on trashiness and cheapness in Houellebecq. The hero, an author named Ollenbeck, calques Houellebecq. He leads a double life through his alias Dr. Zidona, the *Männerwunder* (Wonderman) of the Frankfurt book fair, an ironic echo of the German postwar *Fräuleinwunder* (Wondermiss).

again here, the first time since Ben Abbes's accession to power. Beyond the name, civil war is figured through its conventional tropes: internal divide, twinning, indistinction. The internal divide between Flemish and Walloon lets another moderate Muslim regime come to power in Europe: Belgium turns into France's double. Both are synecdoches for Europe as a whole. François's interpretative breakthrough comes as a lightning bolt of clarity: "j'eus soudain la certitude que je comprenais totalement Huysmans, mieux qu'il ne s'était compris lui-même, et que je pouvais maintenant rédiger ma préface" (279; "all at once I was gripped by the certainty that I understood Huysmans completely, better than he had understood himself, and that I was finally able to redact my preface," 229). We, of course, also understand him better than he understands himself. Now, as the paradigmatic Frenchman, he may complete the conversion of France, and with it Europe, into the permanent civil war of man on woman signified by Rome's return, as empire, as Babylon, as decadence masquerading as renewal.

All the major ethical and aesthetic dichotomies that structure Huysmans's oeuvre break down in François's interpretation: Huysmans champions Impressionism while embracing the Academic style; the ascesis of monastic life is for him indistinct from the *douceur du foyer*, the bourgeois comforts of quotidian good food, affection, snuggling up with a book and a smoke. François's interpretation undoes the decadent author's conversion *qua* Christian conversion and reinscribes the decadence. The figuration of François's interpretation – the lightning bolt of illumination is conversion's trope – undoes his conversion. This tropological unraveling of Christian conversion allows François to move on to a perverted conversion, ostensibly to Islam. Basic distinctions have collapsed; he can now leave his old life behind.

Rediger's name is inscribed into François' undone conversion: "je pouvais maintenant *rédiger* ma préface" (279; "I was finally able to *redact* my preface," 229; our emphasis). He can redact his preface, but Rediger may now redact his life. François has reached the apogee of his intellectual life: This, in his own humble opinion, is his best work, the best interpretation ever written of Huysmans. Now done with the only true friend he ever had, he leaves behind intellectual life to start a new life of the flesh. The tropes of civil war found in Brussels – internal divide, indistinction – sink into François's Islamic conversion and undo it from within. Conversion here does not heal civil war but reenacts it.

François's conversion comes under the sign of Babylon. With Babel's own gibberish, the dead letter occupies the space of the living spirit.

François learns by heart the Arabic formula for conversion and will parrot it without understanding: *"Ach-Hadou ane lâ ilâha illa lahou wa ach-hadou anna Mouhamadane rassouloullahi"* (298; 244–5). He opens himself to a second, if hardly new life. The novel's last lines refer the reader not forward, but back, to an earlier episode where François witnessed his father's second life, and to an earlier, ever-recurring model (299; 246).

His father's death again sets François in Babylon. Without understanding, he records the tropes inscribed in his father's choices. The "new man" François should "put on," in Paul's phrase (Ephesians 4.22), could not be more ancient. He walks on the trail of the father who, despite being estranged from his mother, joins her in an equal repudiation of their only son with an "égoïsme implacable" (73; "completely self-centered," 56) – lovelessnesss is the only thing they still share. Neither would grant refuge to François, he muses, if civil war broke out. This second life on his father's model reveals that François's new oriental conversion reverts to the tropes of the *civitas terrena*, now updated as capitalist globalization, empire's newest manifestation. François's father has transformed from a conventional and tasteful bourgeois, a blond and blue-eyed Hollywood type, into a "baroudeur de banlieu" (189; "suburban adventurer," 155). The transformation, like Ben Abbes's new empire, like François's conversion, unmasks what has always been. This phrase, deriving from the Arabic for gunpowder, denotes the warrior. As a former finance director at Unilever, who could have starred in movies about Wall Street (188–90; 154–6), the capitalist, already a robber baron in disguise, now shows his true face as a militaristic hunter. The suburbs figure simultaneously as bourgeois decadence and the locus of an orientalized threat. "Suburban" is ambivalent: Does he come from the suburbs or hunt them down?

The description of the father's hunting lodge, atop a mountain, parallels the method behind the speaking monuments of Paris. Interior decorating discloses underlying ideologies. American décor – "living room" and open-style kitchen (193; 157), separate bar, privatized public spaces (192; 157) – marks the neoliberal economic register. Dead animal skins strewn over the floor translate neoliberalism into sexual abjection, evoking "un film porno allemand des années 70" (193; "German porno from the '70s," 158). François fails to understand the symbolic register: Pornography figures capitalist exploitation and domination. François takes up his Babylonian, patriarchal inheritance when he literally inherits from his father. The faux-leopard seats of his military-style SUV (an Asian Mitsubishi built for "un milieu hostile," 188; "a hostile milieu," 154), his passion for collecting guns and the hunt (190–2;

155), his new wife's name Sylvia (188; 154),[92] their "chalet," an enormous hunting lodge stuffed with taxidermy trophies (191–2; 156–7), the super size of everything from the parking lot, big enough for ten cars, to the "vast" living room, the dozens of bottles of alcohol on the bar, the setting in some of France's highest mountains, the "massif des Écrins" (73, 193; 56, 158) – this monstrosity figures François's father as the giant Nimrod,[93] a hunter against the Lord and Babylon's notorious founder. Nimrod follows in the footsteps of Cain, the founder, in Augustine, of the *civitas terrena*.[94]

François's conversion by no means ends civil war but refounds Babylon in the *civitas terrena*'s latest realization. François becomes no *civis* of the *civitas Dei* but tracks the founding fathers of the *civitas terrena*. Anointed and enthroned as church father in the secular church of the Sorbonne, elected to the Pantheon of editors of the Pléaide, he becomes a perfect collaborator in the new regime. The novel's last words, "Je n'aurais rien à regretter" (300; "I would have nothing to regret," 246) puts a final twist on the perversion of conversion's tropes. The quotation alludes to Edith Piaf's song "Non, je ne regrette rien" ("No, I regret nothing"): She has nothing to regret, because she will begin a new life of love: "car ma vie, car mes joies, aujourd'hui, ça commence avec toi" ("for my life, my joys, today, it all begins together with you").[95] Without regret, François, lured and seduced, buys into a new life of domination, the new regime's driving force. He has never been able to love nor to understand, why should he start now?

Qu'est-ce que la littérature?

The question is less what *Soumission* is – *What is Literature?* – than what it does. Do all the twists and turns of the satiric screw leave the ideal of conversion intact? Is there any solution to the breakdown – of the social bond, of love – whose figure is civil war? The novel's Roman terms show the collapse of an already-corrupt Republic into a decadent Empire: the eternal French story about France's own history now comes in the guise of Nietzsche, Darwin, Pétain, and fascist collaboration. François's Islamic conversion upends the story of Christian conversion, canonical since Paul,

---

[92] She shares her name, calqued on the Latin *silva* (woods), with the Latin girl in the *Aeneid* whose pet stag Ascanius kills hunting – the catalyst for the violent breaking of the first truce between Latin and Aeneas (7.475–510). The outbreak is a metaphorical civil war.

[93] For the obsession with Nimrod in French literature, particularly Hugo and Flaubert, Vinken (2009a).

[94] For father-son filiation and Augustine in Houellbecq, Viard (2010).

[95] On Houellebecq and popular music, Hussey (2010).

by perverting its tropes: rendering the spirit flesh, turning the living word into a dead letter. François' negative *exemplum* and his perverse conversion alert us to what waits right over the horizon, as soon as 2022, unless we wake up to our own decadence.

The novel speaks back to the Western ideologies it exposes via an encoded, layered palimpsest. Figure over figure, historical layer over historical layer, *Soumission* reduces all ideologies to their perverted other in its resistance to ideology itself. A merely ideological reading, as in much modern interpretation, fails to do justice to the book's unsettling deconstructive force. Literature's art resides in its power to enable us to see, however darkly, the looking glass through which ideology views the world. For Houellebecq, literature provides no restoration, a concept his writings reveal as always already corrupt. He belongs to the same tradition as Vergil and Lucan, as we have shown, and, closer to home, to Flaubert. The model he means to tear down is represented by Augustine and Hugo.

Soumission opens our eyes: We are François, despite all our resistance to him; we are already in the midst of civil war and cannot see; we have already sold out. *Soumission* gives us a model of perverted conversion in its protagonist, and also the model of François's perverted reading of conversion in his understanding of Huysmans. The reader's hypocrisy comes in our failure to recognize our own apathy, our own failures in François, to acknowledge that we, as indifferent secular republicans and lapsed Catholics, are as sinful, blind, and indifferent as he. If we, politically correct and self-important, are prone to judge, to denounce as oriental, as corrupt, as tyrannical, *Soumission* says, before casting the first stone, remember Baudelaire. His line, – "Hypocrite lecteur, – mon semblable, – mon frère!" ("– hypocrite reader, – my fellow – my brother!" 40) from *Au lecteur*, is a governing allusion in *Soumission*.[96] Recognizing our benighted selves in François, that would be the essential first step toward enlightenment. Where we take self-knowledge from there is up to us. Houellebecq manipulates our fears of the Islamic other to show up our own fascistic tendencies, our resistance to self-recognition by externalizing blame for own failures onto the other, whose most recent figuration is no longer the Egyptian, as in ancient Rome, or even the Jew, as perennially in the West, but the Muslim. Whether the traditional model of conversion, crossed out as it is, remains accessible to us dwells, like conversion itself, in the novel's hermeneutic black hole.

---

[96] The repetition of "semblable" ("fellow") and "frère" ("brother") (207–20; 169–80) frames François' failed conversion at Ligugé. The first poem of Baudelaire's *Fleurs du mal* denounces the reader's attraction to vice and incapacity to see it in himself.

Bibliography

Editions

Ahl, F. (ed. and trans.) (2007). *Virgil: Aeneid.* Oxford.

Albouy, P. (ed.) (1964). *Victor Hugo: Oeuvres poétiques* I. *Avant l'exil 1802–1851.* Paris.

(1967). *Victor Hugo: Oeuvres poétiques* II. *Les châtiments, les contemplations.* Paris.

Arnaud-Lindet, M.-P. (ed.) (1990). *Orose: Histoires (contre les païens).* Paris.

Austin, R. G. (ed.) (1964). *P. Vergili Maronis Aeneidos liber secundus.* Oxford.

(1971). *P. Vergili Maronis Aeneidos liber primus.* Oxford.

(1977). *P. Vergili Maronis Aeneidos liber sextus: With a Commentary.* Oxford.

Boudout, J. (ed.) (1957). *Victor Hugo: Quatrevingt-treize.* Paris.

Braudel, F. (ed.) (1978). *Tocqueville: Souvenirs.* Paris.

Bruneau, J. (ed.) (1991). *Flaubert: Correspondance*, vol. III. Paris.

Cambien, M. (ed.) (1972). *Victor Hugo: La preface de "Cromwell."* Paris.

Camus, R. (2011). *Le grand remplacement.* Plieux.

Clausen, W. (ed.) (1994). *Virgil: Eclogues.* Oxford.

Cocteau, J. (1950). "Le mystère laïc," in *Oeuvres complètes*, vol. 10. Lausanne, 9–46.

Cooley, A. E. (ed.) (2009). *Res gestae divi Augusti.* Cambridge.

Daoud, K. (2013). *Meursault, contre-enquête.* Arles.

Diderot, D. (1800). "Les bijoux indiscrèts," in *Oeuvres de Denis Diderot*, vol. 10. Paris.

Dyson, R. W. (ed.) (1998). *Augustine: The City of God against the Pagans.* Cambridge.

Foucault, M. (1977). "*Theatrum Philosophicum*," in *Language, Counter-Memory, Practice: Selected Essays and Interviews*, trans. and ed. D. F. Bouchard and S. Simon. Ithaca, 165–96.

Gide, A. (2002). *Hugo, hélas!* Saint-Clément-de-Rivière.

Giono, J. (1982). *L'homme qui plantait des arbres.* Paris.

(2001). *Virgile ou les palais de l'Atlantide.* Paris.

Gohin, Y. (ed.) (1979). *Victor Hugo: Quatrevingt-treize.* Paris.

Gransden, K. W. (ed.) (1976). *Virgil: "Aeneid" Book* VIII. Cambridge.

Heyworth, S. J. (ed.) (2019). *Ovid, Fasti, Book* III. Cambridge.

Horsfall, N. (ed.) (2013). *Virgil, Aeneid 6: A Commentary.* Berlin.

Houellebecq, M. (2015a). *Soumission.* Paris.

(2015b). *Submission*, trans. L. Stein. New York.

Housman, A. E. (ed.) (1926). *M. Annaei Lucani Belli Civilis.* Oxford.

Hugo, V. (1867). *Paris-Guide de l'exposition universelle.* Paris.

(1889). *Ninety Three*, trans. F. L. Benedict, 2 vols. London and New York.

(1970). *Bug Jargal et le dernier jour d'un condamné*. Paris.

Huysmans, J. K. (1969). *Against the Grain (A Rebours)*. New York.

Jerphagnon, L. (ed.) (1998). *Saint Augustin: Oeuvres. Cité de Dieu*, vol. 2. Paris.

Kirchhoff, B. (2002). *Schundroman*. Frankfurt.

Kroll, W. (ed.) (1989). *Catull*, 6th ed. Stuttgart.

Lankheit, K. (ed.) (1978). *Marc: Schriften*. Cologne.

Leduc-Adine, J.-P. (ed.) (1991). *Zola: Ecrits sur l'art*. Paris.

Marx, K. (1960). *Der achtzehnte Brumaire des Louis Bonaparte*, in K. Marx and F. Engels, *Werke*, vol. 8. Berlin, 111–207.

Mayer, R. (ed.) (1981). *Lucan, Civil War* VIII. Warminster.

Mayer, J. P., and Kerr, P. (eds.) (1970). *Alexis de Tocqueville: Recollections*, trans. G. Lawrence. Garden City, NJ.

Michelet, J. (1966–7). *Histoire de France, 1837–1867*, ed. C. Mettra. Lausanne.

(1952). *Histoire de la Révolution française* I & II, ed. G. Walter. Paris.

Montaigne, M. (2007 [1580]). "De l'amitié," in J. Balsamo and A. Legros (eds.), *Essais*. Paris, 189–202.

Montesquieu, C. L. de Secondat de (1951 [1748]). "De l'esprit des lois," in R. Caillois (ed.), *Œuvres complètes de Montesquieu*, vol. 2. Paris, 225–995.

(1949 [1721]). "Lettres persanes," in R. Caillois (ed.), *Œuvres complètes de Montesquieu*, vol. 1. Paris, 129–373.

Mynors, R. A. B. (ed.) (1969). *P. Vergili Maronis Opera*. Oxford.

(1990). *Virgil: Georgics*. Oxford.

Nisbet, R. G. M., and Hubbard, M. (eds.) (1975). *Horace: Odes Book 1*, corrected edition. Oxford.

Purnal, P., Thierry, J.-J., and Mélèze, J. (eds.) (1963). *Préface de Cromwell*, in *Théâtre complet de Victor Hugo* I. Paris, 409–54.

Seebacher, J., and Rosa, G. (eds.) (1987). *Oeuvres complètes de Victor Hugo*. Paris.

Skutsch, O. (ed.) (1985). *The Annals of Quintius Ennius*. Oxford.

Tarrant, R. J. (ed.) (2012). *Virgil. Aeneid Book* XII. Cambridge.

Thomas, R. F. (ed.) (1988). *Virgil: Georgics*, 2 vols. Cambridge.

Voltaire (1762). *Mahomet*. Brussels.

Watson, L. C. (ed.) (2003). *Horace's Epodes*. Oxford.

West, M. L. (ed.) (1978). *Hesiod: Works and Days*. Oxford.

Woodman, A. J. (ed.) (1983). *Velleius Paterculus: The Caesarian and Augustan Narrative (2.41–93)*. Cambridge.

Zemmour, E. (2014). *Le suicide français*. Paris.

References

Abdurraqib, H. (2017). "Johnny Cash Never Shot a Man in Reno. Or, The Migos: Nice Kids from the Suburbs," *National Post*, November 16: https://national post.com/entertainment/books/johnny-cash-never-shot-a-man-in-reno-or-t he-migos-nice-kids-from-the-suburbs.

Agamben, G. (2015). *Stasis: La guerra civile come paradigma politica.* Turin.

Ahl, F. (1976). *Lucan: An Introduction.* Ithaca, NY.

(1993). "Form Empowered: Lucan's *Pharsalia,*" in Boyle (1993a): 125–42.

Alfaro, M. J. M. (1996). "Intertextuality: Origins and Development of the Concept," *Atlantis* 18/1–2: 268–85.

Al Malik, A. (2013). *L'Islam au secours de la République.* Paris.

Alston, R., and Spentzou, E. (2011). *Reflections of Romanity: Discourses of Subjectivity in Imperial Rome,* Columbus, OH.

Ambuhl, A.-M. (2010). "Lucan's 'Iliupersis': Narrative Patterns from the Fall of Troy in Book 2 of the *Bellum Civile,*" in N. Hömke and C. Reitz (eds.), *Lucan's Bellum Civile Between Epic Tradition and Aesthetic Innovation.* Berlin, 17–38.

(2016). "Thessaly as an Intertextual Landscape of Civil War in Latin Poetry," in J. McInerney and I. Sluiter (eds.), *Valuing Landscape in Classical Antiquity.* Leiden, 297–322.

Anderson, B. (1983). *Imagined Communities: Reflections on the Origin and Spread of Nationalism.* London.

Ando, C. (2015). *Roman Social Imaginaries: Language and Thought in Contexts of Empire.* Toronto.

Ando, C. (ed.) (2016). *Citizenship and Empire in Europe 200–1900: The Antonine Constitution after 1800 Years.* Stuttgart.

André, J. (1993). *La Révolution fratricide: essai de psychanalyse du lien social.* Paris.

Antoine, A. (2003). *L'impensé de la démocratie: Tocqueville, la citoyenneté et la religion.* Paris.

Arasse, D. (1987). *La guillotine et l'imaginaire de la Terreur.* Paris. Translated into English as *The Guillotine and the Terror* (1989), trans. Christopher Miller, London.

Arendt, H. (1958). *The Human Condition.* Chicago.

(1963). *On Revolution.* London. Repr. 1965.

Armitage, D. (2017a). *Civil Wars: A History in Ideas.* New York.

(2017b). "On the Genealogy of Quarrels," *Critical Analysis of Law* 4/2: 178–89.

Armus, S. (2017). "Trying on the Veil: Sexual Autonomy and the End of the French Republic in Michel Houellebecq's *Submission,*" *French Politics, Culture & Society* 35/1: 126–45.

Arquillière, H.-X. (1934). *L'Augustinisme politique.* Paris.

Arum, E. (2020). "Machiavelli's *Principio*: Political Renewal and Innovation in the *Discourses on Livy,*" *The Review of Politics* 82/4: 525–47.

Ash, R. (2009). "Fission and Fusion: Shifting Roman Identities in the *Histories,*" in Woodman (2009): 85–99.

Ashcroft, B., Griffiths, G., and Tiffin, H. (1989). *The Empire Writes Back: Theory and Practice in Post-Colonial Literature.* London.

Asholt, W. (2016). "Vom Terrorismus zum Wandel durch Annäherung: Houellebecqs *Soumission,*" *Romanische Studien* 3: 119–36.

Auer, M. (2019). "Autonomie als Anlass: Die Ode zwischen politischer und literarischer Moderne," dissertation, Ludwig Maximilian University, Munich.

Auerbach, E. (1965). "Sermo humilis," in *Literary Language and Its Public*, trans. R. Manheim, ed. J. M. Ziolkowski. Princeton, NJ, 25–66. Orig. publ. in Auerbach, E. (1958). *Literatursprache und Publikum in der lateinischen Spätantike und im Mittelalter*. Bern.

(2016). *Mimesis und Figura*, ed. F. Balke and H. Engelmeier. Munich.

Austin, J. L. (1962). *How to Do Things with Words*. Cambridge, MA.

Badinter, E. (1984). *Émilie, Émilie: L'amibition féminine au XVIIIe siècle*. Paris.

(2010). *Le conflit: La mère et la femme*. Paris.

Baggesgaard, M. A. (2006). "The Complexities of Honesty: On the Prose of Michel Houellebecq," in Bowd (2010): 159–70.

Bandera, C. (1981). "Sacrificial Levels in Virgil's *Aeneid*," *Arethusa* 14: 217–39.

Bannon, C. (1997). *The Brothers of Romulus: Fraternal Pietas in Roman Law, Literature, and Society*. Princeton, NJ.

Barchiesi, A. (1994). "Rappresentazioni del dolore e interpretazione nell'*Eneide*," *Antike und Abendland* 40: 109–24.

Barchiesi, A., Rüpke, J., and Stephens, S. (eds.) (2004). *Rituals in Ink*. Stuttgart.

Barr, R. R. (1962). "The Two Cities in Saint Augustine," *Laval théologique et philosophique* 18: 211–29.

Barrera, G. (2021). *La guerre civile: Histoire, philosophie, politique*. Paris.

Barrett, A. (1999). *Agrippina: Sex, Power, and Politics in the Early Empire*. New Haven, CT.

Bartleson, J. (2017). "That Brutal Uncivilizer of Nations," *Critical Analysis of Law* 4/2: 153–59.

Bartsch, S. (ed.) (1994). *Actors in the Audience: Theatricality and Doublespeak from Nero to Hadrian*. Cambridge, MA.

(1997). *Ideology in Cold Blood: A Reading of Lucan's Civil War*. Cambridge, MA.

(2012). "The Art of Sincerity: Pliny's *Panegyricus*," in Rees (2012): 148–93. Orig. publ. in Bartsch (1994): 148–87.

(2015). *Persius: A Study in Food, Philosophy, and the Figural*. Chicago.

Bartsch, S. (trans.) (2021). *Vergil: The Aeneid*. New York.

Bartsch, S., and Elsner, J. (eds.) (2007). *Ekphrasis*, special vol. *Classical Philology* 102.

Bastiaensen, A. (2001). "Augustine's Pauline Exegesis and Ambrosiaster," in F. Van Fleteren and J. C. Schnaubelt (eds.), *Augustine: Biblical Exegete*. Pieterlin and Bern, 33–54.

Batinsky, E. E. (1993). "Julia in Lucan's Tripartite Vision of the Dead Republic," in M. DeForest (ed.), *Woman's Power, Man's Game: Essay on Classical Antiquity in Honor of Joy K. King*, Wauconda, IL, 264–78.

Batstone, W. (1997). "Virgilian Didaxis: Value and Meaning in the *Georgics*," in Martindale (1997): 125–44.

Beacham, R. C. (1999). *Spectacle Entertainments of Early Imperial Rome*. New Haven, CT.

Beard, M. (1993). "Looking (Harder) for Roman Myth: Dumézil, Declamation and Problems of Definition," in F. Graf (ed.), *Mythos in mythenloser Gesellschaft: Das Paradigma Roms*. Stuttgart, 44–64.

Bénichou, P. (1973). *Le sacre de l'écrivain 1750–1830: essai sur l'avènement d'un pouvoir spiritual laïque dans la France moderne.* Paris.

(1977). *Le Temps des prophètes: doctrines de l'âge romantique.* Paris.

Benjamin, W. (1982 [1927–1940]). *Gesammelte Schriften,* vol. 5, part 1: *5. Das Passagen-Werk* 1, Frankfurt.

Berest, A. (2015). *Recherche femme parfaite.* Paris.

Bettenworth, A. (2004). *Gastmahlszenen in der Antiken Epik von Homer bis Claudian.* Göttingen.

Beyer de Ryke, B. (1999). "L'apport augustinien: Augustin et l'augustinisme politique," in Renaut (1999): 43–86.

Bhatt, S. (2017). "The Augustan Principate and the Emergence of Biopolitics: A Comparative Historical Perspective," *Foucault Studies* 22: 72–93.

Binder, G. (1971). *Aeneas und Augustus: Interpretationen zum 8. Buch der Aeneis.* Meisenheim am Glan.

Blaschka, K. (2015). *Fiktion im Historischen. Die Bildsprache und die Konzeption der Charaktere in Lucans Bellum Civile.* Rahden.

Bloch, H. (1994). *God's Plagiarist: Being an Account of the Fabulous Industry and Irregular Commerce of the Abbé Migne.* Chicago.

Bloom, H. (1973). *The Anxiety of Influence.* New York.

Blössner, N. (2007). "The City-Soul Analogy," in G. R. F. Ferrari (ed.), *The Cambridge Companion to Plato's Republic.* Cambridge, 345–85.

Blumenberg, H. (1973). *Der Prozeß der theoretischen Neugierde.* Frankfurt.

(1988 [1959]). "Kritik und Rezeption antiker Philosophie in der Patristik," in V. Bohn (ed.), *Typologie: Internationale Beiträge zur Poetik.* Frankfurt.

Bochet, I. (2004). *"Le firmament de l'Écriture": l'herméneutique augustinienne.* Paris.

Boime, A. (1987). *Art in an Age of Revolution, 1750–1800,* vol. 1: *Social History of Modern Art.* Chicago.

Bömer, F. (ed.) (1986). *P. Ovidius Naso: Metamorphosen, Buch XIV–XV.* Heidelberg.

Börm, H., and Havener, W. (2012). "Octavians Rechtsstellung im Januar 27 v. Chr. und das Problem der 'Übertragung' der *res publica,*" *Historia. Zeitschrift für alte Geschichte* 61/2: 202–20.

Börm, H., Mattheis, M., and Wienand, J. (eds.) (2016). *Civil War in Ancient Greece and Rome: Contexts of Disintegration and Reintegration.* Stuttgart.

Borrutta, M. (2010). *Antikatholizismus, Deutschland und Italien im Zeitalter der europäischen Kulturkämpfe.* Göttingen.

Bossuet, J. (1694). *Maximes et réflexions sur la comédie.* Paris.

Bowd, G. (2010). *Le monde de Houellebecq.* Glasgow.

Boyle, A. J. (1986). *The Chaonian Dove: Studies in the Eclogues, Georgics, and Aeneid of Virgil.* Leiden.

Boyle, A. J. (ed.) (1993a). *Roman Epic.* London.

Boyle, A. J. (1993b). "Introduction: The Roman Song," in Boyle (1993a): 1–18.

(1993c). "The Canonic Text: Virgil's *Aeneid,*" in Boyle (1993a): 79–107.

(1999). "*Aeneid* 8: Images of Rome," in Perkell (1999): 148–61.

Bramble, J. C. (1983). "Lucan," in E. J. Kenney (ed.), *Cambridge History of Latin Literature*, vol. 2.4. Cambridge, 37–61. Orig. publ. 1982.

Braund, S. (2012). "Praise and Protreptic in Early Imperial Panegyric," in Rees (2012): 85–108.

Bredekamp, H. (2012). *Thomas Hobbes, der Leviathan: das Urbild des modernen Staates und seine Gegenbilder. 1651 – 2001*. Berlin.

Breed, B., Damon, C., and Rossi, A. (2010). *Citizens of Discord: Rome and Its Civil Wars*. Oxford.

Briant, P. (2012). *Alexandre des lumières: fragments d'histoire européenne*. Paris.

Brier, B. (2016). *Cleopatra's Needles: The Lost Obelisks of Egypt*. London.

Bright, P. (ed. and trans.) (1999). *Augustine and the Bible*. Notre Dame, IN.

Brombert, V. (1984). *Victor Hugo and the Visionary Novel*. Cambridge.

Brooks, C. (1984). "'Recalled to Life': The Christian Myth of *A Tale of Two Cities*," in *Signs of the Times: Symbolic Realism in the Mid-Victorian World*. London, 84–95.

Brooks, P. (2008). "Death in the First Person," *South Atlantic Quarterly* 107/3: 530–46.

Brown, P. R. L. (1967). *Augustine of Hippo*. Berkeley, CA.

(1972). "Political Society," in R. A. Markus (ed.), *Augustine: A Collection of Critical Essays*. New York, 311–29.

(2012). *Through the Eye of a Needle: Wealth, The Fall of Rome, and the Making of Christianity in the West, 350–550 A.D.* Princeton, NJ.

Bruère, R. T. (1951). "Lucan's Cornelia," *Classical Philology* 46: 221–36.

Bruggisser, P. (1987). *Romulus servianus: la légende de Romulus dans les commentaires de Virgile de Servius: mythographie et idéologie à l'époque de la dynastie Théodosienne*. Bonn.

Burton, P. (2012). "Augustine and Language," in Vessey (2012): 113–24.

Bynum, C. W. (1984). *Jesus as Mother: Studies in the Spirituality of the High Middle Ages*. Berkeley, CA.

Cameron, A. (1977). "Paganism and Literature in Late Fourth Century Rome," in *Christianisme et formes littéraires de l'antiquité tardive en Occident: huit exposés suivis de discussions*, Entretiens sur l'antiquité classique 23 (Geneva), 1–40.

Cameron, M. (1999). "The Christological Substructure of Augustine's Exegesis," in Bright (1999): 74–103.

(2012). *Christ Meets Me Everywhere: Augustine's Early Figurative Exegesis*. Oxford.

Campion, P. (2004). "Raisons de la littérature: *Quatrevingt-treize* de Victor Hugo," *Romantisme* 124/2: 103–14.

Cantarella, E. (1995). "Marzia e la locatio ventris," in R. Raffaelli (ed.), *Vicende e figure femminili in Grecia e a Roma. Atti del Convegno Pesaro, 28–30 aprile 1994*. Ancona, 251–58.

Caputo, J. D. (2012). "Augustine and Postmodernism," in Vessey (2012): 492–504.

Caputo, J. D. and Scanlon, M. J. (eds.) (2005). *Augustine and Postmodernism: Confessions and Circumfession*. Bloomington, IN.

Cary, P. (2005). "United Inwardly by Love: Augustine's Social Ontology," in Doody, Hughes, and Paffenroth (2005): 3–33.

Catani, D. (2011). "The French Revolution: Historical Necessity or Historical Evil? Terror and Slavery in Hugo's *Quatrevingt-treize* and Confiant's *L'Archet du colonel*," in D. Evans and K. Griffiths (eds.), *Institutions and Power in Nineteenth-Century French Literature and Culture*. Amsterdam, 51–67.

Celotto, G. (2015). "Lucan's Influence on Tacitus' Account of the Civil War between Otho and Vitellius." Classical Association of the Mid-Western States (abstract at camws.org/sites/default/files/meeting2015/Abstracts2015/033.LucanonTacitus.pdf).

Chamarat-Malandain, G. (1991). "Voix et parole du peuple dans *Quatrevingt-treize*," in André Peyronie (ed.), *Révolution française, peuple et littératures: images du peuple révolutionnaire, théâtralité sans frontières. Actes du XXIIe Congrès de la Société Française de Littérature Générale et Comparée (Nantes-Angers 1989)*. Paris.

(2005). "Langue, parole et savoir dans *Quatrevingt-treize*," in F. Naugrette and G. Rosa (eds.), *Victor Hugo et la langue*. Bréal, 279–97.

Chaplin, J. D. (2000). *Livy's Exemplary History*. Oxford.

Chew, K. (2002). "Ignorance and Aeneas' Identity in the 'Aeneid'," *Latomus* 61/3: 616–27.

Chiu, A. (2010). "The Importance of Being Julia: Civil War, Historical Revision, and the Mutable Past in Lucan's *Pharsalia*," *Classical Journal* 105/4: 343–60.

Cho, M.-A. (1998). "La théorie des deux cités et le pouvoir politique selon saint Augustin," in Jehasse and McKenna (1998): 11–16.

Christgau, R. (2006). "The Psychological Crafts of Marshall Bruce Mathers III," *The Believer*, February: www.robertchristgau.com/xg/music/eminem-06.php.

Citroni, M. (2015). "La vittoria e il tempio: interpretazione del proemio al iii libro delle *Georgiche*," in Fedeli and Günther (2015): 39–88.

Classen, C. J. (1991). "*Virtutes Imperatoriae*," *Arctos* 25: 17–39.

Coates, T.-N. (2013) "Hip-hop Speaks to the Guns." *New York Times*, February 6: www.nytimes.com/2013/02/07/opinion/coates-hip-hop-speaks-to-the-guns.html.

Compagnon, A. (2005). *Les antimodernes: de Joseph de Maistre à Roland Barthes*. Paris.

Connolly, J. (2015). *The Life of Roman Republicanism*. Princeton, NJ.

(2017). "The Romans Tried to Save the Republic from Men like Trump. They Failed." *Village Voice*, January 17.

Connors, C. (1998). *Petronius the Poet: Verse and Literary Tradition in the Satyricon*. Cambridge.

Conte, G. B. (1986). *The Rhetoric of Imitation: Genre and Poetic Memory in Virgil and Other Latin Poets*, trans. and ed. C. Segal. Ithaca, NY.

(1988). *La "guerra civile" di Lucano: studi e prove di commento*. Urbino.

(1992). "Proems in the Middle." *Yale Classical Studies* 29: 147–59.

Cornwell, H. (2017). *Pax and the Politics of Peace: Republic to Principate.* Oxford.

Cramer, T. (2005). "Das Subjekt und sein Widerschein. Beobachtung zum Wandel der Spiegelmetapher in Antike und Mittelalter," in M. Bausch (ed.), *Inszenierungen von Subjektivität in der Literatur des Mittelalters.* Königstein, 213–29.

Creuzer, F. (1837). *Symbolik und Mythologie der alten Völker, besonders der Griechen,* vol. 3. Leipzig.

Curtius, E. R. (2013). *European Literature and the Latin Middles Ages.* Princeton, NJ.

Dahlmann, H. (1954). *Der Bienenstaat in Vergils Georgica.* Mainz.

Damon, C. (2015). *Studies on the Text of Caesar's Bellum Civile.* Oxford.

De Bruyn, T. (1993). "Ambivalences within a Totalizing Discourse: Augustine's Sermons on the Sack of Rome," *Journal of Early Christian Studies* 1: 405–21.

De Maistre, J. (1884). "Éclaircissement sur les Sacrifices," in *Oeuvres complètes de J. de Maistre.* New edition, vol. 5. Lyon, 283–360.

De Man, P. (1979). *Allegories of Reading.* New Haven, CT.

Della Corte, F. (ed.) (1984–91). *Enciclopedia Virgiliana,* 6 vols. Florence.

Denby, D. (1997). "Civil War, Revolution and Justice in Victor Hugo's *Quatrevingt-treize,*" *Romance Studies* 15/2: 7–17.

Derrida, J. (1994). *Politique de l'amitié.* Paris.

(1998). *Demeure: Maurice Blanchot.* Paris.

(2000). *Demeure: Fiction and Testimony.* Stanford, CA.

Dilmac, B. (2014). "Houellebecq's 'Fin de Siècle': Crisis of Society, Crisis of the Novel: Thematic and Poetological Intertextuality between Michel Houellebecq and Joris-Karl Huysmans," in D. Landgraf (ed.), *Decadence in Literature and Intellectual Debate Since 1945.* New York, 153–69.

Dodaro, R. (2004). *Christ and the Just Society in the Thought of Augustine.* Cambridge.

(2012). "Augustine on the Statesman and the Two Cities," in Vessey (2012): 386–97.

D'Onofrio, C. (1967). *Gli obelischi di Roma.* Rome.

Doody, J., Hughes, K. L., and Paffenroth, K. (2005). *Augustine and Politics.* Lanham, MD.

Drinkwater, M. O. (2013). "*Militia amoris*: Fighting in Love's Army," in T. S. Thorsen (ed.), *The Cambridge Companion to Latin Love Elegy.* Cambridge, 194–206.

Drumont, E. (1886). *La France juive devant l'opinion.* Paris.

Dworkin, A. (1981). *Pornography: Men Possessing Women.* London.

Dyson, J. (1996). "Caesi Iuvenci and Pietas Impia in Virgil," *The Classical Journal* 91/3: 277–86.

(2001). *King of the Wood: The Sacrificial Victor in Virgil's Aeneid.* Norman, OK.

Earl, D. C. (1961). *The Political Thought of Sallust.* Cambridge.

(1967). *The Moral and Political Tradition of Rome.* Ithaca, NY.

Eco, U. (2006). "Excess and History in Hugo's *Ninety-three,*" in F. Moretti (ed.), *The Novel,* vol. 2, *Forms and Themes.* Princeton, NJ, 274–94.

Edmunds, L. (1992). *From a Sabine Jar: Reading Horace, Odes 1.9*. Chapel Hill, NC.

Edwards, C. (1993). *The Politics of Immorality in Ancient Rome*. Cambridge.

Edwards, C. (ed.) (1999). *Roman Presences: Receptions of Rome in European Culture, 1789–1945*. Cambridge.

Edwards, C. (2007). *Death in Ancient Rome*. New Haven, CT.

Elm, S. (1996). *The Virgins of God: The Making of Asceticism in Late Antiquity*. Oxford.

(2017). "Signs under the Skin: Flogging Eternal Rome," in I. Därmann and T. Macho (eds.), *Unter die Haut: Tätowierungen als Logo- und Piktogramme*. Paderborn, 51–75.

Elshtain, J. B. (1995). *Augustine and the Limits of Politics*. South Bend, IN.

Engels, D. (2013). *Le déclin: la crise de l'Union européenne et la chute de la République romaine: quelques analogies historiques*. Paris.

Esposito, R. (2011). *Immunitas: The Protection and Negation of Life*, trans. A. Hanafi. Cambridge, MA. Orig. publ. 2002.

Fagen, L. (2017). "Kendrick Lamar goes back to Bangers." *Hyperallergic*, July 22: https://hyperallergic.com/391650/kendrick-lamar-goes-back-to-bangers/.

Fantham, E. (1985). "Caesar and the Mutiny: Lucan's Reshaping of the Historical Tradition in *De bello civili* 5.237–373," *Classical Philology* 80: 119–31.

(1989) "Allecto's First Victim: A Study of Vergil's Amata," in Stahl (1998): 135–53.

(2010). "*Discordia Fratrum*: Aspects of Lucan's Conception of Civil War", in B. W. Breed, C. Damon, and A. Rossi (eds.), *Citizens of Discord: Rome and Its Civil Wars*. Oxford, 207–20.

Farrell, J., and Nelis, D. (eds.) (2013). *Augustan Poetry and the Roman Republic*. Oxford.

Farrell, J., and Putnam, M. C. J. (eds.) (2010). *A Companion to Virgil's Aeneid and Its Tradition*. Malden, MA.

Favier, J. (1971). *Finance et fiscalité au bas Moyen Âge*. Paris.

Fedeli, P., and Günther, H.-C. (eds.) (2015). *Studies on Vergil in Honour of Mario Geymonat (26.1.1941–17. 2.2012)*. Nordhausen.

Feeney, D. C. (1984). "The Reconciliations of Juno," *Classical Quarterly* NS 34: 179–94.

(1991). *The Gods in Epic*. Oxford.

(1998). *Literature and Religion at Rome*. Cambridge.

(2004). "Sacrificial Ritual in Roman Poetry," in Barchiesi, Rüpke, and Stephens (2004): 1–22.

(2017). "Carthage and Rome: An Introduction," *Classical Philology* 112/3: 301–11.

Feldherr, A. (ed.) (2009). *The Cambridge Companion to the Roman Historians*. Cambridge.

(2014). "Viewing Myth and History on the Shield of Aeneas," *Classical Antiquity* 33/2: 281–318.

Felman, S. (1981). "Rereading Femininity," *Yale French Studies* 62: 19–44.

Ferguson, P. P. (1994). *Paris as Revolution: Writing the Nineteenth-Century City.* Berkeley, CA.

(1998). "*Quatrevingt-treize*: Turning the Terror to Account," in R. T. Denommé and R. H. Simon (eds.), *Unfinished Revolutions: Legacies of Upheaval in Modern French Culture.* University Park, PA.

Ferrari, G. R. F. (2005). *City and Soul in Plato's Republic.* Chicago.

Fertik, H. (2018). "Obligation and Devotion: Creating a New Community in Lucan's *Bellum Civile*," *Classical Philology* 113: 449–71.

(2019). *The Ruler's House: Contesting Power and Privacy in Julio-Claudian Rome.* Baltimore, MD.

Flower, H. (2006). *The Art of Forgetting: Disgrace and Oblivion in Roman Political Culture*, Chapel Hill, NC.

(2010). *Roman Republics.* Princeton, NJ.

Fögen, M. T. (2002). *Römische Rechtsgeschichten: Über Ursprung und Evolution eines sozialen Systems.* Göttingen.

Fomin, A. (1977). "*Theatrum Philosophicum*," in *Language, Counter-Memory, Practice: Selected Essays and Interviews*, trans. D. F. Bouchard and S. Simon. Ithaca, NY, 165–96.

(2016). "Speeches in Dio Cassius," in C. J. Lange and J. M. Madsen (eds.), *Cassius Dio: Greek Intellectual and Roman Politician.* Leiden, 217–37.

Fowler, D. P. (1987). "Vergil on Killing Virgins," in M. Whitby *et al.* (eds.), *Homo Viator: Essays for John Bramble.* Bristol, 185–98.

(1990). "Deviant Focalization in Vergil's *Aeneid*," *Proceedings of the Cambridge Philological Society* 216: 42–63.

(1995). "Horace and the Aesthetics of Politics," in S. J. Harrison (ed.), *Homage to Horace: A Bimillenary Celebration.* Oxford, 248–66.

(1998). "Opening the Gates of War: *Aeneid* 7.601–640," in Stahl (1998): 155–74.

(2000). *Roman Constructions: Readings in Postmodern Latin.* Oxford.

Frank, T., Koschorke, A., Lüdemann, S., and Matala de Mazza, E. (2002). *Des Kaisers neue Kleider: Über das Imaginäre politischer Herrschaft.* Frankfurt.

Freccero, J. (1975). "The Fig Tree and the Laurel: Petrarch's Poetics," *Diacritics* 5/1: 34–40.

(1986). *Dante: The Poetics of Conversion.* Cambridge, MA.

Freudenburg, K. (2001). *Satires of Rome: Threatening Poses from Lucilius to Juvenal.* Cambridge.

Freudenburg, K. (ed.) (2005). *The Cambridge Companion to Roman Satire.* Cambridge.

Freudenburg, K. (2014). "*Recusatio* as Political Theatre: Horace's Letter to Augustus," *Journal of Roman Studies* 104: 105–32.

(2018a). "Donald Trump and Rome's Mad Emperors," *Common Dreams*, April 29.

(2018b). "Donald Trump and the Tiberian Lie," *Common Dreams*, December 4.

Frisch, A. (2018). "Emotional Justice in Agrippa d'Aubigné's *Tragiques*," *Forum for Modern Language Studies* 54/1: 73–84.

Fuhrer, T. (2004). *Augustinus.* Darmstadt.

(2011). "Krieg und (Un-)Gerechtigkeit. Augustin zu Ursache und Sinn von Kriegen," in M. Formisano and H. Böhme (eds.), *War in Words: Transformation of War from Antiquity to Clausewitz*. Berlin, 23–36.

Fuhrmann, M. (1959). "Proscriptio," in *Paulys Realencyclopädie der classischen Altertumswissenschaft*, vol. 23.2. Stuttgart, 2439–44.

Fumaroli, M. (2001). "Les abeilles et les araignées," in A.-M. Lecoq (ed.), *La querelle des anciens et des modernes: XVIIe–XVIIIe siècles*. Paris, 7–218.

Funkenstein, A. (1965). *Heilsplan und natürliche Entwicklung: Formen der Gegenwartsbestimmung im Geschichtsdenken des hohen Mittelalters*. Munich.

Gadamer, H.-G. (1975). *Truth and Method*. London.

Gagliardi, D. (1987). "Il banchetto in Lucano (note a Phars. 10.104–71)," *Studi Italiani di Filologia Classica* 5: 186–92.

Gale, M. R. (2000). *Virgil on the Nature of Things*. Cambridge.

(2003). "Poetry and the Backward Glance in Virgil's 'Georgics' and 'Aeneid'," *Transactions of the American Philological Association* 133/2: 323–52.

(2013). "Virgil's Caesar: Intertextuality and Ideology," in Farrell and Nelis (2013): 278–96.

Gauvard, C., de Libera, A., and Zink, M. (2004). *Dictionnaire du Moyen Âge*. Paris.

Geue, T. (2018). "Soft Hands, Hard Power: Sponging Off the Empire of Leisure (Virgil, *Georgics* 4)," *Journal of Roman Studies* 108: 115–40.

Gill, C. (2006). *The Structured Self in Hellenistic and Roman Thought*. Oxford.

Gillis, D. (1983). *Eros and Death in the Aeneid*. Rome.

Ginsberg, L. D. (2011). "*Ingens* as an Etymological Pun in the *Octavia*," *Classical Philology* 106/4: 357–60.

(2017a). *Staging Memory, Staging Strife: Empire and Civil War in the Octavia*. Oxford.

(2017b). "Ut et hostem amarem: Jocasta and the Poetics of Civil War in Seneca's *Phoenissae*," in C. Trinacty and M. Sampson (eds.), *Verba Aliter Instructa: Senecan Poetics*, special volume on Senecan poetics. *Ramus* 46/1–2: 58–74.

Ginsberg, L. D., and Krasne, D. A. (eds.) (2018). *After 69 CE: Writing Civil War in Flavian Rome*. Trends in Classics, supplementary vol. 65. Berlin.

Girard, R. (1972). *La violence et le sacré*. Paris.

Giusti, E. (2018). *Carthage in Virgil's Aeneid: Staging the Enemy under Augustus*. Cambridge.

Gohin, Y. (2002). "Alternance et adherence des contraires dans *Quatrevingt-treize*," in J. A. Hiddleston (ed.), *Victor Hugo: romancier de l'abîme*. Oxford, 156–78.

Gorman, R. J., and Gorman, V. B. (2014). *Corrupting Luxury in Ancient Greek Literature*. Ann Arbor, MI.

Götze, K.-H. (2016). "Sind wir noch zu retten? Überlegungen zur Kulturkritik und Handlungsstruktur in Houellebecqs Unterwerfung," in *Lendemains: Etudes Comparées sur la France / Vergleichende Frankreichforschung* 41: 239–50.

Govrin, J. (2016). *Sex, Gott und Kapital: Houellebecqs "Unterwerfung" zwischen neoreaktionärer Rhetorik und postsäkularen Politiken*. Münster.

Gowing, A. M. (2005). *Empire and Memory: The Representation of the Roman Republic in Imperial Culture.* Cambridge.

(2013). "Afterword," in Farrell and Nelis (2013): 319–32.

Gransden, K. W. (1985). "The Fall of Troy," *Greece and Rome* 32: 60–72.

Grewing, F., and Acosta-Hughes, B. (eds.) (2013). *The Door Ajar: False Closure in Classical Antiquity.* Heidelberg.

Griffin, J. (1985). *Latin Poets and Roman Life.* London.

Grossman, K. (2012). *The Later Novels of Victor Hugo: Variations on the Politics and Poetics of Transcendence.* Oxford.

Gruen, E. (2011). *Rethinking the Other in Antiquity.* Princeton, NJ.

Gurval, R. A. (1995). *Actium and Augustus: The Politics and Emotions of Civil War.* Ann Arbor, MI.

Haarhoff, T. J. (1960). "Vergil and Cornelius Gallus," *Classical Philology* 55: 101–8.

Habinek, T. (1990). "Sacrifice, Society, and Vergil's Ox-Born Bees," in M. Griffith and D. J. Mastronarde (eds.), *Cabinet of the Muses.* Atlanta, 209–23.

Haecker, T. (1931). *Vergil: Vater des Abendlands.* Olten.

Hagendahl, H. (1967). *Augustine and the Latin Classics,* 2 vols. Stockholm.

Hall, J. M. (1997). *Ethnic Identity in Greek Antiquity.* Cambridge.

Hamilton, J. F. (1994). "Terrorizing the 'Feminine' in Hugo, Dickens, and France," *Symposium* 48.3: 204–15.

Hamilton, J. T. (2013). *Security: Politics, Humanity, and the Philology of Care.* Princeton, NJ.

Hammer, D. (2014). *Roman Political Thought: From Cicero to Augustine.* Cambridge.

Hampton, T. (1993). "'Turkish Dogs': Rabelais, Erasmus, and the Rhetoric of Alterity," *Representations* 41: 58–82.

Harder, H. (2018). "Finding Fulfillment through Submission, or How the French Should Stop Worrying and Learn to Love Islam: Michel Houellebecq's *Soumission,*" in Peer, L. H. (ed.), *Transgressive Romanticism.* Newcastle upon Tyne, 76–91.

Hardie, P. (1986). *Virgil's Aeneid: Cosmos and Imperium.* Oxford.

(1993). *The Epic Successors of Virgil: A Study in the Dynamics of a Tradition.* Cambridge.

(2013). "Trojan Palimpsests: The Archaeology of Roman History in *Aeneid* 2," in Farrell and Nelis (2013): 107–23.

(2014). *The Last Cultural Hero: A Cultural History of Virgil's Aeneid.* New York.

(2018). "Augustan and Late Antique Intratextuality: Virgil's *Aeneid* and Prudentius' *Psychomachia,*" in Harrison, Frangoulides, and Papanghelis (2018): 159–70.

Hardt, M., and Negri, A. (2000). *Empire.* Cambridge, MA.

Harich-Schwarzbauer, H., and Pollmann, K. (eds.) (2013). *Der Fall Roms und seine Wiederauferstehungen in Antike und Mittelalter.* Berlin.

Harris, W. (2001). *Restraining Rage: The Ideology of Anger Control in Antiquity.* Cambridge, MA.

Harrison, S. J. (1990a). "Some Views of the Aeneid in the Twentieth Century," in Harrison (1990b): 1–20.

Harrison, S. J. (ed.) (1990b). *Oxford Readings in Vergil's Aeneid*. Oxford.

Harrison, S. J., Frangoulides, S., and Papanghelis, T. D. (eds.) (2018). *Intratextuality and Latin Literature*. Berlin.

Haverkamp, A. (2000). "Allegorie," in K. Barck, M. Fontius, D. Schlenstedt, B. Steinwachs, and F. Wolfzettel (eds.), *Ästhetische Grundbegriffe*, vol. 1. Stuttgart, 49–103.

(2004). *Latenzzeit*. Berlin.

(2009). *Metaphorologie. Zur Praxis von Theorie*. Frankfurt.

Hawkins, P. S. (1975). "Polemical Counterpoint in *De Civitate Dei*," *Augustinian Studies* 6: 97–106.

Heil, A. (2007). "Christliche Deutung der Eklogen Vergils. Die Tityre-Initiale im Codex Klosterneuburg CCl 742," *Antike und Abendland* 53: 100–19.

Heinze, R. (1915). *Virgils Epische Technik*, 2nd ed. Leipzig.

(1993). *Virgil's Epic Technique*, trans. of Heinze 1915 by H. Harvey, D. Harvey, and F. Robertson. Berkeley, CA.

Hellegouarc'h, J. (1963). *Le vocabulaire latin des relations et des partis politiques sous la république*. Paris.

Henderson, J. (1987). "Lucan: The Word at War," *Ramus* 16: 122–64.

(1998). *Fighting for Rome: Poets and Caesars, History and Civil War*. Cambridge.

Henry, P. (1994). "Kénose," in *Supplément au Dictionnaire de la Bible*. Paris.

Hershkowitz, D. (1998). *The Madness of Epic: Reading Insanity from Homer to Lucan*. Oxford.

Heyking, J. von (2001). *Augustine and Politics as Longing in the World*. Columbia, MO.

Hill, T. (2004). *Ambitiosa Mors: Suicide and Self in Roman Thought and Literature*. New York.

Hinds, S. (1998). *Allusion and Intertext: Dynamics of Appropriation in Roman Poetry*. Cambridge.

Hofmann, F. (1933). *Der Kirchenbegriff des heiligen Augustinus in seinen Grundlagen und in seiner Entwicklung*. Munich.

Hollander, A. (1994). *Sex and Suits*. New York.

Hollingworth, M. (2010). *The Pilgrim City: St Augustine of Hippo and His Innovation in Political Thought*. London.

Holsclaw, G. (2016). *Transcending Subjects: Augustine, Hegel, and Theology*. Chichester.

Horne, A. J. (2018). "Georgic Justice," *Vergilius* 64: 3–29.

Horsfall, N. (1995). *A Companion to the Study of Virgil*. Leiden.

Huet, V. (1999). "Napoleon I: A New Augustus?" in C. Edwards (ed.), *Roman Presences: Receptions of Rome in European Culture, 1789–1945*. Cambridge, 53–69.

Hugedé, N. (1957). *La métaphore du miroir dans les épîtres de saint Paul aux Corinthiens*. Paris.

Hunt, L. (1993). *The Family Romance of the French Revolution*. Berkeley, CA.

Huntington, S. P. (1996). *The Clash of Civilizations and the Remaking of World Order*. New York.

Hussey, A. (2010). "*Présence humaine*: Michel Houellebecq, poet-chansonnier," in Bowd (2010): 59–70.

Huysmans, J.-K. (1977 [1884]). *A rebours*, ed. M. Fumaroli. Paris.

Inglebert, H. (1996). *Les Romains chrétiens face à l'histoire de Rome. Histoire, chistianisme et romanité en Occident dans l'Antiquité tardive.* Paris.

(2016). "Christian Reflections on Roman Citizenship (200–430)," in Ando (2016): 99–112.

Jal, P. (1962). "Le rôle des Barbares dans les guerres civiles de Rome, de Sylla à Vespasien," *Latomus* 21: 8–48.

(1963). *La Guerre civile à Rome. Étude littéraire et morale.* Paris.

James, S. (1995). "Establishing Rome with the Sword: *Condere* in the *Aeneid*," *American Journal of Philology* 116/4: 623–37.

Jauss, H. R. (1978). *Toward an Aesthetic of Reception.* Minneapolis.

Jehasse, J., and McKenna, A. (eds.) (1998). *Religion et Politique: Les avatars de l'augustinisme.* Saint-Étienne.

Johnson, P. J. (2008). *Ovid before Exile: Art and Punishment in the "Metamorphoses,"* Madison, WI.

Johnson, W. R. (1965). "Aeneas and the Ironies of *Pietas*," *Classical Journal* 60: 360–4.

(1976). *Darkness Visible: A Study of Vergil's Aeneid.* Berkeley, CA.

(1987). *Momentary Monsters: Lucan and His Heroes.* Ithaca, NY.

Johnston, P. A. (1977). "Eurydice and Proserpina in the *Georgics*," *Transactions of the American Philological Association* 107: 161–72.

(1980). *Virgil's Agricultural Golden Age: A Study of the Georgics.* Leiden.

Joseph, T. A. (2012). *Tacitus the Epic Successor: Virgil, Lucan and the Narrative of Civil War in the Histories.* Leiden.

Josephson, M. (1942). *Victor Hugo: A Realistic Biography of the Great Romantic.* Garden City, NY.

Joshel, S. R. (2002). "The Body Female and the Body Politic: Livy's Lucretia and Verginia," in L. K. McClure (ed.), *Sexuality and Gender in the Classical World.* Oxford, 163–87.

Junkerjürgen, R. (2009). *Haarfarben: Eine Kulturgeschichte in Europa seit der Antike.* Cologne.

Kallendorf, C. (1989). *In Praise of Aeneas: Virgil and Epideictic Rhetoric in the Early Renaissance.* Hanover, NH.

Kalyvas, S. N. (2006). *The Logic of Violence in Civil War.* Cambridge.

Kantorowicz, E. H. (1957). *The King's Two Bodies: A Study in Medieval Political Theology.* Princeton, NJ.

Kapust, D. J. (2011). *Republicanism, Rhetoric, and Roman Political Thought: Sallust, Livy, and Tacitus.* Cambridge.

(2018). "The Founders Hated Excessive Flattery. What Would They Think about the Trump Administration?" *Washington Post*, January 22.

Kasper, J., and Wild, C. (2015). *Rom rückwärts: Europäische Übertragungsschicksale.* Paderborn.

Kaster, R. (1988). *The Guardians of Language.* Berkeley, CA.

Keitel, E. (2010). "The Art of Losing: Tacitus and the Disaster Narrative," in C. S. Kraus, J. Marincola, and C. Pelling (eds.), *Ancient Historiography and Its Contexts: Studies in Honour of A. J. Woodman* (Oxford), 331–52.

Keith, A. (2018). "Engendering Civil War in Flavian Epic," in Ginsberg and Krasne (2018): 295–320.

Kennedy, D. (1992). "'Augustan' and 'Anti-Augustan': Reflections on Terms of Reference," in A. Powell (ed.), *Roman Poetry and Propaganda in the Age of Augustus*. London, 26–58.

Keyser, P. T. (2020). *Recovering a Late-Antique Edition of Pliny's Natural History*. New York.

Kienast, D. (1969). "Augustus und Alexander," *Gymnasium* 76: 430–56.

Kimmerle, N. (2015). *Lucan und der Prinzipat. Inkonsistenz und unzuverlässiges Erzählen im "Bellum Civile."* Berlin.

King, P. (2014). "Augustine on Language," in Meconi and Stump (2014): 292–310.

Kittsteiner, D. (1991). *Die Entstehung des modernen Gewissens.* Frankfurt.

Knauer, G. N. (1964). *Die Aeneis und Homer.* Göttingen.

Knobloch, C. (2016). "Houellebecqs Unterwerfung als kulturkritische Diskursanalyse gelesen," *Lendemains: Etudes Comparées sur la France / Vergleichende Frankreichforschung* 41: 251–63.

Kölmel, W. (1970). *Regimen Christianum: Weg und Ergebnisse des Gewaltenverhältnisses und Gewaltenverständnisses (8. bis 14. Jahrhundert).* Berlin.

Komorowska, A. (2016). "'Mais c'est d'une ambigüité étrange': die Rezeption von Michel Houellebecqs Roman 'Soumission' in Frankreich und Deutschland," *Romanische Studien* 3: 137–69.

Konstan, D. (1977). *Catullus' Indictment of Rome: The Meaning of Catullus 64.* Amsterdam.

(2018). "Praise and Flattery in the Latin Epic: A Case of Intertextuality," in Harrison, Frangoulides, and Papanghelis (2018): 341–52.

Koppenfels, M. von (2012). *Schwarzer Peter: Der Fall Littell, die Leser und die Täter.* Göttingen.

Kopperschmidt, J. (1990). *Rhetorik und Theodizee: Studie zur hermeneutischen Funktionalität der Rhetorik bei Augustin.* Darmstadt.

Koschorke, A., Lüdemann, S., Frank, T., and Matala de Mazza, E. (2007). *Der fiktive Staat: Konstruktionen des politischen Körpers in der Geschichte Europas.* Frankfurt.

Koselleck, R. (2004). *Futures Past: On the Semantics of Historical Time*, trans. K. Tribe. New York.

Kraus, C. S. (1991). "*Initium turbandi omnia a femina ortum est*: Fabia Minor and the Election of 367 B.C.," *Phoenix* 45/4: 314–25.

Kristeva, J. (1980a). *Pouvoir de l'horreur: Essai sur l'abjection.* Paris.

(1980b). "The Bounded Text," in *Desire in Language: A Semiotic Approach to Literature and Art.* New York, 36–63.

(1980c). "Word, Dialogue and Novel," in *Desire in Language: A Semiotic Approach to Literature and Art.* New York, 64–91.

(1982). *Powers of Horror: An Essay on Abjection.* New York.

(1989). *Etrangers à nous-mèmes.* Paris.

Krulic, B. (2011). "Une lecture théologico-politique de l'idée démocratique: Edgar Quinet." www.dogma.lu.

La Bonnaridière, A.-M. (1999). "Augustine's Biblical Initiation," in Bright (1999): 5–25.

La Bua, G. (2013). "Horace's East: Ethics and Politics." *Harvard Studies in Classical Philology* 107: 265–96.

Lacchè, L. (2016). "Expanding Citizenship? The French Experience Surrounding the Code Napoléon," in Ando (2016): 177–98.

Lachmann, R. (1990). *Gedächtnis und Literatur: Intertextualität in der russischen Moderne*. Frankfurt.

Lammel, I. (2015). *Der Toussaint-Louverture-Mythos: Transformationen in der französischen Literatur, 1791–2012*. Bielefeld.

Lange, C. H. (2009). *Res Publica Constituta*. Leiden.

(2013). "Triumph and Civil War in the Late Republic," *Papers of the British School at Rome* 81: 67–90.

(2016a). Review of Börm, Mattheis, and Wienand (2016), *The Classical Review* 66.2: 502–4; long version available at www.academia.edu/18710216/Review_of_Börm_H._Mattheis_M._and_Wienand_J._eds._2015_Civil_War_in_A ncient_Greece_and_Rome_Contexts_of_Disintegration_and_Reintegratio n_Stuttgart_Steiner_The_Classical_Review_forthcoming_long_version (accessed Jan. 25, 2016).

(2016b). *Triumphs in the Age of Civil War: The Late Republic and the Adaptability of Triumphal Tradition*. London.

(2017). "*Stasis* and *Bellum Civile*: A Difference in Scale?," *Critical Analysis of Law* 4/1: 129–40.

(2019). "Augustus, the *Res Gestae*, and the End of Civil War: Unpleasant Events?" in Lange and Vervaet (2019a): 185–209.

Lange, C., and Vervaet, F. (eds.) (2019a). *The Historiography of Late Republican Civil War*. Leiden: 263–91.

(2019b). "Sulla and the Origins of the Concept of *Bellum Civile*," in Lange and Vervaet (2019a): 17–28.

Lange, K. (1966). "Geistliche Speise: Untersuchungen zur Metaphorik der Bibelhermeneutik," *Zeitschrift für deutsches Altertum und deutsche Literatur* 95/2: 81–122.

Langlands, R. (2011). "Roman *Exempla* and Situation Ethics: Valerius Maximus and Cicero *de Officiis*," *Journal of Roman Studies* 101: 100–22.

(2015). "Roman Exemplarity: Mediating between General and Particular," in Lowrie and Lüdemann (2015): 68–80.

(2018). *Exemplary Ethics in Ancient Rome*. Cambridge.

Laurent, F. (2002). "'La guerre civile? Qu'est-ce à dire? Est-ce qu'il y a une guerre étrangère?'" in C. Millet and M. Rebérioux (eds.), *Hugo et la guerre*. Paris, 133–56.

Lavan, M. (2017). "Writing Revolt in the Early Roman Empire," in J. Firnhaber-Baker and D. Schoenars (eds.), *The Routledge History Handbook of Medieval Revolt*. Abingdon, 19–38.

Lear, J. (1997). "Inside and Outside the *Republic*," in R. Kraut (ed.), *Plato's Republic: Critical Essays*. New York, 61–94.

Lee, O. (1979). *Fathers and Sons in Virgil's Aeneid*. Albany, NY.

(1989). "The Golden Age: Eclogue 4," in *Death and Rebirth in Virgil's Arcadia*. Albany, NY, 77–88.

(1996). *Virgil as Orpheus: A Study of the Georgics*. Albany, NY.

Lefèvre, E. (1998). "Vergil as a Republican," in Stahl (1998): 101–18.

Lefort, C. (1981). "Permanence du théologico-politique?" *Le temps de la réflexion* 2: 13–60; reprinted in Lefort (1986): 251–300.

(1986). *Essais sur le politique (XIXe–XXe siècles)*. Paris.

Legendre, P. (1964). *La pénétration du Droit romain dans le Droit canonique classique de Gratien à Innocent IV, 1140–1254*. Paris.

Leigh, M. (1997). *Lucan: Spectacle and Engagement*. Oxford.

Leitao, D. D. (2004). "Ritual? What Ritual?", in Barchiesi, Rüpke, and Stephens (2004): 149–53.

Leopold, S. (2014). "Eros und Polis: Aeneas und die Folgen: von Augustus zu Richelieu," in *Liebe im Ancien Régime: Eros und Polis von Corneille bis Sade*. Paderborn, 62–76.

Leupin, A. (1993). *Fiction et incarnation*. Paris.

Levene, D. (2000). "Sallust's 'Catiline' and Cato the Censor," *Classical Quarterly* NS 50: 170–91.

Lewis, B. (1974). "The Rape of Troy: Infantile Perspective in Book 11 of the *Aeneid*," *Arethusa* 7: 103–13.

Lilla, M. (2015). "Slouching toward Mecca," review of M. Houellebecq, *Soumission, New York Review of Books*, April 2: www.nybooks.com/articles/2015/04/02/slouching-toward-mecca/.

Lim, R. (2012). "Augustine and Roman Spectacles," in Vessey (2012): 138–50.

Lim, W. S. H. (2010). *John Milton, Radical Politics, and Biblical Republicanism*. Cranbury.

Lind, L. R. (1994). "Thought, Life, and Literature at Rome," *Latomus* 227: 5–71.

Lloyd, C. (1999). "The Evander–Anchises Connection: Fathers, Sons, and Homoerotic Desire in Vergil's *Aeneid*," *Vergilius* 45: 3–21.

Lobur, J. A. (2011). "Resuscitating a Text: Velleius' History as Cultural Evidence," in E. Cowan (ed.), *Velleius Paterculus: Making History*. Swansea, 203–18.

Loraux, N. (1997a). "La guerre dans la famille," *Clio* 5: 21–62.

(1997b). *La cité divisée: l'oubli dans la mémoire d'Athènes*. Paris.

Lowrie, M. (1997). *Horace's Narrative Odes*. Oxford.

(2001). "Literature Is a Latin Word," *Vergilius* 2001: 29–38.

(2005). "Vergil and Founding Violence," *Cardozo Law Review* 25: 945–76.

(2007). "Making an Exemplum of Yourself: Cicero and Augustus," in S. J. Heyworth, with P. G. Fowler and S. J. Harrison (eds.), *Classical Constructions: Papers in Memory of Don Fowler, Classicist and Epicurean*. Oxford, 91–112.

(2008). "Evidence and Narrative in Mérimée's *Catilinarian Conspiracy*," *New German Critique* 103: 9–25.

(2009). *Writing, Performance, and Authority in Augustan Rome*. Oxford.

(2010a). "Rom immer wieder gegründet," in T. Döring, B. Vinken, and G. Zöller (eds.), *Übertragene Anfänge: Imperiale Figurationen um 1800*. Paderborn, 23–49.

(2010b). "Horace, *Odes* 4," in G. Davis (ed.), *A Companion to Horace.* Chichester, 210–30.

(2013). "Foundation and Closure," in Grewing and Acosta-Hughes (2013): 83–102.

(2014). "Politics by Other Means: Horace's *Ars Poetica*," in A. Ferenczi and P. Hardie (eds.), *New Approaches to Horace's Ars Poetica, Materiali e Discussioni* 72/1: 121–42.

(2015a). "*Rege incolumi*: Orientalism and Security at *Georgics* 4.212," in Fedeli and Günther (2015): 321–42.

(2015b). "Le corps du chef: transformations dans la sphère publique à l'époque d'Horace," in B. Delignon, N. Le Meur, and O. Thevenaz (eds.), *Le poète lyrique dans la cité antique*. Lyon, 71–86.

(2015c). "The Egyptian Within: A Roman Trope for Civil War," in B. Vinken (ed.), *Translatio Babylonis: Unsere orientalische Moderne*. Paderborn, 13–28.

(2015d). "*Reversio* (Lucan)," in Kasper and Wild (2015): 171–8.

(2018). "Figures of Discord and the Roman Addressee in Horace, *Odes* 3.6," in Harrison, Frangoulides, and Papanghelis (2018): 211–25.

(forthcoming a). "Political Thought," in R. Gibson and C. Whitton (eds.), *Cambridge Critical Guide to Latin Literature*. Cambridge.

(forthcoming b). *Security, Safety, and Care: A Roman Political Discourse*. Cambridge.

Lowrie, M., and Lüdemann, S. (2015). *Exemplarity and Particularity: Thinking through Particulars in Philosophy, Literature, and Law*. London.

Lowrie, M., and Vinken, B. (2018). "Correcting Rome with Rome: Victor Hugo's *Quatrevingt-treize*," in B. Dufallo (ed.), *Roman Error: Classical Reception and the Problem of Rome's Flaws*. Oxford, 179–90.

(2019). "Married to civil war: a Roman trope in Lucan's poetics of history," in C. H. Lange and F. J. Vervaet (eds.), The Historiography of Late Republican Civil War. Leiden, 263–91.

Lubac, H. de (1984). "Augustinisme politique?" in *Théologie d'occasion*. Paris, 255–308.

Lyne, R. O. A. M. (1987). *Further Voices in Vergil's Aeneid*. Oxford.

Mac Góráin, F. (2013). "Virgil's Bacchus and the Roman Republic," in Farrell and Nelis (2013): 124–45.

(2016). "The Poetics of Vision in Virgil's *Aeneid*," *Harvard Studies in Classical Philology* 109: 383–427.

(2018). "Vergil's Sophoclean Thebans," *Vergilius* 64: 131–56.

MacCormack, S. (1998). *The Shadows of Poetry: Vergil in the Mind of Augustine*. Berkeley, CA.

(1999). "Classical Authors," in A. D. Fitzgerald (ed.), *Augustine Through the Ages: An Encyclopedia*. Grand Rapids, MI, 202–6.

MacKinnon, C. A. (1989). "Sexuality, Pornography, and Method: 'Pleasure under Patriarchy'," *Ethics* 99/2: 314–46.

(1996). *Only Words*. Cambridge, MA.

MacRae, D. (2016). *Legible Religion*. Cambridge, MA.

Maltby, R. (1991). *A Lexicon of Ancient Latin Etymologies*. Cambridge.

Mandouze, A., and Fouilheron, J. (eds.) (1985). *Migne et le renouveau des études patristiques*. Paris.

Maraval, P. (ed. and trans.) (2001). *Eusèbe de Césarée: la théologie politique de l'Empire chrétien. Louanges de Constantin (Triakontaétérikos)*. Paris.

Marchesi, S. (2011). *Dante and Augustine*. Toronto.

Marchetta, A. (2013). *Vita agreste e poesia agreste nel finale del* 11 *libro delle Georgiche di Virgilio*. Tivoli.

Marincola, J. (2010). "Eros and Empire: Virgil and the Historians on Civil War," in C. S. Kraus, J. Marincola, and C. Pelling (eds.), *Ancient Historiography and Its Contexts: Studies in Honour of A. J. Woodman* (Oxford), 183–204.

Marion, J.-L. (1977). *L`idole et la distance*. Paris.

Maris, B. (2014). *Houellebecq économiste*. Paris.

Markell, P. (2009). *Bound by Recognition*. Princeton, NJ.

Marrou, H.-I. (1958 [1938]). *Saint Augustin et la fin de la culture antique*. Paris.

Martindale, C. (ed.) (1997). *The Cambridge Companion to Virgil*. Cambridge.

Maschek, D. (2018). *Die römischen Bürgerkriege: Archäologie und Geschichte einer Krisenzeit*. Darmstadt.

Masters, J. (1992). *Poetry and Civil War in Lucan's Bellum Civile*. Cambridge.

Mathy, J.-P. (2017). "Le Terroir, l'Histoire, et la Vierge Noire: ce qui ne passe pas (encore) dans Soumission de Michel Houellebecq," *Contemporary French and Francophone Studies* 21/3: 257–265.

Matthes, M. (2000). *The Rape of Lucretia and the Founding of Republics*. University Park, PA.

Mayer, C. (ed.) (1986–). *Augustinus-Lexikon*, 3 vols. Basel.

Mazzotta, G. (1979). *Dante: Poet of the Desert*. Princeton, NJ.

McAleer, G. (2020). "Victorian Pagans," *Law and Liberty*, October 2: https://lawliberty.org/book-review/victorian-pagans/.

McCormick, J. (2011). *Machiavellian Democracy*. Cambridge.

Mebane, J. (2016). "Pompey's Head and the Body Politic in Lucan's *De bello civili*," *Transactions of the American Philological Association* 146/1: 191–215.

(2017). *The Body Politic and Roman Political Languages*. Chicago.

Mecke, J. (2003). "Der Fall Houellebecq: Zu Formen und Funktionen eines Literaturskandals," in G. Eggeling and S. Segler-Meßner (eds.), *Europäische Verlage und romanische Gegenwartsliteraturen: Profile, Tendenzen, Strategien*. Tübingen, 194–217.

Meconi, D. V., and Stump, E. (2014). *The Cambridge Companion to Augustine*, 2nd ed. Cambridge.

Mehlman, J. (1977). *Revolution and Repetition: Marx/Hugo/Balzac*. Berkeley, CA.

Meizoz, J. (2007). *Postures littéraires: mises en scène modernes de l'auteur*. Geneva.

Mercati, M. (1981). *Gli obelischi di Roma*. Bologna.

Micale, M. S. (1990). "Charcot and the Idea of Hysteria in the Male," *Medical History* 34: 363–411.

Migne, J. P. (1865). *Patrologiae cursus completus. Latina series. Successores*. Paris.

Miles, G. B. (1980). *Virgil's Georgics: A New Interpretation*. Berkeley, CA.

Milnor, K. (2005). *Gender, Domesticity, and the Age of Augustus: Inventing Private Life*. Oxford.

Mitchell, R. N. (1991). "The Violence of Virginity," *Arethusa* 24: 219–38.

Momigliano, A. (1942). "Camillus and Concord," *Classical Quarterly* 36: 111–20.

(1977). "Pagan and Christian Historiography in the Fourth Century A.D.," in *Essays in Ancient and Modern Historiography*. Oxford, 107–26. Orig. publ. A. Momigliano (ed.) (1963). *The Conflict between Paganism and Christianity in the Fourth Century*. Oxford, 79–99.

(1990). "Tacitus and the Tacitist Tradition," in *The Classical Foundations of Modern Historiography*. Berkeley, CA, 109–31.

Morgan, L. (1999). *Patterns of Redemption in Virgil's 'Georgics.'* Cambridge.

Morley, N. (2007). "Civil War and Succession Crisis in Roman Beekeeping," *Historia* 56/4: 462–70.

Morrey, D. (2018). "The Banality of Monstrosity: On Michel Houellebecq's *Soumission*," *Australian Journal of French Studies* 55/2: 202–17.

Morrissey, R. (2010). *Napoléon et l'héritage de la gloire*. Paris.

Muecke, F. (2005). "Ennius and Lucilius," in Freudenburg (2005): 33–47.

Mulhern, E. V. (2017). "Roma(na) Matrona," *Classical Journal* 112/4: 432–59.

Murphy, A. R. (1999). *Jean-François Millet: Drawn into the Light*. New Haven, CT.

Murphy, C. (2007). *Are We Rome? The Fall of an Empire and the Fate of America*. Boston.

Murphy, S. (ed.) (2017). *Lecture de l'éducation sentimentale*. Rennes.

Narducci, E. (2002). *Lucano: Un' epica contro l'impero*. Rome.

Nelis, D. (2004). "From Didactic to Epic: *Georgics* 2.458–3.48," in M. Gale (ed.), *Latin Epic and Didactic Poetry: Genre, Tradition and Individuality*. Swansea, 73–108.

(2013). "Past, Present, and Future in Vergil's *Georgics*," in Farrell and Nelis (2013): 244–62.

Nelsestuen, G. (2015). *Varro the Agronomist: Political Philosophy, Satire, and Agriculture in the Late Republic*. Columbus, OH.

Newman, J. K. (1967). *The Concept of Vates in Augustan Poetry*. Brussels.

Niemeyer, G. (1983). *Augustine's Philosophy in Relation to History and Politics* (VHS recording).

Nirenberg, D. (2013). *Anti-Judaism: The Western Tradition*. New York.

Noiriel, G. (2019). *Le venin dans la plume: Édouard Drumont, Éric Zemmour et la part sombre de la République*. Paris.

Nonnenmacher, K. (2016). "Unterwerfung als Konversion: Als-Ob-Bekehrungen zu Katholizismus und Islam bei Carrère und Houellebecq," *Romanische Studien* 3: 171–98.

O'Donnell, J. J. (1980). "Augustine's Classical Readings," *Recherches Augustiniennes et patristiques* 15: 144–75.

(1991). "The Authority of Augustine," *Augustinian Studies* 22: 7–35.

(2000). "The Next Life of Augustine," in W. E. Klingshirn and M. Vessey (eds.), *The Limits of Ancient Christianity: Essays on Latin Antique Thought and Culture in Honor of R. A. Markus*. Ann Arbor, MI, 215–31.

(2001). "Augustine: His Time and Lives," in Stump and Kretzman (2001): 8–25.

(2005). *Augustine, Sinner and Saint: A New Biography*. London.

O'Gorman, E. (1995). "Shifting Ground: Lucan, Tacitus, and the Landscape of Civil War," *Hermathena* 158: 117–31.

(2000). *Irony and Misreading in the Annals of Tacitus*. Cambridge.

O'Hara, J. (1990). *Death and the Optimistic Prophecy in Vergil's Aeneid*. Princeton, NJ.

Ohly, F. (1977 [1958]). "Vom geistigen Sinn des Wortes im Mittelalter," in *Schriften zur mittelalterlichen Bedeutungsforschung*. Darmstadt, 1–31.

Olender, M. (2002). *Les langues du Paradis: Aryens et Sémites, un couple providentiel*. Paris.

Oliensis, E. (1997). "Sons and Lovers: Sexuality and Gender in Virgil's *Aeneid*," in Martindale (1997): 294–311.

(1998). *Horace and the Rhetoric of Authority*. Cambridge.

(2001). "Freud's *Aeneid*," *Vergilius* 47: 39–63.

(2009). *Freud's Rome: Psychoanalysis and Latin Poetry*. Cambridge.

Orlin, E. (ed.) (2016). *Routledge Encyclopedia of Ancient Mediterranean Religions*. New York.

Osgood, J. (2006). *Caesar's Legacy: Civil War and the Emergence of the Roman Empire*. Cambridge.

(2014). *Turia: A Roman Woman's Civil War*. Oxford.

(2015). "Ending Civil War at Rome: Rhetoric and Reality (88 BCE – 197 CE)," *American Historical Review* 120/5: 1683–95.

(2018). *Rome and the Making of a World State*. Cambridge.

Otis, B. (1964). *Virgil: A Study in Civilized Poetry*. Oxford.

Otten, W., and Pollmann, K. (eds.) (2007). *Poetry and Exegesis in Premodern Latin Christianity: The Encounter between Classical and Christian Strategies of Interpretation*. Leiden.

Owens, P. (2017). "Decolonizing Civil War," *Critical Analysis of Law* 4/2: 160–9.

Ozouf, M. (1989). *L'homme régénéré: essai sur la Révolution française*. Paris.

Pagán, V. (2004). *Conspiracy Narratives in Roman History*. Austin, TX.

(2008). "Toward a Model of Conspiracy Theory for Ancient Rome," in E. Horn (ed.), *Dark Powers: Conspiracy and Conspiracy Theory in History and Literature*, special issue, *New German Critique* 103: 27–49.

Palais de Tokyo (2016). *Magazine Palais* 23.

Pandey, N. (2018). *The Poetics of Power in Augustan Rome: Latin Poetic Response to Imperial Iconography*. Cambridge.

Paris, G., and Buchon, J. A. C. (1827). *Chronique métrique de Philippe-le-Bel suivie de la taille de Paris, en 1313*. Verdière.

Parry, A. (1963). "The Two Voices of Virgil's 'Aeneid'," *Arion* 2/4: 66–80.

Paschalis, M. (1998). *Virgil's Aeneid: Semantic Relations and Proper Names*. Oxford.

Pedullà, G. (2011). *Machiavelli in tumulto: Conquista, cittadinanza e conflitto nei "Discorsi sopra la prima deca di Tito Livio."* Rome.

Peirano, I. (2019). *Persuasion, Rhetoric and Roman Poetry*. Cambridge.

Pellegrini, J. (2007). "Note sur la double description de la 'bugonia' au chant IV des 'Géorgiques' (295–314 et 538–47)," *Latomus* 66/2: 336–41.

Pépin, J. (1976 [1958]). *Mythe et allégorie. Les origines grèques et les contestations judéo-chrétiennes.* Paris.

(1987). *La tradition de l'allégorie de Philon d'Alexandrie à Dante.* Paris.

Perkell, C. G. (1978). "A Reading of Vergil's Fourth Georgic," *Phoenix* 32: 211–22.

(1989). *The Poet's Truth: A Study of the Poet in Virgil's Georgics.* Berkeley, CA.

Perkell, C. G. (ed.) (1999). *Reading Vergil's Aeneid: An Interpretive Guide.* Norman, OK.

Petrey, S. (1980). *History in the Text: Quatrevingt-Treize and the French Revolution.* Amsterdam.

Peyrache-Leborgne, D. (1996). "Roman historique et roman-idylle chez Dickens et Hugo: *A Tale of Two Cities* and *Quatrevingt-treize,*" *Dalhousie French Studies* 36: 51–67.

Piccaluga, G. (1995). "Fondazione della realtà e uscita della storia nel Sermo 'de urbis excidio'," *Augustinianum* 53: 497–510.

Pichon, R. (1912). *Les sources de Lucain.* Paris.

Plass, P. (1988). *Wit and the Writing of History: The Rhetoric of Historiography.* Madison, WI.

Pogorzelski, R. J. (2016). *Virgil and Joyce: Nationalism and Imperialism in the Aeneid and Ulysses.* Madison, WI.

Pollman, K., and Otten, W. (eds.) (2013). *The Oxford Guide to the Historical Reception of Augustine.* Oxford.

Pornschlegel, C. (2015). "Das unerhörte Verlangen: Zu Michel Houellebecqs Roman 'Unterwerfung'," *Stimmen der Zeit* 9: 611–22.

Price, J. J. (2001). *Thucydides and Internal War.* Cambridge.

(2015). "Thucydidean *Stasis* and the Roman Empire in Appian's Interpretation of History," in K. Welch (ed.), *Appian's Roman History.* Swansea, 45–63.

Pugliese Carratelli, G. (ed.) (1992). *Roma e l'Egitto nell'Antichità Classica.* Atti del I Congresso Internazionale Italo-Egiziano, Cairo 6–9 febbraio 1989. Rome.

Putnam, M. C. J. (1965). *The Poetry of the Aeneid.* Cambridge, MA.

(1979). *Virgil's Poem of the Earth.* Princeton, NJ.

(1985). "Possessiveness, Sexuality and Heroism in the 'Aeneid'," *Vergilius* 31: 1–21.

(1994). "Virgil's Danaid Ekphrasis," *Illinois Classical Studies* 19: 171–89.

(1998). *Virgil's Epic Designs.* New Haven, CT.

(1999). "*Aeneid* 12: Unity in Closure," in Perkell (1999): 10–30.

(2000). *Horace's Carmen Saeculare: Ritual Magic and the Poet's Art.* New Haven, CT.

(2008). "Italian Virgil and the Idea of Rome," in Volk (2008): 138–60. Orig. publ. 1975.

Quartarone, L. (2011). "Quantity, Quality, Tension, and Transition: The Dimensions of Vergil's 'Ingens'," *Vergilius* 57: 3–34.

Quint, D. (1993). *Epic and Empire: Politics and Generic Form from Virgil to Milton.* Princeton, NJ.

(2011). "Virgil's Double Cross," *American Journal of Philology* 132/2: 273–300.

(2018). *Virgil's Double Cross: Design and Meaning in the Aeneid.* Princeton, NJ.

Raditsa, L. F. (1980). "Augustus' Legislation concerning Marriage, Procreation, Love Affairs and Adultery," in H. Temporini (ed.), *Aufstieg und Niedergang der römischen Welt,* vol. 2/13. Berlin, 278–339.

Rantala, J. (2013). *Maintaining Loyalty, Declaring Continuity, Legitimizing Power: Ludi Saeculares of Septimius Severus as a Manifestation of the Golden Age.* Tampere.

Ratzinger, J. (1954). *Volk und Haus Gottes in Augustins Lehre von der Kirche.* Munich.

(1961 [1954]). "Herkunft und Sinn der Civitas-Lehre Augustins," in W. Lammers (ed.), *Geschichtsdenken und Geschichtsbild im Mittelalter.* Darmstadt, 55–74.

Rau, K. F. von, and Cronenthal, E. H. H. von (1826). *Der Krieg der Verbündeten gegen Frankreich in den Jahren 1813, 1814, und 1815*, vol. 2. Berlin.

Reckford, K. J. (1958). "Some Appearances of the Golden Age," *The Classical Journal* 54: 79–87.

Reed, J. D. (2007). *Virgil's Gaze: Nation and Poetry in the Aeneid.* Princeton, NJ.

(2010). "Vergil's Roman," in Farrell and Putnam (2010): 66–79.

Rees, R. (ed.) (2012). *Oxford Readings in Classical Studies: Latin Panegyric.* Oxford.

Reggiani, R. (2005). "Presenze femminili in Lucano," in *Varia Latina (satyrica-epica-tragica-historica).* Amsterdam, 83–126.

Rehm, R. (1994). *Marriage to Death: The Conflation of Wedding and Funeral Rituals in Greek Tragedy.* Princeton, NJ.

Renaut, A. (1999). *Naissances de la modernité*, vol. 2. Paris.

Rey, J.-M. (2008). *Paul ou les ambiguïtés.* Paris.

Richards, I. A. (1936). *The Philosophy of Rhetoric.* Oxford.

Richardson, J. (2008). *The Language of Empire: Rome and the Idea of Empire from the Third Century* BC *to the Second Century* AD. Cambridge.

Rieser, M. (2018). *Zolas Naturalismus: Kreuzwege der Rougon-Macquart.* Berlin.

Rimell, V. (2013). "(En)closure and Rupture: Roman Poetry in the Arena," in Grewing and Acosta-Hughes (2013): 103–27.

(2015). *The Closure of Space in Roman Poetics: Empire's Inward Turn.* Cambridge.

Ritte, J. (2016). "Modernes Dandytum: Michel Houellebecqs Junggesellenroman *Soumission*," *Lendemains: Etudes Comparées sur la France / Vergleichende Frankreichforschung* 41: 217–24.

Roberts, M. (1989). *The Jeweled Style: Poetry and Poetics in Late Antiquity.* Ithaca, NY.

Roller, M. B. (1996). "Ethical Contradiction and the Fractured Community in Lucan's *Bellum Civile*," *Classical Antiquity* 15: 319–47.

(2004). "Exemplarity in Roman Culture: The Cases of Horatius Cocles and Cloelia," *Classical Philology* 99: 1–56.

(2009). "The Exemplary Past in Roman Historiography and Culture," in Feldherr (2009): 214–30.

(2018). *Models from the Past in Roman Culture: A World of Exempla.* Baltimore, MD.

Roloff, V. (2016). "Houellebecq und Huysmans: *Soumission* als Lektüreroman," *Lendemains: Etudes Comparées sur la France / Vergleichende Frankreichforschung* 41: 210–16.

Rosa, G. (1974). "Massacrer les massacres," *L'Arc* 57: 72–80.

(1985). "Politique du désastre. Hugo durant 'l'année terrible'," *Europe* 671, March: 170–88.

Rosenberger, V. (1992). *Bella et expeditiones: Die antike Terminologie der Kriege Roms*. Stuttgart.

Rossi, A. (2010). *"Ab Urbe Condita*: Roman History on the Shield of Aeneas," in Breed, Damon, and Rossi (2010): 145–56.

Roulin, J.-M. (2001). "Mothers in Revolution: Political Representations of Maternity in Nineteenth-Century France," *Yale French Studies* 101: 182–200.

Said, E. W. (1978). *Orientalism*. New York.

Salin, E. (1926). *Civitas Dei*. Tübingen.

Salzmann, M. R. (2013). "Memory and Meaning: Pagans and 410," in J. Lipps, C. Machado, and P. von Rummel (eds.), *The Sack of Rome in 410 AD: The Event, Its Context and Its Impact*. Wiesbaden, 295–310.

(2015). "Christian Sermons against Pagans: The Evidence from Augustine's Sermons on the New Year and on the Sack of Rome in 410," in M. Maas (ed.), *The Cambridge Companion to the Age of Attila*. Cambridge, 344–57.

Sannicandro, L. (2010). *I personaggi femminili del Bellum Civile di Lucano*. Rahden.

Saylor, C. F. (1990). *"Lux extrema*: Lucan, *Pharsalia* 4.402–581," *Transactions of the American Philological Association* 120: 291–300.

Scepi, H. (2017)."La barricade renversée: empreintes hugoliennes dans l'Education sentimentale," in Murphy (2017): 335–46.

Scheid, J. (1984). "La spartizione a Roma," *Studi Storici* 4: 945–56.

(1990). *Romulus et ses frères: le collège des frères Arvales, modèle du culte publique dans la Rome des empereurs*. Rome.

(2003). *An Introduction to Roman Religion*. Bloomington, IN.

Schiesaro, A. (1993). "Il destinatario nelle Georgiche," in A. Schiesaro, P. Mitsis, and J. Strauss Clay (eds.), *Mega Nepios: Il destinatario nell'epos didascalico. The Addressee in Didactic Epic*, special issue. *Materiali e discussioni* 31: 129–47.

(1997). "The Boundaries of Knowledge in Virgil's *Georgics*," in T. Habinek and A. Schiesaro (eds.), *The Roman Cultural Revolution*. Cambridge.

Schmidt, M. G. (1986). *Caesar und Cleopatra: Philologischer und historischer Kommentar zu Lucan. 10,1–171*. Frankfurt.

Schmitt, C. (1985). *Political Theology: Four Chapters on the Concept of Sovereignty*, trans. G. Schwab. Cambridge, MA. Orig. publ. 1922, revised 1934.

Schmitzer, U. (2011). "Roman Values in Velleius," in E. Cowan (ed.), *Velleius Paterculus: Making History*. Swansea, 177–202.

Schneider, U. (2016). "'Il n'y a pas de liberté sans une dose de provocation possible': Michel Houellebecqs 'Soumission' oder: die Widerständigkeit der Fiktion," *Romanistisches Jahrbuch* 67: 148–78.

Schober, R. (2002). "Renouveau du réalisme? ou De Zola à Houellebecq?," in M. Gosselin-Noat and A.-S. Dufief (eds.), *La représentation du réel dans le roman: Mélanges offerts à Colette Becker*. Paris, 333–44.

Schönwälder, L. (2015). "Die Ästhetik des Bösen – Banalisierung des Bösen? Zur Funktion literarischer Provokation am Beispiel Michel Houellebecqs," *Romanische Forschungen* 127: 29–51.

Schor, N. (2007). *Reading in Detail: Aesthetics and the Feminine.* New York.

Schrempp, O. (1964). *Prophezeiung und Rückschau in Lucans "Bellum civile."* Winterthur.

Schuhen. G. (2007). *Erotische Maskerade: Sexualität und Geschlecht bei Marcel Proust.* Heidelberg.

Schürmann, R. (1996). *Des hégémonies brisées.* Paris.

Schwindt, J. P. (2013). "The Philology of History. How and What Augustan Poetry Remembers: Horace, Vergil, and Propertius, 1.19, 1.22 and 2.13b," in Farrell and Nelis (2013): 40–56.

Scodel, R., and Thomas, R. (1984). "Vergil and the Euphrates," *American Journal of Philology* 105/3: 339.

Seaford, R. (1989). "Homeric and Tragic Sacrifice," *Transactions of the American Philological Association* 119: 87–95.

Séginger, G. (2017). "Écriture historiographique et fiction romanesque", in Murphy (2017): 279–93.

Seidel, M., and Landau, E. M. (1983). *Altdorfer: Leidensweg, Heilsweg. Der Passionsaltar von Sankt Florian.* Stuttgart.

Seider, A. M. (2013). *Memory in Vergil's Aeneid: Creating the Past.* Cambridge.

Selden, D. (1992). "*Ceveat lector*: Catullus and the Rhetoric of Performance," in R. Hexter and D. Selden (eds.), *Innovations of Antiquity.* New York, 461–512.

Shanzer, D. (2012). "Augustine and the Latin Classics," in Vessey (2012): 161–74.

Siciliano, C. J. (1999). *Labor and Justice: A Pattern of Allusions in Virgil's Georgics.* Chicago.

Siegert, B. (2006). "Ab-Ort Rom. Übertragung als Grund und Abgrund der Referenz," in W. Seitter and C. Vismann (eds.), *Tumult: Schriften zur Verkehrswissenschaft: Römisch*, vol. 30. Zurich and Berlin, 11–18.

Skinner, M. B. (1984). "Rhamnusia Virgo," *Classical Antiquity* 3/1: 134–41.

(2003). *Catullus in Verona: A Reading of the Elegiac Libellus, Poems 65–116.* Columbus, OH.

Sklenár, R. (2003). *The Taste for Nothingness: A Study of Virtus and Related Themes in Lucan's Bellum Civile.* Ann Arbor, MI.

Slimani, L. (2016). *Chanson douce.* Paris.

Smethurst, S. E. (1950). "Women in Livy's History," *Greece and Rome* 19: 80–7.

Smil, V. (2010). *Why America Is Not a New Rome.* Cambridge, MA.

Spence, S. (1991). "Cinching the Text: The Danaids and the End of the *Aeneid*," *Vergilius* 37: 11–19.

(1999). "*Varium et Mutabile*: Voices of Authority in *Aeneid* 4," in Perkell (1999): 80–95.

Spence, S., and Lowrie, M. (eds.) (2006). *The Aesthetics of Empire and the Reception of Vergil. Literary Imagination* 8/3.

Spencer, D. (2005). "Lucan's Follies: Memory and Ruin in a Civil-War Landscape," *Greece and Rome* 52: 46–69.

Spieser-Landes, D. (2017). "Soumission ou simulacre de soumission? Michel Houellebecq et la métaphysique (Baudrillardienne) du radiateur," *French Cultural Studies* 28/1: 42–53.

Spiller, R. (2004). "Sex, Lust and Depression: Michel Houellebecqs Kult elementarer Energien," in R. Freiburg, M. May, *et al.* (eds.), *Kultbücher.* Würzburg, 201–21.

Spiquel, A. (2002). "La double guerre," in C. Millet and M. Rebérioux (eds.), *Hugo et la guerre.* Paris, 227–47.

Staden, H. von (1997). "Inefficacy, Error, and Failure: Galen on δόκιμα φάρμακα ἄπρακτα," in A. Debru (ed.), *Galen on Pharmacology: Philosophy, History and Medicine.* Leiden, 59–83.

Stahl, H.-P. (ed.) (1998). *Vergil's Aeneid: Augustan Epic and Political Context.* London.

Stallybrass, P., and White, A. (1986). *The Politics and Poetics of Transgression.* Ithaca, NY.

Star, C. (2021). *Apocalypse and Golden Age: The End of the World in Greek and Roman Thought.* Baltimore, MD.

Starks, J. H., Jr. (1999). "*Fides Aeneia*: The Transference of Punic Stereotypes in the *Aeneid*," *The Classical Journal* 94.3: 255–83.

Steigerwald, J., and Komorowska, A. (eds.) (2011). "Michel Houellebecq: questions du réalisme d'aujourd'hui," *lendemains* 142/3: 6–17.

Stephens, S. (2004). "Whose Rituals in Ink?", in Barchiesi, Rüpke, and Stephens (2004): 157–60.

Stock, B. (1996). *Augustine the Reader: Meditation, Self-Knowledge, and the Ethics of Interpretation.* Cambridge, MA.

Stover, T. (2008). "Cato and the Intended Scope of Lucan's 'Bellum Civile'," *Classical Quarterly* 58/2: 571–80.

Straumann, B. (2017). "Roman Ideas on the Loose," *Critical Analysis of Law* 4/2: 141–51.

Stroumsa, G. G. (2012). "Augustine and Books," in Vessey (2012): 151–7.

Stump, E., and Kretzman, N. (eds.) (2001). *The Cambridge Companion to Augustine.* Cambridge.

Syed, Y. (2005). *Vergil's Aeneid and the Roman Self: Subject and Nation in Literary Discourse.* Ann Arbor, MI.

Syme, R. (1939). *The Roman Revolution.* Oxford.

Tauber, C. (2016). "Neue Identitäten – neue Genealogien: Jacques-Louis Davids künstlerische Selbstdarstellung nach dem 9. Thermidor 1794," *Zeitschrift für Kunstgeschichte* 79/3: 331–64.

Testard, M. (1958). *Saint Augustin et Cicéron.* Paris.

Thirouin, L. (1998). "La condamnation morale du théâtre: l'autorité morale de saint Augustin," in Jehasse and McKenna (1998): 275–96.

Thomas, R. F. (1982a). "Catullus and the Poetics of Reference (Poem 64.1–18)," *American Journal of Philology* 103: 144–64.

(1982b). *Lands and Peoples in Roman Poetry: The Ethnographical Tradition. Proceedings of the Cambridge Philological Society*, vol. 7., Cambridge.

(1990). "Ideology, Influence, and Future Studies in the 'Georgics'," *Vergilius* 36: 64–73.

(1991). "The 'Sacrifice' at the End of the *Georgics*, Aristaeus, and Vergilian Closure," *Classical Philology* 86/3: 211–18.

(1998). "The Isolation of Turnus," in Stahl (1998): 271–302.

(2000). "A Trope by Any Other Name: 'Polysemy,' Ambiguity, and Significatio in Virgil," *Harvard Studies in Classical Philology* 100: 381–407.

(2001). *Virgil and the Augustan Reception*. Cambridge.

Thomas, Y. (1981). "*Parricidium* I. Le père, la famille et la cité," *Mélanges des écoles françaises de Rome et d'Athènes* 93: 643–715.

Thraede, K. (1983). "Gottesstaat (Civitas Dei)," in T. Klauser *et al.* (eds.), *Reallexikon für Antike und Christentum*, vol. 12. Stuttgart, 58–82.

Todd, E. (2015). *Qui est Charlie? Sociologie d'une crise religieuse*. Paris.

Toll, K. (1997). "Making Roman-ness in the *Aeneid*," *Classical Antiquity* 16: 34–56.

Totelin, L. M. V. (2012). "And to End on a Poetic Note: Galen's Authorial Strategies in the Pharmacological Books," *Studies in History and Philosophy of Science* 43: 307–15.

Tracy, J. (2014). *Lucan's Egyptian Civil War*. Cambridge.

Treggiari, S. (1991). *Roman Marriage: Iusti Coniuges from the Time of Cicero to the Time of Ulpian*. Oxford.

Trump, D., with T. Schwartz (1987). *The Art of the Deal*. New York.

Trüstedt, K. (2018). "Fortress Europe," in *3 Quarks Daily: Science, Arts, Philosophy, Politics, Literature*, June 18: www.3quarksdaily.com/3quarksdaily/2018/06/fo rtress-europe.html.

Tucker, R. A. (1975). "The Banquets of Dido and Cleopatra," *Classical Bulletin* 52: 17–20.

(1990). "Love in Lucan's Civil War," *Classical Bulletin* 66: 43–6.

Tzounakas, S. (2005). "Echoes of Lucan in Tacitus: The *Cohortationes* of Pompey and Calgacus," in C. Deroux (ed.), *Studies in Latin Literature and Roman History*, vol. 12. Brussels, 395–413.

Ubl, R. (2010). "Eugène Delacroix. Mit dem Meer malen," in H. Baader and G. Wolf (eds.), *Das Meer, der Tausch, und die Grenzen der Repräsentation*. Zurich, 95–122.

Uden, J. (2015). *The Invisible Satirist: Juvenal and Second-Century Rome*. Oxford.

Ungelenk, J. (2018). *Literature and Weather: Shakespeare – Goethe – Zola*. Berlin.

Usener, H. (1967). *M. Annaei Lucani Commenta Bernensia*. Hildesheim.

Van Fleteren, F. (2001). "Principles of Augustine's Hermeneutics: An Overview," in Van Fleteren and Schnaubelt (2001): 1–32.

Van Fleteren, F., and Schnaubelt, J. C. (eds.) (2001). *Augustine: Biblical Exegete*. New York.

Veeser, H. A. (1994). *The New Historicism Reader*. New York.

Vessey, M. (2005). "Reading like Angels," in Caputo and Scanlon (2005): 159–211.

Vessey, M. (ed.) (2012). *A Companion to Augustine*. Malden, MA.

Viard, B. (2010). "Les enjeux idéologiques de l'œuvre romanesque de Michel Houellebecq," in Bowd (2010): 171–84.

Vinken, B. (1991a). *Unentrinnbare Neugierde: Die Weltverfallenheit des Romans*. Freiburg.

(1991b). "Zeichenspur, Wortlaut: Paris als Gedächtnisraum. Hugos *A l'Arc de Triomphe*, Baudelaires *Le Cygne*," in A. Haverkamp and R. Lachmann (eds.), *Gedächtniskunst: Raum – Bild – Schrift. Studien zur Mnemotechnik.* Frankfurt, 231–62.

(1992a). *Der Ursprung der Ästhetik aus theologischem Vorbehalt: Theorien des Ästhetischen von Port-Royal bis Rousseau und Sade.* Ann Arbor, MI.

(1992b). "The Concept of Passion and the Dangers of the Theater. Un esthétique avant la lettre: Augustine and Port-Royal," *Romanic Review* 83/1: 45–59.

(1993). "Alle Menschen werden Brüder: Republik, Rhetorik, Differenz der Geschlechter," *Lendemains* 71/2: 112–24.

(2001). *Du Bellay und Petrarca. Das Rom der Renaissance.* Tübingen.

(2004). "Via crucis, via amoris," in B. Menke and B. Vinken (eds.), *Stigmata. Poetiken der Körperinschrift.* Munich, 11–23.

(2006). "Forget Virgil? Baudelaire and the Truth of Modernity," in Spence and Lowrie (2006): 417–40.

(2007). "Wounds of Love: Modern Devotion according to Michelet," *Clio* 36/2: 155–75.

(2009a). *Flaubert: Durchkreuzte Moderne.* Frankfurt; trans. A. Rommens with S. L. Solomon, *Flaubert Postsecular: Modernity Crossed Out* (2015), Stanford, CA.

(2009b). "Blutopfer: Franz Marcs Geheimes Europa und Flauberts Heiliger Julian, Schlächter wider den Herrn," in exhibition catalog *Der große Widerspruch. Franz Marc zwischen Delaunay und Rousseau*, Franz Marc Museum, Kochel am See. Munich: 65–74.

(2011). *Bestien: Kleist und die Deutschen.* Berlin.

(2013). "Eine etwas andere *translatio Romae*," in K. Voigt (ed.), *Unter vier Augen: Sprachen des Porträts.* Bielefeld, 182–9.

(2014a) *Angezogen: Das Geheimnis der Mode.* Stuttgart.

(2014b). "Effekte des Realen: Bildmedien und Literatur im Realismus (G. Flaubert: L'Éducation sentimentale)," in C. Benthien and B. Weingart (eds.), *Handbuch Literatur & Visuelle Kultur.* Berlin, 393–407.

(2015a). "Nana: Venus à Rebours," in S. Goth, H. Berressem, and G. Blamberger (eds.), *Venus as Muse: From Lucretius to Michel Serres.* Amsterdam.

Vinken, B. (ed.) (2015b). *Translatio Babylonis: Unsere orientalische Moderne.* Munich.

Vinken, B. (2015c). "Götzendienst (Émile Zola)," in Kasper and Wild (2015): 60–5.

(2016a). "'Schlusen.' Effi Briest und 'die rechte Liebe'," in U. Haselstein (ed.), *Allegorie. DFG-Symposion 2014.* Berlin, 499–527.

(2016b). "Das Vierte Reich: Houellebecq und Europas innerer Orient," *Zeitschrift für Ideengeschichte* 10/3: 53–68.

Vinken, B. (ed.) (2019). *Gustave Flaubert, Trois contes, nouvelle édition critique de Barbara Vinken, avec trois essais.* Berlin.

Vinken, B. (2020). *Bel Ami: In diesem Babylon leben wir immer noch.* Leipzig.

Volk, K. (ed.) (2008). *Oxford Readings in Classical Studies: Vergil's Georgics*. Oxford.

Wahnich, S. (2002). "De l'économie émotive de la Terreur," *Annales. Histoire, Sciences Sociales* 57/4: 889–913.

Walker, W. (2009). *Paradise Lost and Republican Tradition from Aristotle to Machiavelli*. Turnhout.

Wallace-Hadrill, A. (1981). "The Emperor and His Virtues," *Historia* 30/3: 298–323.

(2008). *Rome's Cultural Revolution*. Cambridge.

Webb, R. (1997). "Mémoire et imagination: le limites de l'*enargeia* dans la théorie rhétorique poétique," in G. Lévy and L. Pernot (eds.), *Dire l'évidence (philosophie et rhétorique antiques)*, Cahiers de philosophie de l'Université de Paris XII–Val de Marne, 2. Paris, 229–47.

Wedeen, L. (1999). *Ambiguities of Domination: Politics, Rhetoric, and Symbols in Contemporary Syria*. Chicago.

(2019). *Authoritarian Apprehensions: Ideology, Judgement, and Mourning in Syria*. Chicago.

Weinstock, S. (1971). *Divus Julius*. Oxford.

Weiser, J. (2013). "Der Autor im Kulturbetrieb: literarisches Self-Fashioning zwischen Selbstvermarktung und Vermarktungsreflexionen (Christine Angot, Frédéric Beigbeder, Michel Houellebecq," *Zeitschrift für französische Sprache und Literatur* 123/3: 225–50.

Weiskel, T. (1976). *The Romantic Sublime: Studies in the Structure and Psychology of Transcendence*. Baltimore, MD.

Weithman, P. (2014). "Augustine's Political Philosophy," in Meconi and Stump (2014): 231–50.

Weitzmann, M. (2015). "Toxicité de Houellebecq", *Le Monde*, January 6, 2015.

Welch, K. (ed.) (2015). *Appian's Roman History: Empire and Civil War*. Swansea.

Westra, H. J. (2007). "Augustine and Poetic Exegesis," in Otten and Pollmann (2007): 11–28.

White, D. E. (2008). "Untimely Revolutions: Victor Hugo and the Spectre of the Date," *Romance Studies* 26/2: 111–25.

White, R. (2008). *Radical Virtues: Moral Wisdom and the Ethics of Contemporary Life*. New York.

Whittaker, T. (2009). "Sex and the Sack of the City," *Greece and Rome* 56: 234–42.

Wilkinson, L. P. (1963). *Golden Latin Artistry*. Cambridge.

(1969). *The Georgics of Virgil: A Critical Survey*. Cambridge.

Williams, B. (1997). "The Analogy of City and Soul in Plato's *Republic*," in R. Kraut (ed.), *Plato's Republic: Critical Essays*. New York.

Wiseman, T. P. (1995). *Remus: A Roman Myth*. Cambridge.

(2010). "The Two-Headed State: How Romans Explained Civil War," in Breed, Damon, and Rossi (2010): 25–44.

Wodianka, S. (2018). "Sommes-nous François? Literatur und Vanitas bei Michel Houellebecq," *Paragrana* 27/2: 291–312.

Woodman, A. J. (1983). "From Hannibal to Hitler: The Literature of War," *University of Leeds Review* 26: 107–24.

Woodman, A. J. (ed.) (2009). *The Cambridge Companion to Tacitus*. Cambridge.

Wyke, M. (1992). "Augustan Cleopatras: Female Power and Poetic Authority," in A. Powell (ed.), *Roman Poetry and Propaganda in the Age of Augustus*. London, 98–140.

(1997). *Projecting the Past: Ancient Rome, Cinema and History*. London.

Xuan, J. (2015). "Ergebung/Erneuerung: Zur Anerkennungsdialektik in Michel Houllebecqs *Soumission*," *Philologie im Netz* 73: 119–31.

Yelle, M. (2019a). *Sovereignty and the Sacred: Secularism and the Political Economy of Religion*, Chicago.

(2019b). "From Sovereignty to Solidarity: Some Transformations in the Politics of Sacrifice from the Reformation to Robertson Smith," *History of Religions* 58/3: 319–46.

Zadro, C. (2007). *Gli obelischi di Roma*. Rome.

Zanker, P. (1988). *The Power of Images in the Age of Augustus*. Ann Arbor, MI; transl. (2003), *Augustus und die Macht der Bilder*, Munich.

Zard, P. (2009). "Raison historique, apocalypse et roman familial dans *Quatrevingt-treize* (Hugo) et *Le Siècle des lumières* (Carpentier)," *Revue de littérature comparée* 329/83: 25–39.

Zeitlin, F. (1965). "The Motif of the Corrupted Sacrifice in Aeschylus' Oresteia," *Transactions and Proceedings of the American Philological Association* 96: 463–508.

Ziolkowski, T. (1993). *Virgil and the Moderns*. Princeton, NJ.

Zollinger, E. (2015). "Monument (Joachim Du Bellay)," in Kasper and Wild (2015): 120–5.

Zwierlein, O. (1974). "Caesar und Kleopatra bei Lucan und späterer Dichtung," *Antike und Abendland* 20: 54–73.

Index

9/11 8

Abel (Bible) 13, 160, 174, 175–7, 180, 181
Abélard and Héloise 320
abject 7, 21, 26, 29, 33, 34, 37–9, 41, 46, 55, 59,
    61–5, 67, 85, 90, 95, 126, 128, 131, 134, 135,
    159, 160, 167, 168, 173, 182, 216, 227, 234,
    244, 251, 292, 310, 317, 318, 323
Abraham 178, 249
absolutism 53, 81, 194, 201, 241, 247, 263, 274,
    283, 285, 288, 305
acedia see indifference (acedia, ennui)
Achilles 92, 95, 118, 136–7, 172, 215, 240
Actium 4–5, 11, 22, 35, 36, 39, 69, 110, 112, 113, 117,
    120, 121, 125–9, 130, 131, 132, 133, 206, 286
Adam (Bible) 87, 182, 225, 226
adultery 5, 24–5, 26, 29, 43–4, 112–17, 118, 119,
    164, 174, 186, 259, 272, 293, 301, 302–3, see
    Lucretia; suicide
aemulatio 87, 146, 171, 238, 242, 251, see imitatio
Aeneas see Vergil: Aeneid
Aeschylus, Oresteia 38, 236
    Agamemnon 257
    Eumenides 38
Agamben, Giorgio 30–2
agriculture 52, 54, 103, 230
Alba Longa 165, 166–7
Alexander, the Great 74, 116–17
Alexandria 7, 89–90, 112–17
allegory see hyponoia; typology
Amata 130, 134–6, 140
America (USA) xiii, 2, 8, 17–19, 20, 56, 263, 265,
    285, 290–2, 323
    American Civil War 8
anagnorisis 220
Anchises 93, 96, 117, 124–6, 137, 188
ancien régime 196, 234, 293, 295–7, 308
anglicism 292
Anglo-American 275, 293
animality 100–1, 217, 232, 237, see animals

animals 23, 38, 54, 58–60, 61, 64, 71, 80, 93,
    95–6, 102, 113, 129, 138, 162, 168, 212, 226,
    228, 233–4, 313, 319, 323, see animality;
    bugonia; sacrifice
bees 5, 35–6, 39, 54, 60–9, 76, 80, 226–30, 256
    see factionism
butterflies 229, 242
horses 56, 70, 90–8, 102, 104, 120, 269
leopard 323
lion 23, 249, 252, 319
nightingale 79, 256
snakes 76–9, 91, 93, 95–6, 134–5, 228, 242
swallows 226
vermin 217, 226, 254
wolf 23, 97, 119–20, 233, 236
Annunciation 229, 231, 313
Antigone 106
antisemitism 259, 262, see Nazism; racism
Antony, Mark 4, 6, 22, 24, 34–6, 50, 53–4, 65,
    99, 112–13, 115, 120, 125, 129–31, 206, 269,
    see Cicero, Marcus Tullius: Philippics
apokatastasis 200, 245
Apollo 95, 98–9, 103, 135, 236
Apollonius, Argonautica 74
apotheosis 131, 132, 161, 226
arabesque 295
Archilochus 268
Arendt, Hannah 17–18, 101
    Eichmann in Jerusalem 263
    On Revolution 226
    The Human Condition 226
Ariadne 110
Aristaeus 59–60, 63–4, 79, 80, 256
Aristophanes, Lysistrata 102
Aristotle 34, 61, 120
    Nicomachean Ethics 28
    Poetics 215
    Politics 28, 212, 234
Assyrian 60, 72, 175, 178
Atwood, Margaret, The Handmaid's Tale 293

Augustine   9–15, 26, 37–44, 89, 141, 195, 200–3, 209, 210, 238, 243–7, 254–5, 263, 288, 313, 325
Ad Pollentium   303
Confessions   41, 147–9, 188, 189, 309, 320–1
De civitate Dei   52, 64, 84, 242, 291, 302, 324
and Introduction, Chapter 4 *passim*
De excidio urbis Romae   147, 157–8
Epistles   145
Expositions of the Psalms   152
Augustus   xiii, 1, 2, 4–6, 12, 13, 17, 22, 24, 26, 27, 32, 35, 36, 47, 48–54, 55, 62, 67, 69–73, 75, 79–82, 85, 86–9, 90, 98, 99, 103, 108, 111–13, 115–18, 120, 121–33, 140, 141–3, 144, 147, 156, 166, 168, 169, 173, 183, 188, 204, 206, 231, 241, 258–62, 266, 276, 280, 281, 286–8, 290, 295, 301–4, 310, 313
Augustan literature   4–5, 15, 23, 48, 50, 53, 69, 71, 85, 108, 114, 126, 225
Augustan period   18, 23, 47, 48, 52, 70, 121, 123, 126, 172
Octavian   12, 35, 39, 65, 218, 269
Res gestae   47, 90, 129, 133
Aury, Dominique, *L'Histoire d'O*   270
Ayatollah Khomeini   276

Babylon   2, 5, 15, 34–8, 41, 45, 67, 117, 141, 144, 160, 165, 168, 172–4, 175, 176, 178–80, 183, 254–5, 261, 263, 272, 277, 303, 310, 311, 318–24
Badinter, Elisabeth
Emilie, Emilie   290
Le conflit. La mère et la femme   290
Balzac, Honoré de   224, 270
Les Chouans   218
Barbey d'Aurevilly, Jules Amadée   278
bastard, bastardization   9, 95, 113, 114, 118
Bataclan   260
Battle of the Nations   282
Baudelaire, Charles   273
Les Fleurs du Mal, Au lecteur   268, 272, 315–17, 325
Befreiungskriege   8
Berest, Anne, *Recherche femme parfaite*   290
Bernard de Clairvaux   214
bestiality *see* animality
Bethlehem   157, 231
Bible *see* Chapters 4 and 5 *passim*; Abel (Bible); Adam (Bible); Eve (Bible); Mary (mother of Christ); Paul; and *passim*
biopolitics   9, 259, 261, 299, 301–2, 303
blasphemy   305, 313
Bloy, Léon   273–4, 278
Blumenberg, Hans   20, 149, 167, *see* metaphorology

body politic   7, 9, 79, 83, 93, 113, 115, 117, 129, 137, 138–9, 158, 162, 167, 185, 207, 216, 269, *see* dismemberment
Boileau, Nicolas, *Art poétique*   271
Bouguereau, William Adolphe   285
Breivik, Anders   257
Bretons   247
Broch, Hermann, *Der Tod des Vergil*   88
Brundisium   205, 209, 269
Brussels   196, 273–5, 321–2
Brutus, Marcus Iunius   49, 124, 170, 176, 207, 219, *see* David, Jacques-Louis
bugonia   5, 39–40, 55, 60–5, 68–9, 80, 128–9, *see* Egypt
butchery   167, 292, 318–20

Cabanel, Alexandre   285
Caesar, Gaius Iulius   4, 5, 6–7, 11, 12, 13, 17, 19, 21, 25–9, 33, 34–8, 43, 61, 65, 74–6, 163–5, 186–7, 201, 205–8, 210, 212, 216, 218–20, 222, 231, 238, 239, 241, 252, 269, *see* Suetonius: *Iulius Caesar*; and Chapter 3 *passim*
Bellum Civile   222
Caesarion   115, 129
Cain   160, 172, 174, 175–7, 180, 181, 218, 324
Camus, Albert, *L'étranger*   320
cannibalism   165
Canova, Antonio   287
capitalism   4, 41, 290–2, 294, 323
Cardinal Mercier   274
carnivalesque   215, *see* grotesque
Carthage   53, 89–90, 98–105, 163, 172, 188
Cassandra   92, 95, 256–7, 268
Cassius Dio   30
castration   92, 94, 120
cataclysm   223
catastrophe   61–2, 163, 168, 197, 198, 202, 246, 250, 251, 257, 281, 289, 318
Catholic   4, 5, 14, 19, 40, 45
and Chapters 4, 5, 6 *passim*
Catilina   20, 84, 222, 287, *see* Cicero, Marcus Tullius: *Orationes in Catilinam*; Sallust: *Bellum Catilinae*
Cato, Marcus Porcius, the Younger   33, 43–4, 105–12, 120, 132, 139, 184–8, 214, 219–20, 232–3; *see* Plutarch: *Cato Minor*; Seneca: *De tranquillitate animi*; Suicide: Cato
Catullus   20–2, 33, 79, 110, 142
Chanson de Roland, La   264
charity   197, 199, 204, 209–13, 220, 235–6, 244, 248, 251–2, 301
Charlie Hebdo   256, 257
chastity   33, 43, 48, 71, 93, 114, 118, 123, 179, 184, 187, 214, 252, 299, *see* Lucretia; rape: suicide; virginity

Christ *see imitatio: imitatio Christi*; Passio
(Passion of Christ); and esp. Chapters 4, 5
passim
chute transfiguration 192, 229, 244, 245, 252
Cicero, Marcus Tullius 53, 146, 153–4, 163, 168,
169, 189, 286
De finibus 233
De imperio Cn. Pompei 26, 164, *see* Pompey,
the Great
De officiis 28
De oratore 87
De re publica 12, 64, 145, 151–3, 154, 155, 182
Epistulae ad familiares 16, 30
Orationes in Catilinam 16, 154, 182, *see*
Catilina
Philippics 35, 159, *see* Antony, Mark
Pro Murena 207
class 65, 71–2, 239
classicism 47, 52, 85
clemency 27, 52, 67, 95, 124, 129, 163, 189, 197,
238–9, 240–1, 247–8, 251–2, *see* Caesar,
Gaius Iulius
Cleopatra 4–7, 9, 22, 24, 34–7, 100, 106, 107–18,
129–31, *see* Horace: Cleopatra Ode
Clichy, Place de 281–5, 287–8, *see* Commune
Cocteau, Jean 203
collaboration 263, 265, 324, *see* Nazism;
occupation; World War II
comedic 236, 261
Commune 14, 20, 40, 194–203, 205, 213, 244–5,
254, 280, 281–8
compassion 166, 184, 188, 204–5, 210, 212–13,
234, 271, 293
Concorde, Place de la 281, 286
concupiscentia 158, 177, 181, 321
conditioning 289, *see* capitalism
Condorcet, Marquis de 273
Congress of Vienna 283
consumerism *see* capitalism
conversion 38–41, 44, 94, 148, 156, 164, 188, 192,
204, 207, 213, 229, 233, 243–4, 247–9
and Chapter 6 *passim*
Corday, Charlotte 217
Cornelia (wife of Pompey) 105–15
coup d'état 16, 195, 198, 206, 280–2
Crassus 108–10, 111, 113
Creusa 92, 96–7, 109, 129
Crusades 222, 264
Cupid 103, 124, 134
curiosity 210, 227, 228
Cybele 97, 120

D'Aubigné, Théodore Agrippa 2
Les Tragiques 225
Danaids 135

dandy 216, 217, 306
Dante 226, 227–8, 231, 309
Divina Commedia 176, 180, 220
Danton, Georges 213–17, 253, 286
Daoud, Kamel, *Meursault, contre-enquête*
320
Darwin, Charles 305–6, 324, *see* Social
Darwinism
Daumier, Honoré 216
David, Jacques-Louis 208
de' Medici, Catherine 223
decadence 2–6, 9, 15, 35, 37, 41, 48, 50–4, 57–9,
105, 217, 220, 263, 268, 272–3, 274, 285,
291, 296, 300, 302–4, 306–7, 312, 319, 321–5
decay, bodily 268–9
Declaration of the Rights of Man 286, 305
Delacroix, Eugène 285
Derrida, Jacques 15
Circonfession 147
Demeure. Maurice Blanchot 9
Politique de l'amitié viii
Specters of Marx 147
Diana 98–9, 103, 134–5
dictatorship 17–18, 47, 216, 266, *see* tyranny
Dido 91, 98–105, 106, 109, 110–11, 112, 114, 118,
130, 134–6, 143, 237, 288, *see* Augustine:
Confessions; suicide: Dido
dismemberment 60, 79, 83, 92, 93, 101, 111, 120,
138, 216, *see* monster; Scaeva
divine right of kings 148, 158, 196, 205–8, 220,
232, 272, 283
division within the soul 29, 83, 100, 136–7, 138,
153, 154–6, 167, 174–88, 189, 216, 241, 249,
251–2, *see* suicide
divorce 106–10, 290, 292
Djebar, Assia 2
Drouet, Juliette 221
Du Bellay, Joachim 217
dystopian 1, 257, 261, 291, 295, 306, 320

Easter 61, 247
Eco, Umberto 203
ecphrasis 11, 69–70, 76–8, 120, 135–6, 223, *see*
Shield, of Aeneas
Egypt 4–7, 34–8, 39, 50, 51, 53, 61–5, 66–7,
68–9, 75, 93, 112, 125–6, 128–31, 135–6, 175,
207, 257–63, 286, 325, *see* Alexandria;
bugonia; Cleopatra; Orientalism
elegy 79, 108, 109–11, 154, 302
emancipation 200, 289–90, 292, 293–4
Empire (French, First) 262, 281–3
Empire, Second 206, 262, 281–2, 285
England 8, 54, 194, 202, 206, 211, 223, 238, 279,
290, 292
English Civil War 8, 202

Ennius 267
  Annales 65, 122, 131, 152
ennui see indifference (*acedia, ennui*)
enslavement 16, 17–18, 24, 26, 97, 102, 132, 152,
  157, 162, 179, 181, 221, 293, 299–300
epic 27, 82, 120, 173, 202, 215, 231, 245
Epicurean 81, 88
equality 6, 16, 17, 35, 38, 41, 71, 99–101, 102, 120,
  151–2, 194, 199–200, 209, 210, 213, 243,
  252, 262–3, 270, 271, 290–1, 292, 294,
  295–300, 303, 304, 307, 312, 323, *see*
  fraternity; liberty
Eumenides 233, 236, *see* Aeschylus, *Oresteia*:
  Eumenides
Eurydice 53, 60, 63–5, 72, 79–81, 128
Eusebius 146, 157, 158–9, 180
Evander 83, 86, 123, 127, 137
Eve (Bible) 182, 227, 228
exegesis *see* interpretation
exemplarity 2–4, 13, 43, 44, 48, 86–9, 90, 101,
  116–17, 120, 138, 145–6, 147–8, 156,
  157–60, 168, 169–72, 180, 184–8, 193, 196,
  207, 238, 240, 248, 259, 261, 269, 277,
  290, 302, 306, 315, 325

factionism 27, 66, 173, 216, 217, 240, 276, 280,
  322, *see* animals: bees, *passim*
familia in Christo 200, 214
farce 13, 216, 262, 273, *see* irony; sarcasm; satire
fascism 6, 14, 19, 268, 271–2, 274, 276, 281, 283,
  301, 308, 324, 325, *see* Nazism;
  totalitarianism; World War II
fashion 266, 285, 307
Faulkner, William, *Absalom Absalom* 2
feminization 92–3, 119, 216–17, 301, *see*
  impotence; Orientalism; rape
Ferrari, Jérôme, *Sermon sur la chute de Rome* 147
Ferry, Jules 273
feudalism 200–1, 205, 207, 209–11, 213, 235,
  247, 296
filicide 186
Flaubert, Gustave 2, 14–15, 193, 194, 224, 263,
  272–3, 278, 281, 300, 325
  L'Éducation sentimentale 254–5, 270, 272
  Madame Bovary 302
Florus, *Epitome* 163
Fontane, Theodor, *Effi Briest* 302
Foucault, Michel 44–5
Fragonard, Jean-Honoré 296
François I 223
Franco-Prussian War 195, 202
fraternity 6, 17, 28, 31, 38, 41, 71, 197, 199–200,
  213, 218, 239, 242, 252, 295–300, 312, 313,
  314, 315–16, *see* equality; liberty

fratricide viii, 13, 21, 22, 23, 26, 27, 28, 29, 32–3,
  43, 56–9, 65, 71–2, 107, 115–16, 119, 121,
  123–5, 128, 136, 138–9, 161, 164, 169, 174,
  175, 176, 185, 195, 197, 216, 238, 247
Freud, Sigmund 269
  The Interpretation of Dreams 83
  The Uncanny 91
furor 23, 53, 58–9, 64, 78, 83, 88, 121, 122–3, 129,
  135, 137, 317
fury 94, 109, 113, 134, 165

gender 10, 24, 100, 117, 120, 135, 138, 262, 292,
  295, 296, 306, 307, *see* women
geography, of Paris 283, *see* Clichy, Place de;
  Concorde, Place de la; Hugo, Victor:
  "A l'arc de triomphe"; Montfermeil;
  Paris; *translatio Romae*
Germany 8, 12, 25, 212, 263, 265, 274–6, 281,
  283, 290, 291–2, 293, 297, 302, 321, *see*
  Nazism
giants 74, 75, 80, 86, 141, 176, 199, 212, 247, 324
Gide, André 203
Gigantomachy *see* giants
Giono, Jean 45
Giraudoux, Jean 45
Golgotha 248
Gourmont, Remy de 278
Gracchi 31, 47, 166, *see* Plutarch: *C. Gracchus*
Great Whore (of Babylon) 303
Greece, cultural model of 11, 25, 27–31, 32, 33,
  38, 103, 106, 110, 115, 125, 126, 135, 175,
  214–15, 297, 299, 310, *see* hyponoia
grotesque 3, 7–8, 15, 33, 38, 39–40, 82, 85, 114,
  153, 159, 161, 163, 185, 191, 202–3, 213,
  232–3, 248, 254, 270, *see* satire
Guénon, René 275
guillotine 40, 197, 199, 215, 217, 221, 233, 237,
  243–52, 286, *see* Concorde, Place de la

Hades 80, 251, *see* katabasis; Underworld
Hamlet 221
Hannibal 104
Hebrew, Jewish 18, 20, 38, 162, 168–9, 173, 174,
  177, 205, 243, 246, 248, 249, 262–3, 289, 307
Hecate 134
Hecuba 91, 92, 130, 233–4
Hegel, G.W.F. 159, 202, 227
  Lectures on Aesthetics 41
  Phenomenology of the Spirit 197, 198, 200, 232
Helen (of Troy) 94–5, 114
Hellenism 25, 49, 52, 53–4, *see* Greece, cultural
  model of
Henri II 223
Hercules 86, 100, 220, 226, 319

hermeneutics 34, 55, 63, 68, 84, 144, 145, 149–50, 153, 159, 160–1, 174, 188–92, 199–201, 205, 218, 225–6, 228, 231, 243, 246, 251, 252, 254, 266, 269, 277–8, 280, 325, *see* typology
Hesiod 125
   Works and Days 21
hieroglyphs 246, *see* Egypt
Hieronymus, *Epistolae* 157
Hobbes, Thomas 31
Hollande, François 286
Holzer, Jenny, *Truisms* 312
Homer 7, 38, 83, 85, 142, 253
   Iliad 92, 95, 99, 120, 136, 172
homme régénéré 304
homoeroticism 79, 135, 136, 299, 307–8, *see* homosexuality
homophobia 306
homosexuality 135, 296, *see* homoeroticism
Horace 35, 49, 131, 171
   Ars poetica 271
   Carmen saeculare 24, 116
   Carmina 116
   Epistulae 11, 69, 114, 171
   Epodes 22–3, 107, 124, 222–3, 268
   Odes 23–4, 56, 95, 118, 119, 313
      Cleopatra Ode 24, 112
   Satires 267–70, *see* satire
Houellebecq, Michel
   Serotonine 295
   Soumission 10, 13–15, 18, 37, 41, 44–5, 48, 84, 89, 153, 175, 203, 255
   and *passim* Introduction, Chapter 6
Hugo, Victor 224, 270, 272–3
   "A l'arc de triomphe" 195
   "Le Verso de la page" 199
   Cromwell 67–8
   Don Juan 236
   Eclogues (translation) 226
   L'année terrible 202, 226, 245
   L'homme qui rit 195, 218
   Le dernier jour d'un condamné 246
   Le Roi s'amuse 218
   Les châtiments 198–9
   Les contemplations 198, 225
   Les misérables 200, 254–5
   Les quatre vents de l'esprit 199
   Notre-Dame de Paris 253
   Preface to Cromwell 14, 41, 191–2, 199, 202–3, 248
   Quatrevingt-treize 10, 13–15, 18, 37–41, 44, 84, 89, 147, 152–3, 175, 272, 273, 308, 312, 325
   and *passim* Introduction, Chapter 5
   William Shakespeare 244–5

humanism 194, 195, 242, 261, 277, 287, 288, 300, 305, 308, 311, *see* Pléiade; university
Huysmans, Joris-Karl 41, 269, 273–8, 288, 308–12, 314, 316–17, 321–3, 325
   A rebours 256
hypocrisy 4, 272, 295, 307, 315, 325
hyponoia 261

idolatry 38–9, 155, 156, 162, 239, 263–4, 288
idyll 52, 56–9, 74, 76–7, 119, 227
Imhoof, Markus, *More Than Honey* 60
imitatio 87, 160, 170–1, 229, 237, 244, *see* aemulatio
   imitatio Christi 40, 44, 156, 220–1, 242, 247–8
imperium 50, 88, 122–3, 124–6, 141–3, 150–1, 153, 159, 258
   passim, *see* Augustus
impotence 92–3, 110, 182, 288–9, *see* sterility
incest 13, 21, 26, 33, 37, 91, 99, 103–4, 107, 113, 114, 130, 134, 165, 178–9, 215, 223, *see* pedophilia
indifference (*acedia*, *ennui*) 191, 270, 287–8, 289, 293, 302, 307, 315–17, 320, 325
indistinction 15, 23, 31, 37, 54, 58, 83, 89, 95–6, 98, 100, 107, 110, 114, 116, 133, 135, 138, 162, 226, 279, 293, 297, 322, *see* animality; indifference
infanticide 115
inner orient *see* Orientalism
insurgency 16–17
insurrection 16–17, 205, 213, 281, 283, 286
interpretation 45, 158, 191, 201, 237, 243, 253, 273, 278, *see* typology
invective tradition 268, *see* satire
Iphigenia 96, 106
irony 8, 17, 43, 53, 60, 76, 94, 99, 115, 118, 132, 133, 148–9, 152, 161–2, 180, 193, 211, 217, 260, 262, 266, 267, 268, 278, 286, 298, 306, 321, *see* farce; sarcasm; satire
Islam 1, 4, 6, 10, 41, 45, 175
   passim Chapter 6; *see* Islamophobia, Orientalism
Islamophobia xiii, 6, 10–11, 14, 271, 289, 307, 309, *see* satire

James, Henry 203
   The Bostonians 2
January 6, 2021 8
Janus 62, 83, 133
Jean de la Croix 318
Jerome 157, 158
   Letters 89
Jewish *see* Hebrew, Jewish
John the Baptist 221, 243

Julia (wife of Pompey)   33, 105–12, 113, 115, 218
Juno   36, 53, 75, 83, 99–100, 102, 105, 122, 123,
     131, 134, 140, 164
Jupiter   50, 54–6, 64–5, 72, 73, 75, 79–83, 88, 90,
     96, 100–3, 105, 119, 121, 122–3, 126, 133,
     139–40, 154, 166, 168, 230, 234, 237, 317
justice   16, 20–1, 40, 52, 60, 63–5, 71, 79, 80, 102,
     128, 141, 151–2, 159, 172, 173, 184, 205, 207,
     209, 215, 242, 253, 298
Juvenal   203, 213, 267, 268

katabasis   215
kenosis   40–1
Kirchhoff, Bodo, *Schundroman*   321
Kleist, Heinrich von, *Hermannsschlacht*   2
Kristeva, Julia   25, 34, 42

labor   5, 9, 50, 56, 73–4, 76–7, 80–1, 137, 141–2,
     143, 222, 226, 230, 231, 263, 292, 297,
     300, 310
laicity   259, 265–6, 272, 274–6, 281, 306
Laocoon   91, 92, 95–6, 98
Laomedon   75, 95
Last Supper   242, 253
Lavinia   33, 100, 104, 129–30, 135, 165
Le Carré, John, *The Most Wanted Man*   2
Le Pen, Marine   35, 280–1, 286–7
Lee, Spike, *Chiraq*   102
liberty   6, 12, 17, 38, 41, 43–4, 48, 66–7, 71, 81–2,
     117, 120, 133, 139, 157, 163, 168, 171, 198–200,
     213, 219–20, 236, 252, 268, 286, 287–9,
     295–300, 304, 311, *see* equality; fraternity
libido dominandi   146, 154, 157, 163, 165, 171, 182
library   222–32, 234–5, 237, 274, 320
literalization   6, 33, 89, 103, 116, 137, 232, 246,
     249, 264, 289, 295, 321
literature   224–32, 267–72, 308–12, 324–5, *see*
     hermeneutics; interpretation; typology,
     passim
Livy   32, 33, 43, 119, 170, 174, 186
     Epitome   32, 185
     Preface   145, 170–1
Longinus   191–2, 203
Loraux, Nicole   7, 25, 26, 28, 30–2
Louis Philippe   194, 286
Louis XIV   224
Louis XV   286
Louis XVI   198, 286
Louis XVII   199
Louverture, Toussaint   17
love *see* marriage, *passim*
     erotic   99, 136, 188, 218, 289, 302, *see* Dido
     failed   154, 288
Lucan, *De bello civili*   9–15, 16, 22, 28–9, 33–4,
     37–41, 135, 153–4, 158, 160–9, 175–6, 184–5,

     191, 194, 195, 205–8, 209, 213, 214, 216,
     218–22, 229, 237, 248, 288, 292, 325
     and *passim* Introduction, Chapter 3
Lucas, George, *Star Wars*   2
Lucilius   267
Lucretia   32, 33, 43–4, 118, 184–8, *see* suicide:
     Lucretia
Lupercalia   120
luxury   12, 54, 57, 60, 69, 70, 72, 76, 98, 104,
     106, 114, 119, 120, 130, 173–4, 188, 231, 285,
     307, 321

Machiavelli   23, 31–2
     Discorsi   24–5
Mahomet *see* Voltaire: *Mahomet*
     in Dante   176
Mallarmé, Stéphane   287
     Hérodiade   287
     L'après-midi d'un faune   287
Marat, Jean Paul   213–17, 227, 242, 253
Marc, Franz   19
Marcia (wife of Cato)   105–9, 111, 113
Marianne   285
Marie-Antoinette   286
Marius, Gaius   65, 90, 138, 140, 167, *see* Plutarch:
     Marius
marriage   23–6, 33, 37, 60, 83, 89–91, 94, 97–120,
     124, 129–30, 135, 154, 164–5, 214, 217, 218,
     259, 288–300, 301–3, *see* adultery; love
Mars   54, 58, 65, 73–6, 117, 118, 119, 164
Martial   135
martyrdom   229, 247–8, 249, 252, 310–11, 318–20
Marx, Karl   17, 245, 254, 281
     *The Eighteenth Brumaire of Louis
          Bonaparte*   13, 216, 262
Mary (mother of Christ)   167, 178–9, 204,
     220–2, 234–5, 301, 314, *see* Rocamadour,
     black Virgin of
masculinist   6, 28, 37, 100, 173, 197, 214, 219, 243,
     270, 280, 291, 293, 300–1, 305–8, 314, *see*
     misogyny; sexism
matricide   33, 101, 165, 166, 167, 179, 200, 246
Maupassant, Guy de   263, 272, 274, 277–8, 300
     Bel-ami   272, 285, 302
media   xiii, 12, 69, 188, 278
Medusa   215
melancholia see indifference (*acedia, ennui*)
Mercury   100
Merula   168
metaphorology   20, *see* Blumenberg, Hans
Michel, Louise   200
Michelet, Jules   272–3
     Histoire de France   195
     History of the French Revolution   195
militia amoris   154, 302, *see* elegy

Millet, Jean-François 56, 204, 231
Milton, John, *Paradise Lost* 172–4, 228
Minerva 91–5, 118, 215
misogyny 270, 283, *see* masculinist; sexism;
  women
Molière, *La critique de l'école des femmes* 267
monarchy 3–4, 5, 38, 48–9, 67, 85, 115, 148, 194,
  195–7, 198–200, 205, 206–8, 213, 214, 217,
  220, 221, 237–8, 246–7, 263, 273–4, 284,
  285, 286, 287, 288, 305
  Bourbon Monarchy 217, 283, 285
monster, monstrosity 46, 62, 64–5, 70, 80, 89,
  91, 92, 93–4, 100, 114, 135, 140, 171, 206,
  212, 214, 216–17, 220–1, 222, 229–30,
  232–3, 236, 237, 239–41, 246, 247, 248,
  252, 296, 315, 316, 324
Montesquieu 48
  Lettres Persanes 263
Montfermeil 282–3
Montmartre 250
murder within the family 21, 26, 28, 32, 138,
  248, 303, *see* Danaids; filicide; fratricide;
  infanticide; matricide; parricide
music 230, 277–8, 324
Mussolini, Benito 307, *see* fascism

Napoleon I 17, 194, 262, 280–3, 286–7
Napoleon III 194, 195, 262, 280–3, 287–8, *see*
  Marx, Karl: *The Eigteenth Brumaire of
  Louis Bonaparte*
narrative persepective *see* speaking voice, first-
  person narrator
Native American 211
naturalism 263, 288
Nazism 6, 55, 56, 263, 273, 276, 281, 291, 298–9,
  302, 306, *see* antisemitism; collaboration;
  racism; World War II
neoliberalism 276, 283, 291, 292, 323
Neptune 22, 95–6
Nero 2, 5, 33, 82, 85, 112, 116, 131–3, 179, 198,
  217
Nietzsche, Friedrich 48, 275–6, 290, 301,
  304–7, 318, 324
  Birth of Tragedy 321
Nimrod 68, 176, 324, *see* giants
Nisus and Euryalus 142–3
Nisus and Scylla 74–5

obelisks 286–7, *see* Egypt
objectification *see* reification (objectification)
occupation 263, *see* World War II
Octavia (sister of Augustus) 129
Oedipus 113
oikos 30–2
Olympian 48, 74, 80–1, 131, 166, 247

Orestes 101, 221
Orientalism 9–11, 14–15, 39, 41, 144, 154, 172–3,
  175, 205, 215, 228, 257, 260–2, 265, 275,
  278, 279–81, 285–6, 288–9, 292–3, 295,
  306–7, 311, 317, 321, 323–4, 325, *see* Egypt;
  luxury, and *passim* Preface, Introduction,
  Chapter 1, Chapter 2
  inner orient 34–8, 131, 259, 263–4, 277, 289
Origen, *contra Celsum* 159
Orosius 158
  Histories against the Pagans 144, 145, 156, 158
Orpheus 60–5, 70, 75, 78–80, 256
Ottoman Empire 260–1
Ovid 123, 302
  Fasti 105
  Metamorphoses 74, 79, 135

Pallas (character in the *Aeneid*) 39, 119, 135–7
Paris (city) 2, 19, 45
  passim Chapter 5, Chapter 6
Paris (lover of Helen) 94–5, 98, 99
parricide 13, 26, 28, 29, 123, 166, 207, 215, 238
Parthians 22, 66–7, 70, 109, 113–14
Passio (Passion of Christ) 156, 178, 188,
  226–9, 247
passion (emotion) 43, 54, 56, 58–60, 74, 76–9,
  81, 100, 101, 103–6, 109, 122, 129–30, 131,
  134–6, 142, 153–5, 171, 178, 182–3, 188–9,
  214, 232, 270, 320, 323, *see* Dido
Paul 68, 150, 157, 181–2, 200, 229, 232, 244, 245,
  246, 248, 254, 316, 324
  Ephesians 40, 323
  Epistle to the Corinthians 192, 243, 294
  Philippians 151, 159, 221
Paulhan, Jean 270
pedophilia 293, 299–300
Péguy, Charles 273, 275, 313–14
Peloponnesian War 13, 215
Penelope 118
Pentheus 101, 136
peripeteia 211
Perusia, Battle of 40, 129, 136
perversion 4, 29, 38–41
  passim
Petronius 203
Pharsalus, Battle of 21, 85, 114, 116, 128, 132, *see*
  Lucan
Philemon and Baucis 211
Philippi, Battle of 24, 72, 75, 105, 117, 128
philology *see* interpretation
Piaf, Edith 324
pied noir 320
pietas 39, 52–3, 67, 128, 138–9, 239
Pisonian Conspiracy 85
plague 54, 56–60, 64

Plato 155, 229
  Menexenus 30, 38
  Republic 7, 151, 181–2, 215
Pléiade 277–8, 310–12, 321–2
Plutarch
  C. Gracchus 166, *see* Gracchi
  Cato Minor 232, *see* Cato, Marcus Porcius, the Younger
  Marius 185, *see* Marius, Gaius
poison 44, 58, 103, 155
Poitiers, Diane de 223
Polis 30–2, 182, 234
political theology 148, 158, 179, 277, 287, 305–6, 313
polygamy 114, 293, 298–9, 300, 303
Pompey, the Great 7, 13, 19, 21, 25–9, 33, 34, 65, 77, 93, 105–12, 124, 131–3, 135, 138, 163–5, 201, 205, 207–8, 218–20, 239, *see* Alexandria; Cicero, Marcus Tullius: *De imperio Cn. Pompei*
pornography 261, 289, 294, 296, 314, 323
postcolonial 11
praeteritio 76
Priam 91–8, 118, 120, 129, 167
pride 22, 98, 125, 129, 154, 170, 172, 184–8, 189, 242, 272, 289
Propertius 35, 115, 302
prophecy, prophets 52, 56, 61, 89, 97, 121, 126, 149, 150, 157–9, 180, 182–4, 202, 215, 225, 242, 256–7, 276, 281
prostitution 23, 46, 117, 119–20, 172–4, 217, 261, 285–6, 289, 293, 299, 306
Proust, Marcel 270, 306
Puccini, Giacomo, *Tosca* 2
Punic Wars 99, 103–5, 131, 140, 163, 166
purple 27, 49, 57, 74, 100, 138, 227
Pygmalion 104, 220

Quinet, Edgar 272
Quintilian 34, 189, 190, 267

racism 257, 259, 267, 270–2, 274–7, 280, 283, *see* antisemitism
rape 26, 33, 58, 79, 90–8, 103–4, 113, 118, 119, 161, 164, 185–7, *see* Lucretia; Rape of the Sabines; Verginia
  Eurydice, attempted rape of 60, 63, 81, *see* Eurydice
  Ilia 64–5, 119
  Pléiades 310
  suicide 184–5, *see* suicide
  Turnus 135–6, *see* Turnus
Rape of the Sabines 29, 33, 71, 79, 120, 164
rationality 85, 88, 213–15, 299

realism 14–15, 148, 236, 254, 255, 263, 270–1, 272, 277, 288, 316
Regulus 177, 180, 186–7, 209
reification (objectification) 93, 106, 289–90, 293, 299, 320
republic *passim*
Republic, Roman xiii, 1, 2–3, 5, 9, 13, 16, 27, 31, 37, 42, 47–9, 65, 145, 151, 154, 169, 173, 185–6, 187, 194, 215, 249, 257, 261, 266, *passim*
Republic, Second 17, 194, 281
repulsion 8, 34, 271, 315–16
resistance 273–4, 315, *see* collaboration; World War II
revolt 15–18, 33, 74, 92, 189, 203, 218
revolution 17–18
  American 17–18
  Haitian 17
  Revolution of 1793 *passim* esp. Chapter 5
  Revolution of 1830 194
  Revolution of 1848 194, 281
Rimbaud, Arthur 273
Risorgimento 8
Robespierre, Maximilien de 213–17, 219, 249, 253, 286
Rocamadour, Black Virgin of 275, 308, 312–14
Romanitas 5, 15, 46, 84, 147, 162, 278
Romanticism 41, 189, 194, 196, 201–3, 212, 225, 227, 229–30, 232–4, 237, 241, 243–52, 253–5, 272, 293, *see* Hugo, Victor: *Preface to Cromwell*
Rome, foundational myths of *see* Alba Longa; Lucretia; Rape of the Sabines; Romulus and Remus; Verginia
Romulus (god) 68
Romulus and Remus 22, 23, 29, 32–3, 65, 71, 83, 86, 87, 98–9, 107, 114, 119, 121–2, 123–8, 136, 161, 164, 172, 174–81, *see* fratricide; Shield, of Aeneas
Rousseau, Jean-Jacques 48, 273
  Confessions 309, 321
  Du contrat social ou Principes du droit politique 28
  Nouvelle Héloïse 320
Rushdie, Salman, *The Golden House* 2
Russia 19, 194, 282–3, 284–5, 287

sacrifice 8, 19, 29, 38–41, 42, 44, 52, 61–5, 67, 93, 95–6, 128, 133–41, 155–6, 159, 162, 165, 167–9, 170, 171–2, 178, 199–200, 220, 232–40, 292, 301, 311–12, 318, 321
  human 38–41, 88, 136, 138–9, 155–6, 162, 167–9, 311, *see* Turnus
  perverted 38, 41, 64, 89–90, 96, 128, 133–4, 136, 139–40, 155–6, 168, *see bugonia*

sacrifice (cont.)
  self-sacrifice 38, 40–1, 44, 67, 139, 156, 168,
    170, 178–9, 196–7, 198, 204, 218–22,
    235–6, 238–9, 243–4, 246, 248, 252, 319, *see*
    imitatio: imitatio Christi
Sallust 33, 53, 68–9, 135, 174
  Bellum Catilinae 16, 30, 33, 69, 104, 154, 182,
    222, *see* Catilina
Sand, George 194
Sappho 110
sarcasm 145, 161, 164, 273, 286, 292, 304, *see*
    farce; irony; satire
Satan 176, 200, 207, 245, 252
satire 8, 14–15, 203, 261–2, 263, 267–72, 312, 314,
    318, 321, *see* farce; irony; sarcasm
Saturn 66, 71, 76, 83, 86, 121, 123, 125–6,
    128–9, 230
Saturnian Age *see* Saturn
Saudi Arabia 19, 265, 276, 280, 287, 298,
    306–8
Scaeva 42, 132, 229
scandal 30, 106, 118, 269, 271
Schmitt, Carl 158, 277
sectarian war 18, *see* factionism
secular, secularization 3–4, 5, 8, 13–14, 18, 31,
    40–1, 44, 88, 146, 158, 159, 166, 193, 197,
    200, 204, 214, 221, 226, 237, 259, 263,
    265–6, 272–7, 280, 288, 297, 301, 306,
    307–9, 310, 314, 324, 325, *see* laicity
security 12, 29, 52, 56–8, 99, 121, 209, 210, 230,
    233, 285, 287, 318
Semiramis 178
Seneca 85, 217
  De clementia 241 *see* clemency
  De tranquillitate animi 43, *see* Cato, Marcus
    Porcius, the Younger
  Phoenissae 28, 91, 125
sentimentality 62, 203, 204, 230–1, 234,
    254
Sermon on the Mount 197, 313
servitude 177, 179, 238
sexism 267, 270–2, *see* masculinist; misogyny
Shakespeare, William 14, *see* Hugo, Victor:
    William Shakespeare
Shield, of Aeneas 11, 36, 39, 49, 53, 86, 98,
    117–20, 126–31, 228, 239
Sibyl 75
Simon, Claude 2, 45
slavery *see* enslavement
Social Darwinism 275, 298, 305, *see* Darwin,
    Charles
sociology 158, 290
Sodom and Gomorrah 158
sodomy 280, 293, 294–5
Sparta 215

speaking voice, first-person narrator 7, 23, 24,
    49, 69, 70, 79–80, 81, 95, 101, 105, 126,
    150, 202, 267–8, 270, 271–2
Spengler, Oswald, *Decline of the West* 301
St. Bartholomew, Massacre of 223, 224–32,
    253
stasis 13, 16, 28, 29–32, 33, 34, 38, 42, 59, 218
Stendhal, *Le rouge et le noir* 320
sterility 33, 64, 79–80, 106–8, 116, 135, 220, 228,
    272, *see* impotence
stillborn 217
Stoicism 99, 106, 107, 110, 141, 187–8, 214–16,
    219–20, 232–3, 234, 237, 248
Strabo, *Geography* 70
sublime 7–8, 38, 40, 191, 202–3, 214, 221,
    229–30, 231–2, 234, 244, 252, 254, 270,
    309, 316, *see* Romanticism
substitute family 105, 213–22, *see familia in*
    Christo
suburbia 291–3
Suetonius 259
  Iulius Caesar 238, *see* Caesar, Gaius Iulius
suicide 23, 26, 29, 39, 43, 44, 67, 83, 85–6, 95,
    111, 124, 130, 133–41, 143, 168, 184–8, 207,
    216–17, 251, 259, 263, 295, 303–4, 315, 319,
    see Cleopatra
  Cato 43–4, 132, 139, 184, 186–7, 220, *see* Cato,
    Marcus Porcius, the Younger
  Cimourdain 40–1, 44, 196–7, 220,
    243–4, 248
  Dido 98–105, 106, 110, 134–6, 188, *see* Dido
  Lucretia 44, 184–8, *see* Lucretia
  Sulla 26, 27, 65, 88, 90, 138, 163, 167
Syrian War 16, 18–19

Tacitus 23, 33, 34, 48, 89, 259
  Annales 112
  Histories 24, 32, 84, 135, 185
Tarquinius Superbus 120, 129, 166
technology 39, 60–1, 64, 69, 70, 75, 76, 80, 206,
    222, 228, 230
Tellmarch 209–13, 233, 235–7, 247
Terror (Terreur) 5, 14, 199, 200–1, 202, 213–19,
    238, 242, 244, 245–9, 283, 286
terrorism 10, 16, 19, 31, 45, 256–7, 264
Tertullian 88
  De corona 155, 159
Thérèse de Lisieux 318
Thermopylae 215
Third Reich *see* antisemitism; fascism; Nazism;
    racism; World War II
Thirty Years War 8
Thucydides 13, 29, 32, 33–4, 42, 59, 310
Tiberius 223
  Senatus consultum de Cn. Pisone patre 133

Tocqueville, Alexis de, *Recollections* 194–5
Todd, Emmanuel, *Qui est Charlie?* 265–6
Tolstoy, Leo, *Anna Karenina* 302
tomb 79, 105–6, 116, 224, 227, 279
totalitarianism 274, 275, 305, 307, *see* fascism; Nazism
Tourgue 222–4, 228, 230, 232–3, 242, 243, 246–7, 249
tragic 3, 13, 33, 82, 85, 106, 114, 165, 214–16, 237, 250, 257, 262, 273, 276, 278, 318, 321
    tragicomic 14, 67
transcendence 2–3, 4, 52–3, 173, 203, 237–40, 242–3, 305–6, 312
translatio Romae 2–4, 15, 46, 146, 168, 201, 205, 224, 258–61
trauma 32, 47, 62, 79, 83–5, 126, 136, 201, 277
Très riches heures du Duc de Berry, Les 316
triangulation 218
tricolor 249, 285
triumvirate 29, 107–8
trompe l'oeil 76, 223
trope xiv, 2, 4–5, 10, 12, 13–15, 16, 18, 20–6, 29, 32, 34, 39, 40–1, 42–4, 50–61, 68, 72, 74–5, 80–1, 82–3, 85, 91, 102–8, 115–16, 117–18, 120, 121–5, 134, 137–9, 149–50, 153, 154, 161, 164–6, 168, 176, 178, 184–6, 191, 195, 199, 205, 207, 212, 214, 216, 218, 240–1, 242, 244, 245, 248, 252, 257, 261–3, 269, 272, 273, 276, 280, 289, 294, 302–3, 305, 319, 320, 322–5
tropes of civil war *see* adultery; animality; Babylon; bastard, bastardization; blasphemy; butchery; cannibalism; castration; cataclysm; catastrophe; curiosity; decadence; decay, bodily; dictatorship; dismemberment; division within the soul; enslavement; factionism; feminization; *furor*; giants; Great Whore (of Babylon); hypocrisy; idolatry; impotence; incest; indistinction; indifference (*acedia, ennui*); inner orient; insurrection; *libido dominandi*; literalization; love: failed; luxury; monster, monstrosity; murder within the family; Orientalism; passion (emotion); pedophilia; polygamy; prostitution; rape; sacrifice: human; sacrifice: perverted; sectarian war; sodomy; sterility; suicide; twinning; tyranny; *see also* perversion
Troy 83, 90–8, 102–4, 118, 122, 123, 129, 137, 165, 168, 172, 313
Tullianum 222

Turnus 33, 39–40, 87–8, 125, 129–30, 133–41, 168, 238, 249–52
twinning 15, 27, 62, 89, 93, 97, 98–9, 107, 108, 113, 114, 116, 119, 127–8, 136, 140, 176, 204, 243, 249, 257, 279–80, 322
typology 86–9, 135, 145–50, 153, 172, 176, 180, 188, 190, 199, 201, 232, 244, 290
tyranny xiii, 3–6, 9, 12, 16, 35–7, 41, 47, 48, 54, 55, 57, 65, 68, 85, 98, 120, 129, 154, 182, 186, 187, 194, 198, 205, 216–17, 222, 224, 241, 257, 263, 272, 276, 286, 304, 306–7, 325, *see* dictatorship; Lucretia; Orientalism

Underworld 49, 60, 75, 83, 94, 109, 120, 124, 129, 215, 251–2, *see* Hades
university 272–3

Valerius Maximus 32, 185
Varro 153–4
    Antiquitates rerum romanarum et divinarum 152
Velleius Paterculus, *Historia Romana* 116, 133, 185
Vendée 196, 198, 207, 209, 217, 218, 223
Venus 77, 94–7, 100, 105, 107, 109, 115, 117–22, 124, 135, 140, 164, 307
Vergil 9–15, 32–3, 34–41, 42, 144–5, 146, 147, 153–4, 157–60, 172–5, 184, 188–9, 200–2, 206, 218, 225, 227–9, 231–2, 244, 256, 262, 269, 312
    and *passim* Introduction
    Aeneid 33, 47–54, 61–2, 65, 66, 69, 74, 75, 157–60, 163, 167–8, 215, 218, 220, 237, 240, 242, 248, 251–2, 261, 270, 288, 313, 325
    and *passim* Chapter 1
    Annales 122
    Eclogues 30, 49, 53, 55, 61, 68, 81, 89, 109, 126, 129, 142, 226–7, 264
    Georgics 21, 27, 82, 95, 123, 126–7, 128–9, 140, 142, 162, 230
    and *passim* Chapter 2
Verginia 32, 33
Vernet, Horace 282
Versailles 220, 223, 283–4
Vesta 68, 93–4, 105, 119, 122–3, 131, 164, 166, 168
Vichy 262–3, 273, 299, 302
virginity 81, 93, 95, 119, 130, 164, 166, 168, 209, 214, 217, 218, 221, *see* Mary (mother of Christ); chastity
virtus 3, 42–3, 52–3, 79, 160, 169–72, 197, 217
Voltaire 117, 224
    Mahomet 263, *see* Mahomet
Volusius, *Annales* 142

Vulcan 117–20, 135
Vulteius 43, 138

Wars of Religion 8, 225, 229
Wilde, Oscar 270
womb 65, 90–8, 106, 302
women 6, 9, 21, 28, 38, 43, 92–3, 96–8, 100, 106,
109, 112, 134–6, 138, 141, 152, 164, 184,
185–7, 197, 209, 212, 223, 241, 259, 262–4,
276, 288–300, 301–3, 304–5, 307, *see*
emancipation; feminization; gender;
misogyny; rape; sexism

World War I 8, 19–20, 55, 274, 319
World War II 8, 18, 19, 54, 263, 265, 314, 315, *see*
collaboration; fascism; Nazism;
occupation; resistance
wound 7, 9–10, 47, 67, 83, 85, 92, 94, 96, 103,
163, 229, 232, 240, 269, 310

Yourcenar, Marguerite 45

Zola, Émile 263, 272–4, 278, 285,
307
L'œuvre 285

Printed in the USA
CPSIA information can be obtained
at www.ICGtesting.com
LVHW011749031123
762994LV00004B/280